STREET ATLAS
West Kent

First published in 1989 by

Philip's, a division of
Octopus Publishing Group Ltd
2-4 Heron Quays, London E14 4JP

Third colour edition 2005
First impression 2005

ISBN-10   0-540-08666-5 (hardback)
ISBN-13   978-0-540-08666-5 (hardback)
ISBN-10   0-540-08667-3 (spiral)
ISBN-13   978-0-540-08667-2 (spiral)

© Philip's 2005

Ordnance Survey®

This product includes mapping data licensed
from Ordnance Survey® with the permission of
the Controller of Her Majesty's Stationery Office.
© Crown copyright 2005. All rights reserved.
Licence number 100011710.

Printed and bound in Spain
by Cayfosa-Quebecor

Contents

III	**Key to map symbols**
IV	**Key to map pages**
VI	**Route planning**
VIII	**Administrative and Postcode boundaries**
1	**Street maps** at 3½ inches to 1 mile
200	**Index** of towns and villages
202	**Index** of streets, hospitals, industrial estates, railway stations, schools, shopping centres, universities and places of interest

Digital Data

The exceptionally high-quality mapping found in this atlas is available as digital data in TIFF format, which is easily convertible to other bitmapped (raster) image formats.

The index is also available in digital form as a standard database table. It contains all the details found in the printed index together with the National Grid reference for the map square in which each entry is named.

For further information and to discuss your requirements, please contact Philip's on 020 7644 6932 or james.mann@philips-maps.co.uk

Key to map symbols

III

Motorway	**Motorway** with junction number (22a)
Primary route	**Primary route** – dual/single carriageway
A road	**A road** – dual/single carriageway
B road	**B road** – dual/single carriageway
Minor road	**Minor road** – dual/single carriageway
Other minor road	**Other minor road** – dual/single carriageway
Road under construction	**Road under construction**
Tunnel, covered road	**Tunnel, covered road**
Rural track	**Rural track, private road or narrow road in urban area**
Gate	**Gate or obstruction to traffic** (restrictions may not apply at all times or to all vehicles)
Path	**Path, bridleway, byway open to all traffic, road used as a public path**
Pedestrianised	**Pedestrianised area**
DY7	**Postcode boundaries**
County boundaries	**County and unitary authority boundaries**
Railway	**Railway, tunnel, railway under construction**
Tramway	**Tramway, tramway under construction**
Miniature railway	**Miniature railway**
Railway station	**Railway station** Walsall
Private railway station	**Private railway station**
DLR station	**Docklands Light Railway station**
Tram stop	**Tram stop, tram stop under construction**
Bus station	**Bus, coach station**

◆	**Ambulance station**
◆	**Coastguard station**
◆	**Fire station**
◆	**Police station**
✚	**Accident and Emergency entrance to hospital**
H	**Hospital**
✛	**Place of worship**
i	**Information Centre** (open all year)
🛒	**Shopping Centre**
P P&R	**Parking, Park and Ride**
PO	**Post Office**
⋀	**Camping site**
⛺	**Caravan site**
▶	**Golf course**
⊠	**Picnic site**
Prim Sch	**Important buildings, schools, colleges, universities and hospitals**
	Built up area
	Woods
River Medway	**Water name**
	River, weir, stream
⟨⟩	**Canal, lock, tunnel**
	Water
	Tidal water
Church	**Non-Roman antiquity**
ROMAN FORT	**Roman antiquity**
87 / 24	**Adjoining page indicators and overlap bands**

Acad	**Academy**	Inst	**Institute**	Recn Gd	**Recreation Ground**
Allot Gdns	**Allotments**	Ct	**Law Court**		
Cemy	**Cemetery**	L Ctr	**Leisure Centre**	Resr	**Reservoir**
C Ctr	**Civic Centre**	LC	**Level Crossing**	Ret Pk	**Retail Park**
CH	**Club House**	Liby	**Library**	Sch	**School**
Coll	**College**	Mkt	**Market**	Sh Ctr	**Shopping Centre**
Crem	**Crematorium**	Meml	**Memorial**	TH	**Town Hall/House**
Ent	**Enterprise**	Mon	**Monument**	Trad Est	**Trading Estate**
Ex H	**Exhibition Hall**	Mus	**Museum**	Univ	**University**
Ind Est	**Industrial Estate**	Obsy	**Observatory**	W Twr	**Water Tower**
IRB Sta	**Inshore Rescue Boat Station**	Pal	**Royal Palace**	Wks	**Works**
		PH	**Public House**	YH	**Youth Hostel**

■ The small numbers around the edges of the maps identify the 1 kilometre National Grid lines

■ The dark grey border on the inside edge of some pages indicates that the mapping does not continue onto the adjacent page

The scale of the maps on the pages numbered in blue is 5.52 cm to 1 km • 3½ inches to 1 mile • 1:18103

0	¼	½	¾	1 mile
0	250m	500m	750m 1 kilometre	

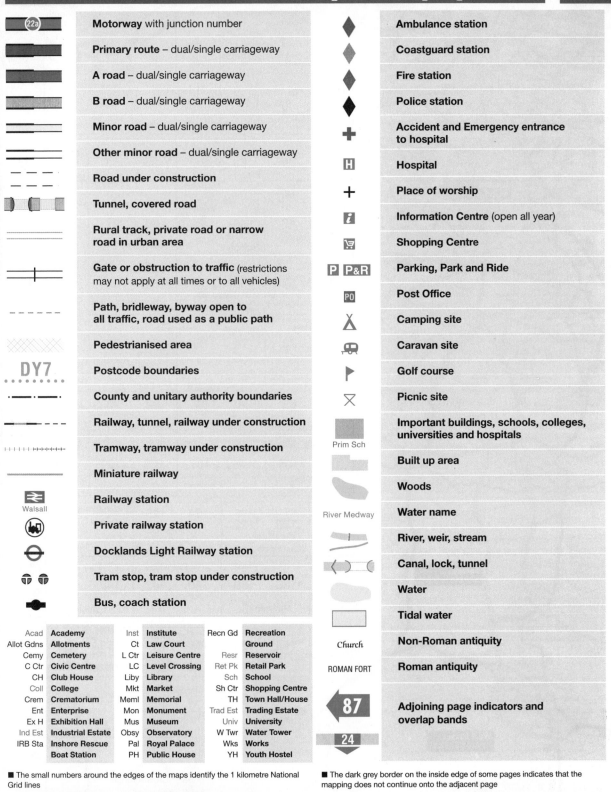

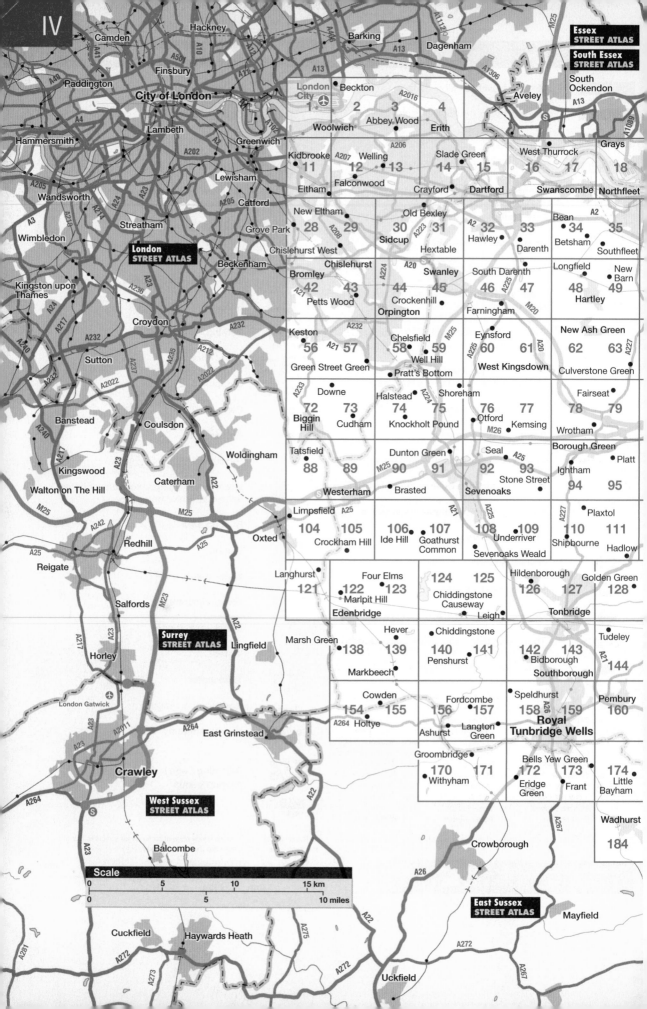

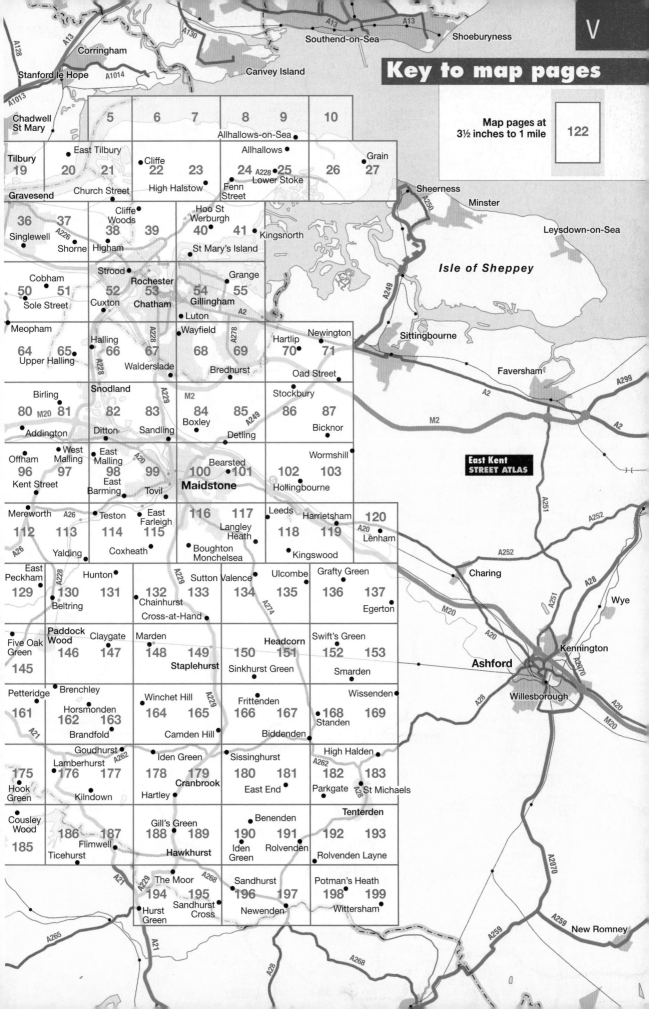

Corringham

Southend-on-Sea

Shoeburyness

A13

A130

A128

Stanford le Hope

A1014

Canvey Island

Chadwell
St Mary

A1013

| 5 | 6 | 7 | 8 | 9 | 10 |

Allhallows-on-Sea

Map pages at
3½ inches to 1 mile | 122

East Tilbury

Allhallows

Grain

Tilbury

19 | **20** | **21** | Cliffe **22** | **23** | **24** A228 **25** Lower Stoke | **26** | **27**

Gravesend

Church Street

High Halstow

Fenn Street

Sheerness

Minster

A250

Cliffe
Woods

Hoo St
Werburgh

Kingsnorth

Leysdown-on-Sea

36 | **37** | **38** | **39** | **40** | **41**

Singlewell

A226

Shorne

Higham

St Mary's Island

Isle of Sheppey

A249

Strood

Grange

Cobham

Rochester

50 | **51** | **52** | **53** | **54** | **55**

Sole Street

Cuxton

Chatham

Gillingham

A2

Luton

Sittingbourne

Faversham

Meopham

Wayfield

Newington

A299

A228

A278

Hartlip

64 | **65** Halling **66** | **67** | **68** | **69** | **70** | **71**

Upper Halling

Walderslade

Bredhurst

Oad Street

A2

A228

M2

A2

Snodland

Stockbury

Birling

M2

80 M20 **81** | **82** | **83** | **84** Boxley | **85** A249 | **86** | **87**

Addington

Ditton

Sandling

Detling

Bicknor

**East Kent
STREET ATLAS**

A29

West
Malling

East
Malling

Wormshill

Offham

A20

Bearsted

A251

96 | **97** | **98** | **99** | **100** | **101** | **102** | **103**

Kent Street

East
Barming

Tovil

Maidstone

Hollingbourne

A252

Mereworth

A26

Leeds

Harrietsham

120

Teston

East
Farleigh

112 | **113** | **114** | **115** | **116** | **117** | **118** | **119** A20 Lenham

Langley
Heath

A251

A28

Yalding

Coxheath

Boughton
Monchelsea

Kingswood

Wye

East
Peckham

Hunton

Sutton Valence

Ulcombe

Grafty Green

Charing

A228

A229

129 | **130** | **131** | **132** | **133** | **134** | **135** | **136** | **137**

Beltring

Chainhurst

A274

Egerton

M20

A251

Cross-at-Hand

Paddock
Wood

Claygate

Marden

Headcorn

Swift's Green

Kennington

Five Oak
Green

146 | **147** | **148** | **149** | **150** | **151** | **152** | **153**

145

Staplehurst

Sinkhurst Green

Smarden

Ashford

A2070

Petteridge

Brenchley

Winchet Hill

Frittenden

Wissenden

Willesborough

Horsmonden

A229

161 | **162** **163** | **164** | **165** | **166** | **167** | **168** | **169**

A21

Brandfold

Camden Hill

Biddenden

Standen

M20

Goudhurst

Iden Green

Sissinghurst

High Halden

Lamberhurst

A262

A262

175 | **176** | **177** | **178** | **179** | **180** | **181** | **182** | **183**

Hook
Green

Kilndown

Cranbrook

East End

Parkgate St Michaels

A28

Hartley

A2070

Cousley
Wood

Benenden

Tenterden

Gill's Green

186 **187** | **188** | **189** | **190** | **191** | **192** | **193**

185

Flimwell

Hawkhurst

Iden
Green

Rolvenden

Rolvenden Layne

A259

Ticehurst

A21

A228

The Moor

A268

Sandhurst

Potman's Heath

194 **195** | **196** | **197** | **198** **199**

Hurst
Green

Sandhurst
Cross

Newenden

Wittersham

New Romney

A265

A21

A28

A268

A259

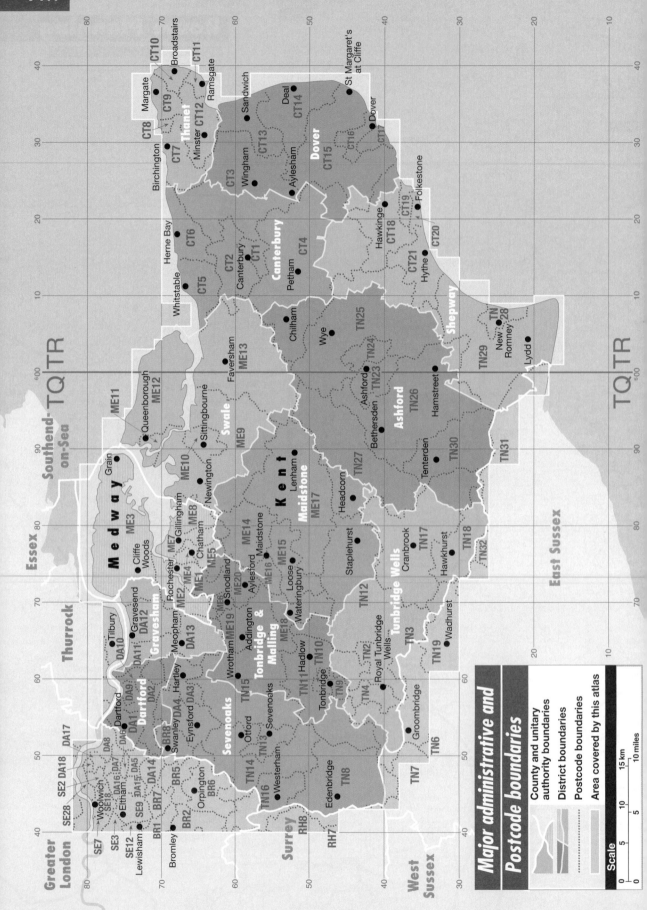

Major administrative and Postcode boundaries

	County and unitary authority boundaries
	District boundaries
	Postcode boundaries
	Area covered by this atlas

Scale

0	5	10	15 km
0	5	10 miles	

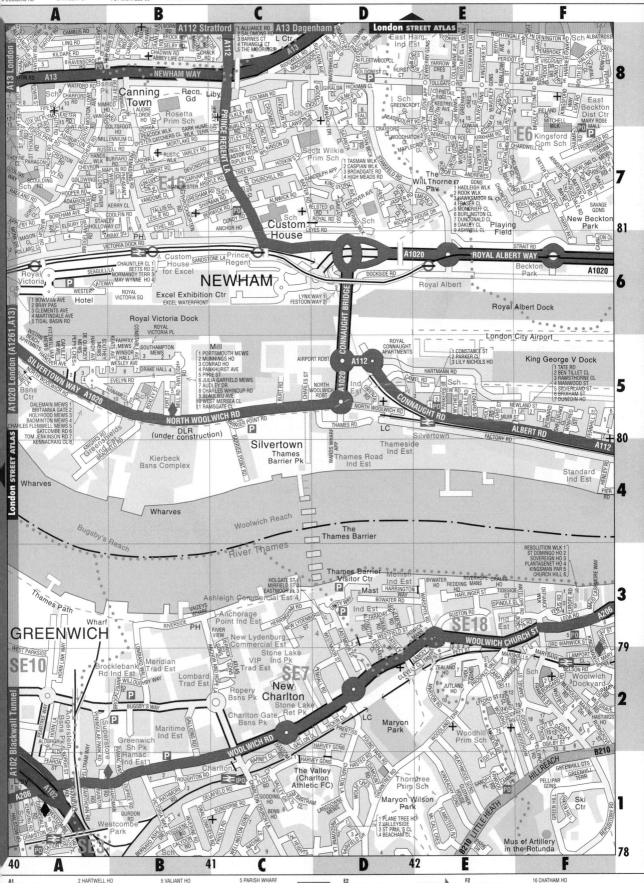

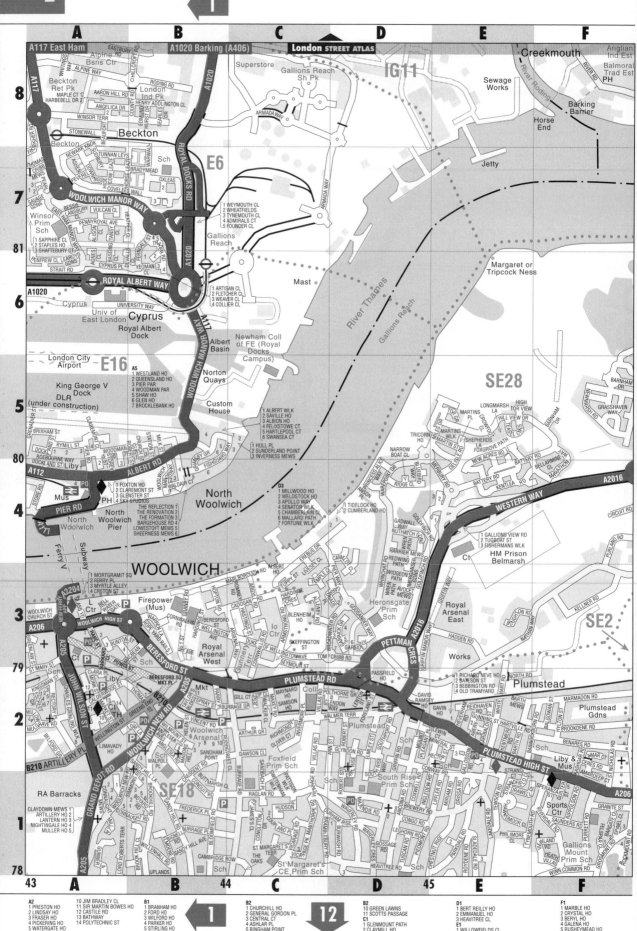

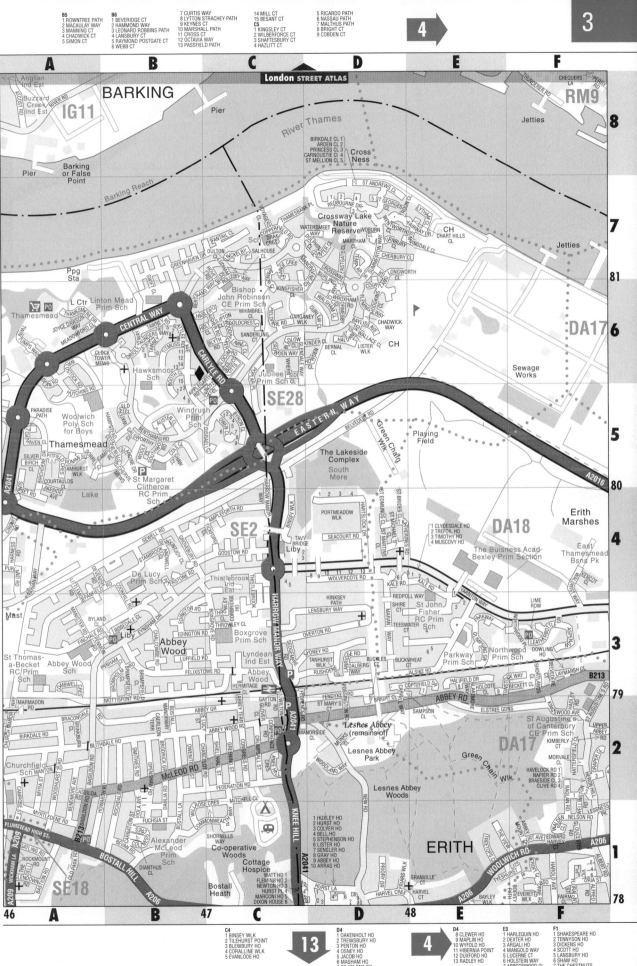

A13 Dagenham, London

RAINHAM

RM9

RM13

DA18

DA17

DA8

Belvedere

ERITH

Lessness
Heath

A1
1 STEVANNE CT
2 TOLCAIRN CT
3 CHALFONT CT
4 ALONSO CT
5 ARIEL CT
6 MIRANDA HO
7 PROSPERO HO
8 SMARDEN CL
9 BERKHAMPSTEAD RD

10 CAMDEN CT
11 THE CHESTNUTS
12 LESSNESS RD
13 HARTFORD WLK
14 WINCHESTER CT
15 BRAMLEY CT
16 RIVERVIEW CT
17 RUSSET CT
18 THE LAURELS

A2
1 BRUSHWOOD LODGE
2 STICKLAND RD
3 BLETCHINGTON CT
4 VENMEAD CT
5 MITRE CT
6 CHAPELSITE CT

A3
1 CRESSINGHAM CT
2 TELFORD HO
3 KELVIN HO
4 JENNER HO
5 MARY MACARTHUR HO
6 LENNOX HO
7 KEIR HARDY HO
8 MONARCH RD
9 ELIZABETH GARRETT ANDERSON HO

A3
10 WILLIAM SMITH HO
11 BADEN POWELL HO
12 BOYLE HO
13 BAIRD HO
14 MARY SLESSOR HO

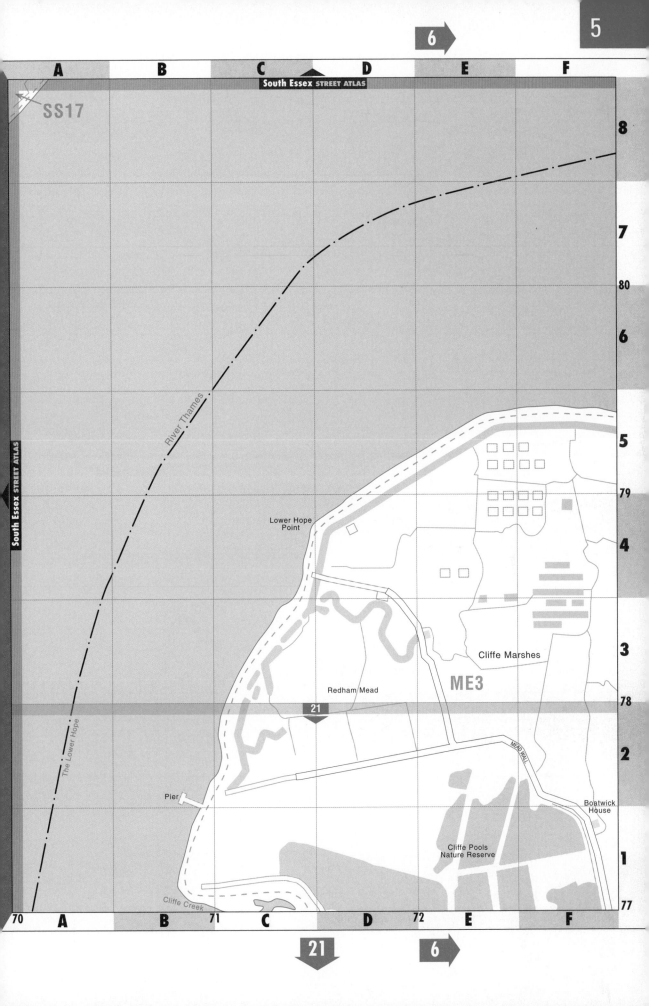

SS17

South Essex STREET ATLAS

River Thames

The Lower Hope

Lower Hope
Point

Cliffe Marshes

ME3

Redham Mead

MEAD WALL

Boatwick
House

Pier

Cliffe Pools
Nature Reserve

Cliffe Creek

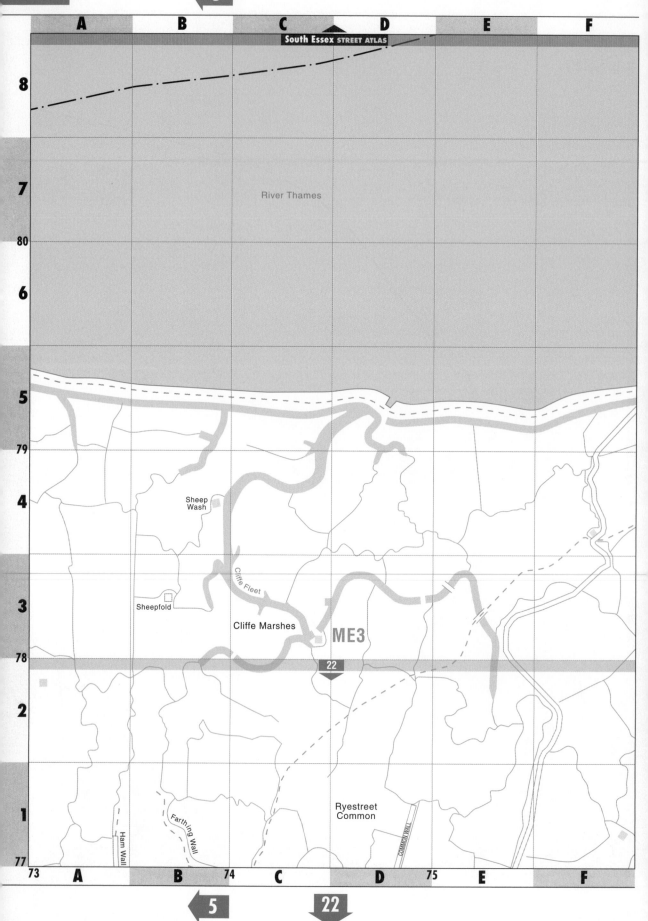

River Thames

Sheep
Wash

Cliffe Fleet

Sheepfold

Cliffe Marshes

ME3

22

Ryestreet
Common

Farthing Wall

Ham Wall

COMMON WALL

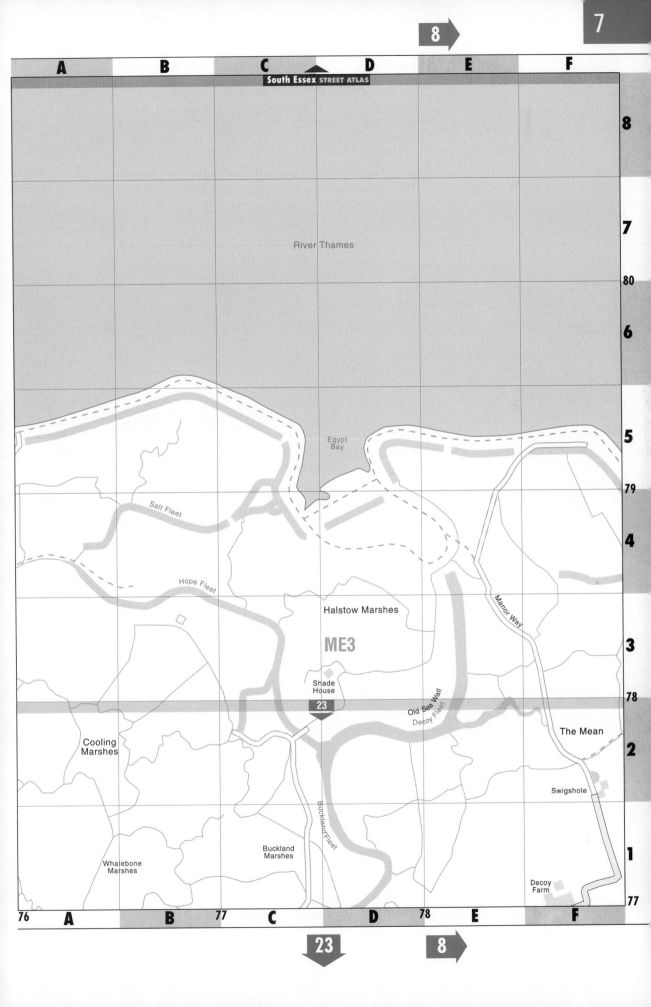

A B C D E F

South Essex STREET ATLAS

8

River Thames

7

80

6

Egypt
Bay

5

79

Salt Fleet

4

Hope Fleet

Manor Way

Halstow Marshes

ME3

3

Shade
House

78

23

Old Sea Wall

Decoy Fleet

The Mean

2

Cooling
Marshes

Swigshole

Buckland Fleet

1

Buckland
Marshes

Whalebone
Marshes

Decoy
Farm

77

76 A 77 B C 77 D 78 E F

7

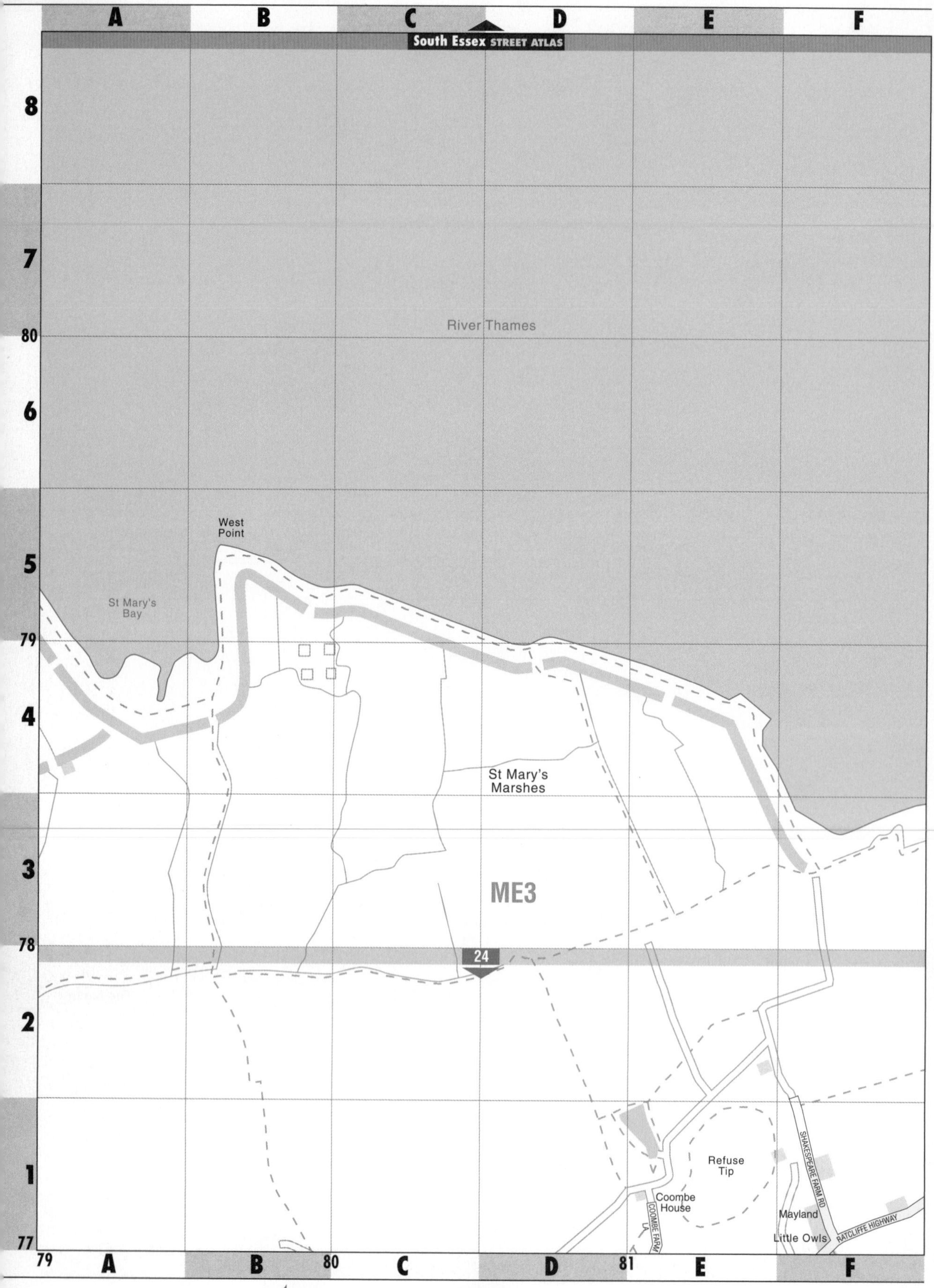
South Essex STREET ATLAS
A
B
C
D
E
F
8
7
80
6
5
79
4
3
78
2
1
77
79
80
81
River Thames
West Point
St Mary's Bay
St Mary's Marshes
ME3
24
Refuse Tip
Coombe House
COOMBE FARM LA
SHAKESPEARE FARM RD
Mayland
Little Owls
RATCLIFFE HIGHWAY

7

24

South Essex STREET ATLAS

River Thames

Dagnam Saltings

Holiday Park

Slough Fort

Allhallows-
on-Sea

ALLHALLOWS-ON-SEA EST

THE BRIMP

QUEENSWAY

Avery
House

British Pilot
(Hotel)

AVERY WAY

PO

AVERY CL

AVERY CT

CH

KINGSMEAD PK

ME3

Allhallows
Prim Sch

HOMEWARDS RD

PARKER'S
CNR

Windhill
Green

Dagnam
Farm

Wr Twr &
Beacon

Rose & Crown
(PH)

Two Rivers

Baytree
Farm

RATCLIFFE HIGHWAY

Brick House
Farm

STOKE RD

BEATTY COTTS

The Chimneys

Allhallows

AVERY WAY

ST LUKE'S WAY

ST GEORGE'S
WLK

ST ANDREW'S
WLK

ST DAVID'S RD

BINNE

RD

ALL... ST MAT...
...EWS
WAY

ST DAVID'S... WAY

Allhallows Marshes

Binney
Farm

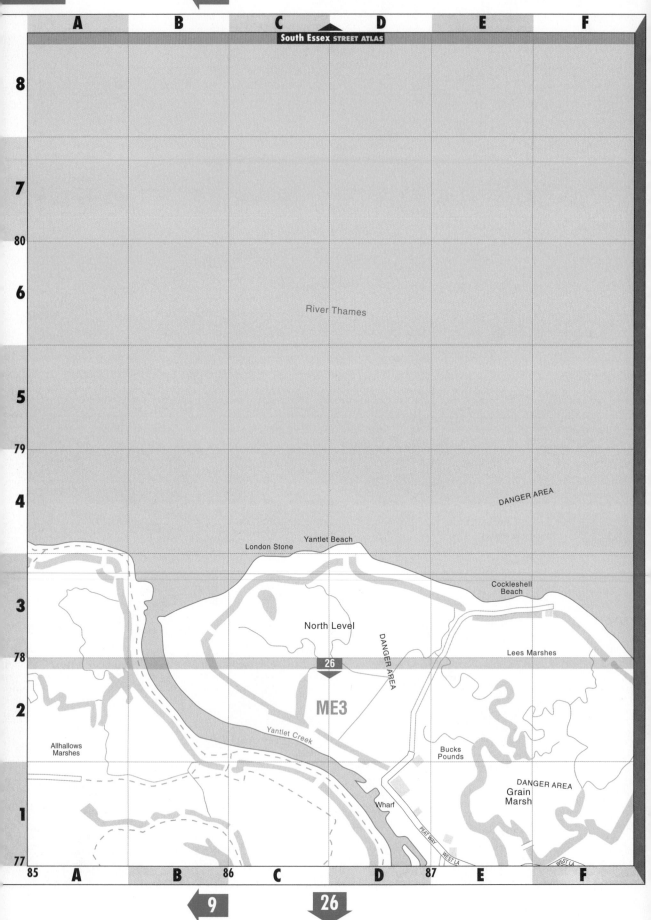

South Essex STREET ATLAS

River Thames

DANGER AREA

Yantlet Beach

London Stone

Cockleshell
Beach

North Level

DANGER AREA

Lees Marshes

26

ME3

Yantlet Creek

Allhallows
Marshes

Bucks
Pounds

DANGER AREA

Grain
Marsh

Wharf

PEAT WAY

WEST LA

WEST LA

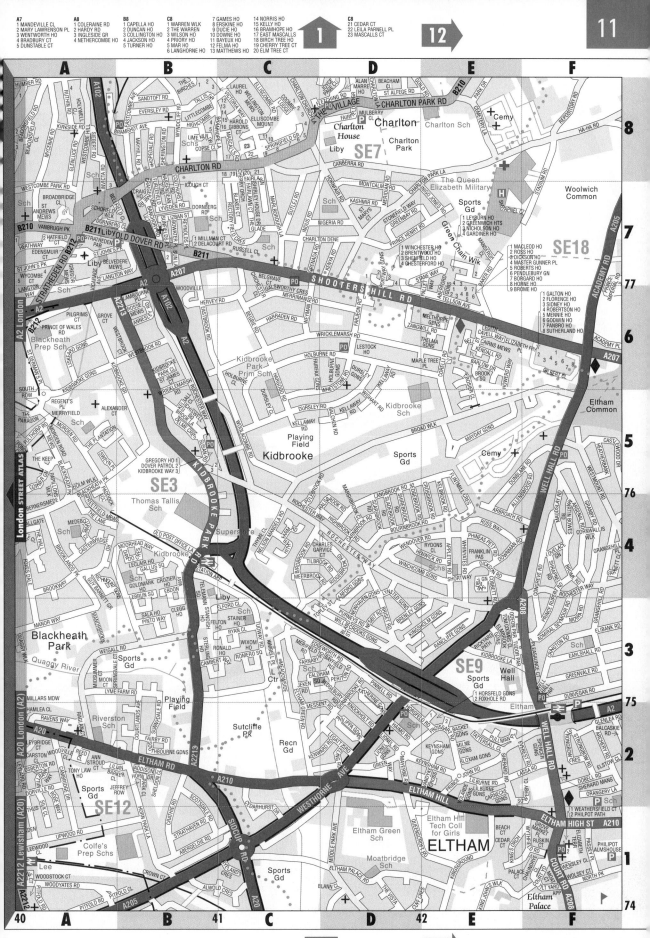

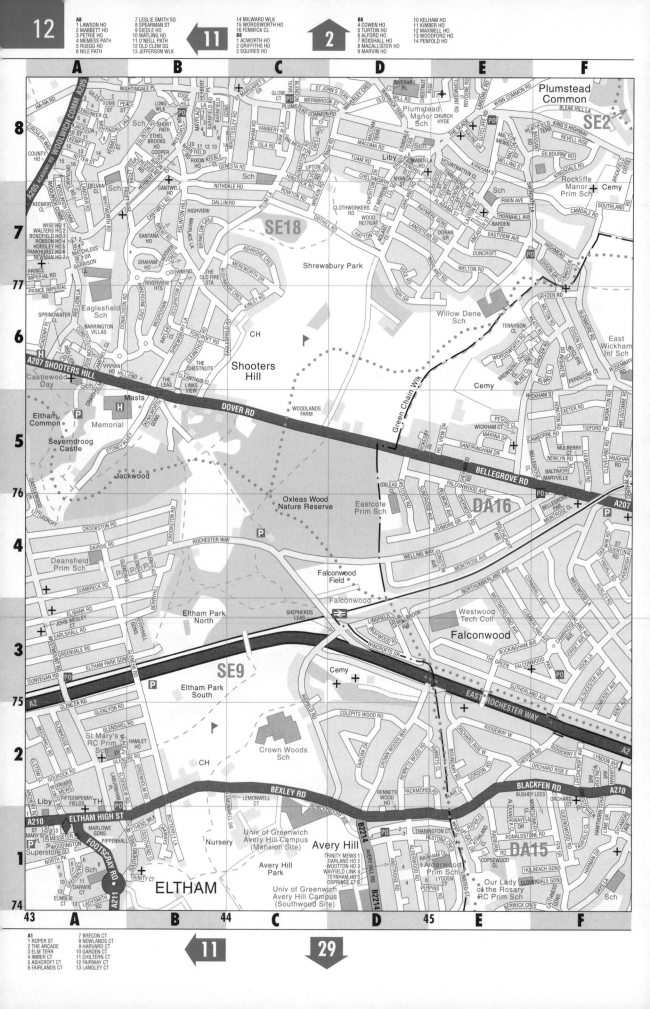

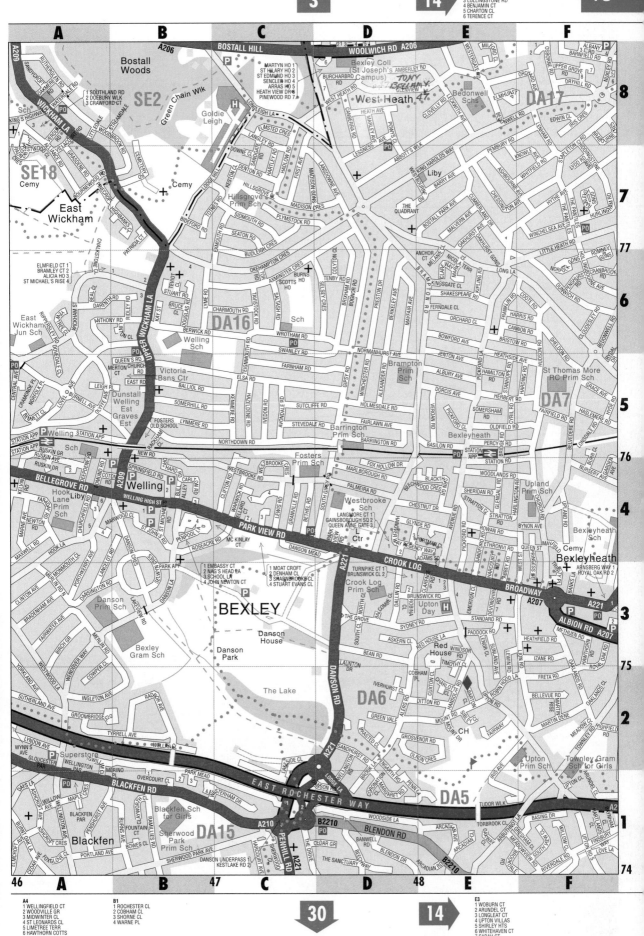

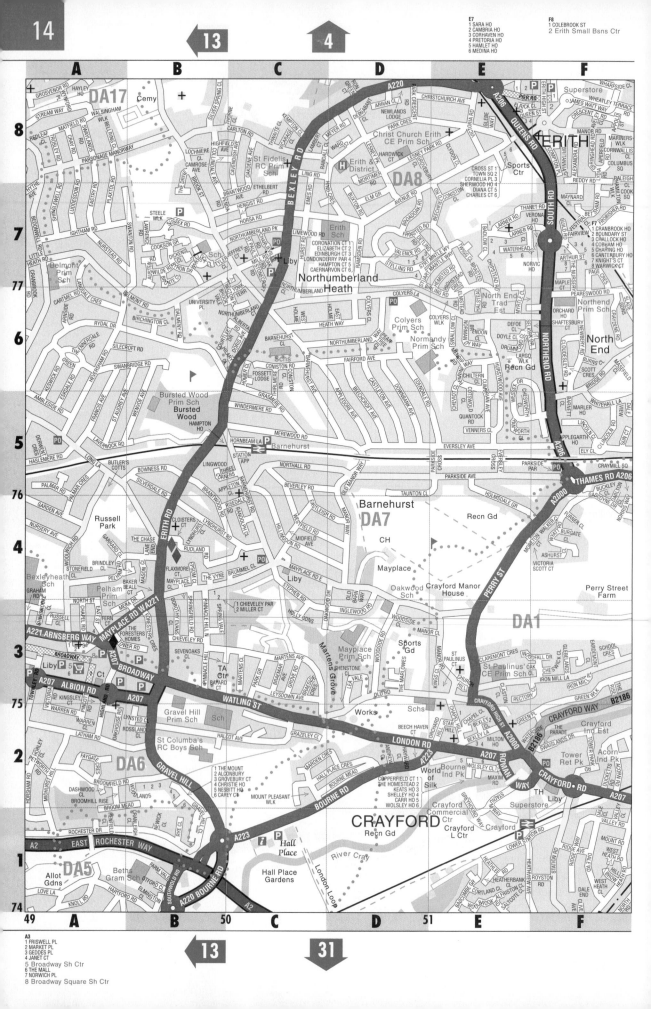

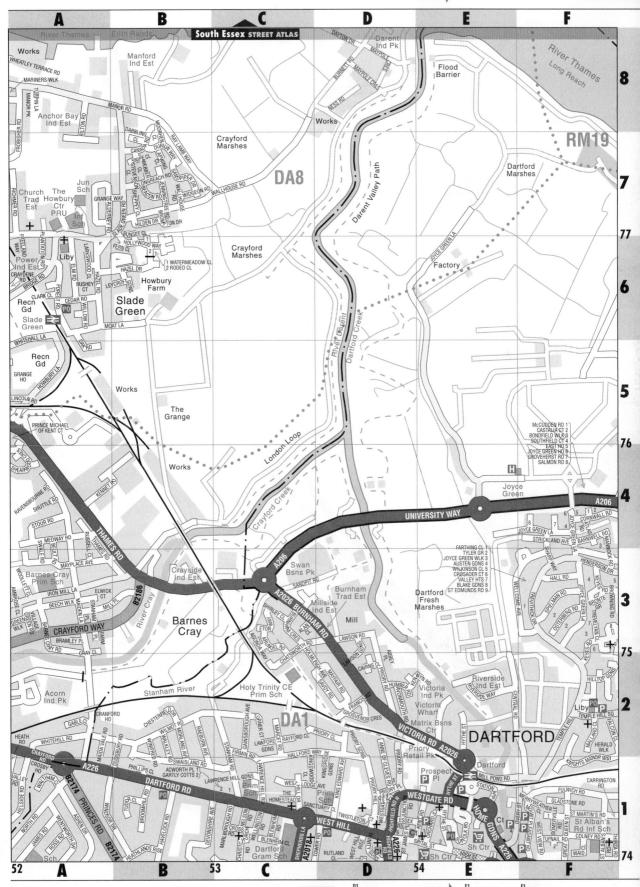

River Thames   Erith Rands

Works
Wheatley Terrace Rd
Mariners Wlk
Turpin La
Manor Pk
Frobisher Rd
Richmer Rd

Anchor Bay Ind Est
Manor Rd
Manford Ind Est

Crayford Marshes

DA8

River Thames Long Reach

RM19

8

Dartford Marshes

7

77

Church Trad Est
The Howbury Ctr PRU
Jun Sch
Inf Sch
Grange Way
Alderney Rd
Hilden Dr
Crayford Marshes
Darent Valley Path

Flood Barrier

Power Ind Est
Fleetland Way
Plantation Rd
Craydene Rd
Bridge Rd
Liby
Larkswood Cl
Hazel Rd
Leycroft Gdns
Willow Rd
1 Watermeadow Cl
2 Rodeo Cl
Howbury Farm

Slade Green

Factory

6

Recn Gd
Slade Green
Whitehall La
Recn Gd
Grange Ho
Howbury La
Lincoln Rd
Oak Rd
Moat La

Works

River Darent
Dartford Creek

McCudden Rd 1
Castalia Ct 2
Bondfield Wlk 3
Southfield Ct 4
East Ho 5
Joyce Green Ho 6
Groveherst Rd 7
Salmon Rd 8

76

Prince Michael of Kent Ct
Shears
Ravensbourne Rd
Shuttle Rd
Stour Rd
Medway Rd
Swale Rd
Kennet Rd

The Grange

Works

London Loop

Joyce Green

H

A206

5

Thames Rd
Russell Cl
Mayplace Ave
Woolley Cl
Iron Mill La
Ambrose Cl
Greenland Wlk
Village Green Row
Barnes Cray Rd
Cray Cl

Barnes Cray Prim Sch

B2186

River Cray

Crayford Way

Bramley Pl

Crayside Ind Est

Crayford Creek

A206

Swan Bsns Pk
Sandpit Rd
Shirley Cl
Eton
Arundel Rd
Chatsworth Rd
Laburnum Way
Burnham Trad Est
Millside Rd
Mill
Lawson Rd

A2026 BURNHAM RD

Dartford Fresh Marshes

FARTHING CL 1
TYLER GR 2
JOYCE GREEN WLK 3
AUSTEN GDNS 4
WILKINSON CL 5
CRUSADER CT 6
VALLEY HTS 7
BLAKE GDNS 8
ST EDMUNDS RD 9

Joyce Green La
Strickland Ave
Cornwall Rd
Barnwell Rd
Mannock Rd
Sharp Way
Henderson Dr
Keyes Rd
Hall Rd
Bronte
Ostlesberg Rd
Spielman Rd
Wellcome Ave

4

3

75

Barnes Cray

Acorn Ind Pk

Stanham River

Holy Trinity CE Prim Sch

Cranford Ho
Gable Cl

Cairns Rd
Priory Rd
Abbey Rd
Royal Eagle Cl
Mayfair Rd
Savoy Rd
Francis Rd
Grosvenor Cres

Victoria Ind Pk
Victoria Wharf
Matrix Bsns Ctr

Riverside Ind Est
Riverside Way
Central Rd

Liby
Temple Hill Sq
Temple Hill
Mallard Rd
Herald Rd

Hilltop Gdns

2

Heath Rd
Whitehill Rd
Crayford Way
Crosby Rd
Maida Vale Rd
Duckworth Rd
B2174

A226
Phillips Cl

DARTFORD RD

DA1

Chesterfield Dr
Wilmot Rd
Morland Ave
Walkley Rd
Winifred Rd
Swaisland Rd
Gartly Cotts 2
Acworth Pl 1
Lawrence Hill Gdns
Prim Sch
Gainsborough Ave
Turner Rd
Rayburn Ave
Firmin Rd
Lawford Gdns
Rayford Cl
Kingsbridge Gdns
Kingsdown Rd
West Lodge Ave
The Homestead
Sanctuary Cl
King Edward Ave
Priory Gdns
Anne of Cleves Rd
Priory Rd
Hyde St
Umber Rd

VICTORIA RD A2026

Priory Retail Pk
Prospect Pl
P

DARTFORD

Mill Pond Rd
Dartford Station
Home Gdns
Carrington Rd
Fulwich Rd
Gladstone Rd
Merryweather Cl
Somerville Rd
St Martin's Rd
Knights Manor Way

1

Valley
Witham
Heathlands Rise
Sch
Hillside Rd
North Rd
James Rd
Ross Rd
Ashen Dr
Wentworth Dr
B2174
Princes Rd

B2174
Tudor Rd
Broomhill Rd
Havelock Rd
Devonshire Ave
Marlborough Rd
Christchurch Rd
Cross Rd
Nelson Rd
Wellington Rd
West La
Blenheim Rd
Shepherds La
A2017
Dartford Gram Sch
PO
West Hill Rise
Rutland Rd
Twistleton Ct
Spital St
High St
A226
St James
Folk Rd
Sh Ctr
Spring Vale
Tufnail Rd
Colney Rd
St Alban's Rd Inf Sch
Great Queen St
Waid
St Alban's Rd

WEST HILL

WESTGATE RD

74

D1
1 ESSEX RD
2 CHADWICK CT
3 FROBISHER CT
4 CLEVES VIEW
5 PRIORY CT
6 WESTGATE HO

E1
1 THE CLOISTERS
2 COPPERFIELDS
3 BULLACE LA
4 CHURCH VIEW

F1
1 LAVINIA RD
2 LAMPLIGHTERS CL

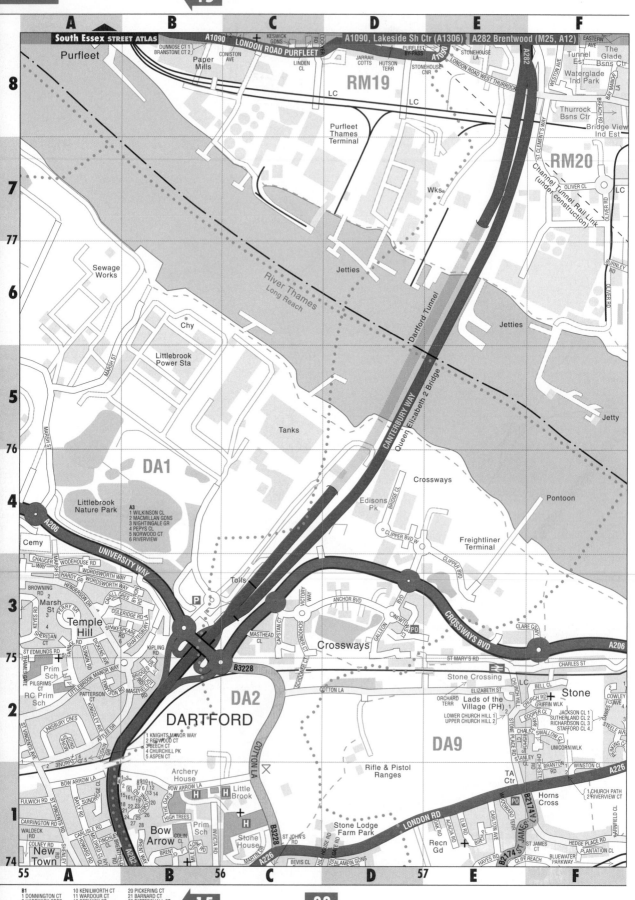

South Essex STREET ATLAS

Purfleet

A1090 DUNNOSE CT 1 KESWICK GDNS A1090, Lakeside Sh Ctr (A1306) A282 Brentwood (M25, A12) EASTERN AVE

LONDON ROAD PURFLEET BRANSTONE CT 2 PURFLEET BY-PASS LONDON ROAD WEST THURROCK STONEHOUSE LA Tunnel Est The Glade Bsns Ctr

CONISTON AVE Paper Mills LINDEN CL JARRAH COTTS HUTSON TERR STONEHOUSE CNR WESTON AVE Waterglade Ind Park BAY MANOR LA

RM19 Thurrock Bsns Ctr

Purfleet Thames Terminal LC LC **RM20** Bridge View Ind Est

ST CLEMENTS WAY OLIVER CL LC OLIVER RD

Channel Tunnel Rail Link (under construction) BURNLEY RD

Wks

Sewage Works Jetties

River Thames Long Reach Jetties

Chy Jetty

Littlebrook Power Sta

DA1 Tanks

Crossways

Littlebrook Nature Park Pontoon

A3 Edisons Pk

1 WILKINSON CL Freightliner Terminal

2 MACMILLAN GDNS

3 NIGHTINGALE GR BRIDGE CL CLIPPER BVD

Cemy 4 PEPYS CL CLIPPER BVD W

5 NORWOOD CT

6 RIVERVIEW

A206 UNIVERSITY WAY

CHAUCER L WAY WODEHOUSE RD WORDSWORTH WAY Tolls VICTORY WAY ANCHOR BVD NEWTOWN WAY CROSSWAYS BVD CLARE C WY A206

BROWNING RD HARDY GR HENDERSON CL MASTHEAD CL CAPSTAN CT SCHOONER WAY GALLEON BVD P O

MARSH ST COLERIDGE LA SHAKESPEARE RD KIPLING RD Crossways ST MARY'S RD CHARLES ST

Temple Hill DICKENS AVE DUNKIN RD BRIDGES RD B3228 Stone Crossing LC BELL CL Stone

ST EDMUNDS RD COTTON LA ELIZABETH ST CHURCH HILL COWLEY

Prim Sch LITTLEBROOK MANOR WAY MASEFIELD RD Lads of the GRIFFIN WLK JAMES ST AVE

PILGRIMS CT PATTERSON RD **DA2** ORCHARD TERR Village (PH) JACKSON CL 1 STEELE AVE

RC Prim Sch **DARTFORD** LOWER CHURCH HILL 1 SUTHERLAND CL 2

UPPER CHURCH HILL 2 RICHARDSON CL 3

1 KNIGHTS MANOR WAY SWALLOW CT STAFFORD CL 4

ST VINCENTS AVE 2 REDWOOD CT UNICORN WLK

3 BEECH CT **DA9**

4 CHURCHILL PK STANLEY RD BRANTON WINSTON CT

5 ASPEN CT Rifle & Pistol CHICHESTER RD A226

BOW ARROW LA Ranges TA Ctr B2174

FULWICH RD SUNDRIDGE BOW ARROW LA Horns Cross

Archery Little 1 CHURCH PATH

CARRINGTON RD High Trees House Brook Stone Lodge LONDON RD 2 RIVERVIEW CT

WALDECK RD Prim Farm Park ELM RD ST JAMES

COLNEY RD Bow Sch Stone B3228 PO CT HEDGE PLACE RD

New Town Arrow House ST JOHN'S CT Recn Gd PLANTATION RD

B202 A226 BEVIS CL B2174 ST JAMES CLIFF REACH BLUEWATER PARKWAY

B1
1 DONNINGTON CT 10 KENILWORTH CT 20 PICKERING CT
2 HARDWICK CRES 11 WARDOUR CT 21 BARNARD CT
3 DENNY CT 12 BERWICK CT 22 TATTERSHALL CT
4 BEESTON CT 13 CONISBOROUGH CT 23 CARISBROOKE CT
5 BROUGHAM CT 14 STOKESAY CT 24 BOWES CT
6 GRANGE CRES 15 PEVERIL CT 25 NORHAM CT
7 ORFORD CT 16 DUNSTER CT 26 MIDDLEHAM CT
8 ALNWICK CT 17 CALSHOT CT 27 PRUDHOE CT
9 BRAMBER CT 18 LYDFORD CT 28 BRIDGE CT
19 LONGTOWN CT

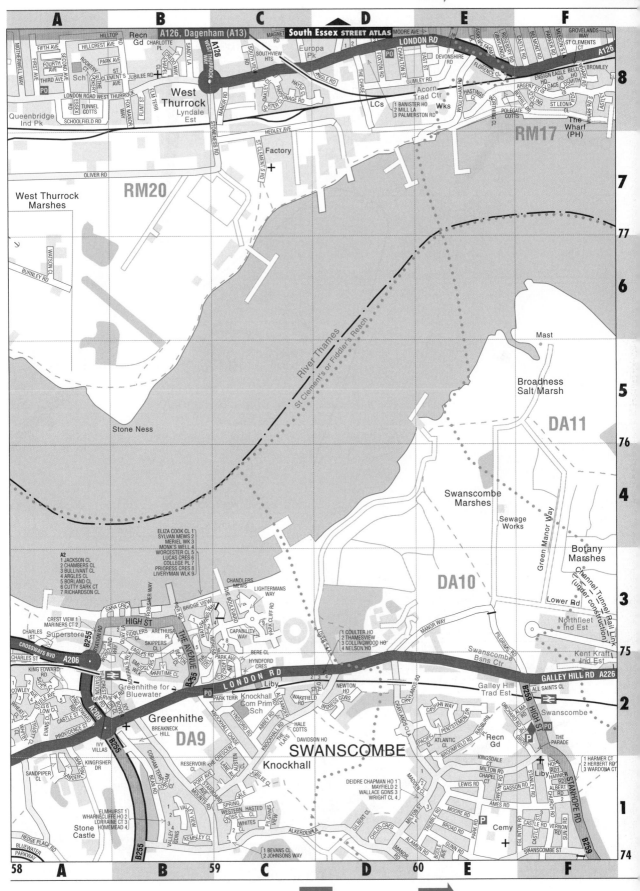

A B C D E F

A126, Dagenham (A13)

South Essex STREET ATLAS

MOORE AVE

LONDON RD

GROVELANDS WAY

ST CLEMENTS CT

A126

8

West Thurrock
Lyndale Est

RM17

The Wharf (PH)

Queenbridge Ind Pk

RM20

7

West Thurrock Marshes

77

BURNLEY RD

6

River Thames

St Clement's or Fiddler's Reach

Stone Ness

Mast

Broadness Salt Marsh

DA11

5

76

Swanscombe Marshes

4

Sewage Works

Botany Marshes

DA10

Green Manor Way

Channel Tunnel Rail Link (under construction)

Lower Rd

Northfleet Ind Est

3

ELIZA COOK CL 1
SYLVAN MEWS 2
MERIEL WK 3
MONK'S WELL 4
WORCESTER CL 5
LUCAS CRES 6
COLLEGE PL 7
PRIORESS CRES 8
LIVERYMAN WLK 9

A2
1 JACKSON CL
2 CHAMBERS CL
3 BULLIVANT CL
4 ARGLES CL
5 BORLAND CL
6 CUTTY SARK CT
7 RICHARDSON CL

CHANDLERS MEWS

LIGHTERMANS WAY

Kent Kraft Ind Est

75

HIGH ST

Superstore

Swanscombe Bsns Ctr

GALLEY HILL RD A226

Galley Hill Trad Est

Swanscombe

2

Greenhithe for Bluewater

LONDON RD

1 COULTER HO
2 THAMESVIEW
3 COLLINGWOOD HO
4 NELSON HO

Knockhall Com Prim Sch

DA9

Greenhithe

SWANSCOMBE

Knockhall

1 HARMER CT
2 HERBERT RD
3 WARDONA CT

Cemy

1

DEIDRE CHAPMAN HO 1
MAYFIELD 2
WALLACE GDNS 3
WRIGHT CL 4

Stone Castle

1 ELMHURST 1
WHARNECLIFFE HO 2
LORRAINE CT 3
HOMEMEAD 4

BLUEWATER PARKWAY

1 BEVANS CL
2 JOHNSONS WAY

SWANSCOMBE ST

74

58 A B 59 C D 60 E F

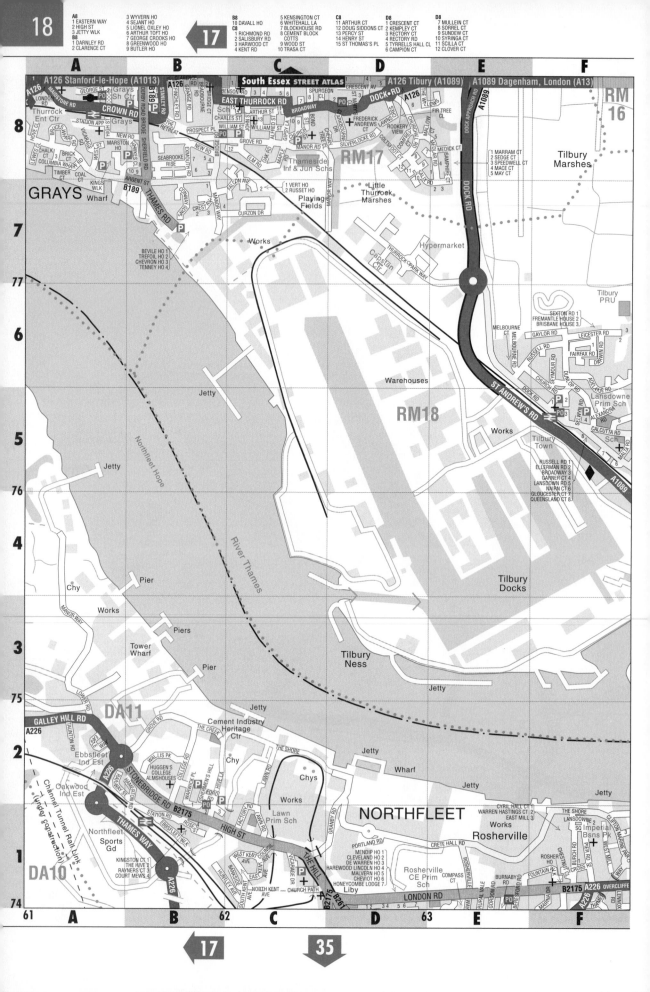

17

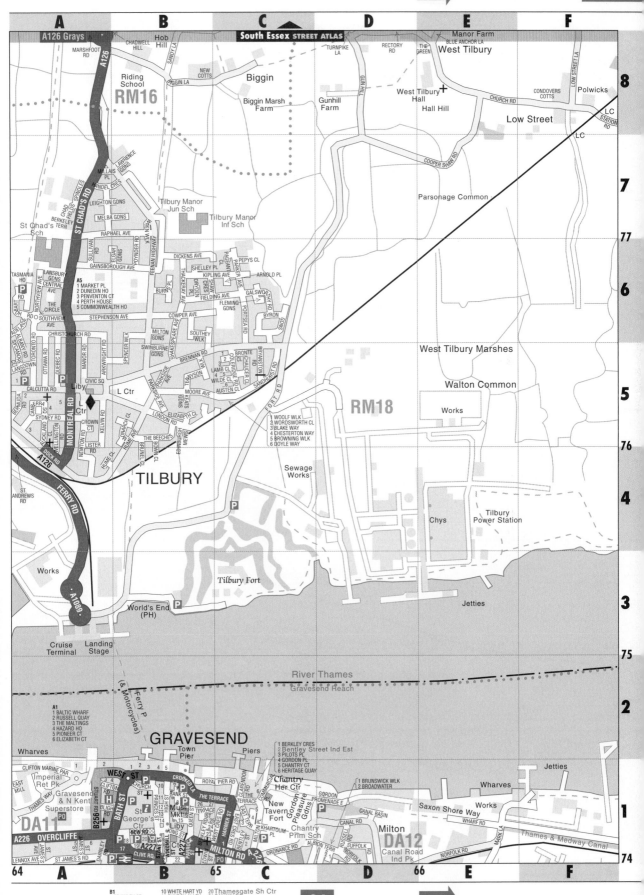

A126 Grays

South Essex STREET ATLAS

RM16

TILBURY

RM18

GRAVESEND

West Tilbury

Low Street

Parsonage Common

West Tilbury Marshes

Walton Common

Tilbury Power Station

Jetties

Tilbury Fort

World's End (PH)

Cruise Terminal

Landing Stage

River Thames
Gravesend Reach

DA11

DA12

Milton

B1
1 CRAWLEY CT
2 MARRIOTTS WHARF
3 REGENTS CT
4 MELBOURNE QUAY
5 TOWN PIER SQ
6 BULL YD
7 HORN YD
8 NEW SWAN YD
9 MARKET ALLEY
10 WHITE HART YD
11 CHURCH ALLEY
12 JURY ST
13 GLOBE YD
14 CHASE SQ
15 BREWHOUSE YD
16 VINE CT
17 BARRACK ROW
18 GARRICK ST
19 ANGLESEA PL
20 Thamesgate Sh Ctr
21 RAILWAY PL
22 MANOR RD
23 WILFRED ST
24 BERNARD ST
25 THE TERRACE
26 ST ANDREWS CT
27 CROSS ST

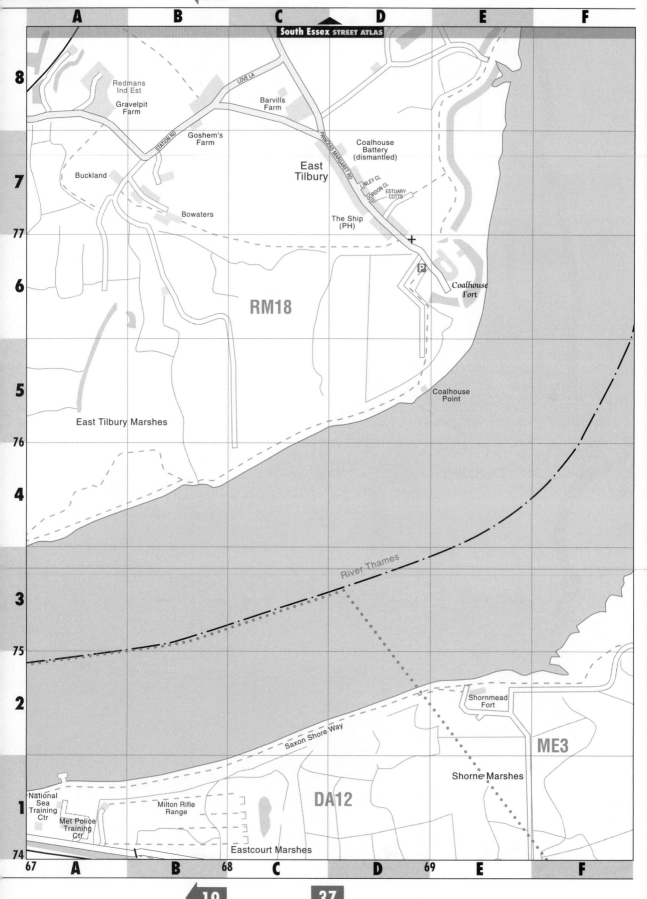

South Essex STREET ATLAS

A   **B**   **C**   **D**   **E**   **F**

8

Redmans
Ind Est

Gravelpit
Farm

LOVE LA

Barvills
Farm

STATION RD

Goshem's
Farm

Buckland

7

East
Tilbury

PRINCESS MARGARET RD

Coalhouse
Battery
(dismantled)

LINLEY CL
GORDON CL
ESTUARY
COTTS

Bowaters

The Ship
(PH)

77

+

P

Coalhouse
Fort

6

RM18

Coalhouse
Point

5

East Tilbury Marshes

76

4

River Thames

3

Shornmead
Fort

75

2

Saxon Shore Way

ME3

Shorne Marshes

National
Sea
Training
Ctr

Milton Rifle
Range

DA12

1

Met Police
Training
Ctr

Eastcourt Marshes

74
67   **A**   **B**   **68**   **C**   **D**   **69**   **E**   **F**

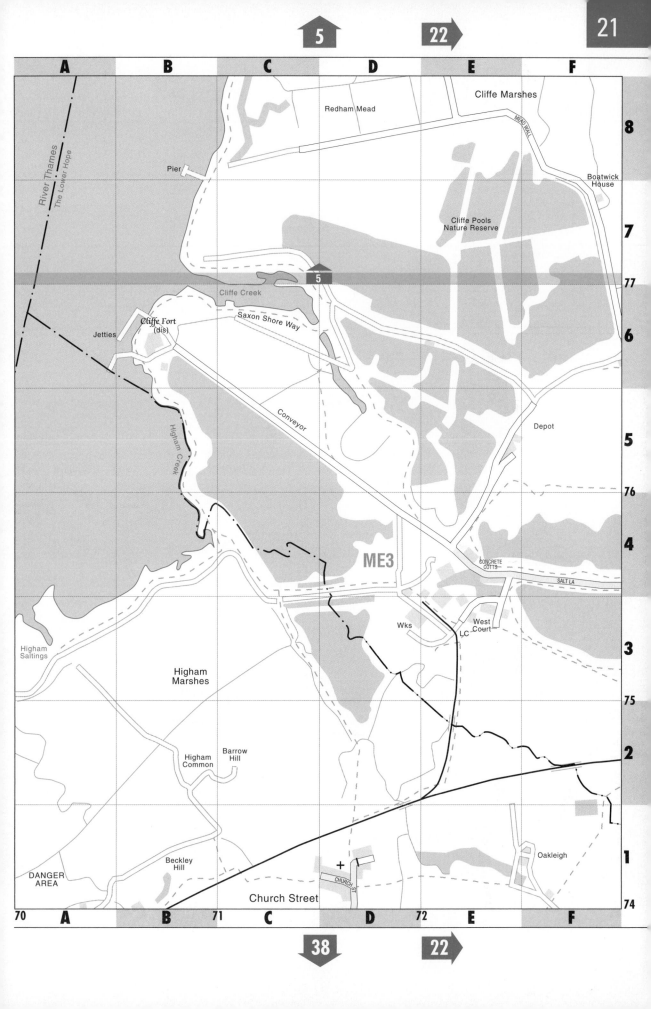

8

Cliffe Marshes

Redham Mead

MEAD WALL

Boatwick House

Pier

River Thames
The Lower Hope

Cliffe Pools
Nature Reserve

7

77

Cliffe Creek

Saxon Shore Way

Cliffe Fort
(dis)

Jetties

6

Higham Creek

Conveyor

Depot

5

76

4

ME3

CONCRETE COTTS

SALT LA

Wks

West Court

LC

Higham Saltings

3

75

Higham Marshes

Barrow Hill

2

Higham Common

DANGER AREA

Beckley Hill

Oakleigh

1

CHURCH ST

Church Street

74

21
6

A B C D E F

8

7

Farthing Wall

Ryestreet Common

77

6

Ham Wall

Pickle's Way

Common Wall

6

Mead Wall

Pond Hill

Church Cl

Marsh La

Glen La

Wharf La

Thorn

Reed St

Thames Terr

PO

B2000

Miskin Cotts

Common La

Mast Allen's Hill

Buttway La

Rookery Cres

Swingate Ave

Shepherd's

Ryestreet Farm

Marshgate

Cliffe Ct

Old Fld

Quickrells Ave

Saxon Shore Way

Cooling

Manor Farm

Wadlands Rd

Rookery Lodge

Cooling Castle Farm

Pip's View

West Street

Church St

St Helens Rd

Chancery Rd

Cliffe

ME3

Cooling Castle

Main Rd

Horseshoe and Castle Inn

5

Chesterton Rd

West Street Farm

Turner St

St Helens CE Prim Sch

76

Millcroft Rd

New Rd

Restmore Cl

Norwood Cl

Cooling Rd

Berry Court Farm

Mount Pleasant

4

Higham Rd

Symonds Rd

Morning Cross Cotts

Redbarn

Salt La

Station Rd

Well Penn Rd

Newlands Farm

Gattons Farm

Cooling Court Farm

3

75

Rectory Rd

Alma House

The Rectory

2

Buckland Farm

South Bank

Cooling Street

New Barn Farm

Buckland Rd

The Grange

Town Rd

Perry Hill

Cooling St

Bell Farm

Castfield Cl

Spendiff Farm

1

Perry Hill Farm

Mortimers Farm

B2000

Rough Shaw

74

73 A B 74 C D 75 E F

21
39

The Mean

Cooling Marshes

Swigshole

Old Sea Wall

Decoy Fleet

Buckland Marshes

Buckland Fleet

Decoy Farm

Whalebone Marshes

7

Masts

Eastborough Farm

Saxon Shore Way

Northward Hill

DECOY HILL RD

Bromhey Farm

Northward Hill Nature Reserve

Clinchstreet Farm

MAIN RD

Childs Farm

Eastborough Bungalow

Buckhole Farm

ME3

MARSH CRES

P

NORTHWOOD AVE

THAMES AVE

LONGFIELD AVE

MEDWAY AVE

WILLOWBANK DR

LIPWELL HILL

BUCKHOLE FARM RD

HARRISON DR

EDEN RD

VALENTINE DR

DRAYTON CL

GOODWOOD CL

RUNGLES CL

TIPLEY DR

THE LEYS

HOLMES CL

JOSH CL

BRITANNIA RD

COOLING RD

High Halstow Prim Sch

THE STREET

NORTHFALL AVE

High Halstow

Dalham Farm

FORGE LA

PH

ST MARGARET'S CT

PO

CARDIGAN CL

GIPSY WAY

HILL FARM CL

CHRISTMAS LA

LC

WYBOURNES LA

Wybournes Farm

Ducks Court

DUX COURT RD

Solomon's Farm

Lodge Hill Wood

Wybornes Wood

RATCLIFFE HIGHWAY A228

A228

76   A   B   77   C   D   78   E   F   74

23
8

A **B** **C** **D** **E** **F**

8

7

77

6

Ramsgreen

Ross
Farm

Moat Farm Rd

Moat
Farm

St Mary Hoo

ROSE
COTTS

Noreland
Cottage

SHAKESPEARE FARM RD

COOMBE FARM LA

Refuse
Tip

Coombe
House

Mayland

Little Owls

HOOPERS LA

5

Newlands
Farm

NEW ARDS FARM RD

ME3

ST MARY'S

RATCLIFFE HIGHWAY

HALL RD

+

76

Walnut Tree
Farm

CLINCH ST

Saxon Shore Way

Bell
Wood

Fenn Bell Inn
(PH)

4

Fenn
Street

FENN ST

BELLWOOD CT

Malmaynes
Hall Farm

JACKSON'S
CNR

BRITANNIA RD

Fenn
Farm

Turkey Hall
Farm

MALMAYNES HALL RD

A228

3

Fisher's
Wood

SHARNAL ST

New Barn
Farm

75

CHRISTMAS LA

RATCLIFFE HIGHWAY

PARBROOK RD

Parbrook
House

2

A228

SHARNAL ST

ROPER'S GREEN LA

Tudor
Farm

1

Sharnal
Street

Cold
Arbour

North
Street

STOKE RD

North Street
Farm

74

Tunbridge
Hill

79 **A** **B** **80** **C** **D** **81** **E** **F**

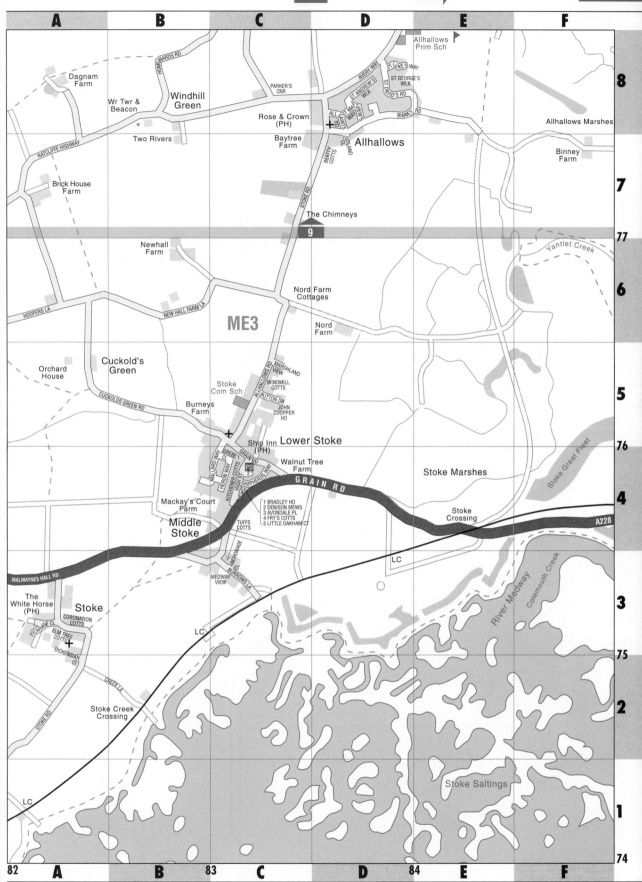

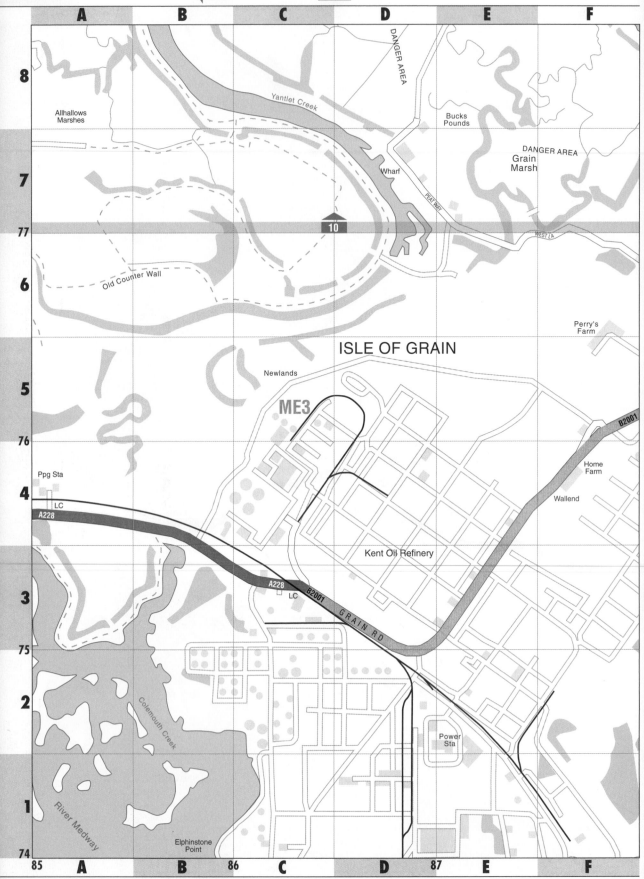

A B C D E F

8

River Thames

Grain Spit

7

The Flats

77

DANGER AREA

Rose Court
Farm

Works

P

B2001

Grain

St James'
CE Prim Sch

6

WEST LA

PINNELL RD
LEVETT CL
FRY CL
PO
PH

HIGH ST

PINTAIL CL
GREEN RD
ST JAMES
CL
TEAL CL

5

EDINBURGH RD

GRAIN RD

CORONATION RD
URBANE AVE
CHAPEL RD
PUFFIN RD

SHELLDRAKE CL

COASTGUARD
COTTS

Grain
Tower

76

CORINTHIAN
CT

LAPWING RD
RIVENDELL CL
CHAPEL RD
SEAVIEW

SMITHFIELD RD

Whitehouse
Farm

ME3

East Kent STREET ATLAS

POWER STATION RD

PORT VICTORIA RD

Garrison
Point

4

Smithfield
Marshes

LB
Sta

GARRISON RD

SLIPWAY RD

BOATHOUSE
RD

ANCHOR LA

Chy

Grain Power
Station

Docks

SHEERNESS

STOREHOUSE
WHARF

3

Jetty

Sheerness
Harbour Est

GREAT BASIN RD

75

2

House Fleet

River Medway

Piers

ME12

Jetty

Cockleshell
Hard

1

The
Lappel

Horseshoe
Point

74

88 A B 89 C D 90 E F

A8
1 WILDWOOD CL
2 ROWAN CT
3 SWALLOW CT
4 HONEYSUCKLE CT
5 ST MILDREDS RD
6 HARROGATE CT

7 LINCHMERE RD
8 WAITE DAVIES RD
9 SUMMERFIELD ST
10 ASKHAM LODGE
11 SYON LODGE
12 CHERITON CT

B5
1 GILLAN CT
2 NAPIER CT
3 OAKCROFT
4 ST JOSEPHS CT
5 HOLM CT
6 ROTHESAY CT

7 CANTERBURY CT
8 CHINBROOK CRES
9 BOLLON CT
10 CAMERON TERR

C5
1 BROOK CT
2 PARK VIEW CT
3 LINCOLN CT
4 MERRYFIELD HO
5 PAXTON CT

11

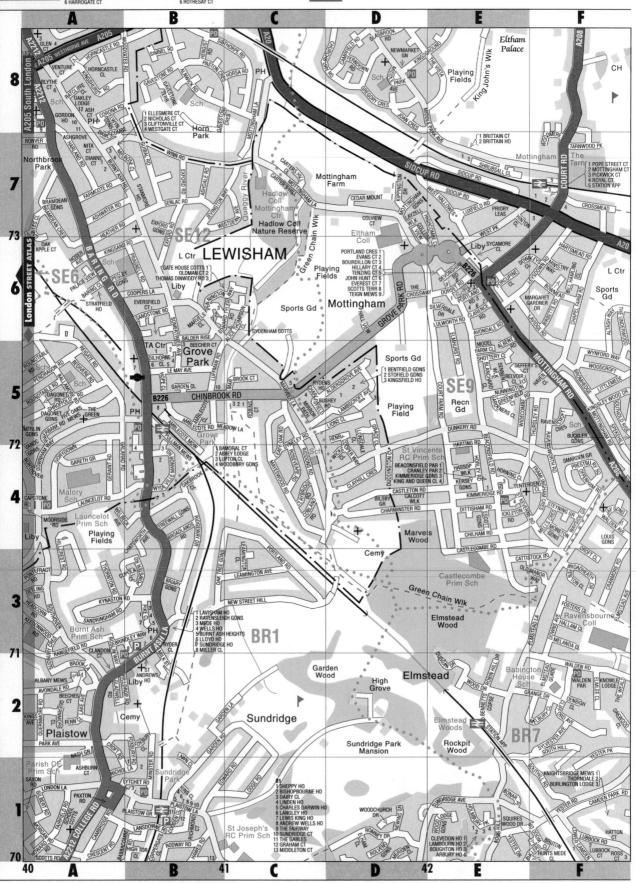

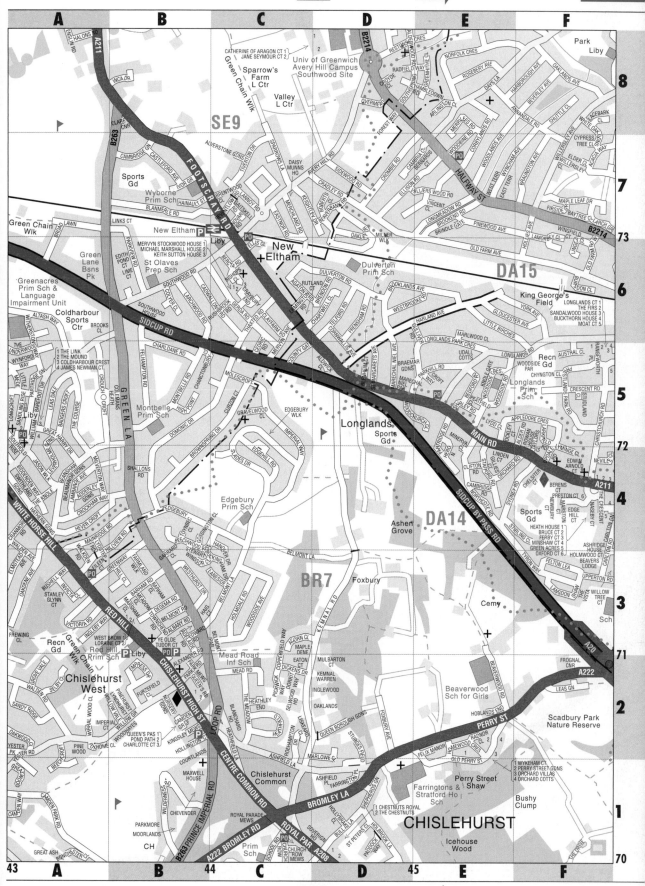

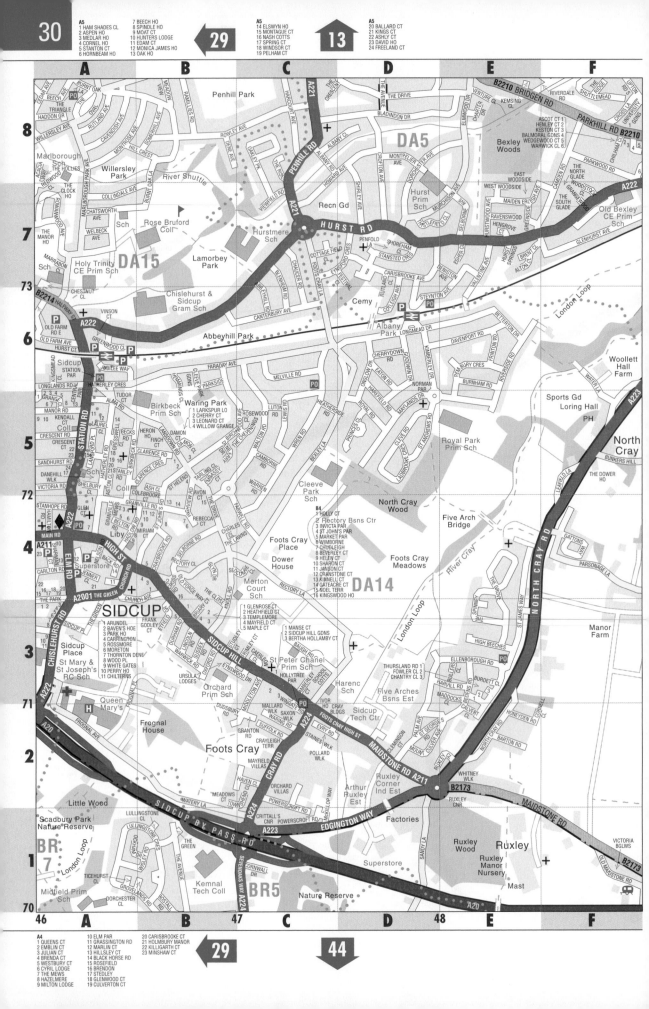

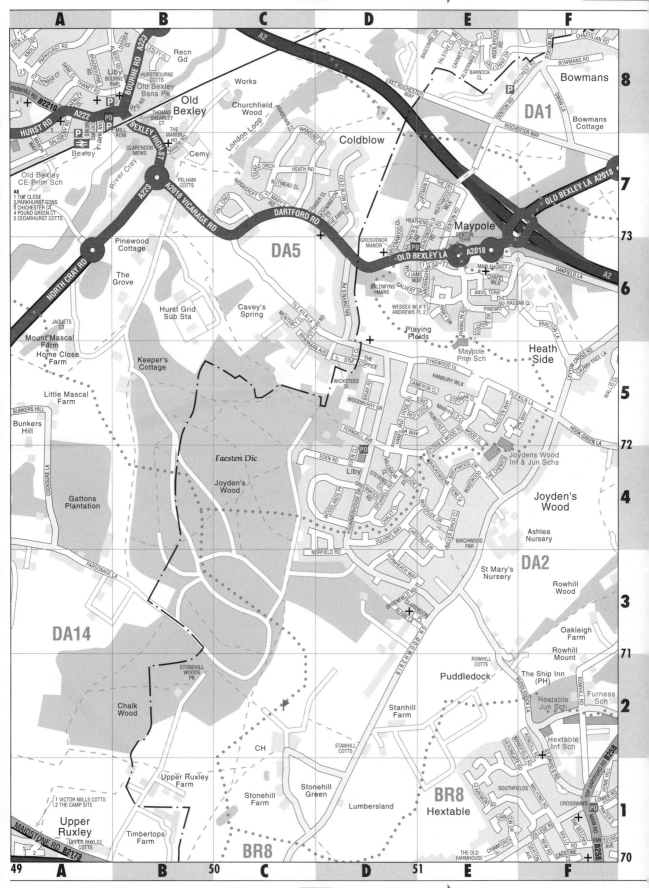

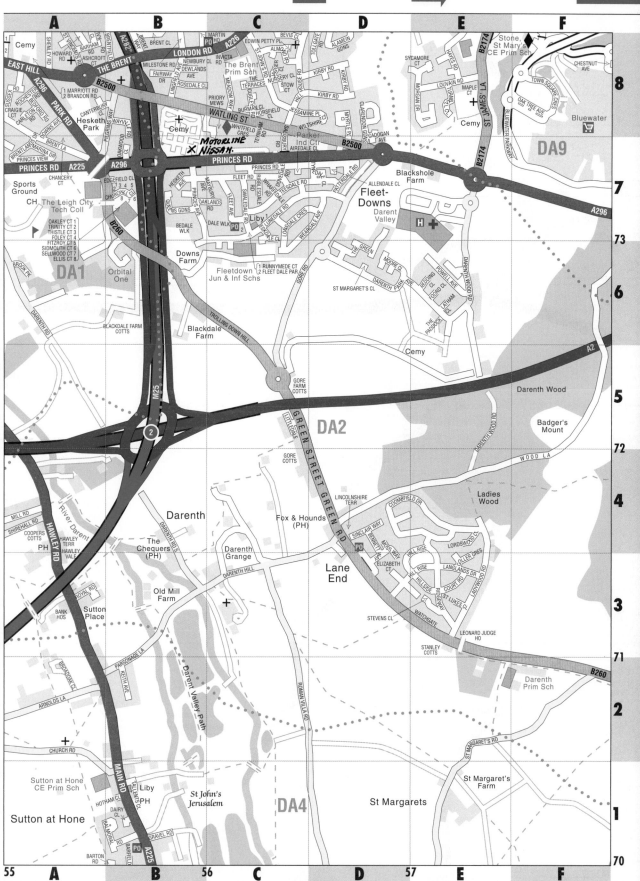

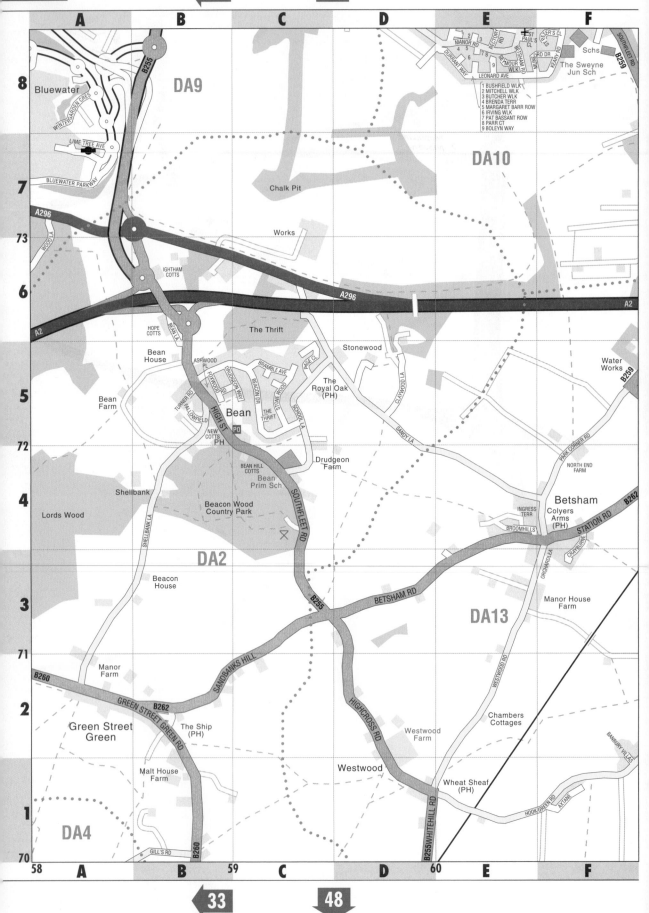

DA9

Bluewater

WINTERGARDEN CRES
LIME TREE AVE
BLUEWATER PARKWAY
WOOD LA

B255

A296

A2

Chalk Pit

Works

DA10

MANOR RD
RECTORY RD
ST PAUL'S CL
DEXTER'S CL
BETSHAM RD
SOUTHFLEET RD
KEARY RD
DURRANT WAY
LEONARD AVE
MOUR WLK
KENTON

Schs

The Sweyne
Jun Sch

1 BUSHFIELD WLK
2 MITCHELL WLK
3 BUTCHER WLK
4 BRENDA TERR
5 MARGARET BARR ROW
6 IRVING WLK
7 PAT BASSANT ROW
8 PARR CT
9 BOLEYN WAY

B259

IGHTHAM
COTTS

HOPE
COTTS

Bean
House

BEAN LA

The Thrift

Stonewood

CLAYWOOD LA

Water
Works

B259

Bean
Farm

ASHWOOD
PL
DRUDGEON WAY
FOXWOOD
TURNER RD
FALLOWFIELD
BRAMBLE AVE
STONE WOOD
BEACON DR
PAGE CL
THE
THRIFT
SCHOOL LA

The
Royal Oak
(PH)

SANDY LA

Bean

HIGH ST
PO

NEW
COTTS
PH

Drudgeon
Farm

PARR CORNER RD

NORTH END
FARM

Shellbank

SHELLBANK LA

BEAN HILL
COTTS
Bean
Prim Sch

SOUTHFLEET RD

Betsham

Colyers
Arms
(PH)

B262

Lords Wood

Beacon Wood
Country Park

INGRESS
TERR
BROOMHILLS

STATION RD

ORCHARD DEA
CRAYBURNE

DA2

Beacon
House

B255

Betsham Rd

Manor House
Farm

DA13

Manor
Farm

B260

GREEN STREET GREEN RD

B262

SANDBANKS HILL

WESTWOOD RD

Chambers
Cottages

Green Street
Green

The Ship
(PH)

HIGHCROSS RD

Westwood
Farm

BANBURY VILLAS

Malt House
Farm

Westwood

Wheat Sheaf
(PH)

B255 WHITEHILL RD

HOOK GREEN RD

LEY LANE

DA4

GILL'S RD

B260

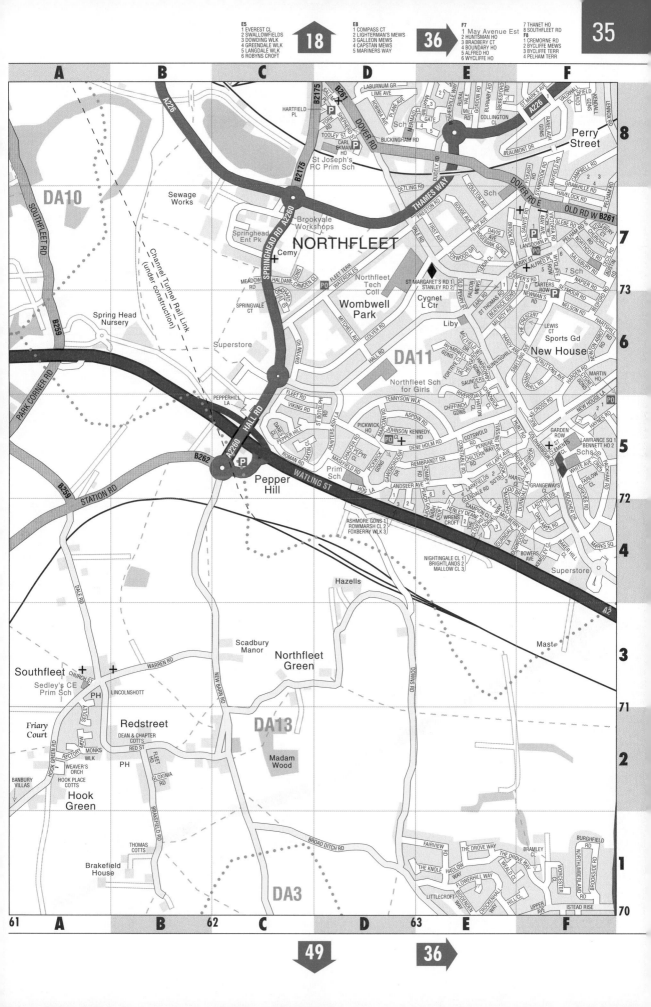

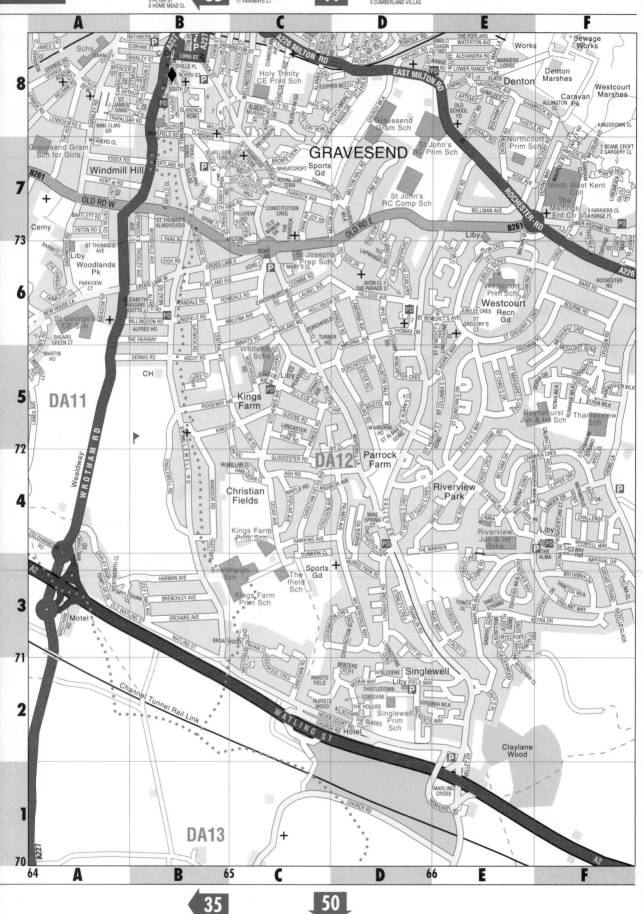

B8
1 CLAREMONT PL
2 LYDIA COTTS
3 VICTORIA AVE
4 WILLIAM HO
5 PETER ST
6 HOME MEAD CL

B8
7 HOMEMEAD
8 GRAVESHAM CT
9 PRESENTATION HO
10 ST ANDREW'S RD
11 FAIRWAYS CT

C8
1 WATERLOO ST
2 CHRIST CHURCH CRES
3 CHRIST CHURCH RD
4 MILTON RD BSNS PK
5 CUMBERLAND VILLAS

D8
1 BRUNSWICK WLK
2 CANAL ROAD IND PK
3 ELLERSLIE CT

35

19

35

50

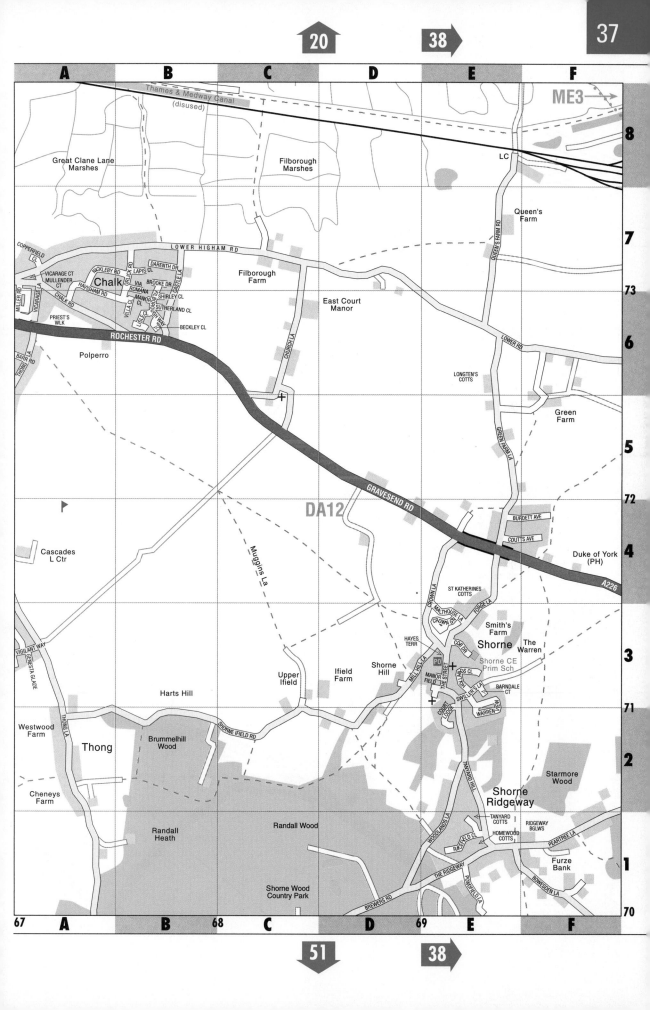

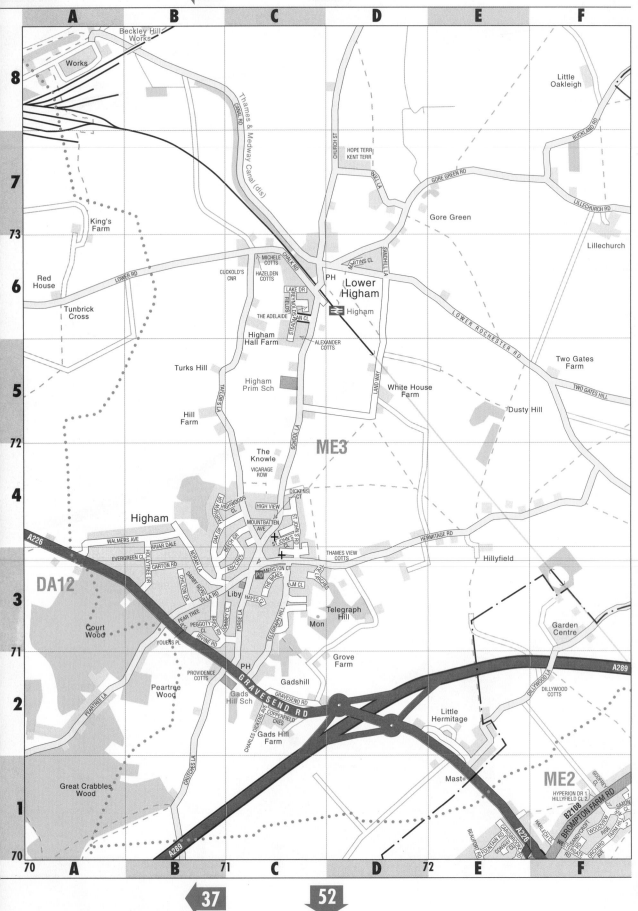

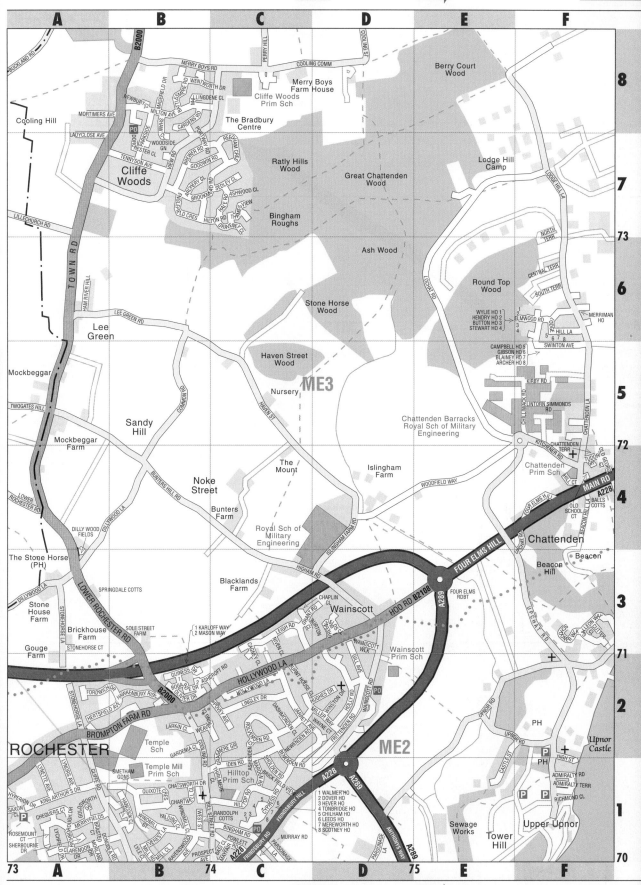

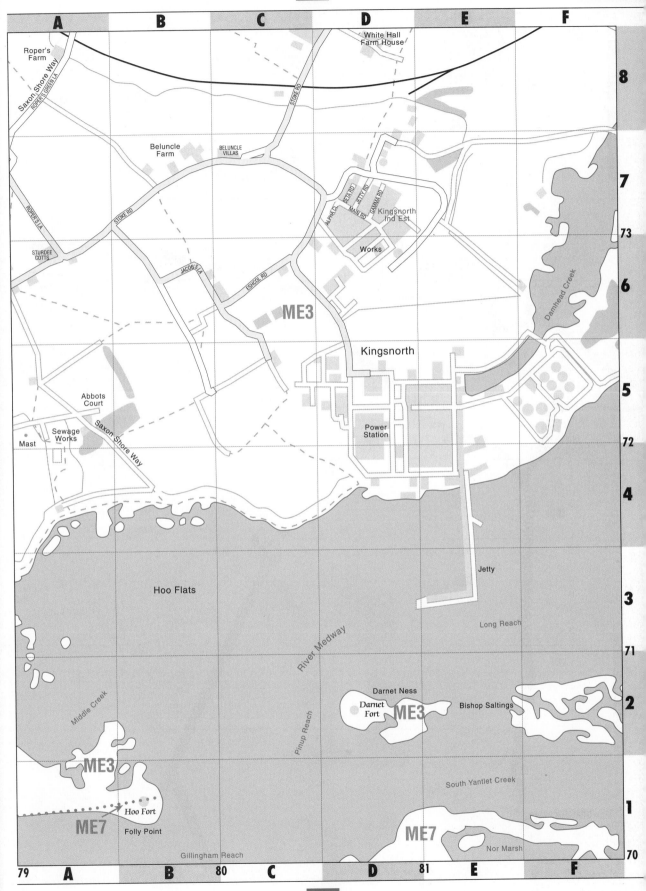

28

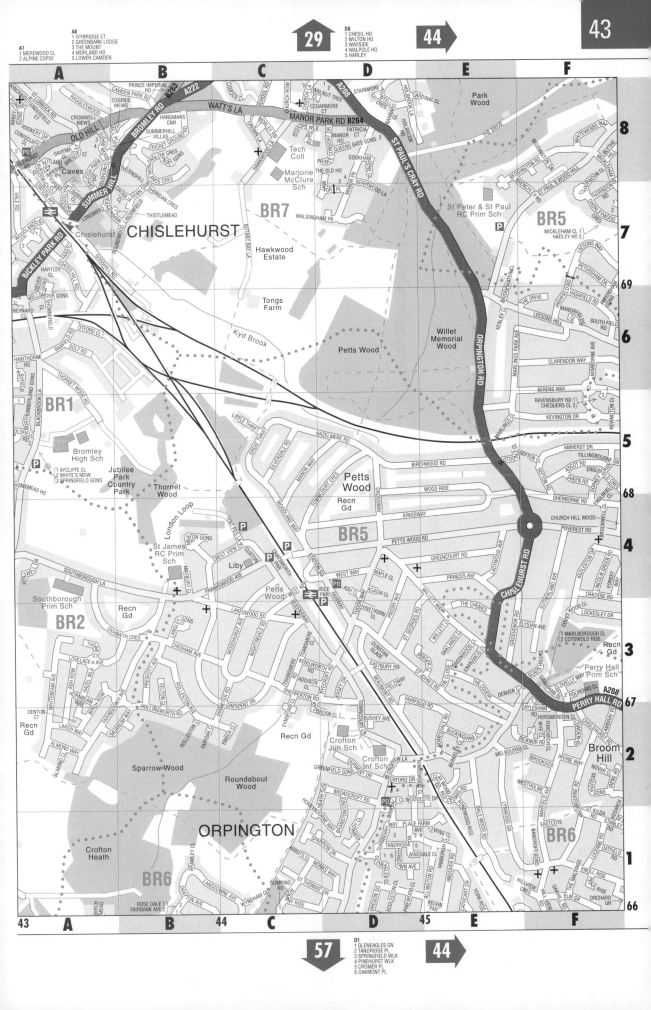

B7
1 SWANSCOMBE HO
2 HAVERSTOCK CT
3 ARRANDENE HO
4 BROOMFIELD HO
5 HEADLEY HO
6 KENLEY HO

7 LADYWELL HO
B6
1 SELWYN PL
2 LEIGH TERR
3 WOULDHAM TERR

← 43

C5
1 MOUNTFIELD WAY
2 HORTON TOWER
3 ELMSTONE TERR
4 TIDEBROOK CT
5 BELGRAVE CT
6 SANDWAY PATH

↑ 30

C5
7 HARBLEDOWN PL
8 BAPCHILD PL
9 ALKHAM TOWER
10 Orpington Trad Est
11 SYDNEY COTTS
12 CAERNARVON CT

C6
1 Sevenoaks Way Ind Est
2 Springvale Ret Pk

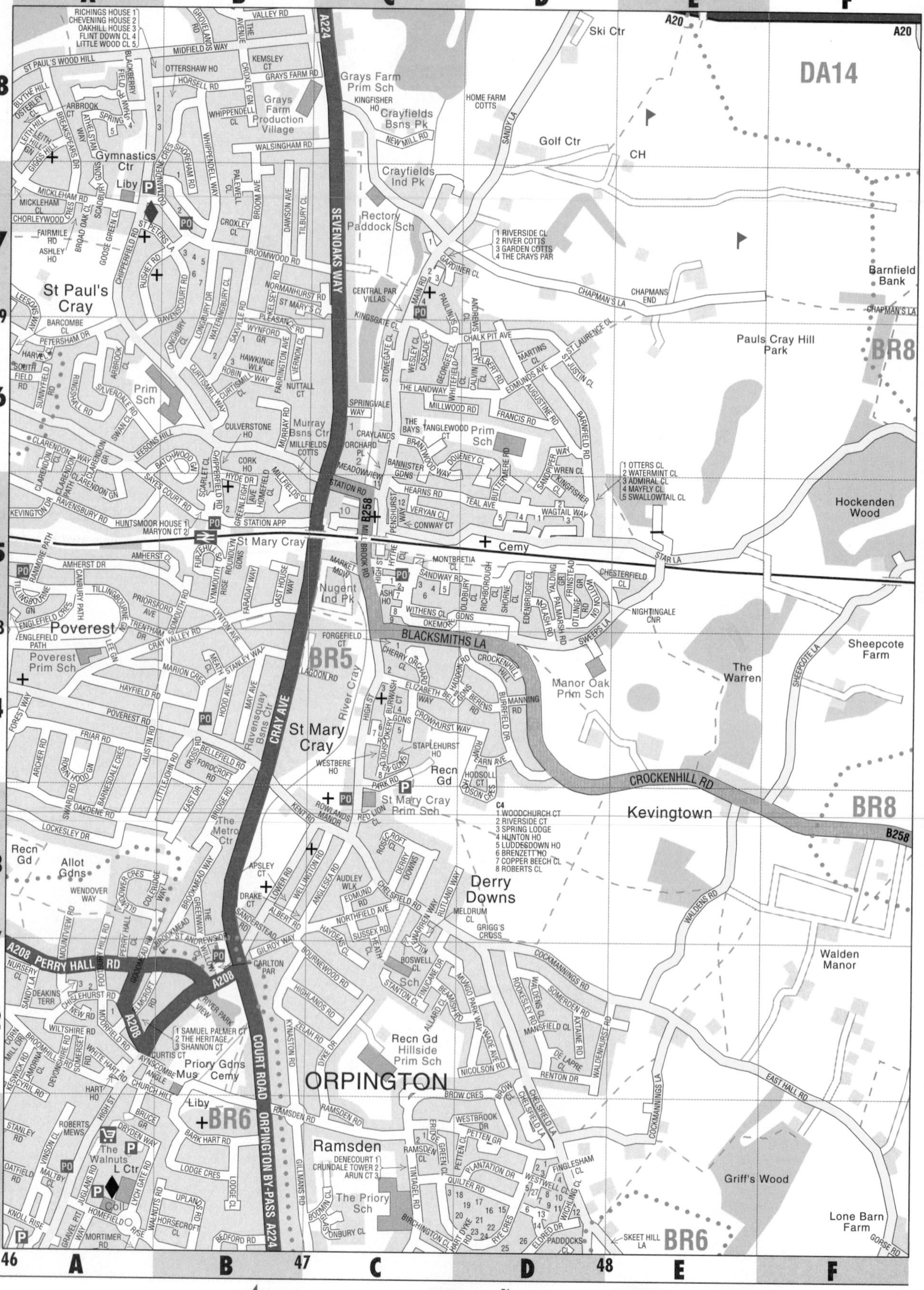

Grid columns: A B C D E F
Grid rows: 8 69 7 6 5 68 4 67 3 2 1 66

Principal labels:
DA14
BR8
St Paul's Cray
Poverest
St Mary Cray
BR5
Derry Downs
Kevingtown
BR8
ORPINGTON
Ramsden
BR6
The Warren
Hockenden Wood
Sheepcote Farm
Walden Manor
Griff's Wood
Lone Barn Farm
Pauls Cray Hill Park
Barnfield Bank

← 43   58 →

D1
1 BREDGAR HO
2 WITTERSHAM HO
3 CHALLOCK HO
4 HOLLINGBOURNE TOWER
5 THURNHAM HO
6 PECKHAM HO
7 STOCKBURY HO
8 EASTLING HO
9 NEWINGTON HO
10 FAWKHAM HO
11 HOUGHAM HO
12 BEKESBOURNE TOWER
13 LENHAM HO
14 LAMBERHURST CL
15 LODDEN HO
16 KENNETT CT
17 EDEN CT
18 CUCKMERE CT
19 DARENTH CT
20 MEDWAY CT
21 MEON CT
22 STOUR CT
23 RAVENSBOURNE CT
24 ROTHER CT
25 RYE FIELD
26 BOX TREE WLK
27 WALTHAM CL

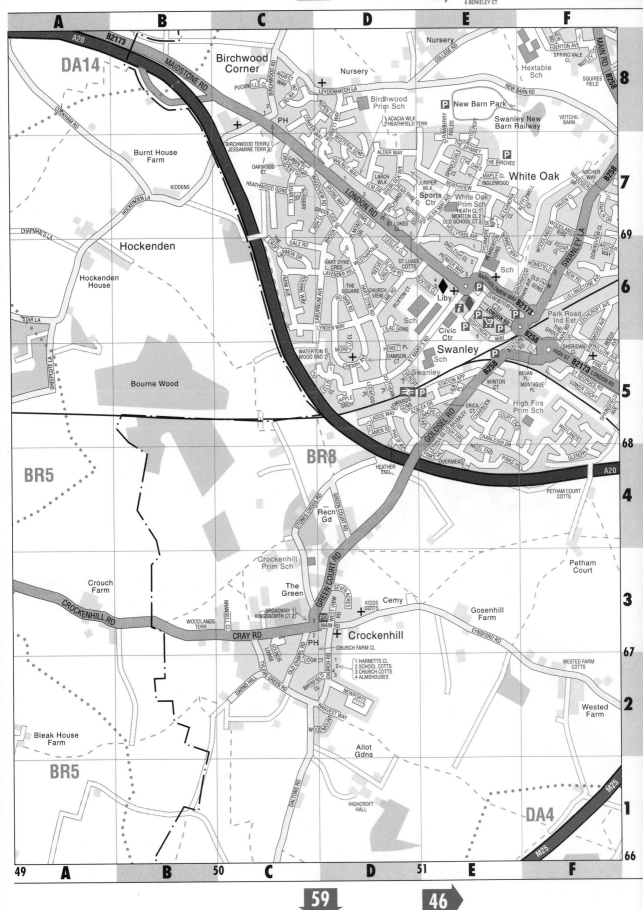

31

46
E6
1 WHITEOAK CT
2 KENNET CT
3 WHITE OAK SQ
4 ST ANDREW'S CT
5 RUXTON CT
6 BERKELEY CT

45

45
32

A **B** **C** **D** **E** **F**

8

VICTORIA HILL RD
MILLBRO
SQUIRES FIELD
Highlands Farm
St Paul's CE Prim Sch
HOGS ORCH
ANTHONYS LA
THE STAPLES
ELM COTTS
SCHOOL LA
HOTHM CL
The Red Lion (PH)
GILDENHILL RD
CHURCH RD
SHIP LA
M25

HIGHLANDS HILL
B258
MAIN RD
SWANLEY LA
FIVE VENTS
SWANLEY VILLAGE RD
WOOD ST
SHIP LA

Swanley Village

7

B258
ARCHER WAY
PARK LA
Ram's Wood

Homefield Farm

69

LEECHCROFT AVE
BEECHEN LA LA

Canada Heights

6

BEECH AVE
Downsview Prim Sch
THE ANNEX
Parkwood Hall Sch

HILLSIDE CT
WILLOW AVE
WEST VIEW RD
SOUTHVIEW CL
L Ctr
Farningham Wood (Nature Reserve)
P
P
CALFSTOCK LA

5

B2173
HIGH CROFT COTTS
SALISBURY AVE
BRENTWOOD
ABBOTTS
ROGERS CT
MANSE WAY
MANSE PAR
ROBINA CT
Broom Hill
BUTTON ST
BR8
DA4

68

MEAD
LONDON RD
3
WOODARD TERR

A20
M20
B2173

4

Moreton Ind Est
MAIN WAY
WESTED LA
1
Hill Farm
The Folly

A20
Teardrop Ctr
FARNINGHAM HILL RD

Pedham Place Est

3

LONDON RD
MAIN RD
A225
A20
M20

67

Little Wested House
ELIZABETH PL
RABLUS PL
LONDON RD
DARTFORD RD
PO
P
The Mill House
HIGH ST
HORTON WAY
SOUTH HILLSIDE TERR

Farningham

2

EYNSFORD RD
Mast
CROCKENHILL LA
Fort Farningham (dis)
SPAREPENNY LA
Darent Valley Path
River Darent
OLIVER CRES
SOUTH ST
TILL
A225
VALLEY VIEW TERR

M25

1

Eynsford Hill
MILL HOUSE CL
OLD MILL LA
EYNSFORD RD

66

52   53   54

A **B** **C** **D** **E** **F**

MILL LA
PRIORY LA
A225

45
60

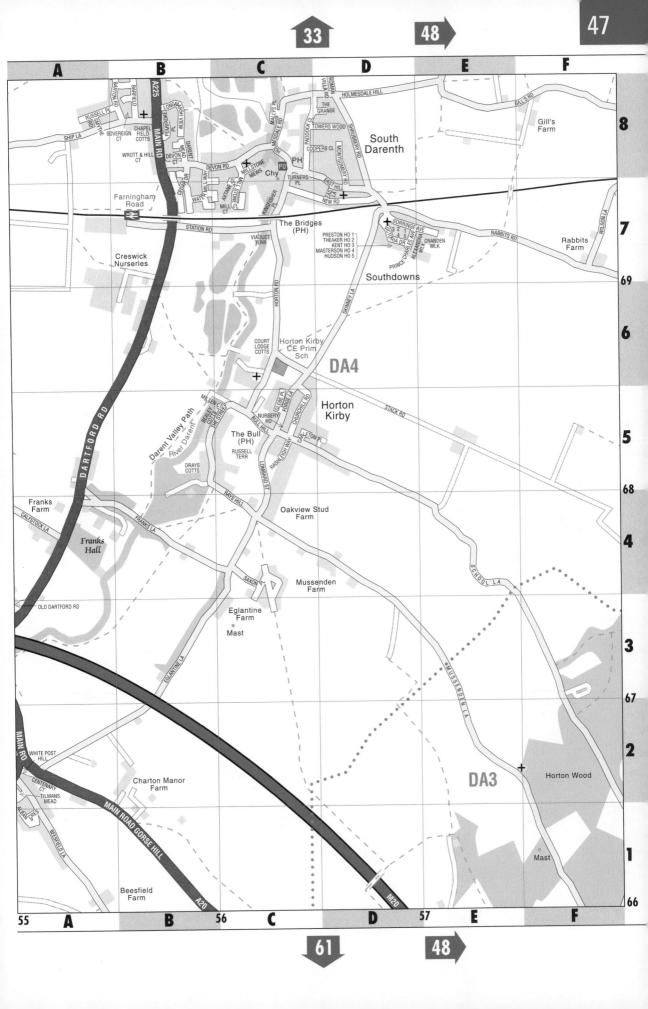

	A	B	C	D	E	F

8

Grubb Street

Ryecroft Farm

B260 GREEN STREET GREEN RD

Ryecrofts Wood

GILL'S RD

WILSON LA

Mile End Green

DA13

WHITEHILL RD

B255

7

DA2

Mile End Green Cotts

Pinden

Pinden End Farm

NORTHDOWN RD

Whitehill

Longfield

Liby

MAIN RD

WEST SHAW

ESSEX RD

PH

69

RABBITS RD

ROWANS CL

FOSTERS MEWS

PO

STATION RD

HARTLEY RD

CHAPEL CL

ST MARY'S WAY

KENT RD

P

DA4

CHEYNE WLK

CAVENDISH SQ

RUSSELL SQ

OAKWOOD RISE

OAKWOOD WLK

P

Longfield

6

Dene Bottom Farm

EATON SQ

THE CRESCENT

BRAMBLEFIELD CL

PARK DR

COPSE SIDE

Axton Chase Sch

B260

Dean Bottom

CANADA FARM RD

FAWKHAM RD

THE MEWS 1
ST JAMES SQ 2
GROSVENOR SQ 3
BEDFORD SQ 4
ST GEORGES SQ 5
SLOANE SQ 6

HOTTSFIELD

FAIRACRE PL

QUAKERS CL

NORTHFIELD

GILCROFT

PITFIELD

CAXTON

P

PORCHESTER

Churchdown Wood

MERTON AVE

HAWTHORNS

BRAMBLEDOWN

WELL FIELD

1 SILVERDALE
2 MERRYFIELDS CL
3 EVERGLADE CL
4 FORTUNA CL

5

BANKSIDE

PARKFIELD

MOSELANDS VIEW

LARKWELL LA

PERRAN CL

LARKS FIELD

Steephill Sch

GRESHAM AVE

GRESHAM AVE

WOODLAND AVE

68

THE OLD DOWNS

OLD DOWNS

WICKHAMS WAY

DICKENS CL

GORSE WOOD RD

JOHNS CL

Beeches Farm

DOWNS VALLEY

SANDSHAW CT

Hill Barn Farm

CASTLE HILL

GREEN HILL

STACK LA

Our Lady of Hartley RC Prim Sch

4

Canada Farm

STACK RD

DA3

Hartley Green

CAMEL TIE WAY

CHURCH RD

BROOMFIELDS

CULVEY CL

PO

CHERRY TREES

GORSE WAY

MANOR DR

Hartley Prim Sch

ROUND ASH WAY

ASH RD

CONYER AVE

OXT WAY

Liby

THE WARRENS

ST JOHN'S LA

BILLINGS HILL SHAW

3

Lane Oak Farm

SCUDDERS HILL

FAIRBY LA

Football Ground

Sports Club

GRANGE WAY

TATES ORCH

Hartley

Pennis Farm

CHANTRY AVE

67

Nursery

VALLEY RD

THREE GATES RD

MANOR LA

2

THE GROVE

Pennis Wood

The Black Lion (PH)

1

Fawkham CE Prim Sch

SCHOOL LA

Parkfield Wood

Fawkham Manor

H

TN15

CH

Chapel Wood

Mast

OLIVER MILL 1
CHAPEL WOOD 2

CALING CROFT

FARM HOLT

CHAPEL WOOD RD

66

58	A	B	59	C	D	60	E	F

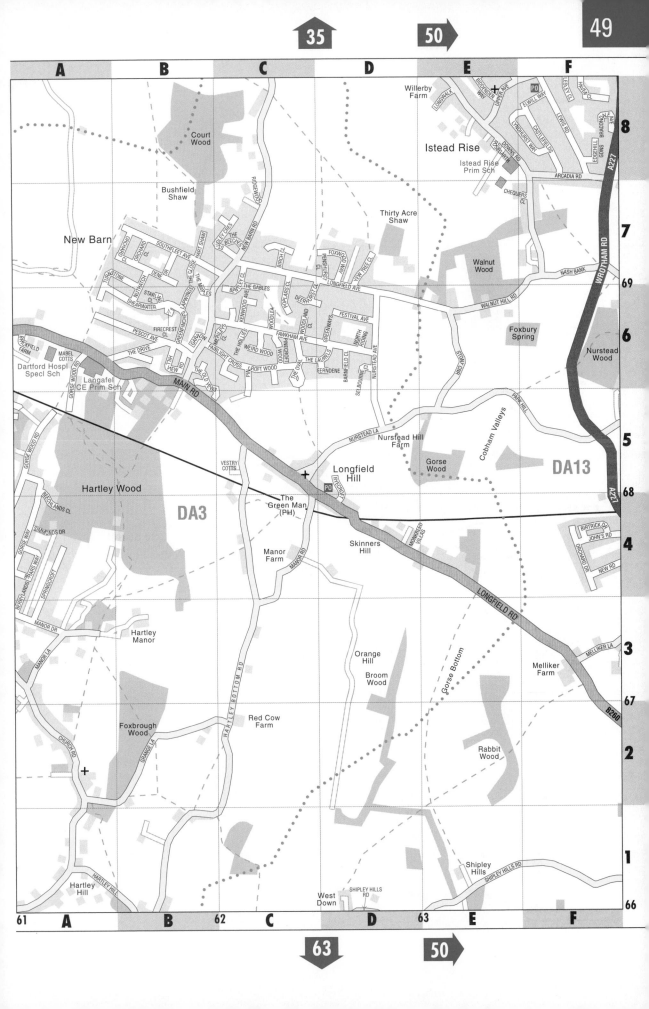

49
36

A   B   C   D   E   F

8

7

69

6

5

68

4

3

67

2

1

66

WROTHAM RD
A227

Huntondown Wood

Ifield Court

New Cottages

Henhurst

Henhurst Dale

CHURCH RD

Nash Street

NASH ST

Cozendon Wood

Tollingtrough Green

Dabbs Place Farm

HENHURST HILL

HENHURST RD

Winstead Hill

Jeskyns Court

Dabbs Place

DA12
Owletts

Cobham

JESKYNS RD

Battle Street

SCOTLAND LA

Nurstead Court

The Park

Mill Hill

COPT HALL RD

Wealdway

ROUND ST

Round Street

Jeskyns Farm

THE STREET

BATTLE ST

SARGENTS CT

Cobham College

NURSTEAD CHURCH LA

WHITE POST LA

Lordscroft Shaw

THE BEECHES

Sweep's Hole

Danes Place

P

Meopham

STATION RD

THE RAILWAY SIDINGS

Sole Street

SALLOWS SHAW

MANOR CT

GRATTON FIELDS

GREENLANDS

SOLE ST

Gold Street

GOLD ST

A227
JOHN'S RD

NEW RD

HOOK GREEN CT

PO

EDMUND CL

NURSERY RD

FAIRVIEW GDNS

Meopham Station

ARBORFIELD

PINE RISE

NORWOOD LA

ROWAN CL

Blundells Shaw

MANOR RD

Sole Street

MAY PL

PO

The Railway Inn (PH)

DA13

The Cock Inn (PH)

Henley Street

HENLEY ST

HAY'S MEAD

Reynold's Farm

CHESTNUT CL

WROTHAM RD

MELLIKER LA

THE MEDLARS

THE PIPPINS

THE RUSSETS

Hook Green

HUNTINGFIELD RD

WALNUT TREE WAY

TRADESCANT DR

POPLAR WALK

DENESWAY

Camer Farm

CAMER RD

CAMER GDNS

CAMER ST

Camer

B260

LONGFIELD RD

LINDEN RD

STRAND

CHINNERY CL

THE WAY

MULBERRY CL

LILAC PL

DORMERS DR

GREEN LA

P

Camer Park Country Park

Henley Wood

Henley Down

Helen Allison Sch

SCHOOL CL

THE PADDOCK

P

Meopham Com Prim Sch

Meopham Court

CAMER PARK RD

Bramble Hall Farm

Oakenden

OAKENDEN RD

DEAN RD

Luddesdown

Luddesdown Court

SHIPLEY HILLS RD

The Old Vicarage

A227

PO

THE STREET

FOXENDOWN LA

BRIMSTONE HILL

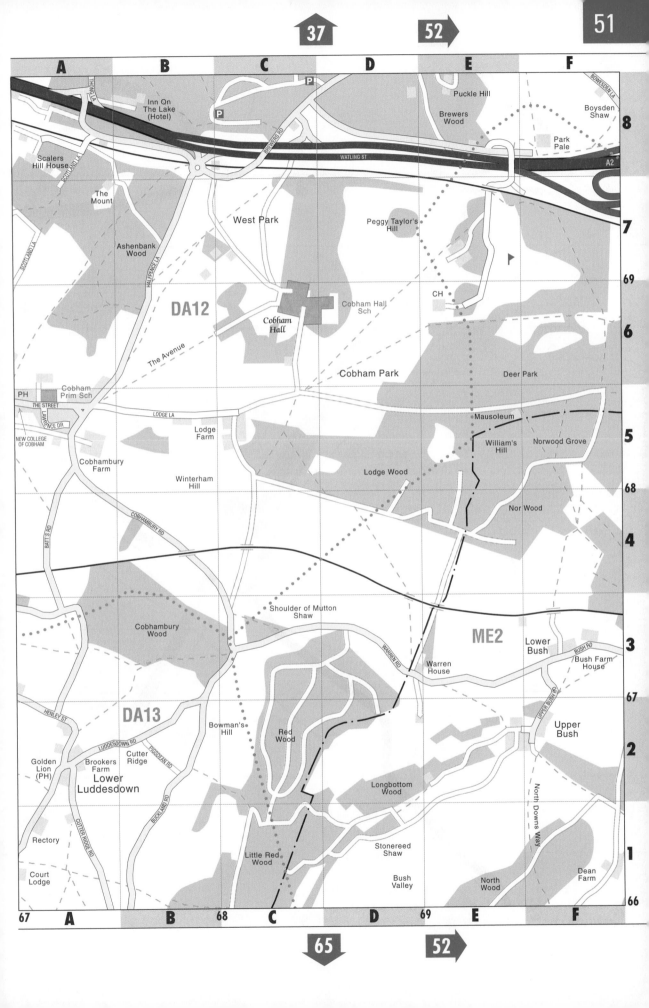

51 38

A B C D E F

8

DA12

A289

Chapter Farm

Crutches Farm

ROSE COTTS

PH

OLD WATLING ST

CRUTCHES LA

ELMWOOD DR

M2

A2

WHITE GATE

REDE COURT RD

Abbey Court Special Sch

B2108

A226

GRAVESEND RD

BURR

SEAFORD

ROMSEY CL

CRISPIN RD

CORB CLINTON AVE

CRISP RD RUSSET CL

BRAMLEY RISE

PARCHMT CLSE

WORCESTER

DUCHESS

ALLINGTON DR

DEACON CL

LETBOURNE DR

COBHAM DR

ABBEY RD

ROAST CL

CHAPTER RD

ST NICHOLAS GDNS

DRAKE'S AVE

BROOMHILL RD

GORSE RD

PEPY'S WAY

A226

A2

7

WATLING ST

B2108

Strood

Sports Ctr

THE SHADES

MILLFORDHOPE RD

Chapter Sch

THURSTON DR

COLUMBINE CL

RIVER DR

HARVEL AVE

P

HUMBER CRES

THE MEWS

WITHAM WAY

SQUIRES DR

WHARF ST

STANGATE RD

PARKFIELDS

SWALE

CHETNEY

COPPERHOUSE

YANTLET

SCHOLARS RESC

CARNATION RD

DAFFODIL CL

COLUMBINE RD

LANCELOT AVE

ELAINE AVE

CLIFTON RD

COBHAM

STOUR CL

TINTAGEL GDNS

DART

69

SEAMEW CT 1
SKUA CT 2
SNIPE CT 3
ARRAN GN 4
NIGHTINGALE CT 5

Bligh Jun & Inf Schs

PO

ORCHID

BLIGH WAY

PESQUER

HYACINTH RD

DARNLEY CL

ST FRAN

ELAINE

GALAHAD AVE

Elaine Prim Sch

DARNLEY RD

MAPLE RD

BEECH RD

ASH RD

Cemy

PO

A228

6

Knights Place

Temple Wood

CORMORANT

ALBATROSS AVE

PELICAN CL

CURLEW CRES

TERN CRES

SOUTHWELL RD

BANGOR

TIDERS

FULMAR RD

WIDGEON RD

PORTSMOUTH RD

SOUTHWARF RD

HAWTHORN RD

OAK RD

CEDAR RD

HOLLY

CHESTNUT RD

Sherwin Knight Jun & Inf Schs

NORTH BANK

HEVER CRES

PINE RD

Broad Oak Wood

Clay Pond Wood

Great Wood

GUILDFORD GDNS 1
CARLISLE CL 2
PETERBOROUGH GDNS 3
WAKEFIELD CL 4
LINCOLN CL 5
ST ALBANS RD 6
NORWICH CL 7
NOTTINGHAM WLK 8

ST PAUL'S

BRISTOL

CHELMSFORD RD

CHESTER CL

COVENTRY

GLAMFORD RD

HIGHLAND

KINSTON RD

WELLS

WELLS RD

LILAC CRES

LILAC RD

LABURNUM RD

POPLAR CL

POPLAR RD

SYCAMORE RD

5

Birch Wood

ME2

THE SPIRES

MERRALS WOOD RD

HILLSHAW CRES

RANSCOMBE CL

RUSHDEAN RD

ELGIN GDNS

BOTHAM

CUXTON RD

Ballard Bsns Pk

SAXON PL

ROMAN WAY

VIKING CL

NORMAN CL

68

RANSCOMBE FARM COTTS

Ranscombe

Pit (dis)

Diggerland

2

CHARIOT WAY

4

Mill Hill

North Downs Way

Longhoes Wood

Merrals Shaw

PH

Wickham Reach

3

POPLICANS RD

NINE ACRES RD

HAROLD RD

REGINALD AVE

WHITELEAVES RD

PETCHARD

PILGRIMS WAY

SUNDRIDGE HILL

Caravan Site

Common Marsh

Medway Bridge

Medway Bridge Marina

CAMBRIA AVE 1
CORDELIA CRES 2
SILVER HILL 3

KENDAL

Kent Centenary Wks

FARMDELL

MANOR LA

AILSA

MEWS

67

Court Lodge

RIGBY CL

DEMELZA CT

BUSH RD

CHARLES DR

LADYWOOD RD

HAYLEY CL

JAMES RD

STAFFORD

WILLIAM RD 1
HOLLYCROFT 2
DOWNSLAND HO 3

Cuxton

PH

STATION RD

LC

River Medway

WARWICK CRES

HILARY GDNS

Sch

2

Cuxton Com Jun & Inf Schs

Liby

PO

MAY ST

WOODHURST RD

THE GLEBE

HILLCREST RD

Cuxton Ind Est

BRAMBLETREE COTTS

Factory Farm

Borstal Court Farm

ME1

Medway Valley Wlk

TASSENDEN FARM LA

1

Church Hill

ROCHESTER RD

A228

Wouldham Marshes

WOULDHAM RD

BURHAM RD

M2

66

Bores Hole

PILGRIMS RD

ME2

Rings Marsh

70 A B 71 C D 72 E F

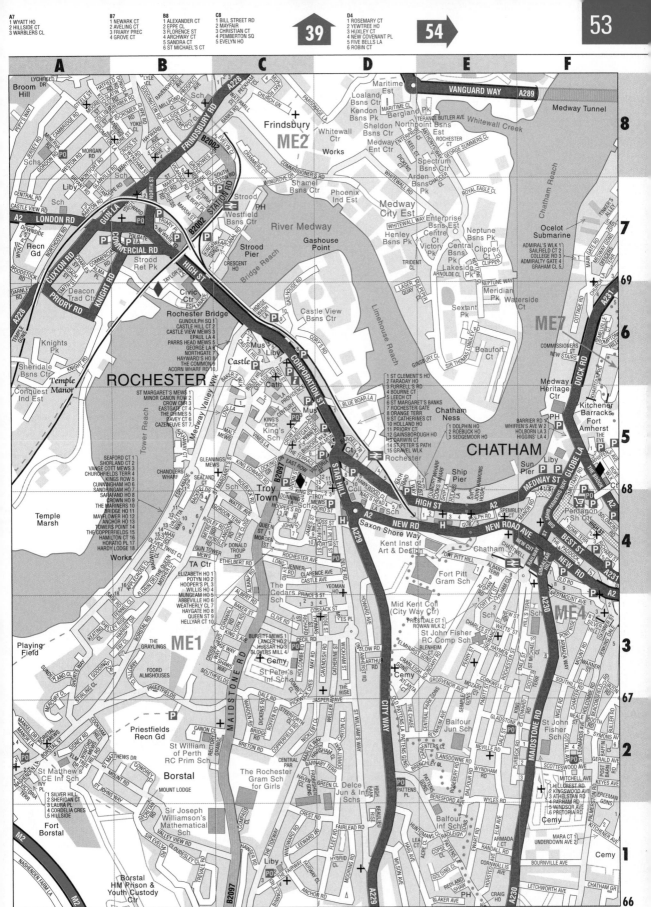

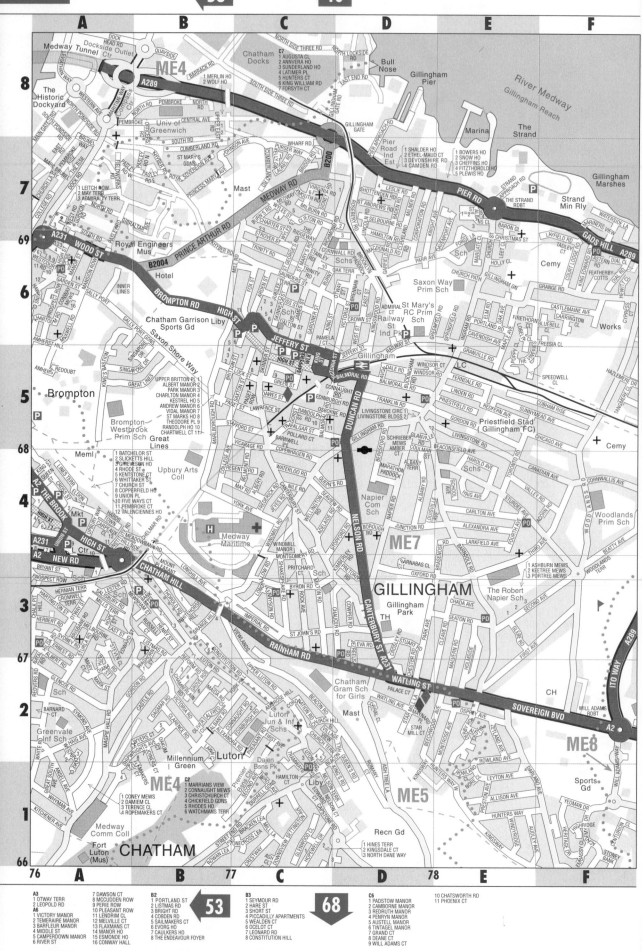

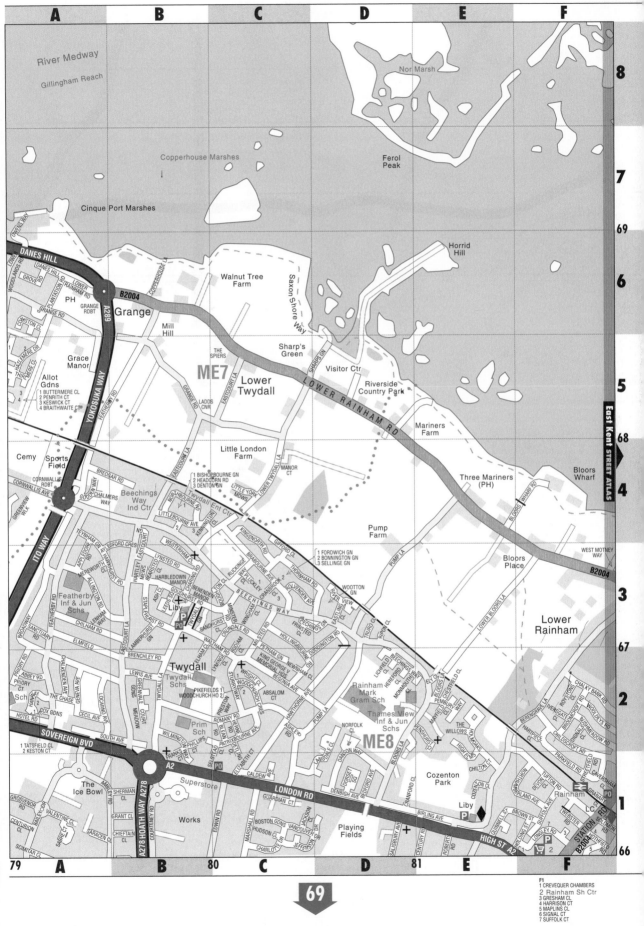

River Medway

Gillingham Reach

Nor Marsh

Copperhouse Marshes

Ferol Peak

Cinque Port Marshes

Horrid Hill

DANES HILL

B2004

Grange

Walnut Tree Farm

Saxon Shore Way

East Kent STREET ATLAS

GRANGE RDBT

PH

GRANGE RD

A289

YOKOSUKA WAY

Mill Hill

THE SPIERS

Sharp's Green

SHARPS GN

Visitor Ctr

LOWER RAINHAM RD

Riverside Country Park

ME7

Lower Twydall

EASTCOURT LA

Grace Manor

Allot Gdns

1 BUTTERMERE CL
2 PENRITH CT
3 KESWICK CT
4 BRAITHWAITE CL

HATHERLEY RD

GRANGE RD

LADDS CNR

Little London Farm

MANOR CT

Mariners Farm

Bloors Wharf

Cemy

Sports Field

Three Mariners (PH)

BLOORS WHARF RD

CORNWALLIS AVE

CORNWALLIS RDBT

GREENVIEW WLK

GOLDERN WAY

CHALMERS WAY

Beechings Way Ind Ctr

1 BISHOPBOURNE GN
2 HEADCORN RD
3 DENTON GN

NORTHBOURNE RD

LITTLE YORK MEWS

TOWER TWYDALL LA

Twydall Ent Ctr

WEST MOTNEY WAY

Bloors Place

B2004

ITO WAY

LITTLEBOURNE AVE

KENILWORTH RD

Pump Farm

PUMP LA

BLOORS LA

Lower Rainham

BREDGAR RD

KINGSNORTH RD

GIFFORD CL

1 FORDWICH GN
2 BONNINGTON GN
3 SELLINGE GN

RIVER VIEW

LOWER BLOORS LA

WOOTTON GN

TEYNHAM GR

APPLEDORE GR

HAMHURST RD

WESTERHAM RD

LYNSTED RD

BRABOURNE AVE

THORNHAM RD

COVENDEN AVE

EASTLING GN

TRURO CT

RIPON CT

Featherby Inf & Jun Schs

MEREWORTH RD

ALLINGTON RD

LENHAM RD

HARBLEDOWN MANOR

GOUDHURST RD

BENENDEN MANOR

RUCKINGE CL

PLUCKLEY RD

CRANBROOK RD 3

BEECHINGS WAY

CUXTON RD

DODDINGTON RD

CHILHAM RD

ASH CT

STAPLEHURST RD

LEEDS SQ

MINSTER CL

WINGHAM CL

HOLLINGBOURNE RD

BEECHINGS WAY

Twydall

ELMFIELD

LAMBERHURST GN

WALTHAM RD

SANDHURST RD

GRUNDEL RD

PETHAM GN

NEWNHAM CL

BEGONIA AVE

LICHFIELD

HEREFORD

FRINSTED

Twydall Schs

BRENCHLEY RD

LEWIS AVE

TWYDALL GN

GREENALL GDNS

CHARING

KING GEORGE V MEMORIAL HO

ELY CT

MONMOUTH CL

CHALKY BANK RD

ROY DENS

INVERGATHER RD

BERENGRAVE LA

Liby

P

PO

ME8

Rainham Mark Gram Sch

PEMBURY CL

MAYFIELD

HARTFIELD

WOOLLEY RD

RUSHMEADOW RD

CHILDSCROFT RD

Prim Sch

PIKEFIELDS 1
WOODCHURCH HO 2

ROMANY RD

WRIGHT CT

HAWTHORNE AVE

ABSALOM CT

PUMP LA

Thames View Inf & Jun Schs

THE WILLOWS

HIGH ST

PARKFIELD RD

CAVERSHAM

HARTPIECE

1 TATSFIELD CL
2 KESTON CT

THE CHASE

GENEVA AVE

WILMINGTON RD

BLEAN

PATRIXBOURNE RD

HENEAGE AVE

NORFOLK CT

LANGDON RD

DANSON WAY

ANSLEY HO

HIGH ST

Cozenton Park

MATFIELD RD

TUFTON RD

SOVEREIGN BVD

A2

HOATH WAY

A278

COURTENAY RD

EDWIN RD

Superstore

LONDON RD

GUARDIAN CT

BEDFORD RD

CRANFORD CL

BIRLING AVE

Liby

P

Rainham

PO

STATION RD

B2004

The Ice Bowl

SHERMAN CL

GRANT CL

CHIEFTAIN CL

Works

MARSHALL RD

BOSTON GDNS

HUDSON RD

VANCOUVER DR

JACKSON RD

DENBIGH AVE

SUNSET CT

DORSET RD

CENTURY RD

ROBERTS RD

Playing Fields

BROWN ST

LONGLEY RD

SOLOMON RD

WEBSTER RD

GRACE

GROSVENOR RD

VALENTINE CL

BAILEY CT

SABRE CT

SARACEN CL

CENTURION CL

SCIMITAR CL

HOTEL RD

COX GDNS

CECIL AVE

LOCARNO RD

SOUTH AVE

PHILLIPS RD

ELIZABETH CT

CALDEW RD

CHARLOTTE CT

JEFFERSON RD

CHARLOTTE RD

HIGH ST A2

QUINNELLS RD

SALISBURY AVE

NITFIELD CL

F1
1 CREVEQUER CHAMBERS
2 Rainham Sh Ctr
3 GRESHAM CL
4 HARRISON CT
5 MAPLINS CL
6 SIGNAL CT
7 SUFFOLK CT

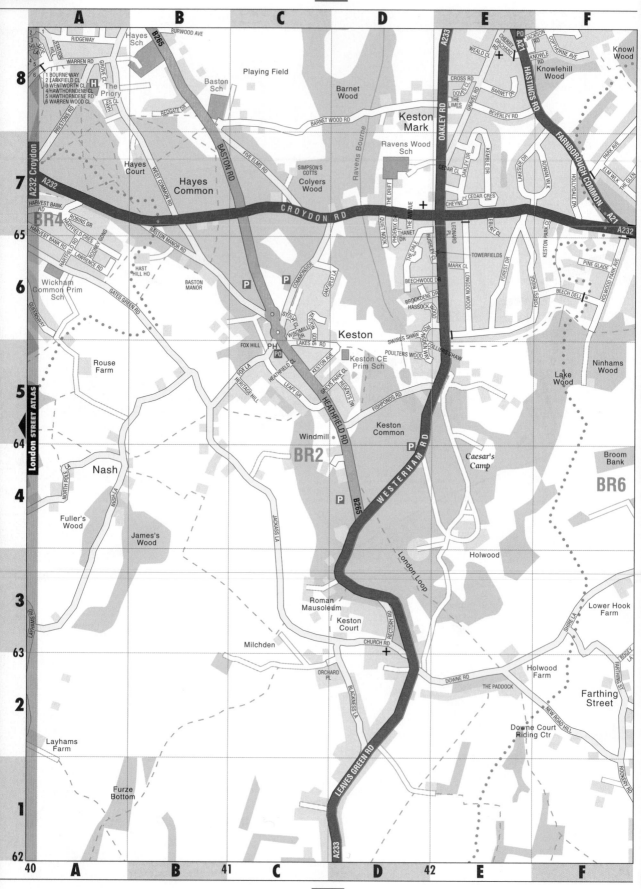

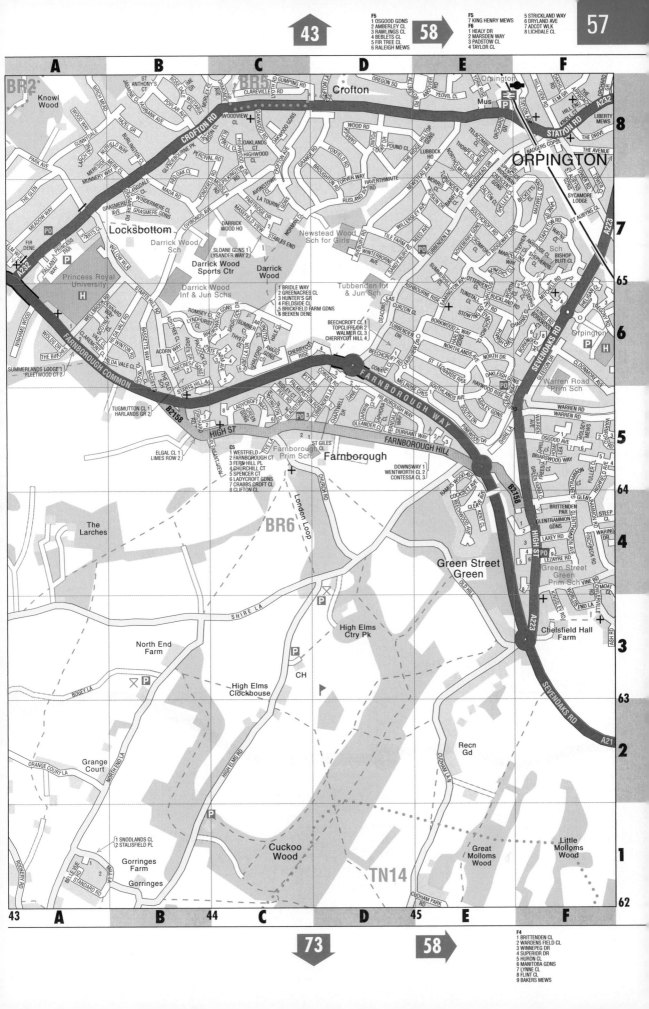

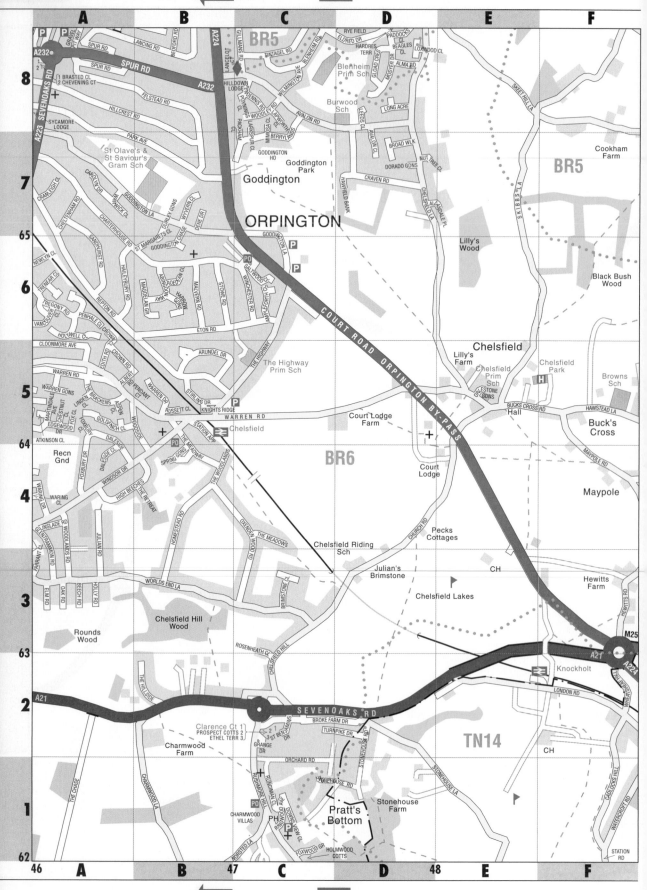

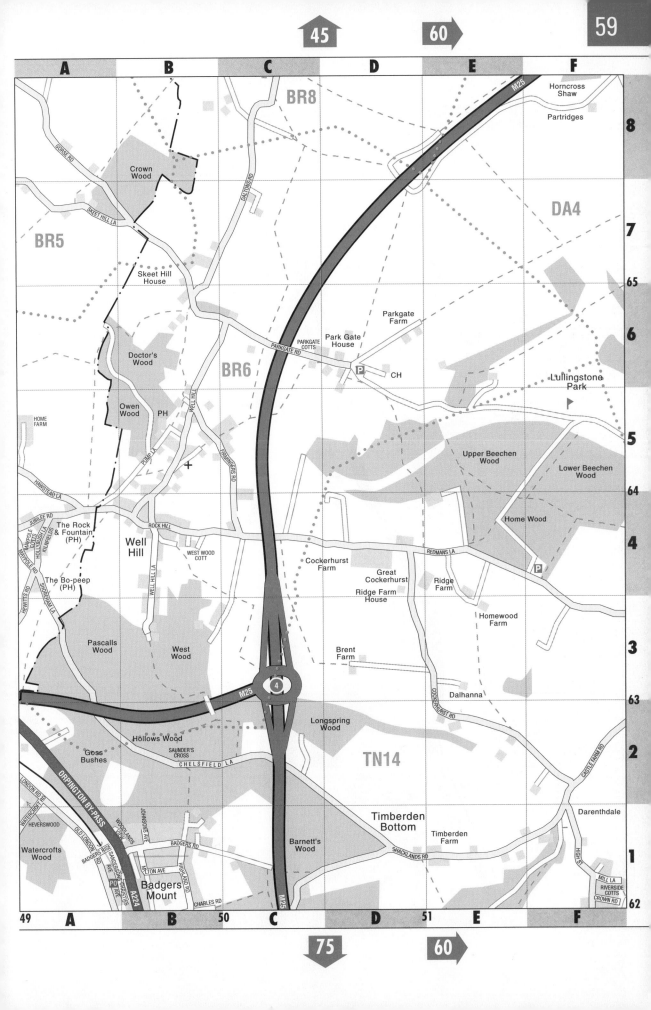

59
46

A | **B** | **C** | **D** | **E** | **F**

8

Hulberry

Eagle Heights
Bird of Prey Ctr

The Anthony
Roper Prim Sch

Eynsford
Castle

HIGH ST

A225

TOWER CROFT

ALTON
COTTS

PRIORY FIELDS

FERN BANK

HULBERRY
FARM

The
Five Bells
(PH)

LULLINGSTONE LA

Home
Farm

Recn
Gd

PO

WILLOW
TERR

ELIZABETH
COTTS

FOUNTAIN
CT

RIVERSIDE

MALT SHOVEL
COTTS

Eynsford

EDWARDS
CT

KNIGHTS
FIELD

7

HILLCROFT

STATION RD

WALNUT CL

CHURCH
WALK

POLLYHAUGH

Pollyhaugh
Farm

LULLINGSTONE
ROMAN VILLA
(rems of)

P

Newbarn
Farm

65

Eynsford

ST MARTIN'S DR

LARCH CL

CKS PK

EYNSFORD RISE

6

Lullingstone Park
Farm

BOWER LA

Lullingstone Park

Chalkhurst

Park
House
Farm

DA4

Chalkhurst
Wood

PARK HOUSE
COTTS

P

Lullingstone
Castle

Park
House

5

Darent Valley Path

River Darent

CASTLE RD

P

Robsacks

UPPER AUSTIN LODGE RD

64

Lullingstone Pk
Visitor Ctr

Lower Austin
Lodge Farm

Hartnips
Wood

4

Castle
Farm

REDMANS LA

CASTLE FARM RD

3

The
Birches

UPPER AUSTIN
LODGE FARM
COTTS

63

Upper Austin
Lodge

2

Rifle
Range

Preston Hill
Plantation

CH

Preston
Farm

1

TN14

DANGER
AREA

Lower
Wood

TN15

Round
Hill

62

52 | **A** | 53 | **B** | **C** | 54 | **D** | **E** | **F**

A225

59
76

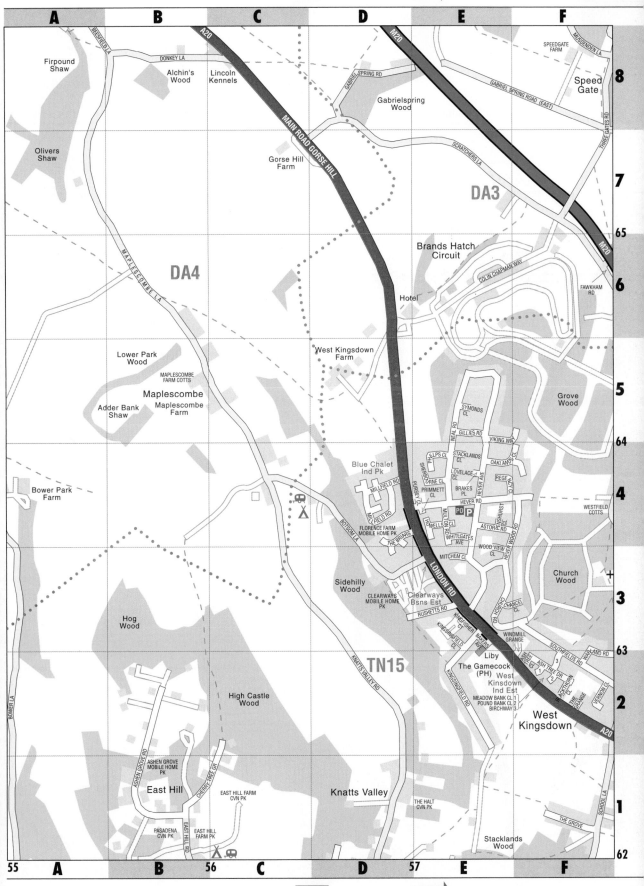

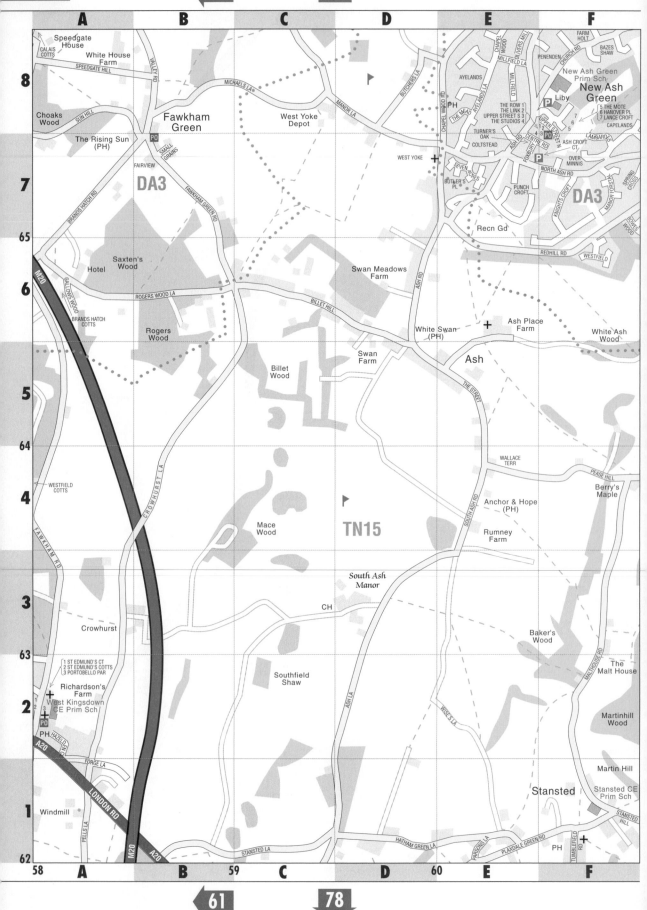

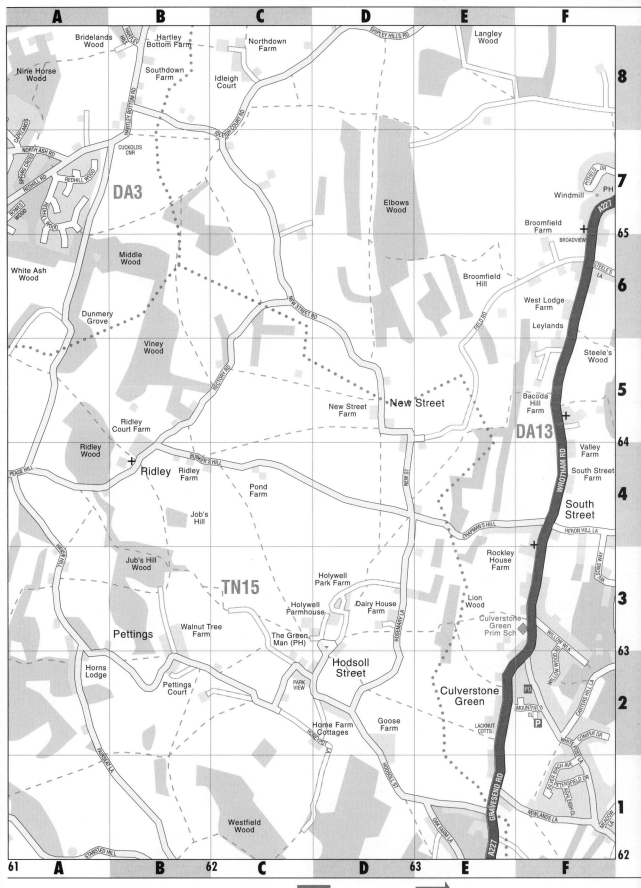

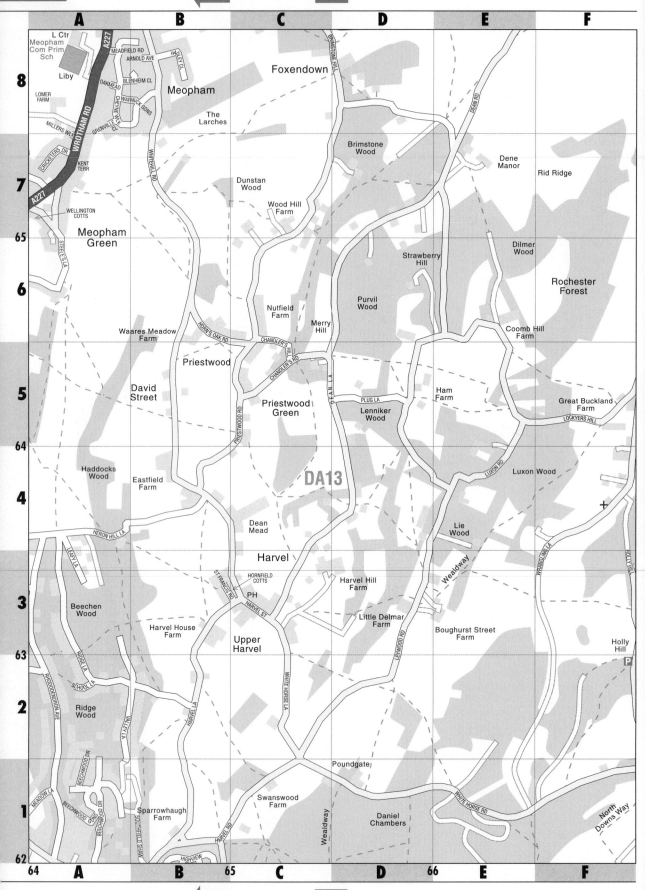

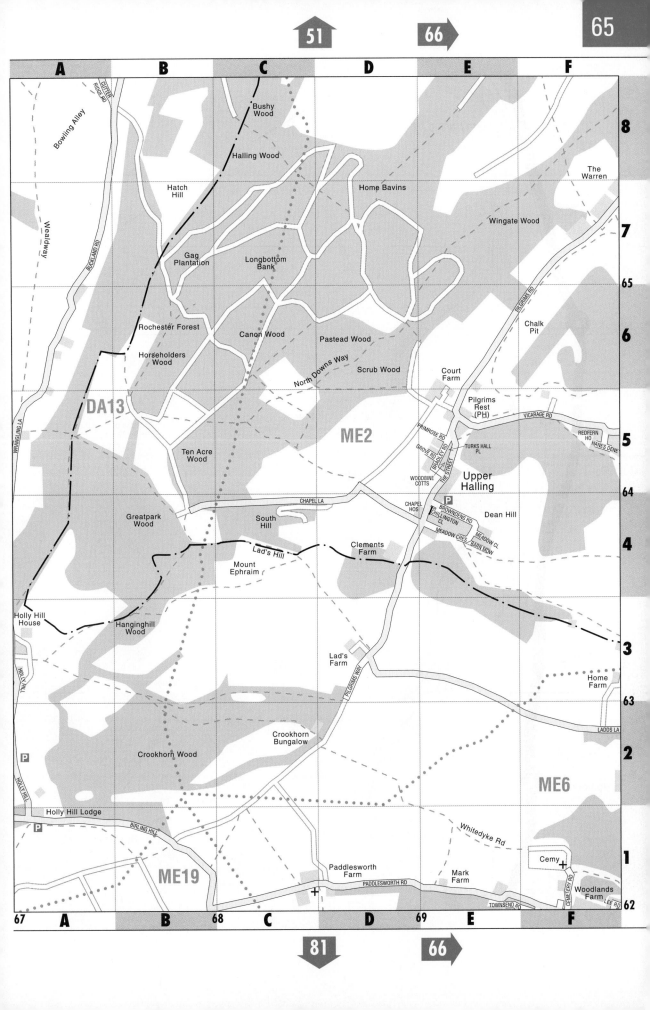

A   B   C   D   E   F

8

Bowling Alley

CUTTER RIDGE RD

Bushy Wood

Halling Wood

The Warren

Hatch Hill

Wingate Wood

7

Wealdway

BUCKLAND RD

Gag Plantation

Home Bavins

65

Chalk Pit

6

Longbottom Bank

PILGRIMS RD

WRANGLING LA

Rochester Forest

Canon Wood

Pastead Wood

Horseholders Wood

North Downs Way

Scrub Wood

Court Farm

Pilgrims Rest (PH)

VICARAGE RD

REDFERN HO

HANES DENE

DA13

ME2

PRIMROSE RD

GROVE RD

BRADLEY RD

THE STREET

TURKS HALL PL

5

Ten Acre Wood

WOODBINE COTTS

Upper Halling

64

CHAPEL LA

CHAPEL HOS

P

BROWNDENS RD

Dean Hill

Greatpark Wood

South Hill

CHILLINGTON CL

MEADOW CL

Clements Farm

MEADOW CRES

BARN MDW

4

Lad's Hill

Mount Ephraim

HOLLY HILL

Holly Hill House

Hanginghill Wood

3

Lad's Farm

Home Farm

63

PILGRIMS WAY

LADDS LA

2

P

Crookhorn Bungalow

ME6

Crookhorn Wood

P

Holly Hill Lodge

BIRLING HILL

Whitedyke Rd

1

Cemy

Cemetery RD

ME19

Paddlesworth Farm

Mark Farm

Woodlands Farm

LEE RD

PADDLESWORTH RD

TOWNSEND RD

62

67   A   B   68   C   D   69   E   F

65
52

A B C D E F

8

May's
Wood

North Halling

Ringshill
Farm

Starkeys

PILGRIMS RD

ROCHESTER RD

A228

LC

BURHAM RD

7

Chy

FORMBY RD

Works

Ivy
Cottage

65

North Downs Way

FORMBY
TERR

6

STAKE LA

JADE HILL

New
Town

Halling
Fresh
Marsh

Halling
Salt
Marsh

Ringshill
Place

KENT RD

ESSEX RD

ME2

Wouldham
All Saints
CE Prim Sch

Medway Valley Wlk

School
Farm

Wouldham
Common

PILGRIMS WAY

STATION APP

Halling

SCHOOL LA

HILL RD

CHARGROVE
MEWS

VICARAGE
CL

MARSH RD

RECTORY CL

PH

5

VICARAGE CT

Cemy

Halling

Halling
Common

MEADOW WAY

OLDFIELD DR

Wouldham

Harris's
Copse

LOW MEADOW WAY

KESTEVEN CL

WENDOVER CL

WALTER
BURKE AVE

TRAFALGAR RD

NELSON RD

HIGH ST

PO

GARDEN CT

64

CEMETERY RD

ASHBY CL

PO

FERRY RD

BENEDICT CL

MAXIMILIAN DR

River Medway

FERRY LA

CASTLE ST

Recn
Gd

ME1

LAMBARDE CL

DALISON CT

Harris
Ho

PORTLAND RD

CORNWALL CR'S

KNOWLE RD

CARROLL CL

SYLVESTRES

ACRE GR

BRITANNIA CL

SCHOLEY CL

HOSIER CL

HERTING CL

Wouldham
Marshes

RAVENS
KNOWLE

Keeper's
Lodge

ME5

4

Whitting's
Farm

HOWLSMERE CL

Halling
Prim Sch

Wouldham
Common

3

Pit
(dis)

Scarborough

63

Holborough
Marshes

HALL RD

2

LADDS LA

Holborough
Marshes

Works

ROCHESTER RD

SCARBOROUGH LA

OLD CHURCH RD

Holborough

Works

ME6

Pit

MARGETTS LA

Burham

1

CLOCK TOWER MEWS 1
WARNETT CT 2

HOLBOROUGH RD

COVEY HALL RD

THOMSON CL

RAYFIELD
CT

CHURCHFIELD

TILGHMAN WAY

Burham
Court

COURT RD

DOWNS VIEW

BRISLEY'S
ROW

CHURCH ST

BAKER ST

ST MARY'S WLK

NEW RD

HODGSON CR'S

WILLOWSIDE

A228

62

70 A B 71 C D 72 E F

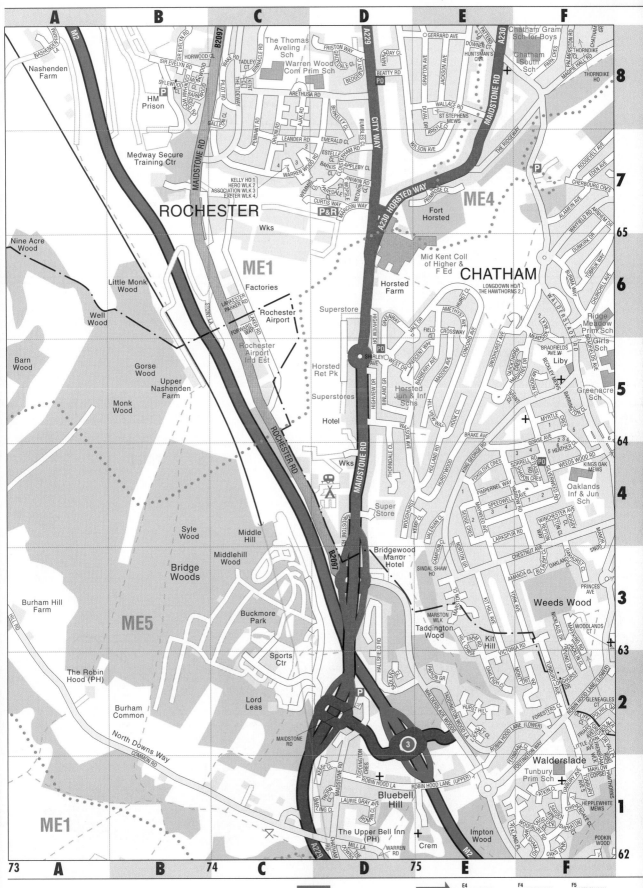

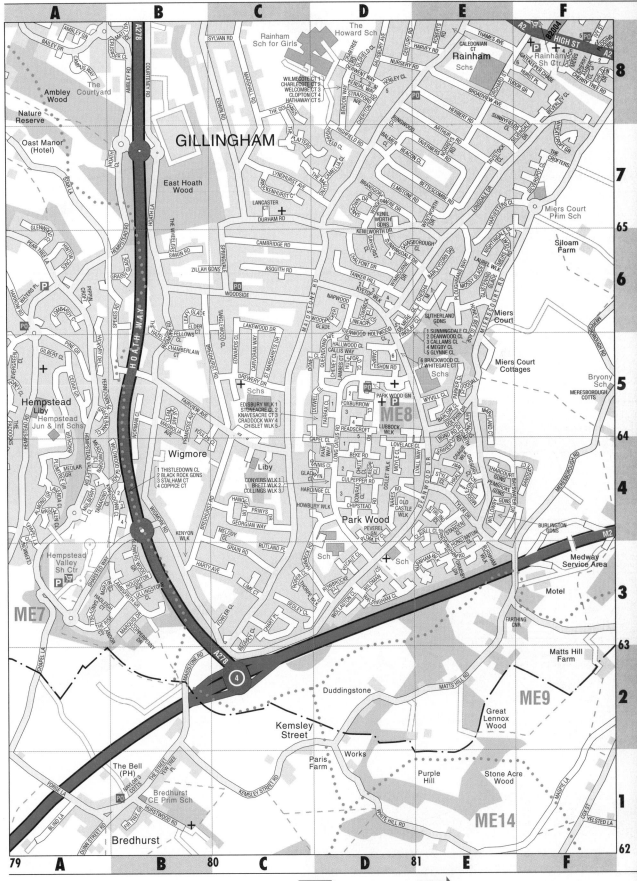

69

East Kent STREET ATLAS

A **B** **C** **D** **E** **F**

8

7

65

6

5

64

4

3

63

2

1

62

82 **A** 83 **B** **C** 84 **D** **E** **F**

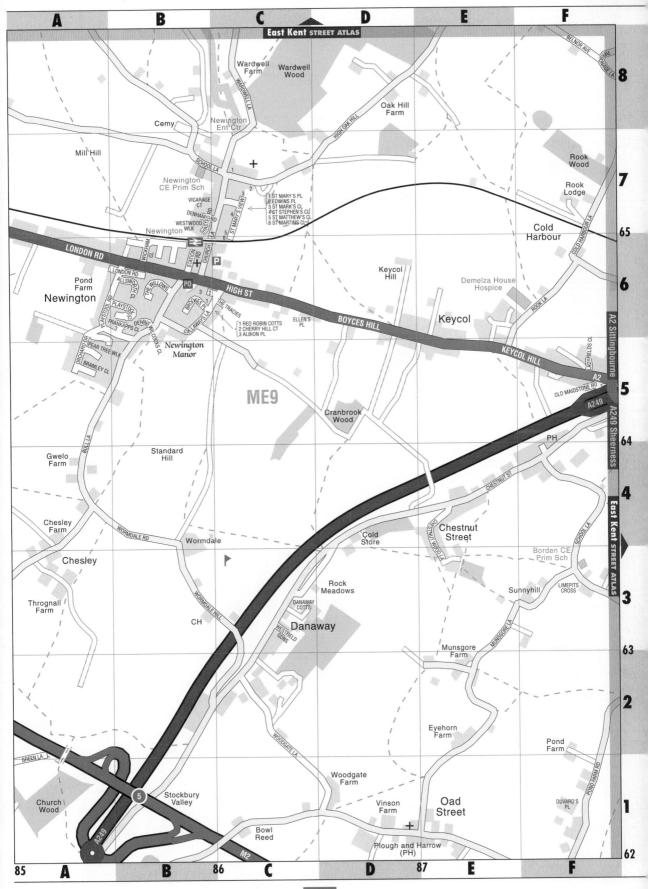

East Kent STREET ATLAS

A B C D E F

8

7

65

6

5

64

4

63

3

2

1

62

Wardwell Farm
Wardwell Wood
Oak Hill Farm
Rook Wood
Rook Lodge
BELNOR AVE
CONIBE LA
Cemy
Newington Ent Ctr
Mill Hill
HIGH OAK HILL
SCHOOL LA
WARDWELL LA
Newington CE Prim Sch
+
VICARAGE CT
DENHAM
WESTWOOD WLK
Newington
FINSTED RD
ST MARY'S VIEW
1 ST MARY'S PL
2 EDWINS PL
3 ST MARK'S CL
4 ST STEPHEN'S CU
5 ST MATTHEW'S CL
6 ST MARTINS CL
Cold Harbour
COLD HARBOUR LA
LONDON RD
WICKHAM CL
STATION RD
CHURCH
P
Pond Farm
LONDON RD
ALLSWORTH
THE WILLOWS
PO
HIGH ST
Newington
PLAYSTOOL RD
PLAYSTOL
FRANKAPPS CL
DENNIS WY
COOKS CL
BROOKES PL
CALLAWAYS LA
2
3
THE TRACIES
ELLEN'S PL
1 RED ROBIN COTTS
2 CHERRY HILL CT
3 ALBION PL
Keycol Hill
BOYCES HILL
Keycol
Demelza House Hospice
ROOK LA
LADYFIELDS CL
KEYCOL HILL
A2
A2 Sittingbourne
ORCHARD DR
PEAR TREE WLK
BRAMLEY CL
Newington Manor
ME9
Cranbrook Wood
OLD MAIDSTONE RD
A249
A249 Sheerness
Gwelo Farm
BULL LA
Standard Hill
PH
Chesley Farm
WORMDALE RD
Wormdale
Cold Store
Chestnut St
Chestnut Street
CHESTNUT LA
Borden CE Prim Sch
SCHOOL LA
East Kent STREET ATLAS
Chesley
WORMDALE HILL
Rock Meadows
Sunnyhill
LIMEPITS CROSS
Thrognall Farm
CH
DANAWAY COTTS
Danaway
WESTFIELD GDNS
Munsgore Farm
MUNSGORE LA
Eyehorn Farm
Pond Farm
POND FARM RD
GREEN LA
WOODGATE LA
Woodgate Farm
Vinson Farm
Oad Street
DUVARD'S PL
5
Church Wood
A249
Stockbury Valley
Bowl Reed
M2
Plough and Harrow (PH)
+

85 A B 86 C D 87 E F

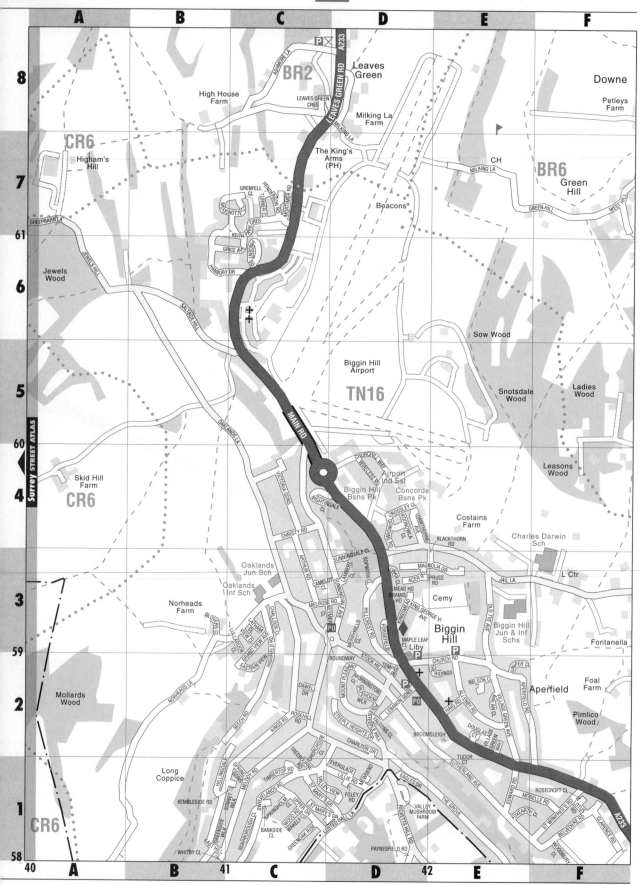

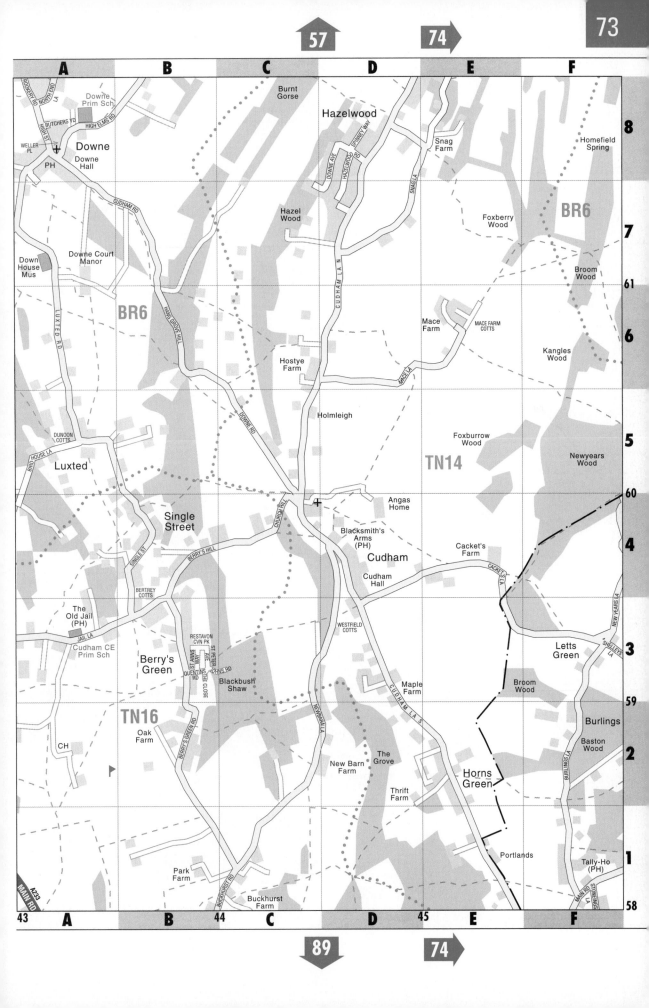

73
58

A B C D E F

8

Charm
Wood

LAMBARDES
CL

Pratts
Bottom
Prim Sch

HOOKWOOD
COTTS

Pratt's
Grove

Birthday
Wood

STONEHOUSE LA

STATION RD

The Old
Rectory

YEW TREE
COTTS

CLARKS LA

Norsted Manor

CHAMWOOD LA

NORSTED LA

PORT HILL

Fairtrough
Farm

BR6

7

Lower Brooms
Wood

FAIRTROUGH RD

BIGGIN'S HILL

HOOKWOOD RD

Hook
Wood

CHURCH RD

Village
House

OTFORD LA

Halstead
Com Prim
Sch

PH

SHOREHAM RD

61

High
Wood

Nurseries

PO

SOUTHDENE

THE MEADOWS

RUSHMORE HILL

6

WASHNEYS RD

PERRYS LA

The
Washneys

Rushmore Hill
Farm

PARKSIDE

KILNWOOD

MEADWAY

Halstead

Perry
Wood

STUBBS HILL

DERLEAP LA

Warren Court
Farm

HALSTEAD LA

5

Hayman's
Wood

Piece
Wood

SINGLE'S CROSS LA

RANDLES LA

Park
Farm

HUNTERS WLK

Curry
Farm

NEW YEARS LA

Newlands
Wood

60

Single's
Cross

TN14

Homevale
Cotts

WAYLANDS CL

4

Jockey's
Wood

Blueberry
Farm

BLUEBERRY LA

POUND LA

Knockholt
Pound

Nurseries

Jubilee
Terr

OLD LONDON RD

HARROW RD

Hampton
Cotts

BIRCHWOOD LA

BVD CL

ELMTREE
COTTS

IVY LA

PH

3

Shelleys

Court
Lodge

MAIN RD

Chine
Farm

Mast

The
Grange

CHEVENING LA

Lees
Wood

STAR HILL RD

CHINE FARM
PL

SHELLEYS LA

59

Knockholt

St Katherine's
Knockholt
CE Prim Sch

North Downs Way

BRASTED LA

2

The Crown
(PH)

SUNDRIDGE LA

Ash
Platt

LORD CHATHAM'S RIDE

Park
House

Minny
Wood

Mast

Sand
Banks

1

The
Mount

SUNDRIDGE HILL

Park
Wood

58

46 A B 47 C D 48 E F

Sundridge
Hill Farm

73
90

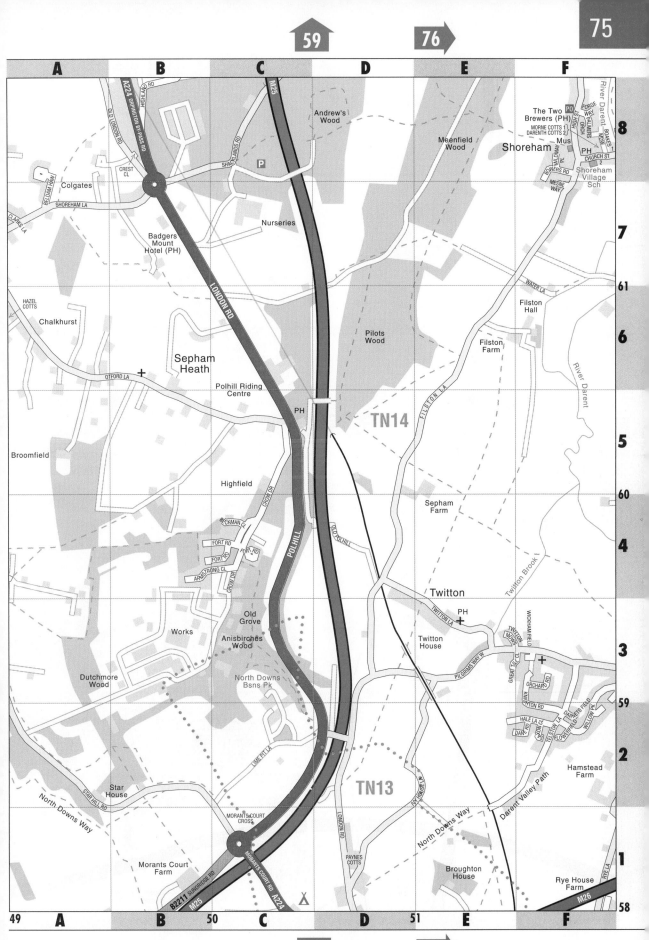

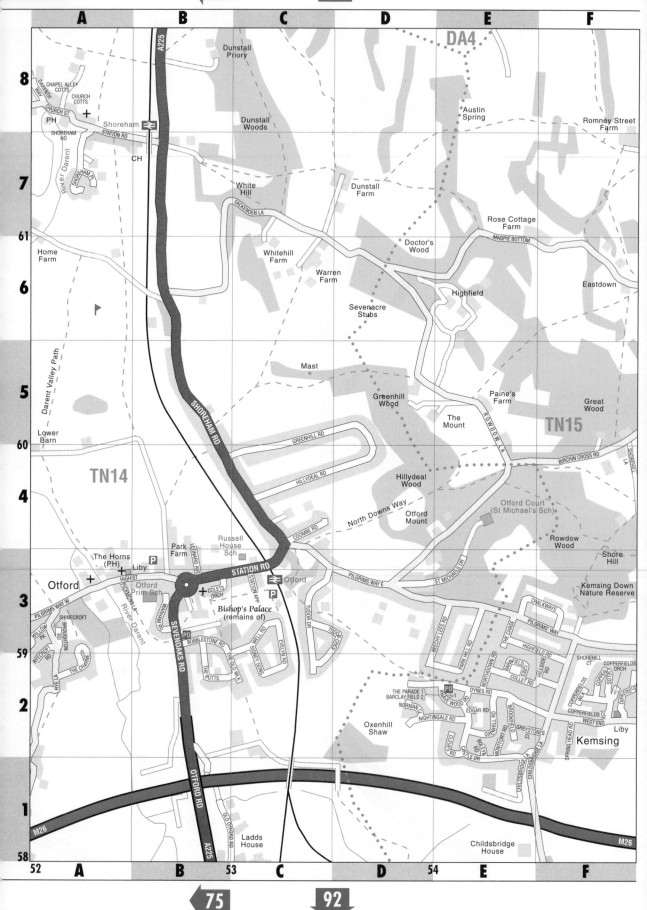

A   **B**   **C**   **D**   **E**   **F**

Broom Wood

Little East Hill Farm

HOLLYWOOD LA

8

Knatts Valley

KNATTS LA

SCHOOL LA

ROMNEY STREET CVN PK
BOWER LA
ROMNEY ST
PH

Leize Wood

EAST HILL RD

Pecken Wood

KNATTS VALLEY RD

Water Wood

Knockmill

MANOR RD

7

Littlehurst Farm

HILLS LA

Knockmill Wood

ST CLERE HILL RD

61

MAGPIE BOTTOM   Mast

Porter's Farm

GOODBURY RD

Goodbury Farm

TINKER POT LA

6

BIRCHIN CROSS RD

CLARKES GREEN RD

Woodlands

CH

Drane Farm

Fernbank Farm

THE POT RISE

TN15

5

Beech Lees Wood

Rising Sun (PH)

COTMAN'S ASH LA

Summeryards Wood

60

Shorehill Farm

Fab's Wood

Ashdown Farm Bungalow

Cotman's Ash

OLD TERRY'S LODGE RD

4

North Downs Way

Kester

Oak Hall

PILGRIMS' WAY

St Clere

3

PILGRIM'S WAY COTTS

59

WHITE LEAM CL
THE LANDWAY
TREETOPS
ORCHARD WAY
SHERBORNE GR
Kemsing Prim Sch
YH
P
MARY BURROWS GDNS
PH
CHURCH LA

HEAVERHAM RD

Crowdleham

Heaverham

Lower St Clere

2

WEST END

HIGH ST

Kemsing

Chequers Inn (PH)

Dynes Farm
OLD BARN CL
EDITH'S RD
CHART VIEW
PO
St Edith's Farmhouse
WULFRED WAY

Hill's Wood

Bushy Wood

WATERY LA

Broughton

1

RUSHYMEAD
PARK LA
THEOBALDS CL
NOAH'S ARK
FAIRFIELD

M26

58

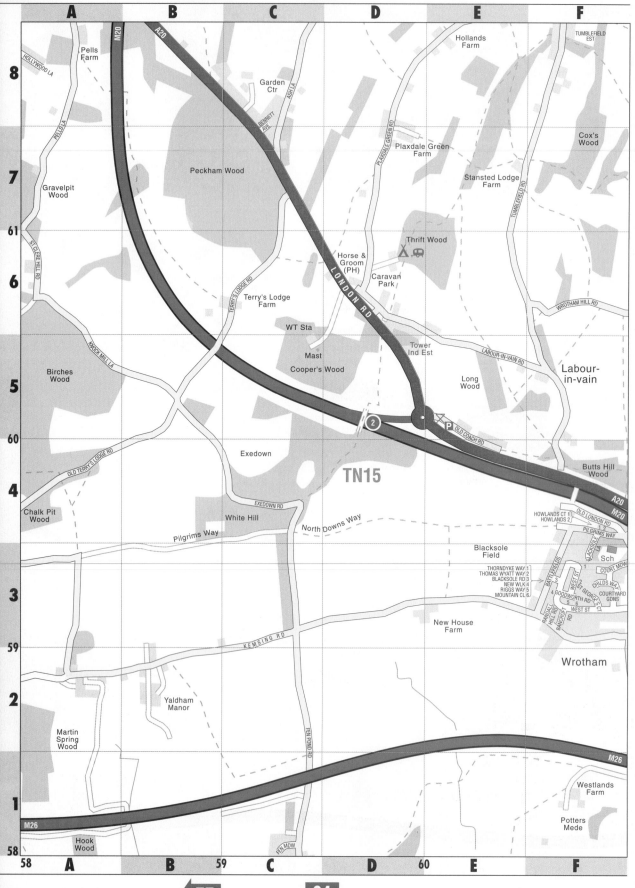

A B C D E F

8

7

61

6

5

60

4

3

59

2

1

58

HOLLYWOOD LA

Pells Farm

PELLS LA

Garden Ctr

BENNETT AVE

ASH LA

M20

A20

ST CLERE HILL RD

Gravelpit Wood

Peckham Wood

Hollands Farm

PLAXDALE GREEN RD

Plaxdale Green Farm

Stansted Lodge Farm

TUMBLEFIELD EST

Cox's Wood

TUMBLEFIELD RD

Thrift Wood

Horse & Groom (PH)

Caravan Park

LONDON RD

TERRY'S LODGE RD

Terry's Lodge Farm

WT Sta

Mast

Cooper's Wood

Tower Ind Est

Long Wood

LABOUR-IN-VAIN RD

WROTHAM HILL RD

Labour-in-vain

KNOCK MILL LA

Birches Wood

2

P

OLD COACH RD

Butts Hill Wood

A20

M20

Exedown

TN15

OLD TERRY'S LODGE RD

Chalk Pit Wood

White Hill

EXEDOWN RD

North Downs Way

Blacksole Field

HOWLANDS CT 1
HOWLANDS 2

OLD LONDON RD

PILGRIMS WAY

BLACKSOLE

Sch

Pilgrims Way

THORNDYKE WAY 1
THOMAS WYATT WAY 2
BLACKSOLE RD 3
NEW WLK 4
RIGGS WAY 5
MOUNTAIN CL 6

BATTLEFIELDS

WEST ST

COURT MDW

CHILDS WAY

COURTYARD GDNS

KEMSING RD

New House Farm

RANDALL HILL RD

BANCROFT RD

GOODWORTH RD

WEST ST

Wrotham

FEN POND RD

Yaldham Manor

Martin Spring Wood

M26

M26

Westlands Farm

Potters Mede

Hook Wood

FEN MDW

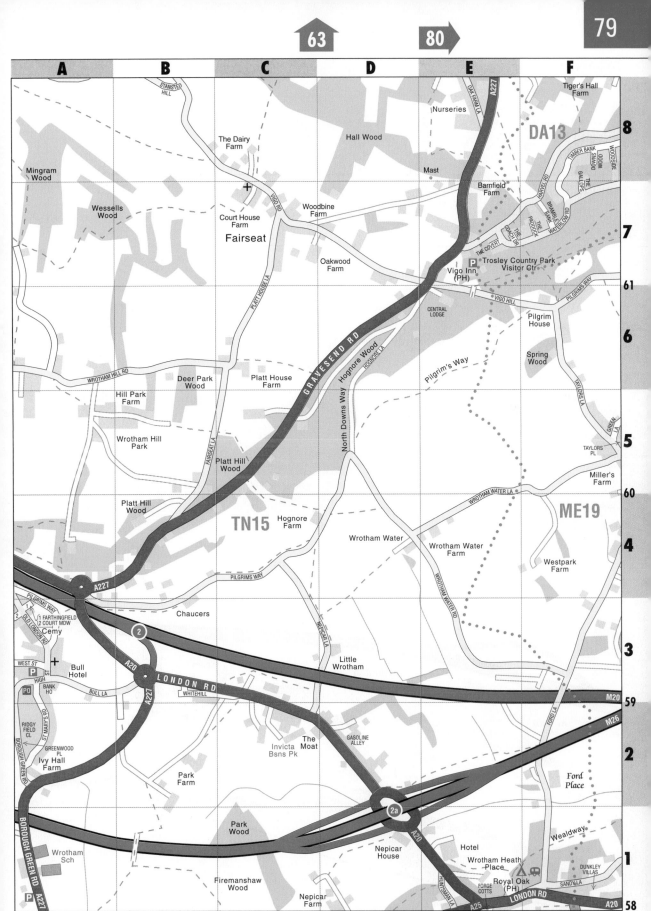

A B C D E F

8

Whitepost La
Vigo Village Sch
HARVEL RD
TIMBER BANK
ASH KEYS
HIGH VIEW
FERN DOWN
BOMBERS WOOD
HYDING FARM
ERSKINE RD
THE COPPICE
CHESTNUT LA
COMMUNITY RD
Harvel Hike
DA13
Whitehorse Wood
THE BAR PO
Liby
STONECROFT
CROFTSIDE
CHURCHSIDE
CHURCHSIDE
WATERLOW RD
Vigo Village

Great Wood

Trosley Country Park
Coney Lodge Farm

7

PILGRIMS WAY
North Downs Way
Park Farm

61

6

P
PINESFIELD LA
Coldrum Long Barrow

Trosley Court
COLDRUM LA
DOWNSVIEW
Trottiscliffe
GREEN LA

CHURCH LA
Chapel St
Cleggett's Farm
CHAPEL CL

5

THE STREET
SCHOOL LA
Trottiscliffe CE Prim Sch
NORTH DOWNS TERR
Ryarsh Wood
WORKHOUSE RD
HOLMES CT
Ryarsh

60

PH
FORD LA
Orchard House
ADDINGTON LA
ME19
Wealdway
THE STREET
OLD SCHOOL LA

4

Leney's Cottages
Woodgate
WOODGATE RD
Little Woodgate
EAST STREET N
Ryarsh Pk

M20

3

Addington
THE CHESTNUTS
TROTTISCLIFFE RD
MILLHOUSE LA
Hazelview
East Street
EAST ST
The Roughetts
ROUGHETTS RD
CHURCH RD
M20

59

M26
PARK RD
CHURCHFIELD
PLOWENDERS CL
THE CLOSE
M20

Westfields Farm

2

ST VINCENTS LA
Addington Park
CH
THE LINKS
GREENWAYS
West Malling Ind Pk
A20

St Vincents
LONDON RD

1

SANDY LA
Wrotham Heath
SHAWHILL HO
ALDON LA
CHURCH RD
Stubberdown Wood
CLEARWAY

58

A20
Aldon

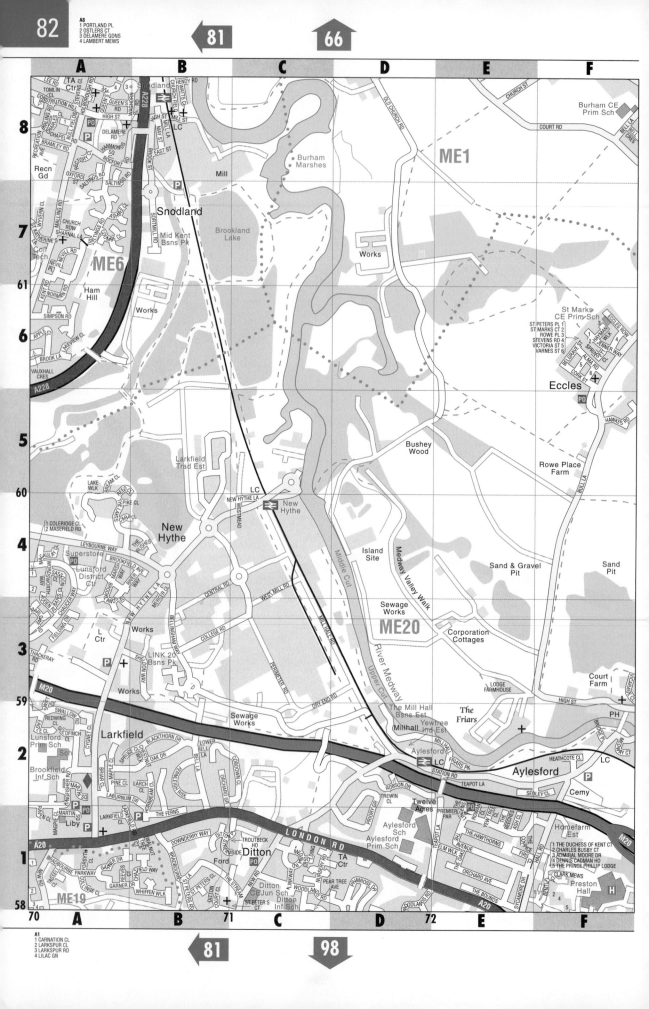

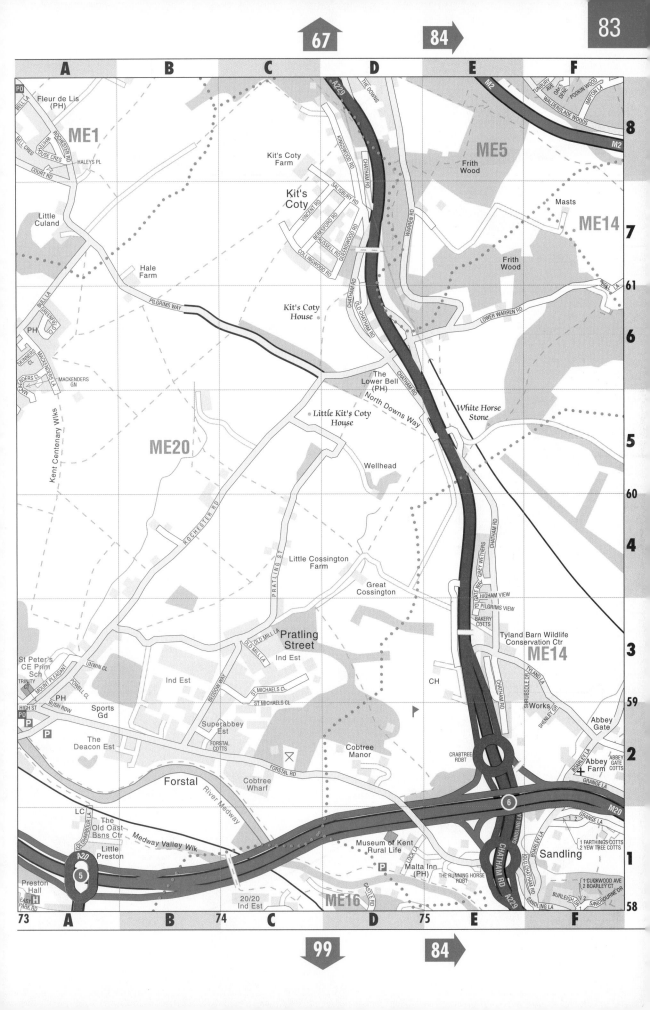

A B C D E F

8

ME1

Fleur de Lis
(PH)

PO

BELL LA

HITHE
HOUSE CRES

BELL CRES

COURT RD

HALEYS PL

Little
Culand

BULL LA

GREENFIELD CL

SKINNERS CL

MACKENDERS LA

MACKENDERS
GN

PH

Kent Centenary Wlks

MACKENDERS LA

Hale
Farm

PILGRIMS WAY

ME20

ROCHESTER RD

PRATLING ST

OLD MILL LA

OLD MILL LA

Kit's Coty
Farm

Kit's
Coty

KINGSWOOD RD

SALISBURY RD

VINCENT RD

BERESFORD RD

BRUSSELL RD

QUEENSWOOD RD

COLLINGWOOD RD

CHATHAM RD

THE DOWNS

A229

WARREN RD

OLD CHATHAM RD

Kit's Coty
House

The
Lower Bell
(PH)

North Downs Way

Little Kit's Coty
House

Wellhead

Little Cossington
Farm

Great
Cossington

M2

ME5

Frith
Wood

Frith
Wood

Masts

ME14

LOWER WARREN RD

White Horse
Stone

CHATHAM RD

CHATHAM RD

GATE WAY

GREY WETHERS

HIGHAM VIEW

PILGRIMS VIEW

BAKERY
COTTS

Tyland Barn Wildlife
Conservation Ctr

ME14

8

7

61

6

5

60

4

3

TUNBURY
AVE

OAKS
BERIE

WALDERSLADE WOODS

PODKIN WOOD

MIPTON LA

M2

SHELL LA

St Peter's
CE Prim
Sch

TRINITY
CT

HIGH ST

PH

BUSH ROW

MOUNT PLEASANT

POWELL CL

UNWIN CL

PO

P

P

Sports
Gd

The
Deacon Est

Pratling
Street

Ind Est

BEDDOW WAY

St Michaels CL

ST MICHAELS CL

Superabbey
Est

FORSTAL
COTTS

Forstal

Cobtree
Wharf

River Medway

FORSTAL RD

Cobtree
Manor

CH

CRABTREE
RDBT

Works

SHRUBSOLE DR

TYLAND LA

SHENLEY GR

Abbey
Gate

ABBEY
GATE
COTTS

Abbey
Farm

BOARLEY LA

GRANGE LA

M20

59

2

LC

A20

Preston
Hall

H

EAST
PARK RD

A20

5

The
Old Oast
Bsns Ctr

Little
Preston

Medway Valley Wlk

20/20
Ind Est

ME16

Museum of Kent
Rural Life

P

CASTLE RD

COCK LA

Malta Inn
(PH)

THE RUNNING HORSE
RDBT

6

CHATHAM RD

SANDLING LA

OLD CHATHAM RD

A229

SANDLING LA

GRANGE LA

1 FARTHINGS COTTS
2 YEW TREE COTTS

1 2

Sandling

1 CUCKWOOD AVE
2 BOARLEY CT

BURLEIGH DR

SANDBOURNE DR

BOARLEY LA

1

58

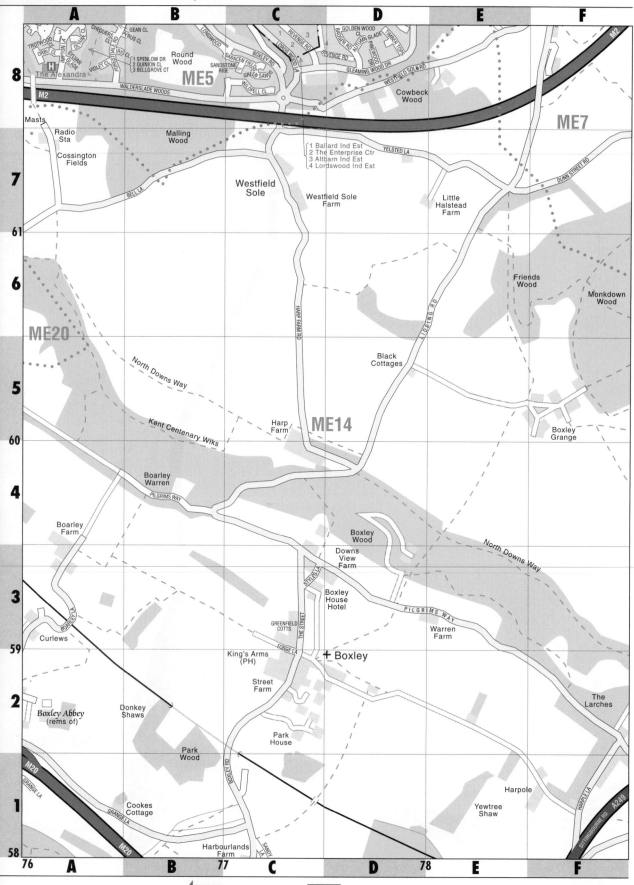

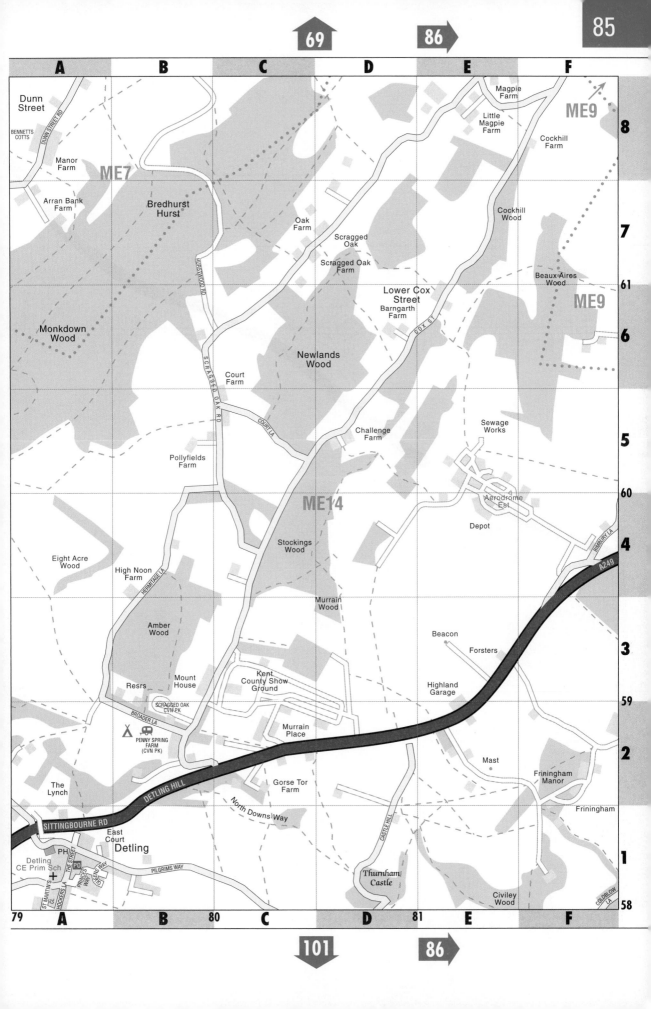

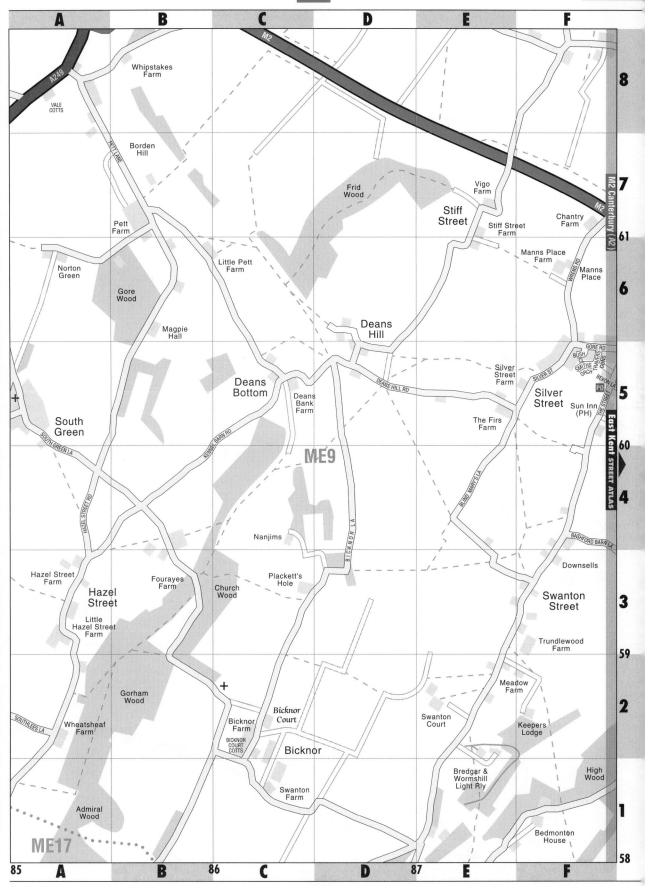

A   B   C   D   E   F

8

VALE COTTS

A249

Whipstakes Farm

Borden Hill

PETT LANE

M2

Frid Wood

Vigo Farm

Stiff Street

Stiff Street Farm

Chantry Farm

M2 Canterbury (A2)

7

61

Pett Farm

Norton Green

Little Pett Farm

Manns Place Farm

WRENS RD

Manns Place

6

Gore Wood

Magpie Hall

Deans Hill

Silver Street Farm

GORE RD
BUSH CL
SMITHS
ORCH
TRAYLERS
GDNS

SILVER ST

BEXON LA

5

Deans Bottom

Deans Bank Farm

DEANS HILL RD

Silver Street

PO

Sun Inn (PH)

THE STREET

East Kent STREET ATLAS

South Green

SOUTH GREEN LA

KENNEL BARN RD

ME9

The Firs Farm

BLIND MARY'S LA

60

4

HAZEL STREET RD

Nanjims

BICKNOR LA

BASHFORD BARN LA

Downsells

Hazel Street Farm

Fourayes Farm

Church Wood

Plackett's Hole

Swanton Street

3

Hazel Street

Little Hazel Street Farm

Trundlewood Farm

59

Gorham Wood

Meadow Farm

2

SOUTHLEES LA

Wheatsheaf Farm

Bicknor Farm

Bicknor Court

Swanton Court

Keepers Lodge

BICKNOR COURT COTTS

Bicknor

High Wood

Admiral Wood

Swanton Farm

Bredgar & Wormshill Light Rly

1

ME17

Bedmonton House

58

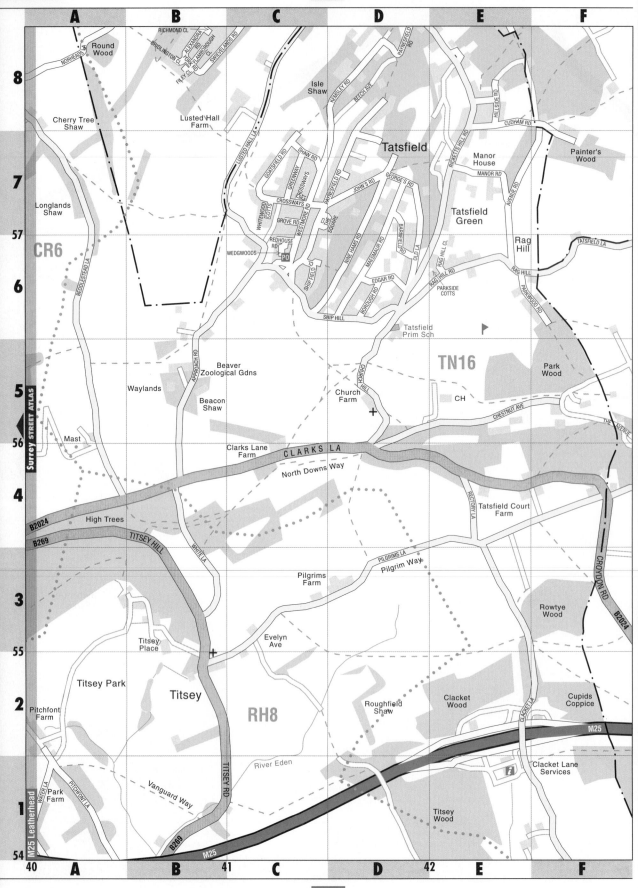

Surrey STREET ATLAS

CR6

Round Wood
NORHEADS
Cherry Tree Shaw
Longlands Shaw
Mast
High Trees
B2024
B269
TITSEY HILL
WHITE LA
Pitchfont Farm
Titsey Park
PITCHFONT LA
WATER LA
Park Farm
M25 Leatherhead
Vanguard Way
TITSEY RD
B269
M25

RICHMOND CL
BRIDLINGTON CL
FILEY CL
ALEXANDRA RD
FLAMBOROUGH CL
SWEVELANDS RD
Lusted Hall Farm
LUSTED HALL LA
GOATSFIELD RD
GREENWAY
WHITEWOOD COTTS
CROSSWAYS
SHAW RD
GROVE RD
WESTMORE RD
REDHOUSE RD
WEDGWOODS
PO
APPROACH RD
Beaver Zoological Gdns
Waylands
Beacon Shaw
Clarks Lane Farm
CLARKS LA
North Downs Way
Pilgrims Farm
Titsey Place
Titsey
RH8
Evelyn Ave
River Eden
Pilgrim Way
PILGRIMS LA

Isle Shaw
KENSLEY RD
BEECH AVE
PAYNESFIELD RD
Tatsfield
JOHN'S RD
PAYNESFIELD RD
GEORGE'S RD
THE SQUARE
NINE ACRES RD
MASSMALIR RD
BARNFIELD
OLD LA
SHIP RD
BOROUGH RD
EDGAR RD
SHIP HILL
CHURCH HILL
Church Farm
CH
Tatsfield Prim Sch
RECTORY LA
Roughfield Shaw
Clacket Wood
CLACKET LA
M25
Titsey Wood

PAYNESFIELD RD
HILLSIDE RD
CUDHAM RD
Manor House
RICKETTS HILL RD
MANOR RD
Tatsfield Green
AVENUE RD
RAG HILL CL
RAG HILL RD
PARKSIDE COTTS
Rag Hill
RAG HILL
TATSFIELD LA
PARKWOOD RD
TN16
CHESTNUT AVE
Park Wood
THE AVENUE
Painter's Wood
Tatsfield Court Farm
CROYDON RD
B2024
Rowtye Wood
Cupids Coppice
Clacket Lane Services
i

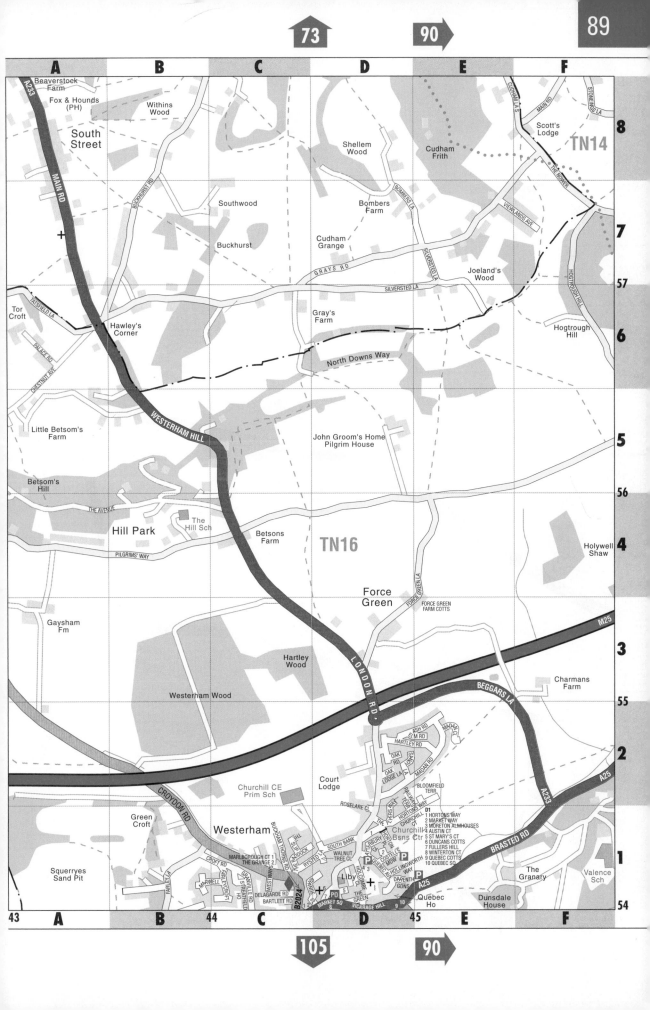

89
74

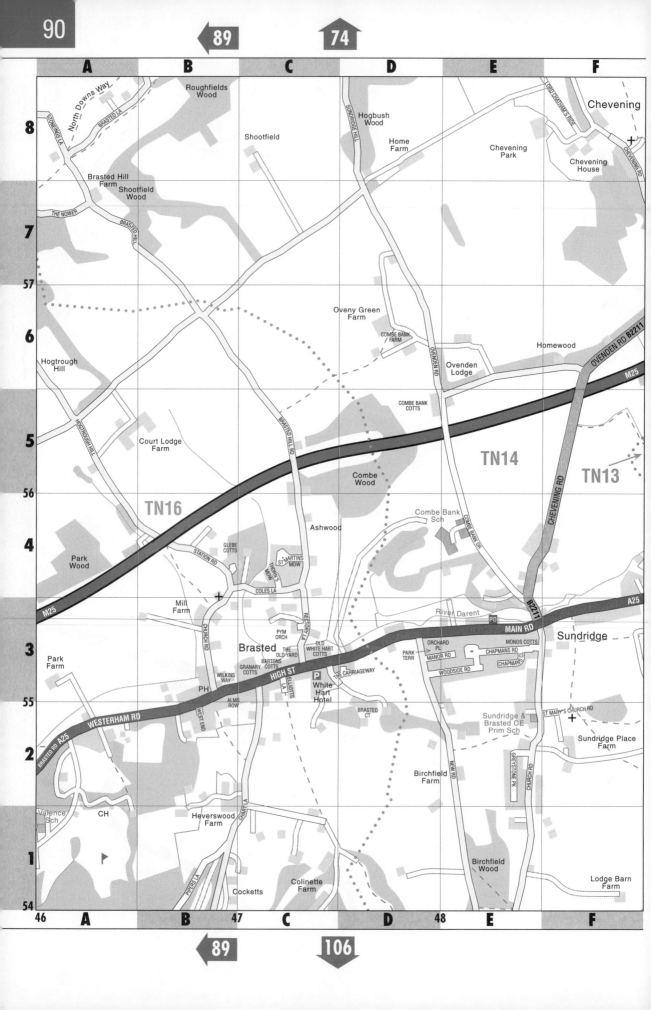

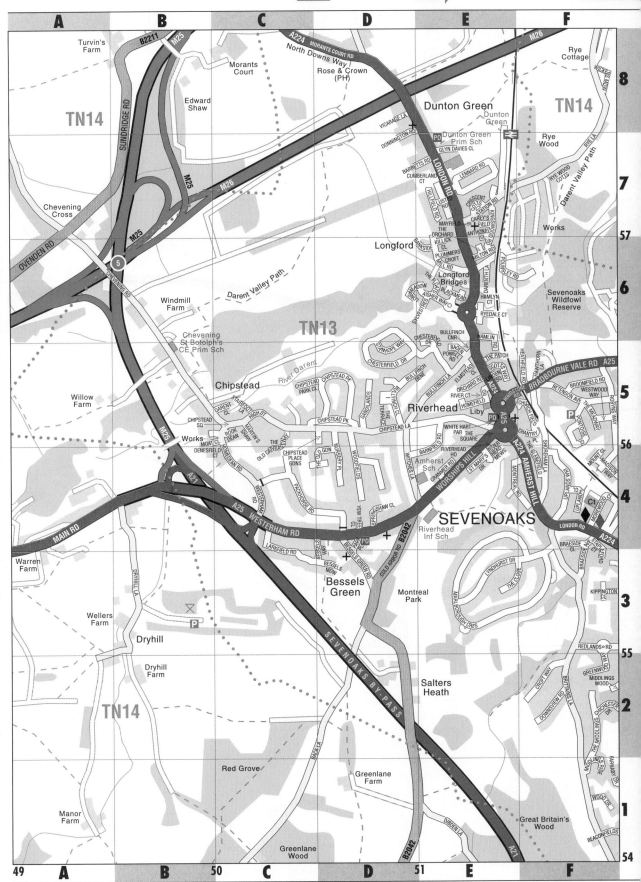

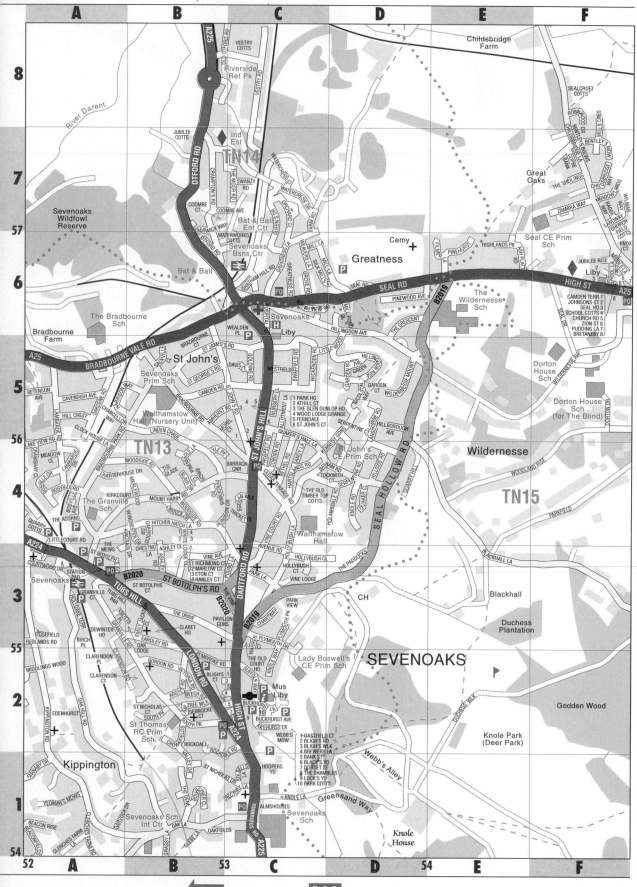

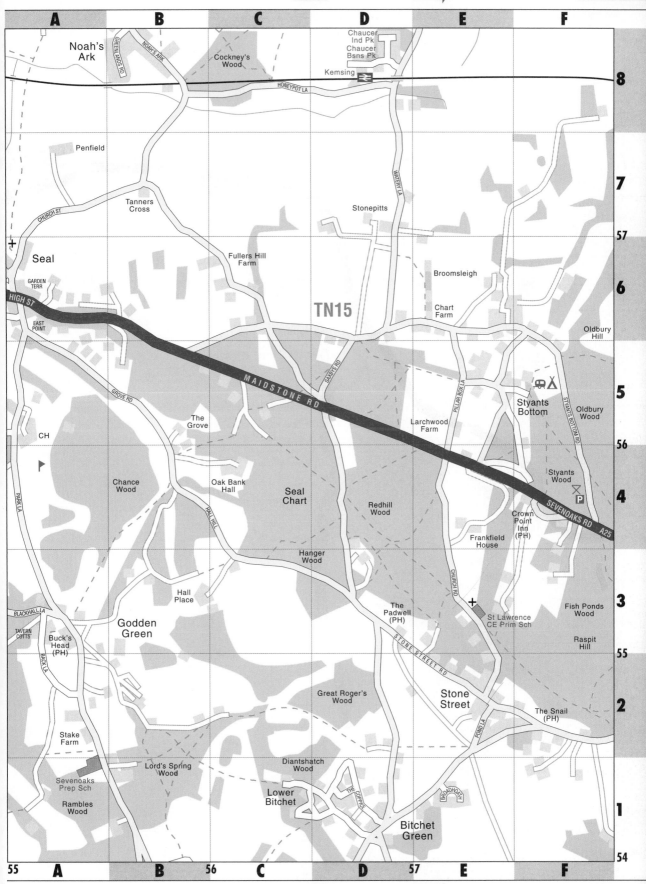

← 93 ↑ 78

A　B　C　D　E　F

8

Borough Green

Sand Pit

Cricketts Farm

Ightham Court

FEN POND RD

Works

STATION CT 1
STATION APP 2
SCHOOL APP 3
CLOKE MEWS 4
FOX LEA 5

Borough Green & Wrotham
LODGE CL

A227　WESTERN RD　SEVENOAKS RD

7

Patchgrove Wood

IGHTHAM BY-PASS

BOROUGH GREEN RD A227

Borough Green Rd

Dark Hill Farm

High St　Liby

MAIDSTONE RD

A25

BELLOWS LA
TAVERN RD
TILTON RD
JASMINE CL
WYATT CL
CONYERD RD
STALEYS RD

THE LANDWAY
ABBOTT RD
HARRISON
CROWHURST RD
DRYLAND RD

57

RUSHMERE CT
WALKER RD

THE CLOSE

DURLINGS ORCH

Trycewell Farm

Works

Basted House

6

Manor Farm Cotts

Manor Farm House

Oldbury

CHAPEL ROW
VIEW RD
COBS CL
PH

THE STREET

BUSTY LA
TRYCEWELL LA

Ightham

QUARRY HILL RD

THOMS LA

BASTED LA

Oldbury Hill

OLDBURY COTTS
OLDBURY LA

Ightham Prim Sch

JUBILEE CRES

BATES HILL

Prestons

MILL LA

5

Oldbury

UPPER SPRING

RECTORY LA

Ightham Warren

56

Oldbury Wood

OLD LA

REDWELL LA

Warren Farm

Crowhurst Farm

Basted

4

SEVENOAKS RD

A25

COPT HALL RD

PH

NUTFIELDS

COMMON RD

SANDY LA

CROWHURST LA

MILL HILL
PLOUGH HILL

The Plough (PH)

SEVEN WENTS

River Bourne

3

Raspit Hill

Ightham Common

ISMATS RD

TEBBS WAY

TONBRIDGE RD

BACK LA

Bewley Farm

WINFIELD LA

Bourne Farm

55

COACH RD

PINE TREE LA

BEWLEY LA

Sheet Hill Farm

Brookside Farm

2

STONE STREET RD

The Golding Hop (PH)

Sheet Hill

YOPPS GN

1

Ivy Hatch

The Plough (PH)

HIGH CROSS RD

Scatt's Dene

Lady's Wood

Yopps Green

Dux Farm

DUX LA

MOTE RD

Scathes Wood

A227

TN11

TN15

54

58　A　B　59　C　D　60　E　F

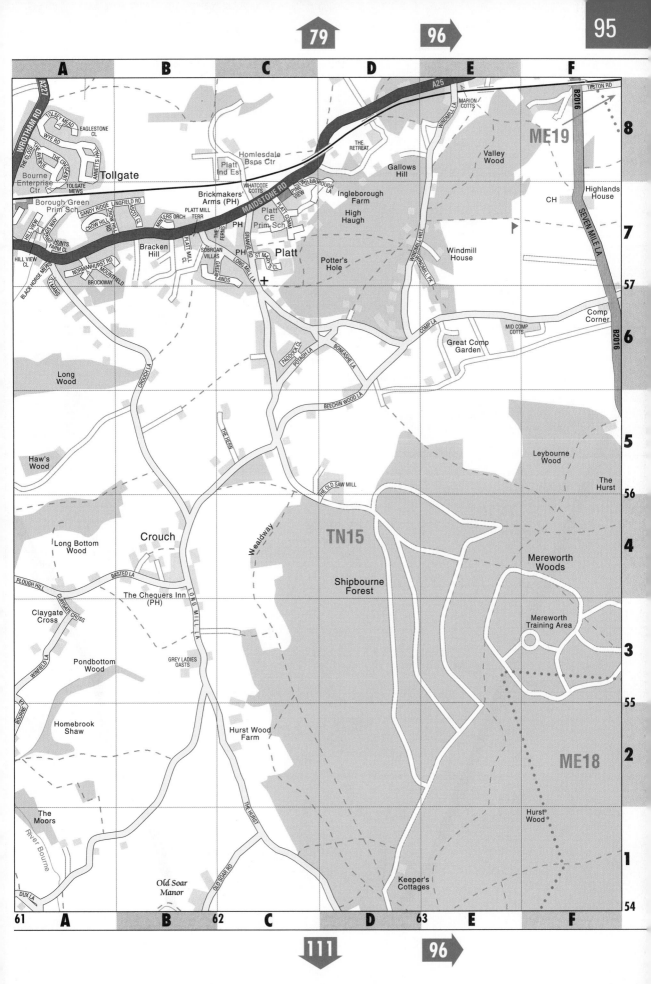

A B C D E F

8 7 57 6 5 56 4 55 2 1 54

A227
WROTHAM RD
TOLSEY MEAD
EAGLESTONE CL
WYE RD
ANNETTS WAY
THE CRESCENT
THE AVENUE
THE CLOSE
Tollgate
Bourne Enterprise Ctr
TOLGATE MEWS
Borough Green Prim Sch
HILL VIEW
SANDY RIDGE
LINGFIELD RD
CROW HILL RD
ASCOT CL
Crow Hill
HUNTS FARM CL
HILL VIEW CL
BLACK HORSE MEWS
LYMANS
NORMANHURST RD
MOUNTFIELD
BROCKWAY
Bracken Hill
MINERS ORCH
PLATT MILL TERR
PLATT MILL CL
SOBRAN VILLAS
THE FERNS
GREENLANDS
Homlesdale Bsps Ctr
Platt Ind Est
Brickmakers' Arms (PH)
WHATCOTE COTTS
PINE VIEW
GLEBOROUGH LA
MAIDSTONE RD
PH
GRANGE RD
ST MARY'S CL
Platt CE Prim Sch
PLATT COMM
Platt
LONG MILL LA
THE HERN
The Retreat
Ingleborough Farm
High Haugh
Potter's Hole
Gallows Hill
MARION COTTS
WINDMILL LA
Valley Wood
Windmill House
WINDMILL PK
ME19
CH
Highlands House
B2016
TESTON RD
SEVEN MILE LA
Comp Corner
B2016
COMP LA
MID COMP COTTS
Great Comp Garden
Long Wood
CROUCH LA
PADDOCK CL
POTASH LA
BONEASHE LA
BEECHIN WOOD LA
Haw's Wood
THE OLD SAW MILL
Wealdway
Crouch
Long Bottom Wood
BASTED LA
The Chequers Inn (PH)
LONG MILL LA
GREY LADIES OASTS
PLOUGH HILL
CLAYGATE CROSS
Claygate Cross
WINFIELD
Pondbottom Wood
BOURNE
Homebrook Shaw
The Moors
River Bourne
DUX LA
Old Soar Manor
OLD SOAR RD
THE HURST
Hurst Wood Farm
TN15
Shipbourne Forest
Mereworth Woods
Leybourne Wood
The Hurst
Mereworth Training Area
ME18
Hurst Wood
Keeper's Cottages
A25

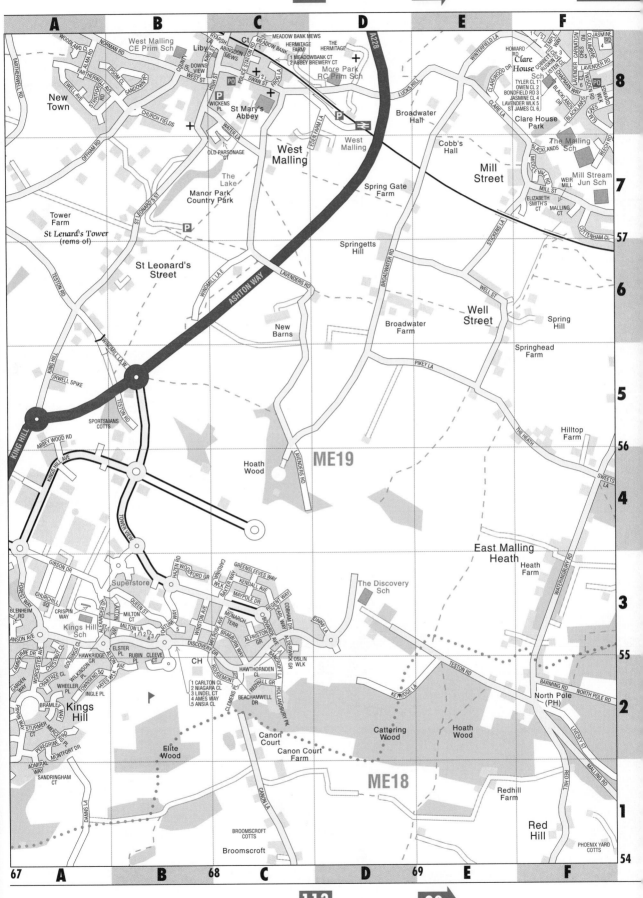

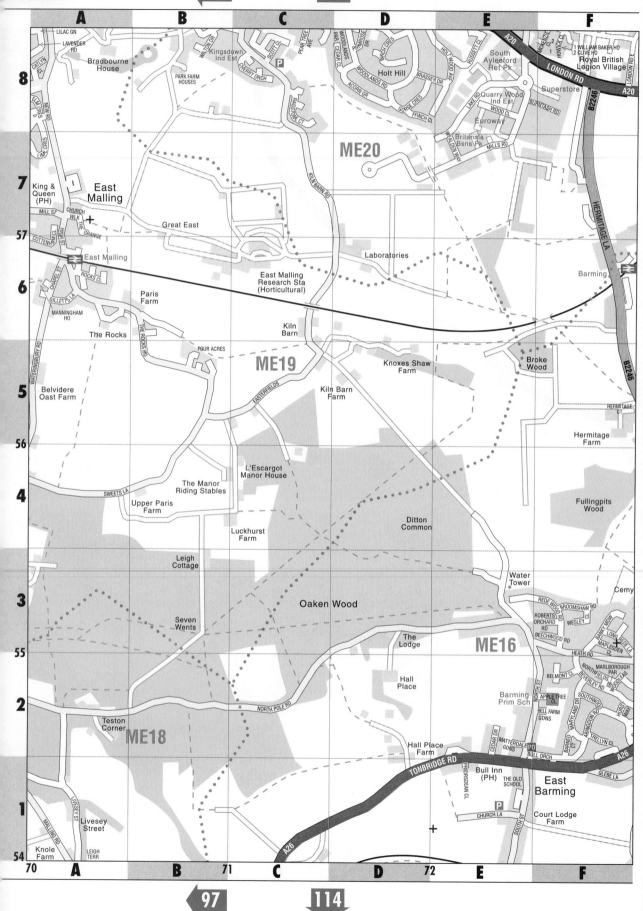

A B C D E F

8
7
57
6
5
56
4
3
55
2
1
54

70 A B 71 C D 72 E F

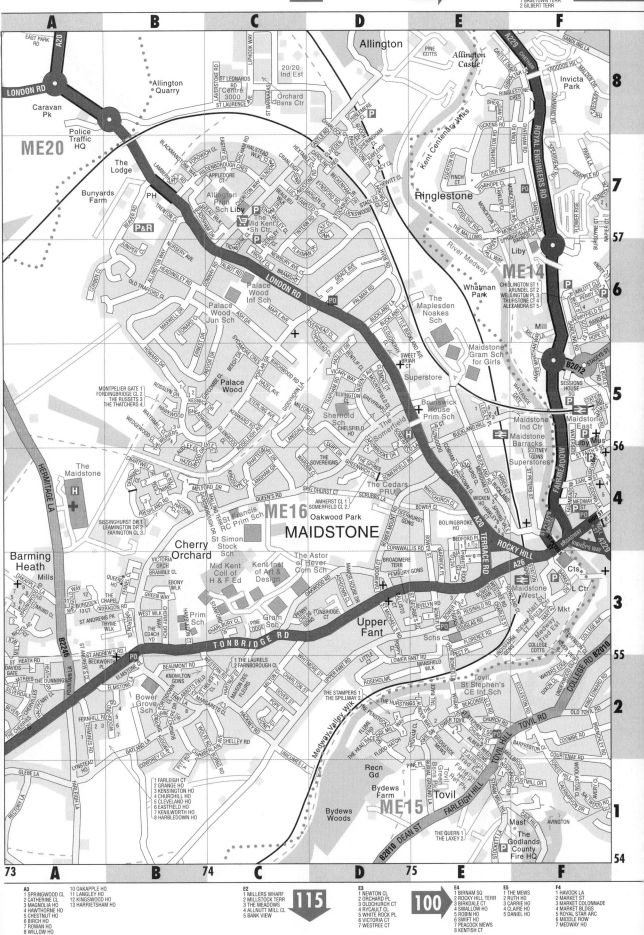

100

A5	
1 MANDEVILLE CT	7 LADBROOKE HO
2 CRUNDALE	8 LAMBARD HO
3 WALMER CT	9 WINCHESTER PL
4 PRIORY GATE	10 LOWER BOXLEY RD
5 STARNES CT	**A6**
6 KILBURN HO	1 TELFORD HO
	2 WALSHAW HO

← 99

A6
3 WALSINGHAM HO
A7
1 ADEN TERR
2 BARBADOS TERR
3 CANADA TERR
4 NORWAY TERR

84

A7
5 MALTA TERR
6 LIBYA TERR
7 KENYA TERR
8 HONDURAS TERR

Harbourland
Sandling Prim Sch
Kiln Wood
Park Wood
SITTINGBOURNE RD
M20
Horish Wood
Viewpoint
Heath Wood
Penenden Heath
Hotel
BEARSTED RD
Newnham Court Farm
Works
PH
Lower Fullingpits Wood
Crem
Gidd's Pond Farm
Pope's Wood
St Pauls Inf Sch
Television Studios
ME14
Weavering Street
Grove Green
Superstore
HM Prison
Vinters Park
St John's Sch
Sch
Invicta Gram Sch
Playing Field
Valley Park Com Sch
ASHFORD RD
A20
LORD ROMNEY'S HILL
Weavering Cotts
Park Villas
Cricket Gd
MAIDSTONE
Mote House
River Len
ME15
Mote Park
Maidstone Gram Sch
Maidstone L Ctr
Prim Sch
Postley Commercial Ctr
Park Way Prim Sch
Mote Cottage
Keepers Cottage
Willington
South Park Bsns Village
South Park
LOOSE RD
A229

A1
1 KINGS ROW
2 NORTH CT
3 WEST CT
4 EAST CT
5 WORSFOLD CT
6 BASIL TERR
7 STONEACRE CT
A3
1 CUTBUSH ALMSHOUSES
2 CUTBUSH HO
3 GREENHITHE
4 COLLEGE WLK
5 CORRALL ALMSHOUSES
6 COLLEGE CT
7 BYCHURCH PL

← 99

A4
1 NEWLYN CT
2 BLOOMSBURY WLK
3 CUTBUSH ALMSHOUSES
4 COLMAN HO
5 EDGER PL
6 WATER LA
7 DUKES WLK
8 GRANADA HO

116

A4
9 GRANADA ST
B4
1 CUTBUSH AND CORRALL CT
2 DAY HO
3 HAYNES HO
4 GULLAND HO
5 PINE HO
6 CLIFFORD HO
7 ELLIS HO
8 RIVER BANK CL
9 BELMONT CT
10 LENHAM CT
11 KINGFISHER CT
12 WILLOWBANK CT

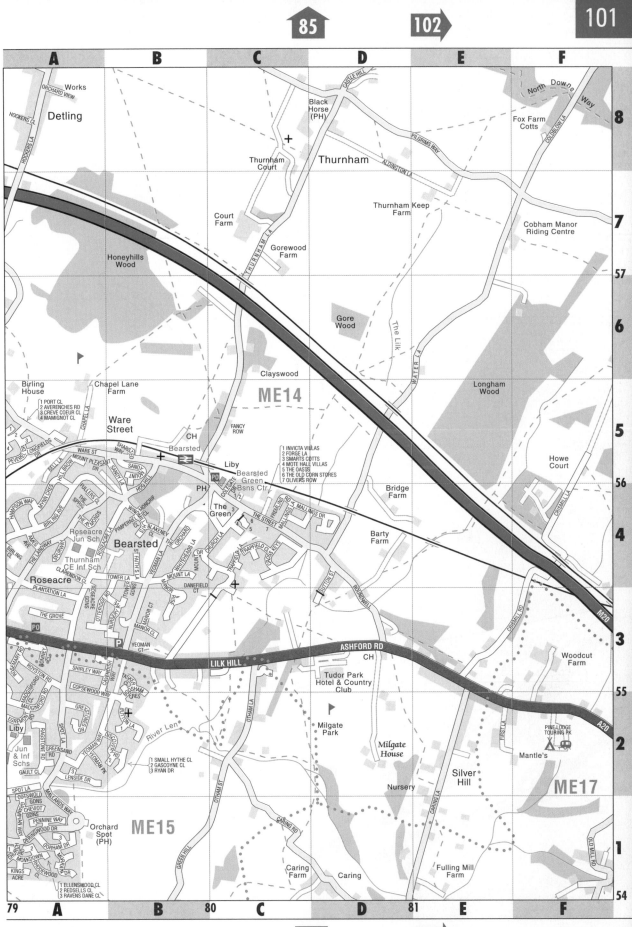

← **101**
↑ **86**

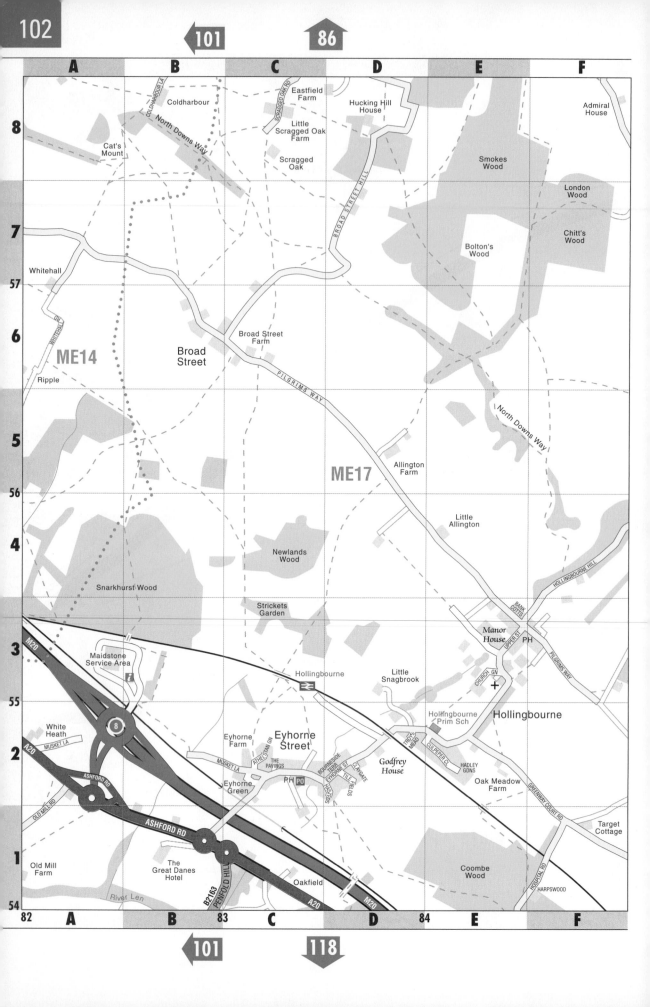

← **101**
↓ **118**

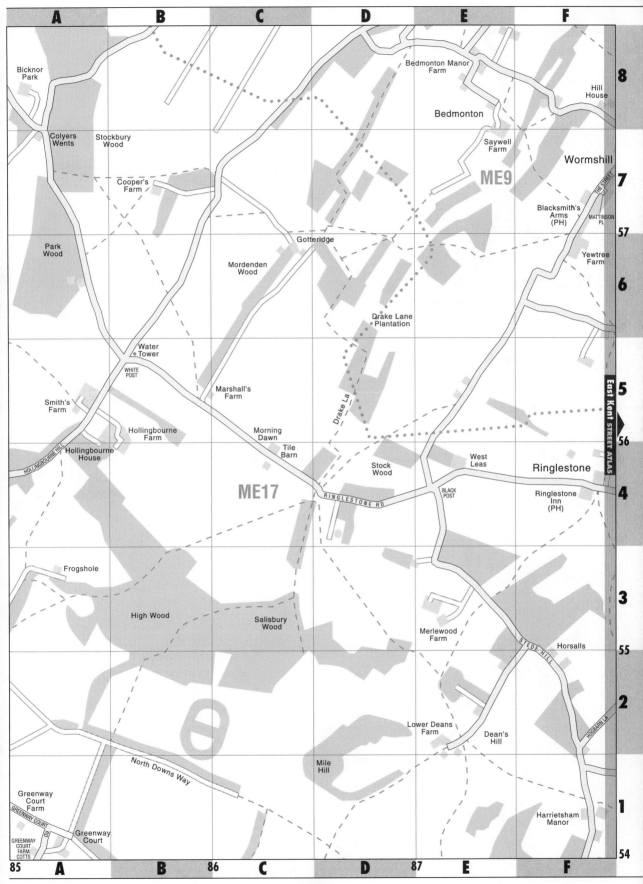

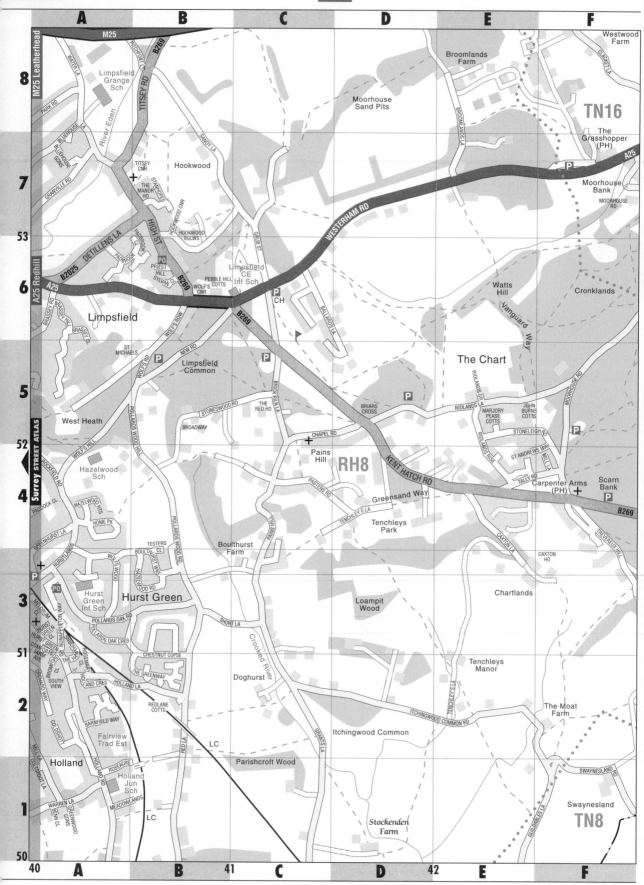

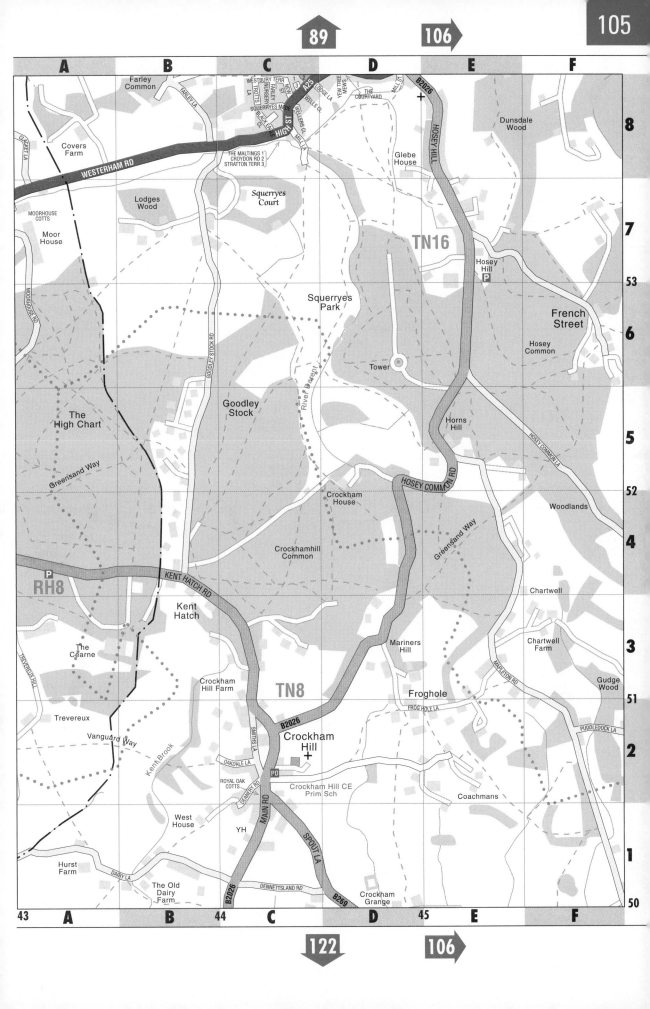

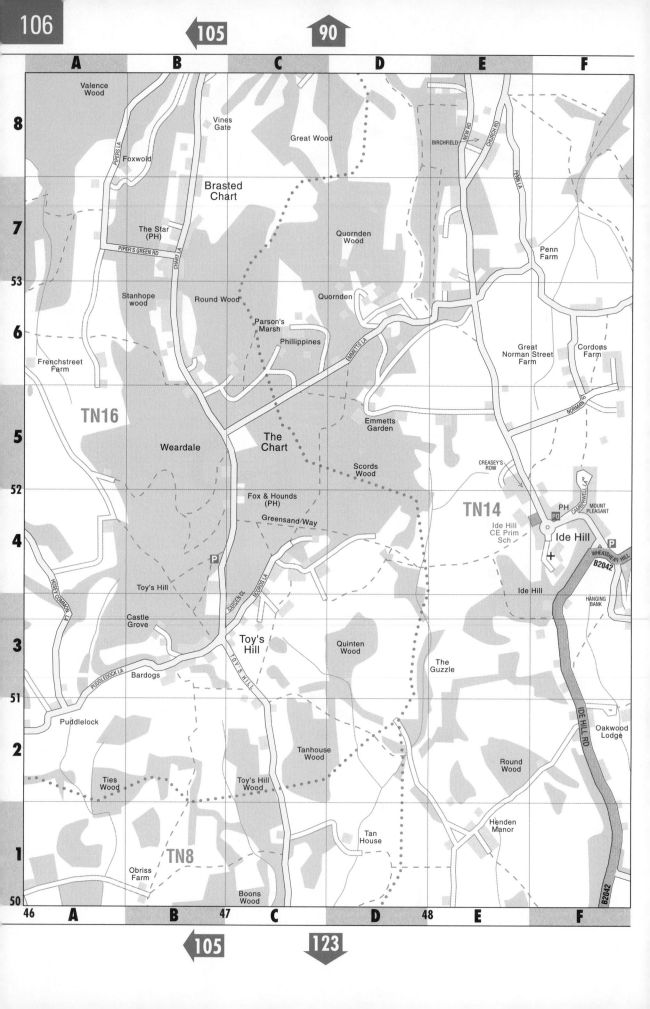

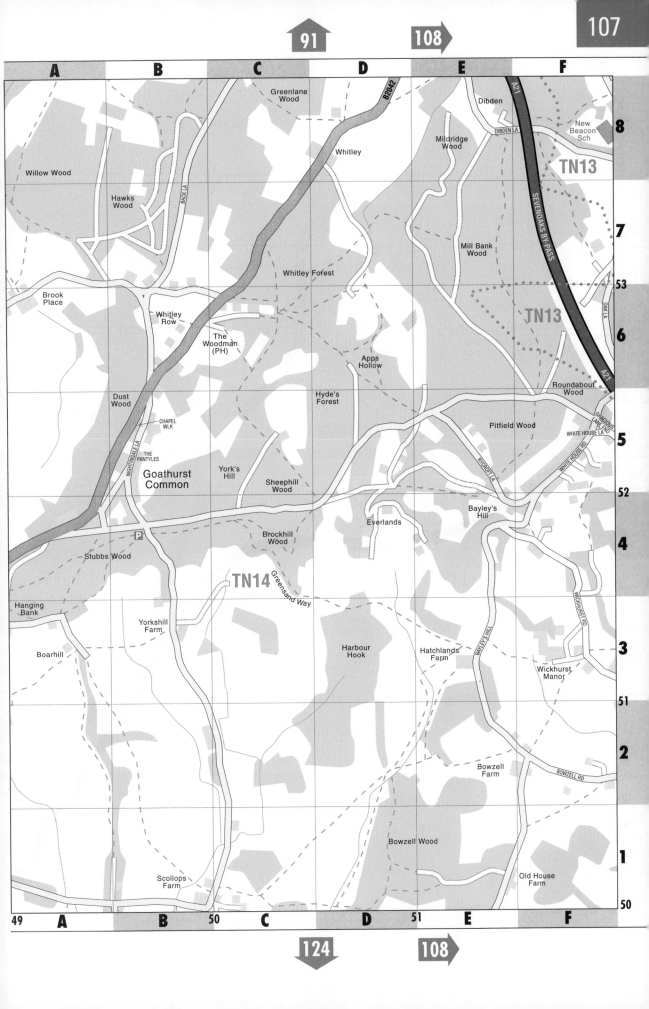

A   B   C   D   E   F

8

Willow Wood

Greenlane Wood

Whitley

Dibden

DIBDEN LA

New Beacon Sch

TN13

Hawks Wood

BACK LA

Mildridge Wood

7

Mill Bank Wood

SEVENOAKS BY-PASS

A21

Brook Place

Whitley Forest

53

Whitley Row

TN13

OAK LA

The Woodman (PH)

Apps Hollow

6

Dust Wood

CHAPEL WLK

Hyde's Forest

A21

Roundabout Wood

NIGHTINGALE LA

THE PANTYLES

York's Hill

Pitfield Wood

GRACIOUS LANE END

WHITE HOUSE LA

5

Goathurst Common

Sheephill Wood

RYCROFT LA

WHITE HOUSE RD

52

Brockhill Wood

Everlands

Bayley's Hill

P

TN14

Greensand Way

4

Stubbs Wood

Hanging Bank

Yorkshill Farm

BAYLEY'S HILL

WICKHURST RD

3

Boarhill

Harbour Hook

Hatchlands Farm

Wickhurst Manor

51

2

Bowzell Farm

BOWZELL RD

Bowzell Wood

1

Scollops Farm

Old House Farm

50

49   A   B   50   C   D   51   E   F

SEVENOAKS

Fig Street

Knole Park

Cedarholme

Deer Park

TN13

The New Sch at West Heath

Sevenoaks Common

St Julian's

Mast

RIVERHILL COTTS

River Hill

TN15

Beechmont Bank

Hubbard's Hill

Riverhill House Gdns

Home Farm

Gracious Lane Bridge

GRACIOUS LANE END

Weald Place

SEVENOAKS BY-PASS

Ash Plat

George's Shaw

Panthurst Farm

Greensand Way

Dale Farm

Mast

Morleys Farm

MORLEY'S RD

LONDON RD

Oakhurst Manor

Weald Com Prim Sch

Hurst Farm Rd

Windmill Rd

THE WICKETS

Victory Cotts

Paiges Farm

Wickhurst Rd

Overdale

Patience Cotts

Sevenoaks Weald

Gilchrist Cotts

TN14

Nizels Wood

Brook Farm

Robsacks Wood

TN11

Nizels

CH

Nizels Farm

The Vineyard

New House Farm

Fletcher's Green

EGGPIE LA

A225

TONBRIDGE RD

SHENDEN WAY

A21

A225

B245

TONBRIDGE BY-PASS

B245

1 ASHBURNHAM CL
2 SOLE FIELDS

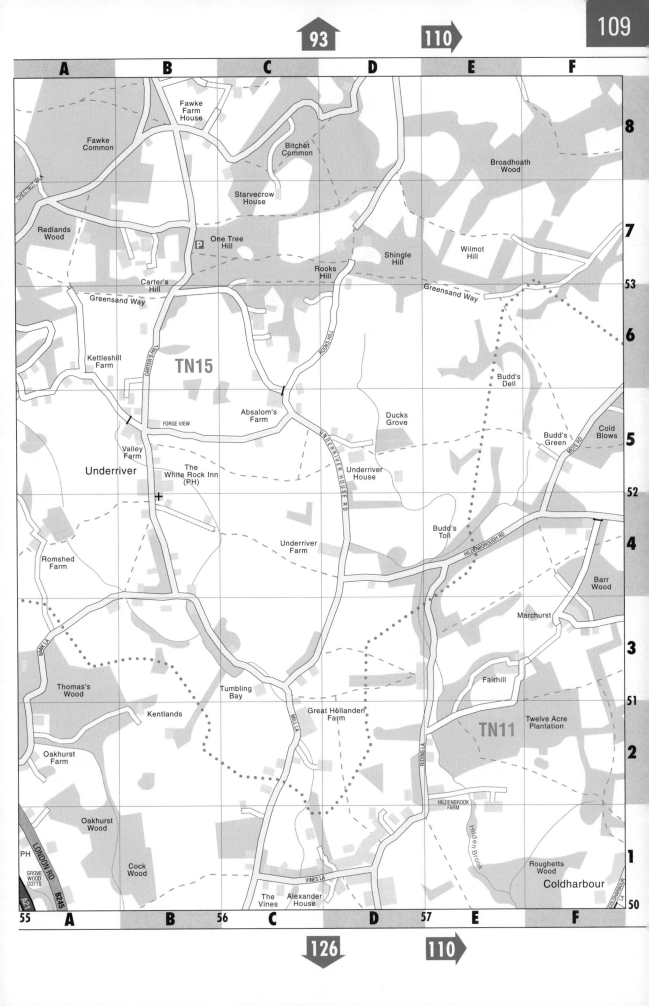

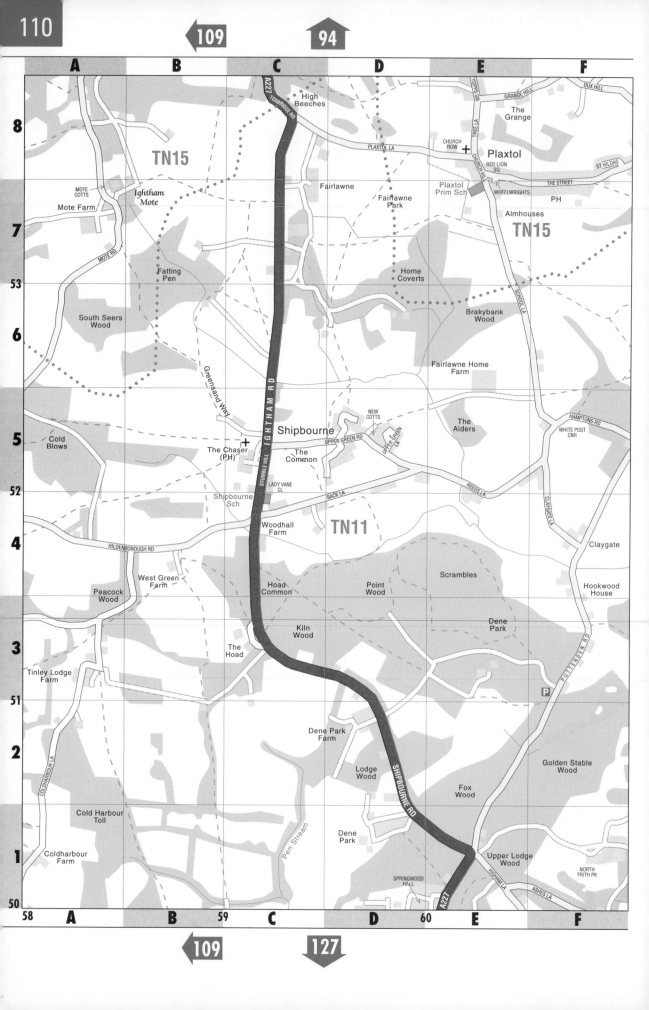

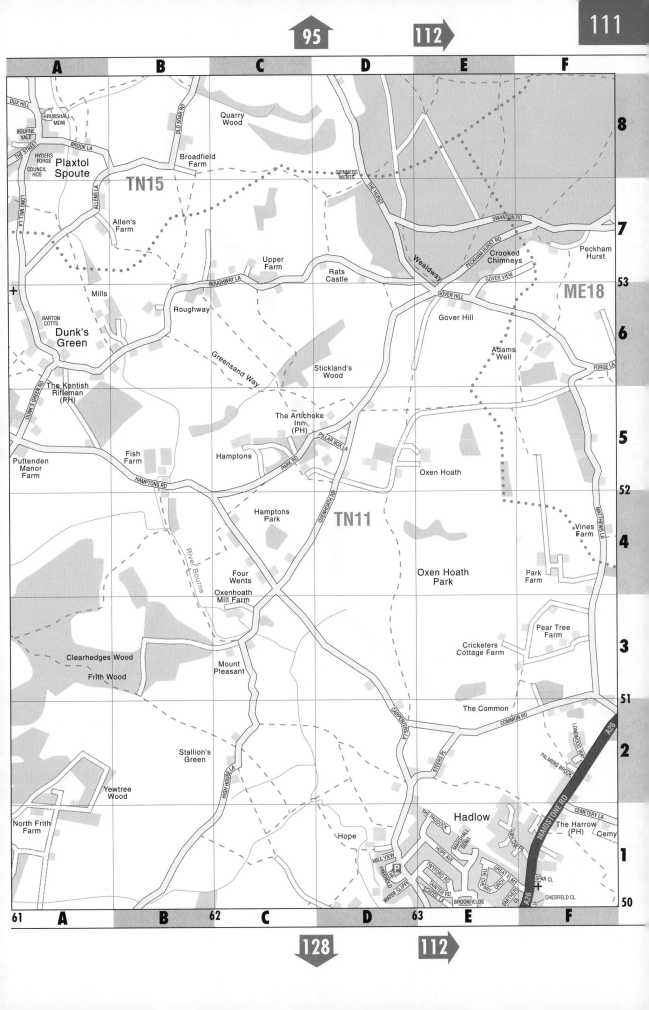

111
96

A B C D E F

8

Swanton Valley

Swanton Rd

World's End Wood

B2016

Seven Mile La

The Street

Church Cl

Torrington Cl

Butcher's La

A228

Malling Rd

A26

Tonbridge Rd

A26

Bull Farm

Mereworth Com Prim Sch

Mereworth

Swanton

7

Bo-peep Shaw

Beech Farm

Stan La

Yates Court

Mereworth Rd

Mere House

Brewer's Hall Farm

ME18

Mereworth Castle

53

6

Forge La

West Peckham

Church Rd

Church Row

The Swan (PH)

Dukes Place

Greensand Way

The Alders

B2016

Alders Wood

A26

A228

Peckham Fields Wood

Park Rd

5

Court Lodge Farm

Forge Farm

Old Church Rd

52

4

Hazel Wood

Killing Grove Wood

Grove Farm

Old Church La

Court Lodge Cotts

The Dover House

Seven Mile La

Roydon Hall

Old Terry's Lodge Rd

3

Hazelwood Farm

Grove Cl

Grove House

Maidstone Rd

Weald Way

TN11

TN12

Mount Pleasant Farm

Martins La

51

A26

Leavers Manor (Hotel)

Goose Green

Stanford La

Peckham Place Farm

Sights

2

Leavers Farm

Pond Farm

Hextall Court

1

Cemetery La

Little Goblands Farm

Bells Farm La

Crowhurst Oast

Bells Farm Rd

Crowhurst Farm

Bullen La

Crowhurst Hop Farm

A228

50

64 A B 65 C D 66 E F

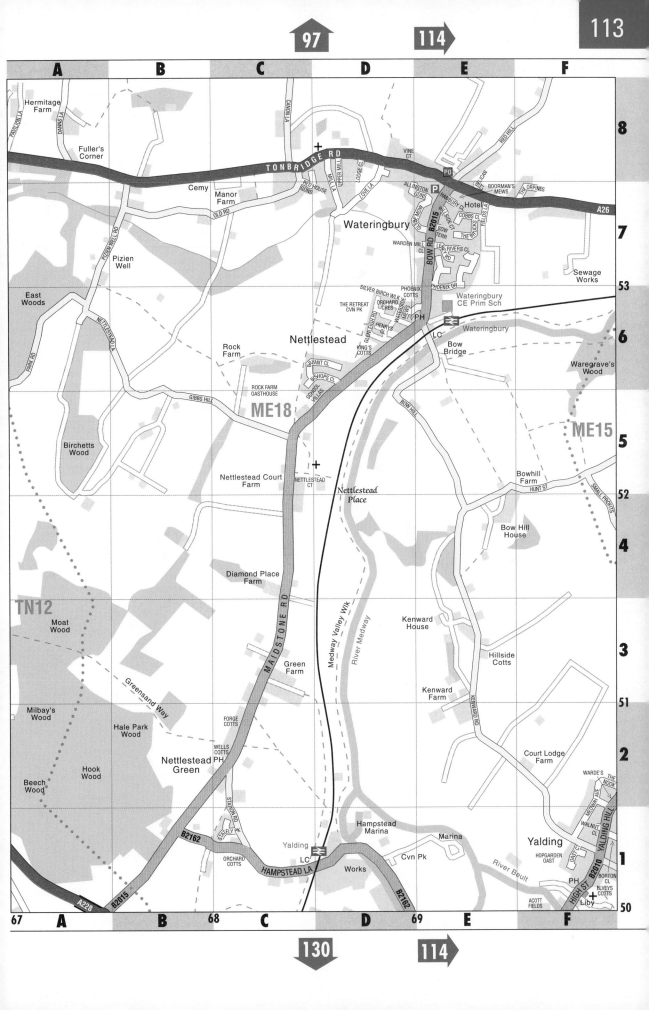

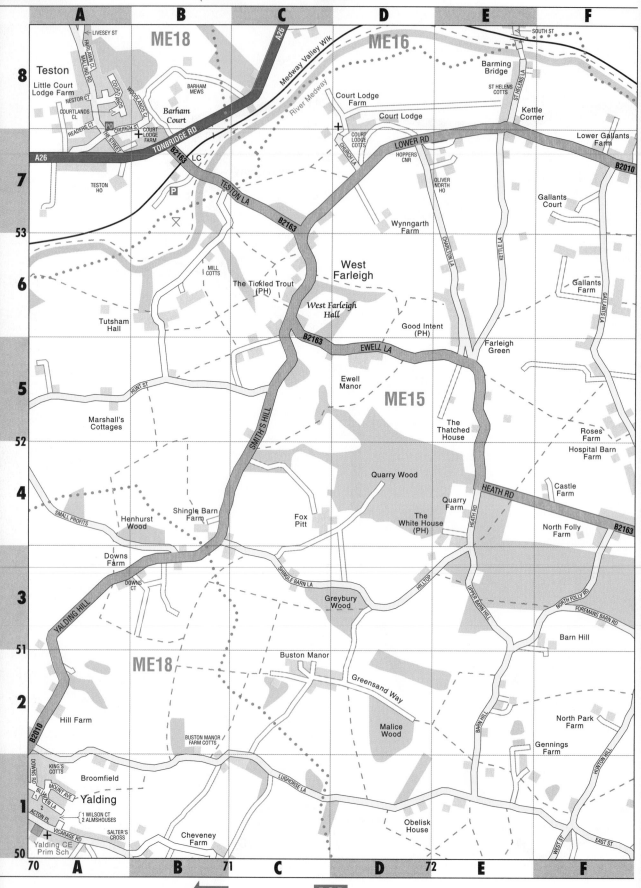

113
98

A B C D E F

ME18

Teston 8
Little Court
Lodge Farm
Nestor Ct
Courtlands
Cl
Readers Ct
PO
Livesey St
Fairlawn Cl
Malling Rd
Court Lands
Woodlands Ct
Church St
Court Lodge
Farm
The Street
Barham
Court
Barham
Mews
A26
Medway Valley Wlk
River Medway
ME16
South St
Barming
Bridge
St Helens
Cotts
St Helens La
Kettle
Corner
Lower Gallants
Farm

TONBRIDGE RD
B2163
LC
A26 7
Teston Ho
P
TESTON LA
B2163
Court Lodge
Farm
Court Lodge
LOWER RD
Court
Lodge
Cotts
Church La
Hoppers
Cnr
Oliver
North
Ho
Charlton La
Kettle La
B2010
Gallants
Court

53
Wynngarth
Farm

Mill
Cotts
The Tickled Trout
(PH)
**West
Farleigh** 6
West Farleigh
Hall
Good Intent
(PH)
Farleigh
Green
Gallants
Farm
Gallants La

Tutsham
Hall
B2163
EWELL LA
Ewell
Manor
ME15

Hunt St 5
Marshall's
Cottages
SMITH'S HILL
The
Thatched
House
Roses
Farm
Hospital Barn
Farm

52
Quarry Wood
Quarry
Farm
HEATH RD
Castle
Farm
B2163

SMALL PROFITS 4
Henhurst
Wood
Shingle Barn
Farm
Fox
Pitt
The
White House
(PH)
Quarry
Farm
Heath Rd
North Folly
Farm

Downs
Farm
Downs
Ct
Shingle Barn La
Greybury
Wood
Hilltop
Upper Barn Hill
North Folly Rd
Foremans Barn Rd

YALDING HILL 3
Barn Hill

51
Buston Manor
Greensand Way
Barn Hill
ME18

B2010 2
Hill Farm
Buston Manor
Farm Cotts
Malice
Wood
North Park
Farm
Gennings
Farm
Hunton Hill

King's
Cotts
Broomfield
Downs Rd
Mount Ave
Buston La
Yalding
Lughorse La

Acton Pl 1
1 Wilson Ct
2 Almshouses
Vicarage Rd
Salter's
Cross
Obelisk
House
West St
East St

Yalding CE
Prim Sch
Cheveney
Farm
50

70 A B 71 C D 72 E F

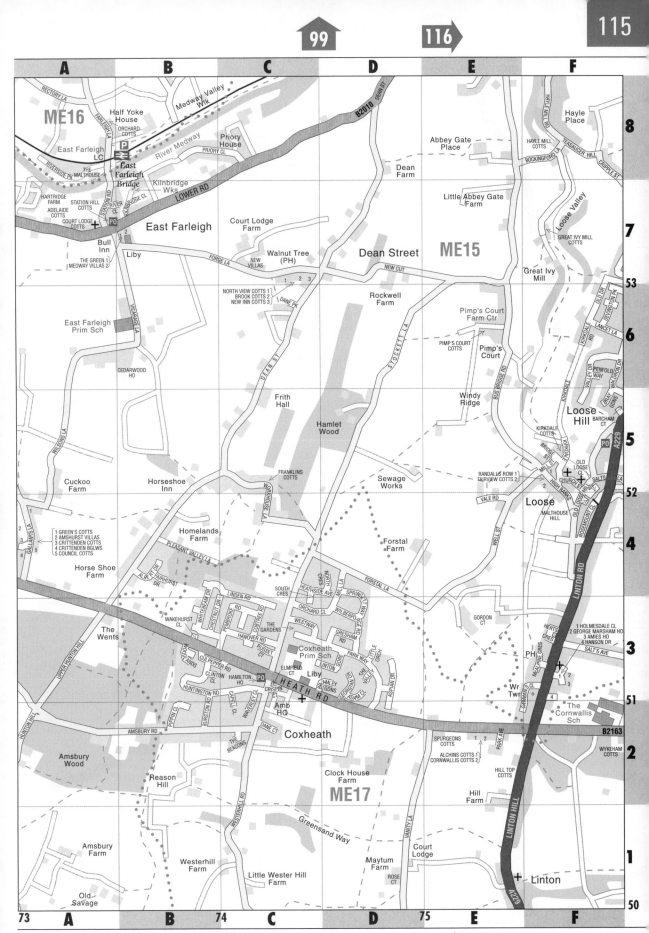

ME16

RECTORY LA

Half Yoke House

Medway Valley Wlk

B2010

DEAN ST

Abbey Gate Place

Hayle Place

East Farleigh LC

ORCHARD COTTS

River Medway

Priory House

Dean Farm

ME15

HAYLE MILL COTTS

TEASAUGER HILL

CRIPPLE ST

HAYLE MILL RD

BOCKINGFORD LA

THE MALTHOUSE

East Farleigh Bridge

Kilnbridge Wks

PRIORY CL

LOWER RD

Little Abbey Gate Farm

Loose Valley

RIVERSIDE PK

HARTRIDGE FARM

STATION HILL COTTS

Dean Street

GREAT IVY MILL COTTS

ADELAIDE COTTS

COURT LODGE COTTS

Bull Inn

East Farleigh

Court Lodge Farm

Dean Street

Great Ivy Mill

OLD DR

SEVINGTON PK

THE GREEN 1
MEDWAY VILLAS 2

Liby

FORGE LA

NEW VILLAS

Walnut Tree (PH)

NEW CUT

Great Ivy Mill

KIRKDALE RD

LANCET LA

East Farleigh Prim Sch

VICARAGE LA

NORTH VIEW COTTS 1
BROOK COTTS 2
NEW INN COTTS 3

DANE PK

Rockwell Farm

Pimp's Court Farm Ctr

VALLEY DR

PENFOLD WAY

CEDARWOOD HO

DEAN ST

Frith Hall

STOCKETT LA

PIMP'S COURT COTTS

Pimp's Court

BUS BRIDGE RD

Loose Hill

BARCHAM CT

WALDRON DR

BRAY GDNS

WILSONS LA

Hamlet Wood

Windy Ridge

KIRKDALE COTTS

BRIDGE ST

KYRKDALE

PO

A229

Cuckoo Farm

Horseshoe Inn

FRANKLINS COTTS

Sewage Works

RANDALL'S ROW 1
FAIRVIEW COTTS 2

MILL ST

OLD LOOSE CL

SALTS

WOODHOUSE LA

VALE RD

HIGH BANKS

Loose

ROSEMOUNT DR

1 GREEN'S COTTS
2 AMSHURST VILLAS
3 CRITTENDEN COTTS
4 CRITTENDEN BGLWS
5 COUNCIL COTTS

GALLANTS LA

Homelands Farm

Forstal Farm

Malthouse Hill

WELL ST

Horse Shoe Farm

PLEASANT VALLEY LA

FAIRHURST DR

ALBE CT

HANOVER RD

NORTH CRES

Little ORCH

HERTS

GORDON CT

LINTON RD

The Wents

UPPER HUNTON HILL

WAKEHURST CL

WHITEBEAM DR

CHESTNUT DR

PEMBROOK RD

COBTREE RD

LINDEN RD

SOUTH CRES

Heathside Ave

SPRINGETT WAY

WILBERFORCE RD

FORSTAL LA

McALPINE CRES

1 HOLMESDALE CL
2 GEORGE MARSHAM HO
3 AMIES HO
4 HANSON DR

The Gardens

WESTWAY

ORCHARD CL

Gresham RD

PARK WAY

PH

SALT'S AVE

HUNTON HILL

WOODLANDS

CULPEPPER RD

RUSSET CT

Coxheath Prim Sch

Liby

GORE

THE VALLEY

ADAM CT

ASPIAN DR

CARMAN'S CL

Wr Twr

CLINTON CL

HAMILTON HO

ELMFIELD CT

LINTON

BROMLEY GDNS

The Cornwallis Sch

HUNTINGTON RD

CAPELL CL

WAFERLEY CL

CRISPIN

PO

HEATH RD

Amb HQ

B2163

BURSTON RD

PIPPIN CL

AMSBURY RD

DANE CT

Coxheath

SPURGEONS COTTS

PARK AVE

WYKEHAM COTTS

Amsbury Wood

THE BEACONS

ALCHINS COTTS 1
CORNWALLIS COTTS 2

HILL TOP COTTS

Reason Hill

WESTERHILL RD

Clock House Farm

ME17

Hill Farm

LINTON HILL

Amsbury Farm

Westerhill Farm

Greensand Way

VANITY LA

Court Lodge

Little Wester Hill Farm

Maytum Farm

ROSE CT

Linton

Old Savage

A229

73   74   75

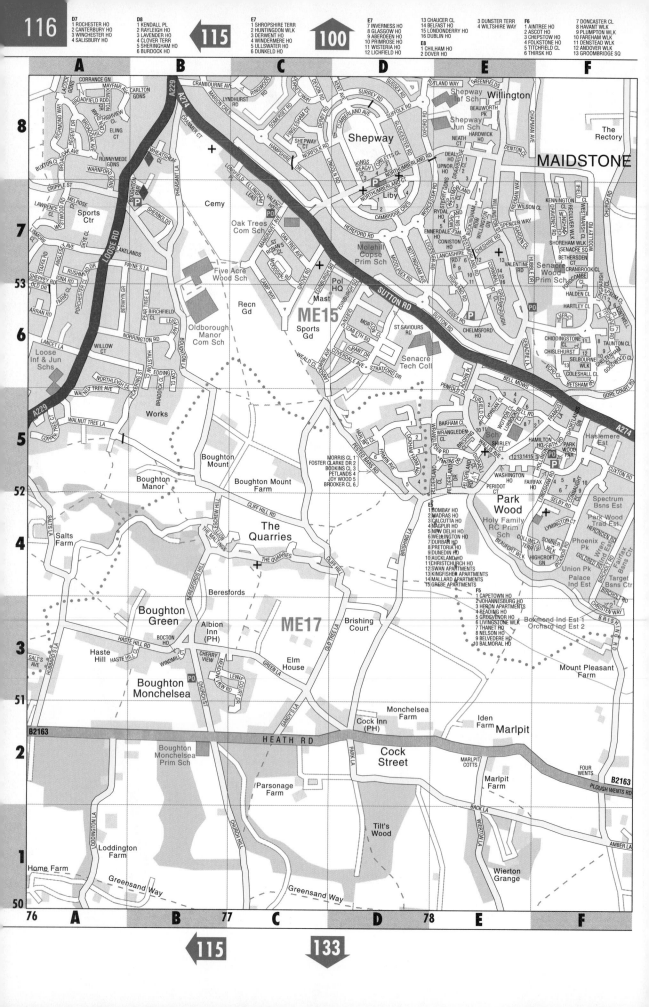

117
102

A B C D E F

8

Sewage
Works

Leeds &
Broomfield
CE Prim Sch

Ashbank

ASHBANK
COTTS

Park Gate
Inn
(PH)

CH

Warren
Wood

HOSPITAL RD

GREENWAY COURT RD

GREENWAY LA

7

Leeds

Battel
Hall

WYKEHAM GR

GEORGE LA

PENFOLD HILL

B2163

Leeds
Castle

A20

M20

ASHFORD RD

Forge
House

A20

M20

53

The George Inn
(PH)

LOWER ST

UPPER ST

B2163

The
Great
Water

River Len

Chegworth

6

Abbey
Farm

FARMER CL

BURBERRY LA

Church
Farm

Broomfield

Roses
Farm

CHEGWORTH RD

Chegworth
Court

5

Park Barn
Farm

PARK BARN RD

BROOMFIELD RD

ME17

52

Scrub
Wood

4

Glebe
Dene

King's
Wood

3

The Apiary
Bsns Pk

The
Apiary

Kingswood

CHARLESFORD AVE

WHITEHALL DR

ASHFORD DR

PO

Kingswood
Prim Sch

Caravan
Site

WATER LA

51

Kingswood
Farm

PITT RD

Works

GRAVELLY BOTTOM RD

CROSS DR

ELDER CL
CHESTNUT DR
THORNEY CREST CL
TALL TREES
LA
COPPERFIELD CL
WYCH CL
THE
IVY CL
BUSH GR
MEWS
IVY
BELL WAY
THE
WALDENS
THE
WALK
CAYSER DR
WILDWOOD CL
HOLLY TREE CL
HEATHERWOOD CL

LENHAM RD

2

Cherry
Tree
Farm

Chartway
Street

1

CHARTWAY ST

Street
Farm

Manor
Farm

MORRY LA

College
Farm

ULCOMBE HILL

50

WORKHOUSE RD

CHARLTON LA

CH

82 A 83 B C 83 D 84 E F

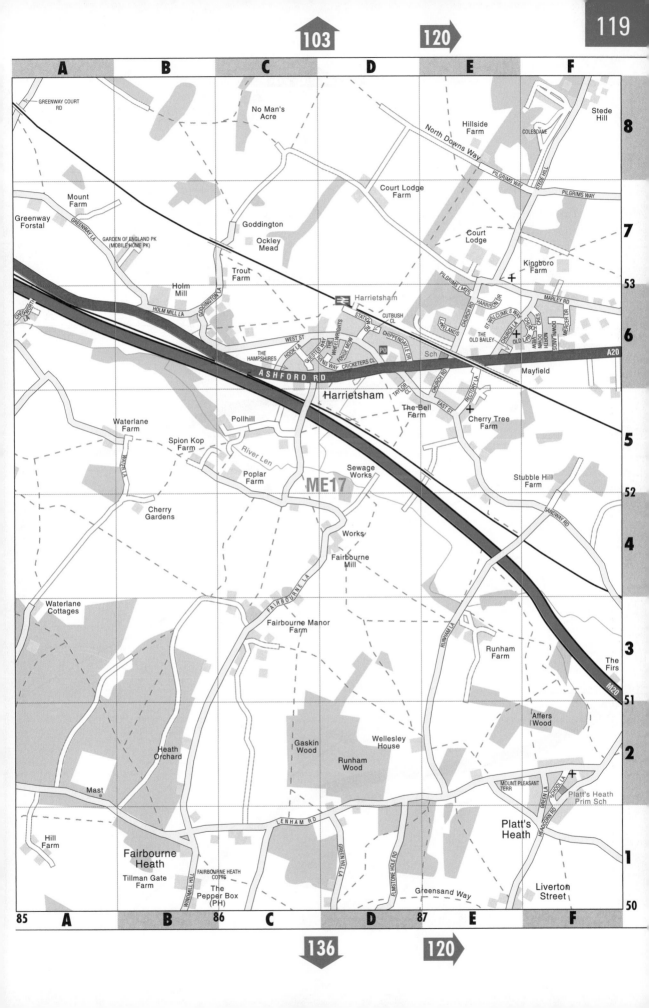

East Kent STREET ATLAS

A20 Ashford · East Kent STREET ATLAS

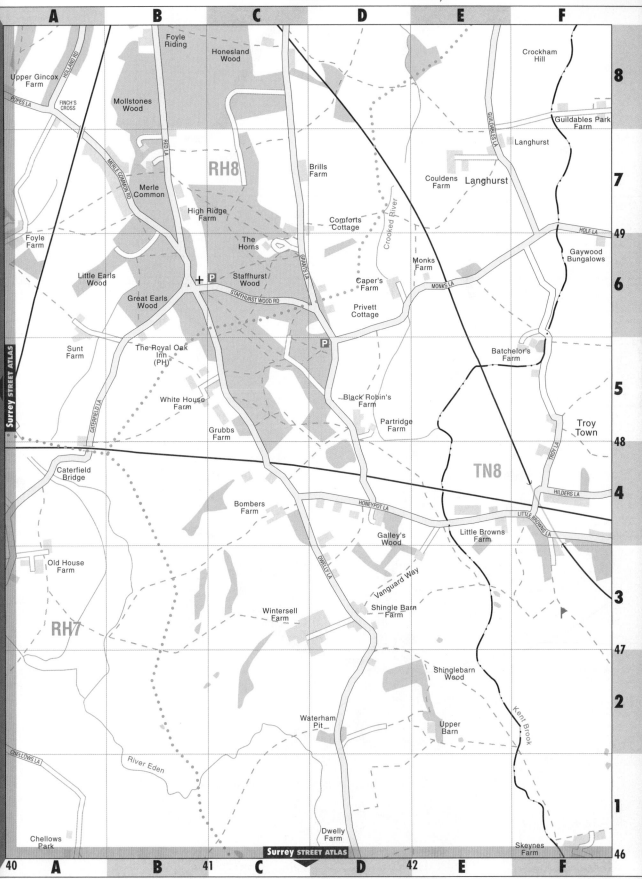

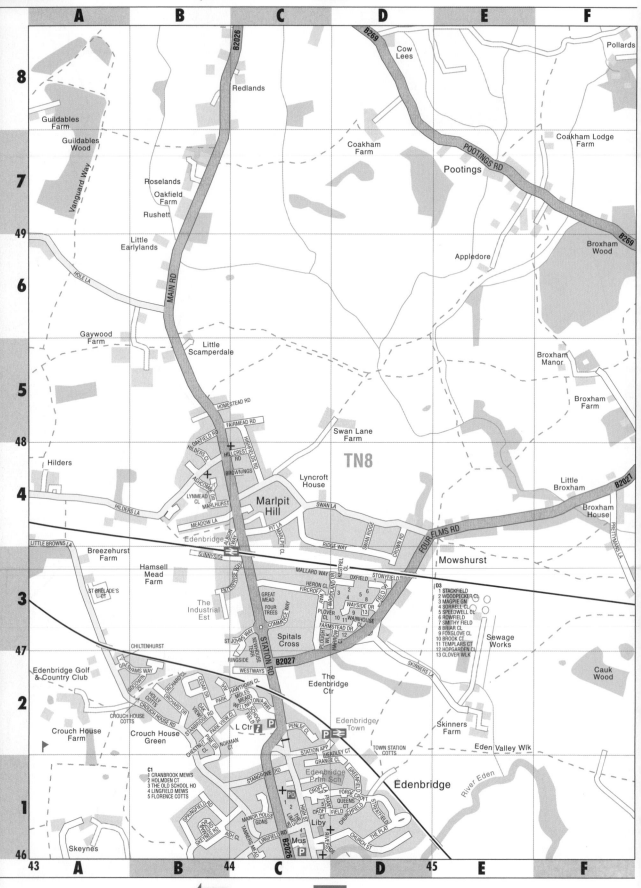

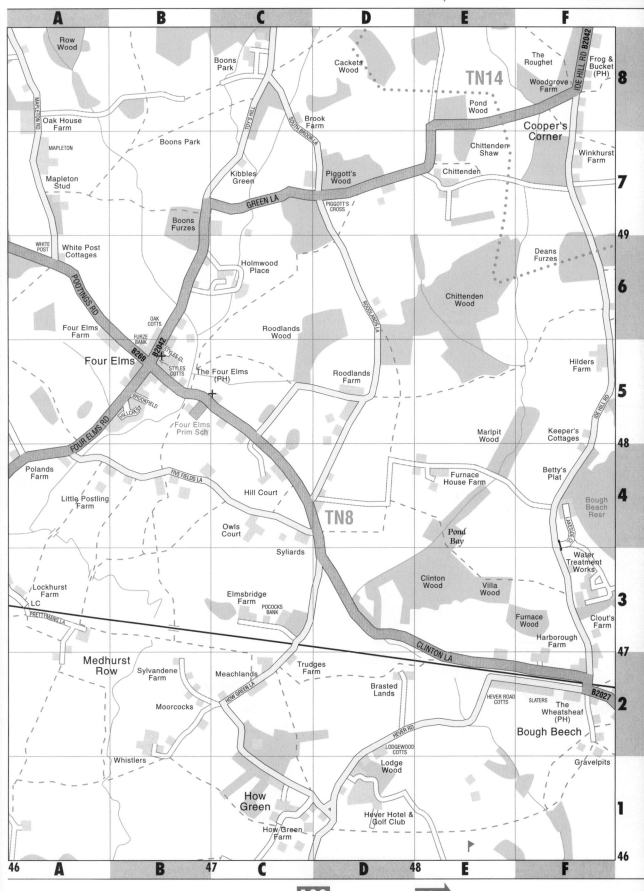

123
107

A B C D E F

8

Faulkners Hill
Farm

TN14

Bushes
Wood

Bushes
Plantation

Bushes
Farm

7

Winkhurst
Green

Nature
Reserve

Bough Beech
Nature Reserve
Visitor Centre

49

Bore Place

Hale
Oak
Farm

Deans
Wood

Field
Trail

Sharp's
Place

6

Batfold
Wood

The Old
Forge

Little
Hale

Kilnhouse
Farm

Little
Sidcup

Hale
Farm

Bough Beech Resr

5

Bushy
Wood

48

Damper's
Wood

Brownings
Cottage

Hickens

Brownings
Farm

CH

Mountjoy
Farm

4

TN8

HALE OAK RD

Polebrook
Farm

3

Cole's
Farm

Breeches
Wood

Birdfield
Plantation

Charcott
Farm

Waterlake

Camp
Hill

Chiddingstone
Causeway

47

The
Horseshoes

Waterlake
Cottage

TN11

CAMP HILL

Somerden

RICHARD'S CL

CAMP HILL
COTTS

CHEQUERS HILL
COTTS
THE CLOSE

Jessop's
Farm

2

Baldocks

DUKES MEADOWS CL

B2027

PO

PO

Trad
Est

B2027

River Eden

Penshurst

STATION HILL

Ppg
Sta

Chested
Farm

Beckett's
Farm

1

Chested

Mill
Farm

Sandhole

46

49 A B 50 C D 51 E F

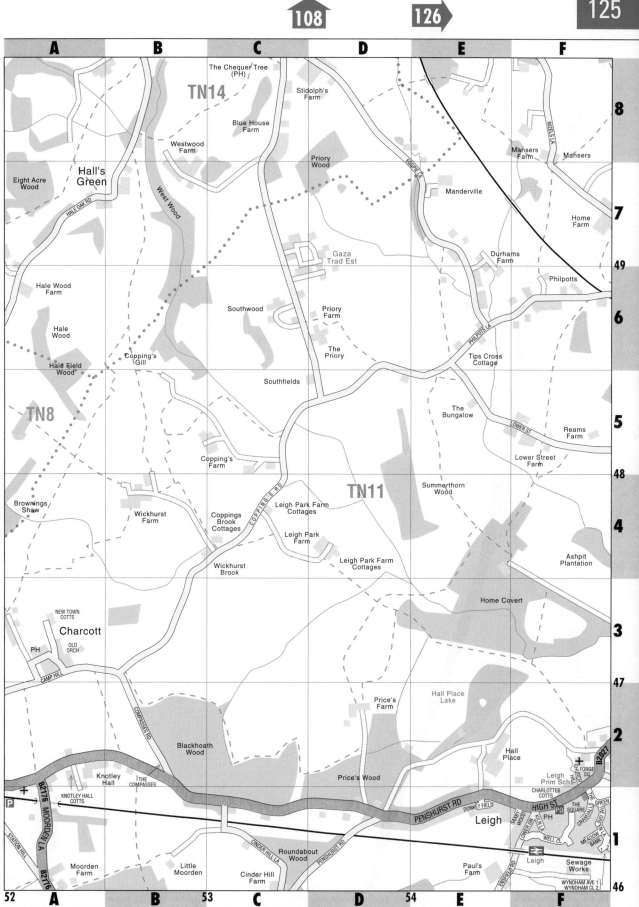

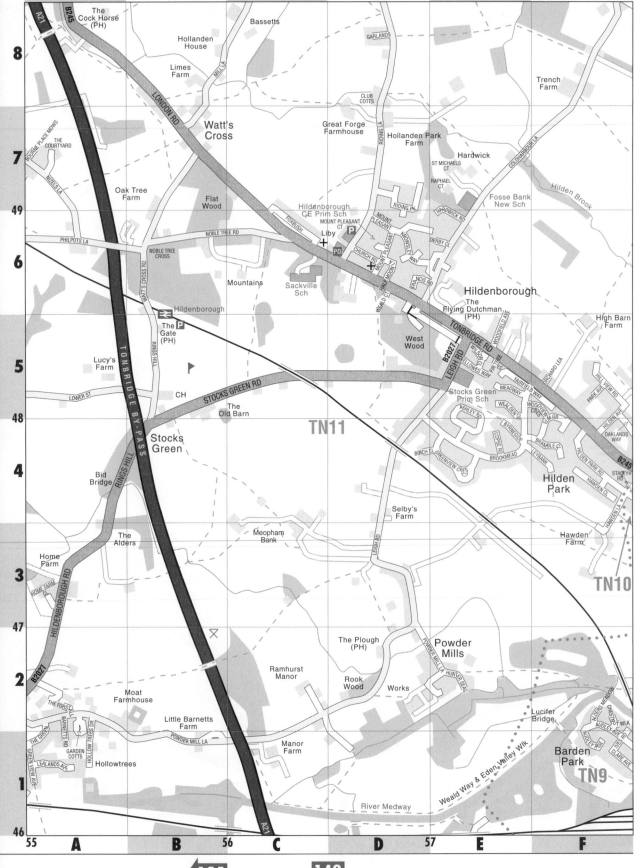

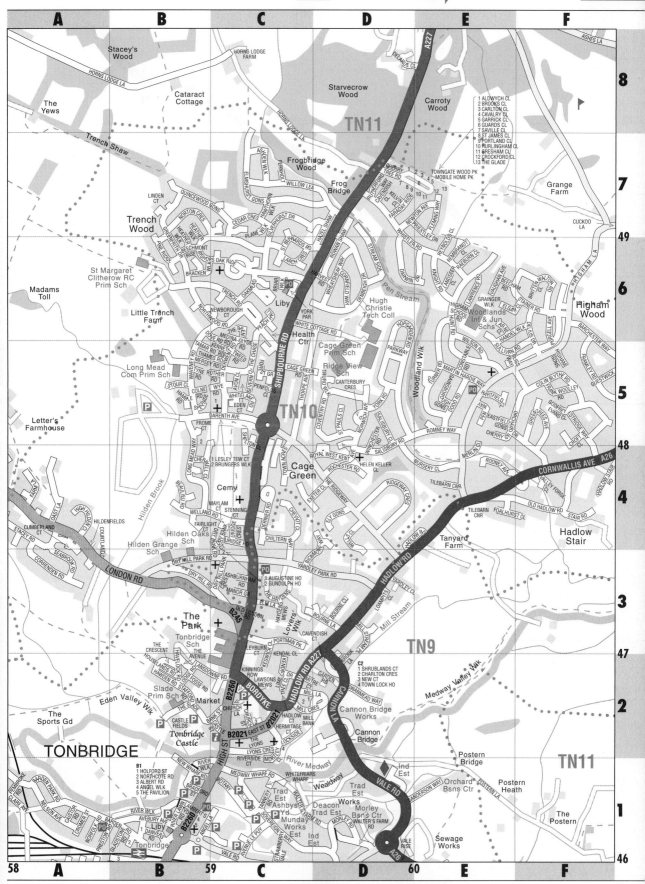

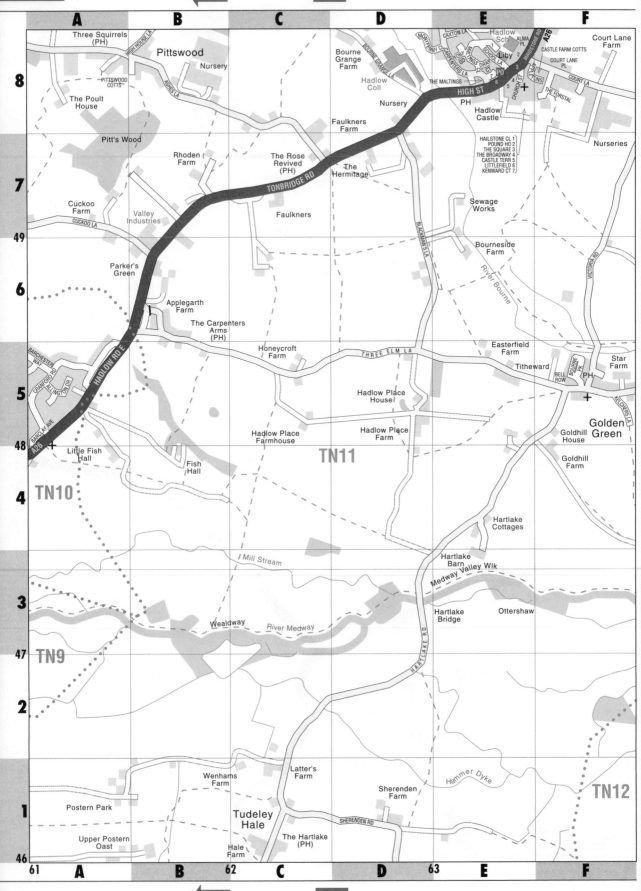

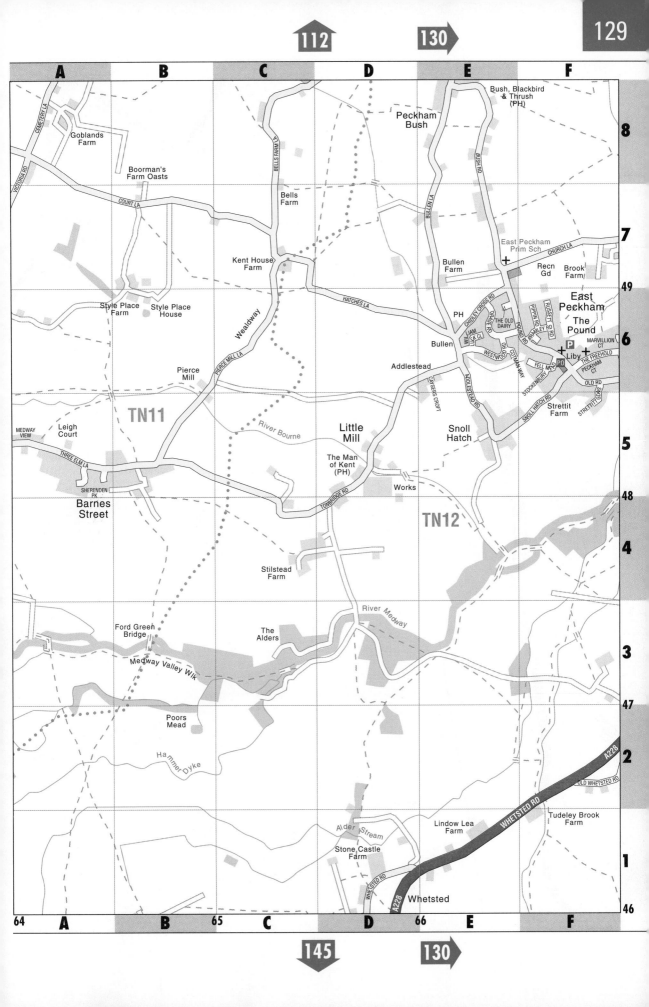

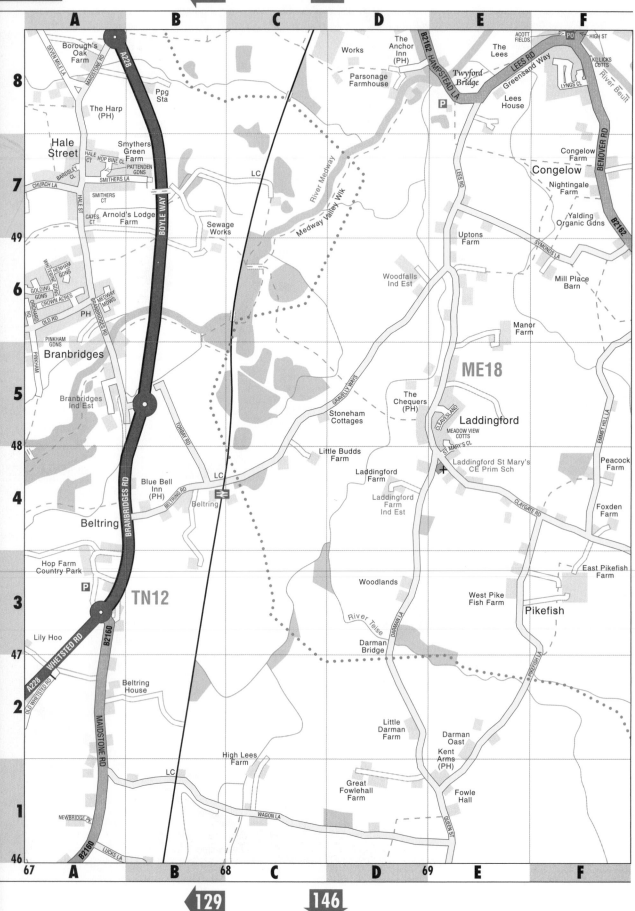

129
113

Borough's Oak Farm

SEVEN MILE LA

MAIDSTONE RD

A228

Ppg Sta

The Harp (PH)

Hale Street

HALE CT

HOP BINE CL

Smythers Green Farm

PATTENDEN GDNS

BOYLE WAY

HALE ST

BARDSLEY CL

CHURCH LA

SMITHERS LA

SMITHERS CT

Arnold's Lodge Farm

CATES CT

Sewage Works

Works

Parsonage Farmhouse

The Anchor Inn (PH)

B2162

HAMPSTEAD LA

Twyford Bridge

P

The Lees

LEES RD

Greensand Way

ACOTT FIELDS

PO

HIGH ST

KILLICKS COTTS

LYNGS CL

River Beult

BENOVER RD

Congelow Farm

Congelow

Nightingale Farm

Lees House

LEES RD

Uptons Farm

SYMONDS LA

Yalding Organic Gdns

B2162

Mill Place Barn

Woodfalls Ind Est

River Medway

Medway Valley Wlk

LC

WHITBORNE GDNS

GOLDING GDNS

ORCHARD RD

OLD RD

HENHAM GDNS

CROWN ACRES

PH

MEDWAY MDWS

BRANBRIDGES RD

PINKHAM GDNS

PINKHAM

Branbridges

Branbridges Ind Est

TORRANT RD

BELTRING RD

Blue Bell Inn (PH)

LC

Beltring

Stoneham Cottages

GRAVELLY WAYS

Little Budds Farm

Laddingford Farm

The Chequers (PH)

ME18

CLEAVES LAND

MEADOW VIEW COTTS

ST MARY'S CL

Laddingford

Laddingford St Mary's CE Prim Sch

EMMET HILL LA

Peacock Farm

Manor Farm

Laddingford Farm Ind Est

CLAYGATE RD

Foxden Farm

BRANBRIDGES RD

Beltring

Hop Farm Country Park

P

TN12

B2160

WHETSTED RD

Lily Hoo

A228

OLD WHETSTED RD

Beltring House

MAIDSTONE RD

Woodlands

River Teise

DARMAN LA

Darman Bridge

West Pike Fish Farm

East Pikefish Farm

PIKEFISH LA

Pikefish

High Lees Farm

LC

Little Darman Farm

Darman Oast

Kent Arms (PH)

Great Fowlehall Farm

Fowle Hall

QUEEN ST

NEWBRIDGE LA

B2160

LUCKS LA

WAGON LA

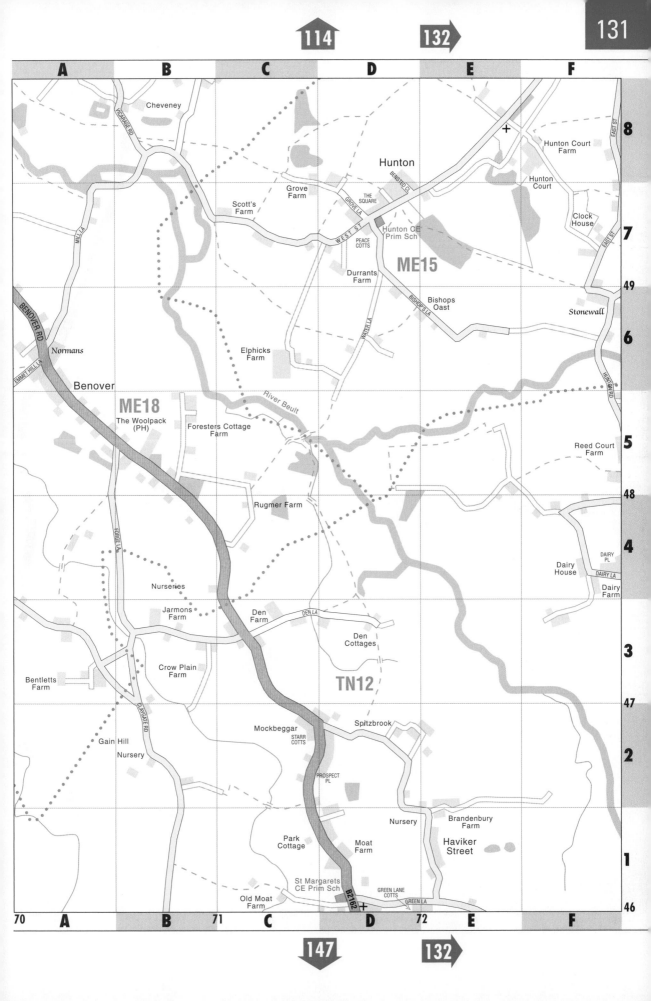

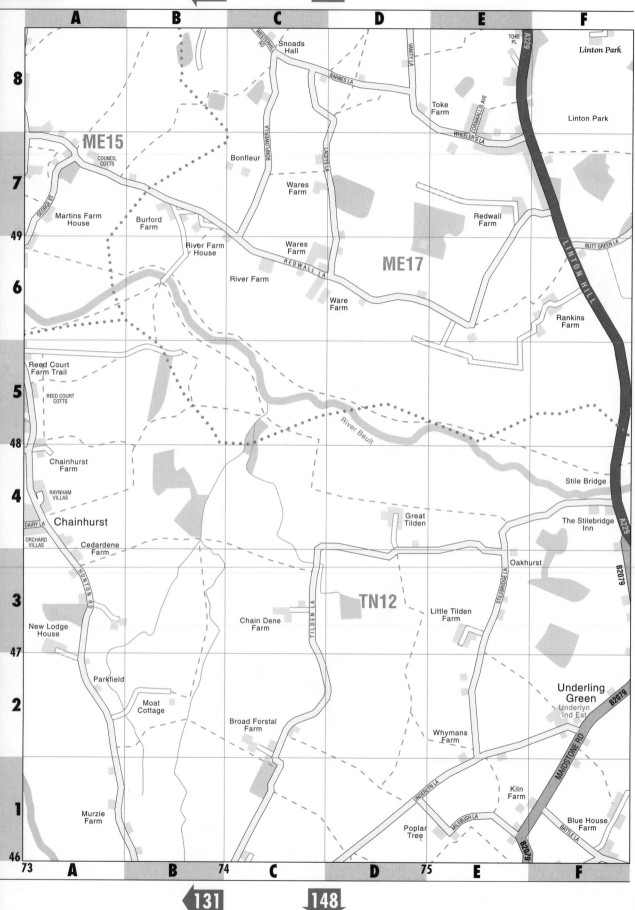

131
115

A · B · C · D · E · F

8

ME15

7

49

6

ME17

5

48

4

3

TN12

47

2

1

46

73 A · B · 74 · C · D · 75 · E · F

Snoads Hall
WESTERHILL RD
BARNES LA
VANITY LA
TOKE PL
Linton Park
Linton Park
Toke Farm
CORNWALLIS AVE
WHEELER'S LA
A229

COUNCIL COTTS
Bonfleur
BONFLOWER LA
LACEYS LA
Wares Farm
Redwall Farm
LINTON HILL
BUTT GREEN LA

GEORGE ST
Martins Farm House
Burford Farm
River Farm House
Wares Farm
REDWALL LA

River Farm
Ware Farm
Rankins Farm

Reed Court Farm Trail
REED COURT COTTS
River Beult
Stile Bridge

Chainhurst Farm
RAYNHAM VILLAS
The Stilebridge Inn

DAIRY LA
Chainhurst
Great Tilden
A229
B2079

ORCHARD VILLAS
Cedardene Farm
Oakhurst

HUNTON RD
New Lodge House
Chain Dene Farm
TILDEN LA
Little Tilden Farm
STILEBRIDGE LA

Parkfield
Moat Cottage
Underling Green
Underlyn Ind Est
B2079

Broad Forstal Farm
Whymans Farm
MAIDSTONE RD

Murzie Farm
Poplar Tree
UNDERLYN LA
MILLBUSH LA
Kiln Farm
Blue House Farm
BATTLE LA
B2079

131
148

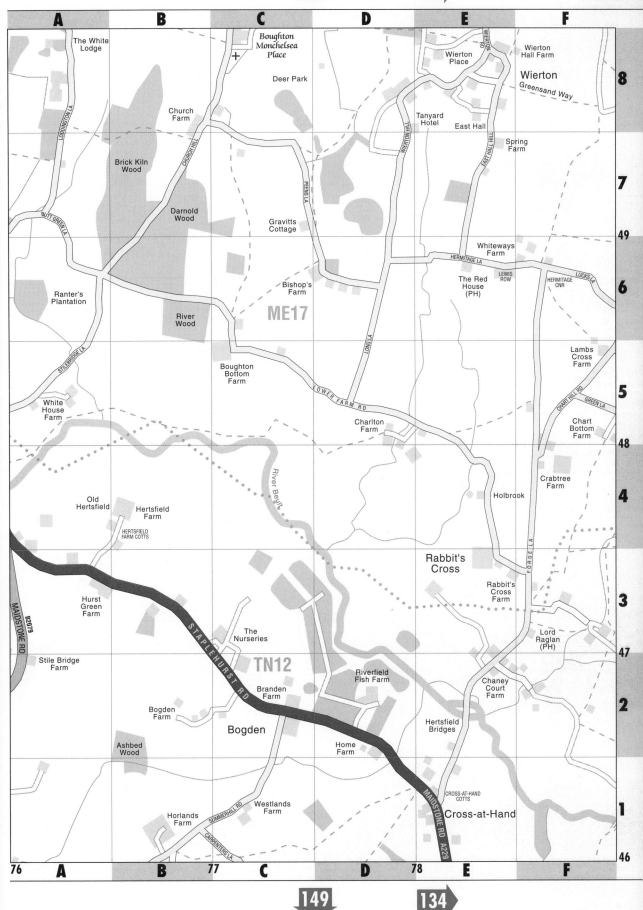

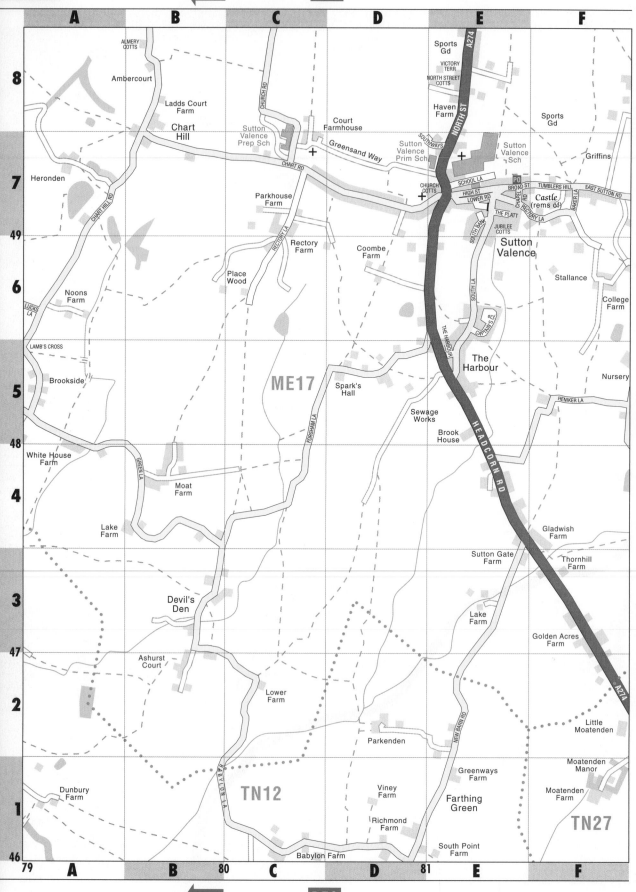

A B C D E F

8

ALMERY COTTS

Ambercourt

Ladds Court Farm

Chart Hill

Sutton Valence Prep Sch

Court Farmhouse

Greensand Way

Sports Gd

VICTORY TERR

NORTH STREET COTTS

NORTH ST

A274

Haven Farm

Sutton Valence Prim Sch

SOUTHWAYS

Sutton Valence Sch

Sports Gd

Griffins

7

Heronden

CHART HILL RD

CHART RD

Parkhouse Farm

RECTORY LA

CHURCH COTTS

SCHOOL LA

HIGH ST

LOWER RD

BROAD ST

CHAPEL RD

THE PLATT

JUBILEE COTTS

TUMBLERS HILL

BAKER LA

EAST SUTTON RD

Castle (rems of)

RECTORY LA

49

Rectory Farm

SOUTH BANK

SOUTH LA

Sutton Valence

6

Noons Farm

Place Wood

Coombe Farm

Stallance

College Farm

LUCKS LA

LAMB'S CROSS

THE HARBOUR

CAPTAIN'S LA

5

Brookside

ME17

FORSHAM LA

Spark's Hall

Sewage Works

Brook House

The Harbour

HENIKER LA

Nursery

48

White House Farm

GREEN LA

Moat Farm

HEADCORN RD

4

Lake Farm

Gladwish Farm

Sutton Gate Farm

Thornhill Farm

3

Devil's Den

Lake Farm

Golden Acres Farm

47

Ashurst Court

Lower Farm

NEW BARN RD

2

BABYLON LA

Parkenden

Little Moatenden

Moatenden Manor

1

Dunbury Farm

TN12

Viney Farm

Greenways Farm

Farthing Green

Moatenden Farm

TN27

46

Richmond Farm

South Point Farm

79 A B 80 C D 81 E F

Babylon Farm

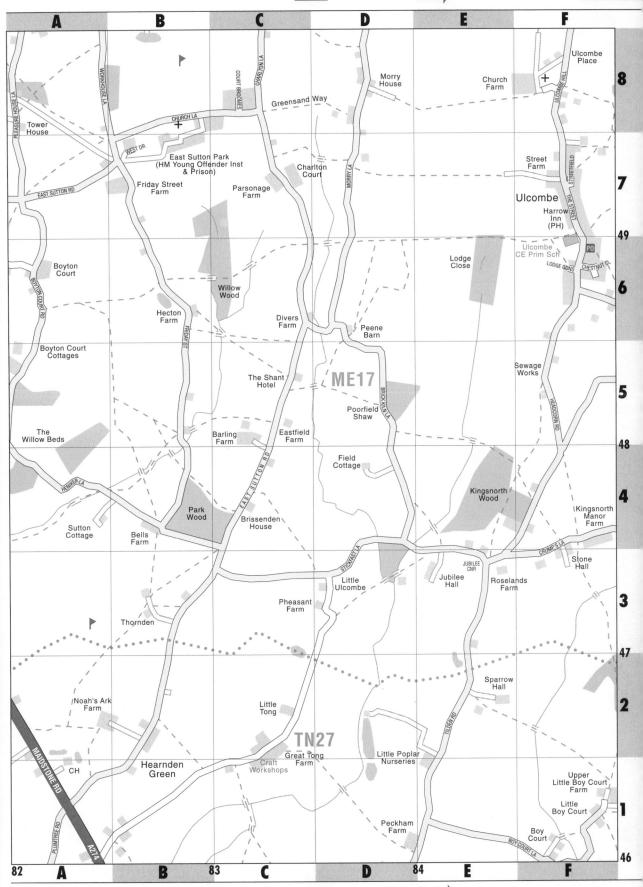

A   B   C   D   E   F

8

7

49

6

5

48

4

3

47

2

1

46

Map labels:

PLEASURE HOUSE LA
WORKHOUSE LA
CHARLTON LA
COURT BROOMES
Greensand Way
Morry House
Church Farm
Ulcombe Place
ULCOMBE HILL
Tower House
CHURCH LA
WEST DR
East Sutton Park
(HM Young Offender Inst & Prison)
Charlton Court
Street Farm
STREETFIELD
THE STREET
Friday Street Farm
Parsonage Farm
MORRY LA
Ulcombe
EAST SUTTON RD
Harrow Inn (PH)
Ulcombe CE Prim Sch
PO
LODGE GDNS
CHESTNUT CL
Boyton Court
Lodge Close
BOYTON COURT RD
Willow Wood
Hecton Farm
Divers Farm
Peene Barn
Sewage Works
FRIDAY ST
ME17
Boyton Court Cottages
The Shant Hotel
Poorfield Shaw
BRICK KILN LA
The Willow Beds
Barling Farm
Eastfield Farm
Field Cottage
Kingsnorth Wood
HEADCORN RD
Kingsnorth Manor Farm
HENIKER LA
EAST SUTTON RD
Park Wood
Brissenden House
Sutton Cottage
Bells Farm
STICKFAST LA
Little Ulcombe
JUBILEE CNR
Jubilee Hall
Roselands Farm
CRUMP'S LA
Stone Hall
Thornden
Pheasant Farm
Sparrow Hall
Noah's Ark Farm
Little Tong
TN27
Great Tong Farm
Little Poplar Nurseries
TILDEN RD
Upper Little Boy Court Farm
MAIDSTONE RD
CH
Hearnden Green
Craft Workshops
Peckham Farm
Little Boy Court
Boy Court
PLUMTREE RD
A274
BOY COURT LA

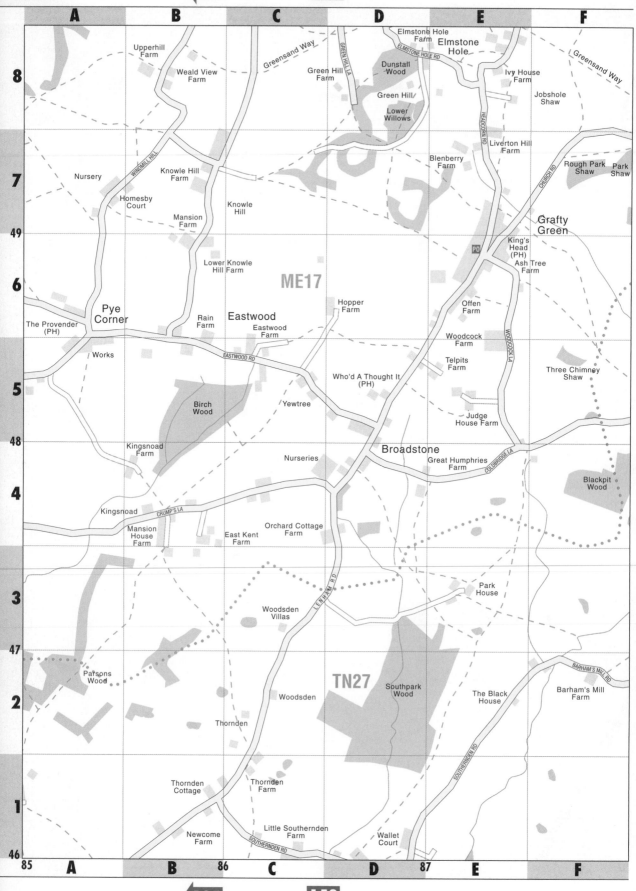

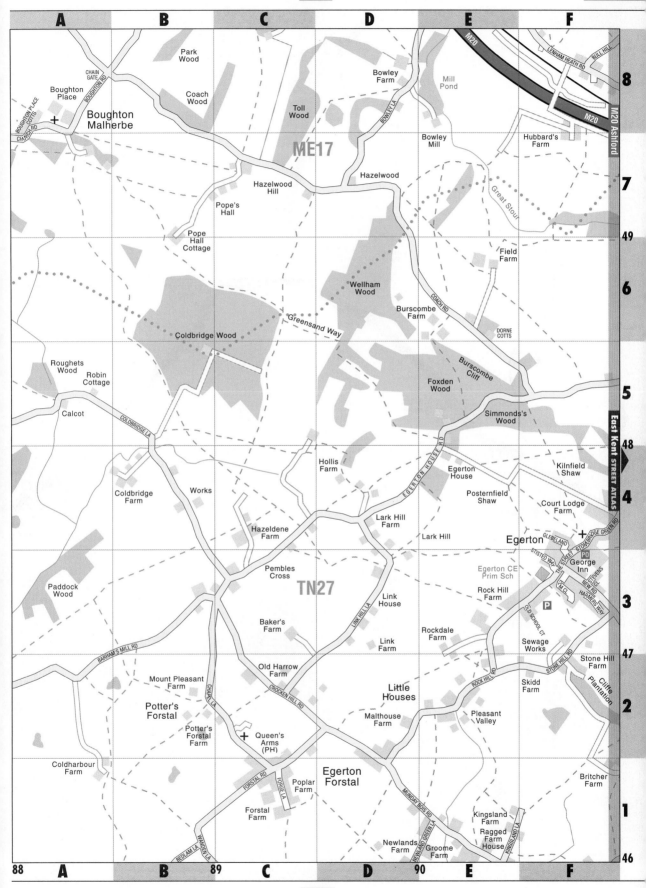

A B C D E F

8

Park
Wood

CHAIN
GATE

Boughton
Place

Coach
Wood

Bowley
Farm

Mill
Pond

LENHAM HEATH RD

BULL HILL

M20

M20 Ashford

Boughton
Malherbe

Toll
Wood

BOWLEY LA

Bowley
Mill

Hubbard's
Farm

BOUGHTON RD

CHART RD
BOUGHTON PLACE
COTTS

ME17

Hazelwood

7

Hazelwood
Hill

Hazelwood

Great Stour

49

Pope's
Hall

Field
Farm

COACH RD

6

Pope
Hall
Cottage

Wellham
Wood

Burscombe
Farm

DORNE
COTTS

Greensand Way

Coldbridge Wood

Roughets
Wood

Robin
Cottage

Foxden
Wood

Burscombe
Cliff

5

Calcot

COLDBRIDGE LA

Simmonds's
Wood

Kilnfield
Shaw

48

East Kent STREET ATLAS

Hollis
Farm

Egerton
House

Court Lodge
Farm

4

Coldbridge
Farm

Works

EGERTON HOUSE RD

Posternfield
Shaw

STONEBRIDGE GREEN RD

Egerton

GLEBELAND

THE STREET

STISTED WAY

PO

George
Inn

NEW RD

STEVENS

Hazeldene
Farm

Lark Hill
Farm

Lark Hill

Egerton CE
Prim Sch

Rock Hill
Farm

Paddock
Wood

Pembles
Cross

TN27

Link
House

OLD SCHOOL CT

HARNESS WAY

P

Baker's
Farm

LINK HILL LA

Rockdale
Farm

Sewage
Works

STONE HILL RD

Stone Hill
Farm

47

BARHAM'S MILL RD

Old Harrow
Farm

Link
Farm

Little
Houses

ROCK HILL RD

Skidd
Farm

Cliffe
Plantation

Mount Pleasant
Farm

CHAPEL LA

CROCKEN HILL RD

Pleasant
Valley

2

Potter's
Forstal

Malthouse
Farm

Potter's
Forstal
Farm

Queen's
Arms
(PH)

Egerton
Forstal

MUNDAY BOIS RD

Kingsland
Farm

Ragged
Farm
House

Coldharbour
Farm

FORGE LA

Poplar
Farm

KINGSLAND LA

Britcher
Farm

1

FORSTAL RD

Forstal
Farm

Newlands
Farm

NEWLAND GREEN LA

Groome
Farm

BEDLAM LA

WARDEN LA

46

122

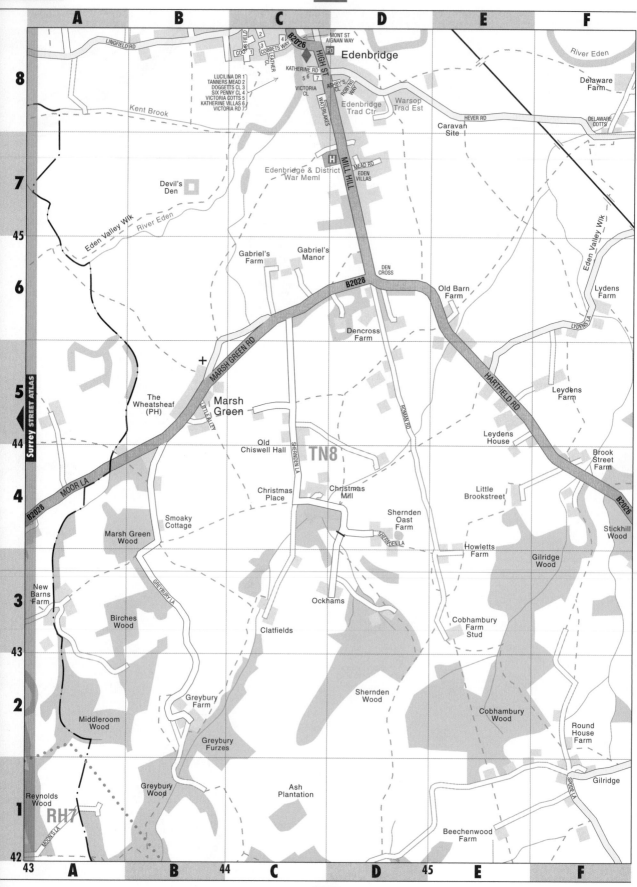

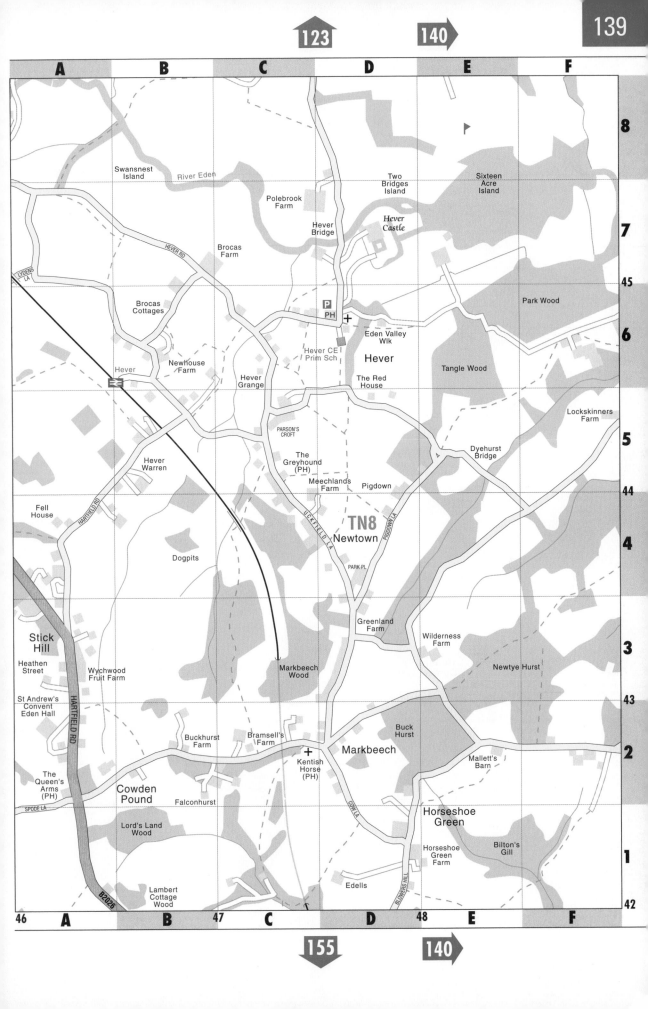

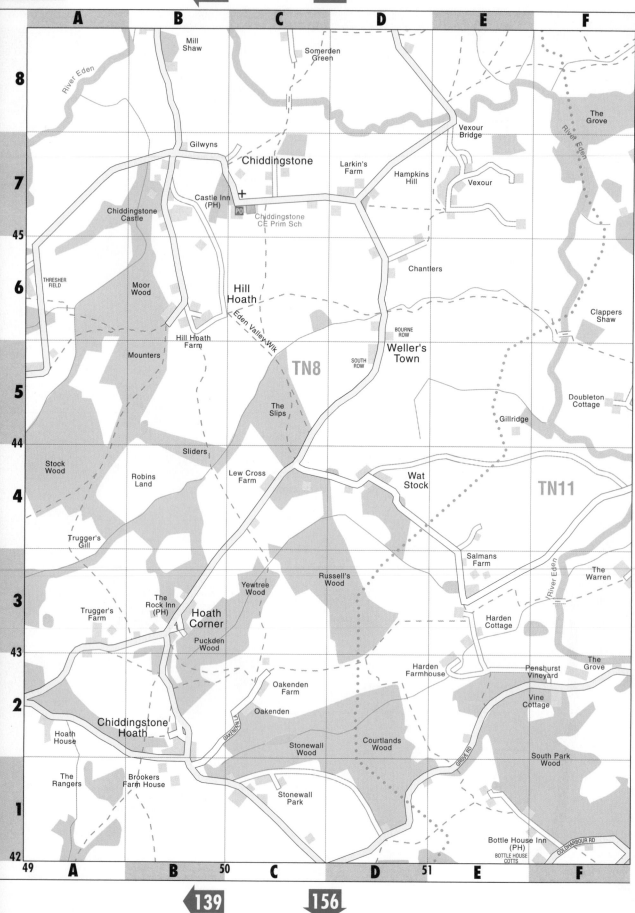

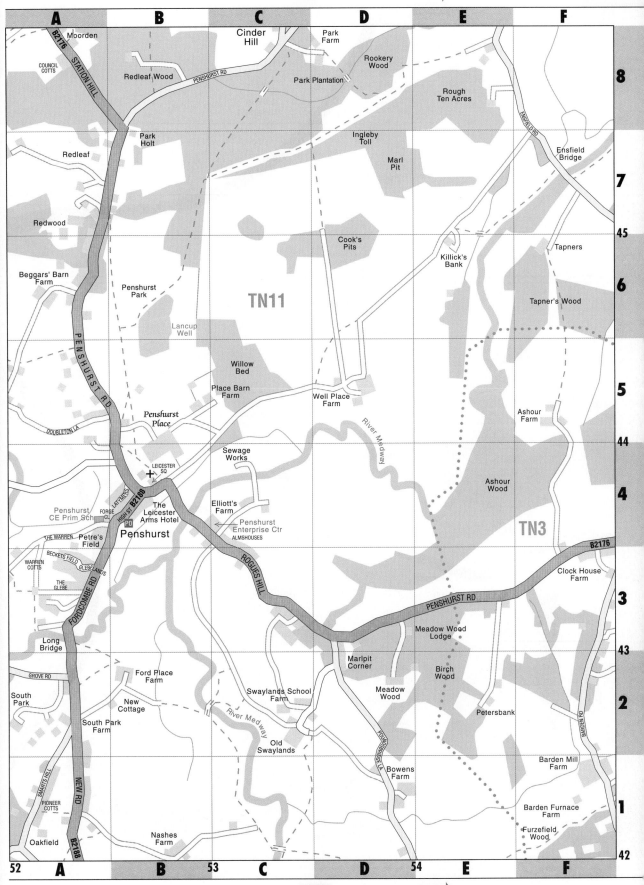

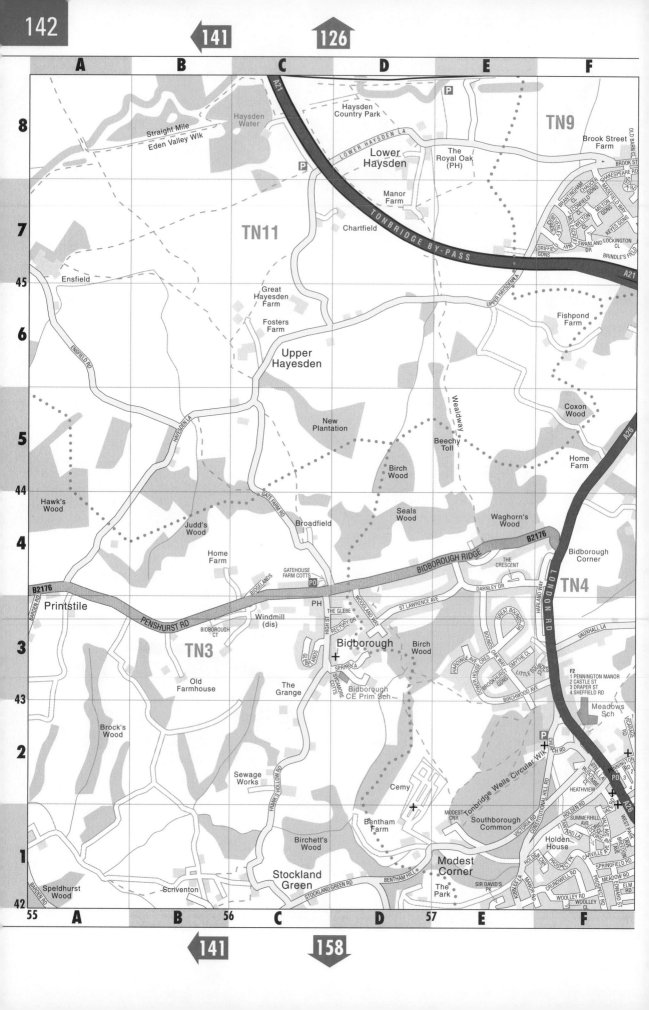

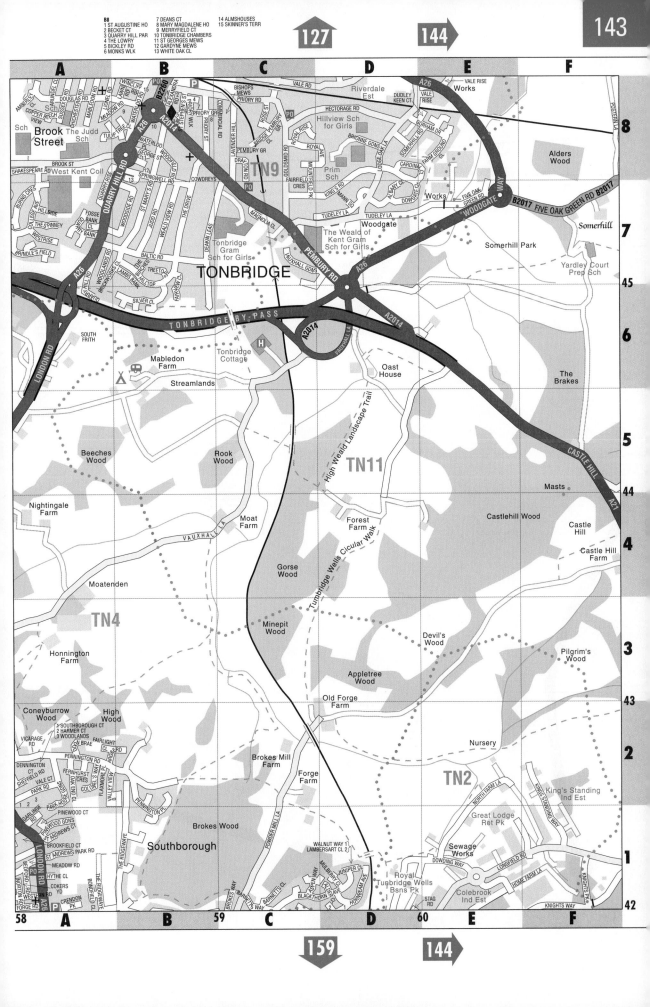

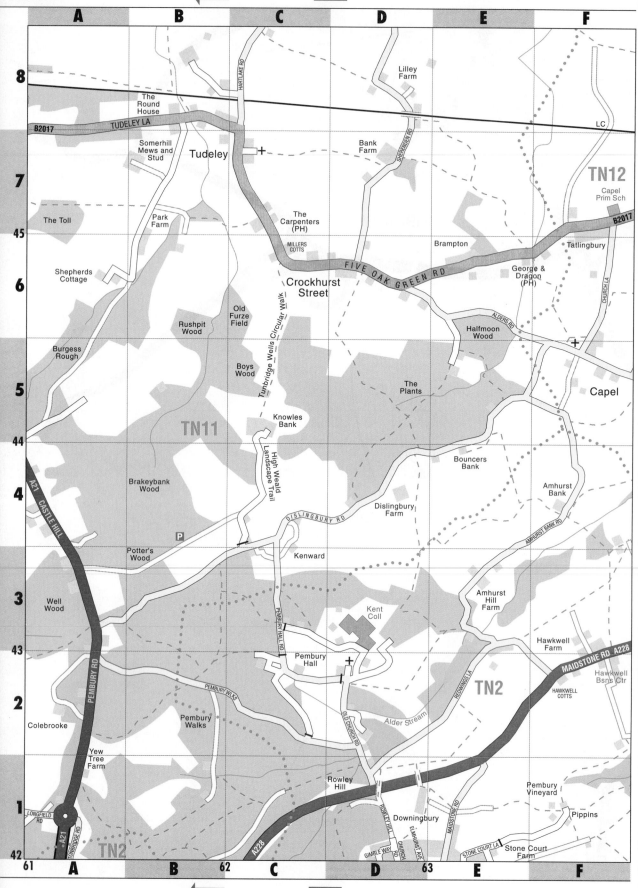

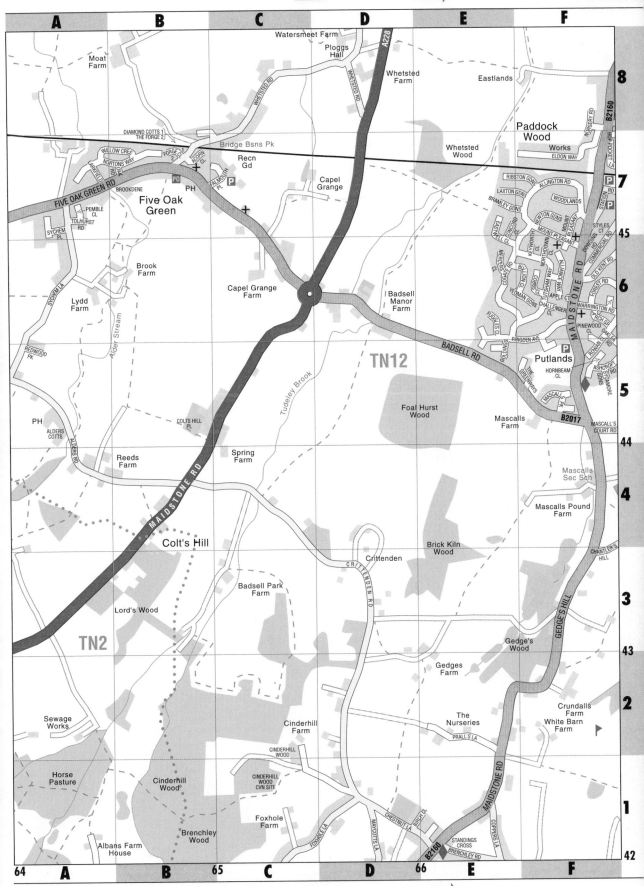

8
B2160
MAIDSTONE RD
Swatlands Farm
LAMB'S MOBILE HOME PK
Orchards Bsns Ctr
LC
NETTLESTEAD COTTS
Depot
Works
LUCKNOW RD
Little Fowle Hall Farm
New Barns Farm
LUCKS LA
Rhoden Farm
Upper Fowle Hall Farm
River Teise

7
HENLEY RD
TRANSFESA RD
Paddock Wood
Superstore
Sewage Works
Little Rhoden Farm
Queen Street
QUEEN ST

45
STATION APP
Bsns Ctr
PO
THE CEDARS
JOHN BRUNT CT
THE SHIRES
BALLARD WAY
BOWLS
CLANMONT RD
THE RIDINGS
FORGE WAY
BEECH CT
TAMARACK CL
LE TEMPLE RD
ST ANDREWS CL
ANCHORAGE FLATS
Cemy
OLD KENT RD
KENT CL
KINGSMEAD PK
GRANARY
CHURCH RD

6
Sch
MACDONALD CT
COLSTHORPE
WARRINGTON RD
WALNUT CL
Recn Gd
Church Farm
Cemy
FOREST RD
BIRCH RD
NEW RD
BLACKBERRY
HEATHER WAY
THE FOXGLOVES
Park Farm
WILLOW LA
Ledger's Farm

5
LINDEN CL
ASHCROFT RD
HAYWAIN CL
THE BINES
CHAFFINCH WAY
BULLFINCH CL
PRIMROSE
BUTTERCUP
THE VIOLETS
GREEN LA
BLUEBELL WAY
CLOVER WAY
TWINE CAVE
GOLDFINCH DR
Knell's Farm
Elm Tree (PH)
TN12
Great Old Hay
Jason's Farm
Oasthouse Farm

44
L Ctr
REDPOLL WAY

4
Mascalls Sec Sch
MASCALL'S COURT RD
Mascall's Court
MASCALL'S COURT LA
CATTS PL
Catts Place
Greenfields Farm
Three Tax Farm

3
CHANTLER'S HILL
Biggenden Farmhouse
Biggenden Barn
WATERMAN'S LA
CH
Mile Oak
MILE OAK RD
KNOWLE LA
Trenches Farm
Longbrooks
KNOWLE RD
Pearson's Green
PEARSON'S GREEN RD
CHURN LA

43
Moatlands Park

2
PIXOT HILL
The Knowle
Latters Toll

1
Parsonage Wood
Hill Top
BRENCHLEY RD
WINDMILL HILL
BROAD OAK
The Crook
PALMERS GREEN LA
Great Wood
CROOK RD
WEALD VIEW PH
Castle Hill
FURNACE LA
Poulhurst
YEW TREE GREEN RD
Poulhurst Farm

PEARSONS GREEN RD

42
67   68   69

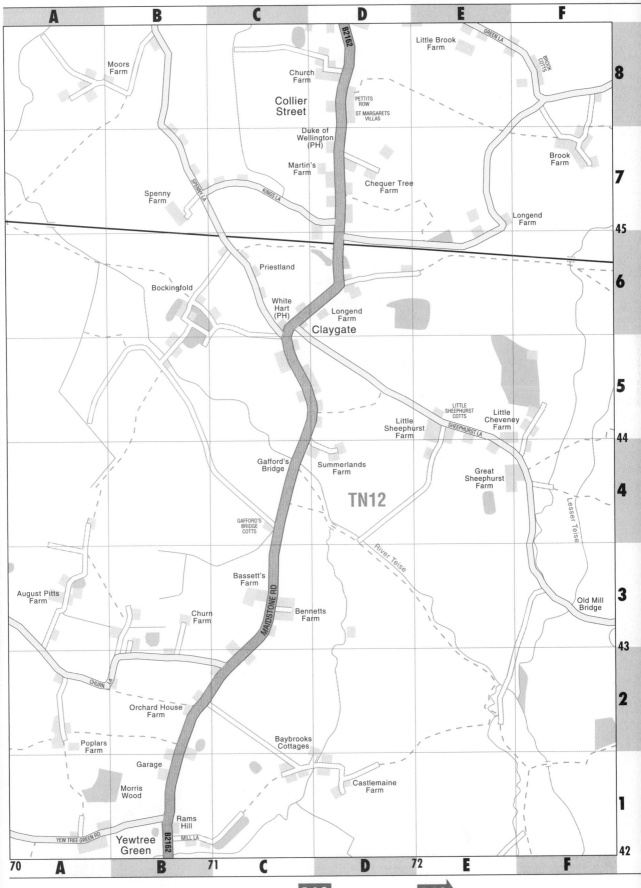

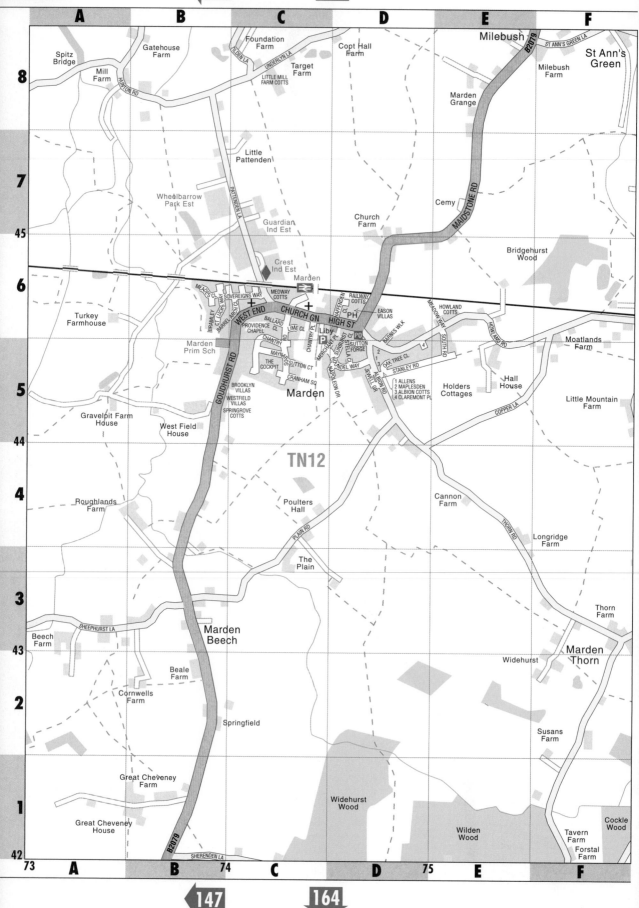

A B C D E F

8

7

45

6

5

44

4

3

43

2

1

42

73 A B 74 C D 75 E F

Spitz Bridge

Mill Farm

HILTON RD

Gatehouse Farm

Foundation Farm

ALDEN LA

UNDERLYN LA

LITTLE MILL FARM COTTS

Target Farm

Copt Hall Farm

Milebush

B2079

St Ann's Green

ST ANN'S GREEN LA

Milebush Farm

Little Pattenden

Marden Grange

PATTENDEN LA

Wheelbarrow Park Est

Cemy

MAIDSTONE RD

Church Farm

Bridgehurst Wood

Guardian Ind Est

Crest Ind Est

Marden

Turkey Farmhouse

MEADS CL

SOVEREIGNS WAY

BRAMLEY CT

CT LUCYS

BARREL ARCH

WEST END

MEDWAY COTTS

BALLARD CL

CHURCH GN

HIGH ST

CHAFFENDEN CL

RAILWAY COTTS

PH

Marden

Railway

EASON VILLAS

HOWLAND COTTS

MEADOW WAY

HOWLAND RD

Moatlands Farm

Marden Prim Sch

PROVIDENCE CHAPEL

CHANTRY CL

LIME CL

CHANTRY PL

MERCHANT PL

Liby

P

SUTTON FORGE

PO

SUNBURST PL

ARUNDEL WAY

NAPOLEON DR

SUTTON CT

1

2

3

BARNES WLK

SOUTH RD

STANLEY RD

COPPER LA

Holders Cottages

Hall House

Little Mountain Farm

MAYNARDS

THE COCKPIT

CRANHAM SQ

Brooklyn Villas

Westfield Villas

Springrove Cotts

Marden

ALBION PL

JEWELL GR

OAK TREE CL

1 ALLENS
2 MAPLESDEN
3 ALBION COTTS
4 CLAREMONT PL

Gravelpit Farm House

West Field House

GOUDHURST RD

TN12

Roughlands Farm

Poulters Hall

PLAIN RD

Cannon Farm

THORN RD

Longridge Farm

The Plain

SHEEPHURST LA

Marden Beech

Beech Farm

Beale Farm

Cornwells Farm

Thorn Farm

Widehurst

Marden Thorn

Springfield

Susans Farm

Great Cheveney Farm

B2079

Great Cheveney House

SHERENDEN LA

Widehurst Wood

Wilden Wood

Tavern Farm

Cockle Wood

Forstal Farm

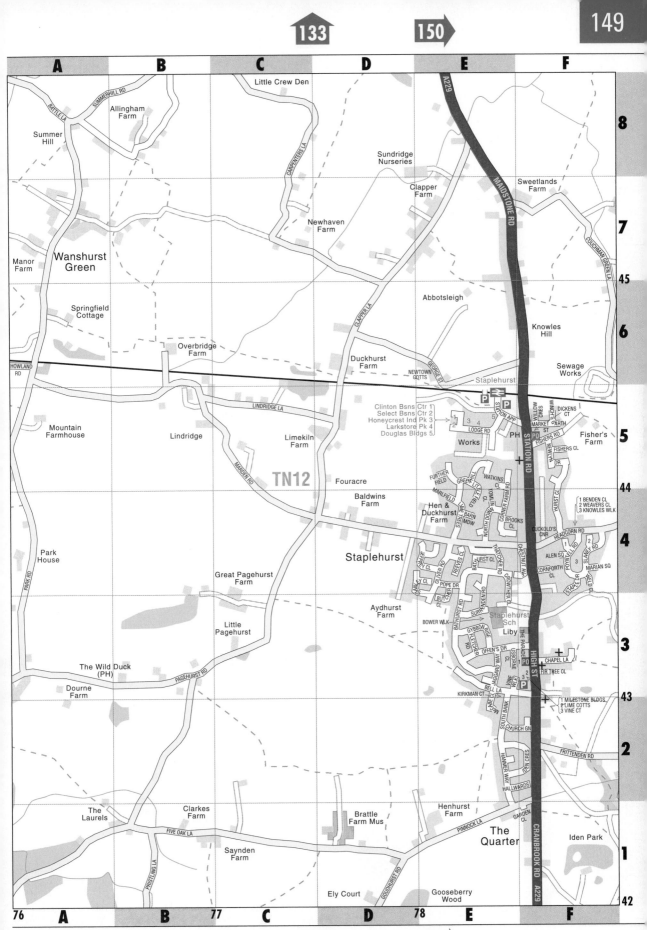

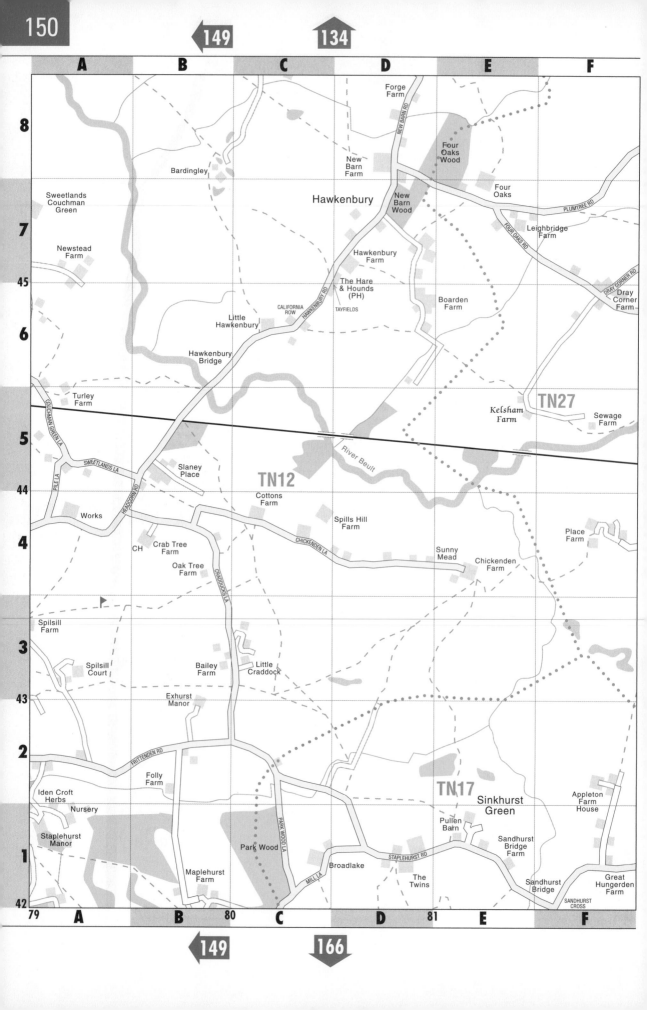

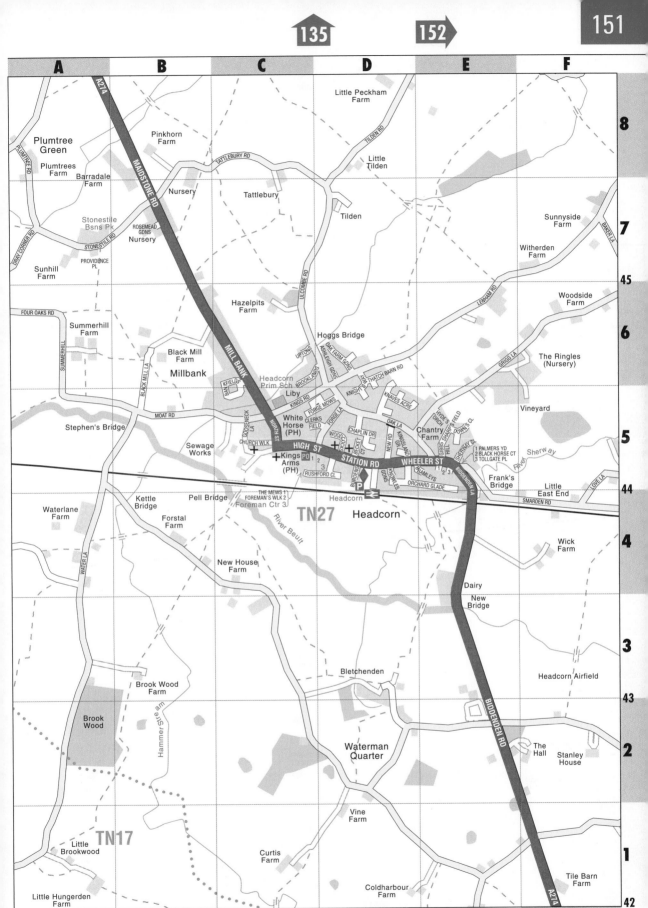

135
152

A B C D E F

8

7

45

6

5

44

4

3

43

2

1

42

Plumtree Green
Plumtrees Farm
Barradale Farm
Pinkhorn Farm
Nursery
Little Peckham Farm
Little Tilden
Tilden
Tattlebury
Sunnyside Farm
Witherden Farm
BAKER LA
A274
MAIDSTONE RD
TATTLEBURY RD
TILDEN RD
Stonestile Bsns Pk
ROSEMEAD GDNS
Nursery
STONESTILE RD
DRAY CORNER RD
PLUMTREE RD
Sunhill Farm
PROVIDENCE PL
ULCOMBE RD
Woodside Farm
LEEMAN RD
FOUR OAKS RD
Summerhill Farm
Hazelpits Farm
Hoggs Bridge
The Ringles (Nursery)
GRIGG LA
SUMMERHILL
BLACK MILL LA
Black Mill Farm
Millbank
MILL BANK
UPTONS
Headcorn Prim Sch
BROOKLANDS
OAK FARM GDNS
ASHLEIGH GDNS
THATCH BARN RD
KNIGHT
Vineyard
BANKFIELD
Liby
KINGS RD
FORGE MDWS
FORGE LA
KNAVES ACRE
HYDE'S FIELD
POWLTS CL
MOAT RD
Stephen's Bridge
GOOSENECK LA
NORTH ST
CHURCH WLK
White Horse (PH)
CLERKS FIELD
WOODCK
CHAPLIN DR
OAK LA
Chantry Farm
CONGY
SHERWAY CL
River Sherway
Sewage Works
Kings Arms (PH)
PO
1 2 3
RUSHFORD CL
HIGH ST
STATION RD
BECKET CT
BURDENS
NEW RD
KINGSLAND GRN
KNOWLES GDNS
WHEELER ST
CRAMLEYS
BIDDENDEN LA
ORCHARD GLADE
1 PALMERS YD
2 BLACK HORSE CT
3 TOLLGATE PL
Frank's Bridge
Little East End
LOVE LA
Waterlane Farm
Kettle Bridge
Pell Bridge
Forstal Farm
THE MEWS 1
FOREMAN'S WLK 2
Foreman Ctr 3
TN27
Headcorn
P
Headcorn
SMARDEN RD
44
Wick Farm
WATER LA
River Beult
New House Farm
Dairy
New Bridge
BIDDENDEN RD
Headcorn Airfield
43
Brook Wood Farm
Hammer Stream
Bletchenden
The Hall
Stanley House
Brook Wood
Waterman Quarter
TN17
Little Brookwood
Vine Farm
Curtis Farm
Coldharbour Farm
Tile Barn Farm
A274
Little Hungerden Farm

82 A B 83 C D 84 E F 42

167
152

151
136

	A	B	C	D	E	F

8

Springfield Farm

Southernden

Southernden Farm

Little Southernden Farm

LENHAM RD

Barling Green Farm

7

Gloversbridge Farm

Glover's Bridge

Little Grigg Farm

45

BAKER LA

GRIGG LA

SHERWAY RD

Burnt House

Grigg Oasts

River Sherway

Old Oak Farm

Grigg Farm

6

Sherway Bridge

Homersham Farm

Swift's Green

BEDLAM LA

Hieland Glen

Little Swift's Green Farm

5

LOVE LA

Little Luckhurst

Luckhurst Farm

ROSEMARY LA

Coldharbour Farm

Homestall Farm

Manor Farm

Malthouse Farm

Suncrest

TN27

44

Abbotts Skreen Farm

East End

SMARDEN RD

Roland House

LC

4

Marley Farm

High Cross Wood

Hegg Hill Farm

MARLEY LA

Watch House

Hegg Hill

HEADCORN RD

3

Munk's Farm

Vane Farm

Westover Farm

Bell Farm

The Roundabout

43

Smarden Bell

The Bell (PH)

Church Farm

Ash Farm

MILL LA

2

Lashenden Air Warfare Mus

Hadman's Place

Oxley Farm

WATER LA

THE OAKS

ASHENDEN

THE ACORNS

Shenley Farm

River Beult

BELL LA

White House

Haylands Farm

Hadman's Bridge

Ebenezer Farm

Sewage Works

1

West Hoy Farm

Braid Farm

Town Bridge

PH

CAGE LA

Snughorn Farm

BURNTHOUSE LA

42

85	A		B	86	C		D	87	E		F

151
168

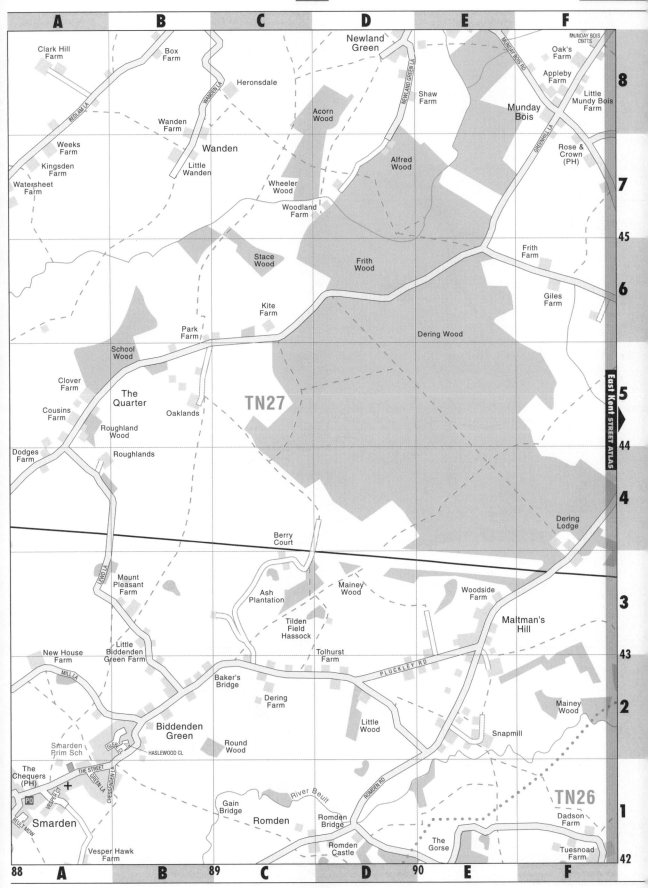

Clark Hill Farm
Box Farm
Newland Green
Munday Bois Cotts
Oak's Farm
WARDEN LA
Heronsdale
Appleby Farm
Shaw Farm
8
Little Mundy Bois Farm
Wanden Farm
Acorn Wood
Munday Bois
BEDLAM LA
Weeks Farm
Wanden
Rose & Crown (PH)
Kingsden Farm
Little Wanden
Alfred Wood
GREENHILL LA
7
Watersheet Farm
Wheeler Wood
Woodland Farm
45
Frith Farm
Stace Wood
Frith Wood
Giles Farm
6
Kite Farm
Dering Wood
Park Farm
School Wood
East Kent STREET ATLAS
Clover Farm
The Quarter
Oaklands
TN27
5
Cousins Farm
Roughland Wood
44
Dodges Farm
Roughlands
Dering Lodge
4
Berry Court
Mount Pleasant Farm
Mainey Wood
Woodside Farm
LEWD LA
Ash Plantation
3
Maltman's Hill
Tilden Field Hassock
Little Biddenden Green Farm
Tolhurst Farm
PLUCKLEY RD
43
New House Farm
Baker's Bridge
MILL LA
Dering Farm
Mainey Wood
2
GLEB... RD
Biddenden Green
Little Wood
Snapmill
Smarden Prim Sch
HASLEWOOD CL
Round Wood
CHESSENDEN LA
TN26
The Chequers (PH)
GREEN LA
THE STREET
River Beult
ROMDEN RD
1
PO
Gain Bridge
Romden
Romden Bridge
Dadson Farm
VESPER LEY
BEULT MDW
Smarden
The Gorse
Tuesnoad Farm
Vesper Hawk Farm
Romden Castle
42

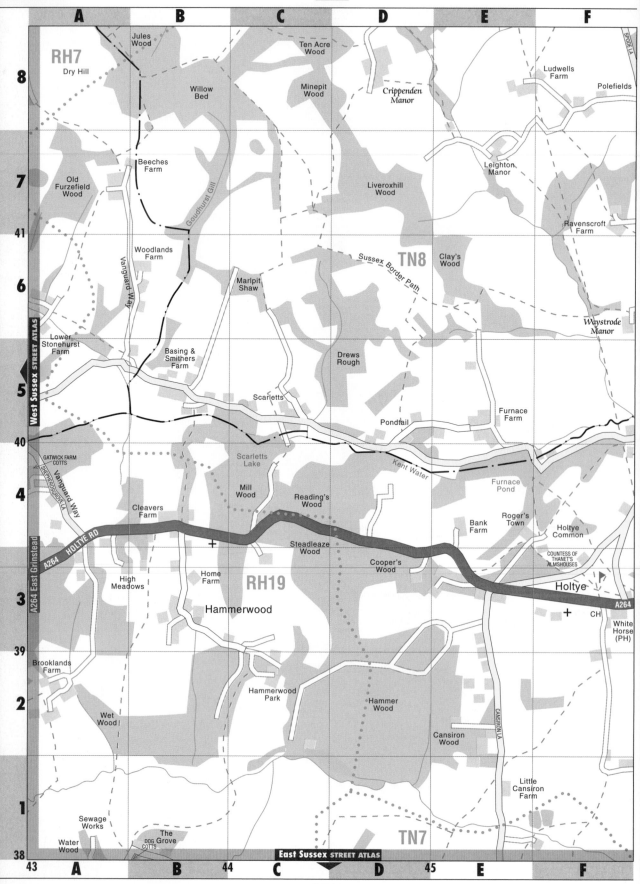

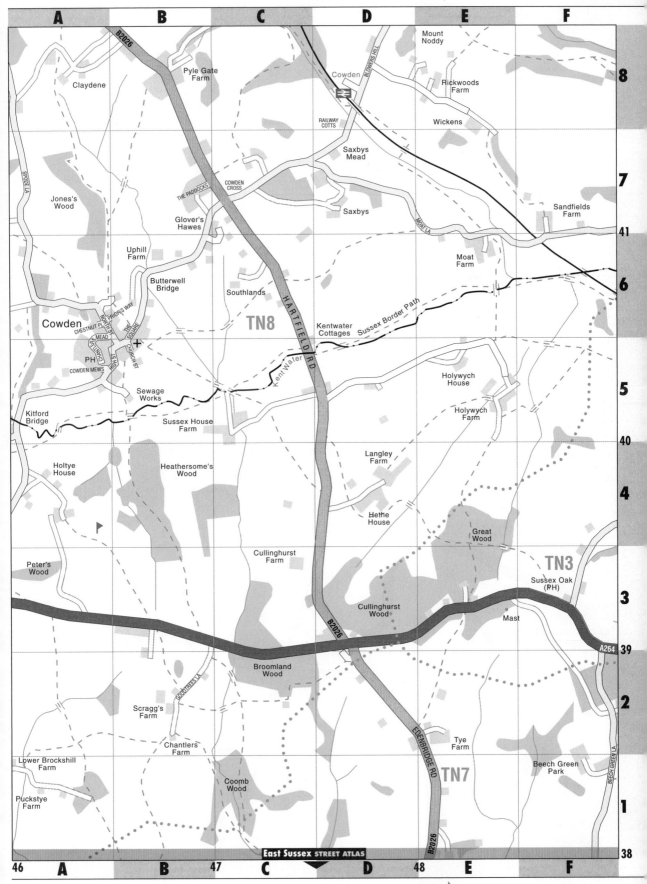

A B C D E F

B2026

8 Claydene
Pyle Gate Farm
Mount Noddy
Cowden
Rickwoods Farm
Wickens

THE PADDOCKS
7 Jones's Wood
Cowden Cross
Saxbys Mead
Saxbys
Sandfields Farm
41

Glover's Hawes
Uphill Farm
MOAT LA
Moat Farm
6
Butterwell Bridge
Southlands
TN8
Kentwater Cottages
Sussex Border Path

HARTFIELD RD

Cowden
CHESTNUT PL
PRIORS WAY
CHANT'S MEAD
NORTH'S
THE SQUARE
CHURCH ST
PH
COWDEN MEWS
HIGH ST

Kent Water
Holywych House
5
Sewage Works
Holywych Farm
Kitford Bridge
Sussex House Farm
40

Holtye House
Heathersome's Wood
Langley Farm
4
Hethe House
Great Wood
TN3

Peter's Wood
Cullinghurst Farm
Sussex Oak (PH)
3
B2026
Cullinghurst Wood
Mast
A264 39

GOODTREES LA
Broomland Wood
2
Scragg's Farm
EDENBRIDGE RD
Tye Farm
Beech Green Park
BEECH GREEN LA

Chantlers Farm
Lower Brockshill Farm
Coomb Wood
TN7
1

Puckstye Farm

SPODE LA

155 140

A B C D E F

8

Birchcope Shaw

Coldharbour

Westfield House

Frienden Gill

TN8

Cook's Wood

COLDHARBOUR RD

NUNNERY LA

Bassett's Mill

Finch Green

White Post

Harts

SANDFIELD RD

7

BASSETTS LA

Frienden Farm

Blacklands Wood

Hartslands Farm

Bassett's Farm

TN11

Prinkham

41

WALTERS GREEN RD

6

Hobbs Hill Farm

Top Hill Wood

Walter's Green

Kent Water

Pilbeams

BRADLEY RD

Sussex Border Path

Nore Farm

CHAFFORD LA

Chafford Bridge

Chafford Cotts

HEDGE BARTON TRAILER PK

THE PADDOCK

THE DRIVE

5

CH

Tollhurst Farm

40

Willett's Farm

Salehurst Farm

Stephnett's Farm

Blackham

River Medway

Chafford Park

Cousins Shaw

4

WILLETTS LA

WILLETTS COTTS

TN3

CARRIERS PL

TEASLEY MEAD

Teasley Mead

Pound Farm

Ashurst Wood

Stable Cottage

3

A264

ASHURST RD

A264

39

ASHURST HILL

The Bald Faced Stag (PH)

Manor Court Farm

Highfields Park

Ashurst Bridge

MILLSTREAM CL

Ashurst

2

Lodgefield Wood

Ashurst

CLAYTON LA

Lodgefield Farm

Jessup's Farm

Lords Wood

Wealdway

1

TN7

Old Woodland Wood

Clay Shaw

Minepit Wood

38

49 A B 50 C D 51 E F

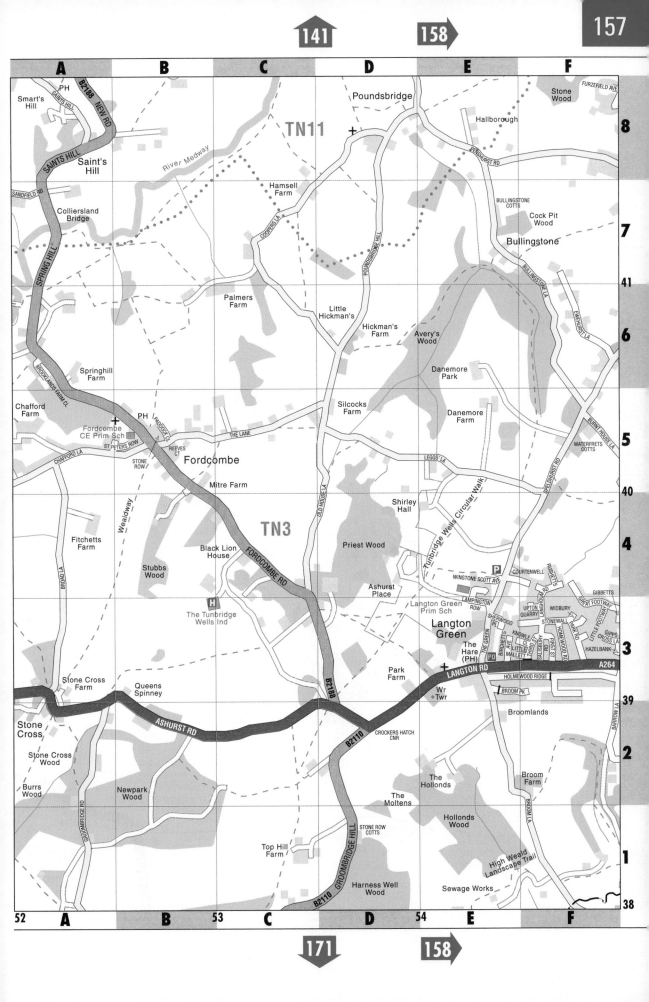

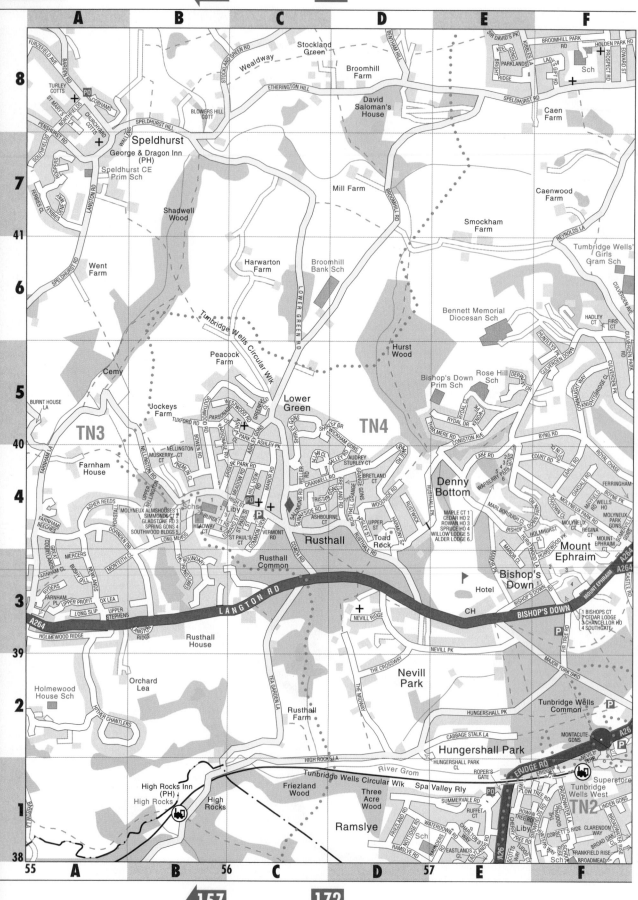

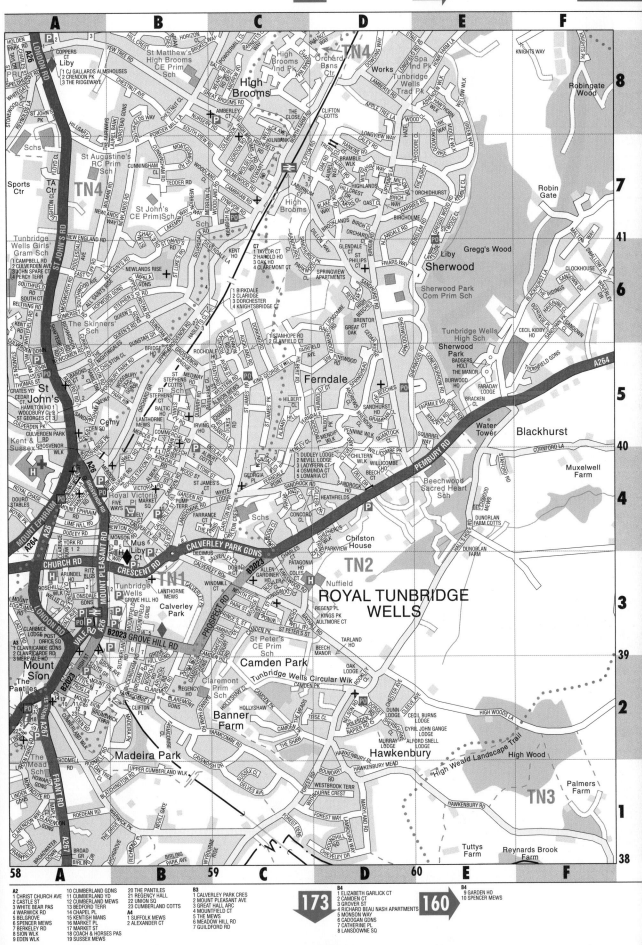

←159 **144**

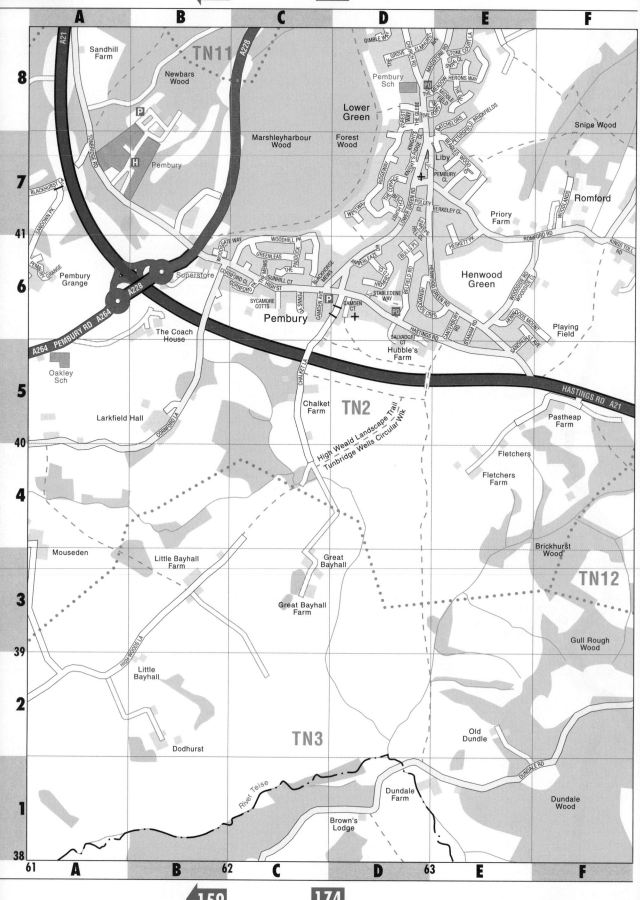

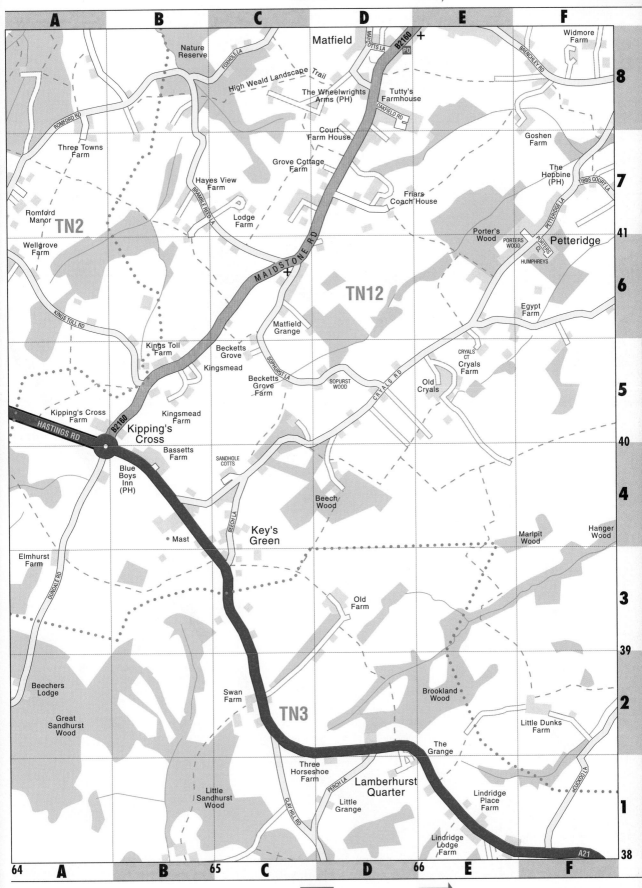

Matfield

Nature Reserve

High Weald Landscape Trail

The Wheelwrights Arms (PH)

Tutty's Farmhouse

Court Farm House

Grove Cottage Farm

Three Towns Farm

Hayes View Farm

Lodge Farm

Friars Coach House

Widmore Farm

Goshen Farm

The Hopbine (PH)

Romford Manor

TN2

Wellgrove Farm

Porter's Wood

PORTERS WOOD

Petteridge

HUMPHREYS

Kings Toll Rd

TN12

Egypt Farm

Kings Toll Farm

Matfield Grange

Becketts Grove

Kingsmead

Becketts Grove Farm

SOPURST WOOD

Cryals Farm

Old Cryals

Kipping's Cross Farm

Kingsmead Farm

HASTINGS RD

Kipping's Cross

Bassetts Farm

SANDHOLE COTTS

Beech Wood

Marlpit Wood

Hanger Wood

Blue Boys Inn (PH)

Elmhurst Farm

Mast

Key's Green

Old Farm

Beechers Lodge

Great Sandhurst Wood

TN3

Swan Farm

Brookland Wood

Little Dunks Farm

Three Horseshoe Farm

Lamberhurst Quarter

The Grange

Lindridge Place Farm

Little Sandhurst Wood

Little Grange

Lindridge Lodge Farm

A21

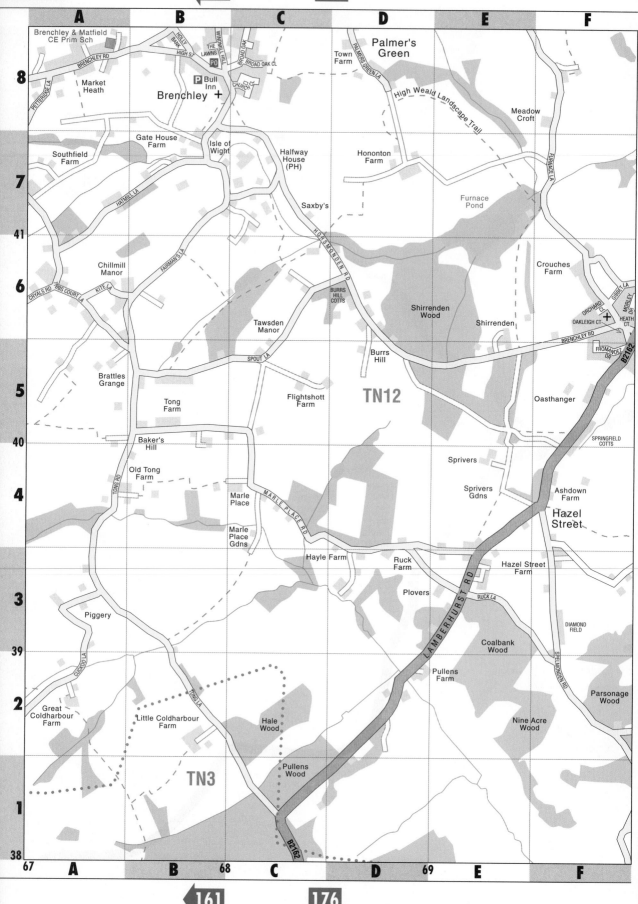

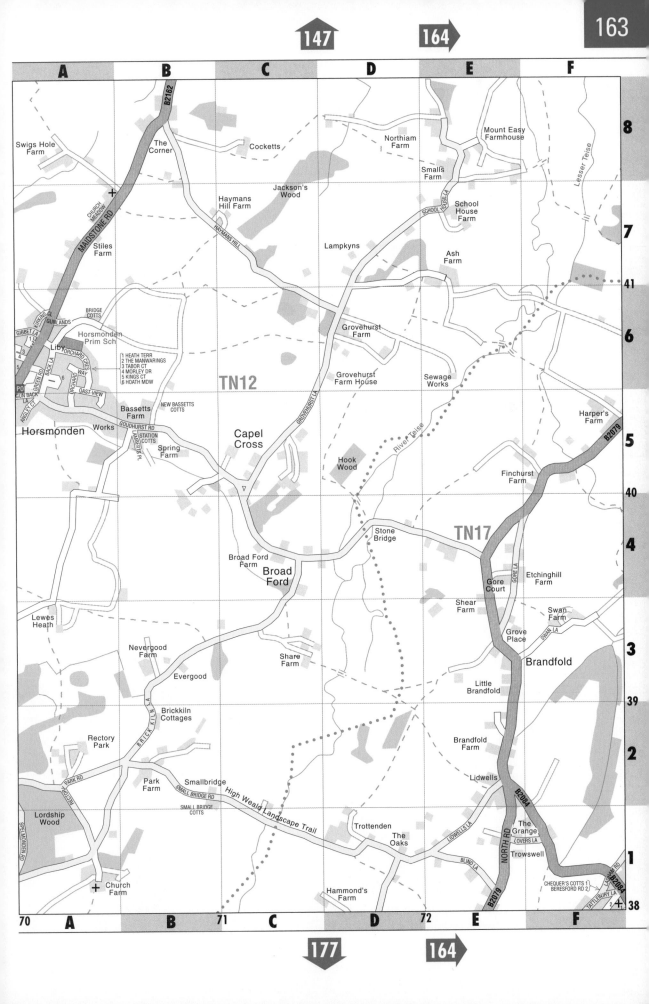

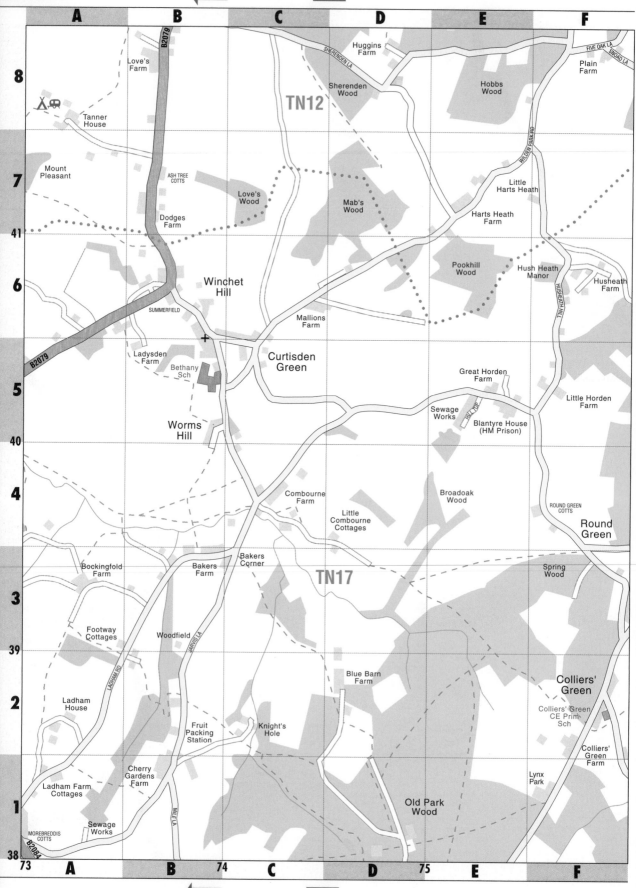

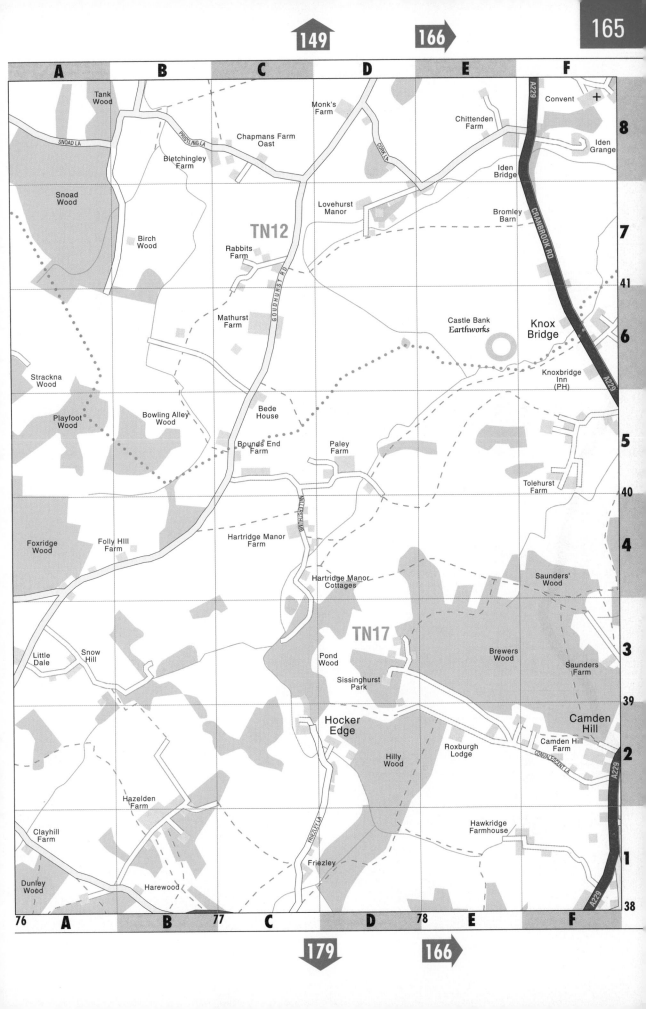

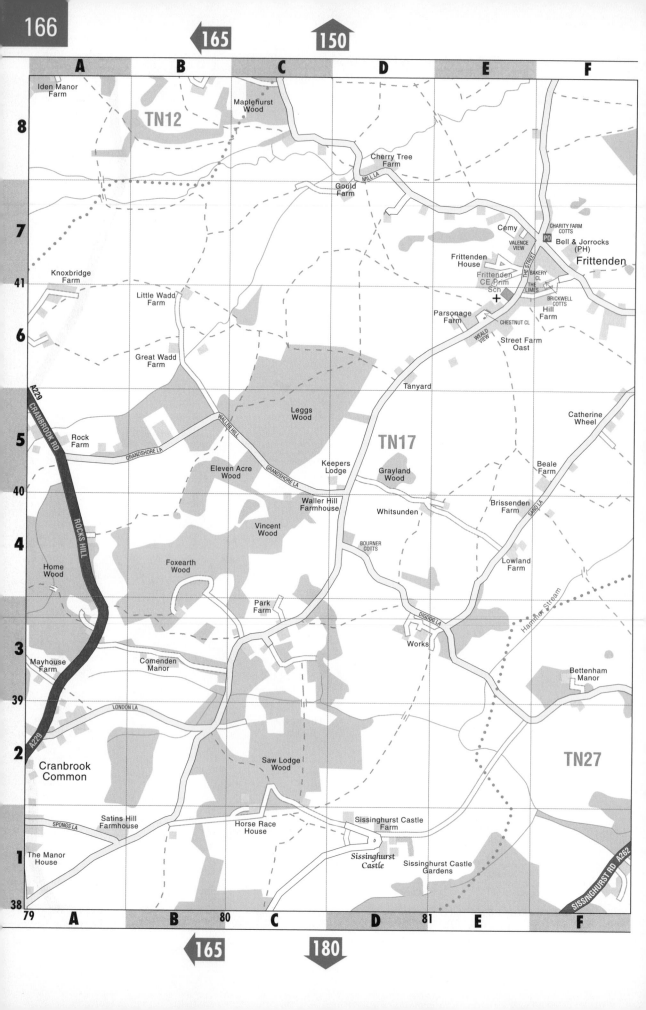

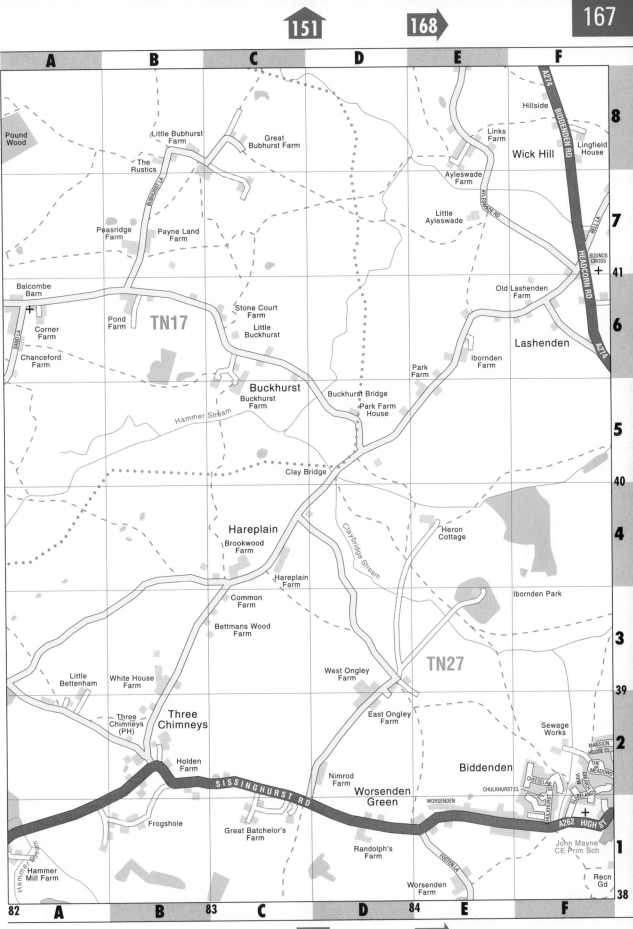

A B C D E F

8

Pound Wood

Little Bubhurst Farm

Great Bubhurst Farm

The Rustics

Hillside

Links Farm

Wick Hill

Lingfield House

Ayleswade Farm

7

Peasridge Farm

Payne Land Farm

Little Ayleswade

41

Balcombe Barn

Old Lashenden Farm

Corner Farm

Pond Farm

TN17

Stone Court Farm

Little Buckhurst

Ibornden Farm

Lashenden

6

Chanceford Farm

Park Farm

Buckhurst

Buckhurst Farm

Buckhurst Bridge

Park Farm House

5

Hammer Stream

Clay Bridge

40

Hareplain

Brookwood Farm

Heron Cottage

4

Hareplain Farm

Claybridge Stream

Common Farm

Ibornden Park

Bettmans Wood Farm

3

Little Bettenham

White House Farm

West Ongley Farm

TN27

39

Three Chimneys (PH)

Three Chimneys

East Ongley Farm

Sewage Works

MANSION HOUSE CL.

2

Holden Farm

Nimrod Farm

Biddenden

THE MEADOWS

CHEESELANE

CHURCH VIEW

GLEBELANDS

CHULKHURST CL.

Frogshole

Great Batchelor's Farm

SISSINGHURST RD

Worsenden Green

WORSENDEN

A262 HIGH ST

John Mayne CE Prim Sch

1

Hammer Mill Farm

Randolph's Farm

FOSTEN LA

Worsenden Farm

Recn Gd

38

82 A 83 B C 84 D E F

A · B · C · D · E · F

8

7

41

6

5

40

4

3

39

2

1

38

85 · 86 · 87

Barnden Farm

Snughorne House

Obeden Farm

BURNTHOUSE LA

BIDDENDEN RD

CAGE LA

Walford House

BETHERSDEN RD

Grigsby Farm

Bardleden Farm

Hill View

Oak Acre

BELL LA

SNUGHORNE LA

THE CUT

Thorn Farm

Stanlash

Limes Farmhouse

Lime Kiln Farm

Tilden Farm

Gilham Land Farm

Monk's Hill

Smarden Bsns Est

Tylden

Priory Farm

Monks Hill Farm

Roberts Farm

Gilham Farm

Lashenden Farm

Standen Wood

SMARDEN RD

Kelsham

Vane Court Farm

Cackle Hill

CH

Vane Court

Deadman's Wood

Great Omenden Farm

Great Omenden Cottages

A274

HEADCORN RD

WEEKS LA

Standen

Ponds Farm

TN27

Standen

40

Newcastle Farm

Forstal Farm

Little Omenden Farm

Apsley

Gorse Farm

POOK LA

Curteis' Corner

COT LA

Omenden Barn

Wagstaff

NORTH ST

Elmstone

39

River Hall

Gallops

MANSION HOUSE CL

Sweet Meadow Farm

STONE CL

SHUTTLE CL

CLOTH HALL GDNS

TEASELS

TOWN LAND CL

THE WEAVERS

A274

PO

HIGH HALDEN RD

Guy House

HIGH ST

A262

Whitfield Farm

Stede Quarter

P

John Mayne CE Prim Sch

HIGH HALDEN RD

Washenden Manor

Podkin Farm

TN26

TENTERDEN RD A262

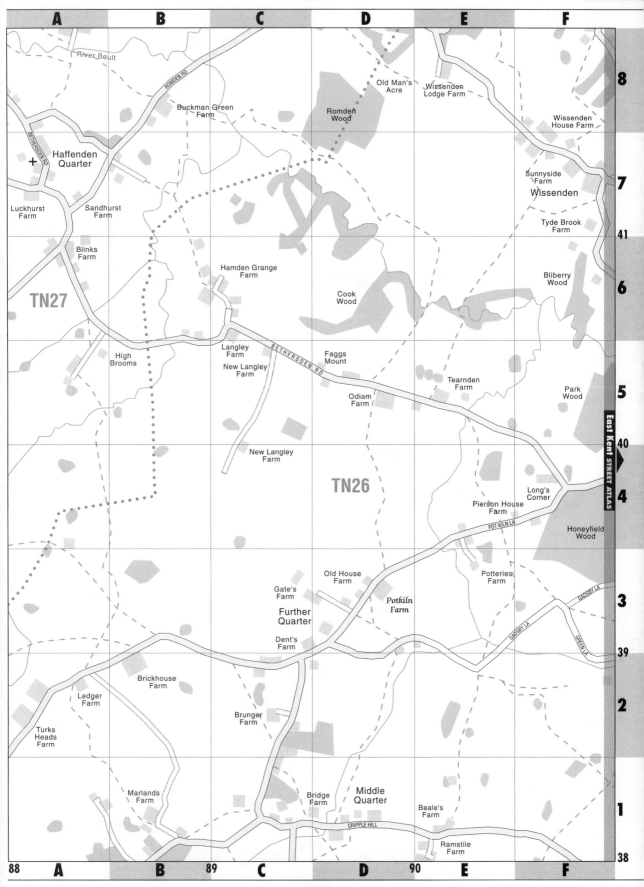

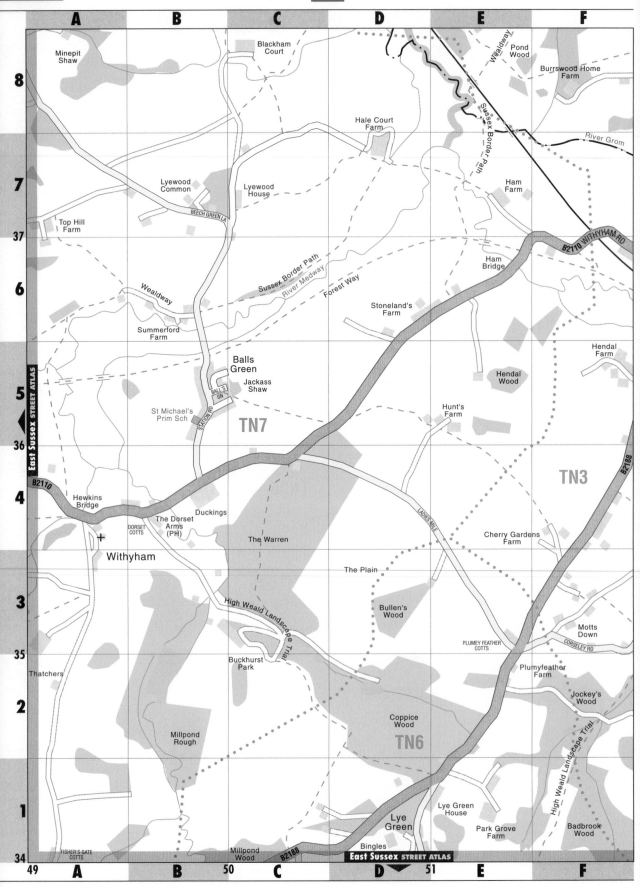

Minepit Shaw

Blackham Court

Burrswood Home Farm

Wealdway

Pond Wood

River Grom

Hale Court Farm

Lyewood Common

Lyewood House

Ham Farm

Top Hill Farm

BEECH GREEN LA

B2110 WITHYHAM RD

Sussex Border Path

River Medway

Forest Way

Ham Bridge

Wealdway

Stoneland's Farm

Hendal Farm

Summerford Farm

Hendal Wood

Balls Green

Jackass Shaw

Hunt's Farm

BALL'S GN

St Michael's Prim Sch

STATION RD

TN7

TN3

B2188

B2110

Hewkins Bridge

Duckings

LADIES MILE

Cherry Gardens Farm

The Dorset Arms (PH)

DORSET COTTS

The Warren

Withyham

The Plain

Bullen's Wood

Motts Down

CORSELEY RD

PLUMEY FEATHER COTTS

High Weald Landscape Trail

Thatchers

Buckhurst Park

Plumyfeather Farm

Jockey's Wood

Millpond Rough

Coppice Wood

TN6

High Weald Landscape Trail

Lye Green House

Park Grove Farm

Badbrook Wood

Lye Green

FISHER'S GATE COTTS

Millpond Wood

B2188

Bingles

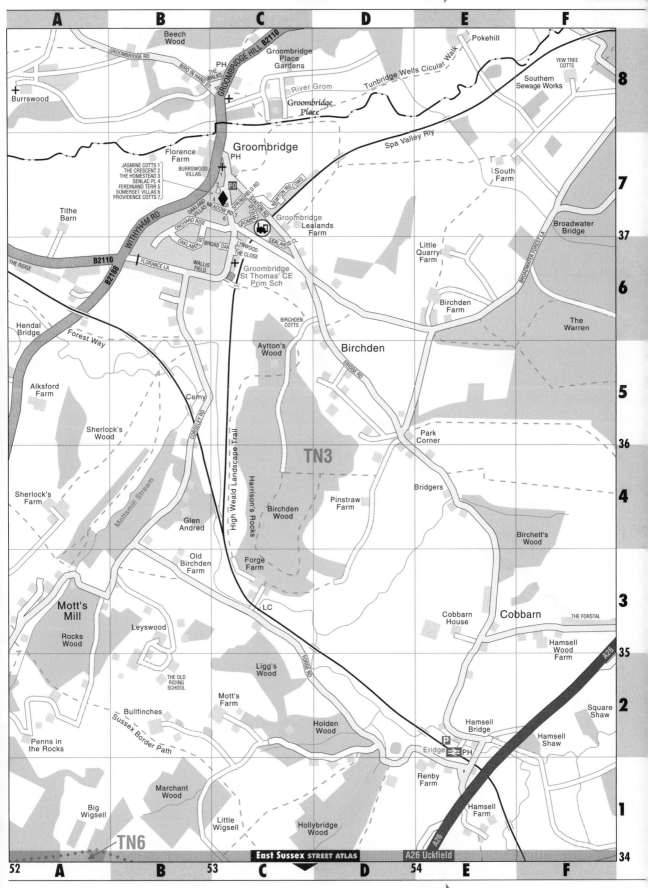

171
158

171

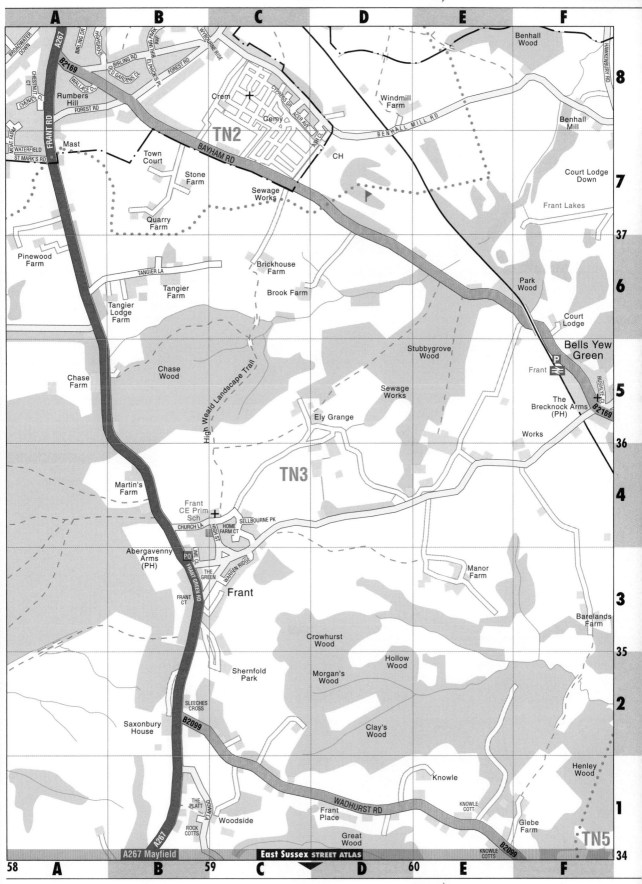

A B C D E F

8

Coker's Down

Brown's Wood

Sunninglye Farmhouse

7

Rushlye Down

Coneyburrow Wood

Furnace Wood

Oxpasture Wood

River Teise

Tollslye

The Bothy

37

6

Bayham Lake

Rushlye Farmhouse

Hollow Wood

Jews Wood

Great Coppice Wood

5

CRICKETERS CL

Highfield

IVY LA

Abbots Down

Diamonds

TN3

MIDDLE RD

B2169

Forest Lodge

Upper Sluice Wood

LITTLE BAYHAM COTTS

36

BAYHAM RD

Burnt Wood

B2169

Little Bayham

4

Higham Wood

Higham Farm

Bartley Mill Wood

BARTLEY MILL LA

Bartley Mill

Wickhurst Farmhouse

Verridge Wood

Churchfield Wood

Little Shoesmiths

Bartley House

BARTLEY MILL RD

3

Sewers Bridge

35

Brookland Wood

Grigg's Wood

Shoesmith's Wood

Brick Kiln Wood

2

Camden Wood

Great Shoesmith Farm

Hewley Wood

Henley Wood

TN5

Sussex Border Path

1

WHITEGATES LA

DENHURST LA

Sewage Works

34

61 A B 62 C D 63 E F

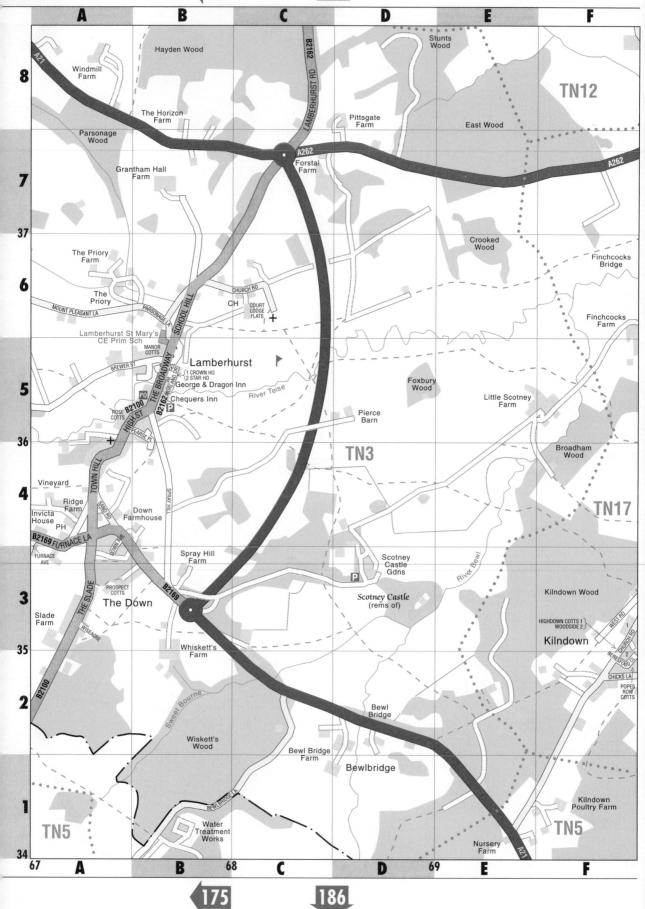

| A | B | C | D | E | F |

8

A21

Windmill Farm

Hayden Wood

LAMBERHURST RD

B2162

Stunts Wood

TN12

The Horizon Farm

Parsonage Wood

Pittsgate Farm

East Wood

7

Grantham Hall Farm

A262

Forstal Farm

A262

37

Crooked Wood

Finchcocks Bridge

6

The Priory Farm

The Priory

SCHOOL HILL

CHURCH RD

CH

COURT LODGE FLATS

Finchcocks Farm

MOUNT PLEASANT LA

PARSONAGE LA

Lamberhurst St Mary's CE Prim Sch

MANOR COTTS

Lamberhurst

5

BREWER ST

THE BROADWAY

1 CROWN HO
2 STAR HO

George & Dragon Inn

River Teise

Foxbury Wood

Little Scotney Farm

PO

B2100

Chequers Inn

NORLAND DR

B2162

P

Pierce Barn

ROSE COTTS

HIGH ST

36

PEARSE PL

TN3

Broadham Wood

4

Vineyard

Ridge Farm

TOWN HILL

SAND RD

Down Farmhouse

SPRAY HILL

TN17

Invicta House

PH

B2169 FURNACE LA

DOWN TYE

FURNACE AVE

Spray Hill Farm

Scotney Castle Gdns

River Bewl

Kilndown Wood

3

THE SLADE

PROSPECT COTTS

B2169

The Down

P

Scotney Castle (rems of)

HIGHDOWN COTTS 1
WOODSIDE 2

WEST RD

CHURCH RD

Kilndown

Slade Farm

WISEACRE

Whiskett's Farm

BERESFORD CL

35

CHICKS LA

POPES ROW COTTS

2

B2100

Sweet Bourne

Bewl Bridge

Bewl Bridge Farm

Bewlbridge

1

Wiskett's Wood

BEWL BRIDGE LA

Kilndown Poultry Farm

TN5

Water Treatment Works

Nursery Farm

A21

TN5

34

| 67 | A | B | 68 | C | D | 69 | E | F |

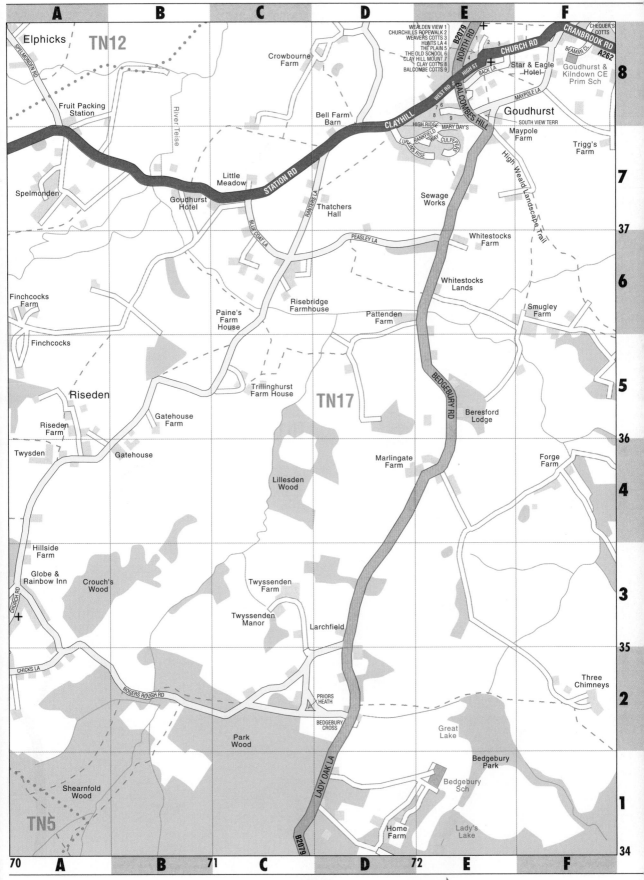

177
164

A **B** **C** **D** **E** **F**

B2084

A262

Chequers Inn (PH)

CRANBROOK RD

Paynetts Oast Farm

Frog's Hole

MILE LA

Lime Tree Farm

Iden Green

IDEN GREEN COTTS

Iden Green Farm

Four Wents

A262

Manor Farm

8

Trigg's Farm

B2085

The Peacock Inn (PH)

CHALK LA

Flishinghurst

7

37

Gill Wood

Glassenbury Park

6

Glassenbury House

Glassenbury

Wenman's Cottage

High Weald Landscape Trail

Little Glassenbury

Saffrons

Beech Hill

Angley Wood

5

TN17

Windmill House

36

Mast

Angley Farm

GLASSENBURY RD

STARVE GOOSE LA

WT Station

4

Wet Wood

Blackbush Wood

Huggin's Hall

TURNDEN RD

3

Furnace Wood

35

Furnace Farm

B2085

HARTLEY RD A229

Bull Farm

2

Pond Bay

BISHOPS LA

STATION COTTS

Three Chimneys Bank

PH

WESTFIELD TERR

THE MEADS

Hartley

HAWKHURST RD A229

1

Iron Latch

Hall Wood Farm

TN18

34

73 **A** **B** **74** **C** **D** **75** **E** **F**

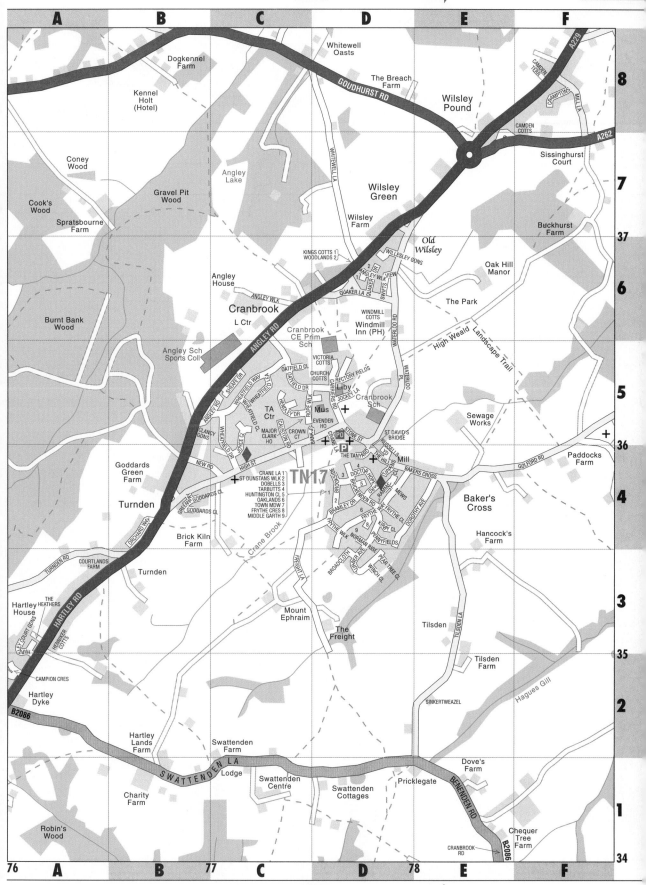

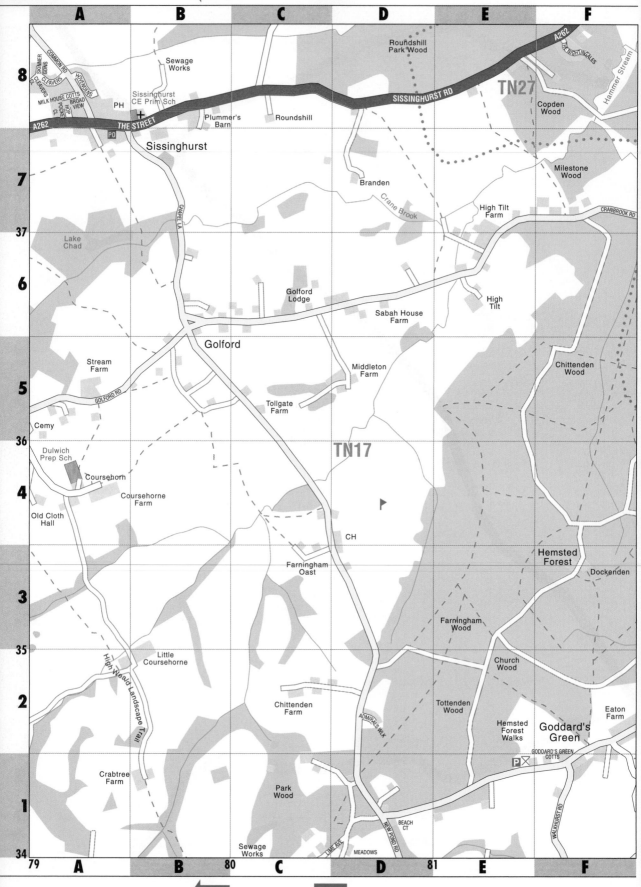

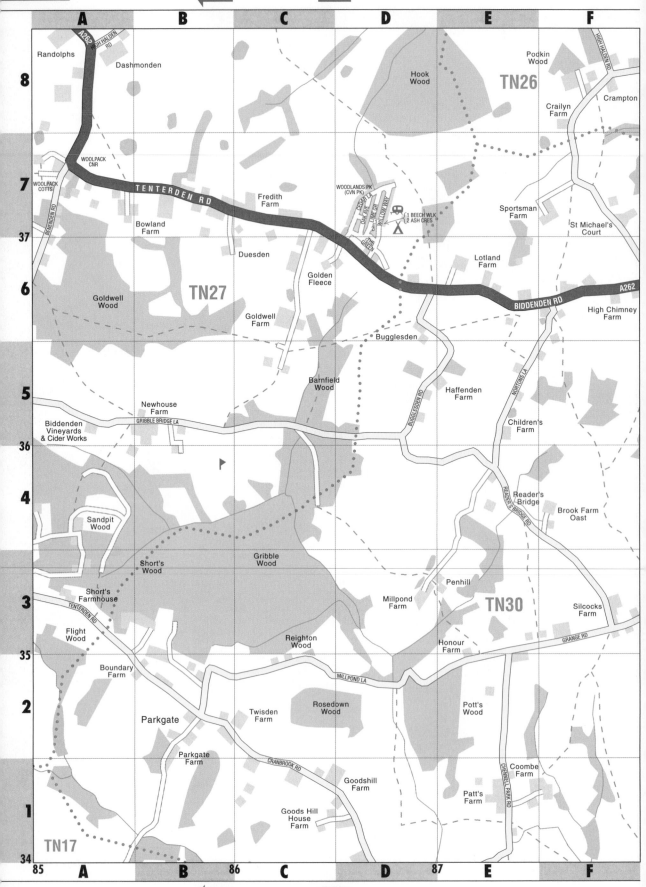

A   B   C   D   E   F

8   Randolphs   Dashmonden   Hook Wood   Podkin Wood   TN26   Crailyn Farm   Crampton

7   WOOLPACK CNR   TENTERDEN RD   Fredith Farm   WOODLANDS PK (CVN PK)   Sportsman Farm   St Michael's Court

WOOLPACK COTTS

37   Bowland Farm   Duesden   1 BEECH WLK 2 ASH CRES

6   Goldwell Wood   TN27   Golden Fleece   Lotland Farm   BIDDENDEN RD   A262   High Chimney Farm

Goldwell Farm   Bugglesden

5   Newhouse Farm   Barnfield Wood   Haffenden Farm   Children's Farm

Biddenden Vineyards & Cider Works   GRIBBLE BRIDGE LA

36

4   Sandpit Wood   Reader's Bridge   Brook Farm Oast

Short's Wood   Gribble Wood   Penhill   TN30   Silcocks Farm

3   Short's Farmhouse   TENTERDEN RD   Millpond Farm   Honour Farm   GRANGE RD

Flight Wood

35   Boundary Farm   Reighton Wood   MILLPOND LA   Pott's Wood

2   Parkgate   Twisden Farm   Rosedown Wood

Parkgate Farm   CRANBROOK RD   Goodshill Farm   Coombe Farm   Patt's Farm

1   Goods Hill House Farm

TN17

34

85   A   B   86   C   D   87   E   F

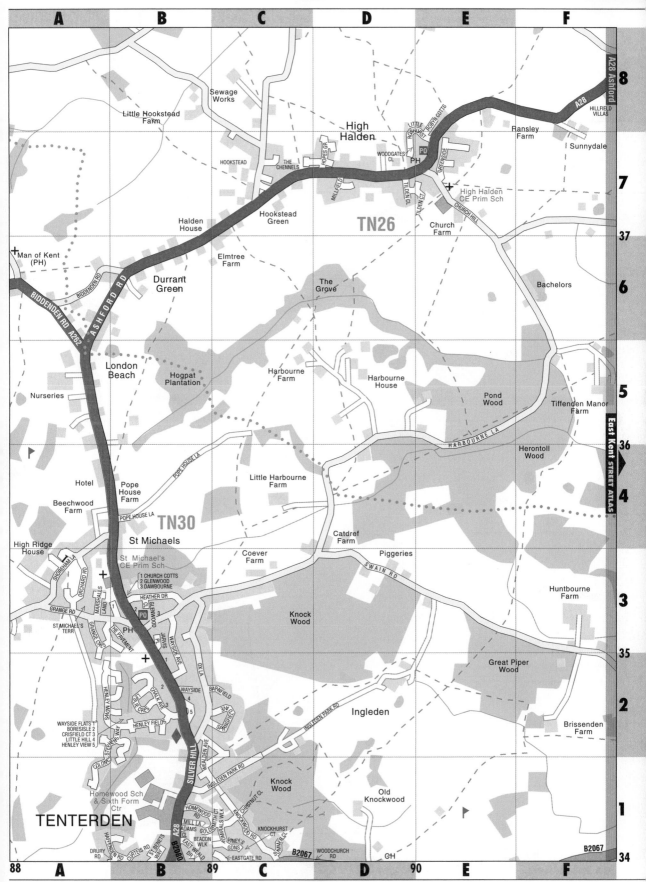

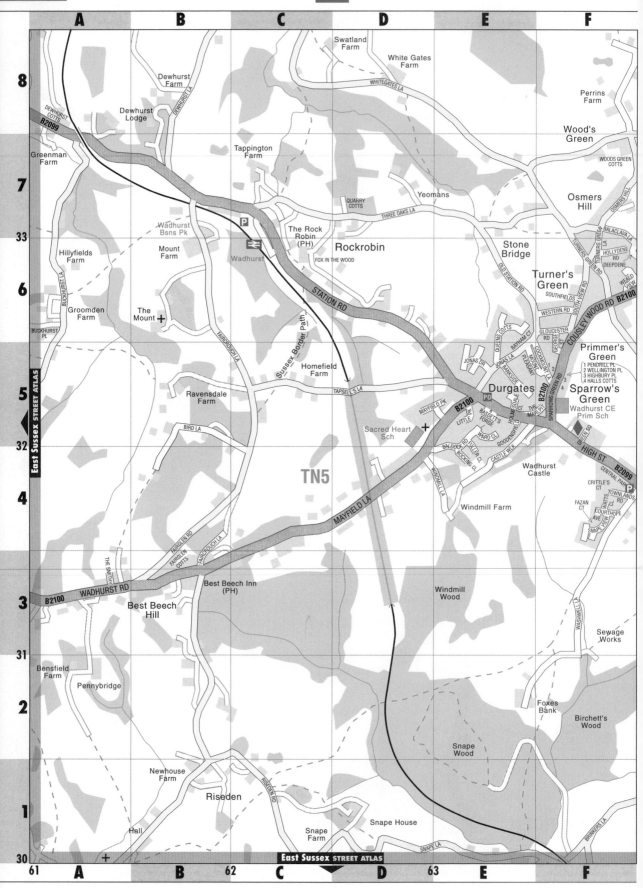

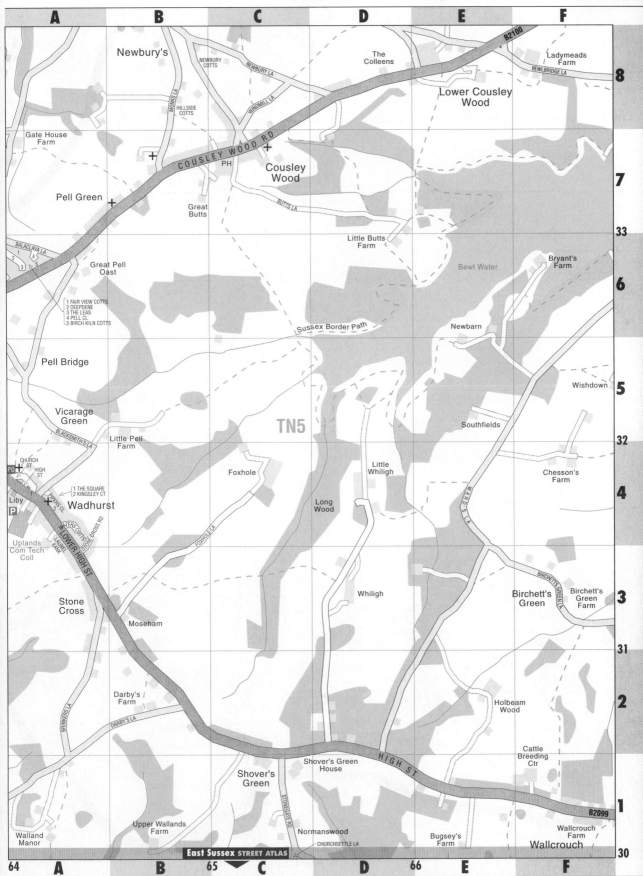

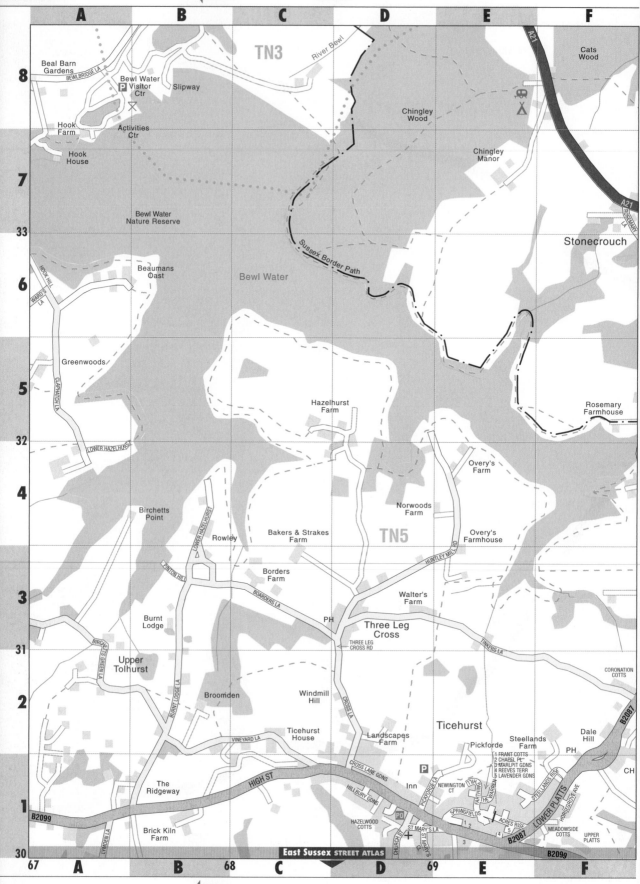

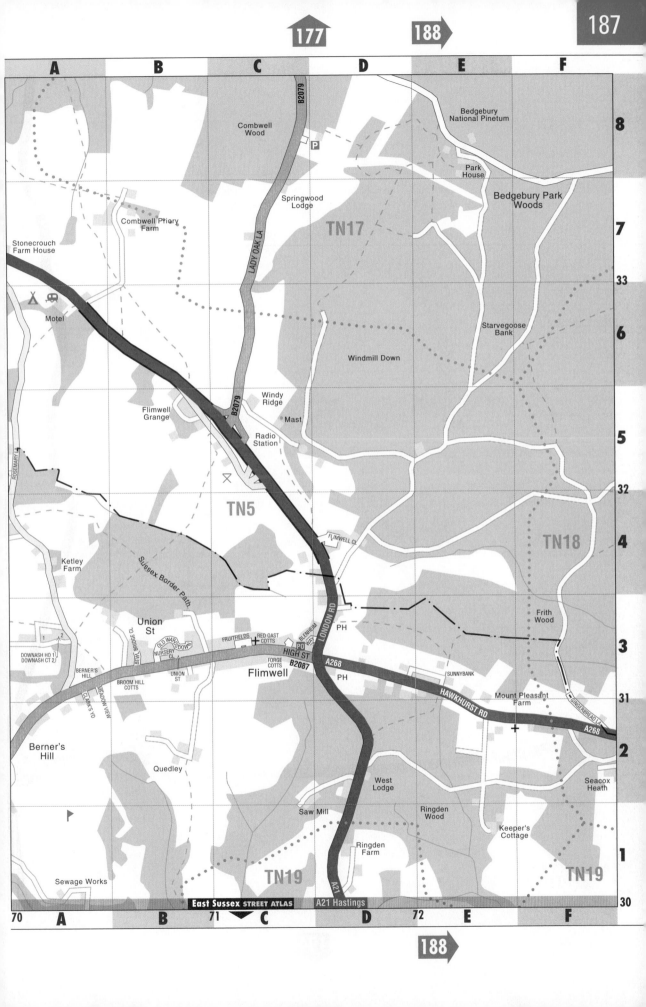

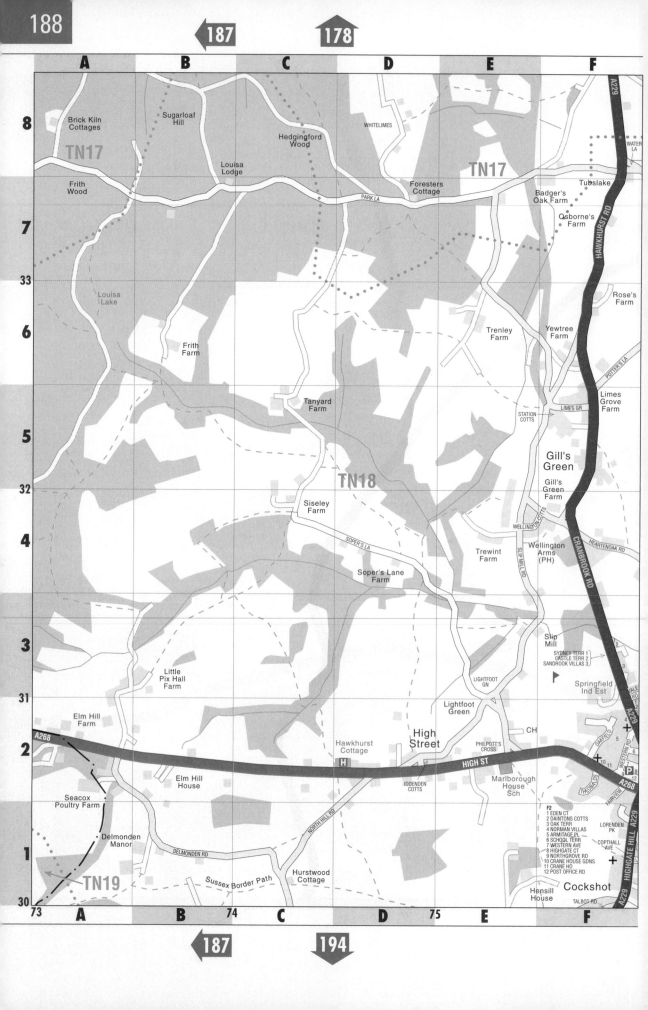

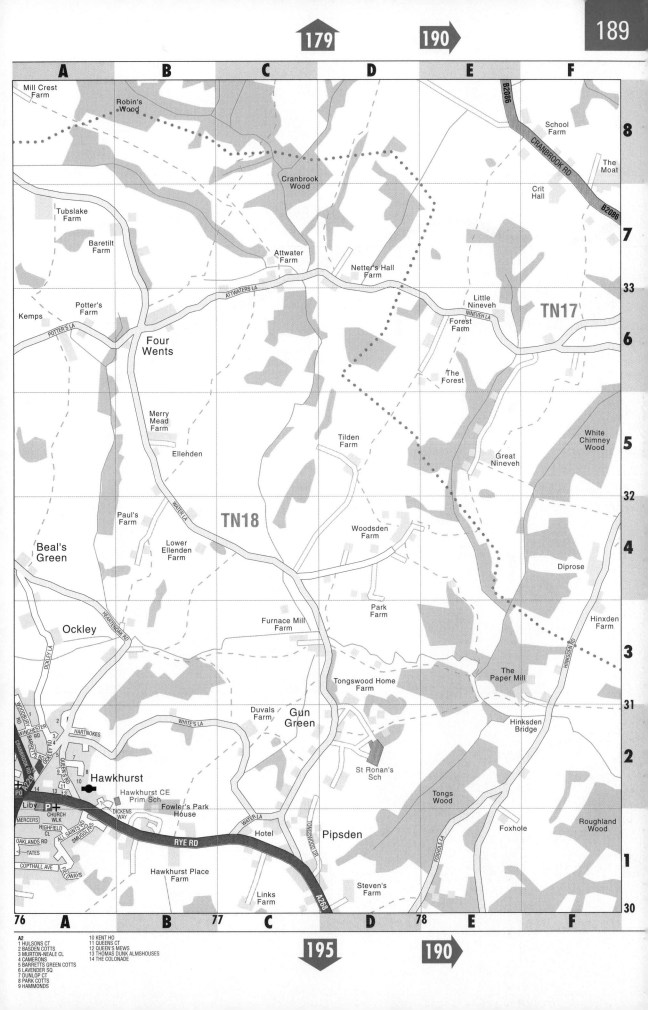

8

7

33

6

5

32

4

3

31

2

1

30

Mill Crest Farm

Robin's Wood

Cranbrook Wood

School Farm

B2086

CRANBROOK RD

B2086

The Moat

Crit Hall

Tubslake Farm

Baretilt Farm

Attwater Farm

Netter's Hall Farm

Little Nineveh

NINEVEH LA

TN17

Kemps

Potter's Farm

POTTER'S LA

ATTWATERS LA

Four Wents

Forest Farm

The Forest

Great Nineveh

White Chimney Wood

Merry Mead Farm

Ellenden

Tilden Farm

Paul's Farm

WATER LA

TN18

Lower Ellenden Farm

Woodsden Farm

Diprose

Hinxden Farm

Beal's Green

Ockley

HEARTENOAK RD

OCKLEY LA

Furnace Mill Farm

Park Farm

The Paper Mill

HINXSDEN RD

Hinksden Bridge

Tongswood Home Farm

WINCHESTER RD

WOODBURY RD

CRANBROOK RD

BARRETT'S RD

OCKLEY RD

QUEENS RD

HARTNOKES

WHITE'S LA

Duvals Farm

Gun Green

St Ronan's Sch

Tongs Wood

Hinksden Bridge

Hawkhurst

Hawkhurst CE Prim Sch

DICKENS WAY

Fowler's Park House

WATER LA

Hotel

TONGSWOOD DR

Pipsden

Foxhole

Roughland Wood

Liby   P

MERCERS

CHURCH WLK

ALL SAINTS RD

SMUGGLERS

HIGHFIELD CL

OAKLANDS RD

TATES

COPTHALL AVE

FIELDWAYS

RYE RD

A268

Hawkhurst Place Farm

Links Farm

A268

Steven's Farm

FOXHOLE LA

A2
1 HULSONS CT
2 BASDEN COTTS
3 MURTON-NEALE CL
4 CAMERONS
5 BARRETTS GREEN COTTS
6 LAVENDER SQ
7 DUNLOP CT
8 PARK COTTS
9 HAMMONDS
10 KENT HO
11 QUEENS CT
12 QUEEN'S MEWS
13 THOMAS DUNK ALMSHOUSES
14 THE COLONADE

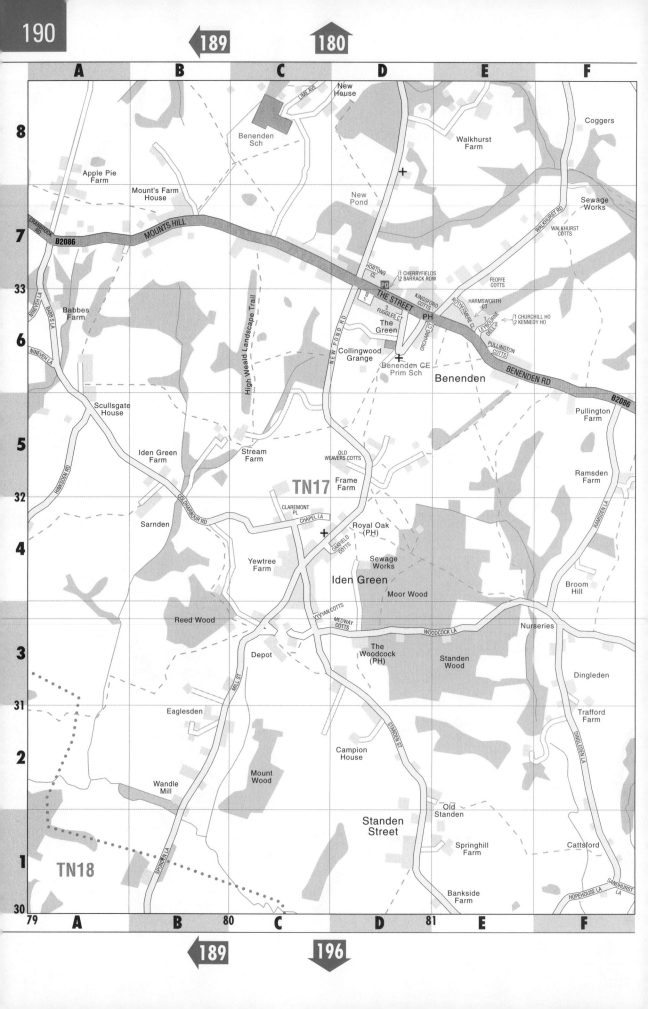

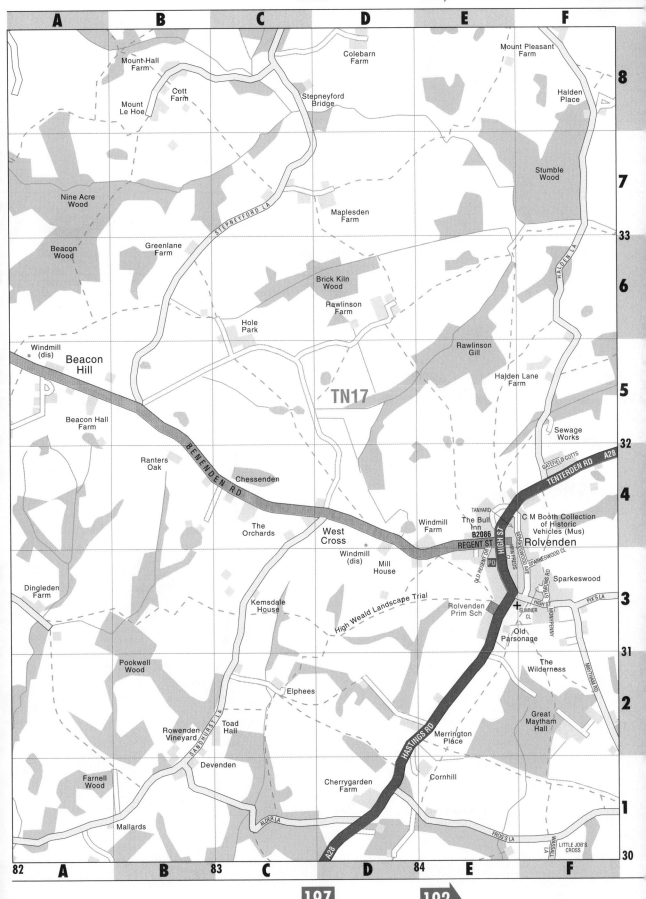

191
182

A B C D E F

8

7

33

6

5

32

4

3

31

2

1

30

Little Halden Place

GOODS HILL

Chennell Park

CHENNELL PARK RD

CRANBROOK RD

LC

Cemy

Ruffets

New Barn Farm

Ashbourne Mill

ROLVENDEN RD

CASTWEAZLE

HURST CL

LAWN CL

WEST CROSS GDNS

WEST CROSS

CLAXTON CL

ROGERSMEAD

A28

B2082

WESTWELL HO

WESTFIELD HOUSE 1
PARKSIDE CT 2
OLD TANNERY CL 3

PLUMMER LA

Old Halden

LC

Rolvenden

West View

H

Heronden Hall

ROLVENDEN HILL

Cold Harbour

Plummer Farm

TN30

Osborn Farm

Folly Farm

Sewage Works

Plummer Wood

Strood

TN17

Kent & East Sussex Rly

TENTERDEN RD

A28

Puddingcake Farmhouse

PUDDINGCAKE LA

Winton Farm

High Weald Landscape Trail

Heronden

Sparkes Gill

MOUNTS LA

Lower Woolwich

Newmill Channel

Gazedown Wood

Morghew Farm

PIX'S LA

Upper Woolwich

Crayfish Lagoons

Kingsgate

Winser Farm

MAYTHAM RD

FRENSHAM RD

OAKFIELD

FROG'S LA

PH

Frensham Manor

WINSER RD

THORNDEN RD

Rolvenden Layne

Friezingham Farm

MAYTHAM BGLWS

85 A B 86 C D 87 E F

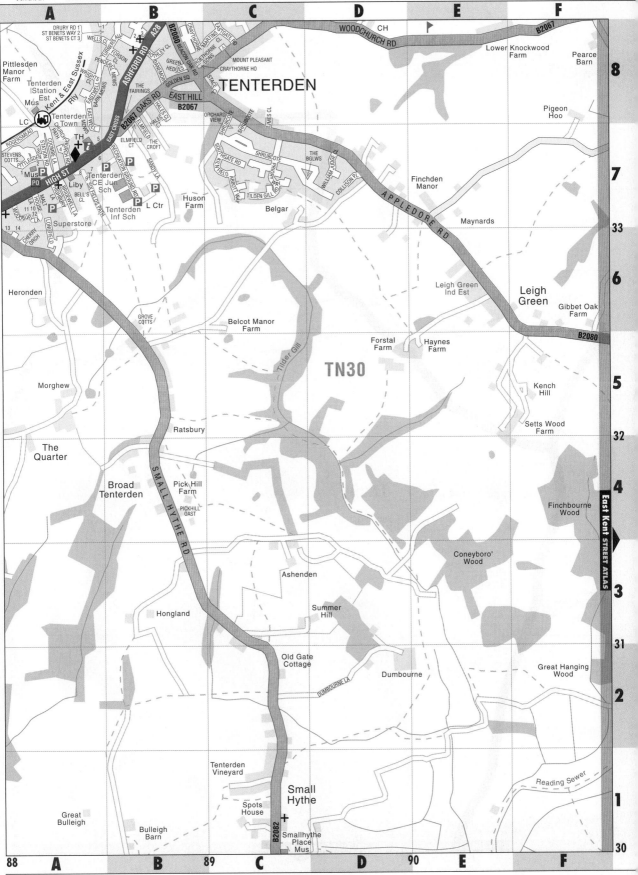

A7
1 PITTLESDEN PL
2 PARK VIEW TERR
3 STATION MEWS
4 ST MILDREDS CL
5 EASTWELL
6 SAYERS LA
7 THEATRE SQ
8 JACKSONS LA
9 BELLS LA
10 BURGESS ROW
11 MAYOR'S PL
12 CEDAR CT
13 BENNETTS MEWS
14 AUSTENS ORCH

TENTERDEN

TN30

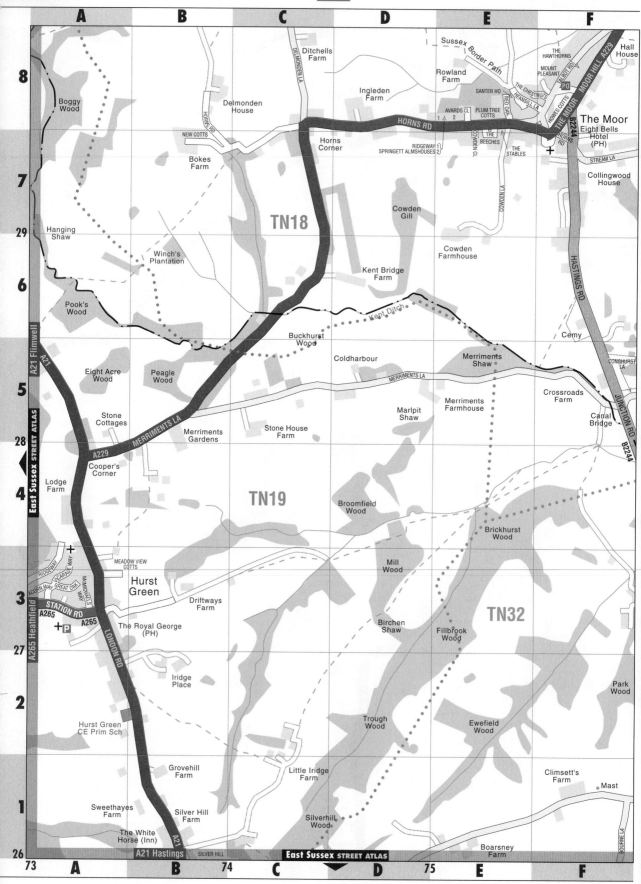

A B C D E F

8

7

29

6

5

28

4

3

27

2

1

26

73 A B 74 C D 75 E F

TN18

TN19

TN32

Boggy Wood

Ditchells Farm

Sussex Border Path

The Hawthorns

Hall House

Delmonden House

Rowland Farm

Mount Pleasant

The Moor

Ingleden Farm

Santer Ho

Heansill La

The Chestnuts

Eight Bells Hotel (PH)

Horns Corner

Avards Cl

Plum Tree Cotts

Red Oak

The Beeches

Collingwood House

Ridgeway

Springett Almshouses

The Stables

Hanging Shaw

New Cotts

Bokes Farm

Horns Rd

Cowden Gill

Winch's Plantation

Cowden Farmhouse

Cemy

Pook's Wood

Kent Bridge Farm

Kent Ditch

Buckhurst Wood

Coldharbour

Merriments Shaw

Crossroads Farm

Conghurst La

Eight Acre Wood

Peagle Wood

Merriments La

Marlpit Shaw

Merriments Farmhouse

Canal Bridge

Stone Cottages

Stone House Farm

Merriments Gardens

A229

Cooper's Corner

Lodge Farm

Broomfield Wood

Brickhurst Wood

Meadow View Cotts

Hurst Green

Mill Wood

Driftways Farm

Birchen Shaw

Fillbrook Wood

Station Rd

The Royal George (PH)

London Rd

Iridge Place

Trough Wood

Ewefield Wood

Park Wood

Hurst Green CE Prim Sch

Climsett's Farm

Mast

Grovehill Farm

Little Iridge Farm

Sweethayes Farm

Silver Hill Farm

Silverhill Wood

Boarsney Farm

The White Horse (Inn)

A21 Hastings

SILVER HILL

Bourne La

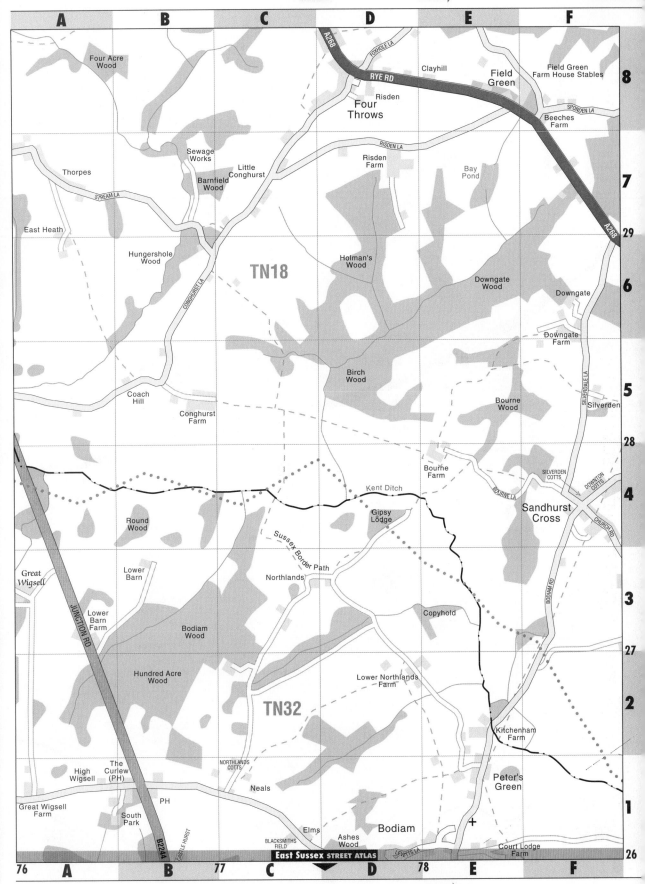

8

Four Acre
Wood

Clayhill

Field
Green

Field Green
Farm House Stables

RYE RD

A268

FOXHOLE LA

SPONDEN LA

Risden

Four
Throws

Beeches
Farm

RISDEN LA

Thorpes

Sewage
Works

Little
Conghurst

Barnfield
Wood

Risden
Farm

Bay
Pond

7

STREAM LA

East Heath

29

Hungershole
Wood

TN18

Holman's
Wood

Downgate
Wood

Downgate

6

CONGHURST LA

Downgate
Farm

Coach
Hill

Birch
Wood

Bourne
Wood

Silverden

5

Conghurst
Farm

SILVERDALE LA

28

Kent Ditch

Bourne
Farm

SILVERDEN
COTTS

DOWNTON
COTTS

4

Round
Wood

Gipsy
Lodge

BOURNE LA

Sandhurst
Cross

CHURCH RD

Great
Wigsell

Sussex Border Path

Northlands

Copyhold

27

JUNCTION RD

Lower
Barn

Lower
Barn
Farm

Bodiam
Wood

Lower Northlands
Farm

BODIAM RD

3

Hundred Acre
Wood

TN32

Kitchenham
Farm

2

NORTHLANDS
COTTS

Peter's
Green

High
Wigsell

The
Curlew
(PH)

Neals

1

Great Wigsell
Farm

PH

South
Park

Elms

Ashes
Wood

Bodiam

Court Lodge
Farm

26

B2244

CASTLE HURST

BLACKSMITHS
FIELD

LEVETTS LA

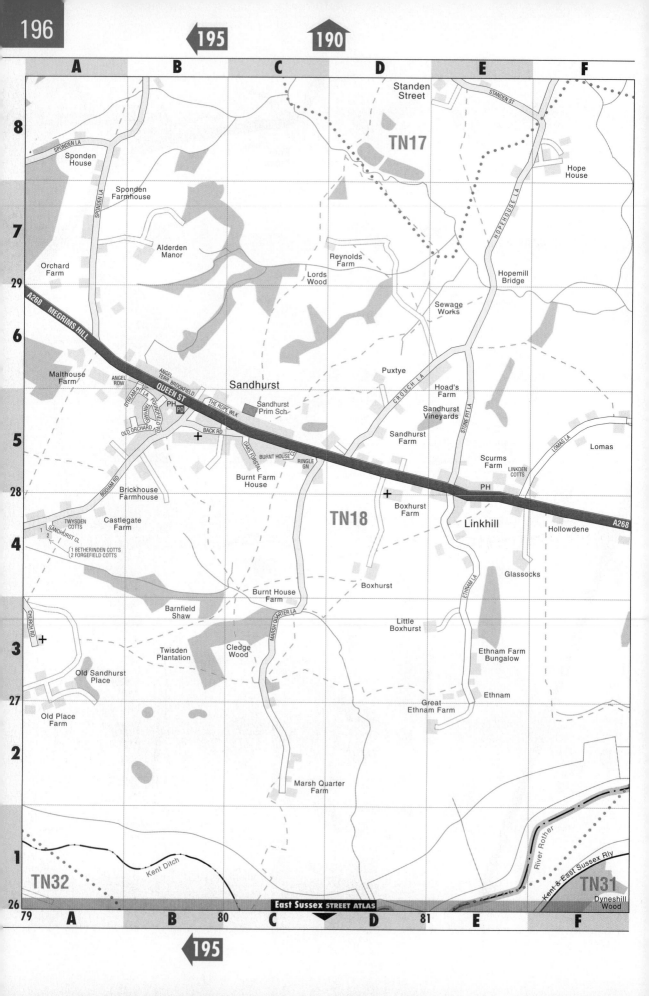

East Sussex STREET ATLAS

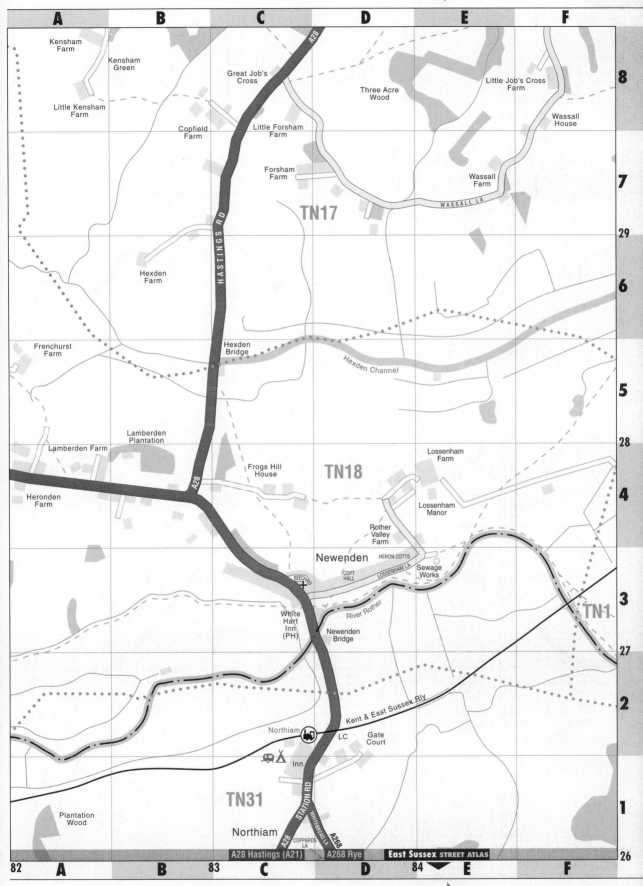

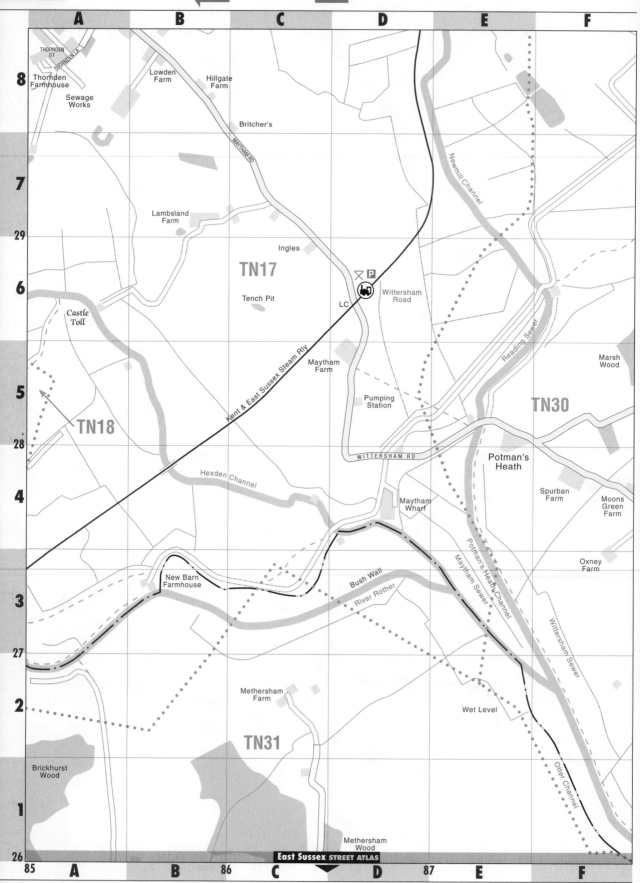

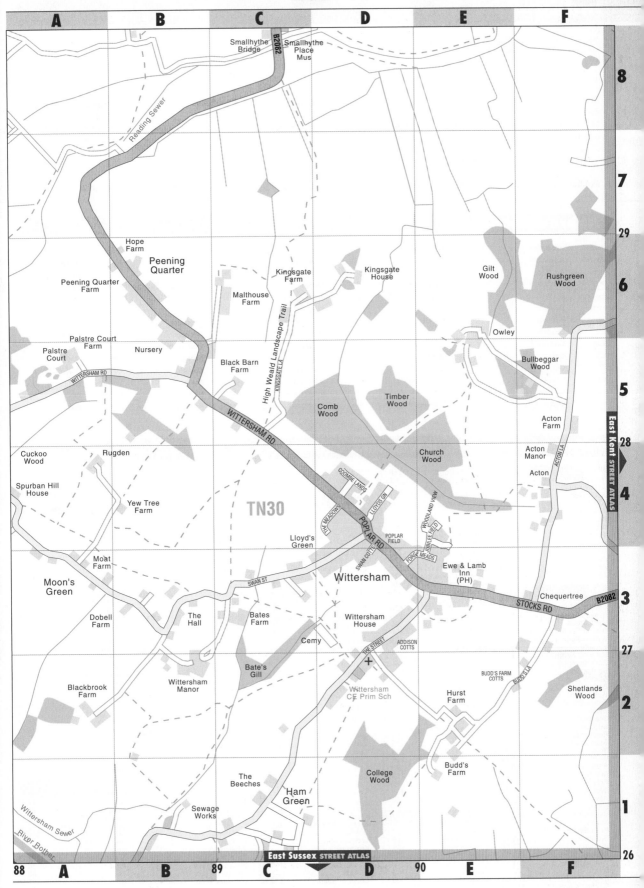

Index

Church Rd [6] Beckenham BR2..........**53** C6

Place name	**Location number**	**Locality, town or village**	**Postcode district**	**Page and grid square**
May be abbreviated on the map	Present when a number indicates the place's position in a crowded area of mapping	Shown when more than one place has the same name	District for the indexed place	Page number and grid reference for the standard mapping

Public and commercial buildings are highlighted in magenta   **Places of interest** are highlighted in blue with a star★

Abbreviations used in the index

Acad	Academy	Comm	Common	Gd	Ground	L	Leisure	Prom	Prom
App	Approach	Cott	Cottage	Gdn	Garden	La	Lane	Rd	Road
Arc	Arcade	Cres	Crescent	Gn	Green	Liby	Library	Recn	Recreation
Ave	Avenue	Cswy	Causeway	Gr	Grove	Mdw	Meadow	Ret	Retail
Bglw	Bungalow	Ct	Court	H	Hall	Meml	Memorial	Sh	Shopping
Bldg	Building	Ctr	Centre	Ho	House	Mkt	Market	Sq	Square
Bsns, Bus	Business	Ctry	Country	Hospl	Hospital	Mus	Museum	St	Street
Bvd	Boulevard	Cty	County	HQ	Headquarters	Orch	Orchard	Sta	Station
Cath	Cathedral	Dr	Drive	Hts	Heights	Pal	Palace	Terr	Terrace
Cir	Circus	Dro	Drove	Ind	Industrial	Par	Parade	TH	Town Hall
Cl	Close	Ed	Education	Inst	Institute	Pas	Passage	Univ	University
Cnr	Corner	Emb	Embankment	Int	International	Pk	Park	Wk, Wlk	Walk
Coll	College	Est	Estate	Intc	Interchange	Pl	Place	Wr	Water
Com	Community	Ex	Exhibition	Junc	Junction	Prec	Precinct	Yd	Yard

Index of localities, towns and villages

A

Abbey Wood 3 B3
Addington 80 C3
Aldon 80 B1
Allhallows 9 D1
Allhallows-on-Sea 9 D3
Allington 99 D8
Aperfield 72 F2
Ash 62 E5
Ashbank 118 B7
Ashurst 156 D2
Avery Hill 12 C1
Aylesford 82 E2

B

Badgers Mount 59 B1
Baker's Cross 179 E4
Balls Green 170 C5
Banner Farm 159 C2
Barden Park 126 F1
Barking 3 B8
Barming Heath 99 A3
Barnehurst 14 D4
Barnes Cray 15 B3
Barnes Street 129 A4
Basted 94 F4
Beacon Hill 191 A5
Beal's Green 189 A4
Bean 34 C5
Bearsted 101 B4
Beckton 2 A8
Bedmonton 103 E8
Bells Yew Green 173 F5
Beltring 130 A4
Belvedere 4 B2
Benenden 190 E6
Benover 131 A6
Berry's Green 73 B3
Bessels Green 91 D3
Best Beech Hill 184 B3
Betsham 34 F4
Bewlbridge 176 D1
Bexley 13 C3
Bexleyheath 13 F4
Bickley 42 F7
Bicknor 87 C2
Bidborough 142 D3
Biddenden 167 E2
Biggin Hill 72 E3
Birchden 171 D5
Birchett's Green 185 F3
Birchwood Corner 45 C8
Birling 81 C6

Bishop's Down – Burham

Bishop's Down 158 E3
Bitchet Green 93 D1
Blackfen 13 A1
Blackheath Park 11 A3
Blackhurst 159 F5
Bluewater 34 A8
Bodiam 195 D1
Bogden 133 C2
Borough Green 94 F8
Borstal 53 B2
Bough Beech 123 F2
Boughton Green 116 B3
Boughton Malherbe ..137 A8
Boughton Monchelsea ..116 B3
Bow Arrow 16 B1
Bowmans 31 F8
Boxley 84 D2
Branbridges 130 A5
Brandfold 163 F3
Brasted 90 C3
Brasted Chart 106 B7
Breach 70 F8
Bredhurst 69 B1
Brenchley 162 B8
Broad Ford 163 C4
Broadstone 136 D4
Broad Street
  Hoo St Werburgh 40 B5
Broad Street Maidstone ..102 B6
Broad Tenterden 193 B4
Broadwater Down 172 E7
Bromley 42 B6
Bromley Common 42 E3
Brompton 54 A5
Brooklands 32 F7
Brook Street 143 A8
Broomfield 118 D5
Broom Hill 43 F2
Buckhurst 167 C5
Buck's Cross 58 F5
Bullingstone 157 F7
Burham 66 E1

C

Cage Green 127 C4
Camden Hill 165 F2
Camden Park 159 C2
Canning Town 1 B8
Capel 144 F5
Capel Cross 163 C5
Capstone 68 E7
Castle Hill 146 E1
Chainhurst 132 A4
Chalk 37 A7

Charcott 125 A3
Charlton 11 D8
Chart Hill 134 B8
Chart Sutton 117 B1
Chartway Street 118 C1
Chatham 53 E5
Chattenden 39 F4
Chelsfield 58 E5
Cherry Orchard 99 B4
Chesley 71 A3
Chestnut Street 71 E4
Chevening 90 F8
Chiddingstone 140 C7
Chiddingstone
  Causeway 124 F2
Chiddingstone Hoath ..140 A2
Chipstead 91 C5
Chislehurst 43 B7
Chislehurst West 29 A2
Christian Fields 36 C4
Church Street 21 C1
Claygate 147 D6
Clement Street 32 D2
Cliffe 22 B5
Cliffe Woods 39 B7
Cobbarn 171 F3
Cobham 50 F6
Cockshot 188 F1
Cock Street 116 D2
Coldblow 31 D7
Coldharbour 109 F1
Cold Harbour 71 F7
Colliers' Green 164 F2
Collier Street 147 C8
Colt's Hill 145 B4
Congelow 130 F7
Cooling 22 F5
Cooling Street 22 D2
Cooper's Corner 123 F8
Cousley Wood 185 C7
Cowden 155 A6
Cowden Pound 139 B2
Coxheath 115 C2
Cranbrook 179 C6
Cranbrook Common 166 A2
Crayford 14 D1
Creekmouth 2 F8
Crockenhill 45 D3
Crockham Hill 105 C2
Crockhurst Street 144 C6
Crofton 57 D8
Cross-at-Hand 133 E1
Crossways 16 D3
Crouch 95 B4
Crowdleham 77 D2

Cudham 73 D4
Culverstone Green 63 E2
Curteis' Corner 168 A3
Curtisden Green 164 C5
Custom House 1 C7
Cuxton 52 B2
Cyprus 2 B6

D

Danaway 71 C3
Darenth 33 B4
Darland 68 E8
Dartford 15 E2
David Street 64 B5
Deans Bottom 87 C5
Deans Hill 87 D6
Dean Street 115 D7
Denny Bottom 158 E4
Denton 36 E8
Derry Downs 44 D3
Detling 85 B1
Devil's Den 134 B3
Ditton 82 C1
Downe 73 A8
Dryhill 91 B3
Dunk's Green 111 A6
Dunn Street 85 A8
Dunton Green 91 E8
Durgates 184 E5
Durrant Green 183 B6

E

East Barming 98 F1
East End Benenden 181 C3
East End Headcorn 152 B4
East Farleigh 115 B7
East Hill 61 B1
East Malling 98 A7
East Malling Heath 97 E4
East Peckham 129 F6
East Street 80 E3
East Tilbury 20 C7
East Wickham 13 A7
Eastwood 136 C6
Eccles 82 F6
Edenbridge 122 D1
Egerton 137 F4
Egerton Forstal 137 D1
Elmstead 28 D2
Elmstone Hole 136 E8
Elphicks 177 A8
Eltham 11 E1
Eridge Green 172 B3

Erith 4 C1
Eyhorne Street 102 C2
Eynsford 60 D7

F

Fairbourne Heath 119 B1
Fairseat 79 C7
Falconwood 12 E3
Farnborough 57 D5
Farningham 46 F2
Farthing Green 134 E1
Farthing Street 56 F2
Fawkham Green 62 B8
Fenn Street 24 B4
Ferndale 159 D5
Field Green 195 E8
Fig Street 108 A7
Fishinghurst 178 F7
Five Oak Green 145 B7
Five Wents 117 D2
Fleet-Downs 33 D7
Flimwell 187 C3
Foots Cray 30 B2
Force Green 89 D4
Fordcombe 157 B5
Forstal 83 B2
Fosten Green 181 D6
Four Elms 123 A4
Four Throws 195 D8
Four Wents 189 B6
Foxendown 64 C8
Frant 173 C3
French Street 105 F6
Frindsbury 53 C8
Frittenden 166 F7
Froghole 105 D3
Further Quarter 169 C3

G

Gillingham 54 D3
Gill's Green 188 F5
Glassenbury 178 E6
Goathurst Common 107 B5
Goddard's Green 180 F2
Godden Green 93 B3
Goddington 58 C7
Golden Green 128 F5
Gold Street 50 E4
Golford 180 B5
Goose Green Biddenden ..181 E8
Goose Green Hadlow ..112 B2
Goudhurst 177 F8
Grafty Green 136 F7

Grain 27 B6
Grange 55 B6
Gravesend 19 B2
Grays 18 A7
Greatness 92 D6
Greenhithe 17 B2
Green Street Green
  Hartley 34 A2
Green Street Green
  Orpington 57 E4
Greenwich 1 A3
Groombridge 171 C7
Grove Green 100 E5
Grove Park 28 B5
Grubb Street 48 B8
Gun Green 189 C2

H

Hadlow 111 E1
Hadlow Stair 127 F4
Haffenden Quarter . . .169 A7
Hale 68 D8
Hale Street 130 A7
Halling 66 B5
Hall's Green 125 A7
Halstead 74 F6
Ham Green 199 C1
Hammerwood 154 B3
Harbourland 100 B8
Hareplain 167 C4
Harrietsham 119 D5
Hartley Cranbrook . . .178 F1
Hartley New Barn 48 F3
Hartley Green 48 E4
Hartlip 70 E5
Harvel 64 C3
Haviker Street 131 E1
Hawkenbury Headcorn .150 D7
Hawkenbury
  Royal Tunbridge Wells .159 D2
Hawkhurst 189 A2
Hawley 32 F3
Hayes 42 A2
Hazel Street Bredgar . . .87 A3
Hazel Street Horsmonden 162 F4
Hazelwood 73 D8
Headcorn 151 D4
Hearnden Green 135 B1
Heath Side 31 F5
Heaverham 77 E2
Hempstead 69 A5
Henhurst 50 E8
Henley Street 50 F3
Henwood Green 160 E6
Herne Pound 96 D2
Hever 139 D6
Hextable 31 E1
Higham 38 B4
Higham Wood 127 F6
High Brooms 159 C8
High Halden 183 D7
High Halstow 23 F4
High Street 188 D2
Hildenborough 126 E6
Hilden Park 126 F4
Hill Green 70 C1
Hill Hoath 140 C6
Hill Park 89 B4
Hill Top 146 B1
Hoath Corner 140 B3
Hockenden 45 B6
Hocker Edge 165 D2
Hodsoll Street 63 D2
Holborough 66 A2
Holland 104 A1
Hollingbourne 102 E2
Holtye 154 F3
Hone Sundridge 90 F3
Hook Green Lamberhurst .175 C4
Hook Green
  Meopham Station 50 A5
Hook Green Northfleet . .35 A2
Hoo St Werburgh 40 F5
Horns Green 73 E2
Horn Street 81 D6
Horseshoe Green 139 E1
Horsmonden 163 A5
Horton Kirby 47 D5
How Green 123 C1
Hucking 86 E1
Hungershall Park 158 E2
Hunton 131 D8
Hurst Green Hawkhurst .194 B3
Hurst Green Oxted 104 B3

I

Ide Hill 106 F4
Iden Green Goudhurst . . .178 C8
Iden Green Hawkhurst . .190 D4
Ightham 94 D6
Ightham Common 94 A3
Istead Rise 49 E8
Ivy Hatch 94 A1

J

Joyden's Wood 31 F4

K

Kemsing 77 B2
Kemsley Street 69 C2
Kent Hatch 105 B3
Kent Street 96 E2
Keston 56 D6
Keston Mark 56 D8

Kevingtown 44 E3
Keycol 71 E6
Key's Green 161 C4
Kidbrooke 11 C5
Kilndown 176 F3
Kings Farm 36 C5
Kings Hill 97 A3
Kingsnorth 41 D5
Kingswood 118 E3
Kipping's Cross 161 B5
Kippington 92 A1
Kit's Coty 83 C7
Knatts Valley 77 D8
Knockhall 17 C1
Knockholt 74 B2
Knockholt Pound 74 D4
Knockmill 77 E7
Knox Bridge 165 F6

L

Labour-in-vain 78 F5
Laddingford 130 E5
Lamberhurst 176 B5
Lamberhurst Quarter . .161 D1
Lane End 33 D3
Langhurst 121 E7
Langley 117 C4
Langley Heath 117 A4
Langton Green 157 E3
Larkfield 82 A2
Lashenden 167 F6
Leadingcross Green . . .120 C3
Leaves Green 72 D8
Leeds 118 A7
Leigh 125 E1
Leigh Green 193 F6
Lenham 120 D5
Lessness Heath 4 B1
Letts Green 73 F3
Lewisham 28 C6
Leybourne 81 D2
Lidsing 68 F1
Limpsfield 104 A6
Linkhill 196 A4
Linton 115 F1
Little Bayham 174 F4
Little Houses 137 D2
Little Mill 129 D5
Liverton Street 119 F1
Locksbottom 57 B7
London Beach 183 B5
Longfield 48 E7
Longfield Hill 49 D5
Longford 91 D6
Longlands 29 D5
Loose 115 F4
Loose Hill 115 F5
Lords Wood 68 C1
Lower Bitchet 93 C1
Lower Bush 51 F3
Lower Cousley Wood . .185 E8
Lower Cox Street 85 D6
Lower Green Pembury . .160 D8
Lower Green Rusthall . .158 C5
Lower Hartlip 70 E4
Lower Haysden 142 D8
Lower Higham 38 D6
Lower Luddesdown . . .51 A2
Lower Rainham 55 F3
Lower Stoke 25 C5
Lower Twydall 55 C5
Lower Upnor 40 A3
Low Street 19 E8
Luddesdown 50 F1
Lunsford 81 E4
Luton 54 B2
Luxted 73 A5
Lye Green 170 D1

M

Madeira Park 159 B2
Maidstone 100 C3
Maplescombe 61 B5
Marden 148 C5
Marden Beech 148 B3
Marden Thorn 148 F3
Markbeech 139 D2
Marlpit 116 E2
Marlpit Hill 122 C4
Marsh Green 138 B5
Matfield 161 D8
Maypole Dartford 31 E7
Maypole Orpington . . .58 F4
Medhurst Row 123 A2
Meopham 64 B8
Meopham Green 64 A7
Meopham Station 50 B4
Meresborough 70 A5
Mereworth 112 D8
Middle Quarter 169 D1
Middle Stoke 25 B4
Milebush 148 E8
Mile Oak 146 C4
Millbank 151 B6
Mill Street 97 E7
Milton 19 D1
Modest Corner 142 E1
Monk's Hill 168 C7
Moon's Green 199 A3
Moor Street 70 B7
Mottingham 28 D6
Mott's Hill 171 A3
Mount Ephraim 158 F4
Mount Sion 159 A2
Mowshurst 122 F3
Munday Bois 153 F8

N

Nash 56 A4
Nash Street 50 A7
Nettlestead 113 D6
Nettlestead Green 113 B2
New Ash Green 62 F8
New Barn 49 A7
Newbury's 185 B8
New Charlton 1 C2
New Eltham 29 C6
Newenden 197 D3
Newham 1 C6
New House 35 F6
New Hythe 82 B4
Newington 71 A6
Newland Green 153 D8
New Street 63 D5
Newtown 139 D4
New Town Dartford 16 A1
New Town Halling 66 A6
New Town West Malling .97 A8
Noah's Ark 93 A8
Noke Street 39 B4
North Cray 30 F5
North End 14 F6
Northfleet 18 D1
Northfleet Green 35 C3
North Halling 66 B8
Northiam 197 C1
North Street 24 E1
Northumberland Heath .14 C7
North Woolwich 2 B4

O

Oad Street 71 E1
Ockley 189 A3
Offham 96 D8
Old Bexley 31 B8
Oldbury 94 B6
Orpington 44 C2
Osmers Hill 184 F7
Otford 76 A3
Otham 117 B7
Otham Hole 117 B6

P

Paddock Wood 145 F8
Palmer's Green 162 D8
Parkgate 182 B2
Park Wood Gillingham . .69 D4
Park Wood Maidstone . .116 E4
Parrock Farm 36 D4
Pearson's Green 146 F3
Peckham Bush 129 E8
Peening Quarter 199 B6
Pell Bridge 185 A5
Pell Green 185 A7
Pembury 160 C6
Penenden Heath 100 B7
Penshurst 141 B4
Pepper Hill 35 C5
Perry Street 35 F8
Petteridge 161 F6
Pettings 63 B3
Petts Wood 43 D5
Pikefish 130 F3
Pinden 48 C7
Pipsden 189 D1
Pittswood 128 B8
Plaistow 28 A2
Platt 95 C7
Platt's Heath 119 E1
Plaxtol 110 E8
Plaxtol Spoute 111 A8
Plumstead 2 E1
Plumtree Green 151 A8
Pootings 122 F7
Potman's Heath 198 E4
Potter's Forstal 137 B2
Poundsbridge 157 D8
Poverest 44 A4
Powder Mills 126 E2
Pratling Street 83 C3
Pratt's Bottom 58 D7
Priestwood 64 B5
Priestwood Green 64 C5
Primmer's Green 184 F5
Princes Park 68 B6
Printstile 142 A3
Puddledock 31 E2
Purfleet 16 A8
Putlands 145 F5
Pye Corner 136 A6

Q

Queen Street 146 D7

R

Rabbit's Cross 133 E3
Rainham Essex 4 F8
Rainham Kent 55 E8
Ramsden 44 C1
Ramslye 158 D1
Red Hill 97 F1
Red Street 35 B2
Ridley 63 B4
Ringlestone Harrietsham .103 F4
Ringlestone Maidstone . .99 E7
Riseden Durgates 184 B1
Riseden Kilndown 177 A5
Riverhead 91 E5
Riverview Park 36 E4

Rochester 53 B6
Rockrobin 184 D6
Rolvenden 191 F4
Rolvenden Layne 192 B1
Romden 153 C1
Romford 160 F7
Roseacre 101 A4
Rosherville 18 E1
Round Green 164 F4
Round Street 50 D5
Royal Tunbridge Wells .159 D3
Rusthall 158 C4
Ruxley 30 E1
Ryarsh 80 E1

S

St Ann's Green 148 F8
St John's
  Royal Tunbridge Wells .159 A5
St John's Sevenoaks . . .92 B5
St Leonard's Street . . .97 B6
St Margarets 33 D1
St Mary Cray 44 B4
St Mary Hoo 24 D6
St Mary's Island 40 C1
St Michaels 183 B4
St Paul's Cray 44 A7
Saint's Hill 157 A8
Sandhurst 196 C6
Sandhurst Cross 195 F4
Sandling 83 F1
Sandway 120 A3
Seal 93 A6
Sepham Heath 75 B6
Sevenoaks 92 D2
Sevenoaks Weald 108 B2
Sheerness 27 F3
Shepway 116 D8
Sherwood 159 E6
Shipbourne 110 C5
Shooters Hill 12 C6
Shoreham 75 F8
Shorne 37 E3
Shorne Ridgeway 37 E2
Shover's Green 185 C1
Sidcup 30 A3
Silver Street 87 F5
Silvertown 1 C4
Single Street 73 B4
Singlewell 36 D2
Sinkhurst Green 150 E2
Sissinghurst 180 B7
Slade Green 15 B6
Small Hythe 193 C1
Smarden 153 A1
Smarden Bell 152 D2
Snodland 82 B7
Snoll Hatch 129 E5
Sole Street 50 C4
Southborough Bromley . .42 F3
Southborough
  Royal Tunbridge Wells .143 B1
South Darenth 47 D8
Southdowns 47 D7
Southernden 152 C8
Southfleet 35 A3
South Green 87 A5
South Street Biggin Hill .89 A8
South Street Meopham . .63 F4
South Street Stockbury . .86 C7
Sparrow's Green 184 F5
Speed Gate 61 F8
Speldhurst 158 B7
Standen 168 B5
Standen Street 190 D1
Stansted 62 F1
Staplehurst 149 D4
Stede Quarter 168 E1
Stick Hill 139 A3
Stiff Street 87 E7
Stockbury 86 E8
Stockland Green 142 C1
Stocks Green 126 B4
Stoke 25 A3
Stone 16 F2
Stone Bridge 184 E6
Stone Cross
  Langton Green 157 A2
Stone Cross Wadhurst . .185 A3
Stonecrouch 186 F6
Stone Street 93 E2
Strood Rochester 52 F7
Strood Tenterden 192 B5
Styants Bottom 93 F5
Sundridge 28 C2
Sutton at Hone 33 A1
Sutton Valence 134 E6
Swanley 45 E5
Swanley Village 46 B7
Swanscombe 17 D2
Swanton 112 A8
Swift's Green 152 E6

T

Tatsfield 88 D7
Teasley Mead 156 C4
Temple Hill 16 A3
Tenterden 193 C8
Teston 114 A8
Thamesmead 3 A5
The Chart Limpsfield . .104 E5
The Chart Toys Hill . . .106 C5
The Crook 146 D1
The Down 176 A3
The Harbour 134 E5
The Moor 194 F8

The Quarries 116 C4
The Quarter Headcorn . .153 B5
The Quarter Staplehurst .149 E1
The Quarter Tenterden .193 A4
Thong 37 A2
Three Chimneys 167 B2
Three Legged Cross . . .186 D3
Thurnham 101 D8
Ticehurst 186 E2
Tilbury 19 B4
Timberden Bottom . . .59 D1
Titsey 88 B2
Tollgate 95 A8
Tonbridge 127 A2
Tovil 99 E1
Toy's Hill 106 C3
Trench Wood 127 B7
Trottiscliffe 80 A5
Troy Town 121 F5
Tudeley 144 B7
Tudeley Hale 128 C1
Turnden 179 B4
Turner's Green 184 F6
Twitton 75 E4
Twydall 55 B2
Tylden 168 E7

U

Ulcombe 135 F7
Underling Green 132 F2
Underriver 109 A5
Union Street 187 B3
Upper Bush 51 F2
Upper Fant 99 D3
Upper Halling 65 E5
Upper Harvel 64 C3
Upper Hayesden 142 C6
Upper Ruxley 31 A1
Upper Tolhurst 186 A2
Upper Upnor 39 F1

V

Vicarage Green 185 A5
Vigo Village 80 B8

W

Wadhurst 185 A4
Wainscott 39 D3
Walderslade 67 F1
Walderslade Bottom . .68 A2
Wallcrouch 185 F1
Walter's Green 156 E6
Wanden 153 B7
Wanshurst Green 149 A7
Ware Street 101 B5
Warmlake 117 D1
Wateringbury 113 D7
Waterman Quarter 151 D2
Watts's Cross 126 B7
Wayfield 68 A8
Weardale 106 B5
Weavering Street 100 F5
Weeds Wood 67 F3
Weller's Town 140 D5
Well Hill 59 B4
Welling 13 B4
Well Street 97 E6
Westcourt 36 E6
West Cross 191 D4
Westerham 89 C1
West Farleigh 114 D6
West Heath 13 D8
West Kingsdown 61 F2
West Malling 97 C7
West Peckham 112 A6
West Street 120 E8
West Thurrock 17 B8
West Tilbury 19 E4
Westwood 34 D1
Whetsted 129 E1
Whitehill 48 D7
White Oak 45 F7
White Post 156 D7
Wick Hill 167 F8
Widmore 42 E7
Wierton 133 F8
Wigmore 69 B4
Willington 100 E1
Wilmington 32 C4
Wilsley Green 179 D7
Wilsley Pound 179 E8
Winchet Hill 164 B6
Windmill Hill 36 A7
Wissenden 169 F7
Withyham 170 A3
Wittersham 199 D3
Wombwell Park 35 D6
Woodlands 77 C6
Wood's Green 184 F6
Woodside Green 120 F8
Woolwich 2 B3
Wormshill 103 F7
Worms Hill 164 B5
Worsenden Green 167 D2
Wouldham 66 D5
Wrotham 78 F2
Wrotham Heath 80 A1

Y

Yalding 113 F1
Yelsted 70 A1
Yewtree Green 147 B1
Yopps Green 94 E1

2

20/20 Ind Est ME16 . . . . . .99 C8

A

Aaron Hill Rd E6 . . . . .2 A8
Abbess Cl **12** E6 . . . . .1 E8
Abbeville Ho ME1 . . . . . . .53 C4
Abbey Brewery Ct ME1 .97 C8
Abbey Court Specl Sch
ME2 . . . . .52 E8
Abbey Cres DA17 . . . . .4 A2
Abbey Dr DA2 . . . . .31 E6
Abbey Gate Cotts ME14 . .83 F2
Abbey Gdns BR7 . . . . .43 A8
Abbey Gr SE2 . . . . .3 B2
Abbey Ho SE2 . . . . .3 D1
Abbey Life Ct E13 . . . . .1 B8
Abbey Lodge SE12 . . . . . .28 B4
Abbey Mount DA17 . . . . . . .3 F1
Abbey Pl DA1 . . . . .15 D2
Abbey Rd Bexley DA6,DA7 .13 E3
Erith DA17 . . . . .3 E3
Gillingham ME8 . . . . .55 A2
Gravesend DA12 . . . . .36 E7
Rochester ME2 . . . . .52 F8
Swanscombe DA9 . . . . . . .17 C2
Abbey Terr SE2 . . . . .3 C1
Abbey Wood Golden Jubilee
Cvn site SE2 . . . . .3 C1
Abbey Wood Rd
Kings Hill ME19 . . . . .97 A5
Woolwich SE2 . . . . .3 C2
Abbey Wood Sch SE2 . . . . .3 A3
Abbey Wood Sta SE2 . . . . .3 C2
Abbeyhill Rd DA15 . . . . . .30 C6
Abbots Cl BR5 . . . . .43 C1
Abbots Court Rd ME3 . . . .40 F4
Abbots Field
Gravesend DA12 . . . . .36 C2
Maidstone ME16 . . . . .99 B2
Abbotswood Cl **7** DA17 . .3 E3
Abbott Rd TN15 . . . . .94 F7
Abbott Way TN30 . . . . . . .193 C7
Abbott's Wlk DA7 . . . . . . .13 D7
Abbotts Cl Rochester ME1 .53 B3
Swanley BR8 . . . . .46 A5
Woolwich SE28 . . . . .3 C6
Aberdeen Ho **9** ME15 . .116 E7
Aberford Gdns SE18 . . . . .11 E6
Abergeldie Rd SE12 . . . . .11 B1
Abery St SE18 . . . . .2 E2
Abigail Cres ME5 . . . . .68 A1
Abingdon Mews ME19 . . . .97 C8
Abingdon Rd ME16 . . . . . .98 F2
Abingdon Way BR6 . . . . . .58 B6
Abinger Cl BR1 . . . . .42 E6
Abinger Dr ME5 . . . . .68 D2
Absalom Ct ME8 . . . . .55 C2
Acacia Cl BR5 . . . . .43 D4
Acacia Ct DA11 . . . . .36 A8
Acacia Rd Dartford DA1 . .32 D7
Stone DA9 . . . . .16 E1
Acacia Way DA15 . . . . . . .29 F7
Acacia Wlk BR8 . . . . .45 D7
Academy Dr ME7 . . . . . . .54 C7
Academy Pl SE18 . . . . . . .12 A6
Academy St SE18 . . . . . . .11 F7
Acer Ave TN2 . . . . .173 C8
Acer Rd TN16 . . . . .72 D3
Achilles Rd ME5 . . . . .68 C2
Acland Cl SE18 . . . . .12 D7
Acorn Cl Chislehurst BR7 .29 C3
Five Oak Green TN12 . . . .145 B7
Acorn Gr ME20 . . . . .98 D8
Acorn Ind Pk DA1 . . . . . . .15 A2
Acorn Pl ME15 . . . . .116 E6
Gillingham ME7 . . . . .54 F4
Acorn Trad Ctr RM20 . . . .17 E8
Acorn Way
Hurst Green TN19 . . . . . . .194 A3
Orpington BR6 . . . . .57 B6
Acorn Wharf Rd ME1 . . . .53 C6
Acorns The
Sevenoaks TN13 . . . . .92 A4
Smarden TN27 . . . . .152 F1
Acott Fields ME18 . . . . . .130 F8
Acre Cl ME1 . . . . .53 E1
Acre Gr ME2 . . . . .66 A4
Acres Rise TN5 . . . . .186 E1
Acton La TN30 . . . . .199 F4
Acton Pl ME18 . . . . .114 A1
Acworth Ho **1** SE18 . . . .12 B8
Acworth Pl DA1 . . . . .15 C1
Adam Cl ME17 . . . . .115 D3
Adams Cl TN30 . . . . .183 B1
Adams Sq DA6 . . . . .13 E4
Adamson Rd E16 . . . . .1 A7
Adbert Dr ME15 . . . . .115 B4
Adcot Wlk **7** BR6 . . . . . .57 F6
Adderley Gdns ME5 . . . . .29 A4
Addington La ME19 . . . . . .80 B4
Addison Cl Orpington BR5 .43 C3
West Malling ME19 . . . . . .81 F1
Addison Cotts TN30 . . . . .199 D3
Addison Dr SE12 . . . . .11 B2
Addison Rd BR2 . . . . .42 D4
Addlestead Rd TN12 . . . .129 E6
Adelaide Rd
Chislehurst BR7 . . . . .29 B3

Adelaide Rd continued
Gillingham ME7 . . . . .54 C4
Tilbury RM18 . . . . .18 F5
Adelaide The ME3 . . . . . . .38 C6
Aden Terr **1** ME14 . . . . .100 A7
Adisham Dr ME16 . . . . . . .99 B7
Admaston Rd SE18 . . . . . .12 C8
Admers Wood ME2 . . . . . .80 B8
Admiral Cl BR5 . . . . .44 D5
Admiral Ct ME7 . . . . .54 D6
Admiral Moore Dr ME20 .82 F1
Admiral Seymour Rd SE9 .11 F3
Admiral Way ME19 . . . . . .97 A1
Admiral's Wlk ME4 . . . . . .53 F7
Admirals Ct E6 . . . . .2 B7
Admirals Wlk
Chatham ME5 . . . . .68 B3
Goddard's Green TN17 . . .180 D2
Swanscombe DA9 . . . . . . .17 B2
Tenterden TN30 . . . . .183 C1
Admiralty Rd ME2 . . . . . . .39 F1
Admiralty Terr
1 Chatham ME7 . . . . . . .54 A7
Rochester ME2 . . . . .39 F1
Aerodrome Est ME14 . . . .85 E4
Afghan Rd ME4 . . . . .53 E4
Agate Cl E16 . . . . .1 D7
Agaton Rd SE9 . . . . .29 C6
Agnes Cl E6 . . . . .2 A6
Ailsa Mews ME1 . . . . .52 F2
Ainsdale Cl BR6 . . . . .43 D1
Aintree Cl DA12 . . . . .36 B5
Aintree Ho **1** ME15 . . . .116 F6
Aintree Rd ME5 . . . . .68 C3
Airedale Cl DA12 . . . . .33 C7
Airport Ind Est TN16 . . . .72 D4
Airport Rdbt E16 . . . . .1 D5
Aisher Rd SE28 . . . . .3 C6
Aisher Way TN13 . . . . .91 E6
Ajax Rd ME1 . . . . .67 C8
Akehurst La TN13 . . . . . . .92 C2
Alabama St SE18 . . . . .12 E7
Alamein Ave ME5 . . . . . . .67 F7
Alamein Gdns DA2 . . . . . .33 D8
Alamein Rd DA10 . . . . . . .17 D1
Alan Cl DA1 . . . . .15 C3
Alan Marre Ho SE7 . . . . . .11 D8
Alanbrooke DA12 . . . . . . .36 C8
Alanthus Cl SE12 . . . . . . .11 A1
Alban Cres DA4 . . . . .47 A1
Albany Cl Sidcup DA5 . . . .30 D8
Tonbridge TN9 . . . . .143 C1
Albany Hill TN2 . . . . .159 C5
Albany Mews BR1 . . . . . . .28 A2
Albany Park Sta DA14 . . .30 D6
Albany Rd Bexley DA17 . . .13 F8
Chatham ME4 . . . . .54 B2
Chislehurst BR7 . . . . .29 B3
Gillingham ME7 . . . . .54 D4
Rochester ME1 . . . . .53 C4
Sidcup DA5 . . . . .30 C8
Tilbury RM18 . . . . .19 A6
Albany St ME14 . . . . .100 B5
Gillingham ME7 . . . . .54 D4
Albany Terr Chatham ME4 .53 E4
Gillingham ME7 . . . . .54 D4
Albatross Ave ME2 . . . . . .52 C6
Albatross Cl E6 . . . . .1 F8
Albatross St SE18 . . . . . . .12 E7
Albemarle Rd ME5 . . . . . .68 C2
Albert Cotts TN1 . . . . . . .159 B4
Albert Ho SE28 . . . . .2 C3
Albert Manor ME4 . . . . . . .54 B5
Albert Murray Cl DA12 . . .36 C8
Albert Pl ME2 . . . . .53 B7
Albert Rd
Bromley,Bromley Common
BR2 . . . . .42 D4
Bromley,Mottingham SE9 .28 C5
Chatham ME4 . . . . .54 A3
Dartford DA2 . . . . .32 C5
Erith DA17 . . . . .3 F1
Gillingham ME7 . . . . .54 C4
Newham E16 . . . . .1 F5
Orpington BR5 . . . . .44 B3
Orpington,Green Street Green
BR6 . . . . .58 A5
Rochester ME1 . . . . .53 C3
Sidcup DA5 . . . . .31 B8
Swanscombe DA10 . . . . . .17 F1
3 Tonbridge TN9 . . . . . .127 B1
Albert Reed Gdns ME15 . .99 E2
Albert St Maidstone ME14 .99 F6
Royal Tunbridge Wells
TN1 . . . . .159 B4
Albert Wlk E16 . . . . .2 B4
Alberta Rd DA8 . . . . .14 C6
Albion Cotts TN12 . . . . . .148 D5
Albion Ct **2** SE18 . . . . . . .1 E2
Albion Ho E16 . . . . .2 B5
Albion Mews TN1 . . . . . . .159 C5
Albion Pl Chattenden ME2 .40 A3
Maidstone ME14 . . . . . . .100 B4
Newington ME9 . . . . .71 B6
Albion Rd Bexley DA6 . . . .14 A3
Chatham ME5 . . . . .68 B2
Gravesend DA12 . . . . .36 C4
Marden TN12 . . . . .148 D5
Royal Tunbridge Wells
TN1 . . . . .159 C5
Albion Terr DA12 . . . . .19 D1
Albion Way TN8 . . . . .122 C4
Albright Ind Est RM13 . . . .4 F8
Albury Ave DA7 . . . . .13 C5
Albury Cl ME5 . . . . .68 D2
Albyfield BR1 . . . . .42 F6
Alchins Cotts ME17 . . . . .115 E2
Alconbury DA6 . . . . .14 B2
Aldeburgh Pl SE10 . . . . . . .1 A2

Aldeburgh St SE10 . . . . . . .1 A1
Alder Cl TN4 . . . . .143 D1
Alder La TN17 . . . . .191 C1
Alder Lodge TN4 . . . . . . .158 E4
Alder Way BR8 . . . . .45 D7
Alderman Cl DA1 . . . . .31 E8
Aldermary Rd BR1 . . . . . .42 A8
Alderney Rd DA8 . . . . .15 A7
Alders Cotts TN12 . . . . . .145 A5
Alders Mdw TN9 . . . . . . .126 F2
Alders Rd TN11,TN12 . . . .144 E6
Alders The ME18 . . . . . . .112 D7
Aldersgrove Ave SE9 . . . .28 D5
Aldershot Rd ME5 . . . . . . .68 A7
Aldershot Gr ME15 . . . . . .97 C3
Aldington Cl ME5 . . . . . . .68 B5
Aldington La ME14 . . . . . .101 D8
Aldington Rd
Greenwich SE18 . . . . .1 D3
Maidstone ME14 . . . . . . .100 F4
Aldon Cl ME14 . . . . .100 C6
Aldon Ct ME14 . . . . .100 C6
Aldon La ME19 . . . . .96 C8
Aldwick Cl SE9 . . . . .29 D5
Aldwych Cl TN10 . . . . . . .127 D7
Alers Rd DA6 . . . . .13 D2
Alestan Beck Rd E16 . . . . .1 D7
Alex Hughes Cl ME5 . . . . .81 F6
Alexander Cotts ME2 . . . .38 C6
Alexander Ct
Greenwich SE3 . . . . .11 B5
1 Rochester ME2 . . . . .53 B8
2 Royal Tunbridge Wells
TN1 . . . . .159 A4
Alexander Gr ME18 . . . . . .97 A3
Alexander McLeod Prim Sch
SE2 . . . . .3 B1
Alexander Rd Bexley DA7 .13 D5
Chislehurst BR7 . . . . .29 B3
Swanscombe DA9 . . . . . . .17 C2
Alexandra Ave ME7 . . . . . .54 C4
Alexandra Cl BR8 . . . . . . .45 E7
Alexandra Glen ME7 . . . . .68 A1
Alexandra Hospl The
ME5 . . . . .84 A8
Alexandra Rd
Biggin Hill TN16 . . . . .88 B8
Chatham ME4 . . . . .54 B2
Erith DA8 . . . . .14 F8
Gravesend DA12 . . . . .36 E8
Tilbury RM18 . . . . .18 F5
Tonbridge TN9 . . . . .143 B8
Alexandra St
Maidstone ME14 . . . . .99 F6
Newham E16 . . . . .1 A8
Alexandra Wlk DA4 . . . . . .47 E7
Alfan La DA2 . . . . .31 D3
Alford Ho **6** SE18 . . . . . .12 B8
Alford Rd DA8 . . . . .4 C1
Alford Snell Lodge TN2 159 D2
Alfred Cl ME4 . . . . .54 B2
Alfred Ho Gravesend DA11 .36 B6
5 Northfleet DA11 . . . . .35 F7
Alfred Pl DA11 . . . . .35 F7
Alfred Rd Erith DA17 . . . . . .3 F1
Gravesend DA11 . . . . .36 B6
Hawley DA2 . . . . .32 F4
Alfred St RM17 . . . . .18 C8
Alfriston Cl DA1 . . . . .14 E1
Alfriston Gr ME19 . . . . . . .97 C3
Alice Thompson Cl SE12 .28 C6
Alicia Ho DA16 . . . . .13 B6
Alison Cl E6 . . . . .2 A7
Alkerden La DA9,DA10 . . .17 C1
Alkham Rd ME14 . . . . . . .100 C5
Alkham Twr **9** BR5 . . . . .44 C5
All Saints CE Prim Sch
ME15 . . . . .100 A3
All Saints Cl DA10 . . . . . . .17 F2
All Saints Rd
Allhallows ME3 . . . . .9 D2
Hawkhurst TN18 . . . . . . .189 A1
Royal Tunbridge Wells
TN4 . . . . .159 B6
All Saints Rise TN4 . . . . .159 A6
All Saints' CE Prim Sch
ME4 . . . . .54 A3
All Saints' Rd DA1 . . . . . . .35 F7
Allan Cl TN4 . . . . .158 C4
Allandale Pl BR6 . . . . .58 D7
Allandale Rd TN2 . . . . . . .159 D7
Allard Cl BR5 . . . . .44 C2
Allen Cl ME5 . . . . .68 C6
Allen Gardiner Ho TN2 . .159 E7
Allen St ME14 . . . . .100 B5
Allenby Rd
Biggin Hill TN16 . . . . .72 E2
Woolwich SE28 . . . . .2 C3
Allendale Cl DA2 . . . . .33 D7
Allens TN12 . . . . .148 D5
Allens La TN15,TN11 . . . .111 A7
Allenswood Rd SE9 . . . . . .11 F5
Allhallows Prim Sch ME3 .9 D2
Allhallows Rd
Lower Stoke ME3 . . . . .25 C5
Newham E6 . . . . .1 E7
Allhallows-on-Sea Est
ME3 . . . . .9 E4
Alliance Rd Newham E13 . .1 C8
Woolwich SE18 . . . . .13 A6
Alliance Way TN12 . . . . . .145 F6
Allington Cl DA12 . . . . . . .36 F7

Allington Dr
Rochester ME2 . . . . .52 E8
Tonbridge TN10 . . . . .128 A5
Allington Gdns ME18 . . . .113 E7
Allington Prim Sch ME16 .99 C7
Allington Rd
Gillingham ME8 . . . . .55 A3
Orpington BR6 . . . . .43 E1
Paddock Wood TN12 . . . .145 F7
Allington Way ME16 . . . . .99 B6
Allison Ave ME7 . . . . .54 E1
Allnutt Mill Cl **4** ME15 . .99 E2
Allotment La ME13 . . . . . .92 C5
Allsworth Cl ME9 . . . . .71 B6
Alma Pl Hadlow TN11 . . . .128 E3
Rochester ME2 . . . . .53 A7
Alma Rd Eccles ME20 . . . .82 F6
Orpington BR5 . . . . .58 D8
Sidcup DA14 . . . . .30 A5
Swanscombe DA10 . . . . . .17 F2
West Malling ME19 . . . . . .97 A8
Alma The DA12 . . . . .36 F4
Almery Cotts ME17 . . . . .134 B8
Almon Pl ME1 . . . . .53 D5
Almond Cl BR2 . . . . .43 A2
Almond Dr BR8 . . . . .45 D7
Almond Gr ME7 . . . . .69 A4
Almond Ho **9** ME5 . . . . .99 A3
Almond Rd DA2 . . . . .33 C8
Almond Way BR2 . . . . . . .43 A2
Almonds The ME14 . . . . .101 A4
Alms Row ME16 . . . . .90 B3
Almshouses
Crockenhill BR8 . . . . .45 D2
Penshurst TN11 . . . . .141 C4
Sevenoaks TN13 . . . . .92 C1
14 Tonbridge TN9 . . . .143 B8
Yalding ME18 . . . . .114 A1
Alnwick Ct **8** DA2 . . . . . .16 B1
Alnwick Rd Eltham SE12 . .28 B8
Newham E16 . . . . .1 C7
Alonso Ho **4** DA17 . . . . . .4 A1
Alpha Cl ME4 . . . . .41 D7
Alpine Bsns Ctr E6 . . . . . . .2 A8
Alpine Copse **2** BR1 . . . .43 A7
Alpine Way E6 . . . . .2 A8
Alsike Rd DA18 . . . . .3 E3
Altash Way SE9 . . . . .29 A6
Altbarn Ind Est ME5 . . . . .84 C8
Alton Ave ME19 . . . . .97 A3
Alton Cl DA5 . . . . .30 E7
Alton Cotts DA4 . . . . .60 E8
Alverstone Gdns SE9 . . . .29 C7
Alwold Cres SE12 . . . . . . .11 C1
Amanda Cl ME5 . . . . .67 F3
Amar Ct SE18 . . . . .2 F1
Amardeep Ct SE18 . . . . . . .2 F1
Ambassador Gdns E6 . . . . .1 F8
Amber Ct ME7 . . . . .54 D5
Amber La ME17 . . . . .117 A1
Amber Way ME17 . . . . . . .117 B1
Amberleaze Dr TN2 . . . .160 D6
Amberley Cl
2 Orpington BR6 . . . . . .57 F5
Tonbridge TN9 . . . . .143 A8
Amberley Ct
Royal Tunbridge Wells
TN4 . . . . .159 C8
Sidcup DA14 . . . . .30 C3
Amberley Rd ME8 . . . . . . .69 B8
Amblecote Cl SE12 . . . . . .28 B5
Amblecote Mdw SE12 . . .28 B5
Amblecote Rd SE12 . . . . .28 B5
Ambleside DA7 . . . . .14 A5
Ambley Gn ME8 . . . . .69 A8
Ambley Rd ME8 . . . . .69 B8
Ambley Wood Nature
Reserve★ ME7,ME8 . . . . .69 A8
Ambrook Rd DA17 . . . . .4 A3
Ambrose Cl Crayford DA1 .15 A3
6 Newham E6 . . . . .1 F8
Orpington BR6 . . . . .57 F7
Ambrose Hill ME5 . . . . . . .54 C2
Amels Hill ME9 . . . . .86 F8
Ames Ave ME14 . . . . .101 A4
Ames Rd DA10 . . . . .17 E1
Ames Way ME18 . . . . .97 B3
Amesbury Rd BR1 . . . . . . .42 D6
Amethyst Ave ME5 . . . . . .67 E6
Amherst Cl
Maidstone ME16 . . . . .99 D4
Orpington BR5 . . . . .44 A5
Amherst Dr BR5 . . . . .44 A5
Amherst Hill
Chatham ME7 . . . . .54 A6
Sevenoaks TN13 . . . . .91 F4
Amherst Prim Sch TN13 .91 E4
Amherst Rd
Rochester ME1 . . . . .53 D3
Royal Tunbridge Wells
TN4 . . . . .159 A5
Sevenoaks TN13 . . . . .92 B5
Amherst Redoubt ME4 . . .54 A7
Amhurst Bank Rd TN2,
TN11,TN12 . . . . .144 F4
Amhurst Wlk SE28 . . . . . . .3 A5
Amies Ho ME15 . . . . .115 F3
Ampleforth Cl BR6 . . . . . .58 C6
Ampleforth Rd SE2 . . . . . . .3 C4
Amsbury Rd ME15,ME17 .115 B2
Amshurst Villas ME15 . . .115 A4
Ancaster St SE18 . . . . . . .12 E7
Anchor & Hope La SE7 . . . .1 C2
Anchor Bay Ind Est DA8 .15 A8
Anchor Bvd DA2 . . . . .16 D3
Anchor Ct DA7 . . . . .13 C6
Anchor Ho Newham E16 . . .1 C7
Rochester ME1 . . . . .53 B4

Anchor La ME12 . . . . .27 F3
Anchor Rd ME1 . . . . .53 C1
Anchorage Cl ME3 . . . . . .25 C3
Anchorage Flats TN12 . .146 A6
Anchorage Point Ind Est
SE7 . . . . .1 C3
Ancona Rd SE18 . . . . .2 D1
Andace Pk BR1 . . . . .42 C8
Anderson Way DA17 . . . . . .4 B4
Andorra Ct BR1 . . . . .42 C8
Andover Ave E16 . . . . .1 D7
Andover Rd BR6 . . . . .43 E1
Andover Wlk **12** ME15 . .116 F6
Andrew Broughton Way
ME14 . . . . .100 B4
Andrew Cl DA1 . . . . .14 D2
Andrew Manor ME7 . . . . .54 C6
Andrew Rd TN4 . . . . .159 C8
Andrew Wells Ho **8** BR1 .28 B1
Andrewes Gdns E6 . . . . . . .1 E7
Andrews Cl Orpington BR5 44 D6
Royal Tunbridge Wells
TN2 . . . . .159 D5
Andrews Pl DA2 . . . . .31 E6
Andringham Lodge **7**
BR1 . . . . .42 B8
Andwell Cl SE2 . . . . .3 B4
Anerley Cl ME16 . . . . .99 D7
Angel La TN9 . . . . .127 B1
Angel Row TN18 . . . . . . .196 B5
Angel Terr TN18 . . . . . . .196 B6
Angel Wlk **4** TN9 . . . . .127 B1
Angelica Dr E6 . . . . .2 A8
Angerstein Bsns Pk SE10 .1 A2
Angle Rd RM20 . . . . .17 D8
Anglesea Ave SE18 . . . . . . .2 B2
Anglesea Pl **19** DA11 . . .19 B1
Anglesea Rd
Orpington BR5 . . . . .44 C3
Woolwich SE18 . . . . .2 B2
Anglesey Ave ME15 . . . . .116 A7
Anglesey Cl ME5 . . . . .68 B7
Angley Ct TN12 . . . . .163 A5
Angley Rd TN17 . . . . .179 C6
Angley Sch Sports Coll
TN17 . . . . .179 C5
Angley Wlk
Cranbrook TN17 . . . . .179 C6
Cranbrook TN17 . . . . .179 C6
Anglia Ctr The RM13 . . . . .4 B4
Anglian Ind Est IG11 . . . . .3 A8
Anglo Saxon Ho DA12 . . .36 F8
Ankerdine Cres SE18 . . . .12 B6
Ann St SE18 . . . . .2 D1
Ann Stroud Ct SE12 . . . . .11 A2
Annandale Rd DA15 . . . . .29 F8
Anne of Cleves Rd DA1 . .15 D1
Annesley Rd SE3 . . . . .11 B6
Annetts Hall TN15 . . . . . . .95 A8
Annex The BR8 . . . . .46 B6
Annie Rd ME6 . . . . .81 F6
Annvera Ho **2** ME7 . . . . .54 C7
Ansell Ave ME4 . . . . .54 A1
Ansia Cl ME18 . . . . .97 B3
Anson Ave ME18,ME19 . . .96 F3
Anson Cl ME5 . . . . .68 C6
Anson Pl SE28 . . . . .2 D4
Anstridge Rd SE9 . . . . . . .12 D1
Antelope Rd SE18 . . . . .1 F3
Anthony Cl TN13 . . . . .91 E7
Anthony Rd DA16 . . . . . . .13 A6
Anthony Roper Prim Sch The
DA4 . . . . .60 B4
Anthonys La BR8 . . . . .46 A8
Anthonys Way ME2 . . . . . .53 E8
Anvil Terr DA2 . . . . .31 E6
Aperfield Rd
Biggin Hill TN16 . . . . .72 F1
Erith DA8 . . . . .14 F8
Apiary Bsns Pk The
ME17 . . . . .118 B3
Apollo Ave BR1 . . . . .42 B8
Apollo Ho ME5 . . . . .68 A6
Apollo Way
St Mary's Island ME4 . . . .40 C2
3 Woolwich SE28 . . . . . .2 D3
Apple Cl ME6 . . . . .82 A6
Apple Ct TN12 . . . . .145 F6
Apple Orch BR8 . . . . .45 D5
Apple Tree Cl ME16 . . . . . .98 F2
Apple Tree La TN2 . . . . . .159 D8
Appleby Cl ME1 . . . . .67 C3
Appleby Rd E16 . . . . .1 A7
Applecross Cl ME1 . . . . . .53 E4
Appledore Ave DA7 . . . . . .14 D5
Appledore Cl BR2 . . . . . . .42 A4
Appledore Cres DA14 . . . .29 F5
Appledore Ct ME16 . . . . . .99 C7
Appledore Rd
Gillingham ME8 . . . . .55 A3
Tenterden TN30 . . . . .193 E7
Applegarth Dr DA1 . . . . . .32 F6
Applegarth Ho DA8 . . . . . .14 F5
Applegarth Rd SE28 . . . . . .3 C6
Appleshaw Cl DA11 . . . . . .36 A3
Appleton Cl DA7 . . . . .14 C5
Appleton Dr DA2 . . . . .32 B5
Appleton Rd SE9 . . . . .11 F4
Appletons TN11 . . . . .128 E8
Appletree Ct **5** ME8 . . . .69 F8
Appold St DA8 . . . . .14 F8
Approach Rd CR6,TN16 . .88 B5
Approach The BR6 . . . . . .57 F6
April Cl BR6 . . . . .57 F5
Apsledene DA12 . . . . .36 D2
Apsley St TN4 . . . . .158 D4
Aragon Cl BR2 . . . . .42 F1

Arborfield DA13 . . . . .50 A4
Arbroath Rd SE9 . . . . . . .11 E4
Arbrook Cl BR5 . . . . .44 A6
Arbrook Ct BR5 . . . . .44 A8
Arbury Ho BR1 . . . . .28 E1
Arbuthnot La DA5 . . . . . .13 E1
Arcade The **2** SE9 . . . . . .12 A1
Arcadia Rd DA13 . . . . . . .49 F8
Arcadian Ave DA5 . . . . . .13 E1
Arcadian Cl DA5 . . . . . . .13 E1
Arcadian Rd DA5 . . . . . . .13 E1
Archer Ho ME5 . . . . .67 F7
Archer Rd Chatham ME5 . .68 B6
  Orpington BR5 . . . . .44 A4
Archer Way BR8 . . . . .46 A7
Archery Cl ME3 . . . . .39 B7
Archery House Hospl
  DA2 . . . . .16 B1
Archery Rd SE9 . . . . .11 F2
Archibald Ho ME14 . . . . .100 A7
Archway Ct Dartford DA1 .32 D8
  4 Rochester ME2 . . . . .53 B8
Arden Bsns Pk ME2 . . . . .53 E7
Arden Cl SE28 . . . . .3 D7
Arden Gr BR6 . . . . .57 B6
Arden Jun Sch ME7 . . . . .54 D6
Arden St ME7 . . . . .54 C6
Ardenlee Dr ME14 . . . . . .100 B5
Arethusa Pl DA9 . . . . . . .17 B3
Arethusa Rd ME1 . . . . . . .67 C8
Argali Ho **3** DA18 . . . . . .3 F2
Argent St RM17 . . . . .18 B7
Argles Cl **4** DA9 . . . . . . .17 A2
Argyle Cl ME1 . . . . .67 E8
Argyle Rd Newham E16 . . .1 B7
  Royal Tunbridge Wells
  TN4 . . . . .143 A2
  Sevenoaks TN13 . . . . . . .92 B2
Argyll Rd SE18 . . . . .2 C3
Ariel Cl DA12 . . . . .36 F4
Ariel Ct **5** DA17 . . . . . . .4 A1
Arkwright Rd RM18 . . . . .19 A5
Arlington Cl DA15 . . . . . .29 E8
Arlott Cl ME14 . . . . .99 F6
Armada Ct ME4 . . . . .53 E1
Armada Way
  Chatham ME4 . . . . .53 F3
  Newham E6 . . . . .2 C7
Armitage Pl **5** TN18 . . . .188 F2
Armoury Dr DA12 . . . . . .36 C8
Armstrong Cl
  Badgers Mount TN14 . . . .75 B4
  Bromley BR1 . . . . .42 E6
  Newham E6 . . . . .1 F7
Armstrong Rd
  Maidstone ME15 . . . . . .100 A1
  Woolwich SE18 . . . . .2 C1
Armytage Cl ME3 . . . . . .40 E4
Arne Cl TN10 . . . . .127 E6
Arne Gr BR6 . . . . .57 F7
Arnhem Dr ME5 . . . . .67 F7
Arnold Ave DA13 . . . . . . .64 B8
Arnold Pl ME18 . . . . .19 C6
Arnold Rd DA12 . . . . .36 D6
Arnolde Cl ME2 . . . . .53 E7
Arnolds La DA4 . . . . .33 A2
Arnott Cl SE28 . . . . .3 C5
Arnsberg Way DA6,DA7 . . .14 A3
Arnside Rd DA7 . . . . .14 A6
Arran Cl DA8 . . . . .14 D8
Arran Gn ME2 . . . . .52 C6
Arran Rd ME15 . . . . .116 A6
Arrandene Ho **3** BR5 . . . .44 B7
  Erith SE2 . . . . .13 D8
Arras Ho Bexley SE2 . . . .13 D8
  Erith SE2 . . . . .3 D1
Arsenal Rd SE9 . . . . .11 F4
Arsenal Way SE18 . . . . . . .2 C3
Artemis Cl DA12 . . . . . . .36 E8
Arthur Ct **11** RM1 . . . . . .18 C8
Arthur Gr SE18 . . . . .2 C2
Arthur Rd Biggin Hill TN16 .72 C5
  Gillingham ME8 . . . . . . .69 E7
  Rochester ME1 . . . . .53 D3
Arthur Ruxley Est DA14 . .30 D2
Arthur St Erith DA8 . . . . .14 F7
  Gravesend DA11 . . . . . . .36 A8
  Grays RM17 . . . . .18 C8
Arthur St W DA11 . . . . . .36 A8
Arthur Toft Ho **6** RM1 . .18 B8
Artillery Ho SE18 . . . . . . .2 A1
Artillery Pl SE18 . . . . .2 A2
Artillery Row DA12 . . . . .36 C8
Artington Cl BR6 . . . . . . .57 C6
Artisan Cl E6 . . . . .2 B6
Arun Ct BR5 . . . . .44 C1
Arundel DA14 . . . . .30 A3
Arundel Cl Bexley DA5 . . .13 F1
  Chatham ME5 . . . . .68 D1
  Tonbridge TN9 . . . . . . .143 D1
Arundel Ct **2** DA6 . . . . .13 E3
Arundel Dr BR6 . . . . .58 B5
Arundel Ho TN1 . . . . . . .159 B5
Arundel Rd Dartford DA1 .15 C3
  Royal Tunbridge Wells
  TN1 . . . . .159 B2
Arundel St ME14 . . . . . . .99 F6
Ascot Cl
  Borough Green TN15 . . . .95 B4
  Chatham ME5 . . . . .68 C2
Ascot Ct Bromley BR1 . . . .42 E7
  Sidcup DA5 . . . . .30 F8
Ascot Ho ME15 . . . . .116 F6
  Orpington BR5 . . . . .43 F5
Ash Cl Aylesford ME20 . . . .82 E1
  Chatham ME5 . . . . .54 C1
  Edenbridge TN8 . . . . . . .122 B1
  Gillingham ME8 . . . . . . .55 B3

Ash Cl continued
  Orpington BR5 . . . . .43 D4
  Royal Tunbridge Wells
  TN2 . . . . .173 D7
  Sidcup DA14 . . . . .30 B5
  Swanley BR8 . . . . .45 D7
Ash Cres Biddenden TN27 182 D7
  Higham ME3 . . . . .38 C3
Ash Croft Ct DA3 . . . . . . .62 F7
Ash Ct SE12 . . . . .28 A8
Ash Gr ME16 . . . . .99 C6
Ash Ho BR5 . . . . .44 C5
Ash Keys DA13 . . . . .80 B8
Ash La TN15 . . . . .62 D2
Ash Platt Rd TN15 . . . . . .92 E6
Ash Rd Dartford DA1 . . . . .32 D7
  Gravesend DA12 . . . . . . .36 C4
  Hartley DA3 . . . . .48 F3
  Hawley DA2 . . . . .27 F4
  New Ash Green DA3,TN15 .62 E7
  Orpington BR6 . . . . .57 F3
  Rochester ME2 . . . . .52 F6
  Westerham TN16 . . . . . . .89 E2
Ash Row BR2 . . . . .43 A3
Ash Tree Cl TN15 . . . . . . .61 B3
Ash Tree Cotts TN15 . . . .164 B7
Ash Tree Dr TN15 . . . . . . .61 B3
Ash Tree La ME5 . . . . . . .54 D1
Ashbank Cotts ME17 . . . .118 B3
Ashbee Cl ME6 . . . . .82 A7
Ashbourne Ave DA7 . . . . .13 E7
Ashbourne Ct TN4 . . . . . .158 D4
Ashbourne Rise BR6 . . . . .57 E6
Ashburn Cl BR1 . . . . .28 A1
Ashburn Mews ME7 . . . . .54 E3
Ashburnham Cl TN13 . . . .108 C8
Ashburnham Rd Erith DA17 4 C2
  Maidstone ME14 . . . . . .100 B8
  Tonbridge TN10 . . . . . . .127 B3
Ashburton Rd E16 . . . . . . .1 A7
Ashby Cl ME2 . . . . .66 A4
Ashby's Cl TN8 . . . . .138 D8
Ashbys Yd TN9 . . . . .127 C5
Ashcombe Dr TN8 . . . . . .122 B4
Ashcroft Ave DA15 . . . . . .13 A1
Ashcroft Cres DA15 . . . . .13 A1
Ashcroft Ct Dartford DA1 .33 A8
  5 Eltham SE9 . . . . . . .12 A1
Ashcroft Rd
  Paddock Wood TN12 . . . .146 A5
  Rochester ME2 . . . . .39 B2
Ashdale Cl SE12 . . . . .28 B7
Ashdown Cl Coldblow DA5 .31 C8
  Maidstone ME16 . . . . . . .99 D3
  Royal Tunbridge Wells
  TN4 . . . . .158 F4
Ashen E6 . . . . .2 A7
Ashen Dr DA1 . . . . .15 A1
Ashen Grove Mobile Home
  Pk TN15 . . . . .61 B1
Ashen Grove Rd TN15 . . . .61 B1
Ashenden TN27 . . . . .152 F2
Ashenden Cl ME2 . . . . . . .39 C2
Ashenden Wlk TN2 . . . . . .159 E8
Asher Reeds TN3 . . . . . . .158 A4
Ashes La Plaxtol TN11 . . .110 F1
  Tonbridge TN11 . . . . . . .128 B8
Ashfield La BR7 . . . . .29 C1
Ashfield Pl BR7 . . . . .29 D1
Ashford Dr ME17 . . . . . . .118 D3
Ashford Rd
  Harrietsham ME17 . . . . .119 C6
  Maidstone ME14 . . . . . .101 D3
  Maidstone,Grove Green
  ME14 . . . . .100 D4
  Tenterden TN30 . . . . . . .193 B6
  Tenterden,Durrant Green
  TN26,TN30 . . . . .183 A6
Ashgrove SE12 . . . . .28 A7
Ashgrove Rd TN13 . . . . . .108 B7
Ashlar Pl **4** SE18 . . . . . . .2 B2
Ashleigh Cl DA13 . . . . . . .63 F1
Ashleigh Commercial Est
  SE18 . . . . .1 D3
Ashleigh Gdns TN27 . . . .151 D6
Ashley Ct TN13 . . . . .92 B3
Ashley Gdns
  Orpington BR6 . . . . .57 E5
  Rusthall TN4 . . . . .158 C5
Ashley Ho BR5 . . . . .44 A7
Ashley Park Cl TN4 . . . . .158 C5
Ashley Pk TN4 . . . . .158 C5
Ashley Rd Gillingham ME8 .55 C2
  Sevenoaks TN13 . . . . . . .92 B3
  Tonbridge TN11 . . . . . . .126 E5
Ashly Ct **22** DA14 . . . . . .30 A5
Ashmead Cl ME5 . . . . . . .68 C3
Ashmead Gate BR1 . . . . .42 C8
Ashmill Bsns Pk ME17 . . .120 F6
Ashmore Gdns DA11 . . . . .35 D5
Ashmore Gr DA16 . . . . . .12 E4
Ashmore La BR2 . . . . . . .72 C8
Ashridge Cres SE18 . . . . .12 C1
Ashridge Ho DA14 . . . . . .29 F4
Ashton Way ME19 . . . . . .97 C6
Ashtree Cl BR6 . . . . .57 B6
Ashurst Cl DA1 . . . . .14 F4
Ashurst Hill TN3 . . . . . . .156 D2
Ashurst Rd
  Maidstone ME14 . . . . . .100 C5
  Stone Cross TN3 . . . . . . .157 B2
Ashurst Sta TN3 . . . . . . .156 D2
Ashwater Rd SE12 . . . . . .28 A7
Ashwell Cl **9** E6 . . . . . . .1 E7
Ashwood Cl ME3 . . . . . . .39 C7
Ashwood Pl DA2 . . . . . . .34 B5
Askern Cl DA6 . . . . .13 D3

Askews Farm La RM17,
  RM20 . . . . .17 E8
Askham Lodge **10** SE12 . .28 A8
Aspdin Rd DA11 . . . . .35 E5
Aspen Cl Orpington BR6 . .58 A5
  Swanley BR8 . . . . .45 D8
Aspen Copse BR1 . . . . . . .42 F7
Aspen Ct DA1 . . . . .16 A2
Aspen Gn DA18 . . . . .3 F3
Aspen Ho **2** DA15 . . . . . .30 A5
Aspen Way
  2 Chatham ME5 . . . . . .67 E4
  Royal Tunbridge Wells
  TN4 . . . . .143 C1
Aspian Dr ME17 . . . . . . .115 D3
Asquith Rd ME8 . . . . .69 C6
Association Wlk ME1 . . . . .67 C7
Aster Rd ME3 . . . . .40 E3
Astley ME17 . . . . .17 F8
Astley St ME14 . . . . .100 A4
Aston Cl Chatham ME5 . . .68 A2
  Sidcup DA14 . . . . .30 A5
Astor Ct E16 . . . . .1 C7
Astor of Hever Com Sch The
  ME16 . . . . .99 C3
Astor Rd TN15 . . . . .61 E4
Astra Dr DA12 . . . . .36 F3
Atcost Rd IG11 . . . . .3 A8
Athelstan Gn ME17 . . . . .102 C2
Athelstan Rd ME4 . . . . . .53 F2
Athelstan Way BR5 . . . . . .44 A8
Athill Ct TN13 . . . . .92 C5
Athol Rd BR8 . . . . .4 C1
Atkinson Cl BR5 . . . . .58 A5
Atkinson Rd E16 . . . . .1 C8
Atlanta Ct ME4 . . . . .53 D3
Atlantic Cl DA10 . . . . . . .17 E2
Atlas Gdns SE7 . . . . .1 C2
Atlas Rd DA1 . . . . .15 F4
Atterbury Rd TN16 . . . . . .89 D1
Attlee Dr DA1 . . . . .16 A2
Attlee Rd SE28 . . . . .3 B6
Attwaters La TN18 . . . . . .189 C1
Atwater Ct ME17 . . . . . . .120 D5
Auckland Cl ME20 . . . . . .82 A3
Auckland Rd ME18 . . . . . .19 A5
Auckland Ho **10** ME15 . . .116 C6
Auckland Rd TN1 . . . . . . .159 C5
Auden Rd ME20 . . . . .82 A3
Audley Ave
  Gillingham ME7 . . . . . . .54 E1
  Tonbridge TN9 . . . . . . .126 F2
Audley Cl ME8 . . . . .69 B5
Audley Dr E16 . . . . .1 B5
Audley Rise TN9 . . . . . . .126 F1
Audley Wlk BR5 . . . . .44 C3
Audre Lorde Ho SE9 . . . . .11 F3
Audrey Sturley Ct TN4 . . .158 D4
Auger Cl ME9 . . . . .70 E5
Augusta Cl **1** ME7 . . . . . .54 C7
Augusta Rd E13 . . . . .1 A8
Augustine Ho TN10 . . . . .127 C3
Augustine Rd
  Gravesend DA12 . . . . . . .36 C8
  Orpington BR6 . . . . .44 D6
Aultmore Ct TN2 . . . . . . .159 D3
Austell Manor **5** ME7 . . .54 C6
Austen Cl
  Swanscombe DA9 . . . . . .17 C1
  Tilbury RM18 . . . . .19 C5
  Woolwich SE28 . . . . .3 B5
Austen Gdns DA1 . . . . . . .15 F3
Austen Rd DA8 . . . . .14 B7
Austen Way ME20 . . . . . .81 F4
Austens Orch **14** TN30 . .193 A7
Austin Ave BR2 . . . . .42 E4
Austin Cl ME5 . . . . .54 E2
Austin Ct **4** TN16 . . . . . .89 C1
Austin Rd Northfleet DA11 .35 F7
  Orpington BR5 . . . . .44 A4
Austral Cl DA15 . . . . .29 F5
Autumn Glade ME5 . . . . .84 D8
Avalon Cl BR6 . . . . .58 D7
Avalon Rd BR5,BR6 . . . . .58 C8
Avard Gdns BR6 . . . . .57 C6
Avards Cl TN18 . . . . .194 E8
Avebury Ave TN9 . . . . . . .127 B1
Avebury Rd BR6 . . . . .57 D7
Aveley Cl DA8 . . . . .14 F8
Aveling Cl ME3 . . . . .40 D6
Aveling Ct **2** ME2 . . . . . .53 B7
Avenons Rd **3** E16 . . . . . .1 A8
Avenue Le Puy TN9 . . . . .127 C1
Avenue Rd Bexley DA7,DA6 13 E4
  Erith DA8 . . . . .14 D7
  Sevenoaks TN13 . . . . . . .92 C3
  Tatsfield TN16 . . . . .88 E7
Avenue The
  Aylesford ME20 . . . . .82 E1
  Biggin Hill TN16 . . . . . . .88 F5
  Borough Green TN15 . . . .95 A8
  Bromley BR1 . . . . .42 D6
  Gravesend DA11 . . . . . . .36 A8
  Hill Park TN16 . . . . .89 A4
  Orpington BR6 . . . . .58 B5
  Orpington,Keston Mark BR2 56 D7
  Orpington,St Paul's Cray
  BR5 . . . . .30 B1
  Sidcup DA14 . . . . .30 D8
  St Mary's Island ME4 . . . .40 A4
  Swanscombe DA9 . . . . . .17 B2
  Tonbridge TN9 . . . . . . .127 B2
Averenches Rd ME14 . . . .100 F5
Avery Cl Allhallows-on-S ME3 9 E4
  Maidstone ME15 . . . . . . .99 F1
Avery Ct ME3 . . . . .9 E3
Avery Hill Rd SE9 . . . . . . .29 D7
Avery La ME15,ME17 . . . .117 D6
Avery Way Allhallows ME3 . .9 D2
  Dartford DA1 . . . . .32 F6

Aviemore Gdns ME14 . . . .100 F4
Avington Cl ME15 . . . . . . .99 F1
Avocet Mews SE28 . . . . . .7 D7
Avocet Wlk ME5 . . . . .68 D2
Avon Cl Gravesend DA12 . .36 D6
  Tonbridge TN10 . . . . . . .127 C5
Avon Ct DA14 . . . . .30 B5
Avon St TN1 . . . . .159 C5
Avondale Ct ME14 . . . . . .100 E5
Avondale Pl ME3 . . . . . . .25 C4
Avondale Rd Bexley DA16 .13 C5
  Bromley,Mottingham SE9 .28 E6
  Bromley,Plaistow BR1 . . . .28 A2
  Gillingham ME7 . . . . . . .54 D5
Avonmouth Rd DA1 . . . . .15 D2
Avonstowe Cl BR6 . . . . . .57 C7
Awliscombe Rd DA16 . . . .12 F5
Axford Ct ME8 . . . . .70 A8
Axminster Cres DA16 . . . .13 C6
Axtaine Rd BR5 . . . . .44 D2
Axtane DA13 . . . . .34 F1
Axtane Cl DA4 . . . . .47 C8
Axton Chase Sch DA3 . . . .48 F6
Aycliffe Cl BR1 . . . . .42 F5
Ayelands DA3 . . . . .62 E8
Ayelands La DA3 . . . . . . .62 E8
Ayers Cotts BR8 . . . . .32 E2
Aylesbury Rd BR2 . . . . . .42 A6
Aylesford Cres ME8 . . . . .55 B4
Aylesford Prim Sch
  ME20 . . . . .82 D1
Aylesford Sch ME20 . . . . .82 D1
Aylesford Sta ME20 . . . . .82 D2
Aylesham Rd BR6 . . . . . . .43 F2
Ayleswade Rd BR7 . . . . .167 E2
Aynscombe Angle BR6 . . .44 A2
Azalea Dr BR8 . . . . .45 E5

B

Babb's La TN17 . . . . .190 A6
Babbacombe Rd BR1 . . . . .28 E1
Babington House Sch
  BR7 . . . . .28 C7
Babylon La ME17,TN12 . . .134 B1
Back La
  Godden Green TN15 . . . . .93 A2
  Goudhurst TN17 . . . . . . .177 E8
  Horsmonden TN12 . . . . .163 A6
  Ightham TN15 . . . . .94 C2
  Maidstone ME17 . . . . . . .116 E1
  Sevenoaks TN13,TN14 . . .91 C1
  Shipbourne TN11 . . . . . .110 D4
  Sidcup DA5 . . . . .31 A8
Back Rd Sandhurst TN18 . .196 B5
  Sidcup DA14 . . . . .30 A4
Back St ME17 . . . . .117 E6
Backfields ME1 . . . . .53 B4
Baden Powell Ho **11** DA17 .4 A3
Baden Powell Rd TN13 . . .76 F1
Baden Rd ME7 . . . . .54 D7
Bader Cres ME5 . . . . .68 A7
Bader Wlk DA11 . . . . .35 F5
Badger Rd ME5 . . . . .68 C1
Badgers Copse BR6 . . . . . .57 F8
Badgers Croft SE9 . . . . . .29 A5
Badgers Holt TN2 . . . . . .159 E5
Badgers Rd TN14 . . . . . . .59 B1
Badgers Rise TN14 . . . . . .59 A1
Badlow Cl DA8 . . . . .14 E7
Badminton Mews E16 . . . . .1 A5
Badsell Park Farm
  TN12 . . . . .145 C3
Badsell Rd TN12 . . . . . . .145 C5
Baffin Cl ME4 . . . . .53 F2
Bagshaw Ho **6** BR1 . . . . .42 A8
Bailey Dr ME7 . . . . .55 A1
Baird Ho **13** DA17 . . . . . .4 A3
Bakenham Ho **11** ME1 . . .53 C1
Baker Beall Ct DA7 . . . . . .14 B4
Baker Hill Cl DA11 . . . . . .35 F4
Baker La Headcorn TN27 . .151 F7
  Sutton Valence ME17 . . . .134 F7
Baker Rd SE18 . . . . .11 E7
Baker St Burham ME1 . . . .66 F1
  Rochester ME1 . . . . .53 C3
Baker's Wlk ME1 . . . . . . .53 C6
Bakers Ave TN15 . . . . . . .61 E3
Bakers Cross TN17 . . . . . .179 E4
Bakers Mews **9** BR6 . . . .57 F4
Bakery Cl TN17 . . . . .166 E2
Bakery Cotts ME14 . . . . . .63 B3
Balaclava La TN5 . . . . . . .185 A6
Balcaskie Rd SE9 . . . . . . .11 F2
Balchen Rd SE3 . . . . .11 D5
Balcombe Cl DA6 . . . . . . .13 D3
Balcombe Cotts TN17 . . . .177 E8
Balcombes Hill TN17 . . . .177 E8
Balder Rise SE12 . . . . . . .28 B6
Baldock Rd TN5 . . . . .184 E4
Baldwyn's Pk DA5 . . . . . .31 D6
Baldwyns Rd DA5 . . . . . . .31 D6
Baldwyns Mans DA2 . . . . .31 D6
Balfour Inf Sch ME1 . . . . .53 E1
Balfour Jun Sch ME4 . . . .53 E2
Balfour Rd Bromley BR2 . .42 D4
  Chatham ME4 . . . . .53 E2
Balgowan St SE18 . . . . . . .2 F2
Ball's Gn TN7 . . . . .170 B5
Ballamore Rd BR1 . . . . . .28 A5
Ballard Bsns Pk ME2 . . . .52 F5
Ballard Ct TN12 . . . . . . .148 C6
Ballard Ct **20** DA14 . . . . .30 A5
Ballard Ind Est ME5 . . . . .84 C8
Ballard Way TN12 . . . . . .146 B7
Ballards La RH8 . . . . .104 C6
Ballens Rd ME5 . . . . .68 C3

Arb – Bar 203

Balliol Rd DA16 . . . . .13 B5
Balls Cotts ME3 . . . . .39 F4
Balmer Cl ME8 . . . . .69 D7
Balmoral Ct SE12 . . . . . . .28 A4
Balmoral Gdns DA5 . . . . .30 F8
Balmoral Ho **10** ME15 . . .116 F5
Balmoral Rd
  Gillingham ME7 . . . . . . .54 D5
  Sutton at H DA4 . . . . . . .33 B1
Balmoral Trad Est E6 . . . . .2 F8
Baltic Ho TN1 . . . . .159 B5
Baltic Rd TN9 . . . . .143 F2
Baltic Wharf **1** DA11 . . . .19 A1
Baltimore Pl DA16 . . . . . .12 F5
Banbury Villas DA13 . . . . .34 F1
Banchory Rd SE3 . . . . . . .11 B7
Banckside DA3 . . . . .48 C5
Bancroft Gdns BR6 . . . . . .43 F1
Bancroft La ME18 . . . . . . .97 C2
Bancroft Rd TN15 . . . . . . .78 F3
Bangor Rd ME2 . . . . .52 D6
Banister Ho RM20 . . . . . .17 D8
Bank Cotts ME17 . . . . . . .102 E3
Bank Ho TN15 . . . . .79 A3
Bank Hos DA2 . . . . .33 A3
Bank La TN11,TN15 . . . . .109 C3
Bank St Chatham ME4 . . . .54 B3
  Cranbrook TN17 . . . . . . .179 C5
  Gravesend DA12 . . . . . . .19 A3
  Maidstone ME14 . . . . . .100 A4
  Sevenoaks TN13 . . . . . . .92 C3
  Tonbridge TN9 . . . . . . .127 C2
Bank View **5** ME15 . . . . .99 E2
Bankfield Way TN17 . . . . .177 E7
Bankfields TN27 . . . . . . .151 C5
Banks La DA6 . . . . .13 F3
Banks Rd ME2 . . . . .53 C8
Bankside Chatham ME5 . . .68 B8
  Durgates TN5 . . . . .184 E5
  Northfleet DA11 . . . . . . .18 C1
  Sevenoaks TN13 . . . . . . .91 E6
Bankside Cl
  Biggin Hill TN16 . . . . . . .72 C1
  Joyden's Wood DA5 . . . . .31 D4
Banky Mdw ME16 . . . . . . .98 F3
Banner Farm Rd TN2 . . . .159 B2
Banning St ME2 . . . . .53 B8
Bannister Gdns BR5 . . . . .44 C6
Bannister Rd ME14 . . . . . .100 A1
Bannockburn Prim Sch
  SE18 . . . . .2 F2
Bannockburn Rd SE18 . . . .2 F2
Banstead Ct **3** BR1 . . . . .42 E6
Banwell Rd DA5 . . . . .13 D1
Bapchild Pl **8** BR5 . . . . . .44 C5
Barbados Terr **2** ME14 . .100 A7
Barberry Ave ME5 . . . . . .67 E5
Barcham Ct ME15 . . . . . .115 F5
Barchester Way TN10 . . . .127 F6
Barclay Ave TN10 . . . . . .128 A5
Barclay Field TN15 . . . . . .76 F3
Barcombe Cl BR5 . . . . . . .44 A6
Bardell Terr ME1 . . . . . . .53 D5
Barden Ct ME14 . . . . . . .100 B5
Barden Park Rd TN9 . . . . .127 A1
Barden Rd Penshurst TN3 .141 F4
  Speldhurst TN3 . . . . . . .158 A8
  Tonbridge TN9 . . . . . . .127 B1
Barden St SE18 . . . . .12 E7
Bardsley Cl TN12 . . . . . . .130 A7
Barfield DA4 . . . . .47 B8
Barfield Rd BR1,BR7 . . . . .43 A6
Barfleur Manor **3** ME7 . .54 C6
Barfreston Cl ME15 . . . . . .99 F2
Bargate SE18 . . . . .2 F1
Bargehouse Rd E16 . . . . . .2 B4
Bargrove Rd ME14 . . . . . .100 C5
Barham Cl Chislehurst BR7 29 B3
  Gravesend DA12 . . . . . . .36 F7
  Maidstone ME15 . . . . . .116 A5
  Orpington BR2 . . . . .42 E1
Barham Ct BR2 . . . . .42 E1
Barham Mews ME18 . . . .114 E2
Barham Rd
  Chislehurst BR7 . . . . . . .29 B3
  Dartford DA1 . . . . .26 B7
Barham's Mill Rd TN27 . .137 B3
Baring Cl SE12 . . . . .28 A6
Baring Prim Sch SE12 . . . .28 A6
Baring Rd SE12 . . . . .28 A6
Bark Hart Rd BR6 . . . . . . .44 B1
Barker Rd ME16 . . . . .99 F3
Barkis Cl ME1 . . . . .67 D7
Barley Fields ME14 . . . . .100 D4
Barleycorn ME14 . . . . . . .81 E1
Barleycorn Dr ME8 . . . . . .69 E6
Barleymow Cl ME5 . . . . . .68 C7
Barling Cl ME5 . . . . .67 D1
Barlow Cl ME8 . . . . .69 E5
Barlow Dr SE18 . . . . .11 E6
Barlow Way RM13 . . . . . . .4 E8
Barlow Way S RM13 . . . . . .4 E8
Barming Prim Sch ME16 . .98 F2
Barming Rd ME18 . . . . . . .97 F2
Barming Sta ME16 . . . . . .98 F6
Barn End Ctr DA2 . . . . . .32 C5
Barn End Dr DA2 . . . . . . .32 C5
Barn End La DA2 . . . . . . .32 C4
Barn Hill ME15 . . . . .114 E2
Barn Mdw
  Staplehurst TN12 . . . . . .149 E4
  Upper Halling ME2 . . . . .65 E4
Barnaby Terr ME1 . . . . . . .53 D2
Barnard Cl
  Chislehurst BR7 . . . . . . .43 D8

Barnard Cl continued
  Woolwich SE18 . . . . .2 A3
Barncroft Ct Chatham ME4 . .54 A2
  21 Dartford DA2 . . . . .16 B1
Barncroft Cl ME14 . . . . . .100 F4
Barncroft Dr ME7 . . . . .68 F4
Barndale Ct DA12 . . . . . . .37 E3
Barned Ct ME16 . . . . .98 F2
Barnehurst Ave DA7,DA8 .14 C6
Barnehurst Cl DA8 . . . . . . .14 C6
Barnehurst Inf Sch DA8 . .14 C6
Barnehurst Jun Sch DA8 .14 C6
Barnehurst Rd DA7 . . . . . .14 C5
Barnehurst Sta DA7 . . . . .14 C5
Barnes Cray Prim Sch
  DA1 . . . . .15 A3
Barnes Cray Rd DA1 . . . . .15 A3
Barnes Ct E16 . . . . .1 C8
Barnes La ME17 . . . . .132 D8
Barnes Wlk TN12 . . . . . . .148 D6
Barnesdale Cres BR5 . . . . .44 A4
Barnet Dr BR2 . . . . .56 E8
Barnet Wood Rd BR2 . . . .56 C8
Barnett Cl DA8 . . . . .14 F5
Barnetts Cl TN4 . . . . .143 C1
Barnetts Rd TN11 . . . . . .126 A2
Barnetts Way TN4 . . . . . .159 C8
Barney Cl SE7 . . . . .1 C1
Barnfield Chatham ME5 . . .68 A8
  Gravesend DA11 . . . . .36 A6
  Royal Tunbridge Wells
   TN2 . . . . .172 F7
  Tenterden TN30 . . . . .183 C2
Barnfield Cl
  Crockenhill BR8 . . . . .45 C2
  New Barn DA3 . . . . .49 D6
  Stone DA9 . . . . .16 F1
Barnfield Cres TN15 . . . . .76 E2
Barnfield Gdns SE18 . . . . .12 B8
Barnfield Rd Bexley DA17 .13 F8
  Orpington BR5 . . . . .44 D6
  Sevenoaks TN13 . . . . .91 E4
  Tatsfield TN16 . . . . .88 C6
  Woolwich SE18 . . . . .12 B8
Barnfield Way RH8 . . . . .104 A2
Barnham Dr SE28 . . . . .2 F5
Barnhill Ave BR2 . . . . .42 A4
Barnock Cl DA1 . . . . .31 E8
Barnsole Inf Sch ME7 . . . .54 C4
Barnsole Jun Sch ME7 . . .54 C4
Barnsole Rd ME7 . . . . .54 E3
Barnwell Pl ME7 . . . . .54 C5
Barnwell Rd DA1 . . . . .15 F4
Barnwood Cl ME1 . . . . .67 B8
Baron Cl Gillingham ME7 . .54 E7
  Maidstone ME14 . . . . .100 F5
Barons Ct TN4 . . . . .159 A5
Barr Rd DA12 . . . . .36 F6
Barrack Cnr TN13 . . . . .92 C4
Barrack Rd ME4 . . . . .54 B4
Barrack Row
  Benenden TN17 . . . . .190 D6
  17 Gravesend DA11 . . . . .19 B1
Barrel Arch Cl TN12 . . . . .148 C6
Barretts Green Cotts **5**
  TN18 . . . . .189 A2
Barretts Rd
  Hawkhurst TN18 . . . . . . .189 A2
  Sevenoaks TN13 . . . . .91 E7
Barrie Dr **7** ME20 . . . . . . .81 F4
Barrier Point Rd E16 . . . . . .1 C5
Barrier Rd ME4 . . . . .53 F5
Barrington Cl ME5 . . . . . . .67 F5
Barrington Prim Sch
  DA7 . . . . .13 D5
Barrington Rd DA7 . . . . . . .13 D5
Barrington Villas SE18 . . .12 A6
Barrow La TN3 . . . . .157 F2
Barrowfields ME5 . . . . .68 D1
Barry Ave DA7 . . . . .13 E7
Barry Cl BR6 . . . . .57 E7
Barry Rd E6 . . . . .1 E7
Barth Mews SE18 . . . . .2 E2
Barth Rd SE18 . . . . .2 E2
Bartholomew Way BR8 . . .45 E6
Bartlett Cl ME5 . . . . .68 C1
Bartlett Rd
  Gravesend DA11 . . . . .36 A7
  Westerham TN16 . . . . .89 C1
Bartley La TN3 . . . . .174 E4
Bartley Mill Rd TN3 . . . . .174 F3
Barton Cl Bexley DA6 . . . . .13 E2
  2 Newham E6 . . . . .1 F7
Barton Cotts TN11 . . . . . .111 A6
Barton Rd
  Maidstone ME15 . . . . . . .100 A2
  Rochester ME2 . . . . .53 A4
  Sidcup DA14 . . . . .30 C4
  Sutton at H DA4 . . . . .47 B8
Bartons Cotts TN16 . . . . . .90 C3
Bascombe Dr DA1 . . . . .14 E1
Basden Cotts **2** TN18 . .189 A2
Baseing Cl E6 . . . . .2 A6
Bashford Barn La ME9 . . . .87 F4
Basi Cl ME2 . . . . .39 C1
Basil Terr **6** ME15 . . . . . .100 A1
Basilon Rd SE2 . . . . .3 A1
Basilon Rd DA7 . . . . .13 E5
Basing Cl ME15 . . . . .100 B3
Basing Dr DA5 . . . . .13 F1
Basket Gdns SE9 . . . . .11 E2
Basmere Cl ME14 . . . . . . .100 C6
Bassant Rd SE18 . . . . .12 F1
Bassett's Forge TN5 . . . . .184 E5

Bassetts Cl BR6 . . . . .57 B6
Bassetts La TN8,TN11 . . .156 C7
Bassetts Way BR6 . . . . . . .57 B6
Basted La Basted TN15 . . . .94 F5
  Crouch TN15 . . . . .95 B4
Bastion Rd SE2 . . . . .3 A1
Baston Manor BR2 . . . . . . .56 B6
Baston Manor Rd BR2,
  BR4 . . . . .56 B6
Baston Rd BR2 . . . . .56 B7
Baston Sch BR2 . . . . .56 B8
Bat & Ball Ent Ctr TN14 . .92 C7
Bat & Ball Sta TN14 . . . . . .92 C6
Batchelor St ME4 . . . . .54 A4
Batchelors TN2 . . . . .160 E8
Batchwood Gn BR5 . . . . . . .44 B6
Bates Cl ME20 . . . . .82 A3
Bates Hill TN15 . . . . .94 C5
Bateson St SE18 . . . . .2 E2
Bath Hard ME1 . . . . .53 D5
Bath Rd DA1 . . . . .32 B8
Baths St DA11 . . . . .19 B1
Baths Rd BR2 . . . . .42 D5
Bathurst Cl TN12 . . . . . . .149 E4
Bathurst Rd TN12 . . . . . . .149 E3
Bathway **18** SE18 . . . . .2 B2
Batt's Rd DA12 . . . . .51 A4
Batten Cl E6 . . . . .1 F7
Battery Rd SE28 . . . . .2 E4
Battle La TN12 . . . . .149 A8
Battle Rd DA8,DA17 . . . . . . .4 B2
Battle St DA12 . . . . .50 F6
Battlefields TN15 . . . . .78 F3
Battlesmere Rd ME3 . . . . . .39 B8
Baugh Rd DA14 . . . . .30 C3
Baxter Rd E16 . . . . .1 C7
Baxter Way ME18 . . . . .97 C3
Bay Manor La RM20 . . . . . .16 F8
Bay The DA13 . . . . .80 A8
Bayard Ct DA6 . . . . .14 B3
Bayeux Ho **11** SE7 . . . . . . .11 C8
Bayfield Rd SE9 . . . . .11 D3
Bayhall Rd TN2 . . . . .159 C3
Bayham Ct TN5 . . . . .184 E6
Bayham Old Abbey ★
  TN3 . . . . .175 B5
Bayham Rd
  Bells Yew Green TN3 . . . .174 B4
  Royal Tunbridge Wells
   TN2,TN3 . . . . .173 C7
  Sevenoaks TN13 . . . . .92 D4
Bayley Wlk SE2 . . . . .3 E1
Bayley's Hill TN14 . . . . . .107 E3
Bayliss Ave SE28 . . . . .3 D6
Bayly Rd DA1 . . . . .16 A1
Bayne Cl E6 . . . . .1 F7
Baynham Cl DA5 . . . . .13 F1
Bays The BR5 . . . . .44 C6
Bayswater Dr ME8 . . . . . . .69 E4
Baytree Cl Bromley BR1 . . .42 D8
  Sidcup DA15 . . . . .29 F7
Baywell ME19 . . . . .81 E2
Bazes Shaw DA3 . . . . .62 F8
Beach Ct Eltham SE9 . . . . . .11 E1
  Goddard's Green TN17 . . .180 D1
Beacham Cl SE7 . . . . .11 E8
Beachamwell Dr ME18 . . . .97 C2
Beacon Cl ME8 . . . . .69 D7
Beacon Dr DA2 . . . . .34 C5
Beacon Hill ME5 . . . . .54 D2
Beacon Hill La ME3 . . . . . . .39 F4
Beacon Oak Rd TN30 . . . .193 B6
Beacon Rd Chatham ME5 . .54 C2
  Erith DA8 . . . . .15 B7
  Lenham ME17 . . . . .120 C5
Beacon Rise TN13 . . . . .92 A1
Beacon Wlk TN30 . . . . . . .183 B1
Beacon Wood Ctry Pk ★
  DA2 . . . . .34 B4
Beaconfields TN13 . . . . . . .92 A1
Beacons Cl **11** E6 . . . . .1 E8
Beacons The ME17 . . . . . .115 C4
Beaconsfield Ave ME7 . . . .54 E5
Beaconsfield Cl SE3 . . . . . .11 A8
Beaconsfield Par SE9 . . . . .28 E4
Beaconsfield Rd
  Bromley,Mottingham SE9 . .28 E4
  Bromley,Widmore BR1 . . . .42 D6
  Chatham ME4 . . . . .53 F3
  Greenwich SE3 . . . . .11 A8
  Maidstone ME15 . . . . .99 E2
  Maypole DA5 . . . . .31 E6
Beadon Rd BR2 . . . . .42 A4
Beagles Cl BR5 . . . . .58 D8
Beagles Wood Rd TN2 . . .160 E2
Beal Cl DA16 . . . . .13 A6
Beaman Cl TN17 . . . . .177 F8
Beamish Rd BR5 . . . . .44 C2
Beams The ME15 . . . . . . .100 F1
Bean Hill Cotts DA2 . . . . . .34 C4
Bean La DA2 . . . . .34 B6
Bean Prim Sch DA2 . . . . . .34 C4
Bean Rd Bexley DA6 . . . . . .13 D3
  Swanscombe DA9 . . . . .17 B1
Beane Croft DA12 . . . . .36 F7
Beanshaw SE9 . . . . .29 A4
Bearsted Green Bsns Ctr
  ME14 . . . . .101 C4
Bearsted Rd ME14 . . . . . .100 E6
Bearsted Sta ME14 . . . . . .101 B5
Beaton Cl DA9 . . . . .17 B2
Beatrice Gdns DA11 . . . . . .35 E6
Beatty Ave ME7 . . . . .54 F4
Beatty Cotts ME3 . . . . .9 D1
Beatty Rd ME1 . . . . .67 D8
Beaufighter Rd ME19 . . . . .96 E3

Beaufort E6 . . . . .2 A8
Beaufort Ct ME2 . . . . .53 E6
Beaufort Rd ME2 . . . . .52 E8
Beaufort Wlk ME15 . . . . .116 E4
Beaulieu Ave E16 . . . . .1 B5
Beaulieu Rd TN10 . . . . . . .127 B4
Beaulieu Rise ME1 . . . . . . .53 D1
Beaulieu Wlk ME16 . . . . . .99 B7
Beaumanor Gdns SE9 . . . .29 A4
Beaumont Dr DA11 . . . . . . .35 F8
Beaumont Rd
  Maidstone ME16 . . . . .99 B2
  Orpington BR5 . . . . .43 D3
Beauworth Pk ME15 . . . .116 E8
Beaver Rd ME16 . . . . .99 B7
Beaver Zoological Gdns ★
  TN16 . . . . .88 B5
Beaverbank Rd SE9 . . . . . .29 D7
Beavers Lodge DA14 . . . . . .29 F3
Beaverwood Rd BR7 . . . . . .29 E2
Beaverwood Sch for Girls
  BR7 . . . . .29 E2
Bebbington Rd SE18 . . . . . .2 E2
Beblets Cl **4** BR6 . . . . .57 F5
Beckenham Dr ME16 . . . . .99 D7
Becket Ct
  Headcorn TN27 . . . . .151 D5
  2 Tonbridge TN9 . . . . . .143 B8
Beckets Field TN11 . . . . . .141 A3
Beckett Cl DA17 . . . . .3 F3
Becketts Ct BR6 . . . . .57 F7
Beckford Dr BR5 . . . . .43 D2
Beckley Cl DA12 . . . . .37 B6
Beckley Hill Works ME2 . .38 B8
Beckley Mews ME5 . . . . . . .67 F5
Beckman Cl TN14 . . . . .75 C4
Becks Rd DA14 . . . . .30 A5
Becksbourne Cl ME14 . . .100 A8
Beckton Park Sta E6 . . . . . .1 F6
Beckton Rd E16 . . . . .1 A8
Beckton Ret Pk E6 . . . . .2 A8
Beckton Sta E6 . . . . .2 A8
Beckworth Pl ME16 . . . . . .99 B2
Becton Pl DA8 . . . . .14 C6
Bedale Wlk DA2 . . . . .33 B7
Beddalls Farm Ct **7** E6 . . .1 B8
Beddington Gn BR5 . . . . . . .43 F8
Beddington Rd BR5 . . . . . . .43 F8
Beddlestead La CR6 . . . . . .88 A6
Beddow Way ME20 . . . . . . .83 B3
Bedens Rd DA14 . . . . .30 E3
Bedford Ave ME8 . . . . .55 D1
Bedford Pl ME16 . . . . .99 E4
Bedford Rd Dartford DA1 . .33 A8
  Northfleet DA11 . . . . .35 F6
  Orpington BR6 . . . . .44 B1
  Royal Tunbridge Wells
   TN4 . . . . .143 A1
  Sidcup DA15 . . . . .29 E5
Bedford Sq DA3 . . . . .48 E6
Bedford Terr **13** TN1 . . . .159 A2
Bedgebury Cl
  Maidstone ME14 . . . . . . .100 C6
  Rochester ME1 . . . . .67 D8
Bedgebury Cross TN17 . .177 D2
Bedgebury National
  Pinetum ★ TN17 . . . . . .187 E8
Bedgebury Rd Eltham SE9 .11 D3
  Goudhurst TN17 . . . . .177 B5
  Bedgebury Sch TN17 . . . .177 E1
Bedivere Rd BR1 . . . . .28 A5
Bedlam La TN27 . . . . .152 E6
Bedonwell Inf Sch DA17 .13 E8
Bedonwell Jun Sch DA17 .13 E8
Bedonwell Rd
  Bexley,Bexleyheath DA7 . . .13 F6
  Bexley,West Heath DA7,
   DA17 . . . . .13 E8
Bedwell Rd DA17 . . . . .4 A1
Bedwin Cl ME1 . . . . .67 D7
Beeby Rd E16 . . . . .1 B8
Beech Ave Sidcup DA15 . . .30 A8
  Swanley BR8 . . . . .45 F5
  Tatsfield TN16 . . . . .88 D8
Beech Copse BR1 . . . . .42 F7
Beech Ct Dartford DA1 . . . .16 A1
  Paddock Wood TN12 . . . .146 A7
  Royal Tunbridge Wells
   TN2 . . . . .159 D4
Beech Dell BR2,BR4 . . . . . .56 F6
Beech Dr ME16 . . . . .99 C5
Beech Gr ME3 . . . . .38 C4
Beech Green La
  Cowden TN7 . . . . .155 F1
  Withyham TN7 . . . . .170 B7
Beech Haven Ct DA1 . . . . .14 D2
Beech Ho DA15 . . . . .30 A5
Beech Hurst TN2 . . . . .160 D7
Beech Hurst Cl ME15 . . . .100 B2
Beech La TN12 . . . . .161 C4
Beech Manor TN2 . . . . . . .159 D3
Beech Mast DA13 . . . . .80 B8
Beech Rd Biggin Hill TN16 .72 C2
  Dartford DA1 . . . . .32 C7
  East Malling ME19 . . . . . . .97 F7
  Herne Pound ME18 . . . . . .96 D3
  Hoo St Werburgh ME3 . . . .40 E3
  Newenden TN18 . . . . .197 C3
  Orpington BR6 . . . . .58 A3
  Rochester ME2 . . . . .52 F6
  Sevenoaks TN13 . . . . .92 B2
Beech St TN1 . . . . .159 B4
Beech Wlk
  Biddenden TN27 . . . . .182 D7
  Crayford DA1 . . . . .15 A3

Beecham Rd TN10 . . . . . . .127 E6
Beechcroft BR7 . . . . .29 A1
Beechcroft Ave DA7 . . . . . .14 D5

Beechcroft Cl BR6 . . . . . . .57 D6
Beechcroft Rd BR6 . . . . . . .57 D6
Beechen Bank Rd ME5 . . . .68 A1
Beechenlea La BR8 . . . . . . .46 B6
Beecher Ct SE12 . . . . .28 B5
Beeches Ct BR1 . . . . .28 A2
Beeches The
  Aylesford ME20 . . . . .82 E1
  Chatham ME5 . . . . .68 A4
  Hextable BR8 . . . . .31 F1
  New Barn DA3 . . . . .49 C7
  Royal Tunbridge Wells
   TN2 . . . . .159 D3
  Sole Street DA13 . . . . .50 D5
  The Moor TN18 . . . . .194 E7
  Tilbury RM18 . . . . .19 B5
Beechfield Cotts **6** BR1 .42 C7
Beechfield Rd
  Bromley BR1 . . . . .42 C7
  Erith DA8 . . . . .14 E7
Beechhill Rd SE9 . . . . .12 A2
Beechin Wood La TN15 . . .95 D5
Beeching Rd ME5 . . . . .68 B3
Beechings Cl ME8 . . . . .55 C3
Beechings Way ME8 . . . . . .55 C3
Beechings Way Ind Ctr
  ME8 . . . . .55 B4
Beechlands Cl DA3 . . . . . . .49 A4
Beechmont Rd TN13 . . . . .108 B6
Beechmont Rise TN10 . . . .127 B6
Beechmore Dr ME5 . . . . . . .68 A2
Beechway
  Meopham Sta DA13 . . . . . .50 B2
  Sidcup DA5 . . . . .13 D1
Beechwood Ave
  Gillingham ME5 . . . . .54 D2
  Orpington BR6 . . . . .57 E4
Beechwood Cres DA7 . . . . .13 E4
Beechwood Dr
  Culverstone Green DA13 . . .64 A1
  Orpington BR2 . . . . .56 D6
Beechwood Gdns DA13 . . . .64 A1
Beechwood Mews TN2 . . .159 E4
Beechwood Rd ME16 . . . . . .98 F3
Beechwood Rise BR7 . . . . .29 B4
Beechwood Sacred Heart Sch
  TN2 . . . . .159 E4
Beechy Lees Rd TN14 . . . . .76 E3
Beeken Dene BR6 . . . . .57 C6
Beesfield La DA4 . . . . .47 A1
Beeston Ct **4** DA1 . . . . .16 B1
Begbie Rd SE3 . . . . .11 C6
Beggars La TN16 . . . . .89 C3
Begonia Ave ME8 . . . . .55 C2
Beke Rd ME8 . . . . .69 D4
Bekesbourne Twr **12**
  BR5 . . . . .44 D1
Beldam Haw TN14 . . . . . . .75 A8
Belfast Ho **14** ME15 . . . . .116 E7
Belfield Rd TN2 . . . . .160 D6
Belford Gr SE18 . . . . .2 A2
Belgrave Cl **5** BR5 . . . . . . .44 C5
Belgrave Ct SE7 . . . . .11 C7
Belgrave Rd TN1 . . . . .159 B4
Belgrave St ME20 . . . . .82 F6
Belgrove **5** TN1 . . . . .159 A2
Bell Cl DA9 . . . . .16 F2
Bell Cres ME1 . . . . .82 F8
Bell Farm Gdns ME16 . . . .98 F2
Bell Gdns BR5 . . . . .44 C4
Bell Ho Erith SE2 . . . . .3 D1
  Grays RM17 . . . . .17 F8
Bell La Burham ME1 . . . . . . .82 F8
  Chatham ME14 . . . . .84 B7
  Larkfield ME20 . . . . .82 B2
  Maidstone ME14 . . . . .101 A5
  Newham E16 . . . . .1 A5
  Standen TN27 . . . . .168 B8
  Staplehurst TN12 . . . . . . .149 E3
Bell Mdw ME15 . . . . .116 E6
Bell Rd ME15 . . . . .116 E6
Bell Row TN11 . . . . .128 F5
Bell St SE18 . . . . .11 E6
Bell Water Gate SE18 . . . . .2 A3
Bell Way ME17 . . . . .118 E2
Bell Wood Prim Sch
  ME15 . . . . .116 E5
Bell's Cl TN30 . . . . .193 A7
Bell's La ME15 . . . . .40 E6
Bellarmine Cl SE28 . . . . . . .2 F4
Belle Vue Rd BR6 . . . . .57 A1
Bellefield Rd BR5 . . . . .44 B4
Bellegrove Cl DA16 . . . . . . .12 F4
Bellegrove Par DA16 . . . . . .12 F4
Bellegrove Rd DA16 . . . . . .12 E5
Bellevue Rd DA6 . . . . .13 F2
Bellfield Cl SE3 . . . . .11 B7
Bellflower Cl **2** E6 . . . . .1 E8
Bellgrove Ct ME5 . . . . .84 A8
Bellingham Way ME20 . . . .82 B3
Bellman Ave DA12 . . . . .36 E7
Bellows La TN15 . . . . .94 F7
Bellring Cl DA17 . . . . .14 A8
Bells Farm La TN11 . . . . . .129 C8
Bells Farm Rd TN11,
  TN12 . . . . .112 D1
Bells La **9** TN30 . . . . .193 A7
Bellwood St ME3 . . . . .24 C3
Belmont Ave DA16 . . . . . . .12 E4
Belmont Cl ME16 . . . . .98 F2
Belmont Ct **9** ME15 . . . . .100 B4
Belmont La BR7 . . . . .29 C3
Belmont Par BR7 . . . . .29 C3
Belmont Prim Sch DA8 . . .14 A7
Belmont Rd
  Chislehurst BR7 . . . . .29 B3
  Erith DA8 . . . . .14 B6
  Gillingham ME7 . . . . .54 C4

Belmont Rd continued
  Grays RM17 . . . . .17 F8
Belnor Ave ME19 . . . . .71 F8
Belson Rd SE18 . . . . .1 F2
Beltana Dr DA12 . . . . .36 E4
Belton Rd DA14 . . . . .30 A4
Beltring Rd
  Beltring TN12,ME18 . . . . .130 E4
  Royal Tunbridge Wells
   TN4 . . . . .159 A6
Beltring Sta TN12 . . . . . . .130 B4
Beltwood Rd DA17 . . . . .4 C2
Beluncle Villas ME3 . . . . . .41 C7
Belvedere Cl DA12 . . . . .36 C7
Belvedere Ct DA17 . . . . .3 F3
Belvedere Ho **9** ME15 . . .116 F5
Belvedere Ind Est DA17 . . .4 C5
Belvedere Inf Sch DA17 . . .4 B3
Belvedere Jun Sch DA17 . .4 B3
Belvedere Link Bsns Pk
  DA17 . . . . .4 C3
Belvedere Mews SE3 . . . . .11 B7
Belvedere Rd Bexley DA7 . .13 F5
  Biggin Hill TN16 . . . . .72 F1
  Erith SE28 . . . . .3 D5
  Erith Station DA17 . . . . .4 B3
Belvoir Cl SE9 . . . . .28 E5
Ben Tillet Cl E16 . . . . .1 F5
Benares Rd SE18 . . . . .2 F2
Benden Cl TN12 . . . . .149 F4
Bendmore Ave SE2 . . . . .3 A2
Bendon Way ME8 . . . . .69 D8
Benedict Cl **9** Erith DA17 . . .3 E3
  Halling ME2 . . . . .66 B4
  Orpington BR6 . . . . .57 E7
Benenden CE Prim Sch
  TN17 . . . . .190 D6
Benenden Gn BR2 . . . . .42 A4
Benenden Hospl TN17 . . .181 C3
Benenden Manor ME8 . . . .55 B3
Benenden Rd
  Benenden TN17 . . . . .191 B4
  Cranbrook TN17 . . . . .179 E1
  Fosten Green TN27 . . . . . .181 F5
  Rochester ME2 . . . . .39 C1
Benenden Sch TN17 . . . . .190 C8
Benhall Mill Rd TN2,
  TN3 . . . . .173 D8
Benjamin Ct **4** DA17 . . . . .13 F8
Benn Cl RH8 . . . . .104 A1
Benn Ho SE7 . . . . .1 C1
Bennett Cl DA16 . . . . .13 A5
Bennett Ho DA11 . . . . .35 F5
Bennett Meml Diocesan Sch
  TN4 . . . . .158 E6
Bennett Way DA2 . . . . .33 D3
Bennetts Ave TN15 . . . . . . .78 C4
Bennetts Copse BR7 . . . . .28 E2
Bennetts Cotts ME7 . . . . . .85 A8
Bennetts Mews **13** TN30 .193 A7
Benover Rd ME18 . . . . .130 F7
Benson Rd RM17 . . . . .18 C8
Bensted Cl ME15 . . . . .131 D7
Bentfield Gdns SE9 . . . . . . .28 B5
Bentham Hill TN3,TN4 . . . .142 D1
Bentham Rd SE28 . . . . .3 D5
Bentley Cl Aylesford ME20 .82 F1
  Chatham ME5 . . . . .68 D2
  New Barn DA3 . . . . .49 C7
Bentley St DA12 . . . . .19 C1
Bentley Street Ind Est
  DA12 . . . . .19 C1
Bentley's Mdw TN15 . . . . . .92 F7
Bentleys Bglws TN15 . . . . .92 F7
Bentlif Cl ME16 . . . . .99 D5
Berber Rd ME2 . . . . .53 B8
Bercta Rd SE9 . . . . .29 C6
Bere Cl DA9 . . . . .17 C2
Berengrave La ME8 . . . . . . .55 F2
Berens Ct DA14 . . . . .29 F4
Berens Rd BR5 . . . . .44 D4
Berens Way BR5 . . . . .43 F6
Beresford Ave ME1 . . . . . . .53 E2
Beresford Cl TN17 . . . . . . .176 F2
Beresford Dr BR1 . . . . .42 E6
Beresford Rd
  Gillingham ME7 . . . . .54 D4
  Goudhurst TN17 . . . . .163 F1
  Kit's Coty ME20 . . . . .83 D7
  Northfleet DA11 . . . . .35 E8
Beresford Square Market Pl
  SE18 . . . . .2 B2
Beresford St SE18 . . . . .2 B3
Beresfords Hill ME17 . . . .116 B4
Berger Cl BR5 . . . . .43 E3
Bergland Pk ME2 . . . . .53 D8
Bering Wlk E16 . . . . .1 D7
Berkeley Ave DA7 . . . . .13 D6
Berkeley Cl Orpington BR5 .43 E2
  Pembury TN2 . . . . .160 E7
  Rochester ME1 . . . . .67 D8
Berkeley Cres DA1 . . . . . . .32 F7
Berkeley Ct **6** BR8 . . . . . . .45 E6
Berkeley Mount **8** ME4 . . .53 F4
Berkeley Rd **7** TN1 . . . . . .159 A2
Berkeley Terr RM18 . . . . . . .19 A7
Berkhampstead Rd **9**
  DA17 . . . . .4 A1
Berkley Cres DA12 . . . . . . .19 C1
Berkley Rd DA12 . . . . .19 B1
Berkshire Cl ME5 . . . . .68 C8
Bermuda Rd RM18 . . . . .19 A5
Bernal Cl SE28 . . . . .3 D6
Bernard Ashley Dr SE7 . . . .1 B1
Bernard St DA12 . . . . .19 B1
Bernards Cl DA15 . . . . .29 E7
Berner's Hill TN5 . . . . .187 A3
Bernersmede SE3 . . . . .11 A4

Berry Rd ME3 . . . . .40 E3
Berry's Green Rd TN16 . .73 B2
Berry's Hill TN16 . . . . . . .73 B4
Berryfield Cl BR1 . . . . . . .42 E7
Berryhill SE9 . . . . .12 B3
Berryhill Gdns SE9 . . . . . .12 B3
Berrylands Hartley DA3 . .49 A3
  Orpington BR6 . . . . .58 C7
Bert Reilly Ho 1 SE18 . . . .2 D1
Bertha Hollamby Ct
  DA14 . . . . .30 C3
Bertha James Ct BR2 . . .42 B5
Bertrand Way SE28 . . . . . .3 C6
Bertrey Cotts TN16 . . . . . .73 B3
Berwick Cres DA15 . . . . .12 E1
Berwick Ct 12 DA2 . . . . .16 B1
Berwick Rd Bexley DA16 . .13 B6
  Newham E16 . . . . .1 C7
Berwick Way TN14 . . . . . .92 B7
Berwyn Gr ME15 . . . . . .116 A6
Beryl Ave E6 . . . . .1 E8
Beryl Ho 3 SE18 . . . . .2 F1
Besant Ct 15 SE28 . . . . . . .3 B6
Bessels Green Rd TN13 . .91 D3
Bessels Mdw TN13 . . . . . .91 D3
Bessels Way TN13 . . . . . .91 D3
Bessie Lansbury Cl E6 . . . .2 A7
Best St ME4 . . . . .53 F4
Beta Rd ME3 . . . . .41 D7
Betenson Ave TN13 . . . . .91 F5
Bethany Sch TN17 . . . . .164 B5
Bethel Rd Bexley DA16 . . .13 C4
  Sevenoaks TN13 . . . . . . .92 C4
Betherinden Cotts
  TN18 . . . . .196 A4
Bethersden Ct ME15 . . . .116 F7
Bethersden Rd TN27,
  TN26 . . . . .169 C5
Beths Gram Sch DA5 . . . .14 B1
Betjeman Cl ME20 . . . . . .81 F3
Betony Gdns ME14 . . . . .100 F5
Betsham Rd
  Betsham DA13 . . . . .34 D3
  Erith DA8 . . . . .14 F7
  Maidstone ME15 . . . . . .116 F6
  Swanscombe DA10 . . . . . .34 E8
Betterton Dr DA14 . . . . . .30 E6
Bettescombe Rd ME8 . . . .69 E7
Betts Rd E16 . . . . .1 B6
Beulah Rd TN1 . . . . .159 C4
Bevan Pl BR8 . . . . .45 F5
Bevan Rd SE2 . . . . .3 B1
Bevans Cl DA9 . . . . .17 C1
Bevercote Wlk 1 DA17 . . .13 F8
Beveridge Ct 1 SE28 . . . . .3 B6
Beverley Ave DA15 . . . . . .29 E8
Beverley Cl ME8 . . . . .69 F8
Beverley Cres TN9 . . . . .142 F7
Beverley Ct 8 DA14 . . . . .30 B4
Beverley Rd Bexley DA7 . .14 C5
  Maidstone ME16 . . . . . . .98 F2
  Orpington BR2 . . . . .56 E8
Beville Ho RM17 . . . . . . .18 B7
Bevis Cl DA2 . . . . .33 C8
Bewl Bridge Cl TN5 . . . .187 B3
Bewl Water Nature Reserve★
  TN5 . . . . .186 B7
Bewl Water Visitor Ctr★
  TN3 . . . . .186 B8
Bewlbridge La
  Lamberhurst TN3,TN5 . . .176 B1
  Lower Cousley Wood TN5 .185 F8
Bewley La TN15 . . . . .94 D2
Bexhill Dr RM17 . . . . . . .17 F8
Bexley Cl ME1 . . . . .14 E2
Bexley Coll Erith DA17 . . . .4 B1
  Erith DA17 . . . . .4 C2
Bexley Coll (St Joseph's
  Campus) SE2 . . . . .13 D8
Bexley Cotts DA4 . . . . . . .47 C5
Bexley Gram Sch DA16 . . .13 B3
Bexley High St DA5 . . . . .31 B7
Bexley La Crayford DA1 . . .14 E2
  Sidcup DA14 . . . . .30 C5
Bexley Rd Eltham SE9 . . . .12 C2
  4 Erith DA8 . . . . .4 E1
  Erith DA8 . . . . .4 F1
  Erith,Northumberland Heath
  DA8 . . . . .14 C8
Bexley Sta DA5 . . . . .31 A7
Bexleyheath Sch DA6 . . . .13 F4
Bexleyheath Sta DA7 . . . .13 E5
Bexon La ME9 . . . . .87 F5
Bglws The TN30 . . . . . . .193 D7
Bickley Cres BR1 . . . . . . .42 E5
Bickley Ct 2 BR1 . . . . . . .42 E6
Bickley Park Rd BR1 . . . . .42 F6
Bickley Park Sch BR1 . . . .42 F6
Bickley Prim Sch BR1 . . . .42 C7
Bickley Rd Bromley BR1 . . .42 E7
  5 Tonbridge TN9 . . . . . .143 B8
Bickley Sta BR1 . . . . .42 E6
Bickmore Way TN9 . . . . .127 D3
Bicknor La ME9 . . . . .87 F5
Bicknor Rd
  Maidstone ME15 . . . . . .116 F4
  Orpington BR6 . . . . .43 F2
Bidborough CE Prim Sch
  TN3 . . . . .142 D3
Bidborough Ct TN3 . . . . .142 B3
Bidborough Ridge TN4 . .142 E4
Biddenden Cl ME15 . . . . .100 C3
Biddenden La TN27 . . . . .151 E5
Biddenden Rd
  Headcorn TN27 . . . . . . .151 E2

Biddenden Rd continued
  Tenterden TN30 . . . . . .182 E6
  Tylden TN27 . . . . .168 F8
Biddenden Vineyards & Cider
  Works★ TN27 . . . . . . .182 A5
Biddenden Way
  Eltham SE9 . . . . .29 A4
  Istead Rise DA13 . . . . . . .35 A1
Biddulph Ho 17 SE18 . . . .1 F2
Bideford Rd SE9 . . . . .28 E5
Biggin Hill Airport TN16 .72 D5
Biggin Hill Bsns Pk TN16 .72 D4
Biggin Hill Jun & Inf Schs
  TN16 . . . . .72 E3
Biggin La RM16 . . . . .19 B8
Bignell Rd SE18 . . . . .2 B1
Bilberry Cl ME14 . . . . . . .100 E5
Bill Hamling Cl SE9 . . . . .28 F6
Bill Street Rd ME2 . . . . . .39 C1
Billet Hill TN15 . . . . .62 C6
Billings DA3 . . . . .48 F3
Bilsby Gr SE9 . . . . .28 D4
Bilsington Cl ME5 . . . . . . .68 B5
Bilton Rd DA8 . . . . .15 A8
Bimbury La ME14,ME9 . . .86 A5
Bines The TN12 . . . . .146 A5
Bingham Point 5 SE18 . . .2 B2
Bingham Rd ME2 . . . . . . .39 C1
Bingley Cl ME6 . . . . .81 F8
Bingley Rd Newham E16 . . .1 C7
  1 Rochester ME1 . . . . . . .53 E4
Binland Gr ME5 . . . . .67 D5
Binnacle Rd ME1 . . . . . . .67 C8
Binney Rd ME3 . . . . .9 D2
Binsey Wlk 1 SE2 . . . . . . .3 C4
Birbetts Rd SE9 . . . . .28 E5
Birch Cl Eynsford DA4 . . . .60 D7
  Matfield TN12 . . . . .145 D1
  New Barn DA3 . . . . .49 C7
  Royal Tunbridge Wells
  TN2 . . . . .159 D7
  Sevenoaks TN13 . . . . . . .92 B4
  Tonbridge TN11 . . . . . . .126 D4
Birch Cres ME20 . . . . .98 D8
Birch Dr ME5 . . . . .68 D1
Birch Gr Bexley DA16 . . . .13 A3
  Gillingham ME7 . . . . .69 A4
Birch Ho 6 ME16 . . . . . . .99 A3
Birch Kiln Cotts TN5 . . . .185 A6
Birch Mead BR6 . . . . .57 A8
Birch Pl Sevenoaks TN13 . .92 A3
  Stone DA9 . . . . .16 E1
Birch Rd
  Hoo St Werburgh ME3 . . . .40 E3
  Paddock Wood TN12 . . . .146 A6
Birch Row BR2 . . . . .43 A3
Birch Tree Ho 18 SE7 . . . .11 C8
Birch Tree Way ME15 . . . .100 B3
Birch Way TN12 . . . . .159 D7
Birchden Cotts TN3 . . . . .171 C6
Birchden Dr SE28 . . . . .3 A5
Birches The
  Greenwich SE7 . . . . .11 B8
  Orpington BR6 . . . . .57 A6
  Swanley BR8 . . . . .45 E7
  Tonbridge TN9 . . . . .143 B7
Birchetts Ave TN3 . . . . . .157 E3
Birchetts Green La TN5 . .186 A2
Birchfield TN11 . . . . .106 E8
Birchfield Cl ME15 . . . . . .116 B6
Birchfields ME5 . . . . .68 A3
Birchin Cross Rd TN15 . . .77 A5
Birchington Cl Bexley DA7 .14 B6
  Maidstone ME14 . . . . . .100 C5
  Orpington BR5 . . . . .44 C1
Bircholme TN2 . . . . .159 D7
Bircholt Rd ME15 . . . . . .116 F4
Birchway TN15 . . . . .61 F2
Birchwood Ave
  Bidborough TN4 . . . . . . .142 E4
  Sidcup DA14 . . . . .30 C5
Birchwood Dr DA2 . . . . . .31 E4
Birchwood La TN14 . . . . . .74 F4
Birchwood Par DA2 . . . . .31 E4
Birchwood Park Ave BR8 .45 E4
Birchwood Prim Sch
  BR8 . . . . .45 D8
Birchwood Rd
  Joyden's Wood DA2,BR8 . .31 D3
  Maidstone ME16 . . . . . . .99 C5
  Orpington BR5 . . . . .43 E5
Birchwood Terr BR8 . . . . .45 C8
Bird House La BR6 . . . . . .73 A5
Bird in Hand La BR1 . . . . .42 D7
Bird in Hand St TN3 . . . .171 B8
Bird La TN5 . . . . .184 B5
Birdbrook Rd SE3 . . . . . . .11 C4
Birdham Ct BR1 . . . . .42 E4
Birkbeck Prim Sch DA14 . .30 B5
Birkbeck Rd DA14 . . . . . .30 A5
Birkdale TN1 . . . . .159 B6
Birkdale Cl Erith SE28 . . . . .3 D7
  Orpington BR6 . . . . .43 D2
Birkdale Ct 3 ME16 . . . . .99 E4
Birkdale Rd SE2 . . . . .3 B2
Birken Rd TN2 . . . . .159 D6
Birkhall Ct ME5 . . . . .68 A5
Birling Ave Gillingham ME8 .55 E1
  Maidstone ME14 . . . . . .101 A4
Birling Cl ME14 . . . . .101 A4
Birling Dr TN2 . . . . .159 A1
Birling Hill DA13,ME19,
  ME6 . . . . .65 B1
Birling Park Ave TN2 . . . .173 B8
Birling Pk ME19 . . . . .81 C5
Birling Rd Bexley DA8 . . . .14 E6
  Leybourne ME19 . . . . . . .81 C3

Birling Rd continued
  Royal Tunbridge Wells
  TN2 . . . . .173 B8
  Ryarsh ME19 . . . . .81 A5
  Snodland ME6 . . . . .81 F7
Birnam Sq 1 ME16 . . . . . .99 E4
Birtrick Dr DA13 . . . . .49 F4
Bishop Butt Cl BR6 . . . . . .57 F7
Bishop John Robinson CE
  Prim Sch SE28 . . . . .3 C6
Bishop's Down TN4 . . . . .158 F3
Bishop's Down Park Rd
  TN4 . . . . .158 F4
Bishop's Down Prim Sch
  TN4 . . . . .158 E5
Bishop's Down Rd TN4 . .158 F3
Bishopbourne Gn ME8 . . .55 B4
Bishops Ave BR1 . . . . .42 C8
Bishops Cl Eltham SE9 . . . .29 C8
  Nettlestead ME18 . . . . . .113 D6
Bishops Ct
  Royal Tunbridge Wells
  TN4 . . . . .158 F3
  Stone DA9 . . . . .16 E2
Bishops Gn BR1 . . . . .42 C8
Bishops La TN17 . . . . . . .178 C2
Bishops Mews TN9 . . . . .143 C8
Bishops Oak Ride TN10 .127 C6
Bishops Way ME15 . . . . . .99 F4
Bishops Wlk
  Chislehurst BR7 . . . . .43 C8
  Rochester ME1 . . . . .53 C5
Bishopsbourne Ho 2
  BR1 . . . . .42 C8
Black Eagle Cl TN16 . . . .105 C8
Black Horse Ct TN27 . . . .151 E5
Black Horse Mews TN15 . .95 A7
Black Horse Rd 14 DA14 . .30 A4
Black Mill La TN27 . . . . .151 B6
Black Post ME17 . . . . . . .103 C4
Black Rock Gdns ME7 . . . .69 A6
Black's Yd TN13 . . . . .92 C2
Blackberry Field BR5 . . . . .44 A8
Blackberry Way TN11 . . . .146 B6
Blackbrook La BR1,BR2 . . .43 A5
Blackdale Farm Cotts
  DA1 . . . . .33 B6
Blackfen Par DA16 . . . . . .13 A1
Blackfen Rd DA15 . . . . . . .13 B1
Blackfen Sch for Girls
  DA15 . . . . .13 B1
Blackhall La TN15 . . . . . . .92 E3
Blackheath Bluecoat CE Sec
  Sch SE3 . . . . .11 B7
Blackheath High Sch
  SE3 . . . . .11 A7
Blackheath High Sch GPDST
  (Jun Dept) SE3 . . . . .11 A5
Blackheath Pk SE3 . . . . . .11 A5
Blackheath Prep Sch
  SE3 . . . . .11 A6
Blackhorse Mews TN2 . . .160 C6
Blackhurst La TN2 . . . . . .159 F6
Blacklands
  East Malling ME19 . . . . . .97 F7
  East Malling ME19 . . . . . .97 F8
Blacklands Dr ME19 . . . . .97 F8
Blackman Cl ME3 . . . . . . .40 D7
Blackman's La TN11 . . . . .128 D6
Blackmans Cl DA1 . . . . . . .32 C7
Blackmanstone Way
  ME16 . . . . .99 B7
Blackmead TN13 . . . . . . .91 E6
Blackness La TN2 . . . . . . .56 D2
Blacksmith Dr ME14 . . . . .100 D5
Blacksmith's La TN5 . . . .185 A5
Blacksmiths Field TN32 . .195 C1
Blacksmiths La BR5 . . . . .44 C4
Blacksole La TN15 . . . . . .78 F3
Blacksole Rd TN15 . . . . . .78 F3
Blackthorn Ave
  Chatham ME5 . . . . .68 A3
  Royal Tunbridge Wells
  TN4 . . . . .143 C1
Blackthorn Cl TN15 . . . . . .61 F2
Blackthorn Dr ME20 . . . . .82 B2
Blackthorn Gr DA7 . . . . . .13 E4
Blackthorne Rd ME8 . . . . .70 B8
Blackwater Cl RM13 . . . . . .4 E8
Bladindon Dr DA5 . . . . . .30 D8
Blainey Ho ME3 . . . . .39 F6
Blair Cl DA15 . . . . .12 E2
Blair Dr TN13 . . . . .92 B4
Blake Cl DA16 . . . . .12 E6
Blake Dr 3 ME20 . . . . . . .81 F4
Blake Gdns DA1 . . . . .15 F3
Blake Way
  Royal Tunbridge Wells
  TN2 . . . . .159 D7
  Tilbury RM18 . . . . .19 C5
Blakemore Way DA17 . . . . .3 F3
Blakeney Cl ME14 . . . . . .101 B4
Blaker Ave ME1 . . . . .53 E1
Blaker Ct SE7 . . . . .11 C7
Blanchard Cl SE9 . . . . . . .28 E5
Blanchard Ho BR7 . . . . . .29 C2
Bland St SE9 . . . . .11 D3
Blanmerle Rd SE9 . . . . . . .29 B7
Blann Cl SE9 . . . . .11 D1
Blatchford Cl ME17 . . . . . .81 F1
Blatchington Rd TN1 . . . .159 B1
Bleak Hill La SE18 . . . . . . .12 F8
Bleakwood Rd 6 ME5 . . . .67 F5
Blean Rd ME8 . . . . .55 C2
Blean Sq ME14 . . . . .100 C6
Bledlow Cl SE28 . . . . .3 C6

Blendon Dr DA5 . . . . .13 D1
Blendon Rd
  Maidstone ME14 . . . . . .100 C5
  Sidcup DA5 . . . . .13 D1
Blendon Terr SE18 . . . . . .12 C8
Blenheim Ave ME4 . . . . . .53 C6
Blenheim Cl Dartford DA1 .15 C1
  Maidstone ME15 . . . . . .100 A3
  Meopham DA13 . . . . .64 B8
Blenheim Ct Chatham ME4 .53 E3
  Sidcup DA15 . . . . .29 D5
Blenheim Dr DA16 . . . . . .12 F6
Blenheim Gr DA12 . . . . . .36 C8
Blenheim Ho SE18 . . . . . . .2 C3
Blenheim Prim Sch BR6 . .58 C8
Blenheim Rd Bromley BR1 .42 E5
  Dartford DA1 . . . . .15 C1
  Orpington BR5,BR6 . . . . .58 C8
  Sidcup DA15 . . . . .30 C7
Blenheim Way TN5 . . . . .187 C3
Bletchingley St DA17 . . . . .4 A2
Blewbury Ho 3 SE2 . . . . . .3 C4
Bligh Inf Sch ME2 . . . . . .52 C7
Bligh Jun Sch ME2 . . . . . .52 C7
Bligh Rd DA11 . . . . .19 A1
Bligh Way ME2 . . . . .52 D6
Blighs Ct TN13 . . . . .92 B2
Bligh's Rd TN13 . . . . .92 B2
Bligh's Wlk TN13 . . . . . . .92 C2
Blind La Bredhurst ME7 . . .69 A1
  Goudhurst TN17 . . . . . . .163 E1
Blind Mary's La ME9 . . . . .87 E4
Bliss Way TN10 . . . . .127 E5
Blithdale Rd SE2 . . . . .3 A2
Blockhouse Rd 7 ME7 . . .18 C8
Blockmakers Ct ME4 . . . . .54 B1
Bloomfield Rd
  Bromley BR2 . . . . .42 D4
  Woolwich SE18 . . . . .2 B1
Bloomfield Terr TN16 . . . .89 E2
Bloomsbury Wlk 2
  ME15 . . . . .100 A4
Bloors La ME8 . . . . .55 D1
Bloors Wharf Rd ME7 . . . .55 F4
Blowers Hil Cott TN3 . . . .158 B8
Blowers Hill TN3 . . . . . . .155 D8
Blowers Wood Gr ME7 . . .69 B3
Bloxam Signs SE9 . . . . . . .11 E2
Blue Anchor La RM18 . . . .19 E8
Blue Boar La ME1 . . . . . . .53 D5
Blue Chalet Ind Pk TN15 .61 A4
Blue Coat La TN17 . . . . . .177 C6
Bluebell Cl Gillingham ME7 .54 F6
  Orpington BR6 . . . . .57 F6
Bluebell Wlks TN12 . . . . .146 A5
Blueberry La TN14 . . . . . .74 C4
Bluebird Way SE28 . . . . . . .2 D4
Bluehouse Gdns RM8 . . . .104 A7
Bluehouse La RH8 . . . . . .104 A8
Bluett St ME14 . . . . .100 A5
Bluewater DA9 . . . . .33 F8
Bluewater Parkway DA9 . .33 E8
Blunden La ME18 . . . . . . .114 A1
Blunts Rd SE9 . . . . .12 A2
Blyth Ho 5 DA8 . . . . .4 E1
Blyth Rd SE28 . . . . .3 C6
Blythe Ct SE12 . . . . .28 A8
Blythe Hill BR5 . . . . .44 A8
Blythe Rd ME15 . . . . . . .100 B4
Boakes Mdw TN14 . . . . . .75 B3
Boarley Ct ME14 . . . . .83 F1
Boarley La ME14 . . . . .83 F2
Boathouse Rd ME12 . . . . .27 F3
Bocking La TN5 . . . . .184 E4
Bockingford La ME15 . . . .115 F8
Bocton Ho ME17 . . . . . . .116 B3
Bodiam Cl ME8 . . . . .55 C3
Bodiam Ct ME16 . . . . .99 F3
Bodiam Rd TN18,TN32 . .195 B3
Bodkins Cl ME17 . . . . . . .116 D5
Bodle Ave DA10 . . . . .17 C1
Bodmin Dr BR5 . . . . .44 C1
Bodsham Cres ME15 . . . .101 B3
Boevey Path
  2 Bexley DA17 . . . . .13 F8
  Erith DA17 . . . . .3 F1
Bogarde Dr ME2 . . . . .39 B2
Bogey La BR6 . . . . .57 A3
Bognor Rd DA16 . . . . .13 D6
Boley Hill ME1 . . . . .53 C6
Boleyn Rd TN15 . . . . .76 E2
Boleyn Way DA10 . . . . . . .34 E8
Bolingbroke Ho ME16 . . . .99 E3
Bollon Ct 9 SE12 . . . . . . .28 B5
Bolner Cl ME5 . . . . .67 F2
Bombay Ho 1 ME15 . . . . .116 E5
Bombers La TN16 . . . . . . .89 D7
Bonar Pl BR7 . . . . .28 E1
Bonaventure Ct DA12 . . . .36 F4
Bonchester Cl BR7 . . . . . .29 A1
Bond Cl TN14 . . . . .74 D4
Bond Rd ME8 . . . . .69 E5
Bond St RM17 . . . . .18 C8
Bondfield Cl TN4 . . . . . . .143 A4
Bondfield Ho SE18 . . . . . .12 A7
Bondfield Rd
  East Malling ME19 . . . . . .97 F8
  4 Newham E6 . . . . .1 F8
Bondfield Wlk DA1 . . . . . .15 F4
Boneashe La TN15 . . . . . . .95 D6
Boneta Rd SE18 . . . . .1 F3
Bonflower La ME17 . . . . . .132 C7
Bonny Way BR8 . . . . .45 E6
Bonnington Gn ME8 . . . . .55 C3
Bonnington Rd ME14 . . . .100 C6
Bonnington Twr BR2 . . . . .42 E3

Ber – Bou 205

Boorman's Mews
  ME18 . . . . .113 E7
Booth Cl SE28 . . . . .3 B6
Booth Rd ME4 . . . . .53 F2
Bootham Ct ME2 . . . . .52 D5
Borden CE Prim Sch ME9 .71 F3
Bordyke TN9 . . . . .127 C2
Boreham Ave E16 . . . . .1 A7
Boresisle TN30 . . . . .183 B2
Borgard Ho SE18 . . . . . . .11 B1
Borgard Rd SE18 . . . . .1 F2
Borkwood Ct BR6 . . . . . . .57 F6
Borkwood Pk BR6 . . . . . . .57 F6
Borkwood Way BR6 . . . . . .57 F6
Borland Cl 5 DA9 . . . . . . .17 A2
Borough Green & Wrotham
  Sta TN15 . . . . .94 F7
Borough Green Prim Sch
  TN15 . . . . .95 A7
Borough Green Rd
  Borough Green TN15 . . . .94 E7
  Ightham TN15 . . . . .94 D6
  Wrotham TN15 . . . . .79 A1
Borough Rd
  Gillingham ME7 . . . . .54 D4
  Tatsfield TN16 . . . . .88 D6
Borstal HM Prison & Youth
  Custody Ctr ME1 . . . . . . .53 B1
Borstal Manor Com Sch
  ME1 . . . . .52 F2
Borstal Mews ME1 . . . . . .53 A3
Borstal Rd ME1 . . . . .53 B3
Borstal St ME1 . . . . .53 A2
Borton Cl ME18 . . . . .113 F1
Boscobel Cl BR1 . . . . .42 F7
Bostall Hill SE2 . . . . .3 B1
Bostall La SE2 . . . . .3 B1
Bostall Manorway SE2 . . . .3 B2
Bostall Park Ave DA7 . . . .13 C7
Bostall Rd BR5 . . . . .30 B1
Boston Gdns ME8 . . . . . . .55 C1
Boston Rd ME5 . . . . .68 C2
Bosville Ave TN13 . . . . . . .92 A4
Bosville Dr TN13 . . . . .92 A4
Bosville Rd TN13 . . . . . . .92 A4
Boswell Cl BR5 . . . . .44 C3
Boswell Ho BR2 . . . . .42 B4
Bosworth Ho 3 DA8 . . . . . .4 E1
Botany TN9 . . . . .127 C1
Botany Bay La BR7 . . . . . .43 C7
Botha Rd E13 . . . . .1 C8
Bothwell Cl 7 E16 . . . . . . .1 A8
Botsom La TN15 . . . . .61 D4
Bott Rd DA2 . . . . .32 F4
Bottle House Cotts
  TN11 . . . . .140 F1
Bottlescrew Hill ME17 . . .116 B4
Boucher Dr DA11 . . . . .35 F4
Bough Beech Nature Reserve
  Visitor Ctr★ TN14 . . . . .124 A7
Boughton Cl ME8 . . . . . . .55 B3
Boughton Ho BR1 . . . . . . .28 E1
Boughton La ME15 . . . . .116 B6
Boughton Monchelsea Prim
  Sch ME17 . . . . .116 B2
Boughton Par ME15 . . . .116 A7
Boughton Place Cotts
  ME17 . . . . .137 A8
Boughton Rd
  Sandway ME17 . . . . . . .120 B2
  Woolwich SE28 . . . . .2 E3
Boulevard The DA9 . . . . . .17 C3
Boulthurst Way RH8 . . . .104 B3
Boultwood Rd E6 . . . . .1 F7
Boundary Ho 4 DA11 . . . .35 A7
Boundary Rd
  Chatham ME1 . . . . .53 E3
  Royal Tunbridge Wells
  TN2 . . . . .159 D1
  Sidcup DA15 . . . . .12 E2
Boundary St 2 DA8 . . . . . .14 F7
Boundary The TN3 . . . . . .158 B3
Bounds Cross TN27 . . . . .167 F7
Bounds Oak Way TN4 . . .142 E3
Bounds The ME20 . . . . . . .82 C1
Bourchier Ct TN13 . . . . . .92 B1
Bourdillon Ct SE9 . . . . . . .28 E6
Bournbrook Rd SE3,SE9 . .11 D4
Bourne Cl TN9 . . . . .127 C2
Bourne Ct ME1 . . . . .53 D5
Bourne Ent Ctr TN15 . . . .95 A7
Bourne Grange La
  TN11 . . . . .128 D8
Bourne Ind Pk DA1 . . . . . .14 E2
Bourne La
  Cranbrook TN32 . . . . . .194 F1
  Plaxtol TN15 . . . . .94 F1
  Sandhurst Cross TN18 . . .195 E4
  Tonbridge TN9 . . . . .127 D3
Bourne Mead DA5 . . . . . .14 D2
Bourne Par DA5 . . . . .31 B8
Bourne Pl DA11 . . . . .128 F5
Bourne Place Mdws
  TN11 . . . . .126 A7
Bourne Rd
  Bexley DA1,DA5 . . . . . . .14 D2
  Bromley BR2 . . . . .42 D5
  Gravesend DA12 . . . . . . .36 F2
  Sidcup DA5 . . . . .31 B8
Bourne Row TN8 . . . . . . .140 D6
Bourne Vale Hayes BR2 . . .42 A2
  Plaxtol Spoute TN15 . . . .111 A8
Bourne Way Hayes BR2 . . .56 A8
  Swanley BR8 . . . . .45 C6
Bourner Cotts TN17 . . . .166 D4

Bourneside Terr ME17 ..102 D2
Bournewood Cl ME15 ..100 F1
Bournewood Rd
Orpington BR5 ...44 C2
Woolwich SE18,SE2 ...13 A7
Bournville Ave ME4 ...53 F1
Bovarde Ave ME19 ...97 C3
Bow Arrow La
Dartford DA2 ...16 A1
Dartford DA2 ...16 B1
Bow Hill ME18 ...113 D5
Bow Rd ME18 ...113 E7
Bow Terr ME18 ...113 E7
Bowater Pl SE3 ...11 B7
Bowater Rd SE18 ...1 D3
Bowen Rd TN4 ...158 B4
Bower Cl ME16 ...99 E4
Bower Gn ME5 ...68 C1
Bower Grove Sch ME16 ..99 B2
Bower La Eynsford DA4 ...60 F6
Maidstone ME16 ...99 E3
Bower Mount Rd ME16 ..99 D4
Bower Pl ME16 ...99 E3
Bower Rd BR8 ...32 A2
Bower St ME16 ...99 E4
Bower Terr ME16 ...99 E3
Bower Wlk TN12 ...149 E3
Bowers Ave DA11 ...35 F4
Bowers Ho ME7 ...54 E7
Bowers Rd TN14 ...75 F8
Bowers Wlk 1 E6 ...1 F7
Bowes Cl DA15 ...13 B1
Bowes Ct 24 DA2 ...16 B1
Bowes Rd ME2 ...53 B8
Bowes Wood DA3 ...62 F7
Bowesden La DA12 ...37 F1
Bowford Ave DA7 ...13 E6
Bowley La ME17 ...137 D8
Bowling Green Row 1
SE18 ...1 F2
Bowls Pl TN12 ...146 A7
Bowman Ave E16 ...1 A6
Bowman Cl ME5 ...68 C5
Bowmans Rd DA1 ...31 F8
Bowmead SE9 ...28 F6
Bown Cl RM18 ...19 B5
Bowness Rd DA7 ...14 B5
Bowyer Cl E6 ...1 F8
Bowzell Rd TN14 ...108 A2
Box Tree Wlk 26 BR5 ...44 D1
Boxgrove Prim Sch SE2 ..3 C3
Boxgrove Rd SE2 ...3 C3
Boxley Cl ME14 ...100 B8
Boxley Rd Chatham ME5 ..68 B2
Maidstone ME14 ...100 B7
Boxley St E16 ...1 B5
Boxmend Ind Est ME15 .116 F3
Boxshall Ho 7 SE18 ...12 B8
Boy Court La TN27 ...135 F1
Boyard Rd SE18 ...2 B1
Boyces Hill ME9 ...71 D6
Boyle Ho 12 DA17 ...4 A3
Boyle Way TN12 ...130 B7
Boyne Pk TN4 ...158 F4
Boyton Court Rd ME17 .135 A6
Brabourne Ave ME8 ...55 C3
Brabourne Cres DA7 ...13 F8
Bracken Cl Newham E6 ...1 F8
Royal Tunbridge Wells
TN2 ...159 E5
Bracken Hill ME5 ...68 A1
Bracken Lea ME5 ...54 C1
Bracken Rd TN2 ...159 E5
Bracken Wlk TN10 ...127 B6
Brackendene DA2,DA5 ...31 E4
Brackens The BR6 ...58 A5
Brackley Cl ME14 ...100 C5
Brackwood Cl ME8 ...69 D5
Bracondale Ave DA13 ...49 F8
Bracondale Rd SE2 ...3 A2
Bracton La DA2 ...31 F6
Bradbery Ct 3 DA11 ...35 F7
Bradbourne Ct TN13 ...92 B6
Bradbourne La ME20 ...82 B1
Bradbourne Park Rd
TN13 ...92 A4
Bradbourne Parkway
ME19 ...82 A1
Bradbourne Rd
Grays RM17 ...18 B8
Sevenoaks TN13 ...92 B5
Sidcup DA5 ...31 A8
Bradbourne Sch The
TN13 ...92 A6
Bradbourne Vale Rd
TN13,TN14 ...92 A5
Bradbury Ct 4 SE3 ...11 A7
Braddick Cl ME15 ...116 B6
Bradenham Ave DA16 ...13 A3
Bradfield Rd E16 ...1 B4
Bradfields Ave ME5 ...67 F5
Bradfields Ave W ME5 ...67 F5
Bradfields Sch ME5 ...68 A6
Bradford Cl BR2 ...42 F1
Bradford St TN9 ...127 B1
Bradfords Cl ME4 ...40 B2
Bradley Ho ME3 ...25 C4
Bradley Rd Ashurst TN3 .156 D5
Upper Halling ME2 ...65 E5
Bradley Stone Rd E6 ...1 F8
Bradymead E6 ...2 B7
Braeburn Way ME19 ...97 C3
Braemar Ave DA7 ...14 C3
Braemar Gdns DA15 ...29 D5
Braes The ME3 ...38 C3
Braeside Ave TN13 ...91 F3
Braeside Cl TN13 ...91 F4
Braeside Cres DA7 ...14 C3
Braesyde Cl DA17 ...3 F2
Braithwaite Ct ME7 ...55 A5
Brake Ave ME5 ...67 E5
Brakefield Rd DA13 ...35 B1
Brakes Pl TN15 ...61 E4
Bramber Ct 9 DA2 ...16 B1
Bramble Ave DA2 ...34 C5
Bramble Bank DA13 ...79 F7
Bramble Cl
Maidstone ME16 ...99 B3
Tonbridge TN11 ...126 F4
Bramble Croft DA8 ...4 C2
Bramble La TN13 ...108 B7
Bramble Reed La TN12 .161 B7
Bramble Wlk TN2 ...159 D7
Bramblebury Rd SE18 ...2 C1
Brambledown
Chatham ME5 ...68 B8
Hartley DA3 ...48 F5
Bramblefield Cl DA3 ...48 E6
Brambletree Cotts ME1 ..52 E2
Brambletree Cres ME1 ..52 F2
Bramdean Cres SE12 ...28 A7
Bramdean Gdns SE12 ...28 A7
Bramhope Ho 16 SE7 ...11 C8
Bramhope La SE7 ...11 B8
Bramis Ho TN16 ...72 D3
Bramley Cl Gillingham ME8 70 B8
Istead Rise DA13 ...35 F1
Newington ME9 ...71 A5
Orpington BR6 ...43 B1
Swanley BR8 ...45 E5
Bramley Cres ME15 ...100 F3
Bramley Ct Bexley DA16 ..13 B6
15 Erith DA17 ...4 A1
Marden TN12 ...148 B6
Bramley Dr TN17 ...179 D4
Bramley Gdns
Coxheath ME17 ...115 C3
Paddock Wood TN12 ...145 E7
Bramley Pl DA1 ...15 A3
Bramley Rd
East Peckham TN12 ...129 F6
Snodland ME6 ...82 A8
Bramley Rise ME2 ...52 E8
Bramley Way ME19 ...97 A2
Bramleys TN27 ...151 D5
Brampton Prim Sch DA7 13 D5
Brampton Rd DA7 ...13 E6
Bramshot Ave SE3,SE7 ..11 B8
Bramshott Cl ME16 ...99 C6
Branbridges Ind Est
TN12 ...130 A5
Branbridges Rd TN12 ..130 B4
Brandon Rd DA1 ...33 A8
Brandon St DA11 ...36 B8
Brandreth Rd E6 ...1 F7
Brands Hatch Circuit★
DA3 ...61 E6
Brands Hatch Cotts DA3 .62 A6
Brands Hatch Rd DA3 ...62 A7
Branham Ho 1 SE18 ...2 B1
Bransell Cl BR8 ...45 C3
Bransgore Cl ME8 ...69 D7
Branston Cres BR5 ...43 D1
Branstone Ct RM19 ...16 B8
Brantingham Cl TN9 ...142 F7
Branton Rd DA9 ...16 F1
Brantwood Ave DA8 ...14 C7
Brantwood Rd DA7 ...14 B4
Brantwood Way BR5 ...44 C6
Brasenose Rd ME7 ...54 E4
Brassey Cl RH8 ...104 A6
Brassey Dr ME20 ...98 D8
Brassey Hill RH8 ...104 A6
Brassey Rd RH8 ...104 A6
Brasted Cl Bexley DA6 ...13 D2
Orpington BR6 ...58 A8
Brasted Ct Brasted TN16 ..90 D2
Rochester ME2 ...39 A1
Brasted Hill TN14 ...90 A7
Brasted Hill Rd TN16 ...90 C5
Brasted La TN14 ...74 A1
Brasted Rd Erith DA8 ...14 E7
Westerham TN16 ...89 E1
Brattle Farm Mus★
TN12 ...149 D1
Brattle Wood TN13 ...108 C6
Braundton Ave DA15 ...29 F7
Braunstone Dr ME16 ...99 D7
Bray Gdns ME15 ...115 F5
Bray Pas E16 ...1 A6
Braywood Rd SE9 ...12 D3
Breach La ME9 ...70 F8
Breach Rd RM20 ...16 F8
Breakneck Hill DA9 ...17 B2
Breakspears Dr BR5 ...44 A8
Bream Cl ME20 ...82 A5
Breaside Prep Sch BR1 ..42 D8
Breckonmead BR1 ...42 C7
Brecon Ct 7 SE9 ...12 A1
Bredgar & Wormshill Light
Rly★ ME9 ...87 E1
Bredgar Cl ME14 ...100 C5
Bredgar Ho 1 BR5 ...44 D1
Bredgar Rd ME8 ...55 B4
Bredhurst CE Prim Sch
ME7 ...69 B1
Bredhurst Rd ME8 ...69 B4
Breedon Ave TN4 ...142 F1
Bremner Cl BR8 ...46 A5
Brenchley & Matfield CE
Prim Sch TN12 ...162 A8
Brenchley Ave DA11 ...36 B3
Brenchley Cl
Chislehurst BR7 ...43 A8
Rochester ME1 ...53 D2
Brenchley Rd
Gillingham ME8 ...55 B2
Horsmonden TN12 ...162 F6
Maidstone ME15 ...99 F2
Matfield TN12 ...161 F8
St Paul's Cray BR5 ...43 F7
Brenda Ct 4 DA14 ...30 A4
Brenda Terr DA10 ...34 E8
Brendon 16 DA14 ...30 A4
Brendon Ave ME5 ...68 A3
Brendon Cl Bexley DA8 ...14 E6
Royal Tunbridge Wells
TN2 ...159 D5
Brendon Rd SE9 ...29 D6
Brenley Gdns SE9 ...11 D3
Brennan Ct ME7 ...54 D6
Brennan Rd RM18 ...19 B5
Brent Cl Chatham ME5 ...67 E5
Dartford DA2 ...16 B1
Sidcup DA5 ...30 E7
Brent La DA1 ...33 A7
Brent Prim Sch The DA2 .33 C8
Brent Rd Newham E16 ...1 A8
Woolwich SE18 ...12 B7
Brent The Dartford DA1 ..33 B8
Tonbridge TN10 ...127 C6
Brent Way DA2 ...16 B1
Brentfield Rd DA1 ...33 B8
Brentlands Dr DA1 ...33 A7
Brentor Ct TN2 ...159 D6
Brentwood Cl SE9 ...29 C7
Brentwood Ho SE18 ...11 D7
Brenzett Cl ME5 ...68 B5
Brenzett Ho 6 BR5 ...44 C4
Bretaneby TN15 ...92 F6
Bretland Ct TN4 ...158 D4
Bretland Rd TN4 ...158 D4
Breton Rd ME1 ...53 C2
Brett Wlk ME8 ...69 D4
Brewer Rd ME3 ...39 B7
Brewer St
Lamberhurst TN3 ...176 A5
Maidstone ME14 ...100 A5
Brewers Field DA2 ...32 C4
Brewers Rd DA12 ...51 C8
Brewery La TN13 ...92 C2
Brewery Rd Orpington BR2 42 E1
Woolwich SE18 ...2 D1
Brewhouse Rd SE18 ...1 F2
Brewhouse Yd 15 DA12 ...19 B1
Brian Cres TN4 ...159 B8
Briar Cl Larkfield ME20 ..82 A2
8 Marlpit Hill TN8 ...122 D3
Briar Dale ME3 ...38 B4
Briar Fields ME14 ...100 E5
Briar Rd DA5 ...31 D5
Briar Wlk TN10 ...127 C6
Briars Cross RH8 ...104 D5
Briars The TN15 ...61 D4
Briars Way DA3 ...49 A4
Briarswood Way BR6 ...57 F5
Briary Ct DA14 ...30 B3
Briary Gdns BR1 ...28 B3
Brice Rd ME3 ...38 B3
Brick Ct RM17 ...18 A8
Brick Field View ME2 ...39 C1
Brick Kiln La
Horsmonden TN12 ...163 B2
Limpsfield RH8 ...104 C5
Ulcombe ME17 ...135 D5
Brickenden Rd TN17 ...179 D4
Brickfield Cotts SE18 ...12 F8
Brickfield Farm DA3 ...49 A6
Brickfield Farm Gdns
BR6 ...57 C6
Brickfields Pembury TN2 .160 E8
West Malling ME19 ...81 B1
Brickwell Cotts TN17 ..166 F6
Brickworks Cl TN9 ...143 B7
Bridewell La TN30 ...193 A7
Bridge Bsns Pk TN12 ..145 C7
Bridge Cl Dartford DA2 ...16 D4
Tonbridge TN9 ...143 C8
Bridge Cotts TN12 ...163 A6
Bridge Ct 28 Dartford DA2 16 B1
Grays RM17 ...18 B8
Bridge Ho Rochester ME1 .53 B4
Royal Tunbridge Wells
TN4 ...159 B5
Bridge Mill Way ME15 ..99 D2
Bridge Pl ME20 ...82 F2
Bridge Rd Bexley DA7 ...13 E5
Erith DA8 ...14 F6
Gillingham ME7 ...54 C7
Grays RM17 ...18 B8
Orpington BR5 ...44 B3
Rochester ME1 ...53 C2
Bridge St ME15 ...115 F5
Bridge View DA9 ...17 B3
Bridge View Ind Est
RM20 ...16 F8
Bridgeland Rd E16 ...1 A6
Bridgen Rd DA5 ...30 E8
Bridges Dr DA1 ...16 B2
Bridgeside Mews ME15 ..99 E2
Bridgewater Cl BR7 ...43 E6
Bridgewater Pl ME19 ...81 E2
Bridle Way BR6 ...57 C6
Bridlington Cl TN16 ...88 B8
Brier Cl ME5 ...68 C8
Bright Cl DA17 ...3 D2
Bright Ct 8 SE28 ...3 C5
Bright Rd 3 ME4 ...54 B2
Bright Ridge TN4 ...158 E8
Brightlands DA11 ...35 E4
Brigstock Rd DA17 ...4 B2
Brimp The ME3 ...9 D3
Brimpsfield Cl SE2 ...3 B3
Brimstone Cl BR6 ...58 C3
Brimstone Hill DA13 ...64 D8
Brindle Gate DA15 ...29 E7
Brindle Way ME5 ...68 C1
Brindle's Field TN9 ...143 A7
Brindley Cl DA7 ...14 B4
Brindley Way BR1 ...28 A3
Brinkburn Cl SE2 ...3 A2
Brinkers La TN5 ...185 A2
Brinklow Cres SE18 ...12 B7
Brionne Gdns TN9 ...143 D8
Brisbane Ho RM18 ...18 F6
Brisbane Rd ME4 ...54 A3
Briset Rd SE9 ...11 D3
Brishing Cl ME15 ...116 E5
Brishing La ME17 ...116 D4
Brishing Rd ME15,ME17 .116 F3
Brisley's Row ME1 ...66 F1
Brissenden Cl ME2 ...40 A3
Bristol Cl ME2 ...52 D5
Bristol Rd DA12 ...36 D5
Bristow Rd DA7 ...13 E6
Britannia Bsns Pk ME20 .98 E7
Britannia Cl Erith DA8 ...14 F8
Halling ME2 ...66 A4
Britannia Dr DA12 ...36 F3
Britannia Gate E16 ...1 A5
Britannia Rd ME3 ...24 A3
Britannia Village Prim Sch
E16 ...1 B5
Brittain Ct SE9 ...28 E7
Brittain Ho SE9 ...28 E7
Brittains La TN13 ...91 F2
Britten Cl TN10 ...127 F6
Brittenden Cl 1 BR6 ...57 F4
Brittenden Par BR6 ...57 F4
Britton St ME7 ...54 B5
Brixham Rd DA16 ...13 D6
Brixham St E16 ...2 A5
Broad Ditch Rd DA13 ...35 D1
Broad Gr TN2 ...159 A1
Broad La Dartford DA2 ...32 B4
Fordcombe TN3 ...157 A4
Broad Lawn SE9 ...29 A7
Broad Oak
Brenchley TN12 ...162 C8
Groombridge TN3 ...171 C6
Broad Oak Cl
Brenchley TN12 ...162 C8
Orpington BR5 ...44 A7
Royal Tunbridge Wells
TN2 ...158 F1
Broad Rd DA10 ...17 E1
Broad St ME17 ...134 E7
Broad Street Hill ME17 .102 D7
Broad View TN17 ...180 A8
Broad Wlk Eltham SE3,SE9 11 E5
Orpington BR6 ...58 D7
Sevenoaks TN15 ...108 E7
Broadbridge Cl SE3 ...11 A7
Broadcloth TN17 ...179 D3
Broadcroft TN2 ...172 F8
Broadcroft Rd BR5 ...43 D2
Broader La ME14 ...85 B2
Broadfield Rd ME15 ...116 A8
Broadgate Rd E16 ...1 D7
Broadheath Dr BR7 ...28 F3
Broadhoath TN15 ...93 E1
Broadlands Dr ME5 ...68 B4
Broadlands Rd BR1 ...28 B4
Broadmead TN2 ...172 F8
Broadmead Ave TN2 ...172 F8
Broadmere Terr ME16 ...99 D3
Broadoak ME19 ...81 E2
Broadoak Ave ME15 ...116 A8
Broadoak Cl DA4 ...33 A2
Broadoak Rd DA8 ...14 D7
Broadview DA13 ...63 F6
Broadview Ave ME8 ...69 E8
Broadwater Ct TN2 ...172 E8
Broadwater Down TN2 .172 F8
Broadwater Down Prim Sch
TN2 ...158 F1
Broadwater Forest La
TN3 ...172 B7
Broadwater Gdns BR6 ...57 C6
Broadwater Ho DA12 ...19 D1
Broadwater La
Royal Tunbridge Wells
TN2 ...172 F8
Royal Tunbridge Wells
TN2,TN4 ...158 F1
Broadwater Rd
East Malling ME19 ...97 D6
Woolwich SE28 ...2 D3
Broadwater Rise TN2 ..158 F1
Broadway Bexley DA6 ...13 F3
Bexley DA6 ...14 A3
Crockenhill BR8 ...45 C3
Gillingham ME8 ...55 A3
Grays RM17 ...18 C8
Limpsfield RH8 ...104 B5
Maidstone ME14 ...99 F4
Tilbury RM18 ...18 F5
Broadway Sh Ctr 5 DA6 .14 A3
Broadway Square Sh Ctr
DA6 ...14 A3
Broadway The
Hadlow TN11 ...128 E8
Lamberhurst TN3 ...176 B5
Broadwood DA11 ...36 B3
Broadwood Rd ME3 ...40 A4
Brock Rd E13 ...1 B8
Brockbank Cl ME5 ...68 A1
Brockdene Dr BR2 ...56 D6
Brockenhurst Ave ME15 100 C1
Brockenhurst Cl ME8 ...69 C7
Brocklebank Ho 7 E16 ..2 A5
Brocklebank Rd SE7 ...1 B2
Brocklebank Rd Ind Est
SE7 ...1 B2
Brockway TN15 ...95 A7
Brockwell Cl BR5 ...43 F4
Brodrick Gr SE2 ...3 B2
Brogden Cres ME17 ...117 F7
Broke Farm Dr BR6 ...58 C2
Brokes Way TN4 ...159 B8
Brome Ho SE18 ...11 E6
Brome Rd SE9 ...11 F4
Bromford Cl RH8 ...104 A2
Bromhedge SE9 ...28 F5
Bromholm Rd SE2 ...3 B3
Bromley RM17 ...17 F8
Bromley Cl ME5 ...68 B4
Bromley Coll 9 BR1 ...42 A8
Bromley Coll of F Ed & H Ed
(Old Town Hall) BR1 ...42 A7
Bromley Coll of F Ed & H Ed
(Rookery Lane Campus)
BR2 ...42 D3
Bromley Comm BR2 ...42 D3
Bromley High Sch BR1 ..43 A5
Bromley Ind Ctr BR1 ...42 D6
Bromley La BR7 ...29 D1
Bromley Manor Mans 3
BR2 ...42 A6
Bromley Mus★ BR6 ...44 B2
Bromley North Sta BR1 ..42 A8
Bromley Rd BR7 ...43 B8
Bromley South Sta BR1 ..42 A6
Bromley Valley Gymnastics
Ctr BR5 ...44 A7
Brompton Dr DA8 ...15 B7
Brompton Farm Rd ME2 .39 A2
Brompton Hill ME4 ...53 F6
Brompton La ME2 ...53 A8
Brompton Rd ME7 ...54 B6
Brompton-Westbrook Prim
Sch ME7 ...54 A5
Bronington Cl ME5 ...68 A5
Bronte Cl Erith DA8 ...14 B7
Lunsford ME20 ...81 F3
Tilbury RM18 ...19 C5
Bronte Gr DA1 ...15 F3
Bronte Sch DA11 ...36 A8
Bronte View DA12 ...36 C7
Bronze Age Way DA8,DA17 4 C3
Brook Cotts
Collier Street TN12 ...147 F8
East Farleigh ME15 ...115 C7
Brook Ct
1 Lewisham SE12 ...28 C5
10 Marlpit Hill TN8 ...122 D3
Brook Hill Cl SE18 ...2 B1
Brook La Bexley DA5 ...13 D2
Bromley BR1 ...28 A2
Greenwich SE3 ...11 B5
Plaxtol Spoute TN15 ...111 A8
Snodland ME6 ...82 A6
Tonbridge TN9 ...127 D2
Brook Pk DA1 ...33 A6
Brook Rd Lunsford ME20 ..81 F4
Northfleet DA11 ...35 E7
Royal Tunbridge Wells
TN2 ...159 D7
Swanley BR8 ...45 D7
Brook Sq SE18 ...11 E6
Brook St Erith DA8 ...14 B7
Snodland ME6 ...82 B8
Tonbridge TN9 ...143 A8
Brook The ME4 ...54 A4
Brook Vale DA8 ...14 B6
Brookbank ME14 ...100 A8
Brookdale Rd DA5 ...13 E1
Brookdene TN12 ...145 B7
Brookdene Rd SE18 ...2 F2
Brooke Dr DA12 ...37 B7
Brookend Rd DA15 ...29 E7
Brooker Cl ME17 ...116 D5
Brookes Pl ME9 ...71 B6
Brookfield Four Elms TN8 123 B5
Kemsing TN15 ...76 E2
Sandhurst TN18 ...196 B5
Brookfield Ave ME20 ...82 A4
Brookfield Ct TN4 ...143 A1
Brookfield Inf Sch ME20 .82 A2
Brookfield Jun Sch
ME20 ...82 A2
Brookfields TN11 ...111 E1
Brookhill Rd SE18 ...2 B1
Brookhurst Gdns TN4 ..142 E3
Brooklands Dartford DA1 .32 E7
Headcorn TN27 ...151 C6
Royal Tunbridge Wells
TN2 ...159 D7
Brooklands Ave DA15 ...29 D6
Brooklands Farm Cl
TN3 ...157 A6
Brooklands Pk SE3 ...11 A4
Brooklands Prim Sch
SE3 ...11 A4
Brooklands Rd ME20 ...82 A4
Brooklyn Paddock ME7 ..54 D6
Brooklyn Rd BR2 ...42 D4
Brooklyn Villas TN12 ..148 C5
Brookmead TN11 ...126 F4
Brookmead Ave BR1 ...42 F4
Brookmead Cl BR5 ...44 B3
Brookmead Rd ME3 ...39 B7
Brookmead Way BR5 ...44 B3
Brooks Cl Eltham SE9 ...29 A6
Staplehurst TN12 ...149 E4
Tonbridge TN10 ...127 E7

Brooks Pl ME14 100 A4
Brookside
Cranbrook TN17 179 D4
Hoo St Werburgh ME3 40 E5
Orpington BR6 43 F2
Brookside Rd DA13 35 F1
Brookvale Workshops DA11 35 C7
Brookway SE3 11 A4
Broom Ave BR5 44 B7
Broom Cl BR2 42 E3
Broom Hill Cotts TN5 187 B3
Broom Hill Rd ME2 52 F8
Broom La TN3 157 F1
Broom Mead DA6 14 A2
Broom Pk TN3 157 E3
Broomcroft Rd ME8 55 F2
Broomfield Ho 4 BR5 44 B7
Broomfield Rd
Bexley DA6 14 A2
Kingswood ME17 118 D4
Sevenoaks TN13 91 F5
Swanscombe DA10 17 E2
Broomfields DA3 48 E4
Broomhill Bank Sch TN3 158 C6
Broomhill Park Rd TN4 158 F8
Broomhill Rd
Dartford DA1 15 B1
Orpington BR6 44 A2
Royal Tunbridge Wells TN3 158 D7
Broomhill Rise DA6 14 A2
Broomhills DA13 34 E4
Broomlands La RH8 104 E8
Broomleigh 3 BR1 42 A8
Broomscroft Cotts ME18 97 C1
Broomshaw Rd ME16 98 F3
Broomsleigh TN16 72 E2
Broomwood Cl DA5 31 D6
Broomwood Rd BR5 44 B7
Brougham Ct 5 DA2 16 B1
Broughton Rd
Orpington BR6 57 D8
Otford TN14 76 A3
Brow Cl BR5 44 D2
Brow Cres BR5 44 D2
Brown Rd DA12 36 E7
Brown St ME8 55 F1
Browndens Rd ME2 65 E4
Brownelow Copse ME5 68 B1
Brownhill Cl ME5 68 A4
Browning Cl Bexley DA16 12 E6
6 Lunsford ME20 81 F4
Browning Rd DA1 15 F3
Browning Wlk RM18 19 C5
Brownings TN8 122 C4
Browns Sch BR6 58 F5
Brownspring Dr SE9 29 B5
Broxbourne Rd BR6 43 F2
Bruce Cl DA16 13 B6
Bruce Ct DA15 29 F4
Bruce Gr BR6 44 A1
Bruces Wharf Rd RM17 18 A8
Brucks The ME18 113 E7
Brummel Cl DA7 14 C4
Brunel Cl RM18 19 B4
Brunel Way ME4 54 A7
Brungers Wlk TN10 127 B5
Brunswick Cl DA6 13 D3
Brunswick House Prim Sch ME16 99 E5
Brunswick Rd DA6 13 E3
Brunswick St ME15 100 A3
Brunswick St E ME15 100 A3
Brunswick Terr TN1 159 A2
Brunswick Wlk 1 DA12 36 D8
Brushwood Lodge 1 DA17 4 A2
Bruton Cl BR7 28 F1
Bryanston Rd RM18 19 C5
Bryant Cl ME18 113 D6
Bryant Rd ME2 53 A7
Bryant St ME4 54 A3
Bryony Sch ME8 69 F5
Bubblestone Rd TN14 76 B3
Bubhurst La TN17 167 B7
Buckden Cl SE12 11 A1
Buckham Thorns Rd TN16 89 C1
Buckhole Farm Rd ME23 23 C4
Buckhurst Ave TN13 92 C2
Buckhurst La
Rockrobin TN5 184 A6
Sevenoaks TN13 92 C2
Buckhurst Pl TN5 184 A6
Buckhurst Rd TN16 89 B7
Buckingham Ave DA16 12 E3
Buckingham Cl BR5 43 E2
Buckingham Dr BR7 29 C3
Buckingham Rd
Gillingham ME7 54 D5
Northfleet DA11 35 D8
Royal Tunbridge Wells TN1 159 B2
Buckingham Row ME15 116 E7
Buckland Cl ME5 68 A2
Buckland Hill ME16 99 E5
Buckland La ME16 99 D6
Buckland Pl ME16 99 E4
Buckland Rd
Cliffe Woods ME3 39 A8
Luddesdown DA13 65 A7
Maidstone ME16 99 E4
Orpington BR6 57 E6
Buckler Gdns SE9 28 F5
Bucklers Cl TN2 159 C3
Buckles Ct DA17 3 D2
Buckley Cl DA1 14 F5
Bucks Cross Rd
Chelsfield BR6 58 E5
Northfleet DA11 35 F5
Buckthorn Ho DA15 29 F5
Buckwheat Ct DA18 3 D3
Budd Ho 4 SE7 1 C1
Budd's Farm Cotts TN30 199 E2
Budd's La TN30 199 F2
Budgin's Hill BR6 74 C8
Budleigh Cres DA16 13 C6
Bugglesden Rd TN27, TN30 182 D5
Bugsby's Way SE10,SE7 1 B2
Bull Alley DA16 13 B4
Bull Fields ME6 82 A8
Bull Hill Horton Kirby DA4 47 C5
Lenham ME17 137 F8
Bull La Chislehurst BR7 29 D1
Eccles ME20 82 F5
Lower Higham ME3 38 D7
Wrotham TN15 79 A3
Yelsted ME9 70 E2
Bull Lane Cotts
Hook Green TN3 175 C4
Yelsted ME9 70 E1
Bull Orch ME16 98 F2
Bull Rd ME19 81 C5
Bull Yd 6 DA11 19 B1
Bullace La 3 DA1 15 E1
Bullbanks Rd DA17 4 C2
Bulldog Rd ME5 68 B2
Bullen La TN12 129 E7
Buller Rd ME4 53 F2
Bullers Cl DA14 30 E3
Bullers Wood Dr BR7 28 F1
Bullers Wood Sch BR7 42 E8
Bullfinch Cl
Paddock Wood TN12 146 A5
Sevenoaks TN13 91 D5
Bullfinch Cnr TN13 91 E5
Bullfinch Dene TN13 91 D5
Bullfinch La TN13 91 E5
Bullingstone Cotts TN3 157 E7
Bullingstone La TN3 157 F7
Bullion Cl TN12 145 F6
Bullivant Cl 3 DA9 17 A2
Bulls Pl TN2 160 D6
Bulrush Cl ME5 67 F3
Bumbles Cl ME1 67 D7
Bunker's Hill Erith DA17 4 A2
New Ash Green TN15 63 B4
Bunkers Hill DA14 30 F5
Bunny La TN3 172 E5
Bunters Hill Rd ME3 39 B4
Bunton St SE18 2 A3
Burberry La ME17 118 B5
Burch Rd DA11 18 F1
Burcharbro Rd SE2 13 D8
Burdens TN27 151 D5
Burdett Ave DA12 37 F4
Burdett Cl DA14 30 E3
Burdett Rd TN4 158 B4
Burdock Ct ME16 99 A3
Burdock Ho 6 ME15 116 D8
Burford Rd BR1 42 E5
Burgate Cl DA1 14 F4
Burgess Hall Dr ME17 117 F6
Burgess Rd ME2 53 B7
Burgess Row 10 TN30 193 A7
Burghclere Dr ME16 99 B2
Burghfield Rd DA13 35 F1
Burgoyne Ct ME14 99 F7
Burham CE Prim Sch ME1 82 F8
Burham Rd ME1 66 E8
Burial Ground La ME15 99 E1
Burleigh Ave DA15 12 F2
Burleigh Cl ME2 52 E8
Burleigh Dr ME14 83 F1
Burley Rd E16 1 C8
Burlings La TN14 73 F2
Burlington Cl
6 Newham E6 1 E7
Orpington BR6 57 B8
Burlington Gdns ME8 69 E4
Burlington Lodge BR7 28 F1
Burma Way ME5 67 F6
Burman Cl DA2 33 C8
Burmarsh Cl ME5 68 B5
Burn's Rd ME7 54 C7
Burnaby Rd DA11 18 E1
Burnell Ave DA16 13 A5
Burnett Rd DA8 15 D8
Burnham Cres DA1 15 C3
Burnham Rd Dartford DA1 15 C3
Sidcup DA14 30 E6
Burnham Trad Est DA1 15 D3
Burnham Wlk ME8 69 E3
Burnley Rd RM20 17 A6
Burns Ave DA15 13 B1
Burns Cl Bexley DA16 12 F6
Erith DA8 14 F6
Burns Cres TN9 143 A7
Burns Ho DA16 13 C6
Burns Pl RM18 19 B6
Burns Rd ME16 99 C2
Burnt Ash Hill SE12 28 A7
Burnt Ash Hts BR1 28 B3
Burnt Ash La BR1,SE12 28 B3
Burnt Ash Prim Sch BR1 28 A3
Burnt House Cl
Rochester ME2 39 C2
Sandhurst TN18 196 C5
Burnt House La
Dartford DA1 32 F5
Hawley DA2 32 F4
Langton Green TN3 158 A5
Burnt Lodge La TN5 186 B2
Burnt Oak Jun Sch DA15 30 A7
Burnt Oak La DA15 13 A1
Burnt Oak Terr ME7 54 D6
Burntash Rd ME20 98 F8
Burnthouse La TN27 152 D1
Burntwood Gr TN13 108 B8
Burntwood Rd TN13 108 B7
Burr Bank Terr DA2 32 C4
Burr Cl DA7 13 F4
Burrage Gr SE18 2 C2
Burrage Pl SE18 2 B1
Burrage Rd SE18 2 C1
Burrard Rd E16 1 B7
Burrfield Dr BR5 44 D4
Burritt Mews ME1 53 C3
Burrows La ME3 25 C3
Burrs Hill Cotts TN12 162 D6
Burrswood Villas TN3 171 B7
Bursdon Cl DA15 29 F6
Burslem Rd TN2 159 E7
Bursted Wood Prim Sch DA7 14 B5
Burston Rd ME17 115 B2
Burt Rd E16 1 C5
Burton Cl ME3 39 C3
Burts Wharf DA17 4 C5
Burwash Ct BR5 44 C4
Burwash Rd SE18 2 D1
Burwood Ave BR2 56 B8
Burwood Ho TN2 159 E5
Burwood Sch BR6 58 D8
Bus Bridge Rd ME15 115 E6
Busbridge Rd ME6 81 E7
Bush Cl ME9 87 F5
Bush Rd Cuxton ME2 52 B2
East Peckham TN12 129 E8
Bush Row ME20 83 A3
Bushell Way BR7 29 A3
Bushey Ave BR5 43 D2
Bushey Ct DA8 15 A6
Bushey Ho SE9 28 C5
Bushey Lees DA15 12 F1
Bushfield Wlk DA10 34 E8
Bushmeadow Rd ME8 55 F2
Bushmoor Cres SE18 12 B6
Bushy Gill TN3 158 A3
Bushy Gr ME17 118 D2
Business Acad Bexley Prim Section The DA18 3 E4
Buston Manor Farm Cotts ME18 114 B2
Busty La TN15 94 D6
Butcher Cl TN12 149 E3
Butcher Wlk DA10 34 E8
Butcher's La ME19 96 D1
Butchers La TN15 62 D8
Butchers Rd E16 1 A7
Butchers Yd BR6 73 A8
Butler Ho 9 RM17 18 B8
Butler's Cotts DA7 14 A5
Butler's Pl DA3 62 E7
Butt Green La ME17 133 A7
Butt Haw Cl ME3 40 E5
Buttercup Cl TN12 146 A5
Butterfield Sq 10 E6 1 F7
Butterfly Ave DA1 32 F6
Butterfly La SE9 12 B1
Buttermere Cl ME7 55 A5
Buttermere Rd BR5 44 D5
Buttmarsh Cl SE18 2 B1
Button Dr ME3 25 C5
Button Ho ME3 39 F6
Button La ME15 101 B2
Button St BR8,DA4 46 C5
Butts La TN5 185 C7
Butts The TN14 76 B2
Buttway La ME3 22 A6
Buxton Cl Chatham ME5 68 D1
Loose ME15 116 A8
Buxton Rd DA8 14 D7
Buzzard Creek Ind Est IG11 3 A8
Bychurch Pl 7 ME15 100 A3
Bycliffe Mews 2 DA11 35 F8
Bycliffe Terr 3 DA11 35 F8
Byland Cl SE2 3 B3
Byng Rd TN4 158 F5
Bynon Ave DA7 13 F4
Byrneside TN11 126 E4
Byron Cl SE28 3 C5
Byron Dr DA8 14 B7
Byron Gdns RM18 19 C6
Byron Prim Sch ME7 54 C3
Byron Rd Dartford DA1 16 B3
Gillingham ME7 54 C3
Maidstone ME14 100 B7
Bywater Ho SE18 1 E3

C

C M Booth Collection of Historic Vehicles (Mus)★ TN17 191 E4
Cabbage Stalk La TN4 158 E2
Cables Cl DA8 4 C3
Cacket's La TN14 73 E4
Cade La TN13 108 C7
Cadlocks Hill TN14 58 F1
Cadnam Cl ME2 52 E8
Cadogan Ave DA2 33 D8
Cadogan Gdns 6 TN1 159 B4
Cadogan Rd SE18 2 C3
Cadwallon Rd SE9 29 C6
Caerleon Cl DA14 30 C3
Caerleon Terr SE2 3 B2
Caernarvon Ct Erith DA8 14 D7
Caernarvon Ct *continued*
12 Orpington BR5 44 C6
Caernarvon Dr ME15 99 F1
Cage Green Prim Sch TN10 127 D5
Cage Green Rd TN10 127 C5
Cage La TN27 152 F1
Cagney Cl ME3 39 C3
Cairns Cl DA1 15 D2
Cairns Mews SE18 11 E6
Caistor Rd TN9 127 A1
Caithness Gdns DA15 12 F1
Calais Cotts DA3 62 A8
Calcott Wlk SE9 28 D4
Calcroft Ave DA9 17 C2
Calcutta Ho 3 ME15 116 E5
Calcutta Rd RM18 19 A5
Calder Rd ME14 99 E7
Calderwood DA12 36 E2
Calderwood St SE18 2 A2
Caldew Ave ME8 55 C1
Caldy Rd DA17 4 B3
Caledonian Ct ME8 69 E8
Calehill Cl ME14 100 C6
Caley Rd TN2 159 D7
Calfstock La DA4 46 F5
California Row TN12 150 C6
Caling Croft DA3 48 F1
Caliph Cl DA12 36 F5
Callams Cl ME8 69 D6
Callaways La ME9 71 B6
Callis Way ME8 69 D5
Callisto Ct ME16 99 D3
Calshot Ct 17 DA2 16 B1
Calverley Ct TN1 159 C3
Calverley Park Cres 1 TN1 159 B3
Calverley Park Gdns TN1 159 C4
Calverley Pk TN1 159 B3
Calverley Rd
Royal Tunbridge Wells TN1 159 B3
Royal Tunbridge Wells TN1 159 B4
Calverley St TN1 159 B4
Calvert Cl Erith DA17 4 B2
Sidcup DA14 30 E2
Calvert Dr DA2 31 D6
Calverton Prim Sch E16 1 D7
Calvin Cl BR5 44 D6
Calydon Rd SE7 1 B1
Cambert Way SE3 11 B3
Camberwell La TN14 106 F4
Camborne Manor 2 ME7 54 C6
Camborne Rd Bexley DA16 12 F5
Sidcup DA14 30 C5
Cambray Rd BR6 43 F2
Cambria Ave ME1 52 F2
Cambria Cl DA15 29 E7
Cambria Cres DA12 36 F4
Cambria Ho 2 DA8 14 E7
Cambrian Gr DA11 36 A8
Cambrian Rd TN4 159 C7
Cambridge Ave DA16 12 F3
Cambridge Barracks Rd 5 SE18 1 F2
Cambridge Cres ME15 116 D7
Cambridge Dr SE12 11 A2
Cambridge Gdns TN2 159 B2
Cambridge Gn SE9 29 B7
Cambridge Ho 7 SE18 1 F2
Cambridge Rd
Bromley BR1 28 A1
Gillingham ME8 69 C6
Rochester ME2 53 A8
Sidcup DA14 29 E4
Cambridge Row SE18 2 B1
Cambridge St TN2 159 C3
Cambridge Terr 1 ME4 53 F4
Cambus Rd E16 1 A8
Camdale Rd SE18 12 F7
Camden Ave TN2 160 C6
Camden Cl Chatham ME5 68 B5
Chislehurst BR7 43 C8
Northfleet DA11 35 C7
Camden Cotts TN17 179 F8
Camden Ct 10 Erith DA17 4 A1
Pembury TN2 160 D6
2 Royal Tunbridge Wells TN1 159 B4
Camden Gr BR7 29 B2
Camden Hill TN2 159 B3
Camden Park Rd BR7 29 A1
Camden Pk TN2 159 C2
Camden Rd
Gillingham ME7 54 D7
Royal Tunbridge Wells TN1 159 B4
Sevenoaks TN13 92 B5
Sidcup DA5 30 F8
Camden St ME14 100 A5
Camden Terr Seal TN15 92 F6
Sissinghurst TN17 179 F8
Camden Way BR7 29 A1
Camel Rd E16 1 E5
Camellia Cl ME8 69 D7
Camelot Cl
Biggin Hill TN16 72 C3
Woolwich SE28 2 D4
Camer Gdns DA13 50 C3
Camer Park Ctry Pk★ DA13 50 C2
Camer Park Rd DA13 50 C2
Camer Rd DA13 50 C3
Camer St DA13 50 C3
Cameron Cl Chatham ME5 68 B8
Cameron Cl *continued*
Joyden's Wood DA5 31 E5
Cameron Rd BR2 42 A4
Cameron Terr 10 SE12 28 B5
Camerons 4 TN18 189 A2
Camomile Dr ME14 100 F5
Camp Hill TN11 125 A3
Camp Hill Cotts TN11 124 F2
Camp Site The DA14 31 A1
Camp Way ME15 116 C6
Campbell Cl SE18 12 A6
Campbell Ho ME3 39 F6
Campbell Rd
Maidstone ME15 100 A3
Northfleet DA11 35 F8
Royal Tunbridge Wells TN4 159 A6
Camperdown Manor 5 ME7 54 A6
Campfield Rd SE9 28 D8
Campion Cl Chatham ME5 67 E3
Newham E6 1 F6
Northfleet DA11 35 E4
Campion Cres TN17 179 A2
Campion Ct 6 RM17 18 D8
Campion Pl SE28 3 B5
Campleshon Rd ME8 69 D5
Campus Way ME8 69 A8
Camrose Ave DA8 14 B8
Camrose St SE2 3 A2
Canada Farm Rd DA4 48 A6
Canada Rd DA8 15 B7
Canada Terr 3 ME14 100 A7
Canadian Ave ME7 54 F4
Canal Basin DA12 19 D1
Canal Rd Gravesend DA12 19 D1
Higham ME3 38 C8
Rochester ME2 53 C7
Canal Road Ind Pk 2 DA12 36 D8
Canberra Rd Bexley DA7 13 D8
Greenwich SE7 11 D8
Canberra Sq RM18 19 A5
Canbury Path BR5 44 A5
Canning St ME14 100 A6
Cannon Bridge Works TN9 127 D2
Cannon La TN9 127 D2
Cannon Pl SE7 1 E1
Cannon Rd DA7 13 F6
Canon Cl ME1 53 B2
Canon La ME18 97 C1
Canon Rd BR1 42 D6
Cansiron La TN7,TN8 154 E2
Canterbury Ave DA15 30 C6
Canterbury Cl
Dartford DA1 33 A8
7 Newham E6 1 F7
Canterbury Cres TN10 127 D5
Canterbury Ct 7 SE12 28 B5
Canterbury Ho
6 Erith DA8 14 F7
2 Maidstone ME15 116 D7
Canterbury Rd
Gravesend DA12 36 C6
Pembury TN2 160 E6
Canterbury St ME7 54 C4
Canterbury Way DA1,DA2, RM20 16 D5
Cantwell Ho SE18 12 B7
Cantwell Rd SE18 12 B7
Capability Way DA9 17 C3
Capel Cl Gillingham ME8 69 D4
Orpington BR2 42 E1
Capel Pl DA2 32 C4
Capel Prim Sch TN12 144 F7
Capelands DA3 63 A8
Capell Cl ME17 115 C3
Capella Ho 1 SE7 11 B8
Capetown Ho 1 ME15 116 F5
Capital Ind Est DA17 4 B3
Capstan Ct DA2 16 C3
Capstan Ctr RM18 18 D7
Capstan Mews 4 DA11 35 E8
Capstone Farm Ctry Pk★ ME7 68 D5
Capstone Rd
Chatham ME5 54 D1
Gillingham ME7 68 F6
Lewisham BR1 28 A4
Captain's Cl ME17 134 E6
Capulet Mews E16 1 A5
Caraway Cl E13 1 B8
Cardens Rd ME3 39 B8
Cardiff St SE18 12 E7
Cardigan Cl ME23 23 F3
Cardinal Cl
Chislehurst BR7 43 D8
Tonbridge TN9 143 D8
Cardinal Wlk ME18 97 C3
Cardwell Prim Sch SE18 1 F2
Carew Ho 18 SE18 1 F2
Carey Ct DA6 14 B2
Carey's Field TN13 91 E7
Caring La ME14,ME17 101 E1
Caring Rd ME15,ME17 101 C1
Carisbrooke Ave DA5 30 D7
Carisbrooke Ct
23 Dartford DA2 16 B1
20 Sidcup DA14 30 A4
Carisbrooke Dr ME16 99 D4
Carisbrooke Rd
Bromley BR2 42 C5
Rochester ME2 38 E1
Carl Ekman Ho DA11 35 D8

Carleton Pl DA4 . . . . . .**47** C5
Carleton Rd DA1 . . . . . .**33** A8
Carlisle Cl ME2 . . . .**52** C6
Carlisle Rd DA1 . . . . . .**16** A1
Carlton Ave
　Gillingham ME7 . . . .**54** E4
　Stone DA9 . . . .**16** E1
Carlton Cl Kings Hill ME18 .**97** B3
　Tonbridge TN10 . . . .**127** E7
Carlton Cres
　Chatham ME5 . . . .**68** D8
　Royal Tunbridge Wells
　TN1 . . . .**159** C4
Carlton Gdns ME15 . . . .**116** B8
Carlton Gn DA14 . . . .**29** F4
Carlton Par BR5 . . . .**44** B7
Carlton Rd Bexley DA16 . .**13** B4
　Erith DA8 . . . .**14** C8
　Royal Tunbridge Wells
　TN1 . . . .**159** C4
　Sidcup DA14 . . . .**29** F3
Carlyle Ave BR1 . . . .**42** D6
Carlyle Rd SE28 . . . .**3** C6
Carman's Cl ME15,ME17 .**115** F3
Carmelite Way DA3 . . . . . .**48** F4
Carnation Cl ◼1 ME19 . . . .**82** A1
Carnation Cres ME19 . . . . .**81** F1
Carnation Rd ME2 . . . .**52** D7
Carnation St SE2 . . . .**3** B1
Carnbrook Rd SE3 . . . . . .**11** D4
Carnecke Gdns SE9 . . . . .**11** E2
Carnet Cl DA1 . . . .**31** E8
Carnoustie Cl SE28 . . . .**3** D7
Caroline Cres ME16 . . . . .**99** D7
Carolyn Dr BR6 . . . .**58** A7
Carp Cl ME20 . . . .**82** A4
Carpeaux Cl ME4 . . . .**54** A4
Carpenters Cl ME1 . . . . . .**53** E2
Carpenters Ct BR1 . . . .**42** D7
Carpenters La
　Hadlow TN11 . . . .**111** D2
　Staplehurst TN12 . . . . . .**149** C8
Carpinus Cl ME5 . . . .**68** B1
Carr Gr SE18 . . . .**1** E2
Carr Ho DA1 . . . .**14** E2
Carrack Ho ◼1 DA8 . . . .**4** E1
Carriageway The TN16 . . . .**90** D3
Carrick Dr TN13 . . . .**92** B4
Carrie Ho ◼3 ME16 . . . . . .**99** E5
Carriers Pl TN3 . . . .**156** B4
Carriers Rd TN17 . . . .**179** D5
Carrill Way DA17 . . . .**3** D3
Carrington DA14 . . . .**30** A3
Carrington Cl ME7 . . . .**54** F6
Carrington Rd DA1 . . . . . .**16** A1
Carroll Cl ME2 . . . .**66** A4
Carroll Gdns ME20 . . . . . .**81** F3
Carronade Pl SE28 . . . .**2** D3
Carsington Gdns DA1 . . . .**32** D6
Carson Rd E16 . . . .**1** A8
Carston Cl SE12 . . . .**11** A2
Carter's Hill Bromley SE9 .**28** C7
　Underriver TN15 . . . .**109** B6
Carters Hill Cl SE9 . . . . . .**28** C7
Carters Hill La DA3 . . . . . .**63** F2
Carters Row DA11 . . . .**35** F6
Cartmel Rd DA7 . . . .**14** A6
Carton Cl ME1 . . . .**53** D2
Carton Rd ME3 . . . .**38** B3
Carville Ave TN4 . . . .**142** F1
Carvoran Way ME8 . . . . . .**69** C5
Cascade Cl BR5 . . . .**44** C6
Caspian Way DA10 . . . . . .**17** E2
Caspian Wlk E16 . . . .**1** D7
Cassilda Rd SE2 . . . .**3** A2
Casstine Cl BR8 . . . .**31** F1
Castalia Ct DA1 . . . .**15** F4
Casterbridge Rd SE3 . . . . .**11** A4
Castfield Cl ME3 . . . .**22** E1
Castile Rd ◼12 SE18 . . . .**2** A2
Castilion Prim Sch SE28 . . .**3** C7
Castle Ave ME1 . . . .**53** C4
Castle Dene ME14 . . . .**99** F8
Castle Dr TN15 . . . .**76** E2
Castle Farm Cotts TN11 **128** F8
Castle Farm Rd TN14 . . . . .**60** A3
Castle Fields TN9 . . . .**127** B2
Castle Hill Hartley DA3 . . .**48** E4
　Rochester ME1 . . . .**53** C6
　Thurnham ME14 . . . .**85** D1
　Tonbridge TN11 . . . .**143** F5
Castle Hill Ct ME1 . . . .**53** C6
Castle Hurst TN32 . . . . . .**195** B1
Castle La DA12 . . . .**37** B6
Castle Rd Chatham ME4 . . .**54** B2
　Eynsford DA4 . . . .**60** C5
　Grays RM17 . . . .**17** F8
　Maidstone ME16 . . . .**99** D7
　Royal Tunbridge Wells
　TN4 . . . .**159** A3
　Swanscombe DA10 . . . . . .**17** F1
Castle St Rochester ME2 . .**39** E1
　◼2 Royal Tunbridge
　Wells,Mount Sion TN1 . .**159** A2
　◼2 Royal Tunbridge
　Wells,Southborough TN4 .**142** F2
　Stone DA9 . . . .**17** A2
　Swanscombe DA10 . . . . . .**17** F1
　Tonbridge TN9 . . . .**127** C2
　Wouldham ME1 . . . .**66** C4
Castle Terr Hadlow TN11 .**128** E8
　Hawkhurst TN18 . . . .**188** F3
Castle View Bsns Ctr
　ME1 . . . .**53** C6
Castle View Mews ME1 . .**53** C6

Castle View Rd ME2 . . . . .**53** A7
Castle Way ME19 . . . .**81** D2
Castle Wlk TN5 . . . .**184** E4
Castlecombe Prim Sch
　SE9 . . . .**28** E3
Castlecombe Rd SE9 . . . . .**28** E4
Castlefields DA13 . . . .**49** F8
Castleford Ave SE9 . . . . . .**29** B7
Castlemaine Ave ME7 . . .**54** F6
Castleton Ave DA7 . . . . . .**14** D5
Castleton Rd SE9 . . . .**28** D4
Castlewood Day Hospl
　SE18 . . . .**12** A6
Castlewood Dr SE9 . . . . . .**11** F5
Castweazle TN30 . . . .**192** E6
Caterfield La RH7,RH8 . .**121** A5
Cates Ct TN12 . . . .**130** A7
Cathcart Dr BR6 . . . .**43** E1
Catherine Cl ME16 . . . . . .**99** A3
Catherine of Aragon Ct
　DA15 . . . .**29** D8
Catherine Pl ◼7 TN1 . . . .**159** B4
Catherine St ME1 . . . .**53** D3
Catkin Cl ME5 . . . .**67** F1
Catlyn Cl ME19 . . . .**98** A8
Catterick Rd ME5 . . . .**68** D2
Cattistock Rd SE9 . . . .**28** F3
Catts Pl TN12 . . . .**146** C4
Caulkers Ho ◼7 ME4 . . . . .**54** B2
Causton Rd TN17 . . . .**179** C5
Cavalry Cl TN10 . . . .**127** E7
Cave Hill ME15 . . . .**99** F1
Cavell Cres DA1 . . . .**16** A3
Cavendish Ave
　Bexley DA16 . . . .**12** F4
　Erith DA8 . . . .**14** C8
　Gillingham ME7 . . . .**54** E6
　Sevenoaks TN13 . . . .**92** A5
　Sidcup DA15 . . . .**30** A8
Cavendish Cl TN10 . . . . .**127** D7
Cavendish Ct TN9 . . . . . .**127** D3
Cavendish Dr TN2 . . . . . .**159** B1
Cavendish Rd ME1 . . . .**53** D3
Cavendish Sq DA3 . . . .**48** D6
Cavendish Way ME15 . . .**101** B3
Caversham Cl ME8 . . . . . .**55** F1
Caveside Cl BR7 . . . .**43** A8
Caxton Cl Hartley DA3 . . .**48** F5
　Tenterden TN30 . . . .**192** F7
Caxton Ho RH8 . . . .**104** F3
Caxton La Hadlow TN11 . .**128** E8
　The Chart RH8 . . . .**104** E4
Cayser Dr ME17 . . . .**118** E2
Caysers Croft TN12 . . . . .**129** E6
Cazeneuve St ME1 . . . . . .**53** C5
Cecil Ave Gillingham ME8 .**55** A2
　Rochester ME2 . . . .**53** B8
Cecil Burns Lodge TN2 .**159** D2
Cecil Kidby Ho TN2 . . . . .**159** F6
Cecil Rd Northfleet DA11 . .**35** F7
　Rochester ME1 . . . .**53** C3
Cecil Road Prim Sch
　DA11 . . . .**35** F7
Cecil Way BR2 . . . .**42** A1
Cedar Ave
　Gravesend DA12 . . . .**36** C4
　Sidcup DA15 . . . .**30** A8
Cedar Cl Ditton ME20 . . . .**98** D8
　Meopham Sta DA13 . . . . .**50** A3
　Orpington BR2 . . . .**56** E7
　Swanley BR8 . . . .**45** C7
Cedar Copse BR1 . . . .**42** F7
Cedar Cres Orpington BR2 .**56** E7
　Tonbridge TN10 . . . .**127** C7
Cedar Ct Eltham SE9 . . . . .**11** E1
　◼21 Greenwich SE7 . . . . . .**11** C8
　Maidstone ME14 . . . . . .**100** B5
　Royal Tunbridge Wells
　TN4 . . . .**159** A5
　◼12 Tenterden TN30 . . . .**193** A7
Cedar Dr Edenbridge TN8 **122** B2
　Maidstone ME16 . . . .**98** E2
　Sutton at H DA4 . . . .**47** B7
Cedar Gdns ME9 . . . .**86** E8
Cedar Gr Gillingham ME7 . .**69** A5
　Sidcup DA15 . . . .**13** D1
Cedar Ho TN4 . . . .**158** E4
Cedar La TN27 . . . .**182** D7
Cedar Lodge TN4 . . . . . .**158** F3
Cedar Mount SE9 . . . .**28** D7
Cedar Pl ◼3 SE7 . . . .**1** C1
Cedar Rd Bromley BR1 . . . .**42** C7
　Dartford DA1 . . . .**32** D7
　Erith DA8 . . . .**15** A6
　Hoo St Werburgh ME3 . . .**40** E3
　Rochester ME2 . . . .**52** F6
Cedar Ridge TN2 . . . .**159** D5
Cedar Terrace Rd TN13 . .**92** A1
Cedarhurst Cotts ◼5 DA5 .**31** A8
Cedarhurst Dr SE9 . . . . . .**11** C2
Cedarmore Ct BR7 . . . . . .**43** D8
Cedars PRU The ME16 . . .**99** D4
Cedars Sch The ME1 . . . . .**53** C4
Cedars The TN12 . . . .**146** A4
Cedarwood Ho ME15 . . . .**115** B6
Cedric Rd SE9 . . . .**29** C5
Celandine Dr SE28 . . . .**3** B5
Celestine Cl ME5 . . . .**68** A1
Cement Block Cotts ◼8
　RM17 . . . .**18** C8
Cement Industry Heritage
　Ctr★ DA11 . . . .**18** B2
Cemetery La
　Hadlow TN11 . . . .**112** A1
　Woolwich SE7 . . . .**11** E8
Cemetery Rd Halling ME2 .**66** A4
　Snodland ME6 . . . .**65** F1
　Woolwich SE7 . . . .**13** B7

Centenary Ct DA4 . . . .**47** A2
Central Ave Bexley DA16 . .**13** A5
　Chatham ME4 . . . .**54** B8
　Gravesend DA12 . . . .**36** B5
　Tilbury RM18 . . . .**19** A6
Central Bsns Pk ME2 . . . . .**53** E7
Central Ct ◼3 SE18 . . . .**2** B2
Central Lodge TN15 . . . . .**79** E6
Central Par
　Rochester ME1 . . . .**53** D2
　Sidcup DA15 . . . .**30** A5
　Wadhurst TN5 . . . .**184** F4
Central Par Villas BR5 . . . .**44** C7
Central Park Gdns ME4 . . .**54** B8
Central Rd Dartford DA1 . .**15** E2
　New Hythe ME20 . . . .**82** B4
　Rochester ME2 . . . .**53** A7
Central Terr ME3 . . . .**39** F6
Central Way SE28 . . . .**3** B5
Centre 2000 ME16 . . . . . .**99** C8
Centre Common Rd BR7 . .**37** C1
Centre Ct ME2 . . . .**53** E7
Centre Rd DA3 . . . .**62** E7
Centurion Way DA18 . . . . .**4** A1
Centurion Cl ME8 . . . .**54** F1
Century Ct ME1 . . . .**53** C5
Century Rd ME8 . . . .**69** D8
Ceres Rd SE18 . . . .**2** F1
Cerne Rd DA12 . . . .**36** E5
Cervia Way DA12 . . . .**36** F5
Chada Ave ME7 . . . .**54** E3
Chadd Dr BR1 . . . .**42** E6
Chadfields RM18 . . . .**19** A7
Chadwell Hill RM17 . . . . . .**19** A8
Chadwick Cl DA11 . . . .**35** E5
Chadwick Ct
　◼2 Dartford DA1 . . . .**15** D1
　◼4 Woolwich SE28 . . . .**3** B5
Chadwick Way SE28 . . . .**3** D6
Chadwin Rd E13 . . . .**1** B8
Chaffey Ho ◼6 SE7 . . . .**1** C1
Chaffinch Cl ME5 . . . .**68** A7
Chaffinch Way TN12 . . . .**146** A5
Chafford Cotts TN3 . . . . .**156** F5
Chafford La TN3 . . . .**156** F5
Chain Gate ME17 . . . .**137** A8
Chalcombe Rd SE2 . . . .**3** B3
Chalet Cl DA5 . . . .**31** D4
Chalfont Ct ◼3 DA17 . . . . . .**4** A1
Chalfont Dr ME8 . . . .**69** D6
Chalgrove Mews ME2 . . . .**66** A5
Chalice Way DA9 . . . .**16** F2
Chalk Ave TN30 . . . .**183** B2
Chalk Ct RM17 . . . .**18** A8
Chalk La TN17 . . . .**178** E7
Chalk Pit Ave BR5 . . . .**44** D6
Chalk Pit Hill ME4 . . . .**54** A3
Chalk Rd Chalk DA12 . . . . .**37** A6
　Lower Higham ME3 . . . . . .**38** C6
　Newham E13 . . . .**1** C8
Chalkenden Ave ME8 . . . . .**55** A2
Chalkers Way ME8 . . . .**55** B4
Chalkstone Cl DA16 . . . . . .**13** A6
Chalkways TN15 . . . .**76** F3
Chalky Bank DA11 . . . .**36** A3
Chalky Bank Rd ME8 . . . . .**55** F2
Chalky Rd ME9 . . . .**86** C6
Challenge Cl DA12 . . . .**36** F4
Challenger Cl TN12 . . . . .**145** F6
Challock Cl TN16 . . . .**72** C3
Challock Ho ◼3 Erith DA8 . . .**7** E7
　◼3 Orpington BR5 . . . .**44** D1
Challock Wlk ME14 . . . . .**100** C6
Chalmers Way ME1 . . . . . .**34** B1
Chamberlain Ave ME16 . . .**99** C2
Chamberlain Cl ◼5 SE28 . . .**2** D3
Chamberlain Rd ME4 . . . . .**54** B2
Chambers Cl ◼2 DA9 . . . . .**17** A2
Chancel Cl TN15 . . . .**61** E3
Chancellor Ho ME4 . . . . .**158** F3
Chancellor Way TN13 . . . .**92** A5
Chancelot Rd SE2 . . . .**3** B2
Chancery Ct DA1 . . . .**33** A7
Chancery La ME15 . . . . . .**100** B3
Chancery Rd ME3 . . . .**22** B5
Chanctonbury Cl SE9 . . . . .**29** B5
Chandler Ave E16 . . . .**1** A8
Chandler's Hill DA13 . . . . .**64** C5
Chandler's Rd DA13 . . . . . .**64** C5
Chandlers Dr DA8 . . . .**4** E2
Chandlers Mews DA9 . . . .**17** C3
Chandlers Wharf ME1 . . . .**53** B5
Chandos Rd TN1 . . . .**159** C5
Chantler's Hill TN12 . . . . .**146** A4
Chantlers Mead TN8 . . . .**155** A5
Chantry Ave DA3 . . . .**48** E3
Chantry Cl DA14 . . . .**30** E3
Chantry Ct DA14 . . . .**30** E3
Chantry Her Ctr★ DA12 . . .**19** C1
Chantry La BR2 . . . .**42** D4
Chantry Pl Marden TN12 .**148** C6
　Sevenoaks TN13 . . . .**91** F5
Chantry Prim Sch DA12 . . .**19** C1
Chantry Rd TN12 . . . .**148** C6
Chapel Alley Cotts TN14 . .**76** A8
Chapel Cl Crayford DA1 . . .**14** E2
　Ryarsh ME19 . . . .**80** F5
　West Thurrock RM20 . . . .**17** B8
Chapel Cotts ME17 . . . . . .**117** C5
Chapel Ct DA10 . . . .**17** C1
Chapel Farm Rd SE9 . . . . .**28** F6
Chapel Field Cotts DA4 . . .**48** B8
Chapel Hill DA1 . . . .**14** E2
Chapel Hos ME2 . . . .**65** E4
Chapel La
　Egerton Forstal TN27 . . . .**137** B2

Chapel La continued
　Gillingham ME7 . . . .**69** A2
　Gillingham ME7 . . . .**69** A4
　Iden Green TN17 . . . .**190** C4
　Maidstone ME14 . . . .**101** A5
　Sissinghurst TN17 . . . . . .**180** B7
　Staplehurst TN12 . . . . . .**149** F3
　Upper Halling ME2 . . . . . .**65** C4
Chapel Pl
　◼14 Royal Tunbridge Wells
　TN1 . . . .**159** A2
　Ticehurst TN5 . . . .**186** E1
Chapel Rd Bexley DA7 . . . .**14** A3
　Grain ME3 . . . .**27** B5
　Limpsfield RH8 . . . .**104** C5
　Snodland ME6 . . . .**82** A8
　Sutton Valence ME17 . . .**134** E7
Chapel Row TN15 . . . .**94** C6
Chapel St
　East Malling ME19 . . . . . .**98** A6
　Ryarsh ME19 . . . .**80** F5
Chapel View TN15 . . . .**94** C6
Chapel Wlk
　Goathurst Common TN14 .**107** B5
　Maypole DA2 . . . .**31** E6
Chapel Wood DA3 . . . .**62** E8
Chapel Wood Rd DA3,
　TN15 . . . .**62** E8
Chapelsite Ct ◼6 DA17 . . . . .**4** A2
Chaplin Cl ME3 . . . .**39** C3
Chaplin Dr TN27 . . . .**151** D5
Chapman Ave ME15 . . . . .**116** E8
Chapman Rd DA17 . . . .**4** B1
Chapman Way
　East Malling ME19 . . . . . .**97** F8
　Royal Tunbridge Wells
　TN2 . . . .**159** C8
Chapman's Hill DA13,
　TN15 . . . .**63** E4
Chapman's La
　Orpington BR5,BR8 . . . . .**44** D7
　Swanley BR8 . . . .**45** A7
Chapmans Cl TN14 . . . . . .**90** E3
Chapmans End BR5 . . . . . .**44** E7
Chapmans Rd TN14 . . . . . .**90** E3
Chapter Rd ME2 . . . .**52** F8
Chapter Sch ME2 . . . .**52** D7
Chardwell Cl E6 . . . .**1** F7
Charford Rd E16 . . . .**1** A8
Charing Cl BR6 . . . .**57** F6
Charing Ho ◼5 DA8 . . . . . .**14** F7
Charing Rd ME8 . . . .**55** B3
Chariot Way ME2 . . . .**52** F4
Charity Farm Cotts
　TN17 . . . .**166** F7
Charlbury Cl ME16 . . . .**99** C3
Charldane Rd SE9 . . . .**29** B5
Charlecote Ct BR1 . . . .**69** D8
Charles Busby Ct ME20 . . .**82** F1
Charles Cl Sidcup DA14 . . .**30** B4
　Snodland ME6 . . . .**82** A8
Charles Ct Erith DA8 . . . . .**14** E8
　Royal Tunbridge Wells
　TN2 . . . .**159** C8
Charles Darwin Ho ◼5
　BR1 . . . .**28** B1
Charles Darwin Sch
　TN16 . . . .**72** F3
Charles Dickens Ave
　ME3 . . . .**38** C2
Charles Dickens Ctr (Mus)★
　ME1 . . . .**53** C5
Charles Dr ME2 . . . .**52** E7
Charles Flemwell Mews
　E16 . . . .**1** A5
Charles Garvice Ct SE3 . . .**11** C4
Charles Grinling Wlk SE18 .**2** A2
Charles Rd TN14 . . . .**59** B1
Charles St Chatham ME4 . .**54** B3
　Grays RM17 . . . .**18** C8
　Maidstone ME16 . . . .**99** E3
　Newham E16 . . . .**1** C5
　Rochester ME2 . . . .**53** A7
　Royal Tunbridge Wells
　TN4 . . . .**159** A8
　Stone DA9 . . . .**16** F2
Charles Street Centre PRU
　The TN4 . . . .**159** A8
Charles Whincup Rd E16 . . .**1** B5
Charlesfield SE9 . . . .**28** C5
Charlesford Ave ME17 . . .**118** D3
Charlieville Rd DA8 . . . . . .**14** C7
Charlock Cl ME16 . . . .**99** D8
Charlotte Cl Bexley DA6 . . .**13** C5
　Chatham ME5 . . . .**68** B6
Charlotte Ct BR7 . . . .**29** B2
Charlotte Dr ME8 . . . .**55** C1
Charlotte Park Ave BR1 . . .**42** E6
Charlotte Pl RM20 . . . .**17** B8
Charlottes Cotts TN11 . . .**125** F1
Charlton Church La SE7 . . . .**1** C1
Charlton Cres ◼2 TN9 . . .**127** C2
Charlton Dene SE7 . . . .**11** D7
Charlton Dr TN16 . . . .**72** D2
Charlton Gate Bsns Pk
　SE7 . . . .**1** C2
Charlton La Greenwich SE7 . .**1** D1
　Sutton Valence ME17 . . .**135** C8
　West Farleigh ME15 . . . .**114** C6
Charlton Manor ME7 . . . . .**54** B5
Charlton Manor Prim Sch
　SE7 . . . .**11** D7
Charlton Park La SE7 . . . . .**11** D7
Charlton Park Rd SE7 . . . . .**11** D8
Charlton Rd SE3,SE7 . . . . .**11** B8
Charlton Sch SE7 . . . .**1** E1
Charlton St Grays RM20 . . .**17** D8

Charlton St continued
　Maidstone ME16 . . . .**99** C2
Charlton Sta SE7 . . . .**1** C1
Charlton's Way TN4 . . . . .**158** E1
Charminster Rd SE9 . . . . . .**28** D4
Charmouth Rd DA16 . . . . .**13** C6
Charnwood La BR6 . . . .**58** B1
Charnwood Villas BR6 . . . .**58** C1
Charne The TN14 . . . .**76** A2
Charnock BR8 . . . .**45** E5
Chart Cnr ME17 . . . .**117** B1
Chart Hill Rd ME17 . . . . . .**134** A7
Chart Hills Cl SE28 . . . .**3** E7
Chart La TN16 . . . .**106** B7
Chart Pl ME8 . . . .**69** C3
Chart Rd ME17 . . . .**134** C7
Chart View TN15 . . . .**77** B2
Charter Dr DA5 . . . .**30** E8
Charter St Chatham ME4 . .**53** F2
　Gillingham ME7 . . . .**54** C7
Charterhouse Dr TN13 . . .**92** A4
Charterhouse Rd BR6 . . . . .**58** A6
Charton Cl ◼5 DA17 . . . . . .**13** F8
Chartway TN13 . . . .**92** C3
Chartway★ St ME17 . . . . .**118** C3
Chartwell★ TN16 . . . .**105** F4
Chartwell Bsns Ctr BR1 . .**42** D6
Chartwell Cl
　Rochester ME2 . . . .**39** B1
　Sidcup SE9 . . . .**29** D6
Chartwell Ct Chatham ME4 .**53** E4
　Maidstone ME15 . . . .**100** B3
Chartwell Dr
　Maidstone ME16 . . . .**99** C2
　Orpington BR6 . . . .**57** D5
Chase Sq ◼14 DA11 . . . . . .**19** B1
Chase The Bexley DA7 . . . .**14** B4
　Bromley BR1 . . . .**42** B6
　Chatham ME4 . . . .**53** D2
　Gillingham ME8 . . . .**55** A2
　Kemsing TN15 . . . .**76** E3
　Pratt's Bottom BR6 . . . . . .**58** A1
　Tonbridge TN10 . . . .**127** C6
　West Thurrock RM20 . . . .**17** D8
Chastilian Rd DA1 . . . .**32** A8
Chatfield Way ME19 . . . . . .**82** B3
Chatham Ave BR2 . . . .**42** A2
Chatham Gr ME4 . . . .**53** F1
Chatham Gram Sch for Boys
　ME4 . . . .**67** F8
Chatham Gram Sch for Girls
　ME5 . . . .**54** C2
Chatham Hill ME4 . . . .**54** B3
Chatham Hill Rd TN14 . . . .**92** C6
Chatham Ho ◼16 SE18 . . . . .**1** F2
Chatham Rd
　Kit's Coty ME20 . . . .**83** D6
　Sandling ME14 . . . .**83** E1
　Sandling ME14 . . . .**83** E4
Chatham Ski Ctr ME7 . . . .**68** C4
Chatham South Sch ME4 . .**67** F8
Chatham Sta ME4 . . . .**53** E4
Chatsworth Ave
　Bromley BR1 . . . .**28** B4
　Sidcup DA15 . . . .**30** A7
Chatsworth Dr ME2 . . . . . .**39** B1
Chatsworth Ho ◼3 BR2 . . .**42** A4
Chatsworth Inf Sch DA15 . .**30** A7
Chatsworth Par BR5 . . . . . .**43** C4
Chatsworth Rd
　Dartford DA1 . . . .**15** C3
　◼10 Gillingham ME7 . . . . . .**54** C6
Chattenden Barracks Royal
　Sch of Military Engineering
　ME3 . . . .**39** F5
Chattenden Ct ME14 . . . .**100** B6
Chattenden La ME3 . . . . . .**39** F5
Chattenden Prim Sch
　ME3 . . . .**39** F4
Chattenden Terr ME3 . . . . .**39** F4
Chatterton Rd BR2 . . . .**42** D4
Chatwell Ct ME7 . . . .**54** C5
Chaucer Bsns Pk TN15 . . .**93** D8
Chaucer Cl
　◼13 Maidstone ME15 . . . .**116** E7
　Rochester ME2 . . . .**53** E8
　Tilbury RM18 . . . .**19** C5
Chaucer Gdns TN9 . . . . . .**142** F7
Chaucer Ind Pk TN15 . . . . .**93** D8
Chaucer Pk DA1 . . . .**32** F8
Chaucer Rd Bexley DA16 . .**12** F6
　Gillingham ME7 . . . .**54** D3
　Northfleet DA11 . . . .**35** D5
　Sidcup DA15 . . . .**30** C7
Chaucer Way
　Dartford DA1 . . . .**16** A3
　New Hythe ME20 . . . .**82** A3
Chaundrye Cl SE9 . . . .**11** F1
Chauntler Cl E16 . . . .**1** B6
Chave Rd DA2 . . . .**32** E5
Cheeselands TN27 . . . . . .**167** F2
Cheffins Ho ME7 . . . .**54** E7
Chegwell Dr ME5 . . . .**68** B4
Chegworth La ME17 . . . . .**119** A6
Chegworth Rd ME17 . . . . .**118** F5
Cheldoc Rise ME4 . . . .**40** C2
Chellows La RH7 . . . .**121** A1
Chelmar Rd ME7 . . . .**54** B4
Chelmsford Cl E6 . . . .**1** F7
Chelmsford Ho ME15 . . . .**116** E6
Chelmsford Rd ME2 . . . . . .**52** D6
Chelsea Ct ◼6 BR1 . . . .**42** E6
Chelsfield Hill BR6 . . . .**58** C2
Chelsfield Ho ME16 . . . . . .**99** D5
Chelsfield La
　Badgers Mount BR6,TN14 . .**59** B2
　Chelsfield BR5,BR6 . . . . . .**58** D7
　Orpington BR5 . . . .**44** D1

Chelsfield Park Hospl
  BR6 ....58 F5
Chelsfield Prim Sch BR6 .58 F5
Chelsfield Rd BR5 ....44 C3
Chelsfield Sta BR6 ....58 B5
Chelsiter Ct DA14 ....29 F4
Chelsworth Dr SE18 ....12 D8
Cheltenham Cl
  Gravesend DA12 ....36 C3
  Maidstone ME15 ....116 F6
Cheltenham Rd BR6 ....58 A7
Cheney Cl ME8 ....69 D5
Chenies Cl TN2 ....173 A8
Chenies The
  Joyden's Wood DA2 ......31 E4
  Orpington BR6 ....43 E3
Chennell Park Rd TN30 .182 E1
Chennels The TN26 ......183 C7
Chepstow Ho **3** ME16 .116 F6
Chequer's Cotts TN17 ...177 F6
Chequers Cl Chatham ME5 84 A8
  Istead Rise DA13 ....49 F7
  Orpington BR5 ....43 F5
Chequers Ct ME2 ....39 A1
Chequers Ctr ME15 ......100 A4
Chequers Hill Cotts
  TN8 ....124 A2
Chequers La RM9 ....3 F8
Cherbourg Cres ME5 ......67 F7
Cherbury Cl SE28 ....3 D7
Cheriton Ave BR2 ....42 A4
Cheriton Ct **12** SE12 ......28 A8
Cheriton Dr SE18 ....12 D8
Cheriton Rd ME8 ....69 D8
Cheriton Way ME16 ....99 C7
Cherries The ME16 ....99 A2
Cherry Amber Cl ME8 .....69 F8
Cherry Ave BR8 ....45 D5
Cherry Cl ME17 ....120 C5
Cherry Ct DA14 ....30 B5
Cherry Gr TN10 ....127 E5
Cherry Hill Ct ME8 ....71 B6
Cherry Orch Ditton ME20 .98 C8
  Greenwich SE7 ....11 C8
  Tenterden TN30 ....193 A8
Cherry Orch The TN11 ...111 E1
Cherry Orchard Cl BR5 ...44 C4
Cherry Orchard Prim Sch
  SE7 ....11 C7
Cherry Orchard Rd BR2 ..56 E8
Cherry Orchard Way
  ME16 ....99 B3
Cherry Rd ME3 ....40 E3
Cherry Tree Cl RM17 .....18 C8
Cherry Tree Gr **19** SE7 ...11 C8
Cherry Tree La DA2 ....31 F5
Cherry Tree Rd
  Gillingham ME8 ....69 F8
  Royal Tunbridge Wells
    TN2 ....158 E1
  Tonbridge TN10 ....127 D7
Cherry Trees DA3 ....48 F4
Cherry View ME17 ....116 B3
Cherry Wlk BR2 ....42 A1
Cherrycot Hill BR6 ....57 D6
Cherrycot Rise BR6 ....57 C6
Cherrydown Rd DA14 .....30 B5
Cherryfields TN17 ....190 D6
Cherrywood Dr DA11 ......35 E5
Chervil Mews SE28 ....3 B5
Cherwell Cl TN10 ....127 B4
Chesfield Cl TN11 ....111 E1
Chesham Ave BR5 ....43 B3
Chesham Dr ME8 ....69 E6
Cheshire Rd
  Maidstone ME15 ....116 E7
  Maidstone,Willington
    ME15 ....100 E2
Cheshunt Cl DA13 ....50 A3
Cheshunt Rd DA17 ....4 A1
Chesil Ho **1** BR7 ....43 D8
Chessenden La ME17 ....153 A1
Chessington Ave DA7 .....13 E7
Chester Ave TN2 ....159 D2
Chester Cl ME2 ....52 D6
Chester Rd
  Gillingham ME7 ....54 D2
  Sidcup DA15 ....12 E2
Chesterfield Dr BR5 ......44 D5
Chesterfield Dr
  Dartford DA1 ....15 B2
  Sevenoaks TN13 ....113 C7
Chesterford Ho SE18 .....11 D7
Chesterton Rd Cliffe ME3 .22 B5
  5 Lunsford ME20 ....81 F4
Chesterton Way RM18 ....19 F5
Chestfield Cl ME8 ....55 E2
Chestnut Ave
  Chatham ME5 ....67 F3
  Hill Park TN16 ....89 A6
  Royal Tunbridge Wells
    TN4 ....159 B8
  Stapleton TN12 ....149 F4
  Stone DA9 ....33 F8
  Tatsfield TN16 ....88 E5
Chestnut Cl
  Edenbridge TN8 ....122 B2
  Frittenden TN17 ....166 E6
  Kings Hill ME19 ....97 A2
  Northfleet DA11 ....18 F1
  Orpington BR6 ....58 A5
  Royal Tunbridge Wells
    TN4 ....159 B8
  Sidcup DA15 ....30 A6
  Tenterden TN30 ....183 C1
  Ulcombe ME17 ....135 F6

Chestnut Copse RH8 ....104 B2
Chestnut Ct TN2 ....173 A8
Chestnut Dr Bexley DA7 ..13 E4
  Coxheath ME17 ....115 B3
  Kingswood ME17 ....118 D2
Chestnut Gr DA2 ....31 E4
Chestnut Ho **5** ME16 ..99 A3
Chestnut La
  Matfield TN12 ....145 D1
  Sevenoaks TN13 ....92 B3
  Vigo Village DA13 ....80 B8
Chestnut Pl TN8 ....155 A6
Chestnut Rd Dartford DA1 32 D7
  Rochester ME2 ....52 E6
Chestnut Rise SE18 ....2 E1
Chestnut St ME9 ....71 E4
Chestnut Wlk
  Larkfield ME20 ....82 B2
  Sevenoaks TN15 ....108 F6
  Tonbridge TN9 ....126 F2
Chestnut Wood La ME9 ..71 E3
Chestnuts Royal BR7 .....29 D1
Chestnuts The
  Addington ME19 ....80 C3
  Chislehurst BR7 ....29 D1
  7 Erith DA17 ....3 F1
  The Moor TN18 ....194 F8
  Woolwich SE18 ....12 B6
Cheswick Cl DA1 ....14 F3
Chesworth Cl DA8 ....14 E5
Chetney Cl ME2 ....52 C7
Chetwood Wlk **15** E6 ....1 E6
Chevender BR7 ....29 B1
Cheveney Wlk **2** BR2 ...42 A6
Chevening CE Prim Sch
  TN13 ....91 B5
Chevening Cl ME5 ....68 A5
Chevening Ct BR6 ....58 A8
Chevening Ho BR5 ....44 A8
Chevening La TN14 ....74 E3
Chevening Rd
  3 Greenwich SE10 ....1 A1
  Sevenoaks TN13,TN14 ...91 B6
  Sundridge TN14 ....90 F4
Chevenings The TN14 .....30 C5
Cheviot Cl Bexley DA7 ....14 E5
  Tonbridge TN9 ....127 C4
Cheviot Gdns ME15 .....101 A1
Cheviot Ho DA11 ....18 D1
Chevron Cl E16 ....1 A7
Chevron Ho RM17 ....18 B7
Cheyne Cl BR2 ....42 A6
Cheyne Wlk Longfield DA3 48 D6
  Meopham DA13 ....64 A8
Chicago Ave ME7 ....54 F5
Chichester Cl
  Gillingham ME8 ....70 A8
  Greenwich SE3 ....11 C6
  Newham E6 ....1 A7
Chichester Ct **3** DA5 ....31 A8
Chichester Dr TN13 ......91 F2
Chichester Rd Stone DA9 16 F1
  Tonbridge TN9 ....143 A8
Chichester Rise DA12 ....36 D4
Chichester Wharf **14** DA8 .4 E1
Chickenden La NT17 ....150 C4
Chickfield Gdns **4** ME5 .54 C2
Chicks La TN17 ....176 F2
Chiddingstone Ave DA7 ..13 F7
Chiddingstone Castle★
  TN8 ....140 B7
Chiddingstone CE Prim Sch
  TN8 ....140 C7
Chiddingstone Cl ME15 .116 F6
Chidley Cross Rd TN12 ..129 E6
Chieftain Cl ME7 ....55 B1
Chieveley Dr TN2 ....159 D1
Chieveley Par DA7 ....14 B4
Chieveley Rd DA7 ....14 B3
Chiffinch Gdns DA11 .....35 E5
Childs Cres DA10 ....17 D1
Childs Way TN15 ....78 F3
Childsbridge La TN15 ....92 F7
Childsbridge Way TN15 ..92 F7
Childscroft Rd ME8 ......55 F2
Chilham Cl Chatham ME4 .53 E4
  Sidcup DA5 ....30 F8
Chilham Ho
  1 Maidstone ME15 ....116 E8
  Rochester ME2 ....39 C1
Chilham Rd Bromley SE9 .28 E4
  Gillingham ME8 ....55 A3
  Maidstone ME16 ....99 C7
Chilham Way BR2 ....42 A2
Chillington Cl ME2 ....65 E4
Chillington St ME14 ......99 F6
Chilliwack Rd ME3 ....39 F5
Chilston Cl TN4 ....159 A5
Chilston Rd
  Lenham ME17 ....120 D5
  Royal Tunbridge Wells
    TN4 ....159 A3
Chiltenhurst TN8 ....122 A2
Chiltern Cl Bexley DA7 ...14 E6
  Maidstone ME15 ....100 F1
Chiltern Ct **11** SE9 ......12 A1
Chiltern Rd DA11 ....35 E5
Chiltern Way TN9 ....127 C4
Chiltern Wlk TN2 ....159 D4
Chilterns DA14 ....30 A3
Chilterns, The BR1 ......42 B7
Chilton Cl ME8 ....55 E1
Chilton Dr ME3 ....38 B3
Chimes The ME1 ....53 C5
Chinbrook Cres **8** SE12 .28 B5
Chinbrook Rd SE12 ......28 B5
Chine Farm Pl TN14 ......74 D3
Chinnery Ct DA13 ....50 A2

Chippendale Cl ME5 .....67 F1
Chippendayle Dr ME17 .119 D6
Chipperfield Rd
  Orpington BR5 ....44 A7
  Orpington BR5 ....44 B5
Chipstead Cl ME16 ....99 D6
Chipstead La TN13 ....91 D5
Chipstead Park Cl TN13 .91 C5
Chipstead Pk TN13 ......91 D5
Chipstead Place Gdns
  TN13 ....91 D5
Chipstead Rd Erith DA8 ..14 E7
  Gillingham ME8 ....69 D4
Chipstead Sq TN13 ......91 C5
Chislehurst & Sidcup Gram
  Sch DA15 ....30 B6
Chislehurst (St Nicholas) CE
  Prim Sch BR7 ....29 C1
Chislehurst Caves★ BR7 .43 A8
Chislehurst Cl ME15 ....116 F6
Chislehurst High St BR7 .29 D2
Chislehurst Rd
  Bromley BR1,BR2 ....42 E8
  Orpington BR6 ....44 A2
  Orpington,Broom Hill BR6 .43 F2
  Orpington,Petts Wood BR5,
    BR6 ....43 E4
  Sidcup DA14 ....30 A3
Chislehurst Sta BR7 .....43 A7
Chislet Wlk ME8 ....69 D5
Chiswell Sq SE3 ....11 B5
Chorleywood Cres BR5 ..44 A7
Christ Church Ave **1**
  TN1 ....159 A2
Christ Church CE Sch
  SE18 ....12 A6
Christ Church Cres **2**
  DA12 ....36 C8
Christ Church Erith CE Prim
  Sch DA8 ....14 D8
Christ Church Rd **3**
  DA12 ....36 C8
Christchurch Ave DA8 ...14 E8
Christchurch Ct **3** ME5 .54 C2
Christchurch Ho **11**
  ME15 ....116 E5
Christchurch Rd
  Dartford DA1 ....15 C1
  Sidcup DA15 ....29 F5
  Tilbury RM18 ....19 A4
Christen Way ME15,
  ME17 ....116 F3
Christian Ct **3** ME2 .....53 C8
Christian Fields Ave
  DA12 ....36 C4
Christie Cl ME5 ....68 B6
Christie Dr **8** ME20 ......81 F4
Christie Ho DA6 ....14 B2
Christies Ave ME14 ....59 B1
Christmas La ME23 ....23 F3
Christmas St ME7 ....54 E7
Christopher Cl DA15 .....12 F2
Christy Rd TN16 ....72 C4
Chudleigh **7** DA14 ....30 B4
Chulkhurst TN27 ....167 F1
Chulkhurst TN27 ....167 F1
Church Alley **11** DA11 ...19 B1
Church Ave DA14 ....30 B3
Church Cl
  Brenchley TN12 ....162 C8
  Cliffe ME3 ....22 B6
  Mereworth ME18 ....112 D8
Church Cotts
  Cranbrook TN17 ....179 D5
  Crockenhill BR8 ....45 D2
  Shoreham TN14 ....76 A8
  Sutton Valence ME17 ..134 E7
  Tenterden TN30 ....183 B3
Church Cres ME17 ......119 F6
Church Ct DA2 ....32 D5
Church Farm Cl
  Crockenhill BR8 ....45 D3
  Hoo St Werburgh ME3 ..40 E4
Church Field
  Dartford DA2 ....32 D6
  Sevenoaks TN13 ....91 F5
  Snodland ME6 ....66 B1
Church Field Cotts TN15 .92 F7
Church Fields ME19 ......97 B8
Church Gn
  Hollingbourne ME17 ...102 E3
  Marden TN12 ....148 C6
  Rochester ME2 ....53 C8
  Staplehurst TN12 ......149 E2
Church Hill Chatham ME5 .54 C2
  Crayford DA1 ....14 E3
  Cudham TN14,TN16 .....73 C4
  Dartford DA2 ....32 D6
  High Halden TN26 .....183 E7
  Leigh TN11 ....125 F2
  Linton ME17 ....133 B7
  Orpington BR6 ....44 A2
  Plaxtol TN15 ....110 E8
  Stockbury ME9 ....86 F7
  Stone DA9 ....16 E2
  Tatsfield TN16 ....88 D5
  Woolwich SE18 ....1 F3
Church Hill Wood BR5 ...43 F4
Church La Capel TN12 ..144 F6
  Chalk DA12 ....37 C6
  Chatham ME4 ....53 F6
  Chislehurst BR7 ....43 C8
  East Peckham TN12 ...129 F7
  Frant TN3 ....173 B4
  Harrietsham ME17 .....119 E6
  Kemsing TN15 ....77 B2
  Maidstone ME16 ....98 E1

Church La continued
  Maidstone,Bearsted ME14 101 C4
  Newington ME9 ....71 B6
  Orpington BR2 ....42 E1
  Stockbury ME9 ....86 E8
  Sutton Valence ME17 ..135 B8
  Tonbridge TN9 ....127 C2
  Trottiscliffe TN15 ....80 B5
  West Farleigh ME15 ...114 D7
Church Manor Way SE18,
  SE2 ....3 A2
Church Manorway DA8 ...4 A3
Church Mdw TN12 ......163 A7
Church Mews ME8 ....69 F8
Church Path
  Gillingham ME7 ....54 E6
  Northfleet DA11 ....18 C1
  Stone DA9 ....16 F1
Church Rd Bexley DA7,DA6 13 B5
  Bexley,Welling DA16 .....13 B5
  Biggin Hill TN16 ....72 E2
  Bitchet Green TN15 .....93 E3
  Brasted TN16 ....90 B3
  Bromley BR1,BR2 ....42 A7
  Chelsfield BR6 ....58 D4
  Crockenhill BR8 ....45 D2
  Erith DA8 ....4 D1
  Goudhurst TN17 ....177 F8
  Grafty Green ME17 ....136 F7
  Gravesend DA12,DA13 ...36 D1
  Halstead TN14 ....74 F7
  Harrietsham ME17 .....119 E6
  Hartley DA3 ....49 A2
  Hawley DA4 ....32 F1
  Henhurst DA13 ....50 C8
  Hucking ME17 ....86 E1
  Kilndown TN17 ....176 F3
  Lamberhurst TN3 ......176 C6
  Maidstone ME15 ....116 C7
  Maidstone,Tovil ME15 ...99 E2
  Offham ME18 ....96 D8
  Orpington BR6 ....57 D5
  Orpington,Keston BR2 ..56 D3
  Paddock Wood TN12 ...146 B6
  Pembury TN2 ....160 D8
  Royal Tunbridge Wells
    TN1 ....159 A3
  Royal Tunbridge
    Wells,Southborough TN4 .142 F2
  Ryarsh ME19 ....81 A3
  Sandhurst Cross TN18 .195 F4
  Seal TN15 ....92 F6
  Sevenoaks Weald TN14 .108 B3
  Sidcup DA14 ....30 A4
  Stone DA9 ....16 F2
  Sundridge TN14 ....90 E2
  Sutton at H DA4 ....33 A2
  Sutton Valence ME17 ..134 C8
  Swanley Village BR8 .....46 D8
  Swanscombe DA10 ......17 F1
  Tenterden TN30 ....193 A7
  Tilbury RM18 ....18 F6
  West Kingsdown TN15 ..61 E3
  West Peckham ME18 ...112 A6
  West Tilbury RM18 ......19 E8
  Pembury TN2 ....144 D1
Church Row
  Chislehurst BR7 ....43 C8
  Plaxtol TN15 ....110 E8
  Snodland ME6 ....82 A7
  West Peckham ME18 ...112 B6
Church Row Mews BR7 ..29 C1
Church Sq ME17 ....120 D5
Church St Burham ME1 ..66 F1
  Chatham ME4 ....54 A4
  Cliffe ME3 ....22 B5
  Cowden TN8 ....155 B5
  Edenbridge TN8 ....122 D1
  Gillingham ME7 ....54 E6
  Grays RM17 ....18 C8
  Hadlow TN11 ....128 E8
  Hoo St Werburgh ME3 ..40 E5
  Loose ME15 ....115 F4
  Lower Higham ME3 .....38 D7
  Maidstone ME14 ....100 A4
  Maidstone, Boughton Monchelsea
    ME17 ....116 B2
  Maidstone,Tovil ME15 ...99 E2
  Newham E16 ....1 A5
  Northfleet DA13 ....35 A3
  Rochester ME1 ....53 D4
  Seal TN15 ....93 A7
  Shoreham TN14 ....76 A8
  Teston ME18 ....114 A8
  Ticehurst TN5 ....186 D1
  Tonbridge TN9 ....127 C2
  Wadhurst TN5 ....185 A4
Church Terr ME5 ....54 C2
Church Trad Est DA8 ....4 A7
Church View
  Biddenden TN27 ....167 F2
  4 Dartford DA1 ....15 E1
  Swanley BR8 ....45 B8
Church Wlk Dartford DA2 .32 D5
  East Malling ME19 ....98 A3
  Eynsford DA4 ....60 E7
  Gravesend DA12 ....36 D7
  Gravesend DA12 ....36 D8
  Hawkhurst TN18 ......189 A1
  Headcorn ME17 ....151 C5
Churchbury Rd SE9 ......28 D8
Churchfield
  Addington ME19 ....80 D3
  Edenbridge TN8 ....122 D1
Churchfield Rd DA16 .....13 A4
Churchfield Sch SE2 .....3 A2

Churchfields Terr ME1 ...53 B4
Churchill Ave ME5 ....68 A7
Churchill Bsns Ctr TN16 .89 D1
Churchill CE Prim Sch
  TN16 ....89 C2
Churchill Cl DA1 ....33 B7
Churchill Cotts ME17 ...117 F6
Churchill Ct
  4 Orpington BR6 ....57 C5
  Westerham TN16 ....89 D1
Churchill Ho
  Benenden TN17 ....190 E6
  Maidstone ME16 ....99 B2
  1 Woolwich SE18 ....2 B2
Churchill Pk DA1 ....16 A2
Churchill Rd Grays RM17 .18 D8
  Horton Kirby DA4 ....47 C5
  Newham E16 ....1 C7
  Northfleet DA11 ....35 F7
Churchill Sq ME19 ....97 A3
Churchill Way
  Biggin Hill TN16 ....72 D4
  Bromley BR1 ....42 A7
Churchills Ropewalk
  TN17 ....177 E8
Churchlands ME14 ......100 B5
Churchsettle La TN5 ...185 C1
Churchside DA13 ....80 A8
Churchside Cl TN16 ......72 C2
Churchyard Cotts TN3 ..158 A8
Churn La TN12 ....147 A2
Chute Cl ME8 ....69 D4
Chyngton Cl DA15 ....29 F5
Cimba Wood DA12 ....36 E4
Cinder Hill La TN11 .....125 C1
Cinderhill Wood TN12 ..145 C1
Cinderhill Wood Cvn Site
  TN12 ....145 C1
Cinnabar Cl ME5 ....68 A1
Circle The RM18 ....19 A6
Circuit Rd SE28 ....3 A4
Circular Way SE18 ....12 A8
Cirrus Cres DA12 ....36 E3
City Way ME1 ....53 D2
Civic Sq RM18 ....19 A5
Civic Way TN1 ....159 A3
CJ Gallards Almshouses
  TN4 ....159 A8
Clacket La Tatsfield TN16 .88 E2
  Westerham TN16 ......105 A8
Clacketts Farm ME19 ....81 B5
Claire Ho **4** ME16 ....99 E5
Clancy Gdns TN17 ......179 B5
Clandon Ct BR1 ....28 A2
Clandon Rd ME5 ....68 D2
Clanricarde Gdns **1**
  TN1 ....159 A3
Clanricarde Rd **2** TN1 .159 A3
Claphatch La TN5 ......186 A5
Clapper La TN12 ....149 D6
Clara Pl SE18 ....2 A2
Clare Ave TN9 ....126 F1
Clare Cnr SE9 ....29 B8
Clare Cswy DA9 ....16 F3
Clare Ct BR7 ....42 F8
Clare La ME19 ....97 E8
Clare Way Bexley DA7 ...13 E6
  Sevenoaks TN13 ....108 C8
Claremont Cl Newham E16 .2 A5
  Orpington BR6 ....57 A6
Claremont Cres DA1 .....14 E3
Claremont Ct **4** TN2 ...159 C7
Claremont Gdns TN2 ...159 B2
Claremont Pl
  1 Gravesend DA11 ......36 B8
  Iden Green TN17 ....190 C4
  Marden TN12 ....148 D4
Claremont Prim Sch
  TN2 ....159 B2
Claremont Rd
  Bromley BR1 ....42 F5
  Hextable BR8 ....31 E1
  Maidstone ME14 ....100 B5
  Royal Tunbridge Wells
    TN1 ....159 B2
Claremont St SE16 ....2 A3
Claremont Way **2** ME4 .53 F3
Clarence Ave Bromley BR1 42 E5
  Rochester ME1 ....53 C4
Clarence Cres DA14 .....30 B5
Clarence Ct
  2 Grays RM17 ....18 B8
  Maidstone ME14 ....100 E4
  Pratt's Bottom BR6 ......58 C2
Clarence Lodge TN1 ....159 A3
Clarence Pl DA12 ....36 B7
Clarence Rd Bexley DA6 .13 E3
  Biggin Hill TN16 ....72 F1
  Bromley,Mottingham SE9 .28 E6
  Bromley,Widmore BR1 ..42 E6
  Chatham ME4 ....54 B2
  Grays RM17 ....18 B8
  Royal Tunbridge Wells
    TN1 ....159 A3
  Sidcup DA14 ....30 B5
Clarence Row
  Gravesend DA12 ....36 B8
  Royal Tunbridge Wells
    TN1 ....159 A3
Clarendon Cl
  Maidstone ME14 ....101 A4
  Orpington BR5 ....44 A5
Clarendon Ct TN13 ......92 A2
Clarendon Dr ME2 ....39 A1

Clarendon Gdns
Dartford DA2 ....33 D8
Royal Tunbridge Wells
TN2 ....159 A1
Clarendon Gn BR5 .....44 A5
Clarendon Gr BR5 .....44 A5
Clarendon Mews DA5 ..31 B7
Clarendon Path BR5 ...44 A5
Clarendon Pl
Joyden's Wood DA2 ....31 E3
Maidstone ME14 ......100 A4
Sevenoaks TN13 ....92 A2
Clarendon Rd
Gravesend DA12 ....19 C1
Sevenoaks TN13 ....92 A2
Clarendon Way
Royal Tunbridge Wells
TN2 ....159 A1
St Paul's Cray BR5,BR7 .43 F6
Claret Ho TN13 ....92 B3
Clareville Rd BR5 ....57 C8
Clarewood Dr ME19 ...97 E8
Claridge TN1 ....159 B6
Claridge Ct ME7 ......68 F4
Clark Cl DA8 ....15 A6
Clark Mews ME20 .....82 F1
Clark's Yd TN5 ......187 A3
Clarkbourne Dr RM17 ..18 D8
Clarkes Green Rd TN15 .77 B5
Clarks La Halstead TN14 .74 F7
Titsey CR6,RH8,TN16 ...88 C4
Claston Cl DA1 ....14 E3
Clavadal Rd TN12 ....146 A7
Clavell Cl ME8 ....69 E4
Clay Cotts TN17 .....177 E8
Clay Hill Mount TN17 .177 E8
Clay Hill Rd TN3 ....175 D6
Clay Wood Cl ME8 ....43 E2
Claybridge Rd SE12 ..28 C4
Claydown Mews SE18 ...2 A1
Clayfarm Rd SE9 .....29 C6
Claygate
Eyhorne Street ME17 .102 D2
Maidstone ME15 ......100 D1
Claygate Cross TN15 ..95 A3
Claygate La TN11 ....110 F4
Claygate Rd TN12 ....131 B2
Clayhill TN17 ....177 D8
Clayhill Cres SE9 ....28 D4
Clayton Cl **3** E6 ......1 F7
Clayton Croft Rd DA2 .32 A6
Clayton's La TN3 ....156 E2
Claytonville Terr DA17 ..4 C4
Claywood La DA2 .....34 D5
Clayworth Cl DA15 ...13 B1
Cleanthus Cl SE18 ...12 B6
Cleanthus Rd SE18 ...12 B6
Clearway ME19 ....80 A1
Clearways Bsns Est TN15 61 E3
Clearways Mobile Home Pk
TN15 ....61 D3
Cleave Ave BR6 ......57 E4
Cleave Rd ME7 ....54 E3
Cleavers TN17 ....180 A8
Cleavers Cl TN17 ....180 A8
Cleavesland ME18 ....130 E5
Cleeve Ave TN2 .....159 D2
Cleeve Ct ME19 ......97 B3
Cleeve Park Gdns DA14 .30 B6
Cleeve Park Sch DA14 .30 C5
Clegg Ho SE3 ....11 B3
Clematis Ave ME8 ....69 B5
Clemens Pl ME18 ....97 C2
Clement Cl ME16 .....99 D5
Clement St BR8,DA4 ..32 E4
Clements Ave E16 .....1 A6
Clenches Farm La TN13 .92 A1
Clenches Farm Rd TN13 .92 A1
Clendon Way SE18 ....2 D2
Clerks Field TN27 ...151 D5
Clermont Cl ME7 .....69 A4
Cleve Rd DA14 ....30 D5
Clevedon Ho BR1 ....28 E1
Cleveland TN2 ......159 C4
Cleveland Ho
Maidstone ME16 ......99 B2
Northfleet DA11 .....18 D1
Cleveland Rd Bexley DA16 12 F5
Gillingham ME7 ......54 D6
Clevely Cl SE7 ....1 D2
Cleves Rd TN15 ......76 E2
Cleves View **4** DA1 ...15 D1
Clewer Ho **8** SE2 ....3 D4
Clewson Rise ME14 ...100 B8
Cliff Hill ME17 .....116 D4
Cliff Hill Rd ME17 ..116 C4
Cliff Reach DA9 .....16 F1
Cliffe Ct ME3 ....22 B5
Cliffe Pools Nature Reserve★
ME3 ....5 E1
Cliffe Rd ME2 ....39 A1
Cliffe Woods Prim Sch
ME3 ....39 C8
Clifford Ave BR7 ....28 F2
Clifford Ho **6** ME14 .100 B4
Clifton Cl
Maidstone ME14 ......100 B5
8 Orpington BR6 .....57 C5
Rochester ME2 ....52 F7
Clifton Cotts TN13 ..159 D8
Clifton Gr DA11 .....36 B8
Clifton Marine Par DA11 .18 F1
Clifton Pl TN1 .....159 B2

Clifton Rd Bexley DA16 .13 C4
Gillingham ME7 ......54 C7
Gravesend DA11 .....19 A1
Royal Tunbridge Wells
TN2 ....159 C7
Sidcup DA14 ....29 E4
Cliftonville Ct SE12 .28 A7
Clinch Ct **15** E16 ....1 A8
Clinch St ME3 ....24 A4
Clinton Ave Bexley DA16 .13 A3
Rochester ME2 ....52 E8
Clinton Cl ME17 ....115 B3
Clinton La TN8 .....123 E3
Clipper Bvd DA9 ....16 E3
Clipper Bvd W DA2 ..16 D4
Clipper Cl ME2 ......53 E7
Clipper Cres DA12 ..36 F4
Clipper Ct ME2 ......53 E7
Clive Ave DA14 ......14 F1
Clive Ho ME20 ......98 F8
Clive Rd Erith DA17 ...4 A2
Gravesend DA11 .....19 B1
Rochester ME1 ......53 C3
Cliveden Cl ME16 ....99 D7
Clock Ho The DA15 ..30 A7
Clock House La TN13 .92 A4
Clock Tower Mews
Snodland ME6 ....66 A1
Woolwich SE28 ....3 B6
Clockhouse TN2 ....159 F6
Cloisterham Rd ME1 .67 D7
Cloisters Ave BR2 ...42 F4
Cloisters Ct DA7 ....14 B4
Cloisters The
1 Dartford DA1 .....15 E1
Lenham ME17 ....120 C5
Cloke Mews TN15 ....94 F7
Cloonmore Ave BR6 ..57 F6
Clopton Ct ME8 .....69 D8
Close The Addington ME19 80 C2
Birling ME19 ....81 B5
Borough Green TN15 ..95 A8
Bough Beech TN8 ...124 A2
Cudham TN16 ....73 B3
Dartford DA2 ....32 D5
Groombridge TN3 ...171 C6
Ightham TN15 ....94 D6
New Barn DA3 ....49 B7
Orpington BR5 ......43 E3
Rochester ME1 ......53 C4
Royal Tunbridge Wells
TN2 ....159 C8
Sevenoaks TN13 .....91 E3
Sidcup DA14 ....30 B3
1 Sidcup,Old Bexley DA5 .31 A8
Cloth Hall Gdns TN27 .168 A2
Clothier Ho SE7 .....1 E1
Clothworkers Rd SE18 .12 D7
Cloudberry ME16 ....99 D6
Cloudesley Cl ME1 ..53 B1
Cloudesley Rd Bexley DA7 13 F6
Erith DA8 ....14 F6
Clovelly Rd DA7 ....13 E8
Clovelly Way BR6 ...43 F3
Clover Bank View ME5 .68 B6
Clover Ct **12** RM17 ..18 D8
Clover Rd ME3 ......40 E3
Clover St **3** ME4 ....53 F4
Clover Terr **4** ME15 .116 D8
Clover Way TN12 ...146 A5
Clover Wlk **13** TN8 ..122 D3
Cloverdale Gdns DA15 .12 F1
Clovers The DA11 ...35 E4
Club Cotts TN11 ...126 D8
Club Gardens Rd BR2 .42 A2
Clyde Rd TN10 .....127 C6
Clydesdale Ho DA18 ..3 E4
Clydon Cl DA8 ......14 E8
Coach & Horses Pas **18**
TN2 ....159 A2
Coach Dr The DA13 ..79 E7
Coach House Mews **8**
BR1 ....42 A6
Coach Rd
Egerton ME17,TN27 ..137 E6
Ightham TN15 ....94 B2
Rusthall TN4 ....158 C3
Coach Yd The ME16 ..99 B3
Coal Ct RM17 ....18 A8
Coalhouse Fort★ RM18 .20 E6
Coastguard Cotts ME3 .27 B5
Coates Hill Rd BR1 ..43 A7
Cob Dr DA12 ....37 E3
Cobb Cl ME2 ....52 D8
Cobbets Way TN8 ...138 C8
Cobbett Cl ME19 ....97 F8
Cobbett Rd SE9 .....11 E4
Cobbett's Ride TN2 .158 F1
Cobbles TN11 ......126 D8
Cobbs Cl
Paddock Wood TN12 ..145 F6
Wateringbury ME18 ..113 E7
Cobden Ct Bromley BR2 .42 C5
9 Woolwich SE28 ....3 C5
Cobden Rd
4 Chatham ME4 ......54 B8
Orpington BR6 ....57 D6
Sevenoaks TN13 .....92 C4
Cobdown Cl ME20 ...82 C2
Cobfield ME17 .....117 A1
Cobham Cl Bromley BR2 .42 E2
Maidstone ME16 .....99 E4
Rochester ME2 ......52 E7
2 Sidcup DA15 ......13 B1
Swanscombe DA9 ....17 B1
Cobham Dr ME18 ....97 C3
Cobham Hall Sch DA12 .51 C6

Cobham Ho **4** DA8 ...14 F7
Cobham Pl DA6 .....13 D2
Cobham Prim Sch DA12 .51 A5
Cobham Rise ME7 ...54 F5
Cobham St DA11 ....36 B8
Cobham Terr DA9 ...17 B1
Cobhambury Rd DA12 .51 B4
Cobhams TN3 ......158 A8
Cobland Rd SE12 ...28 C4
Cobs TN15 ....94 C6
Cobsdene DA12 .....36 D2
Cobtree Cl ME5 ....68 C8
Cobtree Rd ME15 ..115 B8
Cobtree Wharf ME20 .83 C2
Cockerhurst Rd TN14 .59 E2
Cockmannings La BR5 .44 E1
Cockmannings Rd BR5 .44 D2
Cockmount La TN5 ..184 F5
Cockpit The TN12 ..148 C5
Cocksett Ave BR6 ..57 E4
Cocksure La DA14 ..31 A4
Codrington Cres DA12 .36 D3
Codrington Gdns DA12 .36 D3
Cogate Rd TN12 ...145 E6
Cokers Yd TN4 ....143 A1
Colchester Cl ME5 .68 A7
Cold Arbor Rd TN13 .91 D3
Cold Blow Cres DA5 .31 D7
Cold Harbour La ME9 .71 F6
Coldblow La ME14 ..86 A2
Coldharbour La TN27 .137 B5
Coldharbour Crest SE9 .29 A5
Coldharbour La
Aylesford ME20 .....83 A1
Hucking ME14,ME9 ..86 B1
Rainham ME13 ....4 F6
Shipbourne TN11 ...110 A3
Tonbridge TN11 ....126 E7
Coldharbour Rd
Ashurst TN8,TN11 ..156 E8
Gravesend DA11 ....36 A4
Iden Green TN17 ...190 B4
Northfleet DA11 ....35 F5
Coldharbour Sports Ctr
SE9 ....29 A6
Coldred Rd ME15 ..116 F4
Coldrum La ME19 ...80 C6
Coldshott RH8 ....104 A2
Cole Cl SE28 ....3 B5
Cole Terr ME17 ....120 C4
Colebrook Ind Est TN2 .143 E1
Colebrook Rd ME5 ..68 A1
Colebrook St **1** DA8 .14 F8
Colebrooke Ct DA14 .30 B4
Colegate Dr ME14 ..101 C4
Coleman Rd DA17 ....4 A2
Colemans Heath SE9 .29 B5
Colepits Wood Rd SE9 .12 D2
Coleraine Rd **1** SE3 .11 A8
Coleridge Cl **1** ME20 .81 F4
Coleridge Rd
Dartford DA1 ....16 B3
Tilbury RM18 ....19 C5
Coleridge Way BR6 ..44 A3
Coles Ct TN2 ......159 C3
Coles La TN16 ......90 C4
Colesdane ME17 ...119 E8
Coleshall Cl ME15 .116 F6
Colets Orch TN14 ..76 B3
Colewood Dr ME2 ...52 B8
Colfe's Prep Sch SE12 .11 B1
Colin Blythe Rd TN10 .127 F5
Colin Chapman Way DA3 61 E6
Colin Cl DA2 ....16 B1
College Ave
Gillingham ME7 ....54 B4
Maidstone ME15 ....99 F3
Tonbridge TN9 ....143 A7
College Cotts ME16 .99 F3
College Ct **5** ME15 .100 A3
College Dr TN2 ...159 D4
College Gn **10** BR1 ..42 A8
College Rd Bromley BR1 .28 A1
Chatham ME4 ......54 A7
Hextable BR8 ......31 F1
Maidstone ME15 ....99 F2
New Hythe ME20 ....82 B3
Northfleet DA11 ....18 B2
College View SE9 ..28 D7
College Wlk **4** ME15 .100 A3
College Yd ME1 ....53 C6
Coller Cres DA2 ...33 E3
Collet Rd TN15 .....76 E2
Collet Wlk ME8 ....69 D4
Collier Cl E6 ......2 B6
Colliers Shaw BR2 .56 D5
Colliers' Green CE Prim Sch
TN17 ....164 F2
Collindale Ave Erith DA8 14 B8
Sidcup DA15 ....30 A7
Collinge Cl ME19 ..82 A1
Collings Wlk ME8 ..69 D4
Collington Cl DA11 .35 E8
Collington Ho **3** SE7 .11 B8
Collington Terr ME15 .116 D4
Collingwood Ho DA9 .17 D2
Collingwood Ind Ctr
ME17 ....117 E2
Collingwood Rd ME20 .83 C7
Collis St ME2 ......53 A8
Collison Pl TN30 ..193 D7
Colman Ho **4** ME14 ..100 A4
Colman Rd E16 ......1 C8
Colne Rd TN10 ....127 E2
Colney Rd DA1 .....15 F1
Colonade The **14** TN18 .189 A2

Colonel Stephens Way
TN30 ....183 B2
Colonel's Way SE2 ...3 B1
Coltness Cres SE2 ...3 B1
Colts Hill Pl TN12 .145 B5
Coltsfoot Ct RM17 ..18 D8
Coltsfoot Dr ME14 ..100 F4
Coltsfoot Ho E16 ....1 A8
Coltsfoot La RH8 ..104 A1
Coltstead DA2 ......62 E7
Columbia Wharf Rd
RM17 ....18 A8
Columbine Ave E6 ...1 E8
Columbine Cl
Rochester ME2 .....52 E7
West Malling ME19 .81 F1
Columbine Rd
East Malling ME19 .97 F8
Rochester ME2 .....52 E7
Columbus Sq DA8 ..14 F8
Colveiw Ct SE9 ....28 D7
Colyer Cl SE9 .....29 B6
Colyer Ho SE2 ......3 D1
Colyer Rd DA11 ....35 D6
Colyers Cl DA8 ....14 D6
Colyers La DA8 ....14 D6
Colyers Prim Sch DA8 .14 D6
Colyton Cl DA16 ...14 D6
Combe Bank Cotts TN14 .90 D5
Combe Bank Dr TN14 .90 D6
Combe Bank Farm TN14 .90 D6
Combe Bank Sch TN14 .90 E4
Combedale Rd SE10 ..1 A1
Combeside SE18 ....12 F7
Combwell Cres SE9 ..3 A3
Comforts Farm Ave
RH8 ....104 A3
Comfrey Ct RM17 ..18 D8
Command Rd ME14 ..99 F8
Commerce Way TN8 .122 C3
Commercial Pl DA12 .19 C1
Commercial Rd
Paddock Wood TN12 ..145 F6
Rochester ME2 .....53 B7
Royal Tunbridge Wells
TN1 ....159 B5
Tonbridge TN9 ....143 C8
Commissioner's Rd ME2 .53 C8
Commissioners Ct ME4 .53 F6
Commodore Rd ME14 .100 C5
Common La Cliffe ME3 .22 C6
Dartford DA2 ....32 B5
Common Rd Burham ME5 .67 B1
Cliffe Woods ME3 ...39 B5
Hadlow TN11 ......111 E2
Ightham TN15 ......94 B4
Sissinghurst TN17 .180 A8
Common The ME1 ...53 C6
Common View TN4 .158 C4
Common Wall ME3 ..22 D6
Commonside BR2 ...56 C6
Commonwealth Ho **5**
RM16 ....19 A5
Commonwealth Way SE2 .3 C1
Commority Rd DA13 .80 B8
Comp La TN15 ......95 E6
Compass Cl ME1 ...53 C1
Compass Ct DA11 ..18 E1
Compass Ctr ME4 ..54 B8
Compasses Rd TN17 .125 B2
Compasses The TN11 .125 B2
Compton Cl ME5 ...68 D2
Compton Pl DA8 ...14 F8
Concord Ave ME5 ..67 C8
Concord Cl
Paddock Wood TN12 ..145 E7
Royal Tunbridge Wells
TN2 ....159 C4
Concorde Bsns Pk TN16 .72 D4
Concorde Dr E6 .....1 F8
Concrete Cotts ME3 .21 E4
Condover Cres SE18 .12 B7
Condovers Cotts RM18 .19 F8
Conduit Rd SE18 ...12 B5
Coney Mews ME4 ...54 A1
Coneyburrow Rd TN2 .159 E5
Conference Rd SE2 ..3 C2
Conghurst La TN18 .195 B6
Congleton Gr SE18 ..2 C1
Congo Rd SE18 .....2 D1
Congress Rd SE2 ...3 C2
Congreve Rd SE9 ..11 F4
Congreve Wlk **6** E16 .1 D8
Conifer Ave DA3 ...48 E3
Conifer Cl BR6 ....51 D6
Conifer Dr Chatham ME5 .68 C1
Culverstone Green DA13 .63 F2
Conifer Way SE2 ....3 D1
Conisborough Ct **13** DA2 .16 B1
Coniscliffe Cl BR7 .45 A8
Coniston Ave Bexley DA16 12 E4
Purfleet RM19 .....16 C8
Royal Tunbridge Wells
TN4 ....158 E5
Coniston Cl Bexley DA7 .14 C6
Dartford DA1 ......32 B7
Erith DA8 ....14 E7
Gillingham ME7 ....55 A6
Coniston Ho ME15 .116 E1
Coniston Rd DA7 ...14 C6
Connaught Bridge E16 .1 D6
Connaught Cl ME15 .116 H4
Connaught Mews
2 Chatham ME4 .....54 C7
Woolwich SE18 .....2 A1
Connaught Rd
Chatham ME4 ......54 C7

Connaught Rd *continued*
Gillingham ME7 ....54 D5
Newham,Silvertown E16 .1 D5
Woolwich SE18 .....2 B1
Connaught Way TN4 .158 F5
Conquest Ind Est ME2 .53 A5
Conrad Cl ME8 .....69 D4
Consort Cl ME14 ..100 B5
Constable Ave E16 ..1 D5
Constable Rd
Northfleet DA11 ....35 E5
Tonbridge TN10 ...127 C6
Constance St E16 ...1 E5
Constitution Cres DA12 .36 B7
Constitution Hill
8 Chatham ME5 .....54 B3
Gravesend DA12 ....36 C7
Snodland ME6 ......82 A8
Constitution Rd ME5 .54 B2
Constitution Rise SE18 .12 A6
Constitutional Hill Rd
TN4 ....142 F1
Consul Gdns BR8 ..32 A1
Contessa Cl BR6 ..57 E5
Convalescent La TN17 .165 F2
Conway Cl ME2 ....38 E1
Conway Ct BR5 ....44 C5
Conway Gdns RM17 .18 B7
Conway Hall **16** ME7 .54 A6
Conway Mews ME7 .54 A6
Conway Prim Sch SE18 .2 E2
Conway Rd
Maidstone ME16 ....99 C6
Woolwich SE18 .....2 E2
Conyerd Rd TN15 ..94 F6
Conyers Wlk ME8 ..69 D4
Cooden Cl BR1 ....28 B1
Cook Cl ME5 ......68 C6
Cookham Dene Cl BR7 .43 D8
Cookham Hill ME1 ..53 E4
Cookham Rd DA14,BR8 .45 A8
Cookham Wood Rd ME1 .67 B8
Cookhill Rd SE2 ....3 B3
Cooks Wharf ME1 ..53 E4
Cookson Gr DA8 ...14 B7
Coolfin Rd E16 .....1 B7
Cooling Castle★ ME3 .22 B2
Cooling Cl ME14 ..100 C6
Cooling Comm ME3 .39 D8
Cooling Rd Cliffe ME3 .22 C4
High Halstow ME23 .23 C4
Rochester ME2 .....39 B2
Cooling St ME3 ....22 D1
Coomb Field TN8 .138 C8
Coombe Ave TN14 ..92 B3
Coombe Cl Chatham ME5 .68 B3
Snodland ME6 ......82 A4
Coombe Ct TN14 ...92 B7
Coombe Farm La ME3 .24 C8
Coombe La TN30 ..193 A7
Coombe Lands TN30 .199 D8
Coombe Lea BR1 ...42 E6
Coombe Lodge SE7 .11 C8
Coombe Rd
Gravesend DA12 ....36 C6
Hoo St Werburgh ME3 .40 C5
Maidstone ME15 ....99 F2
Otford TN14 ....76 C4
Coombfield Dr DA2 .33 D4
Cooper Cl DA9 ....16 F2
Cooper Ct SE18 ...12 B8
Cooper Rd Chatham ME5 .68 B3
Snodland ME6 ......81 F6
Cooper Shaw Rd RM18 .19 E7
Cooper's Rd DA11 ..35 F7
Coopers Cl DA4 ...47 D8
Coopers Cotts DA12 .33 A4
Coopers Dr DA2 ...31 E6
Coopers La
Lewisham SE12 ....28 B6
Poundsbridge TN11,TN3 .157 C7
Coopers Tech Coll BR7 .43 C8
Coopers' Lane Prim Sch
SE12 ....28 B6
Coote Rd DA7 .....13 F6
Copenhagen Rd ME7 .54 C4
Copley Dene BR1 ..42 B8
Coppards La TN31 .197 D1
Copper Beech Cl
Gravesend DA12 ....36 D8
7 Orpington BR5 .....44 C4
Copper Beech View
TN9 ....143 A6
Copper La TN12 ...148 E5
Copper Tree Ct ME15 .116 A5
Copper Tree Wlk ME5 .68 C1
Copperfield Cl
Chalk DA12 ....37 A7
Kingswood ME17 ..118 D5
Copperfield Cres ME3 .38 C2
Copperfield Ct DA1 .14 E2
Copperfield Dr ME17 .117 E4
Copperfield Ho **6** ME4 .53 F4
Copperfield Rd Erith SE28 .3 C7
Rochester ME2 .....53 C2
Copperfield Way BR7 .29 C2
Copperfields
2 Dartford DA1 .....15 E1
Kemsing TN15 ......76 F2
Copperfields Cl TN15 .76 F2
Copperfields Orch TN15 .76 F2
Copperfields The ME1 .53 B4
Copperfields Wlk TN15 .76 F2
Coppergate ME7 ...68 F5
Coppergate Cl BR1 .42 B8
Copperhouse La ME7 .55 B6
Copperhouse Rd ME2 .52 C7

Copperpenny Dr ME7 ....69 B3
Coppers Ct TN4 ....159 A8
Coppers La TN12 ....145 E1
Coppice Ct ME7 ....69 B4
Coppice Rd ME5 ....68 C2
Coppice The
  Aylesford ME20 ....82 E1
  Bitchet Green TN15 ....93 D1
  Joyden's Wood DA5 ....31 D5
  Pembury TN2 ....160 D7
  Vigo Village DA13 ......80 B8
Coppice View ME14 .....100 E6
Copping's Rd TN11 .....125 C4
Copse Bank TN15 ....92 F7
Copse Cl Greenwich SE7 .11 B8
  Rochester ME1 ....53 C1
Copse Rd TN11 ....126 E4
Copse Side DA3 ....48 E6
Copse The ME3 ....40 E3
Copsehill ME19 ....81 E2
Copsewood Cl DA15 .....12 E1
Copsewood Way ME15 ..101 A3
Copt Hall TN18 ....197 D3
Copt Hall Rd
  Ightham TN15 ....94 A4
  Sole Street DA13 ....50 B5
Coptefield Dr DA17 ....3 E3
Copthall Ave TN18 .....189 A1
Copthorne Ave BR2 ......56 F8
Coralline Wlk 4 SE2 ......3 C4
Corben Cl ME16 ....99 B6
Corbridge Ho SE2 ....3 C3
Corbylands Rd DA15 .....29 E7
Cordelia Cres ME1 ....52 F2
Corelli Rd SE18,SE3 ......11 E6
Corhaven Ho 3 DA8 .....14 E7
Corinthian Ct ME3 ....27 B5
Corinthian Manorway
  DA8 ....4 D2
Corinthian Rd DA8 ....4 D2
Cork Ho BR5 ....44 B6
Cork La TN12 ....165 D8
Cork St ME20 ....82 F6
Corkwell St ME4 ....53 E3
Cormorant Ct ME2 ....52 C7
Corn Mill Dr BR6 ....44 A2
Cornel Ho 4 DA15 ....30 A5
Cornelia Pl DA8 ....14 E8
Cornell Cl DA14 ....30 E2
Corner Farm Rd TN12 ..149 E4
Corner Gn SE3 ....11 A5
Cornfield Way TN10 ....127 D6
Cornflower Cl ME14 ....100 E4
Cornford Cl Hayes BR2 ...42 A4
  Pembury TN2 ....160 B6
Cornford La TN2 ....160 B5
Cornford Pk TN2 ....160 C6
Cornforth Cl TN12 .....149 F4
Cornwall Ave DA16 ......12 F4
Cornwall Cl ME15 ....116 E7
Cornwall Cres ME11 .....66 D4
Cornwall Dr BR5 ....30 C1
Cornwall Rd Dartford DA1 .15 F4
  Gillingham ME7 ....54 D6
  Rochester ME1 ....53 C3
Cornwallis Ave
  Chatham ME4 ....53 E1
  Gillingham ME8 ....55 A4
  Linton ME17 ....132 E8
  Sidcup SE9 ....29 D6
  Tonbridge TN10 ....127 F4
Cornwallis Cl DA8 ....14 F8
Cornwallis Cotts ME17 ..115 E2
Cornwallis Rd
  Maidstone ME16 ....99 D4
  Woolwich SE18 ....2 B1
  Woolwich SE18 ....2 A1
Cornwallis Sch The
  ME15 ....115 F2
Cornwallis Wlk SE9 ......11 F4
Cornwell Ave DA12 ......36 C5
Corona Rd SE12 ....28 A8
Corona Terr ME6 ....81 F6
Coronation Cl DA5 ....13 D1
Coronation Cotts
  Stoke ME3 ....25 A3
  Ticehurst TN5 ....186 F2
Coronation Ct DA8 ......14 D7
Coronation Flats 5 ME4 .53 F3
Coronation Rd
  Chatham ME5 ....54 C2
  Grain ME3 ....27 B5
Corporation Rd ME7 .....54 D7
Corporation St ME1 .....53 C6
Corral Cl ME5 ....54 D2
Corral Hts 13 DA8 ....4 E1
Corrall Almshouses 5
  ME15 ....100 A3
Corrance Gn ME15 .....116 A8
Correnden Rd TN10 ....127 A3
Corseley Rd TN3 ....171 B5
Cortland Cl DA1 ....14 E1
Cory's Rd ME1 ....53 D6
Cossack St ME1 ....53 D3
Cossington Rd ME5 ......68 B1
Costells Mdw TN16 ......89 D1
Cot La TN27 ....168 B3
Cotleigh Ave DA5 ....30 D6
Cotman Way TN12 .....129 E6
Cotman's Ash La TN15 ...77 D4
Cotmandene Cres BR5 ...44 C4
Coton Rd DA16 ....13 A4
Cotswold Cl DA7 ....14 E5
Cotswold Gdns ME15 ...101 A2
Cotswold Rd DA11 ......35 E5
Cotswold Rise BR6 ......43 F3
Cottage Ave BR2 ....42 E1

Cottage Field Cl DA14 ...30 C7
Cottage Rd ME4 ....53 F6
Cottall Ave ME4 ....53 F2
Cottenham Cl ME19 .....97 F7
Cotton La DA2,DA9 ......16 C2
Couchman Green La
  TN12 ....149 F7
Coulman St ME7 ....54 D5
Coulter Ho DA9 ....17 C2
Coulters Cl ME14 ......100 D5
Coulton Ave DA11 ....35 E7
Council Ave DA11 ....18 C1
Council Cotts
  Chainhurst ME15 .....132 A7
  Chiddingstone Causeway
  TN11 ....141 A8
  Coxheath ME15 ....115 A4
Council Hos TN15 ......111 A8
Countess of Thanet's
  Almshouses TN8 ......154 F3
County Gate SE9 ....29 C5
County Gr ME19 ....97 B8
County Ho SE18 ....12 A1
County Rd
  Maidstone ME14 ......100 A5
  Newham E6 ....2 B8
Coupland Pl SE18 ....2 C1
Courier Rd RM13 ....4 D8
Course The SE9 ....29 A5
Court Ave DA17 ....3 F1
Court Broomes ME17 ...135 C8
Court Cres BR8 ....45 E5
Court Dr ME16 ....99 D4
Court Farm Rd SE9 ......28 E5
Court La Detling ME14 ...85 C5
  Hadlow TN11 ....129 B7
Court Lane Pl TN11 ....128 F8
Court Lodge Erith DA17 ...4 A1
  Shorne DA12 ....37 E2
Court Lodge Cotts
  East Farleigh ME15 ...115 A4
  Horton Kirby DA4 ......47 C6
  Mereworth ME18 ......112 E4
  West Farleigh ME15 ...114 D7
Court Lodge Farm
  ME18 ....114 B7
Court Lodge Flats TN3 .176 C6
Court Lodge Rd ME7 ....54 F6
Court Mdw Gillingham ME8 55 B2
  Wrotham TN15 ....78 F3
Court Mews DA11 ....18 B1
Court Rd Burham ME1 ...82 F8
  Dartford DA2 ....33 E3
  Eltham SE9 ....28 F7
  Royal Tunbridge Wells
  TN4 ....158 F4
Court Road (Orpington
  By-Pass)
  Chelsfield BR6,TN14 ....58 D5
  Orpington BR6 ....44 B2
Court Royal TN2 ....172 E8
Court St BR1 ....42 A7
Court Yd SE9 ....11 F1
Courtaulds Cl SE28 ....3 C1
Courtenay Rd ME15 .....99 F2
Courtenay Rd ME8 ......69 B8
Courtenwell TN3 ....157 F4
Courtfield Ave ME5 ......68 B3
Courthope TN12 ....146 A6
Courthope Ave TN5 ....184 F4
Courtland Gr SE28 ....3 D6
Courtlands
  Chislehurst BR7 ....29 B2
  Teston ME18 ....114 B8
  Tonbridge TN10 ....127 A3
Courtlands Ave SE12 ....11 B2
Courtlands Cl ME18 ....114 A8
Courtlands Farm TN17 .179 A3
Courtleet Dr DA8 ....14 B6
Courtwood Dr TN13 .....92 A3
Courtyard Gdns TN15 ...78 F3
Courtyard The
  Gillingham ME8 ....69 A8
  Watts's Cross TN11 ...126 A7
  Westerham TN16 .....105 D8
Cousley Wood Rd TN5 .185 C7
Couthurst Rd SE3 ....11 B7
Coutts Ave DA12 ....37 E4
Covelees Wall E6 ....2 F7
Coventry Cl 9 Newham E6 .1 F7
  Rochester ME2 ....52 D6
Coventry Rd TN10 .....127 D5
Coverdale Ave ME15 ...116 D6
Coverdale Cl ME5 ....68 B7
Covert The Chatham ME5 .68 B4
  Orpington BR6 ....43 E3
  Vigo Village DA13 ......79 E7
Covesfield DA11 ....35 F8
Covet Wood Cl BR5 .....43 F3
Covey Hall Rd ME6 ......66 A1
Cow La TN18 ....139 D1
Cow Leaze E6 ....2 A7
Cowan Cl E6 ....1 E8
Cowbeck Cl ME8 ....69 D6
Cowden Cl TN18 ......194 E8
Cowden La TN18 ......194 E7
Cowden Mews TN8 ....155 A5
Cowden Rd
  Maidstone ME14 ......100 C5
  Orpington BR6 ....43 F7
Cowden Sta TN8 ......155 D8
Cowdrey Cl
  Maidstone ME16 ....99 B2
  Rochester ME1 ....53 B2
Cowdrey Dr DA1 ....32 B8
Cowdreys TN9 ....143 C8
Cowen Ho 4 SE18 ....12 B8

Cowley Ave DA9 ....17 A2
Cowper Ave RM18 ....19 B6
Cowper Cl Bexley DA16 ..13 A1
  Bromley BR2 ....42 D5
Cowper Rd Bromley BR2 .42 D5
  Erith DA17 ....4 A2
  Gillingham ME7 ....54 D3
Cowstead Rd ME9 ....70 D2
Cox Gdns ME8 ....55 A2
Cox St ME14 ....85 E6
Cox's Cl ME6 ....81 F8
Coxheath Prim Sch
  ME17 ....115 C3
Coxmount Rd SE7 ....1 D1
Coxwell Rd SE18 ....2 C1
Cozenton Cl ME8 ....55 E1
Crabbs Croft Cl 7 BR6 ..57 C5
Crabtree Cl ME19 ....97 A2
Crabtree Manorway N
  DA17 ....4 C5
Crabtree Manorway S
  DA17 ....4 C3
Crabtree Rd ME8 ....69 D8
Crabtree Rdbt ME8 .....69 D8
Craddock Way ME8 .....69 D5
Cradducks La TN12 ....150 B4
Cradles Rd ME9 ....70 C2
Cradley Rd SE9 ....29 D7
Craft Workshops TN27 .135 C1
Cragie Wlk ME8 ....69 E4
Craig Ho Greenwich SE3 .11 B7
  Rochester ME1 ....53 E1
Craigerne Rd SE3 ....11 B7
Craigholm SE18 ....12 A6
Craigie Ct DA1 ....33 A8
Craigton Rd SE9 ....11 F3
Crales Ho SE18 ....1 E3
Cramonde Rd DA16 .....13 A5
Crampton's Rd TN14 ....92 B7
Cramptons TN17 ....179 F8
Cranborne Ave ME15 ...100 C1
Cranbourne Ave ME15 ..116 B8
Cranbrook CE Prim Sch
  TN17 ....179 D5
Cranbrook Cl
  Gillingham ME8 ....55 C3
  Hayes BR2 ....42 A3
  Maidstone ME15 ......116 F7
Cranbrook Ho 1 DA8 ...14 F7
Cranbrook Mews 1
  TN8 ....122 C1
Cranbrook Mus★ TN17 .179 D5
Cranbrook Rd
  Benenden TN17 ......189 F8
  Bexley DA7 ....13 F6
  Fosten Green TN27 ...181 C6
  Goudhurst TN17 ......178 A8
  Hawkhurst TN18 .....188 F4
  Knox Bridge TN12,TN17 165 F7
  Parkgate TN30 ....182 C1
  Tenterden TN30 ......192 E7
Cranbrook Sch TN17 ...179 D5
Cranbrook Union Mill★
  TN17 ....179 D4
Crandalls TN11 ....125 F1
Cranden Wlk DA4 ....47 E7
Crane Ho 11 TN18 ....188 F2
Crane House Gdns 10
  TN18 ....188 F2
Crane La TN17 ....179 D5
Cranford Cl ME15 ....55 D1
Cranford Ho DA1 ....15 A2
Cranford Rd Dartford DA1 .32 E7
  Tonbridge TN10 ......128 A5
Cranham Sq TN12 .....148 C5
Cranleigh Cl
  Orpington BR6 ....58 A7
  Sidcup DA5 ....14 B1
Cranleigh Dr BR8 ....45 E5
Cranleigh Gdns
  Chatham ME4 ....53 D3
  Maidstone ME16 ....99 C7
Cranley Par SE9 ....28 E4
Cranley Rd E13 ....1 B8
Cranmer Ct ME15 .....116 B8
Cranmer Rd TN13 ....91 E4
Cranmere Ct ME2 ....53 C8
Cranmore Rd BR7 ....28 F3
Cranstone Ct 12 DA14 ..30 B4
Cranwell Rd TN4 ......158 C4
Crates Yd TN4 ....159 A5
Crathie Rd SE12 ....11 B1
Craven Rd BR6 ....58 D7
Crawford St SE18 ....13 A8
Crawfords BR8 ....31 E1
Crawley Ct 1 DA11 .....19 F1
Crawshay Ct TN13 ......92 A4
Cray Ave BR5 ....44 B4
Cray Bldgs DA14 ....30 C2
Cray Cl DA1 ....15 A3
Cray Rd Crockenhill BR8 ..45 C3
  Erith DA17 ....14 A8
  Sidcup DA14 ....30 C2
Cray Valley Rd BR5 .....44 B4
Craybrooke Rd DA14 ....30 B4
Crayburne DA13 ....34 F4
Craybury End SE9 ......29 C6
Craydene Rd DA8 ....14 F7
Crayfields Bsns Pk BR5 .44 C8
Crayfields Ind Pk BR5 ...44 C7
Crayford Cl
  Maidstone ME14 ......100 C6
  Newham E6 ....1 E7
Crayford Commercial Ctr
  DA1 ....14 E1
Crayford High St DA1 ...14 E2
Crayford Ind Est DA1 ...14 F2
Crayford Rd DA1 ....14 F2

Crayford Sta DA1 ....14 E1
Crayford Way DA1 ......15 A3
Craylands BR5 ....44 C6
Craylands La DA10 ......17 A3
Craylands Sq DA10 .....17 D2
Crayleigh Terr DA14 ....30 C2
Craymill Sq DA1 ....14 F5
Crays Par The BR5 .....44 C7
Crayside Ind Est DA1 ...15 B3
Craythorne TN30 ......193 B8
Craythorne Ho TN30 ..193 B8
Creasey's Row TN14 ...106 E5
Credenhall Dr BR2 ......42 F1
Crediton Rd E16 ....1 A7
Credo Way RM20 ....17 B8
Creek La ME3 ....25 B2
Creek The DA1 ....18 B2
Creek Way RM13 ....4 E8
Cremorne Rd 1 DA11 ...35 F8
Crendon Pk TN4 ....159 A8
Crescent Ave RM17 .....18 D8
Crescent Cotts TN13 ....91 E7
Crescent Ct
  1 Grays RM17 ....18 D8
  Sidcup DA15 ....30 A8
Crescent Dr BR5 ....43 C3
Crescent Gdns BR8 .....45 C7
Crescent Ho ME2 ....53 C7
Crescent Rd Bromley BR1 28 A1
  Erith DA8 ....14 F8
  Royal Tunbridge Wells
  TN1 ....159 B3
  Sidcup DA15 ....29 F5
  Woolwich SE18 ....2 B2
Crescent The
  Bidborough TN4 ......142 E4
  Borough Green TN15 ...95 A8
  Groombridge TN3 ....171 C7
  Longfield DA3 ....48 E6
  Maidstone ME14 ....99 F8
  Northfleet DA11 ....35 F6
  Sevenoaks TN13 ....92 D6
  Sidcup DA15 ....29 F4
  St Mary's Island ME4 ..40 B1
  Swanscombe DA9 ......17 C2
  Tonbridge TN9 ....127 B2
Crescent Way
  Chatham ME5 ....67 D5
  Orpington BR6 ....57 E5
Cressey Ct 7 ME4 ......53 E4
Cressingham Ct 1 DA17 ..4 A1
  27 Gravesend DA12 ....19 B1
  Maidstone ME14 ......100 A6
  Rochester ME2 ....53 B8
Cross Way ME1 ....53 C3
Cross-at-Hand Cotts
  TN12 ....133 E2
Crossbrook Rd SE3 .....11 E4
Crossley Cl TN16 ....72 D4
Crossmead SE9 ....28 E7
Crossway Chatham ME5 .67 E6
  Erith SE28 ....3 D7
  Orpington BR5 ....43 D4
Crossway The
  Bromley SE9 ....28 D6
  Royal Tunbridge Wells
  TN4 ....158 D2
Crossways
  Chart Sutton ME17 ...117 B1
  Hextable BR8 ....31 F1
  Tatsfield TN16 ....88 C7
Crossways Bvd DA2,DA9 .16 E3
Crossways Ct TN16 .....88 C7
Crouch Croft SE9 ....29 A5
Crouch House Cotts
  TN8 ....122 B2
Crouch House Rd TN8 .122 B2
Crouch La Crouch TN15 ..95 B6
  Linkhill TN18 ....196 D6
Crow Cnr ME1 ....53 C5
Crow Dr TN14 ....75 C4
Crow Hill TN15 ....95 A4
Crow Hill Rd TN15 ......95 A7
Crow La ME1 ....53 C5
Crowden Way SE28 ......3 C6
Crowfoot Cl SE28 ....2 E5
Crowhurst La
  Basted TN15 ....94 E4
  West Kingsdown TN15 ..62 B4
Crowhurst Oast TN12 ..112 D1
Crowhurst Rd TN15 .....94 F6
Crowhurst Way BR5 .....44 C4
Crown Acres TN12 ....130 A6
Cronin Cl BR6 ....58 A6
Crown Ct Bromley BR2 ..42 E4
  Cranbrook TN17 ......179 C5
  Eltham SE12 ....11 B1
  Tilbury RM18 ....19 A5
Crown Gn DA12 ....37 B4
Crown Ho
  Lamberhurst TN3 .....176 B5
  Rochester ME1 ....53 B4
Crown La Bromley BR2 ..42 D4
  Chislehurst BR7 ....43 C8
  Shorne DA12 ....37 E4
Crown Lane Spur BR2 ..42 D3
Crown Rd Grays RM17 ..18 A8
  Marlpit Hill TN8 ......122 D4
  Orpington BR6 ....58 A6
  Shoreham TN14 ....59 F1
Crown St ME7 ....54 D6
Crown Woods Sch SE9 ..12 C2
Crown Woods Way SE9 .12 D2
Crownfields
  Maidstone ME14 ......100 F4
  Sevenoaks TN13 ....92 B2
Crowther Cl TN12 .....149 E4
Croxley Cl BR5 ....44 B7

Crofton Rd BR6 ....57 B8
Croftside DA13 ....80 A8
Cromarty Ct 8 BR1 .....42 C7
Crombie Rd DA15 ....29 D7
Cromer Pl 5 BR6 ....43 D1
Cromer Rd ME2 ....53 B8
Cromer St TN9 ....127 A1
Cromford Cl BR6 ....57 E7
Cromlix Cl BR7 ....43 B7
Crompton Gdns ME15 ..100 B3
Cromwell Ave BR2 ......42 B5
Cromwell Cl BR2 ....42 B5
Cromwell Mews BR7 ....43 A8
Cromwell Rd
  Maidstone ME14 ......100 B5
  Royal Tunbridge Wells
  TN2 ....159 C3
Cromwell Terr ME4 .....54 A3
Cronin Cl 2 ME20 ....81 F4
Crook Log DA6 ....13 D3
Crook Log Prim Sch DA6 13 D3
Crook Rd TN12 ....146 D1
Crooked La DA11,DA12 ..19 B1
Crookston Rd SE9 ....12 A4
Croombs Rd E16 ....1 C8
Crosby Ho DA1 ....15 A1
Crosier Cl SE3 ....11 E6
Crosley Rd ME7 ....54 D3
Cross Cl 11 SE28 ....3 B6
Cross Dr ME17 ....118 E1
Cross Keys
  Maidstone ME14 ......101 C4
  Sevenoaks TN13 ......108 A8
Cross Keys Cl TN13 ...108 A8
Cross La Sidcup DA5 ....30 F8
  Ticehurst TN5 ....186 D2
Cross Lane E DA12 .....36 B6
Cross Lane Gdns TN5 .186 D1
Cross Lane W DA11 ....36 B6
Cross Rd Dartford DA1 ..15 C1
  Hawley DA2 ....32 F4
  Northfleet DA11 ....35 F6
  Orpington,Keston Mark BR2 56 E8
  Orpington,St Mary Cray BR5 44 B4
  Sidcup DA14 ....30 B4
Cross St Chatham ME4 ..54 A4
  Erith DA8 ....14 E8
  Gillingham ME7 ....54 C6
  Gravesend DA12 ......19 B1
  Maidstone ME14 ......100 A6
  Rochester ME2 ....53 B8
Cross Way ME1 ....53 C3
Cross-at-Hand Cotts
  TN12 ....133 E2
Crossbrook Rd SE3 .....11 E4
Crossley Cl TN16 ....72 D4
Crossmead SE9 ....28 E7

Croxley Gn BR5 ...44 B8
Croyde Cl DA15 ...29 D8
Croydon Cl ME5 ...68 C4
Croydon Rd
  Hayes BR2,BR4,BR6 ...56 C7
  Tatsfield TN16 ...88 F3
  Westerham TN16 ...89 B2
Crozier Ho SE3 ...11 B4
Cruden Rd DA12 ...36 F6
Crump's La ME17 ...136 B4
Crumpsall St SE2 ...3 C2
Crundale **2** ME14 ...100 A5
Crundale Rd ME8 ...55 C3
Crundale Twr BR5 ...44 C1
Crundwell Rd TN4 ...142 F1
Crusader Cl ME8 ...69 B8
Crusader Ct DA1 ...15 F3
Crusoe Rd ...4 D1
Crutches La ME3,ME2 ...38 B1
Cryals Ct TN12 ...161 E5
Cryals Rd TN12 ...161 D5
Crystal Ho **2** SE18 ...2 F1
Cuckmere Ct **18** BR5 ...44 D1
Cuckold's Cnr ME3 ...38 C6
Cuckold's Cnr TN12 ...149 F4
Cuckolds Cnr DA3 ...63 B7
Cuckolds Green Rd ME3 ...25 B5
Cuckoo La
  Lamberhurst TN12 ...162 A2
  Tonbridge TN11 ...128 A7
Cuckoowood Ave ME14 ...83 F1
Cudham CE Prim Sch
  TN16 ...73 A3
Cudham Cl ME14 ...100 C6
Cudham La N TN14 ...73 D7
Cudham La S TN14 ...73 D2
Cudham Park Rd TN14 ...57 E1
Cudham Rd Downe BR6 ...73 B7
  Tatsfield TN16 ...88 E8
Cuff Cres SE9 ...11 D1
Cugley Rd DA2 ...33 C8
Culcroft DA3 ...48 F6
Culpeper Cl
  Hollingbourne ME17 ...102 E2
  Rochester ME2 ...53 D6
Culpepers TN17 ...177 E7
Culpepper Rd
  Coxheath ME17 ...115 B3
  Gillingham ME8 ...69 D4
Culverden Ave TN4 ...159 A6
Culverden Down TN4 ...158 F5
Culverden Park Rd TN4 ...158 F5
Culverden Pk TN4 ...158 F5
Culverden Sq TN4 ...159 A5
Culverden St TN1 ...159 A4
Culverstone Green Prim Sch
  DA13 ...63 F3
Culverstone Ho BR5 ...44 B6
Culverton Ct **19** DA14 ...30 A4
Culvey Cl DA3 ...48 E4
Cumberland Ave
  Bexley DA16 ...12 F3
  Gravesend DA12 ...36 C8
  Maidstone ME15 ...116 D8
Cumberland Cotts **23** ...159 A2
Cumberland Ct
  Sevenoaks TN13 ...91 E7
  Tonbridge TN10 ...127 A4
Cumberland Dr
  Dartford DA1 ...32 F8
  Erith DA7 ...13 E7
Cumberland Gdns **10**
  TN1 ...159 A2
Cumberland Ho SE28 ...2 D4
Cumberland Mews **12**
  TN1 ...159 A2
Cumberland Rd
  Chatham ME4,ME7 ...54 B7
  Gillingham ME7 ...54 C7
  Newham E13 ...1 B8
Cumberland Sch E16 ...1 A8
Cumberland Villas **5**
  DA12 ...36 C8
Cumberland Wlk TN1 ...159 A2
Cumberland Yd **11** TN1 ...159 A2
Cumbrian Ave DA7 ...14 C5
Cundy Rd E16 ...1 C7
Cunningham Ct TN4 ...159 B7
Cunningham Cres ME5 ...68 A4
Cunningham Ho ME1 ...53 B4
Cunningham Rd TN4 ...159 B7
Cupola Ct BR1 ...28 B3
Curates Wlk DA2 ...32 D5
Curlew Ct SE28 ...3 D6
Curlew Cres ME2 ...52 C6
Curlews The DA12 ...36 D6
Curran Ave DA15 ...12 F2
Currie Rd TN4 ...159 A5
Curteis Rd TN30 ...183 B1
Curtis Ct BR6 ...44 A2
Curtis Way Rochester ME1 ...67 D7
  7 Woolwich SE28 ...3 B6
Curtismill Cl BR5 ...44 B6
Curtismill Way BR5 ...44 B6
Curzon Cl BR6 ...57 D6
Curzon Ct SE9 ...29 C5
Curzon Dr RM17 ...18 C2
Curzon Rd Chatham ME4 ...54 C5
  Maidstone ME14 ...100 A6
Custom House for Excel Sta
  E16 ...1 B6
Cut The TN27 ...168 E8
Cutbush & Corrall Ct **1**
  ME14 ...100 B4

Cutbush Almshouses
  3 Maidstone ME14 ...100 A4
  1 Maidstone ME15 ...100 A3
Cutbush Cl ME17 ...119 D6
Cutbush Ho **2** ME15 ...100 A3
Cutmore St DA11 ...36 B8
Cutter Cl ME2 ...39 F3
Cutter Ho **6** DA8 ...4 E1
Cutter Ridge Rd DA13 ...51 A1
Cutty Sark Ct **6** DA9 ...17 A2
Cuxton BR5 ...43 C4
Cuxton Cl ME5 ...68 C3
Cuxton Com Inf Sch ME2 ...52 B2
Cuxton Com Jun Sch
  ME2 ...52 B2
Cuxton Ind Est ME2 ...52 C2
Cuxton Rd
  Maidstone ME15 ...116 F5
  Rochester ME2 ...52 F5
Cuxton Sta ME2 ...52 C2
Cyclamen Rd BR8 ...45 D5
Cygnet Cl ME20 ...82 A2
Cygnet Gdns DA11 ...35 F6
Cygnet L Ctr DA11 ...35 E6
Cygnet Rd ME5 ...68 C2
Cypress Ave ME3 ...40 E3
Cypress Ct ME7 ...54 F6
Cypress Gr TN2 ...173 C8
Cypress Rd ME2 ...39 C1
Cypress Tree Cl DA15 ...29 C8
Cyprus Pl E6 ...2 A6
Cyprus Sta E6 ...2 A6
Cyril Hall Ct DA1 ...18 F1
Cyril John Gange Lodge
  TN2 ...159 D2
Cyril Lodge **6** DA14 ...30 A4
Cyril Rd Bexley DA7 ...13 E5
  Orpington BR6 ...44 A2

D

D'arcy Pl BR2 ...42 A5
Dabbling Cl DA8 ...15 B7
Daerwood Cl BR2 ...42 F1
Daffodil Rd ME2 ...52 E7
Dagmar Rd ME4 ...54 B2
Dagonet Gdns BR1 ...28 A5
Dagonet Rd BR1 ...28 A5
Dahlia Dr BR8 ...45 F7
Dahlia Rd SE2 ...3 B2
Dainton Cl **2** BR1 ...42 B8
Daintons Cotts **2** TN18 ...188 F2
Dairsie Ct **4** BR1 ...42 C7
Dairsie Rd SE9 ...12 A4
Dairy Cl **3** Bromley BR1 ...28 B1
  Sutton at H DA4 ...33 B1
Dairy La Chainhurst TN12 ...131 F4
  Crockham Hill TN8 ...105 B1
  Woolwich SE18 ...1 F2
Dairy Pl TN12 ...131 F4
Daisy Munns Ho SE9 ...29 C7
Dajen Bsns Pk ME4 ...54 C1
Dalberg Way SE2 ...3 D3
Dale Cl Crayford DA1 ...14 F1
  Greenwich SE3 ...11 A4
Dale Ct Bromley BR1 ...42 D6
  Chatham ME5 ...68 A2
Dale End DA1 ...14 F1
Dale Rd Crayford DA1 ...14 F1
  Northfleet DA13 ...35 A4
  Rochester ME1 ...53 C3
  Swanley BR8 ...45 C6
Dale St Chatham ME4 ...53 E2
  Royal Tunbridge Wells
  TN1 ...159 B4
Dale The BR2 ...56 D6
Dale View DA8 ...14 F5
Dale Wlk DA2 ...33 C7
Dale Wood Rd BR6 ...43 E1
Daleside BR6 ...58 A5
Daleside Cl BR6 ...58 A4
Dalison Ct ME4 ...66 B4
Dallin Rd Bexley DA6 ...13 D3
  Woolwich SE18 ...12 B7
Dalmeny Rd SE9 ...14 B6
Dalton Cl BR6 ...57 E7
Dalton St ME7 ...54 C6
Daltons Rd BR6,BR8 ...59 C7
Damien Cl ME4 ...54 A2
Damigos Rd DA12 ...36 F7
Damon Cl DA14 ...30 B5
Damon Ct DA14 ...30 B5
Damson Ct BR8 ...45 D5
Damson Dr ME3 ...40 E3
Danaway Cotts ME9 ...71 C3
Dando Cres SE3 ...11 B4
Dane Cl Chatham ME5 ...68 C2
  Hartlip ME9 ...70 D6
  Orpington BR6 ...57 D5
  Sidcup DA5 ...31 A8
Dane Ct ME17 ...115 C2
Dane La ME9 ...70 D6
Dane Pk ME15 ...115 C6
Dane Rd TN14 ...75 F2
Danecourt Com Sch ME8 ...55 A2
Danefield Ct ME14 ...101 B4
Danehill Wlk DA14 ...30 A5
Danemore TN30 ...193 B8
Danes Cl DA11 ...35 C5
Danes Hill ME7 ...55 A6
Danescombe SE12 ...28 A7
Daniel Ho **5** ME6 ...99 E5
Danns La ME18,ME19 ...97 A1
Dansington Rd DA16 ...13 A3
Danson Cres DA16 ...13 B4

Danson Ho ★ DA6 ...13 C3
Danson La DA16 ...13 B3
Danson Mead DA16 ...13 C4
Danson Prim Sch DA16 ...13 A3
Danson Rd Bexley DA5 ...13 C1
  Bexley DA5,DA6 ...13 D2
Danson Underpass DA5 ...13 C1
Danson Way ME8 ...55 D2
Danvers Rd TN9 ...127 B1
Darby Gdns ME3 ...38 B3
Darby's La TN5 ...185 B2
Darent Cl TN13 ...91 C5
Darent Ind Pk DA8 ...15 C6
Darent Mead DA4 ...47 B8
Darent Valley Hospl DA2 ...33 D7
Darenth Ave TN10 ...127 C5
Darenth Cotts TN14 ...75 F8
Darenth Ct **19** BR5 ...44 D1
Darenth Dr DA12 ...37 B7
Darenth Gdns TN16 ...89 D1
Darenth Hill DA2 ...33 C3
Darenth La TN13 ...91 C5
Darenth Park Ave DA2 ...33 D6
Darenth Prim Sch DA2 ...33 E2
Darenth Rd Bexley DA16 ...13 A6
  Dartford DA1 ...32 F7
Darenth Rd S DA2 ...33 B4
Darenth Rise ME5 ...68 B3
Darenth Way TN14 ...76 A8
Darenth Wood Rd DA2 ...33 E6
Dargate Cl ME16 ...99 D7
Dargets Rd ME5 ...68 A3
Darland Ave ME7 ...54 E1
Darland Ho SE9 ...12 D1
Darlton Cl DA1 ...14 F4
Darman La TN12,ME18 ...130 D3
Darnets Field TN14 ...75 F2
Darnley Cl ME2 ...52 D6
Darnley Ct DA11 ...36 A8
Darnley Dr TN4 ...142 E4
Darnley Rd
  Gravesend DA11 ...36 A8
  1 Grays RM17 ...18 B8
  Rochester ME2 ...52 E6
Darnley St DA11 ...36 B8
Darns Hill BR8 ...45 C2
Darrick Wood Ho BR6 ...57 C7
Darrick Wood Inf & Jun Schs
  BR6 ...57 B6
Darrick Wood Rd BR6 ...57 B6
Darrick Wood Sch BR6 ...57 B7
Darrick Wood Sports Ctr
  BR6 ...57 B7
Dart Cl ME2 ...52 F7
Dartford Borough Mus ★
  DA1 ...32 E8
Dartford Gram Sch DA1 ...15 C1
Dartford Gram Sch for Girls
  DA1 ...32 C8
Dartford Hospl Specl Sch
  DA3 ...49 A6
Dartford Rd Coldblow DA5 ...31 C7
  Dartford DA1 ...15 B1
  Farningham DA4 ...47 A5
  Sevenoaks TN13 ...92 C3
Dartford Sta DA1 ...15 E1
Dartford Technology Coll
  DA1 ...32 D8
Dartford Trad Pk DA1 ...32 F6
Dartford West Technology
  Coll for Girls DA1 ...32 C8
Dartmouth Rd BR2 ...42 A2
Darwin Cl BR6 ...57 D5
Darwin Ct Eltham SE9 ...12 A1
  Rochester ME4 ...53 D5
Darwin Dr TN10 ...127 D6
Darwin Rd Bexley DA16 ...12 F4
  Tilbury RM18 ...18 F1
Dashmonden Cl ME2 ...39 C2
Dashwood Cl DA6 ...14 A2
Dashwood Rd DA11 ...36 A6
Davall Ho **10** RM17 ...18 B8
Davema Cl ME7 ...43 A8
Davenport Ave ME7 ...54 E7
Davenport Rd DA14 ...30 E6
Davey Cl ME1 ...53 C5
David Coffer Ct DA17 ...4 B7
David Ho **23** DA14 ...30 A5
David Ramsey Ho SE18 ...2 D2
David Saloman's Ho ★
  TN3 ...158 B8
Davidson Ho DA9 ...17 C2
Davis Ave DA11 ...35 E7
Davis Cl TN13 ...92 C5
Davy's Pl DA12 ...36 E2
Dawbourne TN30 ...183 B3
Dawell Dr TN16 ...72 C2
Dawes Cl DA9 ...16 F2
Dawes St ME7 ...54 C5
Dawn La ME18 ...97 D3
Dawson Ave BR5 ...44 B7
Dawson Cl SE18 ...2 C2
Dawson Ct **7** ME7 ...54 A6
Dawson Dr BR8 ...31 E1
Day Ho **2** ME4 ...100 B4
Days La DA15 ...29 E8
Days Lane Prim Sch
  DA15 ...12 F1
Dayton Dr DA8 ...15 D8
De Lapre Cl BR5 ...44 D2
De Luci Rd DA8 ...4 C1
De Lucy Prim Sch SE2 ...3 B4
De Lucy St SE2 ...3 B2
De Mere Cl ME8 ...69 D6
De Quincey Mews E16 ...1 A5
De Warren Ho DA11 ...18 D1
Deacon Cl ME2 ...52 E8
Deacon Est The ME20 ...83 A2

Deacon Trad Ctr ME2 ...53 A6
Deacon Trad Est TN9 ...127 D1
Deacons Leas BR6 ...57 D6
Deakin Leas TN9 ...143 B7
Deakins Terr BR6 ...44 A2
Deal Ho ME15 ...116 E8
Dean & Chapter Cotts
  DA13 ...35 D3
Dean La DA13 ...64 C5
Dean Rd Luddesdown DA13 ...64 C5
  Rochester ME2 ...52 F8
  Woolwich SE28 ...3 A6
Dean St ME15 ...115 C6
Deane Ct **8** ME7 ...54 C6
Deane Rd TN8 ...105 C2
Deans Ct **7** TN9 ...143 B8
Deans Hill Rd ME9 ...87 D5
Deansfield Prim Sch SE9 ...12 A4
Deanwood Cl ME8 ...69 D6
Deanwood Dr ME8 ...69 E4
Deanwood Prim Education
  Tech Sch ME8 ...69 D3
Debrabant Cl DA8 ...14 D8
Decimus Pl TN1 ...159 B4
Decoy Hill Rd ME23 ...23 F6
Deepdene TN5 ...185 A6
Deepdene Rd DA16 ...13 A4
Deerhurst Cl DA3 ...49 C6
Deerhurst Gdns ME16 ...99 D5
Deering Cl ME4 ...40 B2
Deerleap La TN14 ...74 E6
Defiance Wlk SE18 ...1 F3
Defiant Cl ME5 ...68 B6
Defoe Cl Chatham ME5 ...68 B6
  Erith DA8 ...14 F6
Degema Rd BR7 ...29 B3
Deidre Chapman Ho
  DA10 ...17 E1
Delacourt Rd SE3 ...11 B7
Delafield Rd SE7 ...1 C1
Delagarde Rd TN16 ...89 C1
Delamere Gdns **3** ME6 ...82 A8
Delamere Rd ME16 ...99 D5
Delarue Cl TN11 ...127 D8
Delaware Cotts TN8 ...138 F8
Delce Jun & Inf Schs
  ME1 ...53 D2
Delce Rd ME1 ...53 D4
Delisle Rd SE28 ...2 E4
Delius Dr TN10 ...127 F6
Dell Dr Maypole DA5 ...31 E7
  Swanscombe DA9 ...17 B2
Dell The Maypole DA5 ...31 E7
  Swanscombe DA9 ...17 B2
Delmar Cl ME2 ...3 A1
Delmonden Rd TN18 ...188 B1
Delvan Cl SE18 ...12 A7
Delves Ave TN2 ...159 C1
Demelza Cl ME2 ...52 A2
Demelza House Hospice
  ME9 ...71 F6
Den Cross TN8 ...138 D6
Den La TN12 ...131 C3
Denbeigh Dr TN10 ...127 D6
Denberry Dr DA14 ...30 B5
Denbigh Ave ME8 ...55 D1
Denbigh Cl BR7 ...28 F2
Denbigh Rd TN4 ...159 C7
Denbridge Rd BR1 ...42 F7
Dene Ave DA15 ...30 B8
Dene Cl DA2 ...31 E4
Dene Dr New Barn DA3 ...49 B7
  Orpington BR6 ...58 B7
Dene Holm Rd DA11 ...35 E5
Dene Rd DA1 ...32 F8
Dene The TN13 ...92 B1
Dene Way TN3 ...158 A7
Dene Wlk DA3 ...48 E6
Denecourt BR5 ...44 C1
Denefield TN13 ...91 C4
Denesway DA13 ...50 B3
Denham Cl DA16 ...13 C4
Denham Rd ME9 ...71 B7
Denham St **2** SE10 ...1 A1
Denison Mews ME3 ...25 C4
Deniston Ave DA5 ...30 E7
Denmark Ho **10** SE18 ...2 D2
Denmark Rd BR1 ...42 B8
Denmark St E13 ...1 A8
Dennard Way BR6 ...57 A6
Dennettsland Rd TN8 ...105 C1
Denning Cl ME16 ...99 B4
Dennington Ct TN4 ...143 A2
Dennis Cadman Ho ME20 ...82 F1
Dennis Rd DA11 ...36 B5
Dennis Wilcocks Cl ME9 ...71 B6
Denny Cl **13** E6 ...1 E8
Denny Ct **3** DA2 ...16 B1
Denstead Wlk **11** ME15 ...116 F6
Denton Cl ME15 ...116 E8
Denton Court Rd DA12 ...36 E8
Denton Gn ME8 ...55 D2
Denton Gdns Bexley DA16 ...13 C7
  Dartford DA1 ...31 E8
  Maypole DA5 ...31 E7
Denton St DA12 ...36 E8
Denton Terr DA5 ...31 E6
Denver Cl BR6 ...43 E3
Denver Ind Est RM13 ...4 F8
Denver Rd DA1 ...32 A8
Derby Cl TN11 ...126 E6
Derby Rd Gillingham ME5 ...54 E2
  Grays RM17 ...18 B8
  Maidstone ME15 ...116 C8
Derby Road Bridge RM17 ...18 B8

Derifall Cl E6 ...1 F8
Dering Way DA12 ...36 F7
Deringwood Dr ME15 ...100 F1
Dernier Rd TN10,TN9 ...127 C4
Derrick Gdns SE7 ...1 C3
Derry Downs BR5 ...44 C3
Derwent Cl DA1 ...32 B7
Derwent Cres DA7 ...14 A5
Derwent Dr Orpington BR5 ...43 D2
  Royal Tunbridge Wells
  TN4 ...158 E5
Derwent Ho **3** ME15 ...116 E7
Derwent Ho **10** TN10 ...127 C5
Derwent Rd ME8 ...69 D8
Derwent Way ME8 ...69 D8
Detillens La RH8 ...104 A6
Detling CE Prim Sch ME14 ...85 A1
Detling Cl ME8 ...55 C2
Detling Hill ME14 ...85 B2
Detling Rd Bromley BR1 ...28 A3
  Erith DA8 ...14 D7
  Northfleet DA11 ...35 D7
Devalls Cl E6 ...2 A6
Devenish Rd SE2 ...3 A4
Devon Cl Chatham ME5 ...68 C7
  Rainham ME8 ...55 F1
Devon Ct DA4 ...47 B8
Devon Rd
  Maidstone ME15 ...116 C8
  Sutton at H DA4 ...47 C8
Devonshire Ave DA1 ...15 B1
Devonshire Cl TN2 ...172 F8
Devonshire Rd
  Bexley DA16 ...13 E3
  Bromley SE9 ...28 E6
  Gillingham ME7 ...54 D7
  Gravesend DA12 ...36 B6
  Newham E16 ...1 B7
  Orpington BR6 ...44 A2
  West Thurrock RM20 ...17 E8
Devonshire Sq BR2 ...42 B5
Dewberry Gdns E6 ...1 E8
Dewberry Gdns ME4 ...40 B1
Dewhurst Cotts TN5 ...184 A8
Dewhurst La TN5 ...184 B8
DeWinter Ho TN13 ...92 A3
Dewlands Ave DA2 ...33 B8
Dexter Ho **2** DA18 ...3 E3
Dhekelia Cl ME14 ...100 A7
Dial Cl Gillingham ME7 ...54 F6
  Swanscombe DA9 ...17 D2
Dial Rd ME7 ...54 F6
Diameter Rd BR5 ...43 C3
Diamond Cotts TN12 ...145 B7
Diamond Field TN12 ...162 F3
Diana Ct DA8 ...14 E8
Diana Rd ME4 ...54 A2
Dianne Ct SE12 ...28 A7
Dianthus Cl SE2 ...3 B1
Dibden La TN13,TN14 ...107 E8
Dickens Ave Dartford DA1 ...16 A3
  Tilbury RM18 ...19 B6
Dickens Cl Erith DA8 ...14 B7
  Hartley DA3 ...48 F4
  Langley Heath ME17 ...117 E4
Dickens Ct Higham ME3 ...38 C4
  Rochester ME2 ...53 D8
  Staplehurst TN12 ...149 F5
Dickens Dr
  Chislehurst BR7 ...29 C2
  West Malling ME19 ...81 F1
Dickens Ho **3** DA17 ...3 F1
Dickens Rd
  Gravesend DA12 ...36 E7
  Maidstone ME14 ...99 D8
  Rochester ME1 ...53 C2
Dickens Way TN18 ...189 A2
Dickensian Cl ME3 ...25 A2
Dickley La ME17 ...120 A6
Dickson Ho SE18 ...11 E6
Dickson Rd SE9 ...11 E4
Digdog La TN12,TN17 ...166 D2
Diggerland ★ ME2 ...52 F4
Dignals Cl ME8 ...55 F2
Dilhorne Cl SE12 ...28 B5
Dillon Way TN2 ...159 D7
Dilly Wood Fields ME3 ...39 A3
Dillywood Cotts ME3 ...38 F2
Dillywood La ME3 ...38 F2
Dimmock Cl TN12 ...146 B7
Dingleden La TN17 ...190 F2
Dippers TN15 ...76 F2
Discovery Dr TN15 ...97 B3
Discovery Rd ME15 ...101 B2
Discovery Sch The ME18 ...97 D3
Dislingbury Rd TN11 ...144 C3
Disraeli Cl
  Maidstone ME15 ...116 E5
  Woolwich SE28 ...3 C5
Dittisham Rd SE9 ...28 E6
Ditton CE Jun Sch ME20 ...82 C1
Ditton Court Cl ME20 ...82 B1
Ditton Inf Sch ME20 ...82 C1
Ditton Pl ME20 ...82 B1
Ditton Rd DA6 ...13 E2
Dixon Cl Maidstone ME15 ...99 F2
  4 Newham E6 ...1 F8
Dixon Ho SE2 ...3 C1
Dixwell Cl ME8 ...69 D5
Dobell Rd SE9 ...11 F2
Dobells TN17 ...179 D4
Dobson Rd DA12 ...36 E3
Dock Approach Rd RM17 ...18 E8
Dock Head Rd
  Chatham ME4 ...54 A8
  St Mary's Island ME4 ...40 A1
Dock Rd Chatham ME4 ...53 F6
  Chatham ME4 ...54 A7
  Grays RM17 ...18 D8

Dock Rd *continued*
Grays RM17 . . . . .18 E7
Tilbury RM18 . . . . .18 E5
Dockland St E16 . . . . .2 A5
Dockside Outlet Ctr ME4 **54** A8
Dockside Rd E16 . . . . .1 D6
Doctor Hope's Rd TN17 **179** D4
Dodd Rd TN10 . . . . .127 E5
Doddington Cl ME16 . . . . . . .99 E5
Doddington Rd ME8 . . . . . .55 D3
Doebury Wlk SE18 . . . . .11 A8
Dog Cotts RH19 . . . . .154 B1
Doggetts Cl TN8 . . . . .138 C8
Doggetts Row ME15 . . . . .4 A5
Dogwood Cl Chatham ME5 68 D1
Northfleet DA11 . . . . .35 F4
Dolphin Cl SE28 . . . . .3 D7
Dolphin Dr ME8 . . . . .69 E5
Dolphin Ho ME1 . . . . .53 E5
Dombey Cl Higham ME3 . . . .38 C3
Rochester ME1 . . . . .53 C3
Domonic Dr SE9 . . . . .29 B5
Donald Biggs Dr DA12 . . .36 D8
Donald Troup Ho ME1 . . . .53 C4
Donaldson Rd SE18 . . . . . .12 A6
Doncaster Cl 7 ME15 . . .116 F6
Donet Cl ME8 . . . . .69 C5
Dongola Rd ME2 . . . . .39 B1
Donkey Field TN11 . . . . . .125 E1
Donkey La DA4 . . . . .61 B8
Donnington Ct 1 DA2 . . .16 B1
Donnington Rd TN13 . . . . .91 D7
Doon Brae TN4 . . . . .143 A2
Dorado Gdns BR6 . . . . . . .58 D7
Doran Gr SE18 . . . . .12 E7
Dorchester TN1 . . . . .159 B6
Dorchester Ave DA5 . . . .30 D8
Dorchester Cl
Cliffe Woods ME3 . . . . .39 B7
Dartford DA1 . . . . .32 F7
Orpington BR5 . . . . .30 B1
Dorchester Rd DA12 . . . .36 D8
Dorcis Ave DA7 . . . . .13 E5
**Doreen Bird Coll (Birbeck
Ctr)** DA15 . . . . .30 A5
Doreen Bird Coll (Studio Ho)
DA15 . . . . .30 A5
Doria Dr DA12 . . . . .36 F5
Doric Ave TN4 . . . . .142 F1
Doric Cl TN4 . . . . .142 F1
Dorin Ct TN2 . . . . .159 C3
Doris Ave DA8 . . . . .14 C6
Dorking Rd TN1 . . . . .159 C6
Dormers Dr DA13 . . . . .50 B2
Dornberg Cl SE3 . . . . .11 A7
Dornberg Rd SE3 . . . . .11 B7
Dornden Dr TN3 . . . . .158 A4
Dornden Gdns ME5 . . . . . . .68 E2
Dorne Cotts TN27 . . . . . . .137 E6
Dorney Rise BR5 . . . . .43 F5
Dorothy Ave TN17 . . . . . . .179 E4
Dorothy Evans Cl DA7 . . .14 B3
Dorrit Way
Chislehurst BR7 . . . . .29 C2
Rochester ME1 . . . . .53 D2
Dorset Ave DA16 . . . . .12 F3
Dorset Cotts TN7 . . . . . . .170 B4
Dorset Cres DA12 . . . . .36 E4
Dorset Rd Bromley SE9 . . .28 E6
Royal Tunbridge Wells
TN2 . . . . .159 D2
Dorset Road Inf Sch SE9 28 E6
Dorset Sq ME8 . . . . .55 D1
Dorset St TN13 . . . . .92 C2
Dorset Way ME15 . . . . . . .116 C8
Dorton Dr TN15 . . . . .92 F5
**Dorton House (Royal London
Society Sch for the Blind)**
TN15 . . . . .92 F5
Dorton House Sch TN15 . .92 F5
Dorville Rd SE12 . . . . .11 A2
Dothill Rd SE18 . . . . .12 C7
Dotterel Cl ME5 . . . . .68 D2
Doubleton La TN11 . . . . . .141 A5
Doug Siddons Ct 12
RM17 . . . . .18 C8
Douglas Almshouses
ME17 . . . . .120 D5
Douglas Bldgs TN12 . . . .149 E5
Douglas Cl TN16 . . . . .72 E2
Douglas Rd Bexley DA16 . .13 B6
Lenham ME17 . . . . .120 D5
Maidstone ME16 . . . . .99 E3
6 Newham E16 . . . . .1 A8
Tonbridge TN9 . . . . .143 A8
Douro Stables TN4 . . . . . .159 A4
Doust Way ME1 . . . . .53 D5
Dove App E6 . . . . .1 E8
Dove Cl ME5 . . . . .68 B6
Dove Ho TN10 . . . . .127 C6
Dovedale Cl DA16 . . . . .13 A5
Dovedale Rd DA2 . . . . .33 C7
Doveney Cl BR5 . . . . .44 D6
Dover Ho
2 Maidstone ME15 . . . . .116 E8
Rochester ME2 . . . . .39 C1
Dover Patrol SE3 . . . . .5 B5
Dover Rd Northfleet DA11 .35 D8
Woolwich DA11 . . . . .12 C5
Dover Rd E DA11 . . . . .35 F7
Dover Road Com Prim Sch
DA11 . . . . .35 F8
Dover St ME16 . . . . .99 C2
Doves Cl BR2 . . . . .56 E8
Dowding Ho TN12 . . . . . .145 F6
Dowding Rd TN16 . . . . .72 D4
Dowding Way TN2 . . . . . .143 E1
Dowding Wlk 3 DA11 . . . .35 E5

Dower Ho The DA14 . . . . . .30 F5
Dower House Cres TN4 .142 E3
Dowgate Cl TN9 . . . . .143 D7
Dowlerville Rd BR6 . . . . . . .57 F4
Dowling Cl ME6 . . . . .81 E7
Dowling Ho DA17 . . . . .3 F3
Down Ave TN3 . . . . .176 A4
Down La TN3 . . . . .173 B1
Down's Cl TN27 . . . . .151 E5
Downage The DA11 . . . . . .36 A6
Downash Ct TN5 . . . . .187 A3
Downash Ho TN5 . . . . .187 A3
Downbank Ave DA12 . . . . .14 D5
Downderry Way ME20 . . . .82 B1
Downe Ave TN14 . . . . .73 D8
Downe Cl DA16 . . . . .13 C7
Downe Ho 10 SE7 . . . . . . .11 C8
Downe Prim Sch BR6 . . . . .73 A8
Downe Rd
Cudham BR6,TN14 . . . . . . .73 C5
Farthing Street BR2 . . . . . . .56 E2
Downend SE18 . . . . .12 B7
Downer Ct ME1 . . . . .67 E8
Downham Way BR1 . . . . . .28 A4
Downings E6 . . . . .2 A7
Downlands ME17 . . . . .119 F6
Downleys Cl SE9 . . . . .28 F6
Downman Rd SE9 . . . . .11 E4
Downs Ave Bromley BR7 . .28 F3
Dartford DA1 . . . . .33 A8
Downs Cl ME14 . . . . .100 B8
Downs Cl ME18 . . . . .114 B3
Downs Rd
Istead Rise DA13 . . . . .35 D3
Maidstone ME14 . . . . .100 B8
Yalding ME18 . . . . .114 A1
Downs The ME5 . . . . .67 D1
Downs Valley DA3 . . . . .48 E5
Downs View Burham ME1 . .66 F1
West Malling ME19 . . . . . . .97 B8
Downs View Cl ME5 . . . . . .58 C1
Downs View Rd ME14 . . . .100 B8
Downs Wood DA13 . . . . . . .79 F8
Downside ME2 . . . . .53 A7
Downsland Ho ME2 . . . . . .52 C2
Downsview Chatham ME5 . .68 C8
Trottiscliffe ME19 . . . . .80 A5
Downsview Cl BR8 . . . . . . .45 F6
Downsview Prim Sch
BR8 . . . . .46 A6
Downsview Rd TN13 . . . . . .91 F2
Downsway BR6 . . . . .57 E5
Downton Cotts TN18 . . . .195 F4
Doyle Cl DA8 . . . . .14 E6
Doyle Way RM18 . . . . .19 C5
Drage Rd TN12 . . . . .129 E6
Drake Cres SE28 . . . . .3 C7
Drake Ct BR5 . . . . .44 B3
Drake Hall E16 . . . . .1 B5
Drake Mews BR2 . . . . .42 C5
Drake Point 12 DA8 . . . . . . .4 E1
Drake's Ave ME2 . . . . .52 F8
Draper Cl DA17 . . . . .3 F2
Draper Ct BR1 . . . . .42 E5
Draper St 3 TN4 . . . . .142 F2
Drawbridge Cl ME15 . . . . .116 E8
Drawell Cl SE18 . . . . .2 E1
Dray Corner Rd TN27 . . . .150 F7
Dray Ct TN11 . . . . .128 E8
Drays Cotts DA4 . . . . .47 B5
Drayton Ave BR6 . . . . .43 B1
Drayton Cl ME23 . . . . .23 E4
Drayton Rd TN9 . . . . .143 C8
Drew Prim Sch E16 . . . . .1 E5
Drew Rd E16 . . . . .1 E5
Drewery Dr ME8 . . . . .69 C5
Driffield Gdns TN9 . . . . . .142 F7
Drift The BR2 . . . . .56 D7
Drive The Ashurst TN3 . . .156 F5
Bexley DA5 . . . . .30 D8
Chislehurst BR7 . . . . .43 D8
Erith DA8 . . . . .14 B8
Gravesend DA12 . . . . .36 E4
New Barn DA3 . . . . .49 B6
Orpington BR6 . . . . .57 F8
Royal Tunbridge Wells
TN2 . . . . .159 B1
Sevenoaks TN13 . . . . .92 B1
Sidcup DA14 . . . . .30 B4
St Paul's Cray BR7 . . . . .43 F6
Tonbridge TN9 . . . . .143 B7
Drove Way The DA13 . . . . .35 E1
Drudgeon Way DA2 . . . . . .34 B5
Drummond Cl DA8 . . . . . . .14 E6
Drury Rd TN30 . . . . .183 B1
Dry Bank Ct TN10 . . . . . . .127 C4
Dry Bank Rd TN10 . . . . . . .127 C4
Dry End Rd ME20 . . . . .82 C3
Dry Hill Park Cres TN10 127 C3
Dry Hill Park Rd TN10 . . .127 B3
Dry Hill Rd TN9 . . . . .127 B3
Dryden Ho BR2 . . . . .42 D4
Dryden Pl RM18 . . . . .19 B6
Dryden Rd DA16 . . . . .12 F6
Dryden Way BR6 . . . . .44 A1
Dryhill La TN14 . . . . .91 B3
Dryhill Rd DA17 . . . . .13 F8
Dryland Ave 6 BR6 . . . . . .57 F6
Dryland Rd
Borough Green TN15 . . . . . .94 F6
Snodland ME6 . . . . .81 F8
Dublin Ho 16 ME15 . . . . .116 E7
Duchess Cl ME2 . . . . .52 E8
Duchess of Kent Ct The
ME20 . . . . .82 F8
Duchess Of Kent Dr ME5 68 B3
Duchess' Wlk TN15 . . . . . .92 E2

Ducie Ho 9 SE7 . . . . .11 C8
Ducketts Rd DA1 . . . . .14 F2
Duddington Cl SE9 . . . . . .28 D4
Dudely Rd DA11 . . . . .35 E8
Dudley Keen Ct TN9 . . . .143 E8
Dudley Lodge TN2 . . . . . .159 C4
Dudley Rd TN1 . . . . .159 A4
Dudsbury Rd Dartford DA1 15 B2
Sidcup DA14 . . . . .30 B2
Duggan Dr BR7 . . . . .28 E2
Duke Of Wellington Ave
SE18,SE28 . . . . .2 C3
Dukes Mdw TN11 . . . . . . .124 F2
Dukes Meadow Dr ME7 . .68 F6
Dukes Orch DA5 . . . . .31 C7
Dukes Rd TN1 . . . . .159 C5
Dukes Wlk 7 ME15 . . . . .100 A4
Dulverton Prim Sch SE9 .29 D6
Dulverton Rd SE9 . . . . . . .29 D6
Dulwich Prep Sch TN17 180 A4
Dumbourne La TN30 . . . .193 D2
Dumbreck Rd SE9 . . . . . . .12 A4
Dunbar Ct BR2 . . . . .42 A5
Dunbar Rd SE9 . . . . .11 E5
Dunblane Rd SE9 . . . . .11 E5
Duncan Ho 2 SE7 . . . . . . .11 B8
Duncan Rd ME7 . . . . .54 D5
Duncans Cotts 6 TN16 . .89 D1
Duncroft SE18 . . . . .12 E7
Dundale Rd TN12,TN3 . . .161 A3
Dundonald Cl 7 E6 . . . . .1 E7
Dunedin Ho
9 Maidstone ME15 . . . . .116 E5
Newham E16 . . . . .1 F5
2 Tilbury RM18 . . . . .19 A5
Dunera Dr ME14 . . . . .100 A7
Dunk's Green Rd TN11 . . .111 A5
Dunkeld Ho 6 ME15 . . . .116 E7
Dunkery Rd SE9 . . . . .28 E5
Dunkin Rd DA1 . . . . .16 A3
Dunkirk Cl DA12 . . . . .36 C3
Dunkirk Dr ME5 . . . . .67 F6
Dunkley Villas TN15 . . . . .79 F1
Dunlin Dr ME4 . . . . .40 C2
Dunlop Ct 7 TN18 . . . . . .189 A2
Dunlop Rd RM18 . . . . .18 F6
Dunn Lodge TN2 . . . . .159 D2
Dunn Street Rd ME7 . . . . .85 A8
Dunning's La ME1 . . . . . . .53 C4
Dunnings The ME16 . . . . . .99 A2
Dunnock Rd E6 . . . . .1 E8
Dunnose Ct RM19 . . . . .16 B8
Dunoon Cotts BR6 . . . . . . .73 A5
Dunorlan Farm TN2 . . . . .159 E4
Dunorlan Farm Cotts
TN2 . . . . .159 E4
Dunstable Ct 5 SE3 . . . . . .11 A7
Dunstall Welling Est
DA16 . . . . .13 B5
Dunstan Glade BR5 . . . . . .43 D3
Dunstan Gr TN4 . . . . .159 B6
Dunstan Rd TN4 . . . . .159 B6
Dunster Ct 16 DA2 . . . . . .16 B1
Dunster Terr 3 ME15 . . . .116 E8
Dunton Green Prim Sch
TN13 . . . . .91 E7
Dunton Green Sta TN13 . .91 E7
Dunvegan Rd SE9 . . . . .11 F3
Dunwich Rd DA7 . . . . .13 F6
Dupree Rd SE7 . . . . .1 B1
Durant Rd BR8 . . . . .32 A2
Durban Ho 7 ME15 . . . . .116 E5
Durham Cl ME15 . . . . .100 E1
Durham Rd Bromley BR2 . .42 A5
Gillingham ME8 . . . . .69 C7
Sidcup DA14 . . . . .30 B3
Durham Rise SE18 . . . . .2 D1
Duriun Way DA8 . . . . .15 B7
Durley Gdns BR6 . . . . .58 B7
Durlings Orch TN15 . . . . . .94 D6
Durndale La
Northfleet DA11 . . . . .35 E4
Northfleet DA11 . . . . .35 F5
Durrant Way
Orpington BR6 . . . . .57 D5
Swanscombe DA10 . . . . . . .34 C5
Durrell Gdns ME5 . . . . .54 C1
Dursley Cl SE3 . . . . .11 C5
Dursley Gdns SE3 . . . . . . .11 D6
Dursley Rd SE3 . . . . .11 C5
Duval Dr ME1 . . . . .67 E8
Duvard's Pl ME9 . . . . .71 F1
Dux Court Rd ME23 . . . . . .23 D2
Dux Hill TN15 . . . . .110 F8
Dux La TN15 . . . . .94 F1
Duxberry Cl BR2 . . . . .42 E4
Duxford Ho 12 SE2 . . . . . . .3 D4
Dwelly La TN8 . . . . .121 D3
Dyke Dr BR5 . . . . .44 C2
Dykewood Cl DA5 . . . . .31 E5
Dylan Rd DA17 . . . . .4 A3
Dymchurch Cl BR6 . . . . . . .57 E6
Dyneley Rd SE12 . . . . .28 C5
Dynes Rd TN15 . . . . .76 E2
Dynevor Rd TN4 . . . . .159 C7

E

Eagle Cl ME20 . . . . .82 A4
**Eagle Heights Bird of Prey
Ctr** ★ DA4 . . . . .60 B8
Eagle Ho RM17 . . . . .17 F8
Eagle Way ME17 . . . . .18 A2
Eagles Dr TN16 . . . . .72 D1
Eagles Rd DA9 . . . . .17 B2
Eaglesfield Rd SE18 . . . . .12 B6
Eaglesfield Sch SE18 . . . .12 A6
Eaglestone Cl TN15 . . . . . .95 A8

Ealdham Prim Sch SE9 . . .11 C3
Ealdham Sq SE9 . . . . .11 C3
Ealing Cl ME5 . . . . .68 C3
Eardemont Cl DA1 . . . . . . .14 F3
Eardley Point 7 SE18 . . . . .2 B2
Eardley Rd Erith DA17 . . . . .4 A1
Sevenoaks TN13 . . . . .92 B3
Earl Cl ME5 . . . . .68 B4
Earl Rd DA11 . . . . .35 E6
Earl Rise SE18 . . . . .2 D2
Earl St ME14 . . . . .99 F4
Earl's Rd TN4 . . . . .158 F4
Earlshall Rd SE9 . . . . .12 A3
Eason Villas TN12 . . . . . .148 D6
East Beckton District Ctr
E6 . . . . .1 F8
East Borough Prim Sch
ME14 . . . . .100 B5
East Cliff Rd TN4 . . . . .159 A4
East Crescent Rd DA12 . .19 C1
East Cross TN30 . . . . .193 B7
East Ct 4 ME15 . . . . .100 A1
East End Rd ME4,ME7 . . . .54 D8
East Farleigh Prim Sch
ME15 . . . . .115 B6
East Farleigh Sta ME16 . .115 B8
East Hall Hill ME17 . . . . . .133 E7
East Hall Rd BR5 . . . . .44 F2
East Ham Ind Est E6 . . . . . .1 E7
East Ham Manor Way E6 .2 A7
East Hill Biggin Hill TN16 . .72 B1
Dartford DA1 . . . . .32 F8
Sutton at H DA4 . . . . .47 D7
Tenterden TN30 . . . . .193 B8
East Hill Dr DA1 . . . . .32 F8
East Hill Farm Cvn Pk
TN15 . . . . .61 C1
East Hill Farm Pk TN15 . .61 B1
East Hill Rd TN15 . . . . .77 B7
East Ho DA1 . . . . .15 F4
East Holme DA8 . . . . .14 D6
East Kent Ave DA11 . . . . . .18 C1
East La DA4 . . . . .47 F7
**East Malling Research Sta
(Horticultural)** ME19 . . . .98 C6
East Malling Sta ME19 . . . .98 A6
East Mascalls 17 SE7 . . . . .11 C8
East Mill DA11 . . . . .18 C1
East Milton Rd DA12 . . . . .36 D8
East Park Rd ME20 . . . . . . .99 A8
East Peckham Prim Sch
TN12 . . . . .129 E7
East Point TN15 . . . . .93 A6
East Rd Bexley DA16 . . . . . .13 B5
Chatham ME4 . . . . .54 A7
East Rochester Way
Coldblow DA1 . . . . .31 D8
Sidcup DA5,DA15 . . . . .13 C1
East Row ME1 . . . . .53 C5
East St Addington ME19 . . .80 D3
Bexley DA7 . . . . .14 A3
Bromley BR1 . . . . .42 A7
Chatham ME4 . . . . .54 A3
Gillingham ME7 . . . . .54 D6
Grays RM20 . . . . .17 E8
Harrietsham ME17 . . . . . . .119 E5
Hunton ME15 . . . . .131 F7
Snodland ME6 . . . . .82 B8
Tonbridge TN9 . . . . .127 C2
East Street N ME19 . . . . . .80 D3
**East Sutton Park (HM Young
Offender Inst & Prison)**
ME17 . . . . .135 B7
East Sutton Rd
Sutton Valence ME17 . . . .135 A7
Sutton Valence ME17,
TN27 . . . . .135 C4
East Terr Gravesend DA12 .19 C1
Sidcup DA15 . . . . .29 C7
East Thamesmead Bsns Pk
DA18 . . . . .3 F4
East Thurrock Rd RM17 . .18 C8
East Weald Dr TN30 . . . . .183 B1
East Wickham Inf Sch
DA16 . . . . .12 F6
East Wickham Jun Sch
DA16 . . . . .13 A6
East Woodside DA5 . . . . . .30 E7
Eastbrook Rd SE3 . . . . .11 B6
Eastbury Rd Newham E6 . . .2 A8
Orpington BR5 . . . . .43 D3
Eastcombe Ave SE7 . . . . . .11 B8
Eastcote BR6 . . . . .43 F1
Eastcote Prim Sch DA16 .12 D4
Eastcote Rd DA16 . . . . .12 D5
Eastcourt Gn ME8 . . . . . . .55 B4
Eastcourt La
Gillingham ME7,ME8 . . . . . .55 B4
Gillingham ME8 . . . . .55 B3
Easterfields ME19 . . . . .98 C5
Eastern Ave RM20 . . . . . . .16 F8
Eastern Rd ME7 . . . . .54 F6
Eastern View TN16 . . . . . . .72 C2
Eastern Way Erith SE28 . . . .3 D5
1 Grays RM17 . . . . .18 A8
Eastfield Gdns DA12 . . . . .19 C1
Eastfield Ho ME16 . . . . .99 B2
Eastgate ME1 . . . . .53 C5
Eastgate Cl SE28 . . . . .3 D7
Eastgate Ct ME1 . . . . .53 C5
Eastgate Terr ME1 . . . . . . .53 C5
Eastland Ct 3 BR1 . . . . . . .42 C7
Eastlands Cl TN4 . . . . .172 E8
Eastlands Rd TN4 . . . . . . .158 E1
Eastleigh Rd DA7 . . . . .14 C4
Eastling Cl ME8 . . . . .55 D3

Eastling Ho 8 BR5 . . . . . .44 D1
Eastmead Cl BR1 . . . . .42 E7
Eastmoor Pl SE7 . . . . .1 D3
Eastmoor St SE7 . . . . .1 D3
Eastnor Rd SE9 . . . . .29 C7
Eastry Cl ME16 . . . . .99 C7
Eastry Rd DA8 . . . . .14 A7
Eastview Ave SE18 . . . . .12 E7
Eastway BR2 . . . . .42 A2
Eastwell 5 TN30 . . . . .193 A7
Eastwell Barn Mews
TN30 . . . . .193 A8
Eastwell Cl
Maidstone ME14 . . . . .100 C5
Paddock Wood TN12 . . . . .145 E6
Eastwell Mdws TN30 . . . .193 A8
Eastwood Rd ME17 . . . . . .136 C5
Eaton Ct BR7 . . . . .29 C2
Eaton Rd DA14 . . . . .30 D6
Eaton Sq DA3 . . . . .48 D6
Ebbsfleet Ind Est DA11 . .18 A2
Ebbsfleet Wlk DA11 . . . . . .18 B1
Ebdon Way SE3 . . . . .11 B4
Ebony Wlk ME16 . . . . .99 B3
Ebury Ct BR2 . . . . .56 E7
Eccles Row ME20 . . . . .82 F6
Eccleston Cl BR6 . . . . .43 D1
Eccleston Rd ME15 . . . . . . .99 F2
Echo Cl ME15 . . . . .116 F6
Echo Ct DA12 . . . . .36 C6
Echo Sq DA12 . . . . .36 C6
Eclipse Rd E13 . . . . .1 B8
Edam Ct 11 DA14 . . . . . . .30 A5
Eddington Cl ME15 . . . . . .116 B6
Eden Ave ME5 . . . . .68 A7
Eden Cl DA5 . . . . .31 D4
Eden Ct
1 Hawkhurst TN18 . . . . .188 F2
17 Orpington BR5 . . . . . . .44 D1
Tonbridge TN10 . . . . .127 C5
Eden Farm La ME19 . . . . . .97 D8
Eden Pl DA12 . . . . .36 B8
Eden Rd
High Halstow ME23 . . . . . . .23 E4
Joyden's Wood DA5 . . . . . . .31 D4
Royal Tunbridge Wells
TN1 . . . . .159 A2
Eden Valley Mus ★ TN8 .122 C1
Eden Villas TN8 . . . . .138 D7
Eden Wlk 9 TN1 . . . . .159 A2
**Edenbridge & District War
Meml Hospl** TN8 . . . . . .138 D7
Edenbridge Cl BR5 . . . . . .44 D5
Edenbridge Prim Sch
TN8 . . . . .122 D1
Edenbridge Rd TN7 . . . . . .155 E1
Edenbridge Sta TN8 . . . . .122 C3
Edenbridge Town Sta
TN8 . . . . .122 D2
Edenbridge Trad Ctr
TN8 . . . . .138 D8
Edendale Rd DA7 . . . . .14 D5
Edenhurst TN13 . . . . .92 A2
Edensmuir Ct SE3 . . . . .11 A7
Edgar Cl BR8 . . . . .45 F6
Edgar Rd Kemsing TN15 . . .76 E2
Tatsfield TN16 . . . . .88 D6
Edge Hill SE18 . . . . .12 B8
Edge Hill Ct DA14 . . . . .29 F4
Edgeborough Way BR1 . . .42 D8
Edgebury BR7,SE9 . . . . . . .29 B4
Edgebury Prim Sch SE9 . .29 C4
Edgebury Wlk BR7 . . . . . . .29 C5
Edgefield Cl DA1 . . . . .33 B7
Edgehill Gdns DA13 . . . . . .49 F8
Edgehill Rd BR7 . . . . .29 C4
Edgeler Ct ME6 . . . . .81 F7
Edger Pl 5 ME15 . . . . . . .100 A4
Edgeway ME4 . . . . .40 B2
Edgewood Dr BR6 . . . . .58 A5
Edgeworth Rd SE9 . . . . . . .11 D3
Edgington Way DA14 . . . . .30 D1
Edinburgh Ct DA8 . . . . .14 D7
Edinburgh Mews RM18 . . .19 B5
Edinburgh Rd
Chatham ME4 . . . . .54 C2
Gillingham ME7 . . . . .54 D5
Grain ME3 . . . . .27 B5
Edinburgh Sq ME15 . . . . .116 C7
Edington Rd SE2 . . . . .3 B3
Edisbury Wlk ME8 . . . . .69 D5
Edison Gr SE18 . . . . .12 F7
Edison Rd Bexley DA16 . . .12 F6
2 Bromley BR2 . . . . .42 A7
Edith Cavell Way SE18 . . .11 E6
Edith Ct BR1 . . . . .42 D6
Edith Pond Ct SE9 . . . . . . .29 B6
Edith Rd BR6 . . . . .58 A5
Ediva Rd DA13 . . . . .50 A4
Edmund Cl
Maidstone ME16 . . . . .99 A3
Meopham SA DA13 . . . . . . .50 A4
Edmund Hurst Dr E6 . . . . . .2 B8
Edmund Rd Bexley DA16 . .13 A4
Orpington BR5 . . . . .44 C3
Edmunds Ave BR5 . . . . .44 D6
Edna Rd ME14 . . . . .99 F8
Edward Ct Chatham ME5 . .54 C1
2 Newham E16 . . . . .1 A8
Edward Harvey Ct DA17 . . .3 F1
Edward Rd
Biggin Hill TN16 . . . . .72 E1
Bromley BR1 . . . . .28 C1
Chislehurst BR7 . . . . .29 B3
Edward St Chatham ME4 . .54 A3

Edward St continued
Rochester ME2 ....53 B7
Royal Tunbridge Wells
TN4 ....158 F8
Rusthall TN4 ....158 C4
Edward Tyler Rd SE12 ...28 C6
Edward Wlk ME19 ....97 F8
Edwards Cl ME8 ....69 C5
Edwards Ct DA4 ....60 E7
Edwards Gdns BR8 ......45 D5
Edwards Rd DA17 ....4 A2
Edwin Arnold Ct DA15 ...29 F4
Edwin Cl DA7 ....13 F8
Edwin Petty Pl DA2 .....33 C8
Edwin Rd Dartford DA2 ..32 C5
Gillingham ME8 ....69 C8
Edwin St Gravesend DA12 .36 B8
Newham E16 ....1 A8
Edwins Rd ME9 ....71 C7
Egdean Wlk TN13 ....92 C4
Egerton Ave BR8 ....45 F8
Egerton CE Prim Sch
TN27 ....137 F3
Egerton Cl DA1 ....32 B7
Egerton House Rd TN27 137 E4
Egerton Rd ME14 ....99 C7
Eggpie La TN11,TN14 ...125 E7
Egham Rd E13 ....1 B8
Eglantine La DA4 ....47 B3
Eglinton Hill SE18 .....12 B7
Eglinton Prim Sch SE18 .12 A8
Eglinton Rd
Swanscombe DA10 ....17 F1
Woolwich SE18 ....12 B8
Egremont Rd ME15 .....100 F2
Egret Cl ME4 ....40 B2
Eileen Ct BR7 ....29 A3
Eisenhower Dr E6 ....1 E8
Elaine Ave ME2 ....52 E7
Elaine Ct ME2 ....52 E6
Elaine Prim Sch ME2 ....52 E6
Elbourne Trad Est DA17 ...4 B3
Elbury Dr E16 ....1 A7
Elder Cl Kingswood ME17 118 D2
Sidcup DA15 ....29 F7
Elder Ct ME8 ....69 B6
Elderslie Rd SE9 ....12 A4
Eldon St ME4 ....54 A4
Eldon Way TN12 ....145 F7
Eldred Dr BR5 ....58 D8
Eleanor Smith Sch E16 ...1 C8
Eleanor Wlk 19 SE18 ....1 F2
Elford Cl SE3 ....11 C3
Elford Rd ME3 ....22 B5
Elgal Cl BR6 ....57 B5
Elgar Cl TN10 ....127 C6
Elgar Gdns RM18 ....19 B6
Elgin Gdns ME2 ....52 D5
Elham Cl Bromley BR1 ...28 D1
Gillingham ME8 ....55 B3
Elibank Rd SE9 ....12 A3
Eling Ct ME15 ....116 A8
Eliot Rd DA1 ....16 B2
Eliza Cook Cl DA9 ......17 B3
Elizabeth Cl RM18 ......19 B5
Elizabeth Cotts DA4 ....60 E8
Elizabeth Ct Chatham ME5 .68 A7
Dartford DA2 ....33 D3
Erith DA8 ....14 D7
Gillingham ME8 ....55 C1
6 Gravesend DA11 ....19 A1
Elizabeth Fry Pl SE18 ...11 E6
Elizabeth Garlick Ct 1
TN1 ....159 B4
Elizabeth Garrett Anderson
Ho 9 DA17 ....4 A3
Elizabeth Ho
Maidstone ME14 ....100 A6
Rochester ME1 ....53 C4
Elizabeth Huggins Cotts
DA11 ....36 B6
Elizabeth Pl DA4 ....46 E3
Elizabeth Smith's Ct
ME19 ....97 F7
Elizabeth St DA9 ....16 E2
Elizabeth Terr SE9 .....11 F1
Elizabeth Way BR5 .....44 C4
Ellard Ct DA16 ....13 C4
Ellen Cl BR1 ....42 D6
Ellen Wilkinson Prim Sch
E6 ....1 E8
Ellen's Pl ME9 ....71 C6
Ellenborough Rd DA14 ...30 E3
Ellenswood Cl ME15 ....101 A1
Ellerman Rd RM18 ......18 F5
Ellerslie DA12 ....36 D8
Ellerslie Ct 3 DA12 ...36 D8
Ellesmere Ct SE12 ......28 A7
Ellingham Leas ME15 ...116 C7
Elliott Rd BR2 ....42 D5
Elliott St DA12 ....36 D8
Elliotts La TN16 ....90 C3
Ellis Cl Eltham SE9 ....29 C6
Swanley BR8 ....45 D5
Ellis Ct DA1 ....33 B7
Ellis Ho 8 ME14 ......100 B4
Ellis Way DA1 ....32 F6
Elliscombe Mount SE7 ...11 C8
Elliscombe Rd SE7 .....11 C8
Ellison Rd DA15 ....29 D7
Elliston Ho 8 SE18 ......2 A2
Elm Ave Chatham ME4 ...53 E1
Chattenden ME3 ....40 A4
Elm Cl Dartford DA1 ....32 C7
Egerton TN27 ....137 F3

Elm Cl continued
Higham ME3 ....38 C3
Elm Cotts BR8 ....46 B8
Elm Court Ind Est ME7 ..68 E3
Elm Cres ME19 ....97 F8
Elm Dr BR8 ....45 D7
Elm Gr Erith DA8 ....14 D7
Maidstone ME15 ....100 B3
Orpington BR6 ....43 F1
Tonbridge TN11 ....126 F5
Elm La TN10 ....127 C3
Elm Par 10 Dartford DA1 ..30 A4
Elm Rd Dartford DA1 ....32 D7
Erith DA8 ....15 A6
Gillingham ME7 ....54 E6
Gravesend DA12 ....36 C5
Grays RM17 ....18 C8
Hoo St Werburgh ME3 ...40 E3
Orpington BR6 ....58 A3
Royal Tunbridge Wells
TN4 ....142 F1
Sidcup DA14 ....30 A4
Stone DA9 ....16 E1
Westerham TN16 ....89 E2
Elm Terr 3 Eltham SE9 ..12 A1
West Thurrock RM20 ....17 B8
Elm Tree Cotts ME3 .....25 A3
Elm Tree Ct 20 SE7 ....11 C8
Elm Tree Dr ME1 ....53 A2
Elm Wlk Aylesford ME20 .82 E1
Orpington BR6 ....56 F7
Elmbank Dr BR1 ....42 D7
Elmbourne Dr DA17 ......4 B2
Elmbrook Gdns SE9 .....11 E3
Elmcroft Ave DA15 ......13 A1
Elmcroft Rd BR6 ....44 A2
Elmdene Rd SE18 ....2 B1
Elmfield Gillingham ME8 .55 A3
Tenterden TN30 ....193 B8
Elmfield Cl
Gravesend DA11 ....36 B7
Sevenoaks Weald TN14 .108 B2
Elmfield Ct Bexley DA16 .13 B6
Coxheath ME17 ....115 C3
Tenterden TN30 ....193 B8
Elmfield Pk BR1 ....42 A6
Elmfield Rd BR1 ....42 A6
Elmhurst Bexley DA17 ...13 E8
Swanscombe DA10 ......17 B1
Elmhurst Ave TN2 .....160 D8
Elmhurst Gdns ME4 .....53 E3
Elmhurst Rd SE9 ....28 E5
Elmington Cl DA5 ....14 B1
Elmlee Ct ME7 ....28 F2
Elmley Cl 16 E6 ....1 E5
Elmley St SE18 ....2 D2
Elmshurst Gdns TN10 ..127 C7
Elmslie Ct SE9 ....12 A1
Elmstead Ave BR7 ......28 F3
Elmstead Cl TN13 ....91 E5
Elmstead Glade BR7 ....28 F2
Elmstead La BR7 ....28 F3
Elmstead Rd DA8 ....14 E6
Elmstead Woods Sta BR7 28 E2
Elmsted Cres DA16 .....13 C8
Elmstone Cl ME16 ......99 B2
Elmstone Hole Rd
ME17 ....136 D8
Elmstone La ME16 ......99 B2
Elmstone Rd ME8 ....69 D7
Elmstone Terr 3 BR5 ...44 C5
Elmtree Cotts TN14 ....74 D4
Elmwood Dr DA5 ....30 E8
Elmwood Rd ME3 ....39 F6
Elphick's Pl TN2 ......173 B8
Elrick Cl DA8 ....14 E8
Elsa Rd DA16 ....13 C5
Elsinore Ho 8 SE18 ......1 E2
Elster Pl ME19 ....97 B3
Elstow Cl Eltham SE9 ...11 F2
Eltham SE9 ....12 A2
Elstree Gdns DA17 ....3 E2
Elswyn Ho 14 DA14 .....30 A5
Eltham CE Prim Sch SE9 11 F2
Eltham Coll SE9 ....28 C6
Eltham Green Rd SE9 ...11 C3
Eltham Green SE9 ......11 D1
Eltham High St SE9 ....11 F1
Eltham Hill SE9 ....11 E2
Eltham Hill Tech Coll for
Girls SE9 ....11 E1
Eltham Pal★ SE9 ....11 E1
Eltham Palace Rd SE9 ..11 D1
Eltham Park Gdns SE9 ...12 A3
Eltham Rd SE12,SE9 ....11 B2
Eltham Sta SE9 ....11 F2
Elveys Cotts ME18 ....113 F1
Elvington Cl ME16 .....99 D5
Elwick Ct DA1 ....15 A3
Elwill Way DA13 ....49 F8
Elwyn Gdns SE12 ....28 A8
Ely Cl Erith DA8 ....14 F5
Gillingham ME8 ....55 E2
Ely Ct TN1 ....159 B4
Ely Gdns TN10 ....127 D4
Elysian Ave BR5 ....43 F3
Embassy Cl ME7 ....54 F1
Embassy Ct Bexley DA16 .13 B4
Sidcup DA14 ....30 B5
Ember Ct BR5 ....43 C2
Emblin Ct 2 DA14 .....30 A4
Emerald Ct 1 Newham E16 .1 D7
Rochester ME1 ....67 D7
Emersons Ave BR8 ......31 F1
Emerton Rd DA6 ....13 E3
Emes Rd DA8 ....14 C7
Emily Jackson Cl TN13 .92 B3
Emily Jackson Ho TN13 .92 B3

Emily Rd ME5 ....68 B6
Emmanuel Ho 2 SE18 ....2 D1
Emmet Hill La ME8 .....130 F5
Emmetts Garden★
TN14 ....106 D5
Emmetts La TN14,TN16 .106 D6
Empress Dr BR7 ....29 B2
Empress Rd DA12 ....36 E8
Emsworth Gr ME14 ....100 D6
Endeavour Foyer The 8
ME4 ....54 B2
Enderfield St BR7 ......43 A8
Engineer Cl SE18 ....12 A8
Englefield Cl BR5 ......43 F5
Englefield Cres
Cliffe Woods ME3 ....39 B7
Orpington BR5 ....44 A5
Englefield Path BR5 ....44 A5
English Martyrs' RC Prim
Sch ME2 ....53 B8
Ennerdale Ho ME15 ....116 C7
Ennerdale Rd DA7 ......14 A6
Ennis Rd SE18 ....12 C8
Ensfield Rd Leigh TN11 125 E1
Tonbridge TN11 ....142 A6
Ensign Ho RM17 ....17 F8
Enslin Rd SE9 ....29 A8
Enterprise Bsns Est ME2 53 D8
Enterprise Cl ME2 .....53 D8
Enterprise Ctr The ME5 .84 C8
Enterprise Rd ME15 ...100 A1
Enterprise Way TN8 ...122 C3
Epaul La ME1 ....53 C6
Eppe Cl 2 ME2 ....53 B8
Epsom Cl Bexley DA7 ...14 B4
Maidstone ME15 ....116 F6
West Malling ME19 .....97 B8
Epstein Rd SE28 ....3 B5
Erebus Dr SE28 ....2 C4
Erica Ct BR8 ....45 E5
Eridge Ct TN2 ....158 F1
Eridge Green Cl BR5 ...44 C1
Eridge Rd
Groombridge TN3 ......171 D5
Royal Tunbridge Wells
TN2,TN4 ....158 E1
Eridge Sta TN3 ....171 E2
Erindale SE18 ....12 D8
Erindale Terr SE18 ....12 D8
Ermington Rd SE9 .....29 C6
Ernest Dr ME16 ....99 B5
Ernest Rd ME4 ....54 A3
Erskine Ho 8 SE7 ......11 C8
Erskine Park Rd TN4 ..158 C4
Erskine Rd DA13 ....80 B8
Erwood Rd SE7 ....1 E1
Escott Gdns SE9 ....28 E4
Escreet Gr SE18 ....2 A2
Eshcol Rd ME3 ....41 C6
Esher Cl DA5 ....30 E7
Eskdale Cl DA2 ....33 C7
Eskdale Rd DA7 ....14 A6
Esmonde Ho 15 ME7 ....54 A6
Esplanade ME1 ....53 B5
Essenden Rd DA17 ....4 A1
Essex Cl TN2 ....172 F8
Essex Rd 1 Dartford DA1 15 D1
Gravesend DA11 ....36 A7
Halling ME2 ....66 A6
Longfield DA3 ....48 D7
Maidstone ME15 ....116 E6
West Thurrock RM20 ....17 A8
Estelle Cl ME1 ....67 D7
Estridge Way TN10 ....127 D7
Estuary Cotts RM18 ....20 D7
Etfield Gr DA14 ....30 B3
Ethel Brooks Ho SE18 ..12 B8
Ethel Rd E16 ....1 B7
Ethel Terr BR6 ....58 C2
Ethel-Maud Ct ME7 ....54 D7
Ethelbert Rd Bromley BR1 42 A6
Erith DA8 ....14 C7
Hawley DA2 ....32 E3
Orpington BR5 ....44 D6
Rochester ME1 ....53 C4
Etherington Hill TN3 .158 C8
Ethnam La TN18 ......196 E4
Ethronvi Rd DA7 ....13 E4
Eton Cl ME5 ....67 F4
Eton Ct TN13 ....92 B4
Eton Rd BR6 ....58 B6
Eton Way DA1 ....15 C3
Eugenie Mews BR7 .....43 B8
Europa Pk RM20 ....17 C8
Europa Trad Est DA8 ....4 D1
Europe Rd SE18 ....1 F3
Euroway ME20 ....98 E8
Eustace Pl 2 SE18 ......1 F2
Eva Rd ME7 ....54 D3
Evanlode Ho 5 SE2 ......3 C4
Evans Cl DA9 ....17 A2
Evans Ct SE9 ....28 E6
Evelyn Cl ME2 ....53 C8
Evelyn Denington Rd E6 ..1 E8
Evelyn Ho 5 ME2 ......53 C8
Evelyn Rd Maidstone ME16 99 E3
Newham E16 ....1 B5

Evelyn Rd continued
Otford TN14 ....76 C2
Evenden Ho TN17 ......179 D5
Evenden Rd DA13 ....50 A2
Everard Ave BR2 ....42 A1
Everest Cl 1 DA11 .....35 E5
Everest Ct SE9 ....28 E6
Everest Dr ME3 ....40 E4
Everest La ME2 ....39 B1
Everest Mews ME3 ......40 E4
Everest Pl BR8 ....45 D5
Everest Rd SE9 ....11 F2
Everett Wlk DA17 ....3 F1
Everglade BR1 ....72 D1
Everglade Cl DA3 ......48 F5
Everglades The ME7 ....68 F6
Evergreen Cl
Gillingham ME7 ....69 A5
Higham ME3 ....38 B3
Leybourne ME19 ....81 E2
Eversfield Ct SE12 ....28 B6
Eversley Ave DA7,DA8 ..14 C5
Eversley Cl ME16 ......99 C6
Eversley Cross DA7 ....14 C5
Eversley Rd SE7 ....11 B8
Evesham Rd DA12 ......36 D6
Evorg Ho 6 ME4 ....54 B2
Evry Rd DA14 ....30 C2
Ewart Rd ME4 ....53 E1
Ewehurst La TN3 ......157 F6
Ewell Ave ME19 ....97 A8
Ewell La ME15 ....114 D5
Ewin Cl TN12 ....146 A6
Ewins Cl TN12 ....146 A6
Excel Waterfront E16 ...1 B6
Exedown Rd TN15 ......78 C4
Exeter Cl Newham E6 ....1 F7
Tonbridge TN10 ....127 C4
Exeter Rd Bexley DA16 .12 F5
Gravesend DA12 ....36 D5
Newham E16 ....1 A8
Exeter Wlk ME1 ....67 C7
Exford Gdns SE12 ......28 B7
Exford Rd SE12 ....28 B7
Exmouth Rd Bexley DA16 13 C7
Gillingham ME7 ....54 C7
Grays RM17 ....18 B8
Exton Cl ME5 ....68 C2
Exton Gdns ME14 .....100 F5
Eye The ME4 ....53 F5
Eyhorne St ME17 .....102 D2
Eynsford Castle★ DA4 ..60 E8
Eynsford Cl BR5 ....43 C3
Eynsford Cres DA5 .....30 D7
Eynsford Rd
Crockenhill BR8 ....45 E3
Eynsford DA4 ....46 F1
Maidstone ME16 ....99 D7
Swanscombe DA9 ......17 C2
Eynsford Rise DA4 .....60 D6
Eynsford Sta DA4 .....60 D6
Eynsham Dr SE2 ....3 B3
Eynswood Dr DA14 .....30 C3

F

F Ave SE18 ....2 B3
Fackenden La TN14 .....76 C7
Factory Rd Newham E16 ...1 E5
Northfleet DA11 ....18 C1
Faesten Way DA5 ....31 E5
Fagus Cl ME5 ....68 B1
Fair Acres BR2 ....42 A4
Fair View Com Inf Sch
ME8 ....69 C5
Fair View Com Jun Sch
ME8 ....69 C5
Fair View Cotts TN5 ..185 A6
Faircre Pl DA3 ....48 E6
Fairbank Ave BR6 ......57 B8
Fairbourne Heath Cotts
ME17 ....119 B1
Fairbourne La ME17 ...119 C4
Fairby La DA3 ....48 E3
Fairby Rd SE12 ....11 B2
Faircrouch La TN5 ....184 B5
Fairfax Bsns Ctr ME15 116 F4
Fairfax Gdns SE3 ......11 C6
Fairfax Ho ME15 ......116 C5
Fairfax Mews E16 ....1 B5
Fairfield Ave TN2 ....159 C5
Fairfield Cl Kemsing TN15 77 A1
Sidcup DA15 ....12 F1
Fairfield Cres TN9 ...143 C8
Fairfield Gr SE7 ......11 D8
Fairfield Rd Bexley DA7 .13 F5
Borough Green TN15 ....94 F8
Bromley BR1 ....28 A1
Orpington BR5 ....43 D3
Fairfield Way TN11 ...126 F5
Fairfields DA12 ....36 E3
Fairford Ave DA7 ......14 D6
Fairglen Cotts TN5 ...184 B3
Fairglen Rd TN5 ......184 B4
Fairhurst Dr ME15 ....115 B4
Fairings The TN30 ....193 B8
Fairland Ho BR2 ....42 B5
Fairlands Ct 6 SE9 ...12 A1
Fairlawn SE7 ....11 C8
Fairlawn Ave DA7 ......13 D5
Fairlawn Cl ME18 .....114 A8
Fairlawn Ct SE7 ....11 C8
Fairlead Rd ME1 ....53 D1
Fairlight Cl TN4 .....143 A2
Fairlight Cross DA3 ...49 C6
Fairlight Ct TN10 ....127 B4

Fairman's La TN12 ....162 B6
Fairmead BR1 ....42 F5
Fairmead Cl BR1 ......42 F5
Fairmead Rd TN8 .....122 C5
Fairmeadow ME14 ......99 F4
Fairmile Ho BR5 ....44 A7
Fairmile Rd TN2 .....159 E5
Fairmont Ct DA17 ....3 F1
Fairoak Cl BR5 ....43 B2
Fairoak Dr SE9 ....12 D2
Fairseat La Fairseat TN15 .79 B5
Stansted TN15 ....63 A1
Fairthorn Rd SE7 ......1 A1
Fairtrough Rd BR6 ....74 B7
Fairview Erith DA8 ....14 F7
Hawkhurst TN18 ......188 F2
New Ash Green DA3 ....62 B7
Fairview Ave ME8 .....69 B5
Fairview Cl TN9 ......143 B7
Fairview Cotts ME15 .115 F5
Fairview Dr Higham ME3 .38 B4
Orpington BR6 ....57 B6
Fairview Gdns DA5 ....50 A4
Fairview Ind Pk RM13 ...4 D8
Fairview Rd DA13 .....35 E1
Fairview Trad Est RH8 104 A2
Fairwater Ave DA16 ...13 A3
Fairway Bexley DA6 ...13 E2
Orpington BR5 ....43 D4
Fairway Cl ME1 ....53 C1
Fairway Ct 12 SE9 ....12 A1
Fairway Dr Dartford DA2 33 B8
Erith DA8 ....3 E7
Fairway The
Bromley,Southborough BR1 .42 F4
9 Bromley,Sundridge BR1 28 E3
Gravesend DA11 ....36 B6
Rochester ME1 ....53 C1
Fairways Ct 11 DA11 ..36 B8
Fairways The TN4 ....159 A7
Falcon Ave Bromley BR1 42 F5
Grays RM17 ....18 C7
Falcon Cl DA1 ....15 F2
Falcon Gn ME20 ....81 F1
Falcon Mews DA11 .....35 E7
Falcons Cl TN16 ......72 D2
Falconwood Ave DA16 ..12 E5
Falconwood Par DA16 ..12 F3
Falconwood Sta SE9 ...12 D3
Falkland Pl ME5 ......67 E1
Fallowfield Bean DA2 ..34 B5
Chatham ME5 ....68 B8
Fallowfield Cl ME14 .100 E4
Falmouth Pl TN12 ....145 C7
Falstaff Cl DA1 ....31 E8
Fanconi Rd ME5 ....68 B3
Fancy Row ME14 ......101 C5
Fane Way ME8 ....69 D4
Fant La ME16 ....99 B2
Fantail Cl SE28 ....3 C7
Faraday Ave DA14 .....30 B6
Rochester ME1 ....53 D5
Faraday Ho Erith DA17 ..4 A3
Maidstone ME14 ......100 C7
Faraday Lodge TN2 ...159 B3
Faraday Rd Bexley DA16 .13 A4
Maidstone ME14 ......100 C7
Faraday Ride TN10 ...127 D7
Faraday Way
Greenwich SE18 ....1 D3
Orpington BR5 ....44 B5
Fareham Wlk 10 ME15 116 F6
Faringdon Ave BR2 ....43 A3
Farington Cl ME16 ....99 D4
Farjeon Rd SE18,SE3 ..11 D6
Farleigh Ave BR2 .....42 A2
Farleigh Ct ME16 .....99 A2
Farleigh Hill ME15 ...99 E1
Farleigh Hill Ret Pk
ME15 ....99 E1
Farleigh La ME16 .....99 A1
Farleigh Trad Est ME15 .99 E1
Farley La TN16 ....68 D2
Farley Nursery TN16 .105 C8
Farley Rd DA12 ....36 F7
Farleycroft TN16 .....89 C1
Farlow Cl DA11 ....35 F5
Farm Ave BR8 ....45 C6
Farm Ground Cl TN9 .143 C6
Farm Hill Ave ME2 ....38 F1
Farm Holt DA3 ....48 F1
Farm La TN10 ....127 A4
Farm Pl DA1 ....15 A3
Farm Rd Chatham ME5 ..67 C3
Sevenoaks TN14 ....92 C7
Farm Vale DA5 ....14 B1
Farmcombe Cl TN2 ...159 B2
Farmcombe La TN2 ...159 B2
Farmcombe Rd TN2 ...159 C2
Farmcote Rd SE12 .....28 A7
Farmdale Ave ME1 .....52 F2
Farmdale Rd SE10 ......1 A1
Farmer Cl ME17 ......118 A6
Farmland Wlk BR7 .....29 B3
Farmstead Dr TN8 ....122 D6
Farnaby Dr TN13 ......92 A1
Farnaby Rd SE9 ....11 C3
Farnborough Cl ME16 .99 C2
Farnborough Comm BR6 57 A6
Farnborough Ct 2 BR6 .57 C5
Farnborough Hill BR6 .57 C5
Farnborough Prim Sch
BR6 ....57 C5

Farnborough Way BR6 .57 C5
Farne Cl ME15 ....116 A6
Farnham Beeches TN3 .158 A4

Farnham Cl
 Gillingham ME8 ....70 A8
 Langton Green TN3 ....158 A3
Farnham La TN3 ....158 A4
Farnham Pl TN3 ....158 A4
Farnham Rd DA16 ....13 C5
Farningham Cl ME14 ......100 C6
Farningham Hill Rd DA4 .46 D4
Farningham Road Sta
 DA4 ....47 B7
Farningham Wood (Nature
 Reserve)★ BR8,DA4 ......46 D5
Farnol Rd DA1 ....16 A3
Faro Cl BR1 ....43 A7
Farraday Ct ME1 ....67 D8
Farrance Ct TN1 ....159 B4
Farrant Cl TN1 ....58 A3
Farrant Ct BR6 ....58 A3
Farrants Ct BR1 ....42 F7
Farrell Ct DA2 ....32 C5
Farrier Cl Bromley BR1 ..42 D6
 Maidstone ME14 ....100 E5
Farriers Cl DA12 ....36 F7
Farriers Ct ME8 ....70 C8
Farrington Ave BR5 ......38 A5
Farrington Pl BR7 ....29 D1
Farringtons & Stratford Ho
 Sch BR7 ....29 D1
Fartherwell Ave ME19 ....97 A8
Fartherwell Rd ME19 .....97 A8
Farthing Cl DA1 ....15 F3
Farthing Cnr ME9 ....69 E3
Farthing Hill TN5 ....186 E1
Farthing St BR6 ....56 F2
Farthingfield TN15 ......79 A3
Farthings Cotts ME14 ....83 F1
Farwell Rd DA14 ....30 C4
Farwig La BR1 ....42 A8
Fashoda Rd BR2 ....42 D5
Fauchon's Cl ME14 ....100 F3
Fauchon's La ME14 ....100 F4
Faversham Rd ME17 ....120 E7
Fawkes Ave DA1 ....32 F6
Fawkham Ave DA3 ....49 C6
Fawkham CE Prim Sch
 DA3 ....48 B1
Fawkham Green Rd DA3 .62 B7
Fawkham Ho ⑩ BR5 ......44 D1
Fawkham Manor Hospl
 DA3 ....48 C1
Fawkham Rd
 Longfield DA3 ....48 D6
 West Kingsdown TN15 .....48 A8
Fawley Cl ME14 ....99 E7
Fay Cl ME1 ....53 B3
Faygate Cres DA6 ....14 A2
Fazan Ct TN5 ....184 F4
Fearon St SE10 ....1 A1
Featherby Cotts ME7 .....54 F6
Featherby Inf Sch ME8 ...55 A3
Featherby Jun Sch ME8 ..55 A3
Featherby Rd
 Gillingham,Grange ME7 ..55 A5
 Gillingham,Twydall ME8 ..55 A3
Federation Rd SE2 ....3 C2
Feenan Highway RM18 ....19 B6
Felderland Cl ME17 ......116 E5
Felderland Dr ME17 ......116 E5
Felderland Rd ME17 ......116 E5
Feldspar Cl ME5 ....68 A1
Felhampton Rd SE9 ....29 B5
Felix Manor BR7 ....29 E2
Felixstowe Ct E16 ....2 B5
Felixstowe Rd SE2 ....3 B3
Fell Mead TN12 ....129 F6
Fellowes Way TN11 ....126 E5
Fellows Cl ME8 ....69 B6
Felltram Way SE7 ....1 A1
Felma Ho ⑫ ME7 ....11 C8
Felspar Cl SE18 ....2 F1
Felstead Rd ME6 ....58 B8
Felsted Rd E16 ....1 D7
Felton Cl BR5 ....43 B3
Felton Ho SE3 ....11 C3
Felton Lea DA14 ....29 F3
Fen Gr DA15 ....12 F1
Fen Mdw TN15 ....78 C1
Fen Pond Rd TN15 ....94 C7
Fendyke Rd DA17 ....3 D3
Fenn Cl BR1 ....28 A2
Fenn St ME3 ....24 B4
Fennel Ct ME16 ....99 B3
Fennell Cl ME1 ....53 B3
Fennell St SE18 ....12 A8
Fens Way BR8 ....32 A2
Fenton Ct BR7 ....28 F3
Fenwick Ct ⑯ SE18 ....12 A8
Feoffe Cotts TN17 ......190 E7
Ferbies TN3 ....158 A7
Ferbies Cl TN3 ....158 A7
Ferby Ct DA15 ....29 F4
Ferdinand Terr TN1 .....171 C2
Ferguson Ave DA12 .....36 C4
Fern Bank DA4 ....60 E8
Fern Cl DA8 ....15 B6
Fern Ct DA7 ....14 A3
Fern Down DA3 ....80 B8
Fern Hill Pl ❸ BR6 .....57 C5
Fernbank Cl ME14 ......62 C7
Ferndale Bromley BR1 ...42 C7
 Royal Tunbridge Wells
 TN2 ....159 D5
 Sevenoaks TN13 ....92 C5
Ferndale Bexley DA7 ....13 E6
 Royal Tunbridge Wells
 TN2 ....159 C4
Ferndale Point TN2 .....159 C4
Ferndale Rd
 Gillingham ME7 ....54 E5

Ferndale Rd continued
 Gravesend DA12 ....36 B6
Ferndale St E6 ....2 B7
Ferndale Way BR6 ....57 D5
Ferndell Ave DA5 ....31 D5
Ferndene DA3 ....49 D6
Ferndown Ave BR6 ......43 D1
Ferndown Ct ME7 ....69 A5
Ferndown Rd SE9 ....28 D8
Fernheath Way DA2 .....31 D3
Fernhill Rd ME16 ....99 A2
Fernhill St E16 ....1 F5
Fernholt TN10 ....127 C7
Fernhurst Cres TN4 .....143 A2
Fernleigh Rise ME20 ....82 B2
Ferns The Larkfield ME20 .82 B1
 Platt TN15 ....95 C7
 Royal Tunbridge Wells
 TN1 ....159 C4
Fernside La TN13 ....108 D6
Fernwood Cl BR1 ....42 C7
Ferranti Cl SE18 ....1 D3
Ferrier Cl ME8 ....69 E4
Ferrier Point ⑧ E16 ...1 A8
Ferringham La ME14 ....158 F4
 Wouldham ME1 ....66 C4
Ferry La Rainham RM13 ..4 F8
Ferry Pl SE18 ....2 A3
Ferry Rd Halling ME2 ...66 B4
 Tilbury RM18 ....19 A4
Festival Ave DA3 ....49 D6
Festival Erith DA8 .....14 F7
 Sidcup DA5 ....30 D7
Festoon Way E16 ....1 D6
Ffinch Cl ME20 ....98 D8
Fiddlers Cl DA9 ....17 B3
Field Cl Bromley BR1 ...42 C7
 Chatham ME5 ....67 E6
Field Dr TN8 ....122 D3
Field Rd DA13,TN15 ....63 E6
Fieldfare Rd SE28 ......3 C6
Fielding Ave ME18 .....19 B6
Fielding Dr ME20 ....82 A3
Fields La ME18 ....113 E7
Fieldside Cl BR6 ....57 C6
Fieldway BR5 ....43 D3
Fieldways TN18 ....189 A1
Fieldworks Rd ME7 .....54 A7
Fiennes Way TN13 .....108 C8
Fiesta Dr RM9 ....4 C8
Fife Rd E16 ....1 A8
Fifteenpenny Fields SE9 .12 A2
Fifth Ave RM20 ....17 A8
Fiji Terr ME14 ....100 A7
Filborough Way DA12 ...37 B6
Filey Cl TN16 ....88 B8
Filmer La TN14 ....92 E6
Filston La TN14 ....75 E5
Filston Rd DA8 ....4 C1
Finch Ct Maidstone ME14 .99 E7
 Sidcup DA14 ....30 B5
Finch's Cross RH8 .....121 A8
Finchale Rd SE2 ....3 A3
Finchcocks★ TN17 .....177 A5
Finchley Cl DA1 ....16 A1
Finchley Rd RM17 .....18 B8
Findlay Cl ME8 ....69 D6
Finglesham Cl BR5 .....44 D1
Finglesham Ct ME15 ...116 C8
Finsbury Way DA5 .....13 F1
Fintonagh Dr ME14 ....100 B6
Finucane Dr BR5 ......44 C2
Fir Dene BR6 ....57 A7
Fir Tree Cl Grays RM17 .18 D8
 Orpington BR6 ....57 F5
 Staplehurst TN12 ......149 F3
 Tonbridge TN10 ....127 E7
Fir Tree Gr Bredhurst ME7 .69 B1
 Chatham ME5 ....68 D1
Fir Tree Rd TN4 ....158 F3
Firbank Cl E16 ....1 D8
Fircroft Way TN8 .....122 C3
Firecrest Cl SE28 .....49 B6
Firepower (Mus)★ SE18 .2 B3
Firethorn Cl ME7 .....54 E6
Firmin Ave ME17 ......116 D5
Firmin Rd DA1 ....15 C2
Firmingers Rd BR6 ....59 C5
Firs Cl ME20 ....82 E1
Firs Ct TN4 ....158 F6
Firs The Coldblow DA5 .31 D7
 Sidcup DA15 ....29 F5
Firside Gr DA15 ......29 F7
First Ave Bexley DA7 ..13 C7
 Chatham ME4 ....54 C2
 Gillingham ME7 ......54 E3
 Northfleet DA11 ......35 E7
 West Thurrock RM20 ..17 A8
First La ME17 ....101 E2
First St TN3 ....157 F3
Fisher Rd ME5 ....68 B7
Fisher St
 Maidstone ME14 ......100 A6
 Newham E16 ....1 A8
Fisher's Gate Cotts TN7 .170 A1
Fisher's Way DA17 ....4 A7
Fishermans Wlk SE28 ..2 A7
Fishermen's Hill DA11 .18 B2
Fishers Cl TN12 ......149 F5
Fishers Rd TN12 .....149 F5
Fishguard Way E16 ...2 B5
Fishponds Rd BR2 ....56 D5
Fitzroy Ct DA1 ....33 B7
Fitzthorold Ho ME7 ..54 E7
Fitzwilliam Mews E16 .1 A5
Fitzwilliam Rd ME14 ..100 F5

Five Acre Wood Sch
 ME15 ....116 B7
Five Arches Bsns Est
 DA14 ....30 D3
Five Bells La ❺ ME1 ..53 D4
Five Elms Rd BR2 .....56 C7
Five Fields La TN8 ....123 B4
Five Oak Green Rd
 Capel TN11,TN12 ......144 D6
 Tonbridge TN10 ....143 F7
Five Oak La TN12 .....149 B1
Five Oaks Mews BR1 ..28 A5
Five Ways TN1 ....159 B4
Five Ways Ct ME4 ....54 A4
Five Wents BR8 ......46 A7
Fiveash Rd DA11 .....35 F8
Fiveways L Ctr ME4 ..54 A4
Flack Gdns ME3 ......40 E5
Flamborough Cl TN16 .88 B8
Flamingo Cl ME5 .....68 A7
Flamsteed Rd SE7 ...1 E1
Flats The Gravesend DA12 .36 E8
 Swanscombe DA9 .....17 C2
Flaxman Ct
 ⑬ Chatham ME7 .....54 A6
 Erith DA17 ....4 A1
Flaxman Dr ME16 ....99 C6
Flaxmore Ct DA7 .....14 B4
Flaxmore Pl TN4 .....143 A2
Flaxton Rd SE18 .....12 C1
Fleet Ave DA2 ....33 C7
Fleet Dale Par DA2 ..33 C7
Fleet Ho DA13 ....35 B2
Fleet Rd Dartford DA2 .33 C7
 Northfleet DA11 .....35 C6
 Rochester ME1 ......53 D1
Fleet Terr DA11 .....35 D7
Fleetdown Inf Sch DA2 .33 C6
Fleetdown Jun Sch DA2 .33 C6
Fleetwood Cl E16 ....1 D8
Fleetwood Ct
 ❶ Newham E6 ....1 F8
 Orpington BR6 ....57 A6
Fleming Gdns RM18 ..19 C6
Fleming Ho SE2 ......3 C1
Fleming Way Erith SE28 .3 D6
 Tonbridge TN10 .....127 E7
Fletcher Cl E6 ......2 B6
Fletcher Rd TN12 ...149 E3
Fletchers Cl BR2 ...42 B5
Fletching Rd SE7 ...11 D8
Flimwell Cl TN5 ....187 D4
Flint Cl ❽ BR6 .....57 F4
Flint Down Cl BR5 ..44 A8
Flint Gn ME5 ....68 C3
Flint La
 Woodside Green ME17 .120 C8
 Woodside Green ME17 .120 D8
Flint St RM20 ......17 B8
Flintmill Cres SE3,SE9 .11 E5
Floathaven Cl SE28 ..3 A5
Floats The TN13 ....91 E6
Flood Hatch ME15 ..99 D2
Flora St DA17 ......3 F1
Florance La TN3 ....171 B6
Florence Cl RM17,RM20 .17 E8
Florence Cotts ❺ TN8 .122 C1
Florence Farm Mobile Home
 Pk TN15 ....61 D4
Florence Ho SE18 ..11 F6
Florence Rd
 ❹ Bromley BR1 .....42 A8
 Erith DA17,SE2 .....3 C2
 Maidstone ME16 ....99 E3
Florence St ❸ ME2 .53 B8
Florin Dr ME1 ....53 B4
Flower Rise ME14 ..99 F7
Flowerfield TN14 ...75 F2
Flowerhill Way DA13 .35 E1
Floyd Cl TN4 ....159 A7
Floyd Rd SE7 ......1 C1
Flume End ME15 ...99 D2
Flyers Way The TN16 .89 B1
Foalhurst Cl TN10 ..127 E4
Foley Ct DA1 ....33 B7
Foley Rd TN16 ....72 D1
Foley St ME4 ......100 A5
Folkstone Ho ❹ ME15 .116 F6
Fontwell Cl ME15 ..116 F6
Fontwell Dr BR2 ..43 A4
Foord Almshouses ME1 .53 B3
Foord Cl DA2 ......33 E6
Foord Rd ME17 ....120 D5
Foord St ME1 .....53 D4
Footbury Hill Rd BR6 .44 A2
Foots Cray High St DA14 .30 D2
Foots Cray La DA14 .30 C7
Footscray Rd SE9 ..29 C7
Force Green Farm Cotts
 TN16 ....89 E3
Force Green La TN16 .89 E4
Ford Ho ❷ SE18 ..2 B1
Ford La Trottiscliffe ME19 .80 A4
 Wrotham Heath TN15,ME19 .79 F2
Ford Rd DA11 .....18 B2
Fordcombe CE Prim Sch
 TN3 ....157 B5
Fordcombe Cl ME15 .116 F7
Fordcombe Rd
 Fordcombe TN3 ....157 C4
 Penshurst TN11 ...141 D4
Fordcroft Rd BR5 ..44 B4
Forde Ave BR1 ....42 C6
Fordgate Bsns Pk DA17 .4 C4
Fordingbridge Cl ME16 .99 B5
Fords Park Rd E16 .1 A7
Fordwich Cl
 Maidstone ME16 ...99 B7

Fordwich Cl continued
 Orpington BR6 ......43 F2
Fordwich Dr ME2 ...39 A2
Fordwich Gn ME8 ..55 C3
Foreland St SE18 ..2 D2
Foreman Ctr TN27 .151 D5
Foreman's Wlk TN27 .151 D5
Foremans Barn Rd
 ME15 ....114 F3
Forest Cl BR7 .....43 A8
Forest Dene TN2 ..159 C1
Forest Dr Chatham ME5 .67 F2
 Orpington BR2 ....56 E6
Forest Gr TN10 ...127 C5
Forest Hill ME15 ..99 F1
Forest Rd Erith DA8 .15 A6
 Paddock Wood TN12 .146 A6
 Royal Tunbridge Wells
 TN2 ....159 C1
Forest Ridge BR2 .56 F6
Forest Way Eltham DA15 .29 D8
 Kings Hill ME19 ...97 A3
 Orpington BR5 ....43 F4
 Pembury TN2 .....160 D8
 Royal Tunbridge Wells
 TN2 ....159 D1
Forestdale Rd ME5 .84 A8
Foresters Cl ME5 ..67 F2
Foresters Cres DA7 .14 B3
Foresters Homes The
 DA7 ....14 B3
Forge Cl
 Five Oak Green TN12 .145 B7
 Hayes BR2 ....42 A1
 Penshurst TN11 ...141 B4
Forge Cotts Flimwell TN5 .187 C3
 Nettlestead Green ME18 .113 C2
 Wrotham Heath TN15 ..79 F2
Forge Croft TN8 ...122 D1
Forge La Benover ME18 .131 B4
 Boxley ME14 ......84 C2
 Bredhurst ME7 ....69 A1
 East Farleigh ME15 .115 C7
 Egerton Forstal TN27 .137 C1
 Gillingham ME7 ...54 E7
 Gravesend DA12 ..36 F6
 Headcorn ME17 ..151 D5
 High Halstow ME23 .23 E3
 Higham ME3 ....38 C3
 Horton Kirby DA4 ..47 C5
 Leeds ME17 ....117 F7
 Maidstone ME14 ..101 C4
 Rabbit's Cross ME17,
 TN12 ....133 F3
 Shorne DA12 .....37 E3
 West Kingsdown TN15 .62 A1
 West Peckham ME18 .112 A6
Forge Mdw ME17 ..119 D6
Forge Mdws TN27 .151 D5
Forge Meads TN30 .199 E3
Forge Pl DA12 ....36 F7
Forge Rd Cobbarn TN3 .171 C2
 Royal Tunbridge Wells
 TN4 ....143 A1
Forge Sq TN11 ...125 F2
Forge The TN12 ...145 B7
Forge View TN15 .109 B5
Forge Way
 Paddock Wood TN12 .146 A7
 Shoreham TN14 ...75 F8
Forgefield TN16 ..72 D3
Forgefield Cotts TN16 .196 A4
Forgefield Ct BR5 .44 C4
Formation The E16 .2 B4
Formby Rd ME2 ..66 A4
Formby Terr ME2 ..66 A6
Forsham La ME17 .134 C5
Forson Cl TN30 ..193 B8
Forstal Cl BR2 ....42 A6
Forstal Cotts ME20 .83 B2
Forstal La ME17 ..115 D4
Forstal Rd
 Egerton Forstal TN27 .137 C1
 Forstal ME20 ....83 B2
Forstal The Cobbarn TN3 .171 F3
 Hadlow TN11 .....128 F8
 Pembury TN2 ....160 E8
Forstall TN3 .....158 A4
Forstall The TN11 .126 A2
Forsters ME17 ...117 E4
Forsyth Cl ME19 .82 A1
Forsyth Ct ❼ ME7 .54 C7
Fort Amherst Heritage Pk &
 Caverns★ ME4 ..53 D5
Fort Luton (Mus)★ ME4 .54 A1
Fort Pitt Gram Sch ME4 .53 E4
Fort Pitt Hill ME1,ME4 .53 E4
Fort Pitt St ME4 .53 E4
Fort Rd
 Badgers Mount TN14 .75 C4
 Tilbury RM18 ....19 C5
Fort St Newham E16 ..1 B7
 Rochester ME1 ...53 D4
Fortis Cl E16 .....1 C7
Fortrye Cl DA11 ..35 E6
Fortuna Cl DA3 ..48 F5
Fortune Way ME15 .97 B3
Fortune Wlk ❼ SE28 .2 D3
Forty Acre La E16 ..1 A8
Forward Way ME1 ..67 C6
Fossdene Prim Sch SE7 .1 B1
Fossdene Rd SE7 ..1 B1
Fosse Bank Cl TN9 ..143 A7
Fosse Bank New Sch
 TN11 ....126 C2
Fosse Rd TN9 ....127 B2
Fossett Lodge DA7 .14 C6

Fossington Rd DA17 ..3 D2
Fosten La TN27 ....181 E7
Foster Clark Est ME15 .100 B2
Foster Clarke Dr ME17 .116 A2
Foster St ME15 ....100 A3
Fosters Cl BR7 ....28 F3
Fosters Mews DA1 .48 E7
Fosters Old Sch DA16 .13 B5
Fosters Prim Sch DA16 .13 C4
Fostington Way ME5 .67 F1
Foulds Cl ME8 ....69 B5
Founder Cl E6 ....2 B7
Foundry Wharf ME1 .53 E4
Fountain Ct Eynsford DA4 .60 E8
 Sidcup DA15 .....13 B1
Fountain La ME16 .99 A2
Fountain Rd ME2 ..38 C1
Fountain Wlk DA11 .18 F1
Four Acres ME19 ..98 B5
Four Elms Hill ME3 .39 E4
Four Elms Prim Sch
 TN8 ....123 B5
Four Elms Rd TN8 .122 D4
Four Elms Rdbt ME3 .39 E3
Four Oaks Rd TN12,TN27 .150 E7
Four Trees TN8 ...122 C3
Four Wents
 Langley Heath ME17 .117 C3
 Maidstone ME17 ..116 F2
Fouracre Cotts ME9 .70 E6
Fourth Ave Gillingham ME7 .54 E4
 West Thurrock RM20 .17 A8
Fourwents Rd ME3 .40 D7
Fowey Cl ME5 ....68 C5
Fowler Cl Gillingham ME8 .69 C3
 Sidcup DA14 .....30 E3
Fox Cl Newham E16 ..1 A8
 Orpington BR6 ...58 A5
Fox Hill BR2 .....56 C5
Fox Hollow Cl ❷ SE18 .2 E1
Fox Hollow Dr DA7 .13 D4
Fox House Rd DA17 .4 B1
Fox in the Wood TN5 .184 C6
Fox La BR2 ......56 C5
Fox Lea TN15 ....94 F7
Fox Manor Way RM20 .17 B8
Fox St E16 ......54 C6
Foxburrow Cl ME8 .69 D5
Foxbury DA3 .....62 E7
Foxbury Ave BR7 ..29 D2
Foxbury Cl Bromley BR1 .28 B2
 Orpington BR6 ..58 A5
Foxbury Dr BR6 ..58 A4
Foxbury Rd BR1 ..28 B2
Foxbury Wlk DA11 .35 D4
Foxbush TN11 ...126 C6
Foxcroft Rd SE18 .12 B6
Foxden BR5 .....100 F1
Foxearth Cl TN16 .72 E1
Foxes Dale SE3 ..11 A4
Foxfield Prim Sch SE18 .2 C1
Foxfield Rd BR6 ..57 D8
Foxglove Cl
 ❾ Marlpit Hill TN8 .122 D3
 Sidcup DA15 .....13 A1
Foxglove Cres ME5 .67 E4
Foxglove Rise ME14 .99 F7
Foxgloves The TN12 .146 B5
Foxgrove Path SE28 .2 E5
Foxhole La
 Four Throws TN18 .195 D8
 Hawkhurst TN18 ..189 F1
 Matfield TN12 ...161 C8
 Wadhurst TN5 ...185 B4
Foxhole Rd SE9 ..11 E2
Foxhome Cl BR7 ..29 A2
Foxtail Cl ME4 ..40 B2
Foxton Ho E16 ...2 A4
Foxton Rd RM20 .17 D8
Foxwood Gr
 Northfleet DA11 ..35 E7
 Pratt's Bottom BR6 .58 C1
Foxwood Rd DA2 ..34 B5
Foxwood Way DA3 .49 D7
Framley Rd ME14 ..127 F5
Framlingham Cres SE9 .28 F4
Frances St SE18 ..1 F2
Francis Ave DA7 ..14 A5
Francis Ct ❼ DA8 .4 E1
Francis Dr ME5 ..68 A2
Francis La ME15 ..116 F5
Francis Rd Dartford DA1 .15 D2
 Orpington BR5 ..44 D6
 Tonbridge TN11 ..126 D6
Frank Burton Cl ❺ SE7 .1 B1
Frank Godley Ct DA14 .30 B3
Frank Woolley Rd TN10 .127 F5
Frank's Hollow Rd TN3 .142 C2
Frankapps Cl ME7 ..71 B6
Frankfield Rise TN2 ..159 A1
Franklin Dr ME14 ..100 A4
Franklin Pas SE9 ..11 E4
Franklin Rd Bexley DA7 .13 E6
 Gillingham ME7 ..54 D5
 Gravesend DA12 ..36 D3
 Maypole DA2 ....31 E6
Franklins Cotts ME15 .115 C5
Franks Ct ME8 ...55 B2
Franks La ME4 ...47 B4
Frankswood Ave BR5 .43 C4
Frant CE Prim Sch TN3 .173 B4
Frant Cotts TN5 ..186 E1
Frant Ct TN3 ....173 B3
Frant Field TN8 ..122 C1

Frant Green Rd TN3 ....173 B3
Frant Rd TN2,TN3 ....173 A7
Frant Sta TN3 ....173 F5
Fraser Cl Coldblow DA5 ....31 C7
  �4 Newham E6 ....1 E7
Fraser Ho �3 SE18 ....2 A2
Fraser Rd DA8 ....4 D1
Frederick Andrews Ct
  RM17 ....18 D8
Frederick Ho �4 SE18 ....1 E3
Frederick Pl SE18 ....2 B1
Frederick Rd ME7 ....54 C4
Free Heath Rd TN3,TN5 ..175 C3
Freehold The
  East Peckham TN12 ......129 F6
  Hadlow TN11 ....111 D1
Freeland Ct ◢24◣ DA14 ....30 A5
Freeland Way DA8 ....15 A6
Freelands Gr BR1 ....42 B8
Freelands Rd Bromley BR1 42 B8
  Snodland ME6 ....81 F8
Freeman Gdns ME4 ....53 F2
Freeman Rd DA12 ....36 E5
Freeman Way ME15 ....116 E7
Freemasons Rd E16 ....1 B7
Freesia Cl Gillingham ME7 .54 F6
  Orpington BR6 ....57 F5
Freight La TN17 ....179 C3
Fremantle Ho RM18 ....18 F6
Fremantle Rd DA17 ....4 A2
Fremlin Cl TN4 ....158 B4
Fremlins Rd ME14 ....101 C4
Frensham Rd
  Rolvenden TN17 ....192 A1
  Sidcup SE9 ....29 D6
Frensham Wlk ME5 ....67 F1
Freshland Rd ME16 ....99 B4
Freshwater Rd ME5 ....68 B7
Freta Rd DA6 ....13 F2
Frewing Cl BR7 ....29 A3
Friar Rd BR5 ....44 A4
Friars Ave ME15 ....67 F2
Friars Mews SE9 ....12 A2
Friars Pk ME20 ....82 E2
Friars The★ ME20 ....82 E2
Friars Way TN2 ....159 D6
Friars Wlk SE2 ....3 D1
Friary Pl ◢3◣ ME2 ....53 B7
Friary Prec ME2 ....53 B7
Friday Rd DA8 ....4 D1
Friday St ME17 ....135 B6
Friezland Rd TN4 ....158 D1
Friezley La TN17 ....165 C1
Frimley Ct DA14 ....30 C3
Frindsbury Hill ME2 ....39 C1
Frindsbury Rd ME2 ....53 B8
Frinstead Gr BR5 ....44 D5
Frinstead Wlk ME16 ....99 B7
Frinsted Cl ME8 ....55 C3
Frinsted Rd DA8 ....14 D7
Frinton Rd DA14 ....30 E6
Friston Way ME1 ....67 D8
Friswell Pl ◢1◣ DA6 ....14 A3
Frithwood Cl ME15 ....100 F1
Frittenden CE Prim Sch
  TN17 ....166 E6
Frittenden Rd
  Rochester ME2 ....39 D2
  Staplehurst TN12 ....150 B2
Frobisher Ct ◢3◣ DA1 ....15 D1
Frobisher Gdns ME1 ....53 C2
Frobisher Rd Erith DA8 ....15 A7
  Newham E6 ....2 A7
Frobisher Way
  Gravesend DA12 ....36 E3
  Swanscombe DA9 ....17 B3
Frog Hole La TN8,TN16 ..105 D2
Frog La Rainham RM13 ....4 D8
  Royal Tunbridge Wells
  TN1 ....159 A2
  West Malling ME19 ....97 C8
Frog's La TN17 ....191 E1
Frogmore Wlk ME17 ....120 C5
Frognal Ave DA14 ....30 A2
Frognal Cnr BR7 ....29 F2
Frognal Pl DA14 ....30 A3
Frogs Hole La TN17,
  TN27 ....181 E3
Froissart Rd SE9 ....11 E3
Fromandez Dr TN12 ....162 F5
Frome Ct TN10 ....127 B5
Frost Cres ME5 ....68 A7
Froyle Cl ME16 ....99 C6
Fruitfields TN5 ....187 C6
Fry Cl ME3 ....27 A6
Fry's Cotts ME3 ....25 C4
Frythe Cl TN17 ....179 D4
Frythe Cres TN17 ....179 D4
Frythe Way TN17 ....179 D4
Frythe Wlk TN17 ....179 D4
Fuchsia St SE2 ....3 B1
Fuggles Cl TN17 ....145 E6
Fuggles Ct TN17 ....190 D6
Fulbert Dr ME14 ....100 F5
Fuller Cl Durgates TN5 ...184 E5
  Orpington BR6 ....57 F5
Fullers Cl ME14 ....101 A4
Fullers Hill ◢7◣ TN16 ....89 D1
Fulmar Rd ME2 ....52 D6
Fulmer Rd E16 ....1 D8
Fulthorp Rd SE3 ....11 A5
Fulwich Rd DA1 ....15 F1
Furfield Cl ME17 ....116 E5
Furnace Ave TN3 ....176 A3

Furnace La
  Hook Green TN3 ....175 E4
  Horsmonden TN12 ....167 F7
Furner Ct DA1 ....14 F4
Furness Sch BR8 ....31 F2
Furnival Ct TN2 ....172 F8
Furrell's Rd ME1 ....53 D5
Further Field TN12 ....149 E5
Furze Bank TN8 ....123 B8
Furzefield Ave TN8 ....158 A8
Furzefield Cl BR7 ....29 B2
Furzefield Rd SE3 ....11 B7
Furzehill Sq BR5 ....44 B5
Fyfe Way BR1 ....42 A7

G

Gable Cl DA1 ....15 A2
Gables Cl SE12 ....28 A7
Gables The
  ◢11◣ Bromley BR1 ....28 B1
  New Barn DA3 ....49 C6
Gabriel Gdns DA12 ....36 E3
Gabriel Spring Road (East)
  DA3 ....61 F8
Gabriel's Hill ME15 ....100 A4
Gabrielspring Rd DA3 ....61 D8
Gads Hill ME7 ....54 F6
Gads Hill Sch ME3 ....38 C2
Gadsby La TN26 ....169 F3
Gadwall Cl E16 ....1 B7
Gadwall Way SE28 ....2 D4
Gafford's Bridge Cotts
  TN12 ....147 C4
Gagetown Terr ◢1◣ ME14 ..99 F7
Gainsborough Ave
  Dartford DA1 ....15 C2
  Tilbury RM18 ....19 B6
Gainsborough Cl ME8 ....99 B4
Gainsborough Ct ◢3◣ BR2 .42 C5
Gainsborough Dr
  Maidstone ME14 ....99 B4
  Northfleet DA11 ....35 D5
Gainsborough Gdns
  TN10 ....127 A5
Gainsborough Ho ME1 ..53 D5
Gainsborough Sq DA7 ..13 C4
Gaitskell Rd SE9 ....29 C7
Galahad Ave ME2 ....52 E6
Galahad Rd BR1 ....28 A4
Galena Cl ME5 ....68 A1
Galena Ho ◢4◣ SE18 ....2 F1
Gallants La ME15 ....114 F6
Galleon Bvd DA2 ....16 D3
Galleon Cl Erith DA8 ....4 D2
  Rochester ME1 ....67 C8
Galleon Mews ◢3◣ DA11 ..35 E8
Galleon Way ME2 ....53 A8
Galley Hill Rd DA11,DA10 .17 F2
Galley Hill Trad Est DA10 .17 E2
Gallions Mount Prim Sch
  SE18 ....2 F1
Gallions Prim Sch E6 ....2 B7
Gallions Rd SE7 ....1 B2
Gallions Reach Sh Pk E6 .2 C8
Gallions Reach Sta E6 ....2 D8
Gallions View Rd SE28 ....2 E4
Gallon Cl SE7 ....1 C2
Gallops The DA13 ....79 F7
Gallosson Rd SE18 ....2 E2
Gallows Wood DA3 ....62 A6
Gallus Sq SE3 ....11 B4
Galsworthy Cl SE28 ....3 B5
Galsworthy Cres SE3 ....11 C6
Galsworthy Rd RM18 ....19 C6
Galton Ho SE18 ....11 F6
Games Ho ◢7◣ SE7 ....11 C8
Gamma Rd ME3 ....41 D7
Gandy's La ME17 ....116 C2
Garden Ave DA7 ....14 A4
Garden Cl Lewisham SE12 .28 B5
  Maidstone ME15 ....116 E7
  Staplehurst TN12 ....149 F1
  Toy's Hill TN16 ....106 C3
Garden Ct ◢10◣ Eltham SE9 .12 A1
  Sevenoaks TN13 ....92 D5
  Wouldham ME1 ....66 C5
Garden Ho ◢9◣ TN1 ....159 B4
Garden La BR1 ....28 B2
Garden of England Pk
(Mobile Home Pk)
  ME17 ....119 B7
Garden Pl DA2 ....32 D5
Garden Rd Bromley BR1 ..28 B2
  Royal Tunbridge Wells
  TN1 ....159 B4
  Sevenoaks TN13 ....92 D5
  Tonbridge TN9 ....127 D2
Garden Row DA11 ....35 F5
Garden St Chatham ME7 ..54 A6
  Royal Tunbridge Wells
  TN1 ....159 B4
Garden Terr TN15 ....93 A6
Garden Way ME19 ....96 F2
Gardeners Cl SE9 ....28 E5
Gardenia Cl ME2 ....39 B2
Gardens The ME17 ....115 C3
Gardiner Cl BR5 ....44 C7
Gardiner Ho SE18 ....11 F7
Gardiner St ME7 ....54 C6
Gardyne Mews ◢12◣ TN9 .143 B8
Gareth Gr BR1 ....28 A4
Garfield Rd ME7 ....54 D6
Garganey Wlk SE28 ....3 D6

Gargery Cl DA12 ....36 F7
Garibaldi St SE18 ....2 E2
Garland Rd SE18 ....12 D7
Garlands TN11 ....126 D8
Garlinge Rd TN4 ....143 A1
Garner Ct RM18 ....18 F5
Garner Dr ME19 ....82 A1
Garnet Wlk ◢9◣ E6 ....1 E8
Garnett Cl SE9 ....11 F4
Garrard Cl Bexley DA7 ....14 A4
  Chislehurst BR7 ....29 B3
Garrick Cl TN10 ....127 E7
Garrick Dr SE28 ....2 D3
Garrick St ◢18◣ DA11 ....19 B1
Garrington Cl ME14 ....100 C6
Garrison Cl SE18 ....12 A7
Garrison Rd ME12 ....27 F3
Garrolds Cl BR8 ....45 D7
Garrow DA3 ....49 B6
Garside Cl SE28 ....2 D3
Garth Rd TN13 ....108 C7
Gartly Cotts DA1 ....15 C1
Garvary Rd E16 ....1 B7
Garvock Dr TN13 ....92 A1
Gas House Rd ME1 ....53 C6
Gascoyne Cl ME15 ....101 B2
Gascoyne Dr DA1 ....14 F4
Gasoline Alley TN15 ....79 D2
Gasson Rd DA10 ....17 E1
Gassons Rd ME6 ....81 E8
Gatcombe Cl
  Chatham ME5 ....68 A5
  Maidstone ME16 ....99 B5
Gatcombe Rd E16 ....1 A5
Gate Farm Rd TN3,TN11 142 C4
Gate House Cotts SE12 ..28 B6
Gateacre Ct ◢14◣ DA14 ....30 B4
Gatefield Cotts TN17 ....191 F4
Gatehouse Farm Cotts
  TN3 ....142 C4
Gatekeeper Chase ME8 ..69 F8
Gates Green Rd BR2,BR4 .56 A6
Gateway Par DA12 ....36 F4
Gateway Prim Sch The
  DA2 ....16 B1
Gatland La ME16 ....99 B2
Gatling Rd SE2 ....3 A1
Gattons Way DA14 ....30 F4
Gatwick Farm Cotts
  RH19 ....154 A4
Gatwick Rd DA12 ....36 B6
Gault Cl ME15 ....101 A2
Gautrey Sq ◢5◣ E6 ....1 F7
Gavestone Cres SE12 ....28 B8
Gavestone Rd SE12 ....28 B8
Gavestone Terr SE12 ....28 B8
Gavin Ho SE18 ....2 E2
Gayhurst Cl ME8 ....69 D6
Gaylor Rd RM18 ....18 F6
Gayton Rd SE2 ....3 C3
Gaza Trad Est TN11 ....125 D7
Gazelle Glade DA12 ....36 F3
Gean Cl ME5 ....84 A8
Geddes Pl ◢3◣ DA6 ....14 A3
Gedge's Hill TN12 ....145 F3
Geffery's St SE18 ....28 E5
General Gordon Pl ◢2◣
  SE18 ....2 B2
Genesta Glade DA12 ....37 A3
Genesta Rd SE18 ....12 C8
Geneva Ave ME8 ....55 A2
Gentian Cl
  ◢4◣ Chatham ME5 ....67 E4
  Maidstone ME14 ....100 E5
George Akass Ho ◢3◣ SE18 .2 C1
George Crooks Ho ◢7◣
  RM17 ....18 B8
George La Hayes BR2 ....42 B1
  Leeds ME17 ....118 B7
  Rochester ME1 ....53 C6
George Marsham Ho
  ME15 ....115 F3
George St
  Chainhurst ME15 ....132 A7
  Grays RM17 ....18 A8
  Maidstone ME15 ....100 A3
  Royal Tunbridge Wells
  TN2 ....159 C3
  Sparrow's Green TN5 ...184 F5
  Staplehurst TN12 ....149 E6
  Tonbridge TN9 ....143 B8
George Summers Ct ME2 53 E8
George's Rd TN16 ....88 D7
Georges Cl BR5 ....44 C7
Georgia Pl TN2 ....159 C4
Georgian Cl BR2 ....42 B1
Georgian Dr ME17 ....115 D3
Georgian Way ME8 ....69 C4
Geraint Rd BR1 ....28 A4
Gerald Ave ME4 ....53 F2
Gerald Rd DA12 ....36 E8
Gerda Rd SE9 ....29 C6
Gerdview Dr DA2 ....32 C4
Gerrard Ave ME1 ....67 E8
Gerrard Ho ◢4◣ BR2 ....42 C5
Gertrude Rd DA17 ....4 A2
Gibbet La TN12 ....162 F6
Gibbetts TN3 ....157 F3
Gibbs Hill Headcorn TN27 151 E5
  Nettlestead ME18 ....113 B5
Gibraltar Ave ME7 ....54 B7
Gibraltar Hill ME4 ....53 F4
Gibraltar La ME14 ....99 F8
Gibson Cl DA11 ....35 F5
Gibson Dr ME19 ....96 F4
Gibson Ho ME3 ....39 F6
Gidd's Pond Cotts ME14 100 E6
Giddyhorn La ME16 ....99 C5

Gideon Cl DA17 ....4 B2
Gifford Cl ME8 ....55 C3
Giggs Hill BR5 ....44 A8
Gighill Rd ME20 ....81 F4
Gilbert Cl Gillingham ME7 .69 A5
  Swanscombe DA10 ....17 D1
  Woolwich SE18 ....11 F6
Gilbert Rd Bromley BR1 ..28 A1
  Erith DA17 ....4 A3
Gilbert Terr ◢2◣ ME14 ....99 F7
Gilbourne Rd SE18 ....12 F8
Gilchrist Cotts TN14 ....108 C2
Gildenhill Rd BR8 ....32 C1
Gildersome St SE18 ....12 A8
Giles Field DA12 ....36 F7
Gill Ave Newham E16 ....1 A7
  Rochester ME2 ....39 D2
Gill Cres DA11 ....35 F5
Gill Ct SE18 ....2 C2
Gill The TN2 ....160 E8
Gill's Rd
  Green Street Green DA2 ..34 B1
  Sutton at H DA4 ....47 F8
Gillan Ct ◢1◣ SE12 ....28 B5
Gilletts La ME19 ....98 A6
Gillies Ct DA14 ....29 E4
Gillies Rd TN15 ....61 E5
Gillingham Coll The ME7 ..54 F4
Gillingham Gate ME7 ....54 C8
Gillingham Gate Rd ME7 54 C8
Gillingham Gn ME7 ....54 C6
Gillingham Rd ME7 ....54 D5
Gillingham Sta ME7 ....54 D5
Gillmans Rd BR5 ....44 B1
Gilroy Way BR5 ....44 B2
Gimble Way TN2 ....144 D1
Gingerbread La TN18 ....187 F2
Ginsbury Cl ME2 ....53 E6
Gipps Cross La TN3 ....157 F5
Gipsy La RM17 ....18 C8
Gipsy Rd DA16 ....13 D5
Giralda Cl E16 ....1 F8
Glade Bsns Ctr The RM20 16 F8
Glade The Bromley BR1 ..42 D7
  Chatham ME5 ....68 A2
  Greenwich SE7 ....11 C7
  Sevenoaks TN13 ....92 B4
  Tonbridge TN10 ....127 E7
Glades Sh Ctr The BR1 ..42 A7
Glades The DA12 ....36 D2
Gladeswood Rd DA17 ....4 B2
Gladstone Rd
  Chatham ME4 ....53 E2
  Dartford DA1 ....15 F1
  Maidstone ME14 ....100 A6
  Orpington BR6 ....57 C5
  Rusthall TN4 ....158 B4
  Tonbridge TN9 ....127 B1
Gladwell Rd BR1 ....28 A2
Gladwyn Cl ME8 ....69 D4
Glamford Rd ME2 ....52 D5
Glamis Cl ME5 ....68 A5
Glanfield Ct TN1 ....159 C5
Glanville Rd Bromley BR2 .42 B6
  Gillingham ME7 ....54 D5
  Rochester ME2 ....53 A8
Glasbrook Rd SE9 ....28 D8
Glasgow Ho ◢8◣ ME15 ....116 F7
Glass Yd ◢3◣ SE18 ....2 A3
Glassenbury Rd TN17 ....178 E4
Glassmill La BR2 ....42 A7
Glastonbury Cl BR5 ....44 C1
Gleaming Wood Dr ME5 .84 D8
Gleaners Cl ME14 ....100 E4
Gleanings Mews ME1 ....53 C5
Glebe Cl TN27 ....153 C5
Glebe Cotts TN16 ....90 B4
Glebe Gdns ME17 ....120 E5
Glebe Ho ◢7◣ SE18 ....2 A2
Glebe House Dr BR2 ....42 B1
Glebe La Maidstone ME16 .99 A1
  Sevenoaks TN13 ....92 B1
Glebe Mdw ME18 ....113 E7
Glebe Pl DA4 ....47 C5
Glebe Rd Bromley BR1 ..42 A8
  Gillingham ME7 ....54 E3
  Northfleet DA11 ....35 F7
  Sevenoaks Weald TN14 ..108 B3
Glebe The
  Bidborough TN3 ....142 D3
  Chislehurst BR7 ....43 C8
  Cuxton ME2 ....52 C2
  Pembury TN2 ....160 D8
  Penshurst TN11 ....141 A3
Glebe Way DA8 ....14 E8
Glebefield The TN13 ....91 F4
Glebeland TN27 ....137 F4
Glebelands
  Bidborough TN3 ....142 C3
  Biddenden TN27 ....167 F1
  Crayford DA1 ....14 E1
  Penshurst TN11 ....141 A3
Gleeson Dr BR6 ....57 F6
Glen Ct Lewisham SE12 ..28 A8
  Sidcup DA14 ....30 A4
Glen Dunlop Ho The
  TN13 ....92 C5
Glen Ho ◢6◣ E16 ....2 A7
Glen The BR6 ....57 A7
Glen View DA12 ....36 C7
Glen View Rd BR1 ....42 D7
Glenalvon Way ◢7◣ SE18 ..1 F2
Glenbarr Cl SE9 ....12 B4
Glencairne Cl E16 ....1 D8
Glencoe Jun Sch ME4 ....54 A2
Glencoe Rd ME4 ....54 A2
Glendale BR8 ....45 F4
Glendale SE9 ....12 A4

Glendale Ct TN2 ....159 D6
Glendale Rd Erith DA8 ....4 C2
  Northfleet DA11 ....35 E5
Glendale Way SE28 ....3 C6
Glendower Cres BR6 ....44 A3
Glendown Rd SE2 ....3 A1
Gleneagles Cl BR6 ....43 D1
Gleneagles Ct ME15 ....67 F2
Gleneagles Dr ME15 ....100 A1
Gleneagles Gn ◢1◣ BR6 ..43 D1
Glenesk Rd SE9 ....12 B3
Glengall Rd DA7 ....13 C4
Glenhead Cl SE9 ....12 B3
Glenhouse Rd SE9 ....12 A2
Glenhurst Ave DA5 ....30 F7
Glenister St E16 ....2 A4
Glenlea Rd SE9 ....12 A3
Glenleigh Rd ME18 ....113 D6
Glenluce Rd SE3 ....11 A8
Glenlyon Rd SE9 ....12 A3
Glenmore Pk TN2 ....172 F6
Glenmore Rd DA16 ....12 F6
Glenmount Path ◢1◣ SE18 ..2 C1
Glenrose Ct DA14 ....30 B3
Glenshiel Rd SE9 ....12 A4
Glentrammon Ave BR6 ..57 F4
Glentrammon Cl BR6 ....57 F5
Glentrammon Gdns BR6 .57 F4
Glentrammon Rd
  Orpington BR6 ....58 A4
  Orpington BR6 ....57 F4
Glenure Rd SE9 ....12 A2
Glenview SE2 ....13 D8
Glenwood TN30 ....183 B3
Glenwood Cl
  Chatham ME5 ....54 C1
  Gillingham ME7 ....69 A7
  Maidstone ME16 ....99 C5
  Tenterden TN30 ....183 B3
Glenwood Ct ◢18◣ DA14 ....30 A4
Glimpsing Gn DA18 ....3 E3
Glistening Glade ME8 ....69 E6
Gload Cres BR5 ....58 D8
Globe Ct SE18 ....12 C8
Globe La ME4 ....53 F5
Globe Yd ◢18◣ DA11 ....19 B1
Gloucester Ave
  Bexley DA16 ....12 F3
  Sidcup DA15 ....29 E6
Gloucester Cl ME8 ....70 A4
Gloucester Ct RM18 ....18 F5
Gloucester Par DA15 ....13 A2
Gloucester Rd
  Dartford DA1 ....32 B8
  Erith DA17 ....3 F1
  Gravesend DA12 ....36 C4
  Maidstone ME15 ....116 D8
  Turner's Green TN5 ....184 F6
Glover Cl SE2 ....3 C2
Glovers Cl TN16 ....72 B3
Glovers Mill ME4 ....53 D3
Gloxinia Rd DA13 ....35 B2
Glyn Davies Cl TN13 ....91 E7
Glyn Dr DA14 ....30 B4
Glynde Rd DA7 ....13 E4
Glyndebourne Pk BR6 ..57 B8
Glyndon Rd SE18 ....2 D2
Glynne Cl ME8 ....69 D6
Goad Ave ME5 ....68 B3
Goatsfield Rd TN16 ....88 C7
Goddard's Green Cotts
  TN17 ....180 F1
Goddards Cl TN17 ....179 B4
Godden Rd ME6 ....81 F8
Godden Way ME8 ....55 A4
Goddings Dr ME1 ....53 A3
Goddington Chase BR6 ..58 B6
Goddington Ho BR6 ....58 C7
Goddington La
  Harrietsham ME17 ....119 B6
  Orpington BR6 ....58 A7
Goddington Rd ME2 ....53 B8
Godfrey Evans Ho TN10 .127 F5
Godfrey Hill SE18 ....1 E2
Godfrey Rd SE18 ....1 F2
Godstow Rd SE2 ....3 C4
Godwin Ho SE18 ....11 F6
Godwin Rd BR2 ....42 C6
Gold St DA12,DA13 ....50 E4
Goldace RM17 ....17 F8
Goldcrest Cl Newham E16 ..1 D8
  Woolwich SE28 ....3 C6
Goldcrest Dr ME4 ....40 C2
Golden Plover Cl E16 ....1 F7
Golden Sq TN30 ....193 B8
Golden Wood Cl ME5 ....84 D8
Goldfinch Cl
  Larkfield ME20 ....82 A2
  Orpington BR6 ....58 A5
  Paddock Wood TN12 ....146 A5
Goldfinch Rd SE28 ....2 D3
Goldie Leigh Hospl SE2 .13 C8
Golding Cl Ditton ME20 ..82 C1
  Rochester ME1 ....53 E1
Golding Gdns TN12 ....130 A6
Golding Rd TN13 ....92 C5
Goldings TN12 ....145 E5
Goldings Cl ME19 ....97 A3
Goldings The ME8 ....69 C8
Goldmark Ho SE3 ....11 B4
Goldsel Rd BR8 ....45 E5
Goldsmid Rd TN9 ....143 C3
Goldsmid St ◢3◣ SE18 ....2 E1
Goldsmith RM17 ....17 F8
Goldsmith Ct TN30 ....183 B6
Goldsmith Rd ME8 ....69 C5
Goldstone Wlk ME5 ....68 A1

Goldsworth Dr ME2 ... 39 A1
Goldthorne Cl ME14 ... 100 C5
Goldwing Cl E16 ... 1 A7
Golf Links Ave DA11 ... 36 B3
Golf Rd BR1 ... 43 A6
Golford Rd TN17 ... 179 F4
Gollogly Terr 8 SE7 ... 1 C1
Gooch Cl ME16 ... 99 D8
Goodall Cl ME8 ... 69 E5
Goodbury Rd TN15 ... 77 B6
Goodensfield TN5 ... 184 E5
Gooding Ho SE7 ... 1 C1
Goodley Stock Rd TN8, TN16 ... 105 B6
Goodmead Rd BR6 ... 44 A2
Goods Hill TN30 ... 192 D8
Goods Station Rd TN1 ... 159 B4
Goodtrees La TN8 ... 155 B2
Goodwin Cl TN8 ... 122 B2
Goodwin Dr
Maidstone ME14 ... 100 B8
Sidcup DA14 ... 30 D6
Goodwin Rd ME3 ... 39 B7
Goodwins The TN2 ... 158 F1
Goodwood Cl
High Halstow ME23 ... 23 E4
Maidstone ME15 ... 116 F6
Goodwood Cres DA12 ... 36 C2
Goodworth Rd TN15 ... 78 F3
Goosander Way SE28 ... 2 D3
Goose Cl ME5 ... 68 A7
Goose Green Cl BR5 ... 44 A7
Goose Sq 8 E6 ... 1 F7
Gooseneck La TN27 ... 151 C5
Gordon Cl RM18 ... 20 D7
Gordon Ct ME17 ... 115 E3
Gordon Ho SE12 ... 28 A8
Gordon Inf Sch ME2 ... 53 A8
Gordon Jun Sch ME2 ... 53 A8
Gordon Pl DA12 ... 19 C1
Gordon Prim Sch SE9 ... 11 F3
Gordon Promenade E DA12 ... 19 D1
Gordon Rd Chatham ME4 ... 54 A7
Chatham,Luton ME4 ... 54 B2
Dartford DA1 ... 32 D8
Erith DA17 ... 4 C2
Gillingham ME7 ... 54 E5
Hoo St Werburgh ME3 ... 40 D5
Northfleet DA11 ... 35 E8
Rochester ME2 ... 53 A8
Royal Tunbridge Wells TN4 ... 159 C7
Sevenoaks TN13 ... 92 B2
Sidcup DA15 ... 12 E2
Gordon Terr ME1 ... 53 C4
Gordon Way BR1 ... 42 A8
Gore Cotts DA2 ... 33 C4
Gore Court Rd ME15 ... 116 F5
Gore Farm Cotts DA2 ... 33 C5
Gore Green Rd ME3 ... 38 E7
Gore La TN17 ... 163 E4
Gore Rd Dartford DA2 ... 33 C6
Silver Street ME9 ... 87 F5
Gorham Cl ME6 ... 81 F7
Gorham Dr
Maidstone ME15 ... 101 A1
Tonbridge TN9 ... 143 E8
Gorman Rd SE18 ... 1 F2
Gorringe Ave DA4 ... 47 D7
Gorse Ave ME5 ... 67 F5
Gorse Cl E16 ... 1 A7
Gorse Cres ME20 ... 98 D8
Gorse Rd Orpington BR5 ... 59 A8
Rochester ME2 ... 52 F8
Royal Tunbridge Wells TN2 ... 159 E5
Gorse Way DA3 ... 49 A4
Gorse Wood Rd
Hartley DA3 ... 49 A5
New Barn DA3 ... 49 A6
Gorst St ME7 ... 54 C5
Goss Hill BR8,DA2 ... 32 C2
Gossage Rd SE18 ... 2 D1
Gosshill Rd BR7 ... 43 A7
Gossington Cl BR7 ... 29 B4
Gothic Cl DA1 ... 32 D5
Goudhurst & Kilndown CE Prim Sch TN17 ... 177 F8
Goudhurst Cl ME16 ... 99 E4
Goudhurst Rd
Cranbrook TN17 ... 179 D8
Gillingham ME8 ... 55 B3
Horsmonden TN12 ... 163 B5
Knox Bridge TN12,TN17 ... 165 C6
Marden TN12 ... 148 B5
Gouge Ave DA11 ... 35 E7
Gould Rd ME5 ... 68 B3
Gourock Rd SE9 ... 12 A2
Gover Hill TN11,ME18 ... 111 E6
Gover View TN11 ... 111 E7
Gower Ho ME14 ... 100 A6
Grace Ave Bexley DA7 ... 13 F5
Maidstone ME16 ... 99 D6
Grace Cl SE9 ... 28 D5
Gracious La TN13 ... 108 B5
Gracious Lane Bridge TN13 ... 108 A6
Gracious Lane End TN14 ... 107 F5
Grafton Ave ME1 ... 67 E8
Graham Cl ME4 ... 53 F6
Graham Ct 12 BR1 ... 28 B1
Graham Ho SE18 ... 12 B7
Graham Rd DA7 ... 14 A3
Grain Rd Gillingham ME8 ... 69 C3
Grain ME3 ... 26 D3
Grainey Field ME9 ... 70 E4
Grainger Wlk TN10 ... 127 E6
Gram Sch for Girls Wilmington The DA2 ... 32 B5
Grampian Cl
Orpington BR6 ... 43 F3
Royal Tunbridge Wells TN2 ... 159 D5
Grampian Way ME15 ... 101 A1
Granada Ho 8 ME15 ... 100 A4
Granada St 9 ME15 ... 100 A4
Granary TN12 ... 146 B6
Granary Cl
Maidstone ME14 ... 100 E5
Rainham ME8 ... 55 F1
Granary Cotts TN16 ... 90 C3
Granby Ho 8 SE18 ... 1 F2
Granby Rd Eltham SE9 ... 11 F4
Northfleet DA11 ... 18 D1
Woolwich SE18 ... 2 B3
Grand Ct 7 ME7 ... 54 C6
Grand Depot Rd SE18 ... 2 A1
Grand View Ave TN16 ... 72 C3
Grandshore La TN17 ... 166 B5
Grandsire Gdns ME3 ... 40 E6
Grange Cl
Edenbridge TN8 ... 122 C1
Leybourne ME19 ... 81 C2
Sidcup DA15 ... 30 A5
Westerham TN16 ... 89 C1
Grange Cres
6 Dartford DA2 ... 16 B1
Erith SE28 ... 3 C7
Tenterden TN30 ... 183 A3
Grange Dr Bromley BR7 ... 28 F2
Pratt's Bottom BR6 ... 58 C2
Grange Gdns TN4 ... 158 D4
Grange Hill Chatham ME5 ... 54 B3
Plaxtol TN15 ... 110 E8
Grange Ho Erith DA8 ... 15 A5
Gravesend DA11 ... 36 A8
Maidstone ME16 ... 99 A2
Grange La Boxley ME14 ... 84 A1
Hartley DA3 ... 49 B2
Grange Park Sch ME19 ... 81 B3
Grange Rd Gillingham ME7 ... 55 A6
Gravesend DA11 ... 36 A8
Grays RM17 ... 18 B8
Orpington BR6 ... 57 C8
Platt TN15 ... 95 C7
Rochester ME2 ... 53 B7
Rusthall TN4 ... 158 D4
Sevenoaks TN13 ... 108 A8
Tenterden TN30 ... 182 F3
Grange Rdbt ME7 ... 55 A6
Grange The
East Malling ME19 ... 98 A7
Sutton at H DA4 ... 47 D8
West Kingsdown TN15 ... 61 F2
Westerham TN16 ... 89 C1
Grange Way Erith DA8 ... 15 B7
Hartley DA3 ... 48 F3
Rochester ME1 ... 53 C3
Grangehill Pl SE9 ... 11 F4
Grangehill Rd SE9 ... 11 F3
Grangeways Cl DA11 ... 35 F4
Grangewood DA5 ... 30 F7
Granite St SE18 ... 2 F1
Grant Cl ME7 ... 55 B1
Grant Dr ME15 ... 116 D6
Grant Rd ME3 ... 39 C3
Grant's Cotts ME17 ... 120 B5
Granton Rd DA14 ... 30 C2
Grants La TN8,RH8 ... 121 C6
Granville Ct Erith SE2 ... 3 D1
Maidstone ME14 ... 100 A6
Sevenoaks TN13 ... 92 A3
Granville Mews DA14 ... 30 A4
Granville Rd Bexley DA16 ... 13 C4
Gillingham ME7 ... 54 E5
Limpsfield RH8 ... 104 A7
Maidstone ME14 ... 100 A6
Northfleet DA11 ... 35 F7
Royal Tunbridge Wells TN1 ... 159 C5
Sevenoaks TN13 ... 92 A3
Sidcup DA14 ... 30 B4
Westerham TN16 ... 89 C1
Granville Sch The TN13 ... 92 A4
Grapple Rd ME14 ... 100 A7
Grasdene Rd SE18 ... 13 A7
Grasmere Ave BR6 ... 57 B7
Grasmere Gdns BR6 ... 57 B7
Grasmere Gr ME2 ... 39 C2
Grasmere Rd Bexley DA7 ... 14 C5
Orpington BR6 ... 57 B7
Grasshaven Way SE28 ... 2 F5
Grassington Rd 11 DA14 ... 30 A4
Grasslands ME17 ... 117 E4
Grassmere ME19 ... 81 F2
Grassy Glade ME7 ... 69 B6
Grassy La TN13 ... 108 B8
Gravel Hill DA6 ... 14 B2
Gravel Hill Cl DA6 ... 14 B1
Gravel Hill Prim Sch DA6 ... 14 B3
Gravel Pit Way BR6 ... 44 A1
Gravel Rd Orpington BR2 ... 56 E8
Sutton at H DA4 ... 33 B1
Gravel Wlk ME1 ... 53 D5
Gravelly Bottom Rd ME17 ... 118 B2
Gravelly Ways TN12 ... 130 D5
Gravelwood Cl BR7 ... 29 C5
Graveney Cl ME3 ... 39 C7
Graveney Rd ME15 ... 116 F7
Graves Est DA16 ... 13 B5
Gravesend & North Kent Hospl DA11 ... 19 A1
Gravesend Gram Sch DA12 ... 36 D8
Gravesend Gram Sch for Girls DA11 ... 36 A7
Gravesend Rd
Higham ME2,ME3,DA12 ... 38 C2
Rochester ME2 ... 52 F8
Shorne DA12 ... 37 D5
Vigo Village TN15 ... 79 D6
Gravesend Sta DA11 ... 19 B1
Gravesham Ct 8 DA12 ... 36 B8
Gravesham Mus★ DA11 ... 19 B1
Gray Ho SE2 ... 3 D1
Grayland Cl BR1 ... 42 D8
Graylands RM17 ... 17 E8
Graylings The ME1 ... 53 B3
Grayne Ave ME3 ... 27 B5
Grays Farm Prim Sch BR5 ... 44 B8
Grays Farm Production Village BR5 ... 44 B8
Grays Farm Rd BR5 ... 44 B8
Grays Rd TN16 ... 89 D7
Grays Sh Ctr RM17 ... 18 A8
Grays Sta RM17 ... 18 A8
Grazeley Cl DA6 ... 14 C2
Great Ash BR7 ... 29 A1
Great Basin Rd ME12 ... 27 F2
Great Bounds Dr TN4 ... 142 E3
Great Brooms Rd TN4 ... 159 C8
Great Courtlands TN3 ... 158 A3
Great Elms TN11 ... 111 E1
Great Elms Rd BR2 ... 42 C5
Great Footway TN3 ... 157 F3
Great Hall Arc 3 TN1 ... 159 B3
Great Harry Dr SE9 ... 29 A5
Great Ivy Mill Cotts ME15 ... 115 F7
Great Lines ME7 ... 54 B5
Great Lodge Ret Pk TN2 ... 143 E1
Great Maytham Hall★ TN17 ... 191 F2
Great Mead TN8 ... 122 C3
Great Oak
Hurst Green TN19 ... 194 A3
Royal Tunbridge Wells TN2 ... 159 D6
Great Queen St DA1 ... 15 F1
Great South Ave ME4 ... 54 A1
Great Thrift BR5 ... 43 C5
Great Till Cl TN14 ... 75 E3
Greatness La TN14 ... 92 C6
Greatness Rd TN14 ... 92 C6
Greatwood BR7 ... 29 A1
Grebe Apartments 15 ME15 ... 116 E5
Grebe Cl ME3 ... 25 C4
Grebe Ct ME20 ... 81 F1
Grecian Rd TN1 ... 159 B2
Grecian St ME14 ... 100 A6
Green Acres DA14 ... 29 F4
Green Bank Cl ME7 ... 69 A5
Green Cl ME1 ... 53 D2
Green Court Rd BR8 ... 45 D3
Green Farm Cl BR6 ... 57 F5
Green Farm La DA12 ... 37 E5
Green Gdns BR6 ... 57 C5
Green Hedges TN30 ... 193 B8
Green Hill Biggin Hill BR6 ... 72 F7
Maidstone ME15 ... 101 B1
Woolwich SE18 ... 1 F1
Green Hill La ME17 ... 119 D1
Green La Cliffe ME3 ... 22 B6
Collier Street TN12 ... 147 E8
East End TN17 ... 181 C2
Eltham BR7,SE9 ... 29 B5
Four Elms TN8 ... 123 C7
Grain ME3 ... 27 B5
High Halden TN26 ... 169 F3
Langley Heath ME17 ... 117 E3
Maidstone ME17 ... 116 C3
Meopham Sta DA13 ... 50 B2
Paddock Wood TN12 ... 146 A5
Platt's Heath ME17 ... 119 F2
Smarden TN27 ... 153 A1
Sutton Valence ME17 ... 134 B4
Trottiscliffe ME19 ... 80 A5
Yelsted ME9 ... 70 F1
Green La The TN11 ... 125 F1
Green Lane Bsns Pk SE9 ... 29 A6
Green Lane Cotts
Collier Street TN12 ... 131 D1
Langley Heath ME17 ... 117 E3
Green Lawns 10 SE18 ... 2 B2
Green Pl DA1 ... 14 E2
Green Rd TN12 ... 163 A6
Green Sands ME5 ... 84 C8
Green Sq TN5 ... 184 F5
Green St ME7 ... 54 C5
Green Street Green Prim Sch BR6 ... 57 F4
Green Street Green Rd DA1,DA2 ... 33 D4
Green The
Bexley,Bexleyheath DA7 ... 14 A6
Bexley,Falconwood DA16 ... 12 E3
Biddenden TN27 ... 182 D6
Dartford DA2 ... 33 D6
East Farleigh ME15 ... 115 B7
Frant TN3 ... 173 B3
Hayes BR2 ... 42 A2
Langton Green TN3 ... 157 E3
Leigh TN11 ... 125 F1
Lewisham BR1 ... 28 A5
Orpington BR5 ... 30 B1
Sevenoaks TN13 ... 92 D5
Sidcup DA14 ... 30 A4
Green The *continued*
West Tilbury RM18 ... 19 E8
Westerham TN16 ... 89 D1
Green Vale DA6 ... 13 D2
Green View Ave TN11 ... 126 A1
Green Way Bromley BR2 ... 42 E3
Eltham SE9 ... 11 D2
Hartley DA3 ... 48 E4
Maidstone ME16 ... 99 B3
Royal Tunbridge Wells TN2 ... 159 E8
Green Wlk DA1 ... 14 F3
Green's Cotts ME15 ... 115 A4
Greenacre DA1 ... 32 D6
Greenacre Cl
Chatham ME5 ... 68 A5
Swanley BR8 ... 45 E5
Greenacre Sch ME5 ... 67 F5
Greenacres SE9 ... 12 A1
Greenacres Cl BR6 ... 57 C6
Greenacres Prim Sch & Language Impairment Unit SE9 ... 29 A6
Greenbank ME5 ... 68 B8
Greenbank Lodge 2 BR7 ... 43 A8
Greenbanks DA1 ... 32 E6
Greenbay Rd SE7 ... 11 D7
Greenborough Cl ME15 ... 116 E6
Greencourt Rd BR5 ... 43 E4
Greencroft Cl E6 ... 1 D8
Greendale Wlk 4 DA11 ... 35 E5
Greenfield TN8 ... 122 D1
Greenfield Cl Eccles ME20 ... 83 A6
Rusthall TN4 ... 158 C5
Greenfield Cotts ME14 ... 84 C3
Greenfield Ct SE9 ... 28 E5
Greenfield Dr BR1 ... 42 C7
Greenfield Gdns BR5 ... 43 D2
Greenfield Rd
Gillingham ME7 ... 54 D6
Joyden's Wood DA2 ... 31 D3
Greenfields ME15 ... 116 E8
Greenfields Cl ME3 ... 39 D3
Greenfinches
Gillingham ME7 ... 68 F6
New Barn DA3 ... 49 B6
Greenfrith Dr TN10 ... 127 B6
Greenhaven Dr SE28 ... 3 B7
Greenhill TN12 ... 149 E5
Greenhill Cts SE18 ... 1 F1
Greenhill La TN27 ... 153 F7
Greenhill Rd
Northfleet DA11 ... 35 F6
Otford TN14 ... 76 C5
Greenhill Terr SE18 ... 1 F1
Greenhithe 3 ME15 ... 100 A3
Greenhithe Cl DA15 ... 29 E8
Greenhithe for Bluewater Sta DA9 ... 17 A2
Greenholm Rd SE9 ... 12 B2
Greenhurst La
Limpsfield RH8 ... 104 A4
Oxted RH8 ... 104 A3
Greening St SE2 ... 3 C2
Greenlands Platt TN15 ... 95 C7
Sole Street DA12 ... 50 D4
Greenlands Rd TN15 ... 93 B8
Greenlaw St SE18 ... 2 A3
Greenleas TN2 ... 160 C6
Greenleigh Ave BR5 ... 44 B5
Greenoak Rise TN16 ... 72 C1
Greens End SE18 ... 2 B2
Greensand Rd ME15 ... 101 A2
Greenshields Ind Est E16 ... 1 A4
Greenside
High Halden TN26 ... 183 E7
Maidstone ME15 ... 100 B3
Sidcup DA5 ... 30 E7
Swanley BR8 ... 45 D7
Greenside Wlk TN16 ... 72 B1
Greenslade Prim Sch SE18 ... 12 D8
Greensleeves Way ME18 ... 97 C3
Greentrees Ave TN10 ... 127 F5
Greenvale Gdns ME8 ... 55 B2
Greenvale Inf Sch ME4 ... 54 A2
Greenvale Rd SE9 ... 12 A3
Greenview Cres TN11 ... 126 E4
Greenview Wlk ME8 ... 55 A4
Greenway Chatham ME5 ... 67 D6
Chislehurst BR7 ... 29 B3
Cranbrook TN17 ... 179 B4
Tatsfield TN16 ... 88 C7
Greenway Court Farm Cotts ME17 ... 103 A1
Greenway Court Rd ME17 ... 103 A1
Greenway La ME17 ... 119 A7
Greenway The
Orpington BR5 ... 44 B3
Oxted RH8 ... 104 B2
Greenways
Addington ME19 ... 80 E2
Maidstone ME14 ... 100 F5
New Barn DA3 ... 49 D6
Greenways The TN12 ... 145 F5
Greenwich Cl
Chatham ME5 ... 68 B4
Maidstone ME16 ... 99 D4
Greenwich Com Coll SE18 ... 2 C2
Greenwich Cres E6 ... 1 E8
Greenwich Hts SE18 ... 11 E7
Greenwich Sh Pk SE7 ... 1 B2
Greenwood Cl
Orpington BR5 ... 43 E3
Sidcup DA15 ... 30 A6
Greenwood Gdns RH8 ... 104 A1
Greenwood Ho 8 RM17 ... 18 B8
Greenwood Pl TN15 ... 79 A2
Greenwood Rd DA5 ... 31 D4
Greenwood Way TN13 ... 91 F2
Greggs Wood Rd TN2 ... 159 E7
Gregor Mews SE3 ... 11 A7
Gregory Cl ME8 ... 69 E4
Gregory Cres SE9 ... 28 D8
Gregory Ho SE3 ... 11 B5
Grenada Rd SE7 ... 11 C7
Grenadier Cl ME15 ... 100 F2
Grenadier St E16 ... 2 A5
Grenfell Cl TN16 ... 72 C7
Grenville Cl DA13 ... 64 A8
Gresham Ave DA3 ... 48 F4
Gresham Cl
3 Rainham ME8 ... 55 F1
Sidcup DA5 ... 13 F1
Tonbridge TN10 ... 127 E7
Gresham Rd
Coxheath ME17 ... 115 D3
Newham E16 ... 1 B7
Greshams Way TN8 ... 122 A2
Gresswell Cl DA14 ... 30 A5
Grey Ladies Oasts TN15 ... 95 B3
Grey Wethers ME14 ... 83 E4
Greybury La TN8 ... 138 B3
Greyfriars Cl ME16 ... 99 D5
Greyhound Way DA1 ... 14 E1
Greys Park Cl BR2 ... 56 D5
Greystone Pk TN14 ... 90 E2
Greystones Cl TN15 ... 76 E2
Greystones Rd ME15 ... 101 A2
Gribble Bridge La TN27 ... 182 B5
Grice Ave TN16 ... 72 C6
Grieves Rd DA11 ... 35 F5
Grieveson Ho ME4 ... 54 A4
Griffin Manor Way SE28 ... 2 D3
Griffin Rd SE18 ... 2 D2
Griffin Way SE28 ... 2 E3
Griffin Wlk DA9 ... 16 F2
Griffiths Ho 2 SE18 ... 12 B8
Grigg La TN27 ... 152 C7
Grigg's Cross BR5 ... 44 D3
Griggs Way TN15 ... 95 A7
Grimsby Gr E16 ... 2 B4
Grinling Ho 6 SE18 ... 2 A2
Grizedale Cl ME1 ... 67 D8
Gromenfield TN3 ... 171 C7
Groom Cl BR2 ... 42 B5
Groom Way ME17 ... 120 E6
Groombridge Cl DA16 ... 13 A2
Groombridge Hill TN3 ... 157 D1
Groombridge Pl★ TN3 ... 171 C8
Groombridge Place Gdns★ TN3 ... 171 C8
Groombridge Rd TN3 ... 157 A1
Groombridge Sq 13 ME15 ... 116 F6
Groombridge St Thomas' CE Prim Sch TN3 ... 171 C6
Groombridge Sta★ TN3 ... 171 C7
Grosmont Rd SE18 ... 2 F1
Grosvenor Ave ME4 ... 53 E3
Grosvenor Bridge TN1 ... 159 B5
Grosvenor Cres DA1 ... 15 D2
Grosvenor Ho 5 ME15 ... 116 F5
Grosvenor Manor DA5 ... 31 D6
Grosvenor Pk TN1 ... 159 A4
Grosvenor Rd Bexley DA6 ... 13 E2
Erith DA17 ... 14 A8
Gillingham ME7 ... 55 A1
Orpington BR5 ... 43 E3
Royal Tunbridge Wells TN1 ... 159 A4
Grosvenor Sq DA3 ... 48 E6
Grosvenor Wlk TN1 ... 159 A4
Grove Ave TN1 ... 159 A2
Grove Cl
Goose Green TN11 ... 112 C3
Hayes BR2 ... 56 A8
Grove Cotts TN30 ... 193 B6
Grove Ct Greenwich SE3 ... 11 A6
4 Rochester ME2 ... 53 B7
Grove Green La ME14 ... 100 E5
Grove Green Rd ME14 ... 100 F5
Grove Hill Gdns TN1 ... 159 B2
Grove Hill Ho TN1 ... 159 B3
Grove Hill Rd TN1 ... 159 B3
Grove La ME15 ... 131 D7
Grove Market Pl SE9 ... 11 F1
Grove Park Rd SE9 ... 28 D6
Grove Park Sta SE12 ... 28 B5
Grove Rd
Bexley,Bexleyheath DA7 ... 14 C3
8 Bexley,West Heath DA17 ... 13 F8
Chatham ME4 ... 54 B2
Gillingham ME7 ... 55 A6
Grays RM17 ... 18 C8
Maidstone ME15 ... 116 C7
Northfleet DA11 ... 18 B2
Penshurst TN11,TN8 ... 140 E2
Rochester ME2 ... 53 B8
Seal TN15 ... 93 B5
Sevenoaks TN14 ... 92 C6
Tatsfield TN16 ... 88 C7
Upper Halling ME2 ... 65 E5
Grove The Bexley DA6 ... 13 D3
Biggin Hill TN16 ... 72 E1
Fawkham Green DA3 ... 48 A2
Gravesend DA12 ... 36 B8
Maidstone ME14 ... 101 A3
Pembury TN2 ... 160 D8
Sidcup DA14 ... 30 E4
Swanley BR8 ... 45 F6

Grove The continued
Swanscombe DA10 . . . . **17** F2
West Kingsdown TN15 . . . . . **61** F1
Grove Vale BR7 . . . . **29** A2
Grove Wood Cotts TN11 **109** A1
Grovebury Cl DA8 . . . . **14** D8
Grovebury Ct DA6 . . . . **14** B2
Grovebury Rd SE2 . . . . **3** B4
Groveherst Rd DA1 . . . . **15** F4
Grovehurst La TN12 . . . . . . **163** C5
Grovelands ME17 . . . . **120** E5
Grovelands BR5 . . . . **30** A1
Grovelands Way RM17 . . . . . **17** F8
Grover St 3 ME1 . . . . **159** B4
Groves The ME6 . . . . **81** F7
Grovewood Cl ME14 . . . . . . **100** E4
Grovewood Dr ME14 . . . . . . **100** E4
Grub St RH8 . . . . **104** C6
Guardian Ct ME8 . . . . **55** C1
Guardian Ind Est TN12 . . **148** C7
Guards Cl TN10 . . . . **127** E7
Guestwick TN10 . . . . **127** F5
Guibal Rd SE12 . . . . **28** B7
Guild Rd Erith DA8 . . . . **14** F7
Greenwich SE7 . . . . **11** D8
Guildables La RH8,TN8 . . **121** E7
Guildford Gdns ME2 . . . . . . **52** C6
Guildford Rd Newham E6 . . . **1** F7
7 Royal Tunbridge Wells
TN1 . . . . **159** B3
Guildhall Mus The★ ME1 **53** C6
Guiness Dr ME2 . . . . **39** B2
Gulland Ho 4 ME14 . . . . . . **100** B4
Gullands ME17 . . . . **117** E4
Gulliver Rd DA15 . . . . **29** E6
Gumley Rd RM20 . . . . **17** E8
Gumping Rd BR5,BR6 . . . . . **57** C8
Gun Back La TN12 . . . . **163** A5
Gun Hill RM18 . . . . **19** D8
Gun La ME2 . . . . **53** B7
Gun Tower Mews ME1 . . . . **53** A8
Gundulph Ho TN10 . . . . . . **127** C3
Gundulph Rd Bromley BR2 **42** C6
Rochester ME1 . . . . **53** E4
Gundulph Sq ME1 . . . . **53** C6
Gunfleet Cl DA12 . . . . **36** E8
Gunlands TN12 . . . . **163** A6
Gunn Rd ME10 . . . . **17** E1
Gunner La SE18 . . . . **2** A1
Gunnery Terr SE18 . . . . **2** C3
Gunning St SE18 . . . . **2** E2
Gunnis Cl ME8 . . . . **69** D4
Gurdon Rd SE7 . . . . **1** B1
Guston Rd ME14 . . . . **100** C6
Guy Barnett Gr SE3 . . . . . . **11** A4
Gwillim Cl DA15 . . . . **13** A2
Gwynn Rd DA11 . . . . **35** C6
Gybbon Rise TN12 . . . . **149** E3
Gybbons Rd TN17 . . . . **191** F3
Gypsy Way ME23 . . . . **23** E3

H

Ha-Ha Rd SE18 . . . . **11** F8
Hackney Rd ME16 . . . . **99** C2
Hadden St SE28 . . . . **2** E3
Haddon Gr DA15 . . . . **30** A8
Haddon Rd BR5 . . . . **44** C4
Hadleigh Ct ME7 . . . . **69** A3
Hadleigh Wlk 1 E6 . . . . **1** E7
Hadley Cl DA13 . . . . **64** B8
Hadley Ct TN4 . . . . **158** F6
Hadley Gdns ME17 . . . . . . **102** E2
Hadley House BR5 . . . . **43** F7
Hadley Rd DA17 . . . . **3** F2
Hadlow Coll TN11 . . . . **128** D8
Hadlow Coll Mottingham Ctr
SE12 . . . . **28** C7
Hadlow Coll Nature
Reserve★ SE12 . . . . **28** C7
Hadlow Ct TN9 . . . . **127** C2
Hadlow Pk TN11 . . . . **111** E1
Hadlow Rd Bexley DA16 . . . **13** C7
Maidstone ME14 . . . . **100** C5
Sidcup DA14 . . . . **30** A4
Tonbridge TN9 . . . . **127** D3
Hadlow Rd E TN10,TN11 **128** A5
Hadlow Sch TN11 . . . . **128** E8
Hadlow Stair Rd TN10 . . **127** F4
Hadlow Way DA13 . . . . **35** E1
Haffenden Cl TN12 . . . . . . **148** D6
Haffenden Rd TN30 . . . . . **183** B1
Haig Ave Chatham ME1 . . . **53** D1
Chatham ME4 . . . . **54** A2
Gillingham ME7 . . . . **54** E4
Haig Ct BR7 . . . . **29** B3
Haig Gdns DA12 . . . . **36** C8
Haig Rd TN16 . . . . **72** E2
Haig Villas ME3 . . . . **40** A5
Hailey Rd DA18 . . . . **4** A4
Hailey Rd Bsns Pk DA18 . . **4** A4
Haileybury Rd BR6 . . . . **58** A6
Hailing Mews ME2 . . . . **42** B6
Hailstone Cl TN11 . . . . **128** E8
Halcot Ave DA6 . . . . **14** C2
Haldane Gdns DA11 . . . . . . **35** C7
Haldane Rd SE28 . . . . **2** C5
Halden Cl ME15 . . . . **116** F6
Halden La TN30 . . . . **191** F6
Hale Cl BR6 . . . . **57** C6
Hale Cotts DA9 . . . . **17** C2

Hale Ct TN12 . . . . **130** A7
Hale La TN14 . . . . **75** F2
Hale Oak Rd
Hall's Green TN8,TN14 . . **124** E4
Sevenoaks Weald TN14 . . **108** B1
Hale Rd ME3 . . . . **39** C7
Hale St TN12 . . . . **130** A7
Hales Cl TN30 . . . . **193** B8
Hales Ct TN30 . . . . **193** B8
Haleys Pl ME1 . . . . **83** A8
Half Moon La TN11 . . . . . . **126** D6
Half Moon Way ME23 . . . . . **23** E3
Halfpence La DA2 . . . . **51** B7
Halfpenny Cl ME16 . . . . **99** A2
Halfway St DA15 . . . . **29** E7
Halifax Cl ME5 . . . . **68** B6
Halifield Dr DA17 . . . . **3** E3
Hall Hill TN15 . . . . **93** C4
Hall Pl★ TN15 . . . . **93** C4
Hall Place Cres DA1,DA5 . **14** D2
Hall Rd Aylesford ME20 . . . **82** F1
Chatham ME5 . . . . **68** C3
Dartford DA1 . . . . **15** F3
High Halstow ME3 . . . . **24** C6
Northfleet,Pepper Hill DA11 **35** C5
Northfleet,Wombwell Park
DA11 . . . . **35** D6
Wouldham ME1 . . . . **66** C3
Hall The SE3 . . . . **11** A4
Hall View SE9 . . . . **28** D6
Hall's Hole Rd TN2 . . . . . . **159** A4
Hallam Cl BR7 . . . . **28** F3
Hallford Way DA1 . . . . **15** C2
Hallgate SE3 . . . . **11** A4
Halling Prim Sch ME2 . . . . **66** B3
Halling Sta ME2 . . . . **66** A3
Halls Cotts TN5 . . . . **184** F5
Hallsfield Rd ME5 . . . . **67** D2
Halstead Prim Sch E16 . . . **1** A7
Hallwards TN12 . . . . **149** E2
Hallwood Cl ME8 . . . . **69** D5
Hallwood Ho ME5 . . . . **68** C2
Hallywell Cres E6 . . . . **1** F8
Halons Rd SE9 . . . . **29** A8
Halsbrook Rd SE3 . . . . **11** D4
Halstead Com Prim Sch
TN14 . . . . **74** F7
Halstead La TN14 . . . . **74** E5
Halstead Rd DA8 . . . . **14** E6
Halstead Wlk ME16 . . . . **99** C2
Halstow Cl ME15 . . . . **116** B6
Halstow Rd SE10,SE3 . . . . . **1** A1
Halstow Prim Sch SE10 . . . **1** A1
Halt Cvn Pk The TN15 . . . . **61** E1
Halt Robin La DA17 . . . . **4** B2
Halt Robin Rd DA17 . . . . **4** B2
Ham La Gillingham ME7 . . . **68** C3
Lenham ME17 . . . . **120** C5
Ham River Hill ME3 . . . . . . **39** A6
Ham Shades Cl 1 DA15 . . . **30** A5
Hamble Rd TN10 . . . . **127** B5
Hambledon Ct ME16 . . . . . . **99** B3
Hambledown Rd DA15 . . . . **29** E8
Hambro Ave BR2 . . . . **42** A1
Hamelin Rd ME7 . . . . **68** F8
Hamerton Rd DA11 . . . . **18** B2
Hamilton Ct Chatham ME5 **54** C1
Rochester ME1 . . . . **53** B4
Royal Tunbridge Wells
TN4 . . . . **159** A5
Hamilton Ho
Coxheath ME17 . . . . **115** C3
Maidstone ME15 . . . . **116** F5
Royal Tunbridge Wells
TN4 . . . . **159** A5
Hamilton Rd Bexley DA7 . . **13** E5
Gillingham ME7 . . . . **54** D7
Sidcup DA15 . . . . **30** A4
Hamilton Wlk DA8 . . . . **14** F7
Hamlea Cl SE12 . . . . **11** A2
Hamlet Est DA8 . . . . **4** D1
Hamlet Ho Eltham SE9 . . . . **12** A2
5 Erith DA8 . . . . **14** E7
Hamlin Rd TN13 . . . . **91** E6
Hamlyn Ct TN13 . . . . **91** E6
Hammelton Rd 2 BR1 . . . . **42** A8
Hammerwood Pk★
RH19 . . . . **154** C2
Hammond Way 2 SE28 . . . . **3** B6
Hammonds 9 TN18 . . . . . . **189** A2
Hammonds Sq ME4 . . . . **82** A8
Hamond Hill 6 ME4 . . . . . . **53** E4
Hampden Way ME19 . . . . . . **96** F3
Hampshire Cl ME5 . . . . **68** C7
Hampshire Dr ME15 . . . . . **116** C8
Hampshires The ME17 . . . **119** C6
Hampson Way ME14 . . . . . **101** A4
Hampstead Cl SE28 . . . . **3** B5
Hampstead La ME18 . . . . . **113** C1
Hampton Cl ME5 . . . . **68** A5
Hampton Cotts TN14 . . . . . **74** F4
Hampton Cres DA12 . . . . . . **36** E6
Hampton Ct DA8 . . . . **14** D7
Hampton Ho DA7 . . . . **14** B5
Hampton Rd ME14 . . . . . . **100** C6
Hamptons Rd TN11 . . . . . . **111** B5
Hamwick Gn ME5 . . . . **68** C1
Hanameel St E16 . . . . **1** B5
Hanbury Cl ME18 . . . . **113** E7
Hanbury Dr TN16 . . . . **72** B6
Hanbury Wlk DA5 . . . . **31** E5
Hancock Cl ME3 . . . . **39** B1
Handel Cres RM18 . . . . **19** A7
Handel Wlk TN10 . . . . **127** E6
Hands Wlk E16 . . . . **1** A7
Hanes Dene ME2 . . . . **65** F5
Hang Grove Hill BR6 . . . . . . **73** B6
Hanging Bank TN14 . . . . . **106** F3

Hangmans Cnr BR7 . . . . **43** B8
Hanley St TN13 . . . . **92** E6
Hanmer Way TN12 . . . . . . **149** E2
Hanover Ave E16 . . . . **1** A5
Hanover Ct
10 Bromley BR2 . . . . **42** A6
Maidstone ME14 . . . . **100** B5
Hanover Dr
Chislehurst BR7 . . . . **29** C4
Gillingham ME8 . . . . **69** C4
Hanover Gn ME20 . . . . **81** F3
Hanover Pl DA3 . . . . **62** F8
Hanover Rd
Coxheath ME17 . . . . **115** C3
Royal Tunbridge Wells
TN1 . . . . **159** A4
Hanover Way DA7 . . . . **14** C3
Hansol Rd DA6 . . . . **13** E2
Hansom Terr 1 BR1 . . . . . . **42** B8
Hanson Dr ME15 . . . . **115** F3
Hanway ME4 . . . . **55** A2
Harbex Cl DA5 . . . . **31** B8
Harbledown Ho ME16 . . . . . **99** B2
Harbledown Manor ME8 . . **55** B3
Harbledown Pl 7 BR5 . . . . **44** C5
Harborough Ave DA15 . . . . **29** F8
Harbour The ME17 . . . . . . **134** C5
Harbourland Ct ME14 . . . . **100** B8
Harbourne La TN26,
TN30 . . . . **183** E5
Harcourt Ave DA15 . . . . **30** C8
Harcourt Gdns ME8 . . . . . . **69** E4
Harden Ct 1 SE18 . . . . **1** E2
Harden Rd DA11 . . . . **35** F6
Hardie Cl ME19 . . . . **81** F1
Harding Ho 9 SE18 . . . . **1** F2
Harding Rd DA7 . . . . **13** F5
Hardinge Ave TN4 . . . . **142** E3
Hardinge Cl ME8 . . . . **69** D4
Hardinge Cres SE18 . . . . **2** C3
Hardinge St SE18 . . . . **2** B3
Hardman Rd SE7 . . . . **1** B1
Hardres Terr BR5 . . . . **58** D8
Hards Town ME4 . . . . **54** A4
Hardwick Cres 2 DA2 . . . . **16** B1
Hardwick Ct DA8 . . . . **14** D8
Hardwick Ho ME15 . . . . . . **116** E8
Hardwick Rd TN11 . . . . . . **126** E6
Hardy Ave Newham E16 . . . . **1** A5
Northfleet DA11 . . . . **35** F4
Hardy Cl ME5 . . . . **68** B6
Hardy Gr DA1 . . . . **16** A3
Hardy Lodge ME1 . . . . **53** B4
Hardy Rd 2 SE3 . . . . **11** A8
Hardy St ME14 . . . . **100** A6
Hare St 2 Chatham ME4 . . **54** B3
Woolwich SE18 . . . . **2** A3
Harebell Cl
3 Chatham ME5 . . . . **67** F4
Maidstone ME14 . . . . **100** E5
Harebell Dr E6 . . . . **2** A8
Haredale Cl ME1 . . . . **67** D7
Harefield Rd DA14 . . . . **30** D5
Harenc Sch DA14 . . . . **30** C3
Harescroft TN2 . . . . **172** F7
Harewood Lincoln Ho
DA11 . . . . **18** D1
Harfst Way BR8 . . . . **45** C8
Hargate Cl TN2 . . . . **172** F8
Hargood Rd SE3 . . . . **11** C6
Harland Ave DA15 . . . . **29** E6
Harland Rd SE12 . . . . **28** A7
Harland Way TN4 . . . . **142** F4
Harlands Gr BR6 . . . . **57** B6
Harlech Cl ME2 . . . . **38** F1
Harlequin Ho 1 DA18 . . . . . **3** E3
Harley 5 BR7 . . . . **43** D8
Harley Gdns BR6 . . . . **57** E6
Harleyford BR1 . . . . **42** C8
Harling Cl ME17 . . . . **116** D5
Harlinger St SE18 . . . . **1** E3
Harman Ave DA11 . . . . **36** B3
Harman Ct ME5 . . . . **68** B3
Harman Dr DA15 . . . . **12** F1
Harmer Ct
Royal Tunbridge Wells
TN4 . . . . **143** A2
Swanscombe DA10 . . . . . . **17** F1
Harmer Rd DA10 . . . . **17** F1
Harmer St DA12 . . . . **19** C1
Harmers Way TN4 . . . . **137** F3
Harmony St TN4 . . . . **158** D4
Harmony Way 1 BR1,
BR2 . . . . **42** A7
Harmsworth Ct TN17 . . . . **190** E6
Harness Rd SE28 . . . . **3** A4
Harnetts Cl BR8 . . . . **45** D2
Harold Ave Erith DA17 . . . . . **3** F1
Gillingham ME7 . . . . **54** E4
Harold Campbell Ct DA1 **32** D8
Harold Gibbons Ct SE7 . . **11** C8
Harold Ho 2 TN2 . . . . **159** C7
Harold Rd Cuxton ME2 . . . **52** C3
Hawley DA2 . . . . **32** F4
Harp Farm Rd ME14 . . . . . . **84** C6
Harper Rd E6 . . . . **1** F7
Harple La ME14 . . . . **84** F1
Harpswood ME17 . . . . **102** F1
Harptree Dr ME5 . . . . **67** F5
Harraden Rd SE3 . . . . **11** C6
Harrier Mews SE28 . . . . **2** D4
Harrier Way E6 . . . . **1** F8
Harries Rd TN2 . . . . **159** E7
Harrietsham Sta ME17 . . . **119** D6
Harriet Dr ME1 . . . . **53** B3
Harrietsham Ho 13 ME16 **99** A3

Harrietsham Prim Sch
ME17 . . . . **119** E6
Harrington Ho 7 BR1 . . . . . **42** A8
Harrington Way SE18 . . . . . . **1** D3
Harris Cl DA11 . . . . **35** F5
Harris Ho ME2 . . . . **66** B4
Harris Rd DA7 . . . . **13** F6
Harrison Ct 4 ME8 . . . . **55** F1
Harrison Dr
Harrietsham ME17 . . . . . **119** E6
High Halstow ME23 . . . . . . **23** E4
Harrison Rd TN15 . . . . **94** F7
Harrison Way TN13 . . . . **92** A5
Harrogate Ct 6 SE12 . . . . . **28** A8
Harrow Cl TN8 . . . . **122** D3
Harrow Ct Chatham ME5 . . **68** C4
Stockbury ME9 . . . . **86** D8
Harrow Gdns BR6 . . . . **58** B6
Harrow Manor Way SE2 . . . **3** D2
Harrow Rd Gillingham ME7 **68** F6
Halstead TN14 . . . . **74** E4
Harrow Way ME14 . . . . **100** E5
Harrowby Gdns DA11 . . . . . **35** E6
Hart Dyke Cres BR8 . . . . . . **45** D6
Hart Dyke Rd
Orpington BR5 . . . . **44** C1
Swanley BR8 . . . . **45** D6
Hart Ho BR6 . . . . **44** A2
Hart Shaw DA3 . . . . **49** B7
Hart St ME16 . . . . **99** F3
Hart Street Bsns Ctr
ME16 . . . . **99** F3
Hartfield Cl TN10 . . . . **127** E5
Hartfield Cres BR4 . . . . **56** A7
Hartfield Pl DA11 . . . . **35** D8
Hartfield Rd
Cowden TN8 . . . . **155** C6
Hayes BR4 . . . . **56** A6
Hever TN8 . . . . **139** A4
Hartford Rd DA5 . . . . **14** A1
Hartford Wlk 13 DA17 . . . . . **4** A1
Harting Rd SE9 . . . . **28** E5
Hartington Cl BR6 . . . . **57** C5
Hartington Rd E16 . . . . **1** B7
Hartington St ME4 . . . . **54** A3
Hartlake Rd TN11 . . . . **128** D3
Hartlands Cl DA5 . . . . **13** F1
Hartlepool Ct E16 . . . . **2** B4
Hartley Bottom Rd DA3 . . **49** C2
Hartley Court Gdns
TN17 . . . . **179** A3
Hartley Hill DA3 . . . . **49** A1
Hartley Mews ME8 . . . . **55** B3
Hartley Prim Sch DA3 . . . . **48** C4
Hartley Rd Bexley DA16 . . . **13** C7
Hartley TN17 . . . . **179** A3
Longfield DA3 . . . . **48** E7
Westerham TN16 . . . . **89** D2
Hartlip CE Prim Sch ME9 **70** D5
Hartlip Hill ME9 . . . . **70** E6
Hartmann Rd E16 . . . . **1** E5
Hartnokes TN18 . . . . **189** A4
Hartnup St ME16 . . . . **99** C2
Harton Cl BR1 . . . . **42** D8
Hartpiece Cl ME8 . . . . **55** F2
Harts Cottage Farm ME15 **115** A7
Hartshill Rd DA11 . . . . **35** F6
Hartslands Rd TN13 . . . . . . **92** C4
Hartslock Dr DA18,SE2 . . . . **3** D4
Hartsmead Rd SE9 . . . . **28** F6
Hartville Rd SE18 . . . . **2** E2
Hartwell Ho 2 SE7 . . . . **1** B1
Harty Ave ME8 . . . . **69** B3
Harvard Ct 9 SE9 . . . . **12** A1
Harvel Ave ME2 . . . . **52** F7
Harvel Cl BR5,BR7 . . . . **44** A6
Harvel Cres SE2 . . . . **3** D1
Harvel La DA13 . . . . **64** B2
Harvel Rd DA13 . . . . **80** A8
Harvel St DA13 . . . . **64** C3
Harvest Bank Rd BR4 . . . . . **56** A7
Harvest Rd TN10 . . . . **127** D6
Harvest Ridge ME19 . . . . . . **81** D2
Harvest Way BR8 . . . . **45** D2
Harvesters ME8 . . . . **69** E7
Harvesters Way ME14 . . . **100** D4
Harvey Gdns SE7 . . . . **1** C1
Harvey Point 9 E16 . . . . **1** A8
Harvey Rd ME8 . . . . **69** E8
Harvill Rd DA14 . . . . **30** E3
Harwood Ave BR1 . . . . **42** B7
Harwood Ct 3 RM17 . . . . . . **18** C8
Haslemere Est ME15 . . . . **116** F5
Haslemere Rd DA7 . . . . **14** A5
Hasler Cl SE28 . . . . **3** C6
Hasletts Cl TN1 . . . . **159** B6
Haslewood Cl TN27 . . . . . . **153** B2
Hassendean Rd SE3 . . . . . . **11** B7
Hassock Wood BR2 . . . . **56** E6
Hassop Wlk SE9 . . . . **28** E4
Hast Hill Ho BR2 . . . . **56** B6
Haste Hill Cl ME17 . . . . . . **116** B3
Haste Hill Rd ME17 . . . . . . **116** B3
Hasted Cl DA9 . . . . **17** C1
Hasted Rd Greenwich SE7 . . **1** D1
Newington ME9 . . . . **71** B7
Hasteds ME17 . . . . **102** D2
Hastings Cl RM17 . . . . **17** E8
Hastings Ho SE18 . . . . **1** F2
Hastings Rd
Maidstone ME15 . . . . **100** B3
Newenden TN17,TN18 . . . **197** C6
Orpington BR2 . . . . **56** E8
Pembury TN2 . . . . **160** D6
Pembury,Kipping's Cross
TN2 . . . . **160** F5

The Moor TN18 . . . . **194** F6
Hastings St SE18 . . . . **2** C3
Hatch Rd ME17 . . . . **120** C5
Hatches La TN11,TN12 . . . **129** D6
Hatfield Ct SE3 . . . . **11** A7
Hatfield Rd ME2 . . . . **53** A8
Hatham Green La TN15 . . . **62** D1
Hathaway Cl BR2 . . . . **42** F1
Hathaway Ct
Gillingham ME8 . . . . **69** D8
Rochester ME1 . . . . **53** B5
Hatherall Rd ME14 . . . . . . **100** B6
Hatherley Cres DA14 . . . . . **30** A6
Hatherley Rd DA14 . . . . **30** A5
Hathern Gdns SE9 . . . . **29** A4
Hatmill La TN12 . . . . **162** A7
Hattersfield Cl DA17 . . . . **3** F2
Hatton Cl Northfleet DA11 . **35** E5
Woolwich SE18 . . . . **12** D7
Hatton Ct BR7 . . . . **28** F1
Hatton Rd ME5 . . . . **68** C3
Havant Wlk 8 ME15 . . . . . **116** F6
Havelock Rd Bromley BR2 **42** C5
Dartford DA1 . . . . **15** B1
Erith DA8 . . . . **3** F2
Northfleet DA11 . . . . **35** F7
Tonbridge TN9 . . . . **127** B2
Haven Cl Eltham SE9 . . . . . . **28** F5
Istead Rise DA13 . . . . **49** F8
Rochester ME1 . . . . **53** C2
Sidcup DA14 . . . . **30** C2
Swanley BR8 . . . . **45** F7
Haven Hill TN15 . . . . **63** A3
Haven Lodge 9 SE18 . . . . . . **2** B2
Haven St ME3 . . . . **39** C5
Haven Way ME4 . . . . **40** B1
Havengore Ave DA12 . . . . . **36** E8
Havering Cl TN2 . . . . **159** F6
Haverstock Ct 2 BR5 . . . . . **44** B7
Haverthwaite Rd BR6 . . . . . **57** D7
Havisham Cl ME1 . . . . **53** D2
Havisham Rd DA12 . . . . **37** A4
Havock Cl 1 ME14 . . . . **99** F4
Hawbeck Rd ME8 . . . . **69** C3
Hawden Cl TN11 . . . . **126** F4
Hawden La TN11 . . . . **126** F4
Hawden Rd TN9 . . . . **127** B2
Hawes Rd BR1 . . . . **42** B8
Hawfield Bank BR6 . . . . **58** D7
Hawkenbury Cl TN2 . . . . . . **159** D2
Hawkenbury Mead TN2 . . **159** D1
Hawkenbury Rd
Hawkenbury TN2 . . . . **150** C6
Royal Tunbridge Wells
TN2, TN3 . . . . **159** E1
Hawkenbury Rise ME2 . . . . **39** B2
Hawkes Cl RM17 . . . . **18** B8
Hawkes Pl TN13 . . . . **108** A4
Hawkes Rd ME20 . . . . **82** F5
Hawkhurst CE Prim Sch
TN18 . . . . **189** D2
Hawkhurst Cottage Hospl
TN18 . . . . **188** D2
Hawkhurst Rd
Flimwell TN5,TN18 . . . . . **187** D2
Gill's Green TN17,TN18 . . **188** F7
Gillingham ME8 . . . . **55** B3
Hawkinge Wlk BR5 . . . . **44** B6
Hawkins Ave DA12 . . . . **36** C4
Hawkins Cl ME7 . . . . **54** A6
Hawkridge Gr ME18 . . . . **97** A3
Hawksmoor Cl
3 Newham E6 . . . . **1** F7
Woolwich SE18 . . . . **2** E1
Hawksmoor Sch SE28 . . . . . **3** B6
Hawkwell Bsns Ctr TN2 **144** F2
Hawkwell Cotts TN2 . . . . . **144** F2
Hawkwood ME16 . . . . **99** B5
Hawkwood Cl ME1 . . . . **53** D5
Hawkwood La BR7 . . . . **43** C8
Hawley Ct ME16 . . . . **99** C5
Hawley Rd DA1,DA2,DA4 . . **33** A4
Hawley Terr DA2 . . . . **33** A4
Hawley Vale DA2 . . . . **33** A4
Hawser Rd ME1 . . . . **53** C1
Hawstead La BR6 . . . . **58** F5
Hawthorn Cl
Edenbridge TN8 . . . . **122** C2
Gravesend DA12 . . . . **36** C4
Orpington BR5 . . . . **43** D3
Hawthorn Cotts 6 DA16 . **13** A4
Hawthorn Ho 5 ME5 . . . . . . **67** F5
Hawthorn La TN13 . . . . **91** F5
Hawthorn Pl DA8 . . . . **4** C1
Hawthorn Rd Bexley DA6 . **13** F3
Dartford DA1 . . . . **32** C4
Rochester ME2 . . . . **52** E6
Hawthorn Terr DA15 . . . . . . **12** F2
Hawthorn Wlk
Royal Tunbridge Wells
TN2 . . . . **159** E8
Tonbridge TN10 . . . . **127** C5
Hawthornden Cl ME18 . . . **97** C3
Hawthorndene Cl BR2 . . . . **56** A8
Hawthorndene Rd BR2 . . . **56** A8
Hawthorne Ave
Biggin Hill TN16 . . . . **72** D8
Gillingham ME8 . . . . **55** C2
Hawthorne Cl BR1 . . . . **42** F6
Hawthorne Ho 4 ME16 . . . **99** A3
Hawthorne Rd BR1 . . . . **42** F6
Hawthorns Chatham ME5 . . **67** F1
Hartley DA3 . . . . **48** F5
Hawthorns The
Aylesford ME20 . . . . **82** E1
Chatham ME5 . . . . **67** F6
Oxted RH8 . . . . **104** A2

Hawthorns The *continued*
The Moor TN18 194 F8
Haxted Rd BR1 42 B8
Hay's Mead DA13 50 F3
Hayday Rd E16 1 A8
Haydens Cl BR5 44 C3
Haydens Mews TN9 127 C3
Haydens The TN9 127 C3
Haydon Cl ME16 99 B4
Hayes Cl Hayes BR2 56 A8
Higham ME3 38 C3
West Thurrock RM20 17 C8
Hayes Cotts ME19 96 D7
Hayes Gdn BR2 42 A1
Hayes La Hayes BR2 42 A4
Stockbury ME9 86 F6
Hayes Prim Sch BR2 42 B1
Hayes Rd Bromley BR2 42 A5
Stone DA9 33 E8
Hayes Sch BR2 56 B8
Hayes St BR2 42 B1
Hayes Sta BR2 42 A1
Hayes Terr DA12 37 E3
Hayes Wlk ME19 97 A2
Hayes Wood Ave BR2 42 B1
Hayesbrook Sch TN9 143 A8
Hayesden La TN11,TN3 142 B5
Hayesford Park Dr BR2 42 A4
Hayfield ME19 81 E2
Hayfield Rd BR5 44 A4
Hayfields ME5 68 D2
Haygate Ho ME1 53 C4
Hayle Mill Cotts ME15 115 F8
Hayle Mill Rd ME15 115 F8
Hayle Rd ME15 100 A3
Hayley Cl ME2 52 C2
Hayley Ho DA17 14 A8
Hayman Wlk ME20 82 F6
Haymans Hill TN12 163 C7
Haymen St ME4 53 E3
Haynes Ho 3 ME14 100 B4
Haynes Rd
Gravesend DA11 36 A6
Northfleet DA11 35 F5
Hayrick Cl ME14 100 E5
Hays Rd ME6 81 F6
Haysden Ctry Pk★
TN11 142 D8
Haywain Cl
Maidstone ME14 100 F4
Paddock Wood TN12 146 A5
Hayward Ave ME2 53 B8
Hayward Cl DA1 14 D2
Hayward Dr DA1 32 F6
Hayward's Ho ME1 53 C6
Haywood Rd BR2 42 D5
Haywood Rise BR6 57 E5
Hazard Ho 4 DA11 19 A1
Hazel Ave
Hoo St Werburgh ME3 40 E3
Maidstone ME16 99 C5
Hazel Cotts TN14 75 A6
Hazel Dr DA8 15 B6
Hazel End BR8 45 E4
Hazel Gr Chatham ME5 68 B8
Orpington BR6 57 B8
Hazel Rd Dartford DA1 32 D6
Erith DA8 15 A6
Hazel Shaw TN10 127 D7
Hazel Street Rd ME9 87 A4
Hazel Wlk BR2 43 A3
Hazelbank TN3 157 F3
Hazelden Cl TN15 62 A2
Hazelden Cotts ME2 38 C6
Hazeldene Rd DA16 13 C5
Hazelmere 8 DA4 30 A4
Hazelmere Rd BR5 43 D5
Hazelmere Way BR2 42 A3
Hazels The ME8 69 B5
Hazelview ME19 80 E3
Hazelwood Cl TN2 159 D8
Hazelwood Cotts TN5 186 D1
Hazelwood Dr ME16 99 B4
Hazelwood Hts RH8 104 A4
Hazelwood Rd
Downe TN14 73 D8
Oxted RH8 104 B3
Hazelwood Sch RH8 104 A4
Hazen Rd ME18 97 B3
Hazlemere Dr ME7 55 A5
Hazlitt Ct 4 SE28 3 C5
Hazlitt Dr ME16 99 D5
Head Race The ME15 99 D2
Headcorn Prim Sch
TN27 151 C5
Headcorn Rd Bromley BR1 28 A3
Gillingham ME8 55 B4
Lashenden TN27 168 A5
Platt's Heath ME17 119 F1
Smarden Bell TN27 152 C3
Staplehurst TN12 150 B4
Sutton Valence ME17 134 E4
Ulcombe ME17 135 F5
Headcorn Sta TN27 151 D4
Headingley Rd ME16 99 B6
Headley Ct TN8 122 C2
Headley Ho 5 BR5 44 B7
Headway Ct TN4 158 B4
Healy Dr 1 BR6 57 F6
Heansill La TN18 194 E8
Hearns Rd BR5 44 C5
Heartenoak Rd TN18 189 B3
Heath Ave DA7 13 D8
Heath Cl Orpington BR5 44 C3
Swanley BR8 45 E7
Heath Ct TN12 162 F6
Heath Gdns DA1 32 C7
Heath Gr ME16 99 A2
Heath Ho DA15 29 F4
Heath La Dartford DA1 32 C7
Dartford DA1,DA2 32 B7
Heath Park Dr BR1 42 E6
Heath Rd Coldblow DA5 31 C7
Coxheath ME17 115 C3
Crayford DA1 14 F1
East Farleigh ME15 114 E4
Langley Heath ME17 117 E4
Maidstone,Cock Street
ME17 116 C2
Maidstone,East Barming
ME16 98 F3
Heath Rise BR2 42 A3
Heath Side BR5 43 C2
Heath St DA1 32 D8
Heath Terr TN12 163 A6
Heath The ME19 97 F5
Heath View Dr SE2 13 D8
Heath Villas SE18 2 F1
Heath Way DA7,DA8 14 D6
Heathclose Ave DA1 32 B8
Heathclose Rd DA1 32 B7
Heathcote Cl ME20 82 F2
Heathdene Dr DA17 4 B2
Heathend Rd DA5 31 E7
Heather Bank TN12 146 B6
Heather Cl Chatham ME5 67 F4
Newham E6 2 A7
Heather Dr Dartford DA1 32 A8
Maidstone ME15 100 B2
Tenterden TN30 183 B3
Heather End BR8 45 D5
Heather Rd SE12 28 A7
Heather Wlk TN10 127 B6
Heatherbank
Chislehurst BR7 43 A7
Eltham SE9 11 F5
Heatherbank Cl DA1 14 E1
Heathers The TN17 179 A3
Heatherside Rd DA14 30 C5
Heatherwood Cl ME17 118 E2
Heathfield Chislehurst BR7 29 C2
Langley Heath ME17 117 E4
Heathfield Ave ME14 100 C7
Heathfield Cl
Chatham ME5 68 B7
Maidstone ME14 100 B7
Newham E16 1 D8
Orpington BR2 56 C5
Heathfield Ct DA14 30 B3
Heathfield La BR7 29 C2
Heathfield Rd Bexley DA6 13 F3
Maidstone ME14 100 C7
Orpington BR2 56 D5
Sevenoaks TN13 91 F5
Heathfield Terr
Bexley SE18 12 F8
Swanley BR8 45 D7
Heathfields TN2 159 D4
Heathlands Rise DA1 15 B1
Heathlee Rd DA1 14 E1
Heathley End BR7 29 C2
Heathorn St ME14 100 B5
Heathside Ave Bexley DA7 13 E5
Coxheath ME17 115 C4
Heathview TN4 142 F2
Heathview Ave DA1 14 E1
Heathview Cres DA1 32 B7
Heathway SE3 11 A7
Heathwood Gdns
Swanley BR8 45 C7
Woolwich SE7 1 E1
Heathwood Wlk DA5 31 E7
Heaverham Rd TN15 77 C2
Heavitree Cl 3 SE18 2 D1
Heavitree Rd SE18 2 D1
Hector St SE18 2 E2
Hectorage Rd TN9 143 D8
Hedge Barton Trailer Pk
TN3 156 F5
Hedge Place Rd DA9 17 A1
Hedgerow The ME14 100 E5
Hedgerows The DA11 35 E6
Hedges The ME14 100 A7
Hedley Ave RM20 17 C8
Hedley St ME14 100 A5
Heights The SE7 1 C1
Helegan Cl BR6 57 F6
Helen Allison Sch DA13 50 A2
Helen Cl DA1 32 B8
Helen Ct 9 DA14 30 B4
Helen Keller Cl TN10 127 D4
Helen St SE18 2 B2
Hellyar Ct ME1 53 C4
Hemmings Cl DA14 30 B6
Hempstead Inf Sch ME7 69 A5
Hempstead Jun Sch ME7 69 A5
Hempstead Rd
Gillingham ME7 69 A5
Gillingham ME7,ME8 69 B6
Hempstead Valley Dr
ME7 69 A4
Hempstead Valley Sh Ctr
ME7 69 A3
Hemstead Forest Walks★
Fosten Green TN27 181 A7
★ Fosten Green TN27 181 C5
Hemsted Forest Walks★
TN17 180 E2
Hemsted Rd DA8 14 E7
Henbane Cl ME14 100 E5
Henderson Dr DA1 16 A3
Henderson Rd TN16 72 C7
Hendley Dr TN17 179 C5
Hendry Ho ME3 39 F6
Hendy Rd ME6 82 B8
Henfield Cl DA5 14 A1
Hengist Rd Eltham SE12 28 B8
Erith DA8 14 C7
Hengrove Ct DA5 30 E7
Henham Gdns TN12 130 A6
Henhurst Hill DA12 50 D8
Henhurst Rd
Gravesend DA13 36 E1
Henhurst DA12 50 E8
Heniker La ME17 135 A4
Henley Bsns Pk ME2 53 D7
Henley Cl Chatham ME5 68 A6
Gillingham ME8 69 D8
Royal Tunbridge Wells
TN2 159 C4
Henley Ct DA5 30 F8
Henley Deane DA11 35 E4
Henley Fields
Maidstone ME14 100 E6
Tenterden TN30 183 B2
Henley Mdws TN30 183 A2
Henley Rd Newham E16 1 F4
Paddock Wood TN12 146 A7
Henley St DA13 50 F3
Henley View TN30 183 B2
Henniker Cotts TN17 179 A3
Henry Addlington Cl E6 2 B8
Henry Cooper Way SE9 28 D4
Henry St Bromley BR1 42 B8
Chatham ME4 54 B3
14 Grays RM17 18 C8
Henrys Cl ME18 113 D6
Henson Cl BR6 57 B8
Henville Rd BR1 42 B8
Henwick Prim Sch SE9 11 E4
Henwick Rd SE9 11 E4
Henwood Green Rd
TN2 160 E6
Henwoods Cres TN2 160 D6
Henwoods Mount TN2 160 E6
Herald Wlk DA1 15 F2
Herbert Pl SE18 12 B8
Herbert Rd Bexley DA7 13 E5
Bromley BR2 42 E4
Chatham ME4 54 A3
Gillingham ME8 69 E8
Hextable BR8 32 B2
Swanscombe DA10 17 F1
Woolwich SE18 12 B8
Herdsdown ME3 40 D5
Hereford Cl ME8 55 D2
Hereford Rd ME15 116 D7
Heritage Dr ME7 54 F1
Heritage Hill BR2 56 C5
Heritage Quay DA12 19 C1
Heritage Rd ME5 68 A6
Heritage The BR6 44 A2
Herman Terr ME4 54 A3
Hermitage Cl SE2 3 C3
Hermitage Cnr ME17 133 F6
Hermitage Ct
Maidstone ME16 98 F5
Tonbridge TN9 127 C2
Hermitage Farm ME19 97 C8
Hermitage La
Detling ME14 85 B4
Maidstone ME16,ME20 98 F6
Rabbit's Cross ME17 133 E6
Hermitage Rd ME3 38 E4
Hermitage The ME19 97 D8
Hern The TN15 95 C5
Herne Rd ME8 55 C2
Hero Wlk ME1 67 C7
Heron Apartments 3
ME15 116 F5
Heron Cl TN8 122 C3
Heron Cotts TN18 197 D3
Heron Cres DA14 29 E4
Heron Ct BR2 42 C5
Heron Hill DA17 3 F2
Heron Hill La DA13 64 A4
Heron Ho DA14 30 B5
Heron Rd ME20 81 F1
Heron Way Chatham ME5 68 B7
Lower Stoke ME3 25 C4
Heronden Rd ME15 116 F4
Herongate Rd BR8 31 E2
Herons Way TN2 160 E8
Heronsgate Prim Sch
SE28 2 D3
Herringham Rd SE7 1 C3
Herts Cres ME15 115 F3
Hertsfield Ave ME2 39 A2
Hertsfield Farm Cotts
TN12 133 B4
Hervey Rd SE3 11 B6
Herying Cl ME2 66 B4
Hesketh Ave DA2 33 B7
Heskett Pk TN2 160 E6
Hever Ave TN15 61 E4
Hever Castle★ TN8 139 D7
Hever CE Prim Sch TN8 139 D6
Hever Cl ME15 116 F6
Hever Court Rd DA12 36 D2
Hever Croft Eltham SE9 29 A4
Rochester ME2 52 F5
Hever Gdns Bromley BR1 43 A7
Maidstone ME16 99 E3
Hever Ho ME2 39 C1
Hever Rd
Bough Beech TN8 123 D2
Hever TN8 139 B7
West Kingsdown TN15 61 E4
Hever Road Cotts TN8 123 E2
Hever Sta TN8 139 B6
Hever Wood Rd TN15 61 E4
Heverham Rd SE18 2 E2
Heversham Rd DA7 14 A6
Heverswood TN14 59 A2
Hewett Ho 7 SE18 2 B1
Hewett Pl BR8 45 D5
Hewitt Cl Gillingham ME7 54 F6
Maidstone ME16 99 D7
Hewitts Rd BR6,TN14 58 F3
Hextable Cl ME16 99 D7
Hextable Inf Sch BR8 31 F2
Hextable Jun Sch BR8 31 F2
Hextable Sch BR8 45 F8
Hibbs Cl BR8 45 D7
Hibernia Dr DA12 36 F5
Hibernia Point 11 SE2 3 D4
Hickin Cl SE7 1 D2
Hickman Cl E16 1 D8
Hickory Dell ME7 69 A5
Hide E6 2 A7
Higgins' La ME4 53 F5
High Bank ME1 53 D2
High Banks ME15 115 F5
High Beeches
Orpington BR6 58 A4
Royal Tunbridge Wells
TN2 159 D6
Sidcup DA14 30 E3
High Brooms Ind Pk
TN2 159 C8
High Brooms Rd TN4 159 C7
High Brooms Sta TN4 159 C7
High Croft Cotts BR8 46 A5
High Cross Rd TN15 94 B1
High Dewar Rd ME8 70 A8
High Elms ME8 55 E1
High Elms Ctry Pk★ BR6 57 D3
High Elms Rd BR6 57 C2
High Firs BR8 45 E5
High Firs Prim Sch BR8 45 F5
High Gr Bromley BR1 42 D8
Woolwich SE18 12 D6
High Halden CE Prim Sch
TN26 183 E7
High Halden Rd TN26,
TN27 168 C2
High Halstow Prim Sch
ME23 23 E3
High Hilden Cl TN10 127 A4
High House La TN11 111 C2
High Meads Rd E16 1 D7
High Oak Hill ME9 71 D8
High Point SE9 29 B5
High Rd DA2 32 C5
High Ridge TN17 177 E8
High Rocks★ TN3 158 B1
High Rocks La TN3,TN4 158 C1
High Rocks Sta★ TN3 158 B1
High St Aylesford ME20 82 F3
Bean DA2 34 B5
Bidborough TN3 142 C3
Biddenden TN27 167 F1
Borough Green TN15 94 F7
Brasted TN14,TN16 90 C3
Brenchley TN12 162 B8
Bromley BR1 42 A6
Bromley BR1 42 A7
Chatham ME4 54 A4
Chatham ME7 54 A6
Cowden TN8 155 B5
Cranbrook TN17 179 C4
Dartford DA1 15 E1
Downe BR6 73 A8
East Malling ME19 98 A6
Edenbridge TN8 122 C1
Eynsford DA4 60 E8
Farningham DA4 46 F2
Flimwell TN5 187 C3
Frant TN3 173 C4
Gillingham ME7 54 C5
Gillingham,Rainham ME8 69 F8
Goudhurst TN17 177 E8
Grain ME3 27 B6
Gravesend DA11 19 B1
2 Grays RM17 18 A8
Hadlow TN11 128 E8
Halling ME2 66 A4
Hawkhurst TN18 188 E2
Headcorn TN27 151 C5
Kemsing TN15 77 B2
Lamberhurst TN3 176 B5
Leigh TN11 125 F1
Lenham ME17 120 D5
Limpsfield RH8 104 B7
Lower Stoke ME3 25 C4
Maidstone ME14 99 F4
Marden TN12 148 D6
Newington ME9 71 C6
Northfleet DA11 18 C1
Orpington,Broom Hill BR6 44 A1
Orpington,Farnborough BR6 57 C5
Orpington,Green Street Green
BR6 57 F4
Orpington,St Mary Cray BR5 44 C4
Otford TN14 76 A3
Pembury TN2 160 C6
Penshurst TN11 141 B4
Rochester ME1 53 C6
Rochester,Strood ME2 53 B7
Rochester,Upper Upnor
ME2 39 F1
Rolvenden TN17 191 E4
Royal Tunbridge Wells
TN1 159 A2
Rusthall TN4 158 C4
Seal TN15 92 F6
Sevenoaks TN13 92 C2
Sevenoaks,Chipstead TN13 91 C5
Shoreham TN14 59 F1
Sidcup DA14 30 A4
Snodland ME6 82 A8
Staplehurst TN12 149 F3
High St *continued*
Sutton Valence ME17 134 E7
Swanley BR8 45 F5
Swanscombe DA10 17 F2
Swanscombe,Greenhithe
DA9 17 B3
Tenterden TN30 193 A7
Ticehurst TN5 186 C1
Tonbridge TN9 127 C2
Wadhurst TN5 184 F4
West Malling ME19 97 C8
Westerham TN16 105 C8
Wouldham ME1 66 C5
Wrotham TN15 79 A3
Yalding ME18 113 F1
High Tor Cl BR1 28 B1
High Tor View SE28 2 E5
High Trees DA2 16 B1
High View ME3 38 C4
High Woods La TN3 160 B3
Higham Cl ME15 99 E2
Higham Gdns TN10 127 F5
Higham La TN10,TN11 127 F6
Higham Prim Sch ME3 38 C5
Higham Rd Cliffe ME3 22 A4
Rochester ME3 39 C3
Higham School Rd
TN10 127 E6
Higham Sta ME3 38 D6
Higham View ME14 83 E4
Highbanks Cl DA16 13 B7
Highberry ME19 81 E2
Highbrook Rd SE3 11 D4
Highbury La TN30 193 A7
Highbury Pl TN5 184 F5
Highcombe SE7 11 B8
Highcombe Cl SE9 28 E7
Highcroft Gn ME15 116 F4
Highcroft Hall BR8 45 D1
Highcross Rd DA13 34 D2
Highdown Cotts TN17 176 F3
Highfield Ave Erith DA8 14 B8
Orpington BR6 57 F5
Highfield Cl
Gillingham ME8 69 D7
Hawkhurst TN18 189 A1
Pembury TN2 160 D6
Highfield Cotts DA2 32 B2
Highfield Ct DA1 32 D8
Highfield Rd Bexley DA6 13 F2
Biggin Hill TN16 72 C3
Bromley BR1 42 F5
Dartford DA1 32 D8
Gillingham ME8 69 D7
Kemsing TN15 76 F3
Royal Tunbridge Wells
TN4 159 C7
St Paul's Cray BR7 43 F6
Highfield Rd N DA1 15 D1
Highfield Rd S DA1 32 D7
Highfields Rd TN8 122 C4
Highgate Ct 8 TN18 188 F2
Highgate Hill TN18 188 F1
Highgrove TN2 173 A8
Highgrove Cl BR7 42 E8
Highgrove Rd ME5 68 A5
Highland Rd
Badgers Mount TN14 75 B8
Bexley DA6 14 A3
Maidstone ME15 116 E6
Highlands Dartford DA1 32 C8
Royal Tunbridge Wells
TN2 159 D7
Highlands Cl ME2 52 D5
Highlands Hill BR8 46 A8
Highlands Pk TN15 92 E6
Highlands Rd BR5 44 C2
Highmead SE18 12 F7
Highridge ME7 54 F1
Highridge Cl ME14 100 F5
Highstead Cres DA8 14 E7
Highview Vigo Village DA13 80 B8
Woolwich SE18 12 B7
Highview Cl ME15 116 A8
Highview Dr ME5 67 D5
Highview Rd DA14 30 B4
Highway Prim Sch The
BR6 58 C5
Highway The BR6 58 C5
Highwood Cl BR6 57 C8
Highwood Dr BR6 57 C8
Highwoods Cl ME3 38 C4
Hilary Cl DA8 14 C6
Hilary Gdns ME1 52 F1
Hilbert Cl TN2 159 C5
Hilbert Rd TN2 159 C5
Hilborough Way BR6 57 D5
Hilda May Ave BR8 45 E7
Hilda Rd ME4 54 A3
Hilda Vale Cl BR6 57 A6
Hilda Vale Rd BR6 57 B6
Hilden Ave TN11 126 F4
Hilden Dr DA8 15 B7
Hilden Grange Sch
TN10 127 B3
Hilden Oaks Sch TN10 127 B3
Hilden Park Rd TN11 126 F4
Hildenborough CE Prim Sch
TN11 126 D6
Hildenborough Cres
ME16 99 C7
Hildenborough Rd
Leigh TN11 126 A3
Shipbourne TN11,TN15 109 E4

Hildenborough Sta
　TN11 . . . . .126 B6
Hildenbrook Farm TN11 109 E2
Hildenfields TN10 . . . . . .127 A4
Hilders Cl TN8 . . . . .122 B4
Hilders La TN8 . . . . .122 A4
Hill Brow Bromley BR1 . .42 D8
　Crayford DA1 . . . . .14 F1
　Maidstone ME14 . . . . . .101 A5
Hill Chase ME5 . . . . .67 E3
Hill Cl Chislehurst BR7 . . .29 B3
　Istead Rise DA13 . . . . . . .35 E1
Hill Cres Coldblow DA5 . . .31 C7
　Lenham ME17 . . . . .120 D5
Hill Crest
　Royal Tunbridge Wells
　TN4 . . . . .159 B8
　Sevenoaks TN13 . . . . .92 A5
　Sidcup DA15 . . . . .30 B8
Hill Ct ME3 . . . . .39 F4
Hill End Orpington BR6 . . .57 F8
　Woolwich SE18 . . . . .12 A6
Hill Farm Cl ME23 . . . . . .23 E3
Hill Green Rd ME9 . . . . . .86 D8
Hill House Rd DA2 . . . . . .33 C8
Hill Rd Dartford DA2 . . . . .32 E6
　Rochester ME1 . . . . .53 A2
　Wouldham ME1 . . . . .66 F5
Hill Rise DA2 . . . . .33 E3
Hill Sch The TN16 . . . . . .89 B4
Hill Shaw DA3 . . . . .48 F3
Hill St TN1 . . . . .159 B5
Hill The Cranbrook TN17 . .179 D4
　Northfleet DA11 . . . . .18 C1
Hill Top TN17 . . . . .164 D5
Hill Top Cotts ME17 . . . .115 E2
Hill View Basted TN15 . . . .94 F4
　Borough Green TN15 . . . . .95 A7
Hill View Cl TN15 . . . . . . .95 A7
Hill View Dr Bexley DA16 . .12 E5
　Woolwich SE18 . . . . .2 E5
Hill View Rd
　New Barn DA3 . . . . .49 B6
　Orpington BR6 . . . . .57 F8
　Rusthall TN4 . . . . .158 C4
　Tonbridge TN11 . . . . . . .126 F5
Hill View Way ME5 . . . . . .67 E5
Hill's Terr ME4 . . . . .53 F3
Hillary Ave DA11 . . . . . . .35 E4
Hillary Ct SE9 . . . . .28 E6
Hillary Rd ME14 . . . . . . .100 A7
Hillborough Ave TN13 . . . .92 D5
Hillborough Gr ME5 . . . . .68 A3
Hillbrow Cl DA5 . . . . .31 D4
Hillbury Gdns TN5 . . . . .186 D1
Hillcrest TN8 . . . . .123 B8
Hillcrest Ave RM20 . . . . . .17 B8
Hillcrest Dr Cuxton ME2 . . .52 C2
　Royal Tunbridge Wells
　TN2 . . . . .159 D7
　Stone DA9 . . . . .17 A2
Hillcrest Rd
　Biggin Hill TN16 . . . . .72 D3
　Bromley BR1 . . . . .28 A4
　Chatham ME4 . . . . .53 F2
　Dartford DA1 . . . . .31 F8
　Marlpit Hill TN8 . . . . . . .122 C4
　Orpington BR6 . . . . .58 A8
Hillcroft DA4 . . . . .60 D7
Hillcroft Rd E6 . . . . .2 B8
Hillden Shaw ME15 . . . . .116 A8
Hilldown Lodge BR6 . . . . .58 B8
Hilldrop Rd BR1 . . . . .28 B2
Hillfield Rd TN13 . . . . . . .91 E7
Hillfield Villas TN26 . . . .183 F8
Hillgarth TN4 . . . . .159 A8
Hillingdale TN16 . . . . .72 B1
Hillingdon Ave TN16 . . . . .72 B1
Hillingdon Rd Bexley DA7 . .14 C4
　Gravesend DA11 . . . . .36 B6
Hillington Rise TN13 . . . . .92 D5
Hillreach SE18 . . . . .1 F1
Hills La TN15 . . . . .77 C7
Hillsgrove Cl DA16 . . . . . .13 C7
Hillsgrove Prim Sch
　DA16 . . . . .13 C7
Hillshaw Cres BR2 . . . . . .52 D5
Hillside Dartford DA2 . . . . .33 E3
　Erith DA17 . . . . .4 C2
　Farningham DA4 . . . . .46 F2
　Rochester ME1 . . . . .53 A2
　Tonbridge TN9 . . . . .143 A7
Hillside Ave
　Gravesend DA12 . . . . .36 D6
　Rochester ME2 . . . . .53 B8
Hillside Cotts TN5 . . . . . .185 B8
Hillside Ct
　❷ Rochester ME2 . . . . . . .53 A7
　Swanley BR8 . . . . .46 A5
　Wateringbury ME18 . . . . .113 E7
Hillside Dr DA12 . . . . .36 D6
Hillside La BR2 . . . . .56 A8
Hillside Prim Sch BR5 . . . .44 C2
Hillside Rd Chatham ME4 . .54 A4
　Dartford DA1 . . . . .15 A1
　Kemsing TN15 . . . . .76 F2
　Sevenoaks TN13 . . . . .92 D4
　Tatsfield TN16 . . . . .88 E8
Hillside Terr DA12 . . . . . . .36 B7
Hillside The BR6 . . . . .58 B2
Hillsley Ct ❸ DA14 . . . . . .30 A4
Hilltop Tonbridge TN9 . . . .143 B7
　West Farleigh ME15 . . . . . .90 A4
Hilltop Gdns Dartford DA1 15 F2
　Orpington BR6 . . . . .57 E8

Hilltop Prim Sch ME2 . . . .39 C1
Hilltop Rd Rochester ME2 . .39 C1
　West Thurrock RM20 . . . . .17 B8
Hillview Cres BR6 . . . . . . .43 F1
Hillview Ho DA12 . . . . . . .36 C7
Hillview Rd ME2 . . . . .29 A4
Hillview Sch for Girls
　TN9 . . . . .143 D8
Hillydeal Rd TN14 . . . . . . .76 C4
Hillyfield Cl ME2 . . . . .38 F1
Hilton Rd ME3 . . . . .39 B7
Hind Cres DA8 . . . . .14 D7
Hines Terr ME1 . . . . .54 C1
Hinksden Rd TN17,TN18 .189 F3
Hinksey Path SE2 . . . . .3 D3
Hinstock Rd SE18 . . . . . . .12 C7
Hinton Cl SE9 . . . . .28 E7
Hinton Cres ME7 . . . . .69 A6
Historic Dockyard The★
　ME4 . . . . .54 A8
Hitchen Hatch La TN13 . . .92 B4
Hither Chantlers TN3 . . . .158 A2
Hither Farm Rd SE3 . . . . . .11 C4
Hive La DA11 . . . . .18 B2
Hive The DA11 . . . . .18 B1
Hoath Cl ME8 . . . . .69 B7
Hoath La ME8 . . . . .69 B7
Hoath Mdw TN12 . . . . . .163 A6
Hoath Way ME7,ME8 . . . . .69 B8
Hobart Rd ME18 . . . . .19 A6
Hoblands End BR7 . . . . . . .29 E2
Hockenden La BR8 . . . . . .45 B7
Hockers Cl ME14 . . . . . . .101 A8
Hockers La ME14 . . . . . . .101 A8
Hoddesdon Rd DA17 . . . . . .4 A1
Hodgkins Cl SE28 . . . . .3 D6
Hodgson Cres ME6 . . . . . .66 A1
Hodsoll Ct BR5 . . . . .44 D4
Hodsoll St TN15 . . . . .63 D1
Hodson Cres BR5 . . . . . . .44 D3
Hog Hill ME4 . . . . .101 B5
Hog Hole La TN3 . . . . . . .175 F2
Hog La DA11 . . . . .35 D5
Hogarth Cl E16 . . . . .1 D8
Hogbarn La ME17 . . . . . .103 F2
Hognore La TN15 . . . . .79 D6
Hogs Orch BR8 . . . . .46 B8
Hogtrough Hill TN16 . . . . .90 A5
Holbeach Gdns DA15 . . . . .12 F1
Holborn La ME4 . . . . .53 F5
Holborn Rd E13 . . . . .1 B8
Holborough Rd ME6 . . . . .66 A1
Holbrook Ho BR7 . . . . . . .43 D8
Holbrook La BR7 . . . . .29 D1
Holbrook Way BR2 . . . . . .42 F4
Holburne Cl SE3 . . . . .11 C6
Holburne Gdns SE3 . . . . . .11 D6
Holburne Rd SE3 . . . . .11 D6
Holcombe Cl TN16 . . . . . .89 D1
Holcombe Rd
　Chatham ME4 . . . . .53 F2
　Rochester ME1 . . . . .53 C3
Holcote Cl DA17 . . . . .3 A1
Holden Cnr TN4 . . . . .142 F1
Holden Park Rd TN4 . . . .159 A8
Holden Rd TN4 . . . . .142 F1
Holder Cl ME5 . . . . .68 C6
Holding St ME7 . . . . .55 F1
Hole La TN8 . . . . .122 A6
Holford St ❶ TN9 . . . . . .127 B1
Holgate St SE7 . . . . .1 D3
Holland Cres RH8 . . . . . .104 A2
Holland Ho ME1 . . . . .53 D5
Holland Jun Sch RH8 . . . .104 A1
Holland La RH8 . . . . .104 A1
Holland Rd Chatham ME5 . .67 E4
　Maidstone ME14 . . . . . . .100 B5
　Oxted RH8 . . . . .104 A1
Hollandbury Pk ME18 . . . . .97 C2
Hollands Cl DA12 . . . . . . .37 E3
Hollies Ave DA15 . . . . . . .29 F7
Hollies The
　Gravesend DA12 . . . . .36 D2
　New Barn DA3 . . . . .49 C6
　Sidcup DA15 . . . . .30 A8
Holligrave Rd BR1 . . . . . . .42 A8
Hollin Cl TN4 . . . . .158 F4
Hollingbourne Ave DA7 . . .13 F6
Hollingbourne Hill
　ME17 . . . . .102 F4
Hollingbourne Prim Sch
　ME17 . . . . .102 E2
Hollingbourne Rd ME8 . . .55 C2
Hollingbourne Sta
　ME17 . . . . .102 C3
Hollingbourne Twr ❹
　BR5 . . . . .44 D1
Hollington Ct BR7 . . . . . . .29 B2
Hollingworth Ct ME14 . . .100 C3
Hollingworth Rd
　Maidstone ME15 . . . . . . .116 F5
　Orpington BR2,BR5 . . . . . .43 B2
Hollingworth Way TN16 . . .89 D1
Hollow La Hartlip ME9 . . . . .70 E5
　Snodland ME6 . . . . .81 F6
Hollow Trees Dr TN11 . . . .126 A1
Holly Bank TN12 . . . . . . .162 B8
Holly Bush La TN13 . . . . . .92 C3
Holly Cl Chatham ME5 . . . .68 C8
　Gillingham ME7 . . . . .54 E6
Holly Cotts TN8 . . . . .122 B2
Holly Ct ❶ DA14 . . . . .30 B4
Holly Farm Rd ME15 . . . .117 C6
Holly Gdns Bexley DA7 . . . .14 C3
　Maidstone ME14 . . . . . . .100 B7
Holly Hill DA13 . . . . .64 F3
Holly Hill Rd DA8,DA17 . . . .4 B1
Holly Rd Dartford DA1 . . . .32 D7

Holly Rd continued
　Orpington BR6 . . . . .58 A3
Rochester ME2 . . . . .39 D2
Holly Tree Cl ME17 . . . . . .118 E2
Hollybrake Cl BR7 . . . . . . .29 D1
Hollybush Cl TN13 . . . . . . .92 C3
Hollybush Ct TN13 . . . . . . .92 C3
Hollybush La BR6 . . . . . . .59 A4
Hollybush Rd DA12 . . . . . .36 C6
Hollycroft ME2 . . . . .52 C2
Hollydale Dr BR2 . . . . . . .56 F7
Hollydene Rd TN5 . . . . . .184 F6
Hollyshaw TN2 . . . . .159 C2
Hollyshaw Cl TN2 . . . . . .159 C2
Hollytree Ave ME8 . . . . . . .45 E7
Hollytree Dr ME3 . . . . .38 B3
Hollytree Par DA14 . . . . . .30 C2
Hollywood La
　Knockmill TN15 . . . . .77 F8
　Rochester ME2 . . . . .39 D2
Hollywood Way DA8 . . . . .15 B6
Holm Ct ❺ SE12 . . . . . . .28 B5
Holm Mill La ME17 . . . . . .119 B6
Holm Wlk SE3 . . . . .11 A5
Holmbury Manor ❷❶
　DA14 . . . . .30 A4
Holmbury Pk BR7 . . . . . . .28 E1
Holmcroft Way BR2 . . . . . .42 F4
Holmdale Rd BR7 . . . . . . .29 C3
Holmden Ct ❷ TN8 . . . . .122 C1
Holmdene Ct ❺ BR1 . . . . .42 A1
Holmes Ct ME23 . . . . .23 E3
Holmes Rd ME19 . . . . .80 F4
Holmesdale Cl
　Durgates TN5 . . . . .184 E5
　Maidstone ME15 . . . . . . .115 F3
Holmesdale Hill DA4 . . . . .47 D8
Holmesdale Rd
　Bexley DA7 . . . . .13 D5
　Sevenoaks TN13 . . . . .92 D4
　Sutton at H DA4 . . . . .47 C8
Holmesdale Tech Coll
　ME6 . . . . .81 F7
Holmewood House Sch
　TN3 . . . . .158 A2
Holmewood Rd TN4 . . . . .159 C7
Holmewood Ridge TN3 . .157 F3
Holmhurst Cl TN4 . . . . . .158 F4
Holmhurst Rd DA17 . . . . . .4 B1
Holmleigh Ave DA1 . . . . . .15 C2
Holmoaks Gillingham ME8 . .55 E2
　Maidstone ME14 . . . . . . .100 C5
Holmside ME7 . . . . .54 E4
Holmwood Cotts BR6 . . . .58 C1
Holmwood Ct DA14 . . . . . .29 F3
Holstein Way ❻ DA18 . . . . .3 E3
Holt Cl SE28 . . . . .3 C6
Holt Rd E16 . . . . .1 F8
Holt Wood Ave ME20 . . . . .98 E8
Holtwood Cl ME8 . . . . . . .69 D6
Holtye Cres ME15 . . . . . .100 B2
Holtye Rd RH19 . . . . .154 A4
Holwood Park Ave BR2,
　BR4 . . . . .56 F6
Holy Family RC Prim Sch
　Eltham SE3 . . . . .11 C3
　Maidstone ME15 . . . . . . .116 F4
Holy Innocents RC Prim Sch
　BR6 . . . . .57 F7
Holy Trinity CE Prim Sch
　Dartford DA1 . . . . .15 C2
　Gravesend DA12 . . . . .36 C8
Holy Trinity Coll Prep Sch
　BR1 . . . . .42 C8
Holy Trinity Lamorbey CE
　Prim Sch DA15 . . . . .30 A7
Holyhead Ct ❸ E6 . . . . .1 F8
Holyoake Terr TN13 . . . . . .92 A3
Holyrood Mews E16 . . . . . . .1 A5
Holywell Cl Greenwich SE3 11 A8
　Orpington BR6 . . . . .58 A6
Home Farm BR6 . . . . .59 A5
Home Farm Cl TN11 . . . .126 A3
Home Farm Cotts BR5 . . . .44 D8
Home Farm Ct TN3 . . . . .173 C4
Home Farm La TN2 . . . . .159 E8
Home Gdns DA1 . . . . .15 E1
Home Hill BR8 . . . . .31 F1
Home Lea BR6 . . . . .57 F5
Home Mead Cl ❻ DA12 . . .36 B8
Home Pk RH8 . . . . .104 A4
Homedean Rd TN13 . . . . . .91 C4
Homefarm Est ME20 . . . . .82 F1
Homefield Cl
　Orpington BR5 . . . . .44 B5
　Swanley BR8 . . . . .45 F6
Homefield Rd
　Bromley BR1 . . . . .42 C8
　Sevenoaks TN13 . . . . .91 E5
Homefield Rise BR6 . . . . . .44 A1
Homemead
　❼ Gravesend DA12 . . . . . .36 B8
　Swanscombe DA9 . . . . . . .17 B1
Homemead Rd BR2 . . . . . .42 F4
Homer Cl DA7 . . . . .14 C6
Homesdale Bsns Ctr BR1 42 D6
Homesdale Rd
　Bromley BR1,BR2 . . . . . . .42 C6
　Orpington BR5 . . . . .43 C6
Homestead Rd
　Marlpit Hill TN8 . . . . . . .122 B5
　Orpington BR6 . . . . .58 B4
Homestead The
　Crayford DA1 . . . . .14 E2
　Dartford DA1 . . . . .15 C1
　Groombridge TN3 . . . . . .171 C7

Homevale Cotts TN14 . . . .74 E4
Homewards Rd ME3 . . . . . .9 B2
Homewood Cotts DA12 . . .37 E1
Homewood Cres BR7 . . . . .29 E2
Homewood Rd
　Langton Green TN3 . . . . .157 F3
　Tenterden TN30 . . . . . . .183 B1
Homewood Sch & Sixth Form
　Ctr TN30 . . . . .183 B1
Homlesdale Bsns Ctr
　TN15 . . . . .95 C8
Homoepathic Hospl
　TN1 . . . . .159 A3
Honduras Terr ❽ ME14 . .100 A7
Hone St ME2 . . . . .53 B8
Honey Bee Glade ME8 . . . .69 E6
Honey Cl ME7 . . . . .69 A5
Honey La ME17 . . . . .69 A5
Honeybourne Way BR5 . . .43 D1
Honeycombe Lodge
　DA11 . . . . .18 D1
Honeycrest Ind Pk
　TN12 . . . . .149 E5
Honeyden Rd DA14 . . . . . .30 E2
Honeypot Cl ME2 . . . . .53 B8
Honeypot La
　Hodsoll Street TN15 . . . . . .63 D2
　Kemsing TN15 . . . . .93 C8
　Limpsfield TN8 . . . . .121 D4
Honeysuckle Cl
　❸ Chatham ME5 . . . . . . .67 E4
　Gillingham ME7 . . . . .68 F4
Honeysuckle Ct ❹ SE12 . .28 A8
Honiton Rd DA16 . . . . .12 F5
Honywood Rd ME17 . . . .120 C4
Hoo Comm ME3 . . . . .40 A4
Hoo Rd ME2,ME3 . . . . . . .39 D3
Hoo St Werburgh Prim Sch
　ME3 . . . . .40 D5
Hood Ave BR5 . . . . .44 B4
Hook Cl ME5 . . . . .67 E5
Hook Farm Rd BR2 . . . . . .42 D4
Hook Green Ct DA13 . . . . .50 A4
Hook Green La DA2 . . . . . .31 F5
Hook Green Rd DA13 . . . . .34 F1
Hook Hill TN5 . . . . .186 A6
Hook La Bexley DA16 . . . . .13 A4
　Harrietsham ME17 . . . . . .119 C6
Hook Lane Prim Sch
　DA16 . . . . .13 A4
Hook Place Cotts DA13 . . .35 A2
Hook Rd ME6 . . . . .81 F8
Hookfields DA11 . . . . .35 E5
Hookstead TN26 . . . . . . .183 C7
Hookwood Bglws RH8 . . .104 B7
Hookwood Cnr RH8 . . . . .104 B7
Hookwood Cotts TN14 . . . .74 C8
Hookwood Rd BR6,TN14 . .74 C7
Hooper Rd E16 . . . . .1 A7
Hooper's Pl ME1 . . . . .53 B4
Hooper's Rd ME1 . . . . .53 C4
Hoopers La ME3 . . . . .24 F5
Hoopers Yd TN13 . . . . . . .92 C1
Hop Bine TN12 . . . . .130 A7
Hop Farm Ctry Pk★
　TN12 . . . . .130 A3
Hop Pocket Cl TN17 . . . . .180 A8
Hop Pocket La TN12 . . . . .145 F7
Hope Ave TN11 . . . . .111 E1
Hope Cl SE12 . . . . .28 B5
Hope Cotts DA2 . . . . .34 B6
Hope Rd DA10 . . . . .17 F1
Hope St Chatham ME4 . . . .54 A3
　Maidstone ME14 . . . . .99 F6
Hope Terr ME3 . . . . .38 D7
Hopedale Rd SE7 . . . . .11 B8
Hopehouse La TN17,
　TN18 . . . . .196 F2
Hopes Gr TN26 . . . . .183 D7
Hopewell Bsns Ctr ME5 . .68 C8
Hopewell Dr
　Chatham ME5 . . . . .68 C8
　Gravesend DA12 . . . . .36 F3
Hopgarden Cl ❶❷ TN8 . .122 D3
Hopgarden La ME18 . . . . .108 A8
Hopgarden Oast ME18 . . .113 F1
Hopgarden Rd TN10 . . . .127 D6
Hoppers Cnr ME15 . . . . . .114 D7
Hopton Ct BR2 . . . . .42 A1
Hopton Rd SE18 . . . . .2 B3
Hopwood Gdns TN4 . . . .159 A6
Horatio Pl ME1 . . . . .53 B4
Horizon Cl TN4 . . . . .159 B8
Horley Cl DA6 . . . . .14 A2
Horley Rd SE9 . . . . .28 E4
Horn La SE10 . . . . .1 A2
Horn Link Way SE10 . . . . . .1 A2
Horn Park Cl SE12 . . . . . . .11 B2
Horn Park La SE12 . . . . . . .11 B1
Horn Park Prim Sch
　SE12 . . . . .28 B8
Horn Yd ❼ DA11 . . . . . . .19 B1
Horn's Oak Rd DA13 . . . . .64 B6
Hornbeam Ave
　Chatham ME5 . . . . .68 B2
　Royal Tunbridge Wells
　TN4 . . . . .143 D1
Hornbeam Cl
　Larkfield ME20 . . . . .82 B2
　Paddock Wood TN12 . . . .145 F5
Hornbeam Ho ❻ DA15 . . .30 A5
Hornbeam La DA7 . . . . . . .14 C5
Hornbeam Way BR2 . . . . . .43 A3
Hornbeams DA13 . . . . .80 B8
Horncastle Cl SE12 . . . . . .28 A8
Horncastle Rd SE12 . . . . . .28 A8
Horne Ho SE18 . . . . .11 E6

Hornfair Rd SE7 . . . . .11 D7
Hornfield Cotts DA13 . . . . .64 C3
Horning Cl SE9 . . . . .28 E4
Horns La ME18 . . . . .96 D1
Horns Lodge Farm
　TN11 . . . . .127 C8
Horns Lodge La TN11 . . . .127 A8
Horns Rd The Moor TN18 .194 D8
　The Moor TN18 . . . . .194 D8
　The Moor TN18 . . . . .194 F7
Horsa Rd Eltham SE12 . . . .28 C8
　Erith DA8 . . . . .14 C7
Horse Leaze E6 . . . . .2 A7
Horse Wash La ME1 . . . . . .53 C6
Horsecroft Cl BR6 . . . . . . .44 B1
Horsegrove Ave TN5 . . . . .186 F1
Horsell Rd BR5 . . . . .44 B8
Horseshoe Cl
　Gillingham ME7 . . . . .68 F5
　Maidstone ME14 . . . . . . .100 E5
Horseshoes La ME17 . . . .117 E4
Horsfeld Gdns SE9 . . . . . .11 E2
Horsfeld Rd SE9 . . . . .11 D2
Horsfield Cl DA2 . . . . .33 C8
Horsham Rd DA6 . . . . .14 A2
Horsley Ho SE18 . . . . .12 A7
Horsley Rd Bromley BR1 . . .42 B8
　Rochester ME1 . . . . .53 B4
Horsmonden Cl BR6 . . . . .43 F2
Horsmonden Prim Sch
　TN12 . . . . .163 A6
Horsmonden Rd TN12 . . . .162 D6
Horsted Ave ME4 . . . . .53 E1
Horsted Inf Sch ME4 . . . . .67 D5
Horsted Jun Sch ME5 . . . . .67 D5
Horsted Ret Pk ME5 . . . . . .67 D5
Horsted Way ME1 . . . . . . .67 D7
Horton Downs ME15 . . . .100 F1
Horton Kirby CE Prim Sch
　DA4 . . . . .47 C6
Horton Pl TN16 . . . . .89 D1
Horton Rd DA4 . . . . .47 C6
Horton Twr ❷ BR5 . . . . . .44 C5
Horton Way DA4 . . . . .46 F2
Hortons Cl TN17 . . . . . . .190 D1
Hortons Way ❶ TN16 . . . .89 D1
Horwood Cl ME1 . . . . .67 B8
Hoselands View DA3 . . . . .48 F3
Hoser Ave SE12 . . . . .28 A6
Hosey Common La
　TN16 . . . . .105 F5
Hosey Common Rd TN8,
　TN16 . . . . .105 D5
Hosey Hill TN16 . . . . .105 E5
Hoskin's Cl E16 . . . . .1 C1
Hospital La ❸ ME1 . . . . . .53 E4
Hospital Rd
　Hollingbourne ME17 . . . .118 E8
　Sevenoaks TN13 . . . . .92 C6
Hostier Cl ME2 . . . . .66 B4
Hotel Rd ME8 . . . . .55 A2
Hotham Cl Sutton at H DA4 33 B1
　Swanley Village BR8 . . . . . .46 B8
Hothfield Rd ME8 . . . . .55 F1
Hottsfield DA3 . . . . .48 E6
Hougham Ho ❶❶ BR5 . . . .44 D1
Houghton Ave ME7 . . . . . .69 B3
Houselands Rd TN9 . . . . .127 B2
Hove Cl RM17 . . . . .18 A8
Hovendens TN17 . . . . . . .180 A8
Hoveton Rd SE28 . . . . .3 C7
How Green La TN8 . . . . . .123 C2
Howard Ave
　Rochester ME1 . . . . .53 D3
　Sidcup DA5 . . . . .30 C8
Howard Dr ME16 . . . . .99 B5
Howard Gdns TN2 . . . . . .159 A1
Howard Rd Bromley BR1 . . .28 A1
　Dartford DA1 . . . . .16 A1
　East Malling ME19 . . . . . . .97 F8
Howard Sch The ME8 . . . . .69 D8
Howarth Rd SE2 . . . . .3 A2
Howbury Ctr PRU The
　DA8 . . . . .15 A7
Howbury La DA8 . . . . .15 A5
Howbury Wlk ME8 . . . . . . .69 D4
Howden Cl SE28 . . . . .3 D6
Howells Cl TN15 . . . . .61 E4
Howerd Way SE18 . . . . . . .11 E6
Howes Cotts TN18 . . . . . .194 F8
Howick Cl ME20 . . . . .98 F8
Howland Cotts TN12 . . . .148 E6
Howland Rd TN12 . . . . . .148 E6
Howlands TN15 . . . . .78 F4
Howlands Ct TN15 . . . . . . .78 F4
Howlsmere Cl ME2 . . . . . .66 B3
Hubbard's Hill TN13,
　TN14 . . . . .108 B4
Hubbard's La ME15 . . . . .116 A3
Hubble Dr ME15 . . . . . . .116 E2
Huckleberry Cl ME5 . . . . . .68 B3
Hudson Cl ME8 . . . . .55 C1
Hudson Ho DA4 . . . . .47 D7
Hudson Pl SE18 . . . . .2 C1
Hudson Rd DA7 . . . . .13 F6
Huggen's College
　Almshouses DA11 . . . . . .18 B2
Hugh Christie Tech Coll
　TN10 . . . . .127 D6
Hughes Dr ME2 . . . . .39 D2
Hulberry Farm DA4 . . . . . .60 B8
Hulkes La ME1 . . . . .53 E4
Hull Pl E16 . . . . .2 C5
Hulsewood Cl DA2 . . . . . . .32 B5
Hulsons Ct ❶ TN18 . . . . .189 A2
Humber Cres ME2 . . . . . . .52 F7
Humber Rd Dartford DA1 . .15 D2

Humber Rd continued
  Greenwich SE3 ....11 A8
Humboldt Ct TN2 .....159 D5
Hume Ave RM18 ....19 B5
Hume Cl RM18 ....19 A4
Hume Terr E16 ....1 B7
Humphreys TN12 ......161 F6
Hundred of Hoo Comp Sch
  The ME3 ....40 C5
Hungershall Park Cl
  TN4 ....158 E1
Hungershall Pk TN4 ...158 E2
Hunsdon Dr TN13 ......92 B4
Hunstanton Cl ME8 ....69 E3
Hunt Rd Northfleet DA11 .35 F5
  Tonbridge TN10 ....127 E6
Hunt St
  Nettlestead ME15,ME18 .113 F5
  West Farleigh ME15 ...114 B5
Hunter Seal TN11 .....126 E2
Hunter's Gr BR6 ....57 C6
Hunters Cl DA5 ....31 E5
Hunters Ct 5 ME7 .....54 C7
Hunters Lodge 10 DA15 .30 A5
Hunters Way
  Gillingham ME7 ....54 E1
  Royal Tunbridge Wells
  TN2 ....158 F1
Hunters Way W ME5 ...54 E1
Hunters Wlk TN14 .....74 E5
Huntersfield Cl ME5 ...68 C1
Huntingdon Wlk 2
  ME15 ....116 E7
Huntingfield Rd DA13 ..50 A2
Huntington Cl TN17 ...179 D4
Huntington Rd ME17 ..115 B3
Huntley Ave DA11 .....18 C1
Huntley Mill Rd TN5 ..186 E3
Huntleys Pk TN4 ......158 F5
Hunton CE Prim Sch
  ME15 ....131 D7
Hunton Hill ME15 .....114 F1
Hunton Ho 4 BR5 .....44 C4
Hunton Rd TN12 ......132 A3
Hunts Farm Cl TN15 ...95 A7
Hunts La TN17 ....177 E8
Hunts Mede Cl ME7 ...28 F1
Huntsman Ho 2 DA11 .35 F8
Huntsman La
  Maidstone ME14 ......100 B4
  Wrotham Heath TN15 ..79 E1
Huntsman's Cnr ME4 ..67 E8
Huntsmans Cl ME1 ....53 E1
Huntsmoor Ho BR5 ...44 B5
Hurlfield DA2 ....32 C5
Hurlingham Cl TN10 ..127 E7
Hurlingham Rd DA7 ...13 F7
Huron Cl 5 BR6 ....57 F4
Hurricane Rd ME19 ...96 F3
Hurst Cl Chatham ME5 .67 E6
  Staplehurst TN12 .....149 F4
  Tenterden TN30 ......192 F7
Hurst Ct Newham E6 ....1 D8
  Sidcup DA15 ....30 A6
Hurst Farm Rd TN14 ..108 B3
Hurst Green CE Prim Sch
  TN19 ....194 A2
Hurst Green Inf Sch
  RH8 ....104 A3
Hurst Green Rd RH8 ..104 A3
Hurst Hill ME5 ....67 E2
Hurst Ho SE2 ....3 D1
Hurst La Erith SE2 ......3 D1
  Sevenoaks Weald TN14 .108 B2
  Woolwich SE2 ....3 D1
Hurst Pl Gillingham ME8 .69 F8
Hurst Prim Sch DA5 ...30 D7
Hurst Rd Erith DA8 ....30 D7
  Sidcup DA5 ....30 D7
Hurst Springs DA5 ....30 E7
Hurst The Crouch TN11 .111 D7
  Plaxtol Spoute TN15 ...95 C1
  Royal Tunbridge Wells
  TN2 ....159 E7
Hurst Way
  Maidstone ME16 ....98 F2
  Sevenoaks TN13 ......108 C3
Hurstbourne Cotts DA5 .31 B8
Hurstfield BR2 ....42 A4
Hurstings The ME15 ...99 D2
Hurstlands RH8 ......104 A3
Hurstmere Foundation Sch
  for Boys DA15 ....30 C7
Hurstwood ME5 ....67 E4
Hurstwood Ave
  Bexley DA7,DA8 ....14 E6
  Sidcup DA5 ....30 E7
Hurstwood Dr BR1 ....42 F6
Hurstwood La TN4 ....158 F3
Hurstwood Pk TN4 ...158 F3
Hurstwood Rd
  Bredhurst ME7 ....69 B1
  Bredhurst,Bredhurst Hurst
  ME14 ....85 B7
Husheath Hill TN17 ...164 F6
Hussar Ho ME1 ....53 C3
Husseywell Cres BR2 ..42 A1
Hutchins Rd SE28 ......3 A5
Hutsford Cl ME8 ......69 D5
Hutson Terr RM19 ....16 D8
Huxley Cl 3 ME1 ......53 D4
Huxley Ho SE2 ....3 D1
Huxley Rd DA16 ....12 F4
Hyacinth Rd ME2 ......52 E6
Hybrid Cl ME1 ....53 D1
Hyde Dr BR5 ....44 B5
Hyde Rd Bexley DA7 ...13 F5

Hyde Rd continued
  Maidstone ME14 ....99 D6
Hyde's Orch TN27 ....151 E5
Hyders Forge TN15 ...111 A8
Hylton St SE18 ....2 F2
Hyndford Cres DA9 ...17 C2
Hyperion Dr ME2 ......38 F1
Hythe Ave DA7 ....13 F7
Hythe Cl Orpington BR5 .44 C5
  Royal Tunbridge Wells
  TN4 ....143 A1
Hythe St Dartford DA1 .15 E1
  Dartford DA1 ....15 D1

I

Ice Bowl The★ ME8 ...55 A1
Ickleton Ct SE9 ....28 E4
Icough Ct SE3 ....11 B7
Iddenden Cotts TN18 .188 D2
Ide Hill CE Prim Sch
  TN14 ....106 F4
Ide Hill Rd
  Bough Beech TN8,TN14 .123 F5
  Ide Hill TN14 ....106 F2
Iden Cres TN12 ....149 F2
Iden Croft Herbs★
  TN12 ....150 A1
Iden Green Cotts TN17 .178 C8
Iden Rd ME2 ....39 C1
Idenwood Cl ME8 .....69 D6
Idleigh Court Rd DA3,
  DA13 ....63 C8
Ifield Cl ME15 ....116 F7
Ifield Sch The DA12 ...36 C3
Ifield Way DA12 ......36 D2
Ightham By-Pass TN15 .94 C7
Ightham Cotts DA2 ...34 B6
Ightham Mote★ TN15 .110 C5
Ightham Prim Sch TN15 .94 B6
Ightham Rd Bexley DA8 .14 A7
  Shipbourne TN11,TN15 .110 C5
Ilkley Rd E16 ....1 C8
Illustrious Cl ME5 .....68 A6
Imber Ct 4 SE9 ....12 A1
Impala Gdns TN4 .....159 B6
Imperial Bsns Pk 18 F1
Imperial Ct BR7 ......29 B2
Imperial Dr DA12 .....36 F3
Imperial Pl BR7 ......43 A8
Imperial Rd ME7 ......54 C3
Imperial Ret Pk DA11 ..19 A1
Imperial Way BR7 ....29 C5
Impton La ME5 ....68 A1
Inca Dr SE9 ....28 B8
Indus Rd SE7 ....11 C7
Industrial Est The TN8 .122 B3
Ingle Pl ME18 ....97 E4
Ingle Rd ME4 ....53 F2
Ingleborough La TN15 .95 C8
Ingleby Way BR7 .....29 A3
Ingleden Park Rd TN30 .183 C1
Ingledew Rd SE18 ......2 D1
Ingleside 3 SE3 ....11 A8
Ingleton Ave DA16 ...13 C6
Inglewood Chislehurst BR7 29 D2
  Swanley BR8 ....45 E7
Inglewood Copse BR1 .42 F7
Inglewood Rd DA7 ...14 D3
Ingoldsby Rd DA12 ...36 F7
Ingram Rd Dartford DA1 .32 E7
  Gillingham ME7 ....54 E6
Ingress Gdns DA9 ....17 D2
Ingress Park Ave DA9 .17 C3
Ingress Terr DA13 ....34 E4
Inigo Jones Rd SE7 ...11 E7
Inner Lines ME7 ......54 A6
Institute Rd ME4 .....54 A4
Instone Rd DA1 ....32 D8
Inveraray Pl SE18 .....12 D8
Inverine Rd SE7 ....1 B1
Invermore Pl SE18 .....2 C2
Inverness Ho 7 ME15 .116 E7
Inverness Mews E16 ...2 C5
Invicta Bsns Pk TN15 .79 C2
Invicta Cl BR7 ....29 A3
Invicta Gram Sch ME14 .100 A5
Invicta Par 3 DA14 ...30 B4
Invicta Prim Sch SE3 ..11 A7
Invicta Rd Dartford DA2 .16 B8
  Greenwich SE3 ....11 A8
Invicta Villas ME14 ...101 C4
Io Ctr SE18 ....2 C3
Iona Cl ME5 ....68 D1
Iona Rd ME5 ....116 A7
Ionia Wlk DA12 ....36 F5
Ireland Cl E6 ....1 F8
Irene Rd BR6 ....43 E7
Iris Ave DA5 ....13 E1
Iris Cl ME5 ....84 A8
Iris Cres DA7 ....13 F8
Iron Mill La DA1 ......14 F3
Iron Mill Pl DA1 ......14 F3
Ironside Cl ME5 ......68 A8
Ironstones TN3 ......158 B3
Irvine Rd ME3 ....38 B3
Irvine Way BR6 ....43 F2
Irving Ho TN1 ....159 B5
Irving Way BR8 ....45 D7
Irving Wlk DA10 ......34 E8
Irwin Ave SE18 ....12 E7
Isabella Dr BR6 ......57 C6
Isla Rd SE18 ....2 C1
Island Way E ME4 ....40 C1
Island Way W ME4 ...40 B2
Islehurst Cl BR7 ......43 A8
Islingham Farm Rd ME3 .39 D4

Ismays Rd TN15 ....94 C3
Istead Rise DA13 ......35 F1
Istead Rise Prim Sch
  DA13 ....49 E8
Itchingwood Common Rd
  RH8 ....104 E2
Ito Way ME8 ....55 A3
Ivedon Rd DA16 ......13 C5
Ivens Way ME17 .....119 D6
Iverhurst Cl DA6 ......13 D2
Iversgate Cl ME8 .....55 F2
Ives Rd TN9 ....126 F1
Ivor Gr SE9 ....29 B7
Ivor Ho DA14 ....30 C3
Ivorydown BR1 ....28 A4
Ivy Bower Cl DA9 .....17 B2
Ivy Cl Dartford DA1 ...33 A8
  Gravesend DA12 ......36 D5
Ivy House La TN13,TN14 .75 C3
Ivy La
  Bells Yew Green TN3 .174 A5
  Knockholt TN14 ......74 C3
Ivy Mews ME17 ......118 C2
Ivy Pl ME1 ....53 A2
Ivy Rd E16 ....1 A7
Ivy St ME8 ....69 F8
Ivy Villas DA1 ....17 A2
Ivybridge Ct 1 BR7 ...43 A8
Izane Rd DA6 ....13 F3

J

Jackass La BR2 ....56 C4
Jacklin Cl ME5 ....67 F2
Jackson Cl ME1 ....67 E8
Jackson Cl Rainham ME8 .55 C1
  1 Stone DA9 ....17 A2
Jackson Ho 4 SE7 .....11 B8
Jackson Rd BR2 ....56 F8
Jackson St SE18 ....12 A8
Jackson Way TN17 ...181 C3
Jackson's Cnr ME1 ....24 A3
Jacksons La 8 TN30 ..193 A4
Jacob Ho 5 DA18 ......3 D4
Jacob's La ME3 ....41 B6
Jade Cl E16 ....1 D7
Jade Hill ME2 ....66 A6
Jaffray Rd BR2 ....42 B5
Jaggard Way TN12 ...149 E3
Jagger Cl DA2 ....33 C8
Jago Cl SE18 ....12 C8
Jail La Biggin Hill TN16 .72 E3
  Cudham TN16 ....73 A3
Jamaica Terr ME14 ...100 A7
James Newman Ct SE9 .29 A5
James Rd Cuxton ME2 .52 C2
  Dartford DA1 ....15 A1
James St 5 Chatham ME4 .53 F4
  Gillingham ME7 ....54 C6
  Maidstone ME14 ......100 A5
  Rochester ME1 ....53 C4
James Watt Way DA8 .14 F8
James Whatman Way
  ME14 ....99 F5
Jane Seymour Ct DA15 .29 D8
Janet Ct 4 DA7 ....14 A3
Janson Ct 11 DA14 ...30 B4
Japonica Cl ME5 ......68 C2
Jaquets Ct DA5 ....31 A6
Jarrah Cotts RM19 ....16 D8
Jarrett Ave ME2 ......39 C2
Jarvis La TN17 ....164 B3
Jarvis Pl TN30 ....183 B3
Jasmine Cl
  2 Chatham ME5 ....67 F4
  East Malling ME19 ....97 E8
  Orpington BR6 ....57 B8
Jasmine Cotts
  Borough Green TN15 ..94 F7
  Groombridge TN3 ....171 C7
Jasmine Ct SE12 ......11 A1
Jasmine Rd ME19 .....97 F8
Jason Wlk SE9 ....29 A4
Jasper Ave ME1 ......53 D2
Jasper Rd E16 ....1 D7
Javelin Rd ME19 ......96 F3
Jay Gdns BR7 ....28 F4
Jefferson Dr ME8 .....55 C1
Jefferson Wlk 18 SE18 .12 A8
Jeffery St ME7 ....54 C6
Jeffrey Cl TN12 ......149 E4
Jeffrey Cl DA8 ....14 C7
Jeffrey Row SE12 .....11 B2
Jeffrey St ME14 ......100 A5
Jeken Rd SE9 ....11 C3
Jellicoe Ave ME7 .....36 C5
Jellicoe Ave W DA12 .36 C5
Jenkins Dr ME15 .....116 E5
Jenkins' Dale ME4 ....53 F3
Jenner Cl DA14 ....30 A4
Jenner Ho 4 DA17 .....4 A3
Jenner Rd ME1 ....53 C4
Jenner Way ME20 ....82 F6
Jennifer Ct ME3 ......40 F5
Jenningtree Rd DA8 ..15 B7
Jenningtree Way DA17 .4 C4
Jenton Ave DA7 ......13 E5
Jerome Rd ME20 .....81 F4
Jersey Dr BR5 ....43 D3
Jersey Rd Newham E16 ..1 C8
  Rochester ME2 ....53 A4
Jeskyns Rd DA12 .....50 E6
Jessamine Pl DA2 ....33 C8
Jessamine Terr BR8 ..45 C8
Jessett Cl SE18 ....4 D2
Jessup Cl SE18 ....2 C2

K

K9 Est RM13 ....4 E7
Kale Rd DA18 ....3 E4
Karloff Way ME2 .....39 B2
Kashgar Rd SE18 ......2 F2
Kashmir Rd SE7 ......11 D7
Katherine Ct ME5 ....68 B2
Katherine Gdns SE9 ..11 D3
Katherine Rd TN8 ...138 C8
Katherine Villas TN8 .138 C8

Jetty Rd Kingsnorth ME3 .41 D7
  Sheerness ME12 ......27 F3
Jetty Wlk 3 RM17 ....18 A8
Jevington Way SE12 ..28 B7
Jewell Gr TN12 ......148 D5
Jewels Hill TN16 .....72 A6
Jeyes Rd ME7 ....54 C4
Jezreels Rd ME7 ......54 D3
Jiniwin Rd ME1 ....67 D7
Joan Cres SE9 ....28 D8
Jockey La TN17 ......179 D5
Johannesburg Ho 2
  ME15 ....116 F5
John Brunt Ct TN12 ..146 A7
John Burns Cotts RH8 .104 E5
John Cooper Ho ME3 .25 C5
John Hunt Ct SE9 ....28 E6
John Mayne CE Prim Sch
  TN27 ....167 F1
John Newton Ct DA16 .13 B4
John Spare Ct TN4 ...159 A6
John St Grays RM17 ..18 C8
  Maidstone ME14 ......100 A6
  Rochester ME1 ....53 C4
  Royal Tunbridge Wells
  TN4 ....159 A5
John Wesley Ct SE9 ..12 A3
John Wilson St SE18 ...2 A2
John's Rd
  Meopham Sta DA13 ...49 F4
  Tatsfield TN16 ....88 D7
Johns Cl DA3 ....48 F4
Johns Rd TN16 ....73 B3
Johnson Ave ME7 ....54 C7
Johnson Cl DA11 .....35 D5
Johnson Rd BR2 ......42 D4
Johnsons Ave TN14 ..59 B1
Johnsons Ct TN15 ....92 F6
Johnsons Way DA9 ...17 D5
Joiners Ct ME4 ....54 B2
Jonas Dr TN5 ....184 E5
Jonas La TN5 ....184 E5
Jordan Cl ME15 .....116 E5
Josling Cl RM17 ......17 F8
Joy Rd DA12 ....36 C7
Joy Wood ME7 ......116 D5
Joyce Cl TN17 ....179 C5
Joyce Dawson Way SE28 .3 A6
Joyce Green Ho DA1 ..15 F4
Joyce Green Hspl DA1 .15 E4
Joyce Green La
  Dartford DA1 ....15 E6
  Dartford,Temple Hill DA1 .15 E5
Joyce Page Cl SE7 ....11 D8
Joyden's Wood Rd DA5 .31 E5
Joydens Wood Inf Sch
  DA5 ....31 E4
Joydens Wood Jun Sch
  DA5 ....31 E4
Jubilee Cl DA9 ....17 C1
Jubilee Cnr ME17 ....135 E3
Jubilee Cotts
  Sevenoaks TN14 ......92 B7
  Sutton Valence ME17 .134 E7
Jubilee Cres
  Gravesend DA12 ......36 E6
  Ightham TN15 ....94 C6
Jubilee Field TN30 ...199 E4
Jubilee Park Ctry Pk★
  BR1,BR5 ....43 B5
Jubilee Prim Sch SE28 ..3 A6
Jubilee Rd Chelsfield BR6 .59 A4
  West Thurrock RM20 ..17 B8
Jubilee Rise TN15 ....92 F6
Jubilee Terr
  Gillingham ME7 ....54 C6
  Knockholt TN14 ......74 E4
Jubilee Way DA14 ....30 A6
Judd Rd TN9 ....143 B7
Judd Sch The TN9 ...143 A8
Judeth Gdns DA12 ...36 E3
Judkins Cl ME5 ......68 C6
Juglans Rd BR6 ......44 A1
Julia Garfield Mews E16 .1 B5
Julian Cl 3 DA14 .....30 A4
Julian Rd BR6 ....58 A4
Julians Cl TN13 .....108 A8
Julians Way TN13 ...108 A8
Junction Rd
  Bodiam TN18,TN32 ..195 A3
  Dartford DA1 ....15 D1
  Gillingham ME7 ....54 C6
Juniper Cl Biggin Hill TN16 72 C2
  Chatham ME5 ....68 A4
  Maidstone ME16 ......99 B6
  Royal Tunbridge Wells
  TN4 ....143 D1
Juniper La E6 ....1 E8
Juniper Wlk BR8 .....45 D7
Jury St 12 DA11 ......19 B1
Jutland Cl ME3 ....9 D1
Jutland Ho SE18 ....1 E2

Kay St DA16 ....13 B6
Keary Rd DA10 ....34 F8
Keats Ave E16 ....1 B5
Keats Gdns RM18 ....19 B5
Keats Ho DA1 ....14 C2
Keats Rd Bexley DA16 .12 F6
  Erith DA17 ....4 C3
  Lunsford ME20 ....81 F3
Kechill Gdns BR2 .....42 A2
Kedleston Dr BR5 ....43 F4
Keeble Cl SE18 ....12 B8
Keedonwood Rd BR1 ..28 A3
Keefe Cl ME5 ....67 D1
Keel Gdns TN4 ......158 E8
Keeley Mews ME7 ....54 E3
Keeling Rd SE9 ....11 D2
Keemor Cl SE18 ......12 A7
Keep The SE3 ....11 A5
Keightley Dr SE9 .....29 C8
Keir Hardie Prim Sch E16 .1 A8
Keir Hardy Ho 7 DA17 .4 A3
Keith Ave DA4 ....33 B2
Keith Park Cres TN16 .72 C7
Keith Sutton Ho SE9 ..29 C6
Kelbrook Rd SE3 .....11 E4
Kelchers La TN11 ....128 F5
Kelham Ho 10 SE18 ...12 B8
Kellaway Rd Chatham ME5 68 A2
  Greenwich SE3 ....11 D5
Kellner Rd SE28 ....2 F3
Kelly Dr ME7 ....54 F8
Kelly Ho 15 Greenwich SE7 11 C8
  Rochester ME1 ....67 C7
Kelsall Ct SE3 ....11 B5
Kelsey Rd BR5 ....44 B7
Kelso Dr DA12 ....36 F4
Kelvin Cl TN10 ......127 D7
Kelvin Ho 3 DA17 .....4 A3
Kelvin Par BR6 ....43 E1
Kelvin Rd Bexley DA16 .13 A4
  Tilbury RM18 ....19 A5
Kemble Cl TN2 ......159 E7
Kemble Dr BR2 ......56 E7
Kembleside Rd TN16 .72 C1
Kemnal Rd BR7 ......29 D3
Kemnal Tech Coll BR5 .30 B1
Kemnal Warren BR7 ..29 D2
Kemp Cl ME5 ....67 E4
Kempley Ct 2 RM17 .18 C8
Kempt St SE18 ....12 A8
Kempton Cl Chatham ME5 .68 C2
  Erith DA8 ....14 C8
Kemsing Cl DA5 ......30 E8
Kemsing Prim Sch TN15 .77 A2
Kemsing Rd
  Greenwich SE10 ....1 A1
  Wrotham TN15 ....78 C3
Kemsing Sta TN15 ....93 D8
Kemsley Cl
  Northfleet DA11 ......35 F4
  Swanscombe DA9 ....17 B1
Kemsley Ct BR5 ......44 B8
Kemsley Rd TN16 ....44 B8
Kemsley Street Rd ME7 .69 C1
Kencot Cl DA18 ....3 F4
Kendal Cl TN9 ......127 C2
Kendal Dr TN9 ......127 C2
Kendal Pk TN4 ......158 E5
Kendal Way ME8 .....69 D8
Kendall Ave ME18 ....97 C3
Kendall Ct DA15 ......30 A5
Kendall Gdns DA11 ...35 F8
Kendall Lodge 9 BR1 .42 B8
Kendall Pl 1 ME15 ..116 D8
Kendall Rd SE18 ......11 E6
Kendon Bsns Pk ME2 .53 D8
Kenia Wlk DA12 ......36 F5
Kenilworth Ct 10 DA2 .16 B1
Kenilworth Dr ME8 ...69 D6
Kenilworth Gdns
  Gillingham ME8 ....69 D7
  Woolwich SE18 ....12 B5
Kenilworth Ho ME16 .99 B2
Kenilworth Rd BR5 ...43 C3
Kenley Cl Sidcup BR7 .31 A8
  St Paul's Cray BR7 ...43 E6
Kenley Ho 6 BR5 .....44 B7
Kenmere Rd DA16 ...13 C5
Kennacraig Cl E16 .....1 A5
Kennard Cl ME1 ......52 F2
Kennard St E16 ....1 C5
Kennedy Cl BR5 ......43 D1
Kennedy Gdns TN13 .92 D5
Kennedy Ho
  Benenden TN17 ......190 E6
  Northfleet DA11 ......35 D5
Kennel Barn Rd ME9 .87 C5
Kennet Ct 2 BR8 .....45 C6
Kennet Rd Crayford DA1 .15 A4
  Tonbridge TN10 .....127 C5
Kennett Ct 16 BR5 ...44 D1
Kennington Cl
  Gillingham ME8 ....55 B4
  Maidstone ME15 .....116 F7
Kensington Ct 5 RM17 .18 B8
Kensington Ho ME16 .99 A2
Kent & East Sussex Rly★
  TN17 ....192 D5
Kent & East Sussex Rly Mus★
  TN30 ....193 A8
Kent & East Sussex Steam
  Rly★ TN17 ....198 C5
Kent & Sussex Hospl
  TN4 ....159 A4

Kent Ave Bexley DA16 ....12 F2
Maidstone ME15 ....100 C1
Kent Cl Orpington BR6 ....57 E4
Paddock Wood TN12 ...146 A6
Rochester ME1 ....67 C8
Kent Coll TN2 ....144 D2
Kent County Optholmic &
Aural Hospl ME14 .....100 A4
Kent County Show Gd
ME14 ....85 C3
Kent Hatch Rd
Crockham Hill RH8,TN8 ..105 D4
The Chart RH8,TN8 ....104 D4
Kent Ho
10 Hawkhurst TN18 ....189 A2
Royal Tunbridge Wells
TN1 ....159 C6
Sutton at H DA4 ......47 D7
Kent Inst of Art & Design
Maidstone ME16 ....99 C3
Rochester ME1 ....53 E4
Kent Kraft Ind Est DA11 ..17 F2
Kent Rd Dartford DA1 ....15 E1
Gravesend DA11 ....36 A7
4 Grays RM17 ....18 C8
Halling ME2 ....66 A6
Longfield DA3 ....48 D7
Orpington BR5 ....44 B3
Royal Tunbridge Wells
TN4 ....159 A6
Snodland ME6 ....82 A6
Kent St ME18 ....96 E2
Kent Terr
Lower Higham ME3 .....38 D7
Meopham DA13 ....64 A7
Kentish Ct **8** ME16 ....99 E4
Kentish Gdns TN2 .....172 E8
Kentish Mans **15** TN1 ..159 A2
Kentish Rd DA17 ....4 A2
Kentish Way BR1,BR2 ...42 B6
Kentlea Rd SE28 ....2 E4
Kentmere Rd SE18 ......2 E2
Kentstone Ct ME4 ......54 A4
Kenward Ct TN11 ......128 E8
Kenward Rd Eltham SE9 ..11 D2
Maidstone ME16 ....99 C5
Yalding ME18 ....113 E2
Kenwood Ave
Chatham ME5 ....68 A4
New Barn DA3 ....49 C6
Kenwyn Rd DA1 ....15 D2
Kenya Rd SE7 ....11 D7
Kenya Terr **11** ME14 ..100 A7
Kenyon Wlk ME8 ....69 B3
Kerry Cl E16 ....1 B7
Kerry Hill Way ME14 ...99 E6
Kersey Gdns SE9 ....28 E4
Kesteven Cl ME2 ....66 B5
Kestlake Rd DA5 ....13 C1
Keston Ave BR2 ....56 B6
Keston CE Prim Sch BR2 56 D5
Keston Cl DA16 ....13 C7
Keston Ct Gillingham ME8 55 A2
Sidcup DA5 ....30 F8
Keston Gdns BR2 ......56 C6
Keston Park Cl BR2 ....56 F7
Kestrel Ave E6 ....1 E8
Kestrel Cl TN8 ....122 D3
Kestrel Ho ME7 ....54 B6
Kestrel Rd ME5 ....68 C4
Keswick Cl TN9 ....127 C2
Keswick Ct ME7 ....55 A5
Keswick Dr ME16 ....99 B5
Keswick Gdns RM19 ....16 C8
Keswick Rd Bexley DA7 ..14 A6
Orpington BR6 ....44 A2
Ketridge La ME18 ......97 D2
Kettle La ME15 ....114 E6
Kettlewell Ct BR8 .....45 F7
Kevington Cl BR5 ......43 F5
Kevington Dr BR7 ......43 F5
Kewlands ME14 ....100 C6
Keycol Hill ME9 ....71 F5
Keyes Ave ME4 ....53 F2
Keyes Gdns TN9 ......142 F7
Keyes Rd DA1 ....16 A3
Keymer Cl TN16 ....72 D3
Keynes Ct **9** SE28 ....3 B6
Keynsham Gdns SE9 ...11 E2
Keynsham Rd SE9 ......11 E2
Keyworth Cl ME12 ....145 F6
Khalsa Ave TN9 ....36 C8
Khartoum Pl DA12 .....19 C1
Khartoum Rd ME4 .....53 F6
Khyber Rd ME4,ME7 ...54 B7
Kibbles La TN4 ....158 E8
Kidbrooke Gdns SE3 ...11 A6
Kidbrooke Gr SE3 .....11 B6
Kidbrooke La SE9 .....11 C5
Kidbrooke Park Cl SE3 ..11 B6
Kidbrooke Park Prim Sch
SE3 ....11 C6
Kidbrooke Park Rd SE12,
SE3 ....11 B4
Kidbrooke Sch SE3 ....11 D5
Kidbrooke Sta SE3 ....11 B4
Kidbrooke Way SE3 ....11 B5
Kidd Pl SE7 ....1 E1
Kiddens ME8 ....45 B7
Kidds Cotts BR8 ......45 D3
Kierbeck Bsns Complex
E16 ....1 B4
Kilburn Ho **6** ME14 ..100 A5
Kildare Rd E16 ....1 A8
Killewarren Way BR5 ...44 C3

Killick Cl TN13 ....91 E6
Killick Rd ME3 ....40 D5
Killicks Cotts ME18 ...130 F8
Killigarth Ct **22** DA14 ..30 A4
Kiln Barn Rd ME19,ME 20 .98 C7
Kiln Field TN30 ......193 C7
Kiln La TN11 ....125 F1
Kiln Way TN12 ....146 A6
Kilnbank TN2 ....159 C7
Kilnbridge Cl ME15 ...115 B7
Kilnbridge Wks ME15 ..115 B7
Kildown DA12 ....36 D2
Kildown Cl ME16 ......99 C7
Kilnfields BR5 ....59 A4
Kilnwood TN14 ....74 F6
Kimbell Rd SE13 ......11 C3
Kimber Ho **11** SE18 ....12 B8
Kimberley Dr DA14 ....30 D6
Kimberley Rd ME7 .....54 D3
Kimberly Ct DA17 .....3 F2
Kimmeridge Gdns SE9 ..28 E4
Kimmeridge Rd SE9 ...28 E4
Kincraig BR7 ....43 A8
Kincraig Dr TN13 ......92 B4
Kinder Cl SE28 ....3 D6
King & Queen Cl SE9 ..28 E4
King Arthur's Dr ME2 ..39 A1
King Edward Ave DA1 ..15 D1
King Edward Rd
Chatham ME4 ....53 F2
Gillingham ME7 ....54 F6
Maidstone ME15 ....99 F2
Rochester ME1 ....53 C5
Stone DA9 ....17 A2
King George Ave E16 ...1 D7
King George Rd ME5 ...67 E4
King George V Hill TN1 .159 C5
King George V Meml Houses
ME8 ....55 C2
King George VI Ave
TN16 ....72 D3
King Harolds Way DA7 ..13 E7
King Henry Mews **7** BR6 57 F5
King Hill ME19 ....97 A5
King John's Wlk SE9 ...11 E1
King St Chatham ME4 ..54 A4
Gillingham ME7 ....54 C6
Gravesend DA12 ....19 B1
Maidstone ME14 ......100 A4
Rochester ME1 ....53 C4
West Malling ME19 ....97 C8
King William Rd **6** ME7 54 C7
King's Ave ME1 ....53 C3
King's Bastion ME7 ...54 A5
King's Cotts
Wateringbury ME18 ...113 D6
Yalding ME18 ....114 A1
King's Highway SE18,SE2 12 F8
King's Orch Eltham SE9 ..11 E1
Rochester ME1 ....53 C5
King's Rd Chatham ME5 .54 D1
Tonbridge TN9 ....143 D7
King's Standing Ind Est
TN2 ....143 F2
Kingfisher Apartments **13**
ME15 ....116 E5
Kingfisher Cl Erith SE28 ..3 C4
Orpington BR5 ....44 D5
Kingfisher Com Prim Sch
ME5 ....68 B7
Kingfisher Ct
11 Maidstone ME15 ...100 B4
West Kingsdown TN15 ..61 E3
Kingfisher Dr
Chatham ME5 ....68 C7
Swanscombe ME2 .....17 A1
Kingfisher Ho BR5 ....44 C8
Kingfisher Pl DA4 .....47 C7
Kingfisher Rd ME20 ...82 A2
Kingfisher St E6 ....1 E8
Kings Acre ME15 .....101 A1
Kings Ave BR1 ....28 A2
Kings Cl DA1 ....14 E3
Kings Cotts
Cranbrook TN17 ......179 D6
Leeds ME17 ....117 F6
Kings Ct
Horsmonden TN12 ....163 A6
21 Sidcup DA14 ....30 A5
Kings Dr DA12 ....36 B5
Kings Farm Prim Sch
DA11 ....36 C3
Kings Hill Ave ME19 ...97 A4
Kings Hill Sch ME19 ...97 A4
Kings La TN12 ....147 C7
Kings Oak Mews ME5 ..67 F4
Kings Pk TN2 ....159 D3
Kings Rd Biggin Hill TN16 ..72 C2
Headcorn TN27 ......151 C5
Orpington BR6 ....57 F6
Kings Reach ME15 ....116 D8
Kings Row
1 Maidstone ME15 ....100 A1
Rochester ME1 ....53 B4
Kings Standing Way
TN2 ....143 F1
Kings Toll Rd TN2 ....161 A6
Kings Wlk Grays RM17 ..18 A8
Maidstone ME14 ......100 B5
Kingsand Rd SE12 .....28 A6
Kingsdale Ct
Chatham ME5 ....54 C1
Swanscombe ME10 ....17 E1
Kingsdale Rd SE18 ....12 F8
Kingsdown Cl
Gillingham ME7 ....69 B4
Gravesend DA12 ....36 F7

Kingsdown Cl continued
Maidstone ME16 ....99 E4
Kingsdown Ind Est ME20 .98 B8
Kingsdown Way BR2 ...42 A3
Kingsfield Ho SE9 .....28 D5
Kingsford Com Sch E6 ...1 F7
Kingsford Cotts TN17 ..190 D6
Kingsford Way E6 .....1 F8
Kingsgate Cl Bexley DA7 ..13 E6
Maidstone ME16 ....99 C4
Orpington BR5 ....44 C6
Kingsground SE9 ....11 E1
Kingshill Dr ME3 ......40 D6
Kingsholm Gdns SE9 ..11 E3
Kingshurst Rd SE12 ...28 A8
Kingsingfield Cl TN15 ..61 E3
Kingsingfield Rd TN15 ..61 E2
Kingsland Gr TN27 ...151 D5
Kingsland La TN27 ...137 C3
Kingsley Ave DA1 .....16 A2
Kingsley Ct Bexley DA6 ..14 A3
Wadhurst TN5 ....185 A4
1 Woolwich SE28 .....3 C5
Kingsley Mews BR7 ...29 B2
Kingsley Rd
Maidstone ME15 ......100 A3
Orpington BR6 ....57 F3
Kingsley Wood Dr SE9 ..28 F5
Kingsman Par SE18 ....1 F2
Kingsman St SE18 .....1 F2
Kingsmead TN16 ......72 D3
Kingsmead Cl DA15 ...30 A6
Kingsmead Cotts BR2 ..42 E1
Kingsmead Pk
Allhallows-on-S ME3 ...9 E3
Paddock Wood TN12 ..146 A6
Kingsmere BR7 ....42 E8
Kingsnorth Cl ME3 ....40 E6
Kingsnorth Ct BR8 ....45 C3
Kingsnorth Ind Est ME3 ..41 D7
Kingsnorth Rd ME8 ...55 C4
Kingsridge Gdns DA1 ..15 C4
Kingston Cres ME5 ....68 C4
Kingston Ct DA11 .....18 B1
Kingston Dr ME15 ...116 A8
Kingsway Chatham ME5 ..54 D1
Gillingham ME7 ....54 E1
Orpington BR5 ....43 D4
Kingswear Gdns ME2 ..53 C7
Kingswood Ave
Chatham ME4 ....53 F2
Erith DA17 ....3 F2
Swanley BR8 ....45 F6
Kingswood Cl
Dartford DA1 ....15 C1
Orpington BR6 ....43 D2
Royal Tunbridge Wells
TN2 ....159 C3
Kingswood Ho
12 Maidstone ME16 ...99 A3
10 Sidcup DA14 ....30 B4
Kingswood Prim Sch
ME17 ....118 E2
Kingswood Rd
Gillingham ME7 ....54 D6
Kit's Coty ME20 ....83 D8
Royal Tunbridge Wells
TN2 ....159 C3
Sevenoaks TN13 ......91 E7
Kinlet Rd SE18 ....12 C6
Kinnell Ct **18** DA14 ...30 B4
Kinnings Row TN9 ....127 C2
Kinross Cl ME5 ....68 B7
Kinveachy Gdns SE7 ...1 E1
Kipling Ave RM18 .....19 C6
Kipling Dr ME20 ......81 F4
Kipling Rd Bexley DA7 ..13 E6
Dartford DA1 ....16 B2
Kippington Cl TN13 ...91 F3
Kippington Dr SE9 ....28 D7
Kippington Rd TN13 ...92 A7
Kirby Cl TN17 ....179 D4
Kirby Rd Chattenden ME3 ..39 F5
Dartford DA2 ....33 D8
Kirk La SE18 ....12 C8
Kirkcourt TN13 ....92 A4
Kirkdale ME15 ....115 F5
Kirkdale Cl ME5 ......68 D1
Kirkdale Cotts ME15 ..115 F5
Kirkdale Rd
Maidstone ME15 ......115 F6
Royal Tunbridge Wells
TN1 ....159 B4
Kirkham Rd E6 ....1 E7
Kirkham St SE18 ......12 E8
Kirkins Cl TN12 ......163 A6
Kirkland Cl DA15 .....12 E1
Kirkman Ct TN12 ....149 E3
Kirkside Rd SE3 ......11 A8
Kit Hill Ave ME5 ......67 E4
Kit's Coty Ho★ ME20 ..83 C6
Kitchener Ave
Chatham ME4 ....54 A1
Gravesend DA12 ....36 C5
Kitchener Cotts ME3 ..25 C4
Kitchener Rd
Chattenden ME3 ......39 F4
Rochester ME2 ....53 A8
Kite La TN12 ....162 A6
Knatts La TN15 ....77 E8
Knatts Valley Rd TN15 ..61 D2
Knave Wood Rd TN15 ..76 E2
Knaves Acre TN27 ...151 D5
Knavesacre Ct ME8 ...69 D5
Knee Hill SE2 ....3 C2
Knee Hill Cres SE2 ....3 C2
Knight Ave ME7 ....54 D7

Knight Rd Rochester ME2 .53 A6
Tonbridge TN10 ......127 E6
Knight's Ct **7** DA8 ....14 F7
Knight's Ridge TN2 ...160 D7
Knight's Way TN27 ...151 D6
Knighton Rd TN14 ....75 F2
Knightrider Cl ME15 ..100 A3
Knightrider St ME15 ..100 A3
Knights Cl
Hoo St Werburgh ME3 ..40 E5
Pembury TN2 ....160 D7
Knights Croft DA3 ....62 F7
Knights Field DA4 ....60 E7
Knights Manor Way DA1 .15 F1
Knights Pk Rochester ME2 53 A6
Royal Tunbridge Wells
TN11 ....143 F1
Knights Rd
Hoo St Werburgh ME3 ..40 D5
Newham E16 ....1 A4
Knights Ridge BR6 ....58 B5
Knights Way TN2,TN11 .143 F1
Knightsbridge Cl TN4 .158 F5
Knightsbridge Ct TN1 .159 B6
Knightsbridge Mews BR7 28 F1
Knock Mill La TN15 ...78 A5
Knockhall Chase DA9 ..17 C2
Knockhall Com Prim Sch
DA9 ....17 C2
Knockhall Rd DA9 ....17 C2
Knockholt Rd Eltham SE9 .11 D2
Halstead TN14 ....74 F6
Knockholt Sta TN14 ...58 E2
Knockhurst Ct TN30 ..183 C1
Knockwood Rd TN30 ..183 C1
Knole Cl TN14 ....108 B2
Knole Gate DA15 .....29 E5
Knole Ho★ TN15 ......92 D1
Knole La TN13,TN15 ...92 C1
Knole Rd Chatham ME5 ..68 C3
Sevenoaks TN13 ......92 D4
Knole The Eltham SE9 ..29 A4
Istead Rise DA13 ......35 E1
Knole Way TN13 ......92 D1
Knoll Cl BR6 ....57 F8
Knoll Rd Sidcup DA14 ..30 B4
Sidcup,Old Bexley DA5 ..14 A1
Knoll Rise BR6 ....43 F1
Knoll The BR2 ....42 A1
Knotley Hall Cotts TN11 125 A2
Knott Ct TN14 ....99 F6
Knotts Pl TN13 ....92 A3
Knowle Ave DA7 ......13 F7
Knowle Cl TN3 ....157 F3
Knowle Cott TN3 .....173 E1
Knowle Cotts TN3 ....173 E1
Knowle La TN12 .....146 C3
Knowle Lodge BR7 ...28 F2
Knowle Rd
Maidstone ME14 ......100 B6
Orpington BR2 ....56 E8
Paddock Wood TN12 ..146 D3
Wouldham ME1 ....66 D4
Knowles Gdns TN27 ..151 D5
Knowles Wlk TN12 ..149 F4
Knowlton Gdns ME16 ..99 B2
Knowlton Gn BR2 .....42 A4
Knowsley Way TN11 ..126 D6
Knox Ct TN15 ....92 F6
Koonowla Cl TN16 ....72 D4
Kydbrook Cl BR5 .....43 C2
Kyetop Wlk ME8 ......69 D6
Kynaston Rd Bromley BR1 28 A3
Orpington BR5 ....44 B2

L

La Providence ME1 ....53 C5
La Tourne Gdns BR6 ..57 C7
Labour-in-vain Rd TN15 .78 E5
Laburnham Pl SE9 ....12 A2
Laburnum Ave
Dartford DA1 ....32 D7
Swanley BR8 ....45 D6
Laburnum Ct TN2 ....159 C7
Laburnum Dr ME20 ...82 A2
Laburnum Gr DA11 ...35 D8
Laburnum Rd ME2 ....52 E5
Laburnum Way BR2 ...43 B2
Lacebark Cl DA15 .....29 F8
Lacey Cl ME17 ....117 E4
Laceys La ME17 ......132 C5
Lacknut Cotts DA13 ...63 E2
Lacock Gdns
Loose ME15 ....116 A8
Maidstone ME15 ......100 A1
Lacy Cl ME16 ....99 D7
Ladbrooke Cres DA14 ..30 D5
Ladbrooke Ho **7** ME14 100 A5
Laddingford Farm Ind Est
ME18 ....130 D4
Laddingford St Mary's CE
Prim Sch ME18 ......130 E4
Ladds Cnr ME7 ....55 B5
Ladds La ME6 ....66 A2
Ladds Way BR8 ....45 D5
Ladham Rd TN17 .....164 A2
Ladies Mile TN6,TN7 ..170 D4
Lady Boswell's CE Prim Sch
TN13 ....92 C2
Lady Oak La TN5,TN17 .187 C2
Lady Vane Cl TN11 ...110 C5
Lady's Gift Rd TN4 ...158 F8
Ladyclose Ave ME4 ...39 A7
Ladycroft Gdns **6** BR6 ..57 C5
Ladycroft Way BR6 ....57 C5

Ladyfern Ct TN2 .....159 C4
Ladyfields Chatham ME5 ..68 D2
Northfleet DA11 ....35 F4
Ladyfields Cl ME9 ....71 F5
Ladysmith Rd SE9 ....12 A1
Ladywell Ho **7** BR5 ..44 B7
Ladywood Ave BR5 ...43 E4
Ladywood Rd Cuxton ME2 .52 B2
Dartford DA2 ....33 E3
Lagonda Way DA1 ....15 C3
Lagoon Rd BR5 ....44 B4
Lake Ave BR1 ....28 A2
Lake Dr ME3 ....38 C6
Lake Rd Ditton ME20 ..98 B8
Royal Tunbridge Wells
TN4 ....158 E4
Lake View Rd TN13 ...92 A3
Lake Wlk ME20 ....82 A5
Lakelands
Harrietsham ME17 ...119 E6
Loose ME15 ....116 A3
Lakeman Way TN4 ...159 B7
Laker Ho ME14 ......100 A6
Laker Rd ME1 ....67 C6
Lakes Rd BR2 ....56 C5
Lakes The ME20 ......82 A4
Lakeside
Royal Tunbridge Wells
TN2 ....159 C6
Snodland ME6 ....81 F6
Lakeside Ave SE28 ....3 A5
Lakeside Cl
Bexley DA5,DA15 .....13 C2
Bough Beech TN8 ....123 F4
Lakeside Dr BR2 ......56 E7
Lakeside Pk ME2 .....53 E7
Lakeswood Rd BR5 ...43 C3
Lakeview Cl ME6 .....82 A6
Lakeview Rd DA16 ...13 B3
Lakewood Dr ME8 ....69 C6
Lamb Cl RM18 ....19 C5
Lamb's Cross ME17 ..134 A5
Lamb's Mobile Home Pk
TN12 ....146 A7
Lambard Ho **8** ME14 ..100 A1
Lambarde Ave SE9 ...29 A4
Lambarde Cl ME2 ....66 A4
Lambarde Dr TN13 ...92 A4
Lambarde Rd TN13 ...92 A5
Lambardes DA3 ......62 F7
Lambardes Cl TN14 ..74 C8
Lamberhurst Cl **14** BR5 .44 D1
Lamberhurst Gn ME8 ..55 B3
Lamberhurst Rd
Horsmonden TN2,TN3 ..162 E3
Lamberhurst TN3,TN12 ..176 C8
Maidstone ME15 ......115 F6
Lamberhurst St Mary's CE
Prim Sch TN3 ......176 B6
Lamberhurst Vineyard★
TN3 ....176 A4
Lambersart Cl TN14 ..143 D1
Lambert Cl TN16 ......72 D3
Lambert Ct DA8 ......14 C8
Lambert Mews **4** ME6 .82 A8
Lambert Rd E16 ....1 B7
Lambert's Yd TN9 ...127 B1
Lambert's Pl TN12 ...163 B5
Lamberts Rd TN2 ....159 D8
Lambes Ct ME8 ......69 D5
Lambeth Cl ME5 ......68 B4
Lambourn Dr ME19 ..97 A2
Lambourn Ho BR1 ...28 E1
Lambourn Way
Chatham ME5 ....68 C2
Royal Tunbridge Wells
TN2 ....159 D1
Lambourne Pl SE3 ....11 B6
Lambourne Rd ME15 ..100 F2
Lambs Bank TN9 .....143 B7
Lambscroft Ave SE9 ..28 D5
Lambsfrith Gr ME7 ...69 B3
Lamorbey Cl DA15 ...29 F6
Lamorna Ave DA12 ...36 D6
Lamorna Cl BR6 ......44 A2
Lampington Row TN3 .157 E3
Lamplighters Cl
2 Dartford DA1 ......15 F1
Gillingham ME7 ....68 F5
Lamport Cl SE18 ......1 F2
Lamson Rd RM13 .....4 F8
Lancashire Rd ME15 ..116 E7
Lancaster Ct
Gillingham ME8 ....69 C7
Gravesend DA12 ......36 C5
Lancaster Gdns BR1 ..42 E4
Lancaster Way ME19 ..96 F3
Lance Croft DA3 ......62 F8
Lancelot Ave ME2 ....52 E7
Lancelot Cl ME2 ......52 E6
Lancelot Ct BR6 ......58 B8
Lancelot Rd DA16 ....13 A4
Lancer Ho ME1 ....53 C3
Lances Cl DA13 ......50 A2
Lancet La ME15 .....116 A6
Lancey Cl SE7 ....1 F2
Lancing Rd BR6 ......58 B8
Land Way ME3 ....38 D5
Landale Gdns DA1 ...32 C8
Landor Ct ME7 ....69 A3
Landseer Ave DA11 ...35 D5
Landseer Cl TN10 ...127 E6
Landstead Rd SE18 ...12 D7
Landway TN15 ....92 F7
Landway The
Borough Green TN15 ..94 F7
Kemsing TN15 ....77 A2

Landway The *continued*
Maidstone ME14 . . . . .101 A4
Orpington BR5 . . . . .44 C6
Lane Ave DA9 . . . . .17 C1
Lane End DA7 . . . . .14 B4
Lane The Fordcombe TN3 .157 C5
Greenwich SE3 . . . . .11 A4
Lanes Ave DA11 . . . . .36 A5
Laneside BR7 . . . . .29 C3
Langafel CE Prim Sch
DA3 . . . . .49 A6
Langafel Cl DA3 . . . . .48 E7
Langbrook Rd SE3 . . . . .11 D5
Langdale Cl
Gillingham ME8 . . . . .55 D1
Orpington BR6 . . . . .57 B7
Langdale Cres DA7 . . . . .14 B4
Langdale Rise ME16 . . . . . . .99 C5
Langdale Wlk 5 DA11 . . . . .35 C5
Langdon Rd Bromley BR2 . .42 B6
Rochester ME1 . . . . .53 C4
Langdon Shaw DA14 . . . . . . .29 F3
Langford Pl DA14 . . . . .30 A5
Langham Gr ME16 . . . . .99 C4
Langholm Rd TN3 . . . . .157 F3
Langhorne Rd 6 SE7 . . . . .11 C8
Langlands Dr DA2 . . . . .33 C4
Langley Ct 13 SE9 . . . . .12 A1
Langley Gdns
2 Bromley BR2 . . . . .42 C5
Orpington BR5 . . . . .43 B3
Langley Ho
6 Bromley BR1 . . . . .28 B1
11 Maidstone ME16 . . . . . .99 A3
Langley Rd DA16 . . . . .13 C8
Langmore Ct DA7 . . . . .13 D4
Langton Cl ME14 . . . . .100 C5
Langton Green Prim Sch
TN3 . . . . .157 E4
Langton Rd
Rusthall TN3,TN4 . . . . . . .158 C3
Speldhurst TN3 . . . . .158 A7
Langton Ridge TN3 . . . . . . .158 B3
Langton Way SE3 . . . . .11 B7
Langworth Cl DA2 . . . . .32 D5
Lankester Parker Rd
ME1 . . . . .67 C6
Lannoy Rd SE9 . . . . .29 C7
Lanridge Rd SE2 . . . . .3 D3
Lansbury Cres DA1 . . . . .16 A2
Lansbury Ct 4 SE28 . . . . . . .3 B6
Lansbury Gdns RM18 . . . . . .19 B6
Lansbury Ho 5 DA17 . . . . . . .3 F1
Lansdown Pl DA11 . . . . .36 C7
Lansdown Rd Sidcup DA14 30 B5
Tilbury RM18 . . . . .18 F5
Lansdowne Ave
Bexley DA7 . . . . .13 D7
Maidstone ME15 . . . . .116 C6
Orpington BR6 . . . . .43 B1
Lansdowne Ct 8 ME4 . . . . .53 F4
Lansdowne La SE7 . . . . .1 D1
Lansdowne Mews SE7 . . . . .1 D1
Lansdowne Prim Sch
RM18 . . . . .18 F5
Lansdowne Rd
Bromley BR1 . . . . .28 B1
Chatham ME4 . . . . .53 E2
Royal Tunbridge Wells
TN1 . . . . .159 B4
Sevenoaks TN13 . . . . .92 D5
Tonbridge TN9 . . . . .127 B2
Lansdowne Sq
Northfleet DA11 . . . . .18 F1
8 Royal Tunbridge Wells
TN1 . . . . .159 B4
Lantern Cl BR6 . . . . .2 A1
Lanthorne Mews
Royal Tunbridge Wells
TN1 . . . . .159 B5
Royal Tunbridge
Wells,Calverley Park TN1 159 B3
Lapins La ME19 . . . . .96 F2
Lapis Cl DA12 . . . . .37 B7
Lapwing Cl DA8 . . . . .15 B7
Lapwing Rd ME3 . . . . .27 B5
Lapwings DA3 . . . . .49 B6
Lapwings The DA12 . . . . . . .36 D6
Lapworth Ct BR6 . . . . .58 C8
Larch Cl ME20 . . . . .82 B2
Larch Cres
Hoo St Werburgh ME3 . . . .40 E3
Tonbridge TN10 . . . . .127 C6
Larch Dene BR6 . . . . .57 A8
Larch Gr
Paddock Wood TN12 . . . . .145 F6
Sidcup DA15 . . . . .29 F7
Larch Rd DA1 . . . . .32 D7
Larch Way BR2 . . . . .43 A2
Larch Wlk BR8 . . . . .45 D7
Larch Wood Cl ME5 . . . . . . .68 D1
Larchcroft ME5 . . . . .68 A4
Larches The ME4 . . . . .38 C3
Larchwood Rd SE9 . . . . .29 B6
Largo Wlk DA8 . . . . .14 E6
Larkfield Ave ME7 . . . . .54 E4
Larkfield Cl Hayes BR2 . . . . .56 A8
Larkfield ME20 . . . . .82 A1
Larkfield Rd
Larkfield ME20 . . . . .82 B1
Sevenoaks TN13 . . . . .91 C4
Sidcup DA14 . . . . .29 F5
Larkfield Trad Est ME20 . . .82 B5
Larkfields DA11 . . . . .35 E5
Larkin Cl ME2 . . . . .39 B2
Larkspur Dr ME16 . . . . .99 D7
Larks Field DA3 . . . . .48 F5

Larkspur Cl
2 East Malling ME19 . . . . .82 A1
4 Newham E6 . . . . .1 E8
Orpington BR6 . . . . .58 C7
Larkspur Lodge DA14 . . . . .30 B5
Larkspur Rd Chatham ME5 67 E4
West Malling ME19 . . . . . . .81 F1
Larkstore Pk TN12 . . . . . . .149 E5
Larkswood Cl DA8 . . . . .15 A6
Larkwell La DA3 . . . . .48 F5
Larner Rd DA8 . . . . .14 E7
Laser Quay ME2 . . . . .47 C5
Lashenden Air Warfare Mus ★
TN27 . . . . .152 A2
Lassa Rd SE9 . . . . .11 F2
Latham Cl Biggin Hill TN16 72 C3
Dartford DA2 . . . . .33 E6
Newham E6 . . . . .1 E7
Latham Rd DA6 . . . . .14 A2
Latimer Pl 4 ME7 . . . . .54 C7
Latona Dr DA12 . . . . .36 F3
Latymers TN11 . . . . .141 B4
Launcelot Prim Sch BR1 . . .28 A4
Launcelot Rd BR1 . . . . .28 A4
Launder Way ME15 . . . . . . .99 E2
Launton Dr DA6 . . . . .13 D3
Laura Dr BR8 . . . . .32 A1
Laura Pl ME1 . . . . .53 A2
Laurel Ave DA12 . . . . .36 C6
Laurel Bank
Royal Tunbridge Wells
TN4 . . . . .159 B8
Wadhurst TN5 . . . . .185 A4
Laurel Cl Dartford DA1 . . . . .32 C7
Sidcup DA15 . . . . .30 A5
Laurel Gdns BR1 . . . . .42 E5
Laurel Gr ME17 . . . . .118 D2
Laurel Ho SE7 . . . . .11 C8
Laurel Rd Gillingham ME7 . .54 C7
Royal Tunbridge Wells
TN2 . . . . .159 B3
Laurel Way TN2 . . . . .159 D7
Laurel Wlk ME8 . . . . .69 E6
Laurels The
12 Bromley BR1 . . . . .42 B8
Bromley BR2 . . . . .42 A5
Dartford DA2 . . . . .32 C5
18 Erith DA17 . . . . .4 A1
Maidstone ME16 . . . . .99 C2
New Barn DA3 . . . . .49 D6
Laurie Gray Ave ME5 . . . . . .67 D1
Lavenda Cl ME7 . . . . .69 A4
Lavender Cl Bromley BR2 . .42 E3
1 Chatham ME5 . . . . .67 E4
East Malling ME19 . . . . . . .97 F8
Lavender Gdns TN5 . . . . . .186 E1
Lavender Hill
Swanley BR8 . . . . .45 D6
Tonbridge TN9 . . . . .143 C8
Lavender Ho 3 ME15 . . . . .116 D8
Lavender Rd ME19 . . . . .97 F8
Lavender Sq 6 TN18 . . . . .189 A2
Lavender Wlk ME19 . . . . . . .97 F8
Lavenders Rd ME19 . . . . . . .97 C6
Lavernock Rd DA7 . . . . .14 A5
Laverstoke Rd ME16 . . . . . .99 C8
Lavidge Rd SE9 . . . . .28 F6
Lavinia Rd 1 DA1 . . . . .15 F1
Lavisham Ho BR1 . . . . .28 B3
Lawford Gdns DA1 . . . . .15 C2
Lawn Cl Bromley BR1 . . . . . .28 B1
Chatham ME4 . . . . .54 B2
Swanley BR8 . . . . .45 C7
Tenterden TN30 . . . . .192 F7
Lawn Pk TN13 . . . . .108 B8
Lawn Prim Sch DA11 . . . . . .18 C1
Lawn Rd Northfleet DA11 . . .18 C1
Tonbridge TN9 . . . . .143 B8
Lawns Cres RM17 . . . . .18 D3
Lawns The
Brenchley TN12 . . . . .162 B8
Sidcup DA14 . . . . .30 B4
Lawrance Sq DA11 . . . . .35 F5
Lawrence Cl ME15 . . . . . . .116 A7
Lawrence Dr DA12 . . . . .51 A5
Lawrence Gdns RM18 . . . . . .19 B7
Lawrence Hill Gdns DA1 . . .15 C1
Lawrence Hill Rd DA1 . . . . .15 C1
Lawrence Rd Erith DA8 . . . .14 B7
Hayes BR4 . . . . .56 A6
Tonbridge TN10 . . . . .127 C6
Lawrence St ME7 . . . . .54 C5
Lawson Cl E16 . . . . .1 C8
Lawson Gdns DA1 . . . . .15 D3
Lawson Ho 1 SE18 . . . . . . .12 A8
Lawson Rd DA1 . . . . .15 D3
Lawsons Mews TN9 . . . . . .127 C2
Laxey Rd BR6 . . . . .57 F4
Laxey The ME15 . . . . .99 E1
Laxton Cl ME15 . . . . .100 F3
Laxton Ct ME17 . . . . .117 A1
Laxton Gdns TN12 . . . . . . .145 E7
Laxton Wk ME18 . . . . .97 B3
Layfield Ho 4 SE10 . . . . . . .1 A1
Layfield Rd ME7 . . . . .54 F7
Layhams Rd BR2 . . . . .56 A3
Laymarsh Cl DA17 . . . . .3 F3
Layzell Wlk SE9 . . . . .28 D7
Le May Ave SE12 . . . . .28 B5
Le Temple Rd TN12 . . . . . .146 B6
Lea Ct ME4 . . . . .53 E1
Lea Rd TN13 . . . . .108 C8
Lea Vale DA1 . . . . .14 D3
Leafield La DA14 . . . . .30 F5
Leafy Glade ME8 . . . . .69 B6
Leafy Gr BR2 . . . . .56 C5
Leafy La DA13 . . . . .64 A3
Leafy Oak Rd SE12 . . . . . . .28 C5

Leake Ho 2 ME1 . . . . .53 C1
Lealands Ave TN11 . . . . . . .126 A1
Lealands Cl TN3 . . . . .171 C6
Leaman Cl ME23 . . . . .23 E4
Leamington Ave
Bromley BR1 . . . . .28 C3
Orpington BR6 . . . . .57 E6
Leamington Cl BR1 . . . . .28 C3
Leamington Dr ME16 . . . . . .99 B4
Leamouth Rd E6 . . . . .1 E8
Leander Dr DA12 . . . . .36 F4
Leander Rd ME1 . . . . .67 C7
Learoyd Gdns E6 . . . . .2 A6
Leas Dale SE9 . . . . .29 A5
Leas Gn BR7 . . . . .29 F2
Leas The
Turner's Green TN5 . . . . . .185 A6
Woolwich SE18 . . . . .12 B6
Leather Cl TN8 . . . . .138 C8
Leatherbottle Gn DA18 . . . . .3 F3
Leaves Gn BR2 . . . . .72 D8
Leaves Green Cres BR2 . . . .72 C8
Leaves Green Rd
Biggin Hill BR2 . . . . .72 D8
Keston BR2 . . . . .56 D1
Lebanon Gdns TN16 . . . . . . .72 D2
Lebrun Sq SE3 . . . . .11 B4
Leckwith Ave DA7 . . . . .13 E8
Leclair Ho SE3 . . . . .11 B4
Leconfield Cl TN9 . . . . .142 F7
Leda Rd SE18 . . . . .1 F3
Lee Gn BR5 . . . . .44 A4
Lee Green Rd ME3 . . . . .39 B6
Lee Rd ME6 . . . . .82 A8
Lee Sta SE12 . . . . .11 A1
Leech Ct ME1 . . . . .53 D5
Leechcroft Ave
Sidcup DA15 . . . . .12 F2
Swanley BR8 . . . . .45 F6
Leeds & Broomfield CE Prim
Sch ME17 . . . . .118 A7
Leeds Castle ★ ME17 . . . . .118 D7
Leeds Ho BR6 . . . . .58 D8
Leeds Ho ME2 . . . . .39 C1
Leeds Rd ME17 . . . . .117 E3
Leeds Sq ME8 . . . . .55 B3
Lees Rd ME18 . . . . .130 E7
Leesons Hill BR5,BR7 . . . . . .44 A6
Leesons Prim Sch BR5 . . . . .44 B6
Leesons Way BR5 . . . . .43 F7
Leet Cl ME7 . . . . .54 E6
Leeward Rd ME1 . . . . .53 C1
Leewood Cl SE12 . . . . .11 A1
Leewood Pl BR8 . . . . .45 D5
Legatt Rd SE9 . . . . .11 D2
Leggatt Rd E15 . . . . .1 A8
Leggs' La TN3 . . . . .157 C5
Leghorn Rd SE18 . . . . .2 D1
Leicester Dr TN2 . . . . .172 F8
Leicester Rd
Maidstone ME15 . . . . .116 D7
Tilbury RM18 . . . . .18 F6
Leicester Sq TN11 . . . . . . .141 B4
Leigh Ave ME15 . . . . .116 B6
Leigh City Tech Coll The
DA1 . . . . .33 A7
Leigh Green Ind Est
TN30 . . . . .193 E6
Leigh Halt TN11 . . . . .125 C1
Leigh Pl DA16 . . . . .13 A5
Leigh Prim Sch TN11 . . . . .125 F1
Leigh Rd Gravesend DA11 . .36 B6
Rochester ME3 . . . . .39 C3
Tonbridge TN11 . . . . .126 D3
Leigh Terr
2 Orpington BR5 . . . . .44 B8
Teston ME18 . . . . .98 A1
Leighton Cl TN4 . . . . .159 A4
Leighton Gdns RM18 . . . . . .19 A7
Leila Parnell Pl 22 SE7 . . .11 C8
Leitch Row 6 ME7 . . . . . . .54 A7
Leith Hill BR5 . . . . .44 A8
Leith Hill Gn BR5 . . . . .44 A8
Leith Park Rd DA12 . . . . . . .36 B7
Lemonwell Ct SE9 . . . . .12 C2
Lemonwell Dr SE9 . . . . .12 C2
Len Clifton Ho 6 SE18 . . . . .1 F2
Len Valley Wlk ME15 . . . . .100 F1
Lenderyou Ct DA1 . . . . .32 E8
Lendon Rd TN15 . . . . .94 F6
Lendrim Cl 11 ME7 . . . . . . .54 A6
Leney Rd ME18 . . . . .113 E7
Lenfield Ave ME14 . . . . .100 B4
Lenham Ct 10 ME15 . . . . . .100 B4
Lenham Heath Rd ME17 120 C2
Lenham Ho
Lenham ME17 . . . . .120 E5
13 Orpington BR5 . . . . . . .44 D1
Lenham Prim Sch ME17 120 C5
Lenham Rd Bexley DA7 . . . .13 F8
Broadstone TN27,ME17 . . .136 D3
Fairbourne Heath ME17 . . .119 C1
Headcorn ME17 . . . . .151 E6
Lenham Sta ME17 . . . . . . .120 C4
Lenham Way ME8 . . . . .55 A3
Lennard Rd Orpington BR2 42 F1
Sevenoaks TN13 . . . . .91 E7
Lennox Ave DA11 . . . . .19 A1
Lennox Ho 6 DA17 . . . . .4 A3
Lennox Rd Northfleet DA11 35 F8
Gravesend DA11 . . . . .36 A8
Lennox Rd E DA11 . . . . .36 A8
Lenor Cl DA6 . . . . .13 E3
Lensbury Way SE2 . . . . .3 D3
Lenside Dr ME15 . . . . .101 A2
Lenton St SE18 . . . . .2 D2
Leonard Ave Otford TN14 . .76 D3

Leonard Ave *continued*
Swanscombe DA10 . . . . . . .34 E8
Leonard Cl ME16 . . . . .99 B6
Leonard Ct DA14 . . . . .30 B5
Leonard Judge Ho DA2 . . . .33 E3
Leonard Pl BR2 . . . . .56 E7
Leonard Rd 7 ME4 . . . . . . .54 A3
Leonard Robbins Path 3
SE28 . . . . .3 B6
Leonard St E16 . . . . .1 E5
Leopold Rd 2 ME4 . . . . . . .54 A3
Lesley Cl Istead Rise DA13 . .49 F8
Sidcup DA5 . . . . .31 B8
Swanley BR8 . . . . .45 D6
Lesley Pl ME16 . . . . .99 E5
Lesley Tew Ct TN10 . . . . . .127 C5
Leslie Cres TN30 . . . . .183 B2
Leslie Rd Gillingham ME7 . . .54 D7
Leslie Smith Sq 7 SE18 . .12 A8
Lesnes Abbey (remains of) ★
SE2 . . . . .3 E2
Lesney Park Rd DA8 . . . . . . .14 D8
Lesney Pk DA8 . . . . .14 D8
Lessness Ave DA7 . . . . .13 D7
Lessness Heath Prim Sch
DA17 . . . . .4 A1
Lessness Pk DA17 . . . . .4 A1
Lessness Rd 12 DA17 . . . . . .4 A1
Lested La ME17 . . . . .117 B1
Lester Rd ME4 . . . . .54 A3
Lestock Ho SE3 . . . . .11 D6
Letchford Ave ME4 . . . . .53 F1
Letchworth Cl BR2 . . . . .42 A4
Letchworth Dr BR2 . . . . .42 A4
Letter Box La TN13 . . . . . . .108 C6
Leverholme Gdns SE9 . . . . . .29 A4
Levett Cl ME3 . . . . .27 B6
Levetts La TN32 . . . . .195 D1
Leviathan Way ME4 . . . . . . .40 A1
Lewd La TN27 . . . . .153 A3
Lewes Cl RM17 . . . . .18 A8
Lewes Rd BR1 . . . . .42 D7
Lewin Cl SE18 . . . . .2 E2
Lewin Rd DA6 . . . . .13 E3
Lewing Cl BR6 . . . . .43 E1
Lewis Ave ME8 . . . . .55 B2
Lewis Court Dr ME17 . . . . .116 C3
Lewis Ct DA11 . . . . .19 A1
Lewis King Ho 7 BR1 . . . . .28 B1
Lewis Mews ME7 . . . . .54 F7
Lewis Rd Bexley DA16 . . . . .13 C4
Istead Rise DA13 . . . . .49 F8
Sidcup DA14 . . . . .30 C5
Swanscombe DA10 . . . . . . .17 E1
Lewis Row ME17 . . . . .133 E6
Leybank TN11 . . . . .126 F4
Leybourne Cl
Chatham ME5 . . . . .68 A2
Hayes BR2 . . . . .42 A3
Leybourne Dell TN17 . . . . .190 E6
Leybourne Rd ME2 . . . . .52 F8
Leybourne Way BR2 . . . . . . .81 E2
Leybourne, St Peter & St
Paul CE Prim Sch ME19 .81 E2
Leybridge Ct SE12 . . . . .11 A2
Leyburn Ct TN9 . . . . .127 C3
Leyburn Ho SE18 . . . . .1 E7
Leycroft Gdns DA8 . . . . .15 B6
Leydenhatch La BR8 . . . . . . .45 D8
Leyes Rd E16 . . . . .1 D7
Leyhill Cl BR8 . . . . .45 E4
Leyland Rd SE12 . . . . .11 A2
Leysdown Ave DA7 . . . . .14 C3
Leysdown Rd SE9 . . . . .28 F6
Lezayre Rd BR6 . . . . .57 F4
Liberty Mews BR6 . . . . .57 F8
Libya Terr 6 ME14 . . . . . . .100 F4
Lichdale Cl 8 BR6 . . . . .57 F6
Lichfield Cl ME4 . . . . .53 D2
Lichfield Ho 12 ME15 . . . . .116 F7
Liddon Rd BR1 . . . . .42 D6
Lidsing Rd ME14 . . . . .84 E6
Lidwells La TN17 . . . . .163 E1
Lieth Park Rd DA12 . . . . . . .2 E1
Liffler Rd SE18 . . . . .2 E1
Lighterman's Mews 2
DA11 . . . . .35 E8
Lightermans Way DA9 . . . . .17 C3
Lightfoot Gn TN18 . . . . . . .188 E3
Lila Pl BR8 . . . . .45 E5
Lilac Cres ME2 . . . . .52 E6
Lilac Gdns BR8 . . . . .45 D6
Lilac Gn 4 ME19 . . . . .82 A1
Lilac Pl DA13 . . . . .50 B2
Lilac Rd ME2 . . . . .52 E5
Lilburne Gdns SE9 . . . . .11 E2
Lilburne Rd SE9 . . . . .11 E2
Lilian Barker Cl SE12 . . . . . .11 A2
Lilk Hill ME14 . . . . .101 C3
Lillechurch Rd ME3 . . . . . . .38 F7
Lillie Rd TN16 . . . . .72 D1
Lillieburn ME19 . . . . .81 D2
Lily Nichols Ho E16 . . . . . . .1 E5
Limavady Ho SE18 . . . . .2 A2
Lime Ave Benenden TN17 .190 C6
Northfleet DA11 . . . . .35 D8
Lime Cl Bromley BR1 . . . . . .42 E5
Frant TN3 . . . . .173 B3
Marden TN12 . . . . .148 C6
Lime Cotts TN12 . . . . .149 F3
Lime Cres ME19 . . . . .98 A7
Lime Ct Eltham SE9 . . . . . . .29 B6
Gillingham ME8 . . . . .69 C3

Lime Gr Biddenden TN27 .182 D7
Orpington BR6 . . . . .57 B8
Sidcup DA15 . . . . .12 F1
Lime Hill Rd TN1 . . . . .159 A4
Lime Kiln Dr SE7 . . . . .11 B8
Lime Pit La TN13,TN14 . . . .75 C2
Lime Rd BR8 . . . . .45 D6
Lime Row DA18 . . . . .3 F3
Lime Tree Ave DA9 . . . . .34 A7
Lime Tree Cl TN9 . . . . .127 C2
Lime Tree Wlk TN13 . . . . . .92 B2
Lime Trees TN12 . . . . .149 E4
Limepits Cross ME9 . . . . . . .71 F3
Limes Cl TN30 . . . . .193 C8
Limes Gr TN18 . . . . .188 F5
Limes Row BR6 . . . . .57 B5
Limes The
Edenbridge TN8 . . . . .122 C1
Frittenden TN17 . . . . .166 E6
Lenham ME17 . . . . .120 D5
Orpington BR2 . . . . .56 E8
Limetree Cl ME5 . . . . .68 B8
Limetree Terr
5 Bexley DA16 . . . . .13 A4
Lenham ME17 . . . . .120 E6
Limewood Rd DA8 . . . . .14 C7
Limpsfield CE Inf Sch
RH8 . . . . .104 C6
Limpsfield Grange Sch
RH8 . . . . .104 A8
Linchmere Rd 7 SE12 . . . . .28 A8
Lincol n Rd ME7 . . . . .54 D7
Rochester ME2 . . . . .52 D6
Lincoln Ct 3 SE12 . . . . . . .28 C5
Lincoln Green Rd BR5 . . . . .43 F4
Lincoln Rd Erith DA8 . . . . . .14 F5
Maidstone ME15 . . . . .116 D8
Sidcup DA14 . . . . .30 B3
Lincolnshire Terr DA2 . . . . .33 D4
Lincolnshott DA13 . . . . .35 B3
Lindel Cl ME18 . . . . .97 B3
Linden Ave DA1 . . . . .32 C7
Linden Chase TN13 . . . . . . .92 B5
Linden Cl Orpington BR6 . . .58 A5
Paddock Wood TN12 . . . . .146 A6
Purfleet RM19 . . . . .16 C8
Royal Tunbridge Wells
TN4 . . . . .159 A2
Linden Ct Sidcup DA14 . . . .29 E4
Tonbridge TN10 . . . . .127 B7
Linden Gdns TN2 . . . . .158 F1
Linden Ho 4 Bromley BR1 .28 B1
5 Chatham ME5 . . . . .67 E4
Linden Park Rd TN2 . . . . . .159 A2
Linden Rd
Coxheath ME17 . . . . .115 C4
Gillingham ME7 . . . . .54 E5
Linden Sq TN13 . . . . .91 E5
Lindenfield BR7 . . . . .43 B7
Lindens The ME20 . . . . .82 C1
Lindisfarne Cl DA12 . . . . . . .36 E6
Lindisfarne Gdns ME16 . . . .99 E3
Lindridge La TN12 . . . . . . .149 C5
Lindsay Ho 2 SE18 . . . . .2 A2
Lindsey Cl BR1 . . . . .42 E6
Lindwood Cl 8 E6 . . . . .1 F8
Lineacre Cl ME8 . . . . .69 D6
Lines Terr ME4 . . . . .54 A4
Ling Rd Erith DA8 . . . . .14 C8
Newham E16 . . . . .1 A8
Lingey Cl DA15 . . . . .29 A6
Lingfield Ave DA2 . . . . .33 B8
Lingfield Cres SE9 . . . . .12 D3
Lingfield Mews 4 TN8 . . . .122 C1
Lingfield Rd
Borough Green TN15 . . . . . .95 B7
Edenbridge TN8 . . . . .138 A8
Gravesend DA12 . . . . .36 B6
Lingley Dr ME2 . . . . .39 C2
Lingwood DA7 . . . . .14 B5
LINK 20 Bsns Pk ME20 . . . .82 B3
Link Field BR2 . . . . .42 A3
Link Hill La TN27 . . . . .137 D3
Link The Eltham SE9 . . . . . .29 A5
New Ash Green DA3 . . . . . .62 F8
Link Way Bromley BR2 . . . . .42 E2
Royal Tunbridge Wells
TN2 . . . . .159 E8
Linkden Cotts TN18 . . . . . .196 E5
Links Ct 29 B7
Links The Addington ME19 .80 E2
Chatham ME5 . . . . .68 B8
Links View Dartford DA1 . . .32 C7
Woolwich SE18 . . . . .12 B6
Linkway ME20 . . . . .82 C1
Linley Ct RM18 . . . . .20 D7
Linnet Ave TN12 . . . . .146 A5
Linnet Cl SE28 . . . . .3 C6
Linsted Ct SE9 . . . . .12 E1
Linton Cl Bexley DA16 . . . . .13 B6
2 Greenwich SE7 . . . . .1 C1
Linton Dann Cl ME3 . . . . . . .40 D6
Linton Gdns E6 . . . . .1 E7
Linton Gore ME17 . . . . .115 D3
Linton Hill TN12 . . . . .132 F6
Linton Mead Prim Sch
SE28 . . . . .3 B6
Linton Rd ME15 . . . . .115 F4
Lintorn Symonds Rd ME3 39 F5
Linwood Ave ME2 . . . . .52 E8
Lion Rd Bexley DA6 . . . . . . .13 F3
Newham E6 . . . . .1 F8
Lionel Gdns SE9 . . . . .11 D2

Lionel Oxley Ho **5** RM17 . .18 B8
Lionel Rd Eltham SE9 . . . . .11 D2
Tonbridge TN9 . . . . .143 A8
Lions Cl SE9 . . . . .28 D5
Liphook Way ME16 . . . . . .99 C8
Lipscombe Rd TN2 . . . . . .159 D6
Lipton Cl SE28 . . . . .3 C6
Liptraps La TN2 . . . . .159 D7
Lipwell Hill ME23 . . . . .23 B4
Liskeard Cl BR7 . . . . .29 C2
Liskeard Gdns SE3 . . . . . . .11 A6
Lisle Cl DA12 . . . . .37 B6
Lismore Rd ME15 . . . . . . .116 A4
Lister Cl ME19 . . . . .97 F8
Lister Ho SE2 . . . . .3 D1
Lister Rd RM18 . . . . .19 A5
Lister Wlk SE28 . . . . .3 D6
Listmas Rd ME4 . . . . .54 B3
Little Alley TN8 . . . . .138 B5
Little Bayham Cotts
  TN3 . . . . .174 F4
Little Birches DA15 . . . . . .29 E6
Little Boundes Cl TN4 . .142 F3
Little Brook Hospl DA2 . .16 C1
Little Browns La TN8 . . .121 F4
Little Buckland Ave
  ME16 . . . . .99 D6
Little Ct ME16 . . . . .99 D2
Little Field TN12 . . . . . . .149 E5
Little Footway TN3 . . . . . .157 F3
Little Heath SE7 . . . . .1 E1
Little Heath Rd DA7 . . . . .13 F7
Little Hill TN30 . . . . .183 B8
Little Job's Cross TN17 . .191 F1
Little John Ave ME5 . . . . . .67 F2
Little Julians Hill TN13 . .108 A8
Little Kit's Coty Ho★
  ME20 . . . . .83 C5
Little Mallett TN3 . . . . . . .157 F3
Little Market Row ME19 . .81 E2
Little Mill Farm Cotts
  TN12 . . . . .148 C8
Little Mount Sion TN1 . . .159 A2
Little Oakham Ct ME3 . . . .25 C4
Little Orch ME17 . . . . .115 D3
Little Oxley ME19 . . . . .81 E2
Little Pk TN5 . . . . .184 E5
Little Queen St DA1 . . . . . .32 F8
Little Redlands BR1 . . . . . .42 E7
Little Robhurst TN26 . . .183 D8
Little Sheephurst Cotts
  TN12 . . . . .147 E5
Little Thrift BR5 . . . . .43 C5
Little Wood TN13 . . . . .92 D5
Little Wood Cl BR5 . . . . . . .44 A8
Little York Mdws ME7 . . . .55 C4
Littlebourne Ave ME8 . . . .55 B4
Littlebourne Rd ME14 . .100 C6
Littlebrook Manor Way
  DA1 . . . . .16 A2
Littlecombe SE7 . . . . .11 B8
Littlecourt Rd TN13 . . . . . .92 A3
Littlecroft Eltham SE9 . . . .12 A4
  Istead Rise DA13 . . . . . . .35 E1
Littledale Dartford DA2 . . .33 C5
  Woolwich SE2 . . . . .13 A8
Littlefield TN11 . . . . .128 E8
Littlejohn Rd BR5 . . . . .44 B4
Littlemede SE5 . . . . .28 F5
Littlemore Rd SE2 . . . . .3 A4
Liveryman Wlk DA9 . . . . . .17 C3
Livesey Cl SE28 . . . . .2 C3
Livesey St ME18 . . . . .98 A1
Livingstone Bldgs ME4 . . .54 D5
Livingstone Circ ME7 . . . .54 D5
Livingstone Gdns DA12 . .36 D3
Livingstone Hospl DA1 . . .32 F8
Livingstone Rd
  Gillingham ME7 . . . . .54 E5
  Gravesend DA12 . . . . . . .36 D3
Livingstone Wlk **6**
  ME15 . . . . .116 F5
Lizban St SE3 . . . . .11 B7
Llanover Rd SE18 . . . . .12 A7
Lloyd Ho BR1 . . . . .28 B3
Lloyds Gn TN30 . . . . .199 D4
Loaland Bsns Ctr ME2 . . . .53 D8
Loam Ct DA1 . . . . .32 E7
Loampits Cl TN9 . . . . .127 D3
Lobelia Cl Gillingham ME7 . .54 E6
  5 Newham E6 . . . . .1 E8
Locarno Ave ME8 . . . . .55 A2
Lochat Rd ME3 . . . . .39 E6
Lochmere Cl DA8 . . . . .14 B8
Lock La ME14 . . . . .83 D1
Lock St ME7 . . . . .54 C5
Lock's Yd TN13 . . . . .92 C2
Lockesley Dr BR5 . . . . .44 A3
Lockham Farm Ave
  ME17 . . . . .116 D5
Lockington Cl TN9 . . . . . .142 F7
Lockington Gr ME1 . . . . . . .53 C5
Lockside TN9 . . . . .127 C2
Locksley Cl ME5 . . . . .67 E2
Lockswood ME16 . . . . .99 D7
Lockyer Rd RM19 . . . . .16 C4
Lockyers Hill ME3 . . . . . . .64 F5
Lodden Ct **15** BR5 . . . . . . .44 D1
Loddington La ME17 . . . .133 A8
Loder Cl ME17 . . . . .120 B5
Lodge Cl Orpington BR6 . . .44 B1
  Wateringbury ME18 . . . .113 D4
Lodge Cres BR6 . . . . .44 B1
Lodge Farmhouse ME20 . .82 E3

Lodge Gdns ME17 . . . . . .135 F6
Lodge Hill DA16 . . . . .13 B7
Lodge Hill La ME3 . . . . .39 F7
Lodge La Cobham DA12 . . .51 B5
  Royal Tunbridge Wells
  TN3 . . . . .172 A8
  Sidcup DA5 . . . . .13 D1
  Westerham TN16 . . . . . .105 C8
Lodge Oak La TN9 . . . . . .143 D8
Lodge Rd Bromley BR1 . . .28 C1
  Maidstone ME14 . . . . . .100 D5
  Staplehurst TN12 . . . . . .149 E5
  Tonbridge TN9 . . . . .127 B2
Lodgewood Cotts TN8 . .123 D2
Logs Hill BR1,BR2 . . . . . . .42 E8
Logs Hill Cl BR7 . . . . .42 E8
Lolland Ho **9** SE18 . . . . . .1 E2
Lomaria Ct TN2 . . . . .159 C4
Lomas La TN5 . . . . .196 F5
Lombard St DA4 . . . . .47 C5
Lombard Trad Est SE7 . . . .1 B2
Lombard Wall SE7 . . . . .1 B2
Lombardy Cl ME7 . . . . .69 A6
Lombardy Dr ME14 . . . . .100 C5
London City Airport E16 . .1 E7
London Inn Pk E6 . . . . .2 B8
London La Bromley BR1 . . .28 A1
  Sissinghurst TN17 . . . . . .166 A2
London Rd
  Addington ME19 . . . . . . .80 D7
  Badgers Mount TN14 . . . .75 C6
  Bidborough TN4 . . . . . . .142 F3
  Bromley BR1 . . . . .42 A8
  Chelsfield TN14 . . . . .58 F2
  Crayford DA1 . . . . .14 D2
  Ditton ME20 . . . . .82 C1
  Farningham BR8,DA4 . . . .46 D3
  Flimwell TN5 . . . . .187 D3
  Grays RM17,RM20 . . . . . .17 E8
  Hartlip ME8 . . . . .70 D7
  Hildenborough TN11,TN13,
  TN15 . . . . .126 B7
  Hurst Green TN19 . . . . .194 A3
  Maidstone ME16 . . . . . . .99 C6
  Newington ME9 . . . . .71 A6
  Northfleet DA11 . . . . .18 E1
  Otford TN15 . . . . .75 D1
  Rochester ME2 . . . . .53 A7
  Royal Tunbridge Wells
  TN4 . . . . .159 A3
  Royal Tunbridge Wells,Mount Sion
  TN1 . . . . .159 A3
  Sevenoaks TN13 . . . . .92 B2
  Sevenoaks,Dunton Green
  TN13 . . . . .91 E7
  Stone DA2,DA9 . . . . .16 E1
  Swanley BR8 . . . . .45 D7
  Swanley BR8 . . . . .45 E6
  Swanscombe DA9 . . . . . .17 C2
  Tilbury RM18 . . . . .19 B5
  Tonbridge TN10,TN11 . . .127 B3
  West Kingsdown TN15 . . .62 A1
  Wrotham TN15 . . . . .79 B3
  Wrotham Heath TN15,ME19 .79 F1
London Rd E ME20 . . . . . . .98 F8
London Road Purfleet
  RM19 . . . . .16 C8
London Road West Thurrock
  RM20 . . . . .17 A8
Londonderry Ho **16**
  ME15 . . . . .116 E7
Londonderry Par DA8 . . . .14 D7
Lonewood Way TN11 . . . .111 F2
Long Acre BR6 . . . . .58 D8
Long Barn Rd TN14 . . . . .108 B2
Long Catlis Rd ME8 . . . . . .69 D4
Long La Bexley DA7 . . . . . .13 C6
  Rabbit's Cross ME17 . . . .133 C5
Long Mark Rd **5** E16 . . . . .1 D8
Long Mead Com Prim Sch
  TN10 . . . . .127 B5
Long Mead Way TN10 . . .127 B4
Long Meads TN3 . . . . . . .158 B4
Long Mill La Crouch TN15 .95 B3
  Platt TN15 . . . . .95 C7
Long Rede La ME16 . . . . . .98 F3
Long Slip TN3 . . . . .158 A3
Long Wlk SE18 . . . . .12 B8
Longbury Cl BR5 . . . . .44 B6
Longbury Dr BR5 . . . . .44 B7
Longcroft SE9 . . . . .29 A5
Longdon Wood BR2 . . . . . .56 E6
Longdown Ho ME5 . . . . . . .67 F6
Longfellow Rd ME4 . . . . . .54 C3
Longfield TN30 . . . . .193 A6
Longfield Ave
  High Halstow ME23 . . . . . .23 E4
  New Barn DA3,DA13 . . . . .49 D7
Longfield Pl ME15 . . . . . .116 C8
Longfield Rd
  Meopham Sta DA3,DA13 . .49 E3
  Royal Tunbridge Wells
  TN1,TN2,TN11 . . . . .143 E1
Longfield Sta DA3 . . . . . . .48 E6
Longfields Dr ME14 . . . . .101 A5
Longford Cl ME8 . . . . .70 A8
Longford Ct ME8 . . . . .70 A8
Longham Copse ME15 . . .100 F1
Longhill Ave ME5 . . . . .54 B3
Longhurst Dr ME5 . . . . . . .67 F2
Longlands Ct DA15 . . . . . .29 F5
Longlands Park Cres
  DA15 . . . . .29 E6
Longlands Prim Sch
  DA15 . . . . .29 E5
Longlands Rd DA15 . . . . . .29 F5

Longleat Ct **3** DA6 . . . . . .13 E3
Longleigh La SE2,DA7 . . . .13 C8
Longley Rd Rainham ME8 . .55 C4
  Rochester ME1 . . . . .53 C4
Longmarsh La SE28 . . . . . . .2 E5
Longmarsh View DA4 . . . .47 B8
Longmead BR7 . . . . .43 A7
Longmead Dr DA14 . . . . . .30 D6
Longmeade DA12 . . . . .36 F7
Longmeadow TN13 . . . . . .91 D6
Longmeadow Rd DA15 . . .29 E7
Longparish Cl ME15 . . . . .116 F6
Longreach Rd DA8 . . . . . . .15 B7
Longshaw Rd ME15 . . . . .116 F5
Longten's Cotts DA12 . . . .37 E6
Longtown Ct **19** DA2 . . . .16 B1
Longview Way TN2 . . . . . .159 D7
Longwalk DA13 . . . . .49 E8
Longwood ME5 . . . . .68 B1
Longworth Cl SE28 . . . . . . .3 D7
Lonsdale Cl SE9 . . . . .28 D5
Lonsdale Cres DA2 . . . . . . .33 C7
Lonsdale Dr ME8 . . . . .69 E7
Lonsdale Gdns TN1 . . . . .159 A3
Lonsdale Rd DA7 . . . . .13 F5
Loop Rd BR7 . . . . .29 C2
Loose Inf & Jun Schs
  ME15 . . . . .116 A6
Loose Rd ME15 . . . . .116 A7
Loraine Ct BR7 . . . . .29 B3
Lord Chatham's Ride
  TN14 . . . . .74 D2
Lord Roberts Terr SE18 . . .2 A1
Lord Romney's Hill
  ME14 . . . . .100 F3
Lord St Gravesend DA12 . .36 B8
  Newham E16 . . . . .1 E5
Lord Warwick St SE18 . . . .1 F3
Lords Wood Cl ME5 . . . . . .68 B2
Lords Wood La ME5 . . . . . .68 B2
Lordswood Cl DA2 . . . . . . .33 E4
Lordswood Ind Est ME5 . .84 C8
Lordswood Inf & Jun Sch
  ME5 . . . . .68 B3
Lorenden Pk TN18 . . . . . .188 F1
Lorimar Bsns Ctr RM13 . . . .4 E8
Lorraine Ct DA9 . . . . .17 B1
Lorton Cl DA12 . . . . .36 E6
Lossenham La TN18 . . . . .197 D3
Lotus Rd TN16 . . . . .72 F1
Louis Gdns BR7 . . . . .28 F4
Louise Ct **8** DA6 . . . . . . .13 E3
Louisville Ave ME7 . . . . . . .54 D4
Louvain Rd DA9 . . . . .33 E8
Lovage App E6 . . . . .1 E8
Love La East Tilbury RM18 .20 C8
  Rochester ME1 . . . . .53 C5
  Sidcup DA5 . . . . .14 A1
  Swift's Green TN27 . . . . .152 B5
  Wateringbury ME18 . . . .113 D7
  Woolwich SE18 . . . . .2 B2
Lovel Ave DA16 . . . . .13 A5
Lovelace Ave BR2 . . . . .43 A3
Lovelace Cl
  Gillingham ME8 . . . . .69 D4
  West Kingsdown TN15 . . .61 E4
Lovelace Gn SE9 . . . . .11 F4
Lover's La DA9,DA10 . . . . .17 D3
Lovers La TN17 . . . . .163 F1
Lovibonds Ave BR6 . . . . . . .57 B7
Low Cl DA9 . . . . .17 A2
Low Mdw ME2 . . . . .66 B5
Low Street La RM18 . . . . . .19 F8
Lowe Ave E16 . . . . .1 A8
Lower Bell La ME20 . . . . . .82 B2
Lower Bloors La ME8 . . . . .55 E3
Lower Boxley Rd **10**
  ME14 . . . . .100 A5
Lower Camden BR7 . . . . . .42 F8
Lower Church Hill DA9 . . .16 E2
Lower Croft BR8 . . . . .45 F5
Lower Fant Rd ME16 . . . . .99 D2
Lower Farm Rd ME17 . . . .133 D5
Lower Gn TN11 . . . . .125 F1
Lower Gravel Rd BR2 . . . .42 F1
Lower Green Rd
  Pembury TN2 . . . . .160 D7
  Rusthall TN3,TN4 . . . . . .158 C6
Lower Hartlip Rd ME9 . . . .70 E5
Lower Haysden La
  TN11,TN9 . . . . .142 D8
Lower Hazelhurst
  Ticehurst TN5 . . . . .186 A4
  Ticehurst TN5 . . . . .186 B4
Lower High St TN5 . . . . . .185 A4
Lower Higham Rd DA12 . . .37 B7
Lower Park Rd DA17 . . . . . .4 A2
Lower Platts TN5 . . . . .186 B1
Lower Rainham Rd ME7 . . .55 D5
Lower Range Rd DA12 . . . .36 E8
Lower Rd
  East Farleigh ME15 . . . . .115 B7
  Erith DA17 . . . . .4 B3
  Erith DA8 . . . . .4 D2
  Hextable BR8 . . . . .32 B1
  Higham DA12,ME3 . . . . . .38 B6
  Maidstone ME15 . . . . . . .100 B3
  Northfleet DA11 . . . . .18 A3
  Orpington BR5 . . . . .44 B3
  Shorne DA12 . . . . .37 E6
  Sutton Valence ME17 . . . .134 E7
  West Farleigh ME15 . . . . .116 C8
Lower Rochester Rd ME3 .38 C6
Lower St Leeds ME17 . . . .118 A7
  Tonbridge TN11 . . . . . . .125 F5
Lower Station Rd DA1 . . . .14 E1
Lower Stone St ME15 . . . .100 A3
Lower Tovil ME15 . . . . .99 E2

Lower Twydall La ME7,
  ME8 . . . . .55 C4
Lower Warren Rd ME20 . . .83 E6
Lower Woodlands Rd
  ME7 . . . . .55 A6
Lowestoft Mews E16 . . . . . .2 B4
Lowfield St DA1 . . . . .32 E8
Lownds Ct BR1 . . . . .42 A7
Lowry Cl DA8 . . . . .4 D2
Lowry The **4** TN9 . . . . . .143 B8
Loxwood Cl BR5,BR6 . . . . .58 D8
Lubbock Cl ME15 . . . . . . .116 C5
Lubbock Ct BR7 . . . . .28 F1
Lubbock Ho BR6 . . . . .57 E8
Lubbock Rd BR7 . . . . .28 F1
Lubbock Wlk ME8 . . . . . . .69 D5
Lucas Cres DA9 . . . . .17 C3
Lucas Rd ME6 . . . . .81 E7
Lucerne Ct **5** DA18 . . . . . .3 E3
Lucerne Rd BR6 . . . . .43 F1
Lucerne St ME14 . . . . . . .100 A5
Lucilina Dr TN8 . . . . .138 C8
Lucknow Rd TN12 . . . . . . .146 A8
Lucknow St SE18 . . . . .12 E7
Lucks Hill ME19 . . . . .97 D3
Lucks La
  Paddock Wood TN12 . . . .146 B8
  Rabbit's Cross ME17 . . . .133 F6
Lucks Way TN12 . . . . .148 B6
Luddenham Cl ME14 . . . .100 C6
Luddesdon Rd DA8 . . . . . .14 A7
Luddesdon Ho **5** BR5 . . .44 C4
Luddesdown Rd DA13 . . . .51 A2
Ludham Cl SE28 . . . . .3 C7
Ludlow Cl BR2 . . . . .42 A6
Ludwig Mews SE12 . . . . . . .5 A2
Luffield Rd SE2 . . . . .3 B3
Luffman Rd SE12 . . . . .28 B5
Lughorse La ME15,ME18 . .114 C1
Lullarook Cl TN16 . . . . . . .72 C3
Lullingstone Ave BR8 . . . . .45 F6
Lullingstone Castle★
  DA4 . . . . .60 B5
Lullingstone Cl
  Gillingham ME7 . . . . .69 B3
  Orpington BR5 . . . . .30 B1
Lullingstone Cres BR5 . . . .30 B1
Lullingstone La DA4 . . . . . .60 C8
Lullingstone Pk★ DA4 . . . .59 F6
Lullingstone Pk Visitor Ctr★
  DA4 . . . . .60 B4
Lullingstone Rd
  3 Bexley DA17 . . . . .13 F8
  Maidstone ME16 . . . . . . .99 C7
Lullingstone Roman Villa
  (rems of)★ DA4 . . . . .60 B7
Lulworth Rd Bexley DA16 . .12 F5
  Bromley SE9 . . . . .28 E6
Lumley Cl DA5 . . . . .4 A1
Lumsden Terr **8** ME4 . . . .53 E4
Lunar Cl TN16 . . . . .72 D3
Lunedale Rd DA2 . . . . .33 C7
Lunsford District Ctr
  ME20 . . . . .82 A4
Lunsford La ME20 . . . . . . .81 F2
Lunsford Prim Sch ME20 . .82 A2
Lupton Cl SE12 . . . . .28 B4
Lurkins Rise TN17 . . . . . . .177 D7
Lushington Rd ME14 . . . . .99 E7
Lusted Hall La TN16 . . . . . .88 C7
Lusted Rd TN13 . . . . .91 E7
Luton High St ME5 . . . . . . .54 C2
Luton Inf Sch ME5 . . . . . . .54 C2
Luton Jun Sch ME4 . . . . . . .54 C2
Luton Rd
  Chatham ME4,ME5 . . . . . .54 B2
  Sidcup DA14 . . . . .30 C4
Luxfield Rd SE9 . . . . .28 E7
Luxon Rd DA13 . . . . .64 E4
Luxted Rd BR6 . . . . .73 A6
Lyall Way ME8 . . . . .69 E4
Lych Gate Rd BR6 . . . . .44 A1
Lychfield Dr ME2 . . . . .53 A8
Lydd Cl DA14 . . . . .29 E5
Lydd Rd Bexley DA7 . . . . . .13 F7
  Chatham ME5 . . . . .68 B5
Lydden Ct SE9 . . . . .12 E1
Lydens La TN8 . . . . .138 F6
Lydford Ct **18** DA2 . . . . . .16 B1
Lydia Cotts **2** DA11 . . . . .36 B8
Lydia Rd DA8 . . . . .14 F8
Lydstep Rd BR7 . . . . .29 A4
Lyford St SE18 . . . . .1 E2
Lyle Cl ME2 . . . . .53 B8
Lyle Ct ME16 . . . . .99 C5
Lyle Pk TN13 . . . . .92 B4
Lyme Farm Rd SE12 . . . . . .11 B3
Lyme Rd DA16 . . . . .13 B6
Lyminge Cl
  Gillingham ME8 . . . . .55 C2
  Sidcup DA14 . . . . .29 F4
Lymington Cl **2** E6 . . . . . . .1 F8
Lymington Ct ME15 . . . . .116 F4
Lyndale Est ME20 . . . . .17 B8
Lyndean Ind Est SE2 . . . . . .3 C3
Lynden Way BR8 . . . . .45 D6
Lyndhurst Ave ME8 . . . . . .69 C7
Lyndhurst Cl Bexley DA7 . .14 C4
  Orpington BR6 . . . . .57 B6
Lyndhurst Rd TN13 . . . . . .91 E3
Lyndhurst Rd Bexley DA7 . .14 C4
  Maidstone ME15 . . . . . . .116 C8
Lyndhurst Way DA13 . . . . .49 F8
Lyndon Ave DA15 . . . . .12 F2
Lyndon Rd DA17 . . . . .4 A2
Lynette Ave ME2 . . . . .39 A1
Lyngs Cl ME18 . . . . .130 F8
Lynmead Cl TN8 . . . . .122 B4

Lynmere Rd DA16 . . . . . . .13 B5
Lynmouth Rise BR5 . . . . . .44 B5
Lynne Cl **7** BR6 . . . . .57 F4
Lynors Ave ME2 . . . . .39 A1
Lynstead Cl BR1 . . . . .42 C7
Lynstead Ho ME16 . . . . . . .99 A1
Lynsted Cl DA6 . . . . .14 B2
Lynsted Gdns SE9 . . . . . . .11 C5
Lynsted Rd ME8 . . . . .55 B5
Lynton Ave BR5 . . . . .44 B5
Lynton Dr ME5 . . . . .68 B3
Lynton Rd ME11 . . . . .36 A7
Lynton Rd S DA11 . . . . . . .36 A7
Lynwood TN3 . . . . .171 C6
Lynwood Gr BR6 . . . . .43 E1
Lynx Way E16 . . . . .1 D6
Lyons Cres TN9 . . . . .127 C2
Lyons The TN9 . . . . .127 C2
Lyoth Rd BR5 . . . . .57 C8
Lysander Rd ME19 . . . . . . .96 F3
Lysander Way BR6 . . . . . . .57 C7
Lytchet Rd BR1 . . . . .28 B1
Lytham Cl SE28 . . . . .3 E7
Lytton Strachey Path **8**
  SE28 . . . . .3 B6
Lyveden Rd SE3 . . . . .11 B7

M

Mabbett Ho **2** SE18 . . . . .12 A8
Mabel Cotts DA3 . . . . .49 A6
Mabel Rd BR8 . . . . .32 A2
Mabledon Rd TN9 . . . . . .143 B8
Macallister Ho **8** SE18 . . .12 B8
Macaulay ME20 . . . . .82 A4
Macaulay Way **2** SE28 . . . .3 B5
Macbean St SE18 . . . . .2 B3
Macdonald Ct TN12 . . . . .146 A4
Macdonald Rd ME7 . . . . . .54 D6
Mace Ct RM17 . . . . .18 E8
Mace Farm Cotts TN14 . . .73 E6
Mace La TN14 . . . . .73 D6
Macgregor Rd E16 . . . . .1 C8
Mackenders Cl ME20 . . . . .83 A6
Mackenders Gn ME20 . . . .83 A6
Mackenders La ME20 . . . . .83 A6
Mackenzie Way DA12 . . . .36 D2
Mackintosh Cl ME23 . . . . .23 F3
Macleod Ho SE18 . . . . .11 F5
Macmillan Gdns **2** DA1 . .16 A3
Macoma Rd SE18 . . . . .12 D8
Macoma Terr SE18 . . . . . . .12 D8
Mada Rd BR6 . . . . .57 B7
Madan Cl TN16 . . . . .89 E2
Madan Rd TN16 . . . . .89 E2
Madden Ave ME5 . . . . .67 E5
Madden Cl DA10 . . . . .17 E1
Maddocks Cl DA14 . . . . . . .30 E3
Madeira Pk TN2 . . . . .159 B2
Madginford Cl ME15 . . . . .101 A2
Madginford Park Inf Sch
  ME15 . . . . .101 A2
Madginford Park Jun Sch
  ME15 . . . . .101 A2
Madginford Rd ME15 . . . .100 F2
Madison Cres DA7 . . . . . . .13 C7
Madison Gdns DA7 . . . . . . .13 C7
Madison Way TN13 . . . . . .91 F4
Madras Ho **2** ME15 . . . . .116 E5
Maesmaur Rd TN16 . . . . . .88 C4
Mafeking Rd ME5 . . . . .67 F3
Magdalen Cl ME7 . . . . .69 A4
Magdelan Gr BR6 . . . . .58 B6
Magnet Rd RM20 . . . . .17 C8
Magnolia Ave ME8 . . . . . . .69 B5
Magnolia Cl TN9 . . . . .143 C7
Magnolia Dr TN16 . . . . . . .72 E3
Magnolia Ho **3** ME16 . . . .99 A3
Magpie Bottom TN15 . . . . .76 E6
Magpie Cl ME20 . . . . .82 A1
Magpie Gn **3** TN8 . . . . . .122 D3
Magpie Hall Cl BR2 . . . . . .42 E3
Magpie Hall La BR2 . . . . . .42 F3
Magpie Hall Rd ME4 . . . . . .54 A2
Magpie La ME9,ME14 . . . . .69 F1
Magwitch Cl ME1 . . . . .53 B4
Maida Rd Chatham ME4 . . .54 B2
  Erith DA17 . . . . .4 A3
Maida Vale Rd DA1 . . . . . . .15 A2
Maiden Erlegh Ave DA5 . . .30 E7
Maiden La DA1 . . . . .15 A3
Maidstone Barracks Sta
  ME16 . . . . .99 B5
Maidstone East Sta ME14 .99 F5
Maidstone Gram Sch
  ME15 . . . . .100 B2
Maidstone Gram Sch for Girls
  ME16 . . . . .99 E5
Maidstone Hospl The
  ME16 . . . . .99 A4
Maidstone Ind Ctr ME14 . .99 F5
Maidstone L Ctr ME15 . . .100 C2
Maidstone Mus & Bentlif Art
  Gallery★ ME14 . . . . .99 F5
Maidstone Rd
  Bredhurst ME7,ME8 . . . . .69 B2
  Chatham ME4 . . . . .53 F2
  Chatham ME5 . . . . .67 D4
  Colt's Hill TN12,TN2 . . . .145 B4
  Danaway ME9 . . . . .71 D4
  Five Wents ME17 . . . . . . .117 E2
  Gillingham ME8 . . . . .69 C6
  Goose Green ME18,TN11 . .112 C3
  Grays RM17 . . . . .18 A8
  Headcorn TN27 . . . . .151 B7
  Horsmonden TN12 . . . . . .163 A7

Maidstone Rd *continued*
Horsmonden,Claygate TN12 ....147 C3
Lenham ME17 ....120 D5
Matfield TN12 ....161 C6
Nettlestead Green ME18 ..113 C3
Pembury TN2 ....144 E1
Platt TN15 ....95 C7
Rochester ME1 ....53 C3
Seal TN15 ....93 C5
Sevenoaks TN13 ....91 E5
Sidcup DA14 ....30 F1
Staplehurst TN12 ....149 E7
Swanley DA14,BR8 ....45 B8
Underling Green TN12 ....132 F2
Maidstone St Michaels CE Jun Sch ME16 ....99 E3
Maidstone West Sta ME16 ....99 F3
Mailyns The ME8 ....69 D7
Main Gate Rd ME4 ....53 F7
Main Rd Biggin Hill TN16 ..72 C5
Chattenden ME3 ....39 F4
Cooling ME3 ....22 F4
Crockenhill BR8 ....45 D3
Crockham Hill TN8 ....105 C1
Cudham TN16 ....89 A7
Farningham DA4 ....46 F3
Halstead TN14 ....74 C3
Hoo St Werburgh ME3 ....40 C5
Kingsnorth ME3 ....41 D7
Longfield DA3 ....48 E7
Marlpit Hill TN8 ....122 B6
Orpington BR5 ....44 C7
Sidcup DA14,DA15 ....29 E5
Sundridge TN14 ....90 E3
Sutton at H DA4 ....33 B1
Swanley BR8 ....45 F8
Main Road Gorse Hill DA4 ....61 D7
Main St ME4 ....40 B2
Mainridge Rd BR7 ....29 A4
Maison Des Fleurs ME16 99 C2
Majendie Rd SE18 ....2 D1
Major Clark Ho TN17 ..179 C5
Major York's Rd TN4 ..158 F2
Malan Cl TN16 ....72 E2
Malden Dr ME14 ....100 A8
Mall The 6 Bexley DA6 ..14 A3
4 Bromley BR1 ....42 A6
Mallard Apartments 14 ME15 ....116 E5
Mallard Cl DA1 ....15 F2
Mallard Path 6 SE28 ....2 D3
Mallard Way
Lower Stoke ME3 ....25 C4
Marlpit Hill TN8 ....122 C3
Mallard Wlk
Larkfield ME20 ....81 F2
Sidcup DA14 ....30 C2
Mallards Way ME15 ....101 A1
Malling Ct ME19 ....97 F7
Malling Rd
Kings Hill M18,ME19 ....96 F2
Lunsford ME6,ME20 ....81 F5
Snodland ME6 ....82 A7
Teston ME18 ....98 A1
Malling Sch The ME19 ..97 F7
Malling Terr ME16 ....99 C4
Mallingdene Cl ME3 ....39 B8
Mallings Dr ME14 ....101 C4
Mallings La ME14 ....101 C4
Mallow Cl DA11 ....35 E4
Mallow Ct RM17 ....18 D8
Mallow Way 1 ME5 ....67 F4
Mallows The ME14 ....99 E7
Mallys Pl DA4 ....47 C8
Malmaynes Hall Rd ME3 .24 D3
Malory Sch BR1 ....28 A4
Malt House La TN30 ..193 A7
Malt Mews ME1 ....53 C5
Malt Shovel Cotts DA4 ..60 D7
Malta Ave ME5 ....68 A7
Malta Rd RM18 ....18 F5
Malta Terr 5 ME14 ....100 A7
Maltby Cl BR6 ....44 A1
Malthouse Cl ME17 ....120 D5
Malthouse Hill ME15 ..115 F4
Malthouse La DA12 ....37 E3
Malthouse Rd TN15 ....62 F2
Malthouse The ME16 ..115 A8
Malthus Path 7 SE28 ....3 C5
Maltings Cl TN11 ....128 E8
Maltings Ent Ctr The DA12 ....36 F7
Maltings The
Gillingham ME8 ....70 A8
3 Gravesend DA11 ....19 A1
Hadlow TN11 ....128 E8
Loose ME17 ....116 B4
Maidstone, Grove Green ME14 ....100 E5
Orpington BR6 ....43 F1
Westerham TN16 ....105 C8
Malton Mews SE18 ....12 E8
Malton St SE18 ....12 E8
Malton Way TN2 ....159 F7
Malus Cl ME5 ....68 B1
Malvern Ave DA7 ....13 E7
Malvern Ho DA11 ....18 D1
Malvern Rd
Gillingham ME7 ....54 E3
Orpington BR6 ....58 B6
Malvina Ave DA12 ....36 C6
Malyons Rd BR8 ....31 F1
Mamignot Cl ME14 ....101 A5
Manchester Cl ME5 ....68 C6
Manchester Ct E16 ....1 B7
Mandela Ho SE18 ....12 D8
Mandela Rd E16 ....1 A7
Mandeville Cl 1 SE3 ....11 A7
Mandeville Ct 1 ME14 .100 A5
Manford Ind Est DA8 ....15 B8
Mangold Way 4 DA18 ....3 E3
Mangravet Ave ME15 ..116 C7
Manister Rd SE2 ....3 A3
Manitoba Gdns 6 BR6 ..57 F4
Mann Sq TN9 ....143 D7
Manning Ct 3 SE28 ....3 B5
Manning Rd BR5 ....44 D4
Manningham Ho ME19 ..98 A6
Mannock Rd DA1 ....15 F4
Manor Cl Chalk DA12 ....37 B6
Crayford DA1 ....14 E3
Dartford DA2 ....32 A5
Erith SE28 ....3 C7
Maidstone ME14 ....101 B3
Royal Tunbridge Wells TN4 ....158 E3
Manor Cotts
Lamberhurst TN3 ....176 B5
Langley ME17 ....117 C5
Manor Ct Gillingham ME7 .55 C4
Maidstone ME14 ....101 B3
Sole Street DA13 ....50 D4
Manor Dr DA3 ....49 A3
Manor Farm Cotts TN15 .94 A6
Manor Field DA12 ....37 E3
Manor Forstal DA3 ....62 F7
Manor Gdns ME5 ....67 F4
Manor Gr TN10 ....127 C3
Manor Ho
14 Chatham ME7 ....54 A6
Chislehurst BR7 ....43 D8
Manor Ho The
Limpsfield RH8 ....104 B7
Sidcup DA15 ....30 A7
Sidcup,Old Bexley DA5 ....31 B7
Manor House Dr ME16 ..99 D3
Manor House Gdns TN8 122 C1
Manor La
Fawkham Green DA3 ....48 C2
Hartley DA3 ....49 A3
Rochester ME1 ....52 F3
Manor Oak Prim Sch BR5 ....44 D4
Manor Park Ctry Pk★ ME19 ....97 B7
Manor Park Rd BR7 ....43 D8
Manor Pk Chislehurst BR7 .43 D8
Erith DA8 ....15 A8
Royal Tunbridge Wells TN4 ....158 E3
Manor Pl Bromley BR1 ....42 E8
Chislehurst BR7 ....43 D7
Manor Rd Chatham ME4 ..53 F4
Crayford DA1 ....14 E3
Edenbridge TN8 ....122 B1
Erith DA8 ....15 B8
22 Gravesend DA12 ....19 B1
Grays RM17 ....18 C8
Knockmill TN15 ....77 F8
New Barn DA3 ....49 C4
Royal Tunbridge Wells TN4 ....142 E1
Rusthall TN4 ....158 C4
Sidcup DA15 ....30 A5
Sidcup,Old Bexley DA5 ....31 B7
Sole Street DA13 ....50 D4
Sundridge TN14 ....90 D3
Swanscombe DA10 ....34 E8
Tatsfield TN16 ....88 E7
Tilbury RM18 ....19 A5
West Thurrock RM20 ....17 C8
Manor Rise ME14 ....101 B3
Manor St ME7 ....54 A6
Manor The TN2 ....159 E5
Manor Way Bexley DA7 ..14 D4
Bromley BR2 ....42 E3
Eltham SE3 ....11 A3
Grays RM17 ....18 B7
Grays RM17 ....18 D7
Northfleet DA11 ....18 A3
Orpington BR5 ....43 C5
Sidcup DA5 ....31 A7
Swanscombe DA10 ....17 E3
Manor Way Bsns Ctr RM13 ....4 D8
Manorbrook SE3 ....11 A3
Manordene Rd SE28 ....3 D7
Manorfields Cl BR7 ....43 F6
Manorside Cl SE2 ....3 D2
Manse Ct DA14 ....30 C3
Manse Par BR8 ....46 A5
Manse Way BR8 ....46 A5
Mansel Dr ME1 ....53 A2
Mansergh Cl SE18 ....11 E7
Mansfield Cl BR5 ....44 D2
Mansfield Rd BR8 ....31 F2
Mansfield Wlk ME16 ....99 E2
Mansion House Cl TN27 168 A2
Mansion Row ME7 ....54 A6
Manthorpe Rd SE18 ....2 C1
Manton Rd SE2 ....3 A2
Manwarings The TN12 ..163 A6
Manwood St E16 ....1 F5
Maple Ave Gillingham ME7 .54 E6
Maidstone ME16 ....99 C6
Maple Cl Larkfield ME20 ..82 A2
Orpington BR5 ....43 D4
Royal Tunbridge Wells TN2 ....159 A1
Swanley BR8 ....45 E7
Maple Cres DA15 ....13 A1
Maple Ct Erith DA8 ....14 F7
Newham E6 ....2 A8
Maple Ct *continued*
Royal Tunbridge Wells TN4 ....158 E4
Sidcup DA14 ....30 B3
Stone DA9 ....33 E8
Maple Leaf Cl TN16 ....72 D3
Maple Leaf Dr DA15 ....29 F7
Maple Rd Dartford DA1 ..32 C7
Gravesend DA12 ....36 C4
Grays RM17 ....18 C8
Hoo St Werburgh ME3 ....40 E3
Rochester ME2 ....52 F6
Maple Tree Pl SE3 ....11 E6
Maplecroft Cl E6 ....1 E7
Mapledene BR7 ....29 C3
Maplehurst Cl DA2 ....31 E6
Maples The DA3 ....49 B6
Maplescombe Farm Cotts DA4 ....61 B5
Maplescombe La DA4 ..61 B6
Maplesden TN12 ....148 D5
Maplesden Cl ME16 ....98 F3
Maplesden Noakes Sch The ME16 ....99 E6
Mapleton TN8 ....123 A7
Mapleton Cl BR2 ....42 A3
Mapleton Rd
Four Elms TN8 ....123 A8
Westerham TN8,TN16 ....105 E3
Maplin Ho 9 SE2 ....3 D4
Maplin Rd E16 ....1 B7
Maplins Cl 5 ME8 ....55 F1
Mar Ho 5 SE7 ....11 C8
Mara Ct ME4 ....53 F1
Maran Way DA18 ....3 D3
Marathon Paddock ME7 .54 D4
Marathon Way SE28 ....2 F4
Marble Ho 1 SE18 ....2 F1
Marbrook Ct SE12 ....28 C5
Marc Brunel Way ME4 ..54 A7
Marcellina Way BR6 ....57 F7
Marcet Rd DA1 ....15 C2
Marconi Ho SE2 ....3 C1
Marconi Rd DA11 ....35 D5
Marconi Way ME1 ....67 D7
Marcus Rd DA1 ....32 A8
Marden Ave BR2 ....42 A3
Marden Cres DA5 ....14 C2
Marden Prim Sch TN12 .148 B5
Marden Rd Rochester ME2 39 C1
Staplehurst TN12 ....149 C5
Marden Sta TN12 ....148 C6
Marechal Niel Ave DA15 .29 D5
Marechal Niel Par DA15 .29 D5
Margaret Barr Row DA10 34 E8
Margaret Gardner Dr SE9 ....28 F6
Margaret Rd DA5 ....13 D1
Margate Cl ME7 ....54 E6
Margetts La ME1 ....66 D1
Margetts Pl ME2 ....40 A3
Marian Sq TN12 ....149 F4
Marigold Way ME16 ....99 A3
Marina Cl 1 BR2 ....42 A6
Marina Dr Bexley DA16 ..12 E5
Dartford DA1 ....33 A7
Northfleet DA11 ....18 F1
Marine Dr
Hoo St Werburgh ME3 ....40 E3
Woolwich SE18 ....1 F2
Marine View ME4 ....40 B1
Mariners Ct DA9 ....17 B3
Mariners The ME1 ....53 B4
Mariners View ME7 ....54 F7
Mariners Way 5 DA11 ..35 E8
Mariners Wlk DA8 ....14 F8
Marion Cl ME5 ....68 A2
Marion Cotts TN15 ....95 E8
Marion Cres
Maidstone ME15 ....116 B8
Orpington BR5 ....44 B4
Maritime Cl
Rochester ME2 ....53 D8
Swanscombe DA9 ....17 B2
Maritime Est ME2 ....53 D8
Maritime Gate DA11 ....35 E8
Maritime Ind Est SE7 ....1 B2
Maritime Way ME4 ....54 A8
Marjorie McClure Sch BR7 ....43 C8
Marjory Pease Cotts RH8 ....104 E5
Mark Cl Bexley DA7 ....13 E6
Orpington BR2 ....56 E6
Mark La DA12 ....19 E1
Mark St ME4 ....54 A2
Mark Way BR8 ....46 A4
Markers Lodge DA12 ....36 E8
Market Alley 9 DA11 ....19 B1
Market Bldgs 4 ME14 ..99 F4
Market Colonnade 3 ME14 ....99 F4
Market Mdw BR5 ....44 C5
Market Par Bromley BR1 ..42 A8
5 Sidcup DA14 ....30 B4
Market Pl 2 Bexley DA6 ..14 A3
Dartford DA1 ....32 E8
16 Royal Tunbridge Wells TN2 ....159 A2
1 Tilbury RM18 ....19 A5
Market Sq Bromley BR1 ..42 A7
Royal Tunbridge Wells TN1 ....159 B4
Westerham TN16 ....89 D1
Market St Dartford DA1 ..32 E8
2 Maidstone ME14 ....99 F4
17 Royal Tunbridge Wells TN2 ....159 A2
Market St *continued*
Staplehurst TN12 ....149 F5
Woolwich SE18 ....2 A2
Market Way 2 TN16 ....89 D1
Marks Sq DA11 ....35 F4
Marlborough Cl
Orpington BR6 ....43 F3
Royal Tunbridge Wells TN4 ....158 E4
Marlborough Cres TN13 .91 E3
Marlborough Ct TN16 ..89 C1
Marlborough Ho 4 ME8 .69 F8
Marlborough House Sch TN18 ....188 E2
Marlborough La SE7 ....11 C7
Marlborough Par ME16 ..98 F2
Marlborough Park Ave DA15 ....30 A7
Marlborough Rd
Bexley DA7 ....13 D4
Bromley BR2 ....42 C5
Dartford DA1 ....15 C1
Gillingham ME7 ....54 B5
Woolwich SE18 ....2 C3
Marlborough Sch DA15 ..30 A8
Marle Place Gdns★ TN12 ....162 C4
Marle Place Rd TN12 ..162 C4
Marler Ho DA8 ....14 F5
Marley Ave DA7 ....13 D8
Marley La TN27 ....152 C3
Marley Rd
Harrietsham ME17 ....119 F6
Hoo St Werburgh ME3 ....40 D6
Marley Way ME1 ....53 C2
Marlfield TN12 ....149 E4
Marlhurst TN8 ....122 B4
Marlin Ct 12 DA14 ....30 A4
Marling Cross DA12 ....36 E1
Marling Way DA12 ....36 E3
Marlings Cl BR7 ....43 E5
Marlings Park Ave BR7 ..43 E6
Marlow Copse ME5 ....67 F1
Marlow Ct TN13 ....92 B4
Marlowe Cl BR7 ....29 D2
Marlowe Gdns SE9 ....12 A1
Marlowe Rd ME20 ....82 A3
Marlowes The DA1 ....14 D3
Marlpit Cl TN8 ....122 C4
Marlpit Cotts ME17 ....116 E2
Marlpit Gdns TN5 ....186 E1
Marlpit The TN5 ....184 E5
Marlwood Cl DA15 ....29 E6
Marmadon Rd SE18 ....2 F2
Marne Ave DA16 ....13 A4
Marquis Dr ME7 ....69 B3
Marrabon Cl DA15 ....30 A7
Marram Ct RM17 ....18 E8
Marrians View 1 ME5 ..54 C2
Marriott Rd DA1 ....33 A8
Marriotts Wharf 2 DA11 .19 B1
Marsden Way 2 BR6 ....57 F6
Marsh Cres ME23 ....23 E4
Marsh Green Rd TN8 ..138 C5
Marsh La ME3 ....22 B6
Marsh Quarter La TN18 196 C3
Marsh Rd ME2 ....66 B5
Marsh St Dartford DA1 ..16 A3
Dartford DA1 ....16 A5
Rochester ME2 ....53 B7
Marsh View DA12 ....36 F7
Marsh Way
New Hythe ME20 ....82 A4
Rainham RM13 ....4 D8
Marshall Gdns TN11 ....111 E1
Marshall Path 10 SE28 ....3 B6
Marshall Rd ME8 ....69 C8
Marshalls Gr SE18 ....1 E2
Marshalls Land TN30 ..183 A3
Marsham Cl BR7 ....29 B3
Marsham Cres ME17 ..117 B1
Marsham St ME14 ....100 A4
Marsham Way ME2 ....66 A5
Marshbrook Cl SE3 ....11 D4
Marshland View ME3 ....25 C5
Marston Cl ME5 ....67 E3
Marston Ct DA14 ....29 F4
Marston Dr ME14 ....100 C5
Marston Ho RM17 ....18 A8
Marston Wlk ME5 ....67 E3
Martens Ave DA7 ....14 C3
Martens Cl DA7 ....14 C3
Martham Cl SE28 ....3 D6
Martin Bowes Rd SE9 ....11 F4
Martin Ct ME7 ....69 A3
Martin Dene DA6 ....13 F2
Martin Dr DA2 ....16 C1
Martin Hardie Way TN10 ....127 E5
Martin Ho Dartford DA2 ..33 C8
Gravesend DA11 ....36 A5
Northfleet DA11 ....35 F6
Martin Rd Dartford DA2 ..32 C5
Rochester ME2 ....53 B8
Martin Rise DA6 ....13 F2
Martin Sq ME20 ....82 A2
Martin St SE28 ....2 E5
Martin's Shaw TN13 ....91 C5
Martindale Ave
Newham E16 ....1 A6
Orpington BR6 ....58 A5
Martins Cl
Lower Higham ME3 ....38 D6
Orpington BR5 ....44 D6
Tenterden TN30 ....193 C8
Martins La TN12 ....112 E2
Martins Pl SE28 ....2 E5
Martins Wlk SE28 ....2 E5
Martyn Ho SE2 ....13 D8
Marvels Cl SE12 ....28 B6
Marvels La SE12 ....28 C5
Marvels Lane Prim Sch SE12 ....28 C4
Marvillion Ct TN12 ....129 F6
Marvin Ho 9 SE18 ....12 B8
Marwell TN16 ....89 B1
Marwood Cl DA16 ....13 B4
Mary Burrows Gdns TN15 ....77 B2
Mary Ct ME4 ....54 A2
Mary Day's TN17 ....177 E7
Mary Last Cl ME6 ....81 E7
Mary Lawrenson Pl 2 SE3 ....11 A7
Mary Macarthur Ho 5 DA17 ....4 A3
Mary Magdalene Ho 8 TN9 ....143 B8
Mary Rose Mall E6 ....1 F8
Mary Slessor Ho 14 DA17 .4 A3
Marybank SE18 ....1 F2
Maryfield Cl DA5 ....31 E5
Maryland Ct ME8 ....69 E5
Maryland Dr ME16 ....98 F2
Maryland Rd TN2 ....159 D1
Maryon Ct BR5 ....44 B5
Maryon Gr SE7 ....1 E2
Maryon Rd SE7,SE18 ....1 E2
Maryville DA16 ....12 F5
Mascall's Court La TN12 146 B4
Mascall's Court Rd TN12 ....146 A4
Mascalls Ct 23 SE7 ....11 C8
Mascalls Pk TN12 ....145 F5
Mascalls Rd SE7 ....11 C8
Mascalls Sec Sch TN12 .146 A4
Masefield Cl DA8 ....14 F6
Masefield Dr ME3 ....39 B8
Masefield Rd
Dartford DA1 ....16 B2
Lunsford ME20 ....81 F4
Northfleet DA11 ....35 D5
Masefield View BR6 ....57 C7
Masefield Way TN9 ....142 F7
Masham Ho 6 DA18 ....3 D4
Mason Cl Bexley DA7 ....14 B4
Newham E16 ....1 A6
Mason Way ME2 ....39 B2
Masons Hill Bromley BR2 .42 B5
Woolwich SE18 ....2 B2
Master Gunner Pl SE18 ..11 E6
Masters La ME19 ....81 B5
Masterson Ho DA4 ....47 D7
Masthead Cl DA2 ....16 C3
Matchless Dr SE18 ....12 A7
Matfield Cl BR2 ....42 A4
Matfield Cres ME14 ....100 C5
Matfield Rd DA17 ....14 A8
Matilda Cl ME8 ....69 B8
Matrix Bsns Ctr DA1 ....15 E2
Matterdale Gdns ME16 ..98 E2
Matthews Ho 13 SE7 ....11 C8
Matthews La TN11,ME18 111 F4
Mattinson Pl ME9 ....103 F7
Matts Hill Rd ME9 ....69 E2
Maud Cashmore Way SE18 ....1 F3
Maude Rd BR8 ....32 A2
Maudslay Rd SE9 ....11 F4
Maundene Sch ME5 ....68 B5
Maunders Cl ME5 ....68 C8
Mavelstone Cl BR1 ....42 E8
Mavelstone Rd BR1 ....42 E8
Mavis Wlk 10 E6 ....1 E8
Maxey Rd SE18 ....2 C2
Maxim Rd Crayford DA1 ..14 E2
Erith DA8 ....4 E2
Maximfeldt Rd DA8 ....4 E1
Maximilian Dr ME2 ....66 B4
Maxton Cl ME14 ....100 F5
Maxwell Dr ME16 ....99 B6
Maxwell Gdns BR6 ....57 F7
Maxwell Ho
Chislehurst BR7 ....29 B1
12 Woolwich SE18 ....12 B8
Maxwell Rd Bexley DA16 ..13 A4
Chatham ME7 ....54 A6
May Ave Northfleet DA11 ..35 F7
Orpington BR5 ....44 B4
May Avenue Est 1 DA11 .35 F7
May Ct RM17 ....18 E8
May Pl DA12 ....50 D4
May Rd Gillingham ME7 ..54 C4
Hawley DA2 ....32 F4
Rochester ME1 ....53 C3
May St Cuxton ME2 ....52 B2
Snodland ME6 ....82 B8
May Terr 2 ME7 ....54 A7
May Wynne Ho E16 ....1 B7
Maybury Ave DA2 ....33 C7
Maybury Cl BR5 ....43 B4
Maycotts La TN12 ....145 D1
Mayday Gdns SE3 ....11 E5
Mayerne Rd SE9 ....11 D2
Mayes Cl BR8 ....46 A5
Mayeswood Rd SE12 ....28 C4
Mayfair 2 ME2 ....53 C8
Mayfair Ave Bexley DA7 ..13 D6
Loose ME15 ....116 A8
Mayfair Rd DA1 ....15 D2
Mayfield Bexley DA7 ....13 F4
Sevenoaks TN13 ....91 E7
Swanscombe DA10 ....17 E1

Mayfield Ave BR6 ......43 F2
Mayfield Cl Chatham ME5 .68 A1
 Gillingham ME8 ....55 E2
Mayfield Ct DA14 ......30 B3
Mayfield La TN5 ......184 D4
Mayfield Pk TN5 ......184 E5
Mayfield Rd Bromley BR1 .42 E4
 Erith DA17 ....4 C2
 Northfleet DA11 ......35 F8
 Royal Tunbridge Wells
 TN4 ....158 F4
Mayfield Villas DA14 ...30 C2
Mayflower Ho ME1 .....53 B4
Mayfly Cl BR5 ....44 D5
Mayford Rd ME5 ......68 D2
Mayhill Rd SE7 ....11 B8
Maylam Ct TN10 ......127 C4
Maylands Dr DA14 .....30 D5
Maynard Cl DA8 ....14 F7
Maynard Ho SE18 ....2 C2
Maynard Pl ME5 ....54 D2
Maynards TN12 ....148 C5
Mayor's La DA2 ....32 C3
Mayor's Pl **11** TN30 ...193 A7
Mayplace Ave DA1 .....15 A3
Mayplace Cl DA7 ......14 B4
Mayplace La
 Woolwich SE18 ....12 B7
 Woolwich SE18 ....12 B8
Mayplace Prim Sch DA7 .14 D3
Mayplace Rd E DA7 ....14 C4
Mayplace Rd W DA7 ....14 A3
Maypole Cotts BR6 .....59 A4
Maypole Cres DA8 .....15 D8
Maypole Dr ME18 ......97 C3
Maypole La TN17 .....177 F8
Maypole Prim Sch DA5 .31 E5
Maypole Rd Chelsfield BR6 58 F4
 Gravesend DA12 ....36 F7
Mayston Mews **6** SE10 ...1 A1
Maytham Bglws TN17 .192 A1
Maytham Rd TN17 ....198 C7
Mayview DA1 ....32 E7
Mayweed Ave ME5 .....67 E4
Mc Call Cres SE7 ....1 E1
Mc Kenzie Rd ME5 .....68 A3
Mc Kinlay Ct DA16 ....13 C4
McAlpine Cres ME15 ..115 F3
McAuley Cl SE9 ....12 A2
McCabe Cl TN12 ......149 E2
McCudden Rd DA1 .....15 F4
McCudden Row **8** ME7 .54 A6
McDermott Rd TN15 ...94 F7
McDowall Cl **11** E16 .....1 A8
McIntyre Ct **6** SE18 ....1 E2
McKenzie Cl ME20 .....98 F8
McKillop Way DA14 ....30 C1
McLeod Rd SE2 ....3 B2
McMichaels Way TN19 .194 A3
McMillan Cl DA12 ......36 C4
Mead Cl BR8 ....46 A4
Mead Cres DA1 ....32 D7
Mead Gn ME5 ....68 C3
Mead Ho TN16 ....72 D3
Mead Rd Chislehurst BR7 .29 C2
 Dartford DA1 ....32 D7
 Edenbridge TN8 ......138 D7
 Gravesend DA11 ......36 B6
Mead Road Inf Sch BR7 .29 C2
Mead Sch The TN2 ....159 A1
Mead The Leybourne ME19 81 E2
 New Ash Green DA3 ...62 E8
Mead Wall ME3 ....5 F2
Mead Way BR2 ....42 A3
Meades Ct TN12 ......148 B6
Meadfield Rd DA13 ....64 A8
Meadow Bank
 Leigh TN11 ....125 F1
 West Malling ME19 ...97 C8
Meadow Bank Mews
 ME19 ....97 C8
Meadow Cl Bexley DA6 .13 F2
 Chatham ME5 ....67 F5
 Chislehurst BR7 ....29 B3
 Sevenoaks TN13 ....92 A4
 Upper Halling ME2 ....65 E4
Meadow Cres ME2 .....65 E4
Meadow Croft BR1 .....42 F6
Meadow Hill Rd **6** TN1 .159 B3
Meadow La
 Culverstone Green DA13 ..64 A1
 Lewisham SE12 ....28 B5
 Marlpit Hill TN8 .....122 B4
Meadow Rd
 Gravesend DA11 ......36 A6
 Groombridge TN3 ....171 C2
 Northfleet DA11 ....35 C7
 Royal Tunbridge Wells
 TN1 ....159 A4
 Royal Tunbridge
 Wells,Southborough TN4 .142 F1
 Rusthall TN4 ....158 C4
 Tonbridge TN9 ......143 B8
Meadow The
 Chislehurst BR7 ....29 C2
 Pembury TN2 ....160 E8
Meadow View
 Flimwell TN5 ....187 A3
 Sidcup DA15 ....30 B8
Meadow View Cotts
 Hurst Green TN19 ....194 A3
 Laddingford ME18 ...130 E5
Meadow View Rd ME17 .116 B3

Meadow Way
 Dartford DA2 ....33 C8
 Marden TN12 ....148 E6
 Orpington BR6 ....57 A7
 Wouldham ME1 ....66 C5
Meadow Wlk
 Dartford DA2 ....32 C4
 Maidstone ME15 ......100 B3
 Snodland ME6 ....81 F7
Meadowbank Ct ME19 ..97 C8
Meadowbank Rd ME4 ..54 A4
Meadowdown ME14 ...100 E4
Meadowdown Cl ME7 ..69 A4
Meadowford Cl SE28 ...3 C8
Meadowlands
 Oxted RH8 ....104 A1
 Seal TN15 ....92 F7
Meadows TN17 ....180 D1
Meadows Ct DA14 .....30 B2
Meadows Sch TN4 ....142 F2
Meadows The
 Biddenden TN27 .....167 F2
 Halstead TN14 ....74 F6
 3 Maidstone ME15 ...99 E2
 Orpington BR6 ....58 C4
 Wittersham TN30 ....199 D4
Meadowside Dartford DA1 32 E7
 Eltham SE3,SE9 ....11 C3
Meadowside Cotts TN5 .186 F1
Meadowsweet Cl **3** E16 ..1 D8
Meadowsweet View ME4 .40 B2
Meadowview BR5 ....44 C6
Meadowview Rd DA5 ...13 F1
Meads The Hartley TN17 .178 F1
 Royal Tunbridge Wells
 TN2 ....159 C2
Meadside Wlk ME5 .....67 F6
Meadway Halstead TN14 .74 F6
 Tonbridge TN11 ......126 E3
Meadway The
 Orpington BR6 ....58 B4
 Sevenoaks TN13 ....91 F5
Meath Cl BR5 ....44 B4
Medbury Rd DA12 .....36 F7
Mede Ho BR1 ....28 B3
Medebourne Cl SE3 ...11 A4
Medhurst Cres DA12 ...36 F6
Medhurst Gdns DA12 ..36 F5
Medick Ct RM17 ....18 E8
Medina Ho **6** DA8 ....14 E7
Medina Rd Ditton ME20 ..82 C1
 Tonbridge TN10 ......127 C6
Medlar Gr ME7 ....69 A4
Medlar Ho **3** DA15 ....30 A5
Medlar Rd RM17 ....18 E8
Medlars The
 Maidstone ME14 .....100 D6
 Meopham Sta DA13 ...50 A3
Medway Ave
 High Halstow ME23 ...23 E4
 Yalding ME18 ....113 F1
Medway City Est ME2 ..53 D7
Medway Com Coll ME4 .54 A1
Medway Cotts
 Iden Green TN17 .....190 D3
 Marden TN12 ....148 C6
Medway Ct Aylesford ME20 82 F2
 20 Orpington BR5 .....44 D1
Medway Ent Ctr ME2 ..53 D8
Medway Gdns ME4 ....53 F7
Medway Heritage Ctr★
 ME4 ....53 F5
Medway Ho **7** ME14 ..99 F4
Medway Hts **5** ME4 ...53 E4
Medway Maritime Hospl
 ME7 ....54 B4
Medway Mdws TN12 ..130 A6
Medway Rd Crayford DA1 .15 A4
 Gillingham ME7 ....54 C7
 Royal Tunbridge Wells
 TN1 ....159 B5
Medway St Chatham ME4 .53 F7
 Maidstone ME14 ......99 C1
Medway Trad Est ME16 ..99 F3
Medway View
 Barnes Street TN11 ..129 A5
 Middle Stoke ME3 .....25 C3
Medway Villas ME5 ...115 B7
Medway Wharf Rd TN9 .127 C1
Meerbrook Rd SE3 ....11 C4
Meeson's La RM17 .....17 F8
Meeting House La **2**
 ME4 ....53 F4
Megby Cl ME8 ....69 D6
Megrims Hill TN18 ....196 A6
Meirs Court Rd ME8 ...69 E6
Melanda Cl BR7 ....28 F3
Melanie Cl DA7 ....13 E6
Melba Gdns RM18 .....19 A7
Melbourne Cl BR6 .....43 E2
Melbourne Ct RM18 ...18 E6
Melbourne Quay **4** DA11 19 B1
Melbourne Rd
 Chatham ME4 ....54 A3
 Tilbury RM18 ....18 E6
Melbury Cl BR7 ....28 F2
Melbury Grange BR1 ..42 E8
Meldrum Cl Orpington BR5 44 C3
 Oxted RH8 ....104 A3
Melford Dr ME16 ......99 C4
Melliker La DA13 ......50 A3
Melling St SE18 ....12 E8
Mellish Ind Est SE18 ...1 D3
Mells Cres SE9 ....28 F4
Melody Cl ME8 ....69 C4
Melody Rd TN16 ......72 C1
Melrose Ave Dartford DA1 31 E8
 Kings Hill ME19 ....97 C3

Melrose Cl Lewisham SE12 28 B7
 Loose ME15 ....116 A7
Melrose Cres BR6 .....57 D5
Melrose Rd TN16 ......72 C3
Melthorpe Gdns SE3 ..11 E6
Melville Ct ME4 ....53 F6
Melville Rd
 Maidstone ME15 .....100 A3
 Sidcup DA14 ....30 C6
Memess Path **4** SE18 ..12 A8
Memorial Hospl SE18 ..12 A5
Mendip Ho DA11 ......18 D1
Mendip Rd DA7 ....14 E6
Mendip Wlk TN2 .....159 D5
Mennie Ho SE18 ......11 F6
Meon Ct **21** BR5 ......44 D1
Meopham Com Prim Sch
 Meopham DA13 ....64 A8
 Meopham Sta DA13 ...50 A2
Meopham Sta DA13 ....50 A4
Mera Dr DA7 ....14 A3
Merbury Rd SE28 ....2 E4
Mercer Cl ME20 ....82 B4
Mercer Dr ME17 ......119 F6
Mercer St TN1 ....159 B5
Mercer Way ME17 ....117 B1
Mercers Hawkhurst TN18 .189 A1
 Langton Green TN3 ..158 A3
Mercers Cl TN12 .....145 E6
Mercers Pl ME19 ......97 A2
Merchant Pl TN12 ....148 C5
Merchland Rd SE9 .....29 C7
Mercury Cl ME1 ....53 A3
Mere Cl BR6 ....57 B8
Meredith Cl ME17 ....117 F7
Meresborough Cotts
 ME8 ....69 F5
Meresborough La ME8,
 ME9 ....70 B5
Meresborough Rd ME8 .70 A4
Mereside BR6 ....57 A8
Merevale Ho **3** TN1 ..159 A3
Merewood Cl **1** BR1 ..43 A7
Merewood Rd DA7 ....14 C5
Mereworth Cl ME8 ....55 A3
Mereworth Com Prim Sch
 ME18 ....112 D8
Mereworth Dr SE18 ...12 C7
Mereworth Ho ME2 ...39 C1
Mereworth Rd
 Royal Tunbridge Wells
 TN4 ....159 A6
 West Peckham ME18 ..112 C7
Merganser Gdns SE28 ...2 D3
Meriden Cl BR1 ....28 D1
Meridian Ct ME16 .....99 E4
Meridian Pk ME2 ......53 E6
Meridian Rd SE7 ......11 D7
Meridian Trad Est SE7 ...1 B2
Meriel Wlk DA9 ....17 B3
Merifield Rd SE9 ......11 C3
Merileys Cl DA3 ......49 C6
Merino Pl DA15 ....13 A2
Merivale Gr ME5 ......68 B4
Merle Common Rd RH8 .194 B4
Merlewood TN13 ......92 B4
Merlewood Dr BR7 ....42 F8
Merlin Ave ME20 ......81 F2
Merlin Cl TN10 ......127 E4
Merlin Gdns BR1 ......28 A5
Merlin Ho ME4 ....54 B8
Merlin Prim Sch BR1 ..28 A5
Merlin Rd DA16 ....13 A3
Merlin Rd N DA16 .....13 A3
Mermaid Ct Chatham ME5 .68 A6
 Northfleet DA11 ......35 D8
Mermerus Gdns DA12 ..36 F4
Merrals Wood Rd ME2 .52 D5
Merrilees Rd DA15 ....29 E8
Merrivale Gr ME5 .....68 B4
Merriman Ho ME3 .....39 F6
Merriman Rd SE3 .....11 C6
Merriments Gdns★
 TN19 ....194 B5
Merriments La
 Hurst Green TN18, TN19 .194 D5
 Hurst Green TN19 ...194 B5
Merrion Cl TN4 ......159 B7
Merrion Way TN4 ....159 B7
Merry Boys Rd ME3 ...39 B8
Merrydown Way BR7 ..42 F8
Merryfield SE3 ....11 A5
Merryfield Ct **9** TN9 ..143 B8
Merryfield Ho **4** SE9 ..28 C5
Merryfields ME2 ......39 A1
Merryfields Cl DA3 ....48 F5
Merryhills Cl TN16 ....72 D3
Merryweather Cl DA1 ..15 F1
Mersey Rd TN10 .....127 B5
Merston Ct ME3 ....38 C4
Merton Ave DA3 ......48 F5
Merton Cl ME5 ....68 C5
Merton Court Sch DA14 .30 C4
Merton Ct DA16 ....13 B5
Merton Gdns BR5 .....43 B4
Merton Rd ME15 .....100 F2
Mervyn Ave SE9 ......29 C6
Mervyn Stockwood Ho
 SE9 ....29 C6
Mesne Way TN14 ......75 F7
Messent Rd SE9 ....11 D2
Messeter Pl SE9 ....12 A1
Meteor Rd ME5 ....96 F3
Methuen Rd Bexley DA16 .13 F3
 Erith DA17 ....4 C2
Metro Ctr The BR5 .....44 B3
Mews The
 Headcorn TN27 ......151 C5
 Longfield DA3 ....48 E6

Mews The continued
 1 Maidstone ME16 ....99 E5
 Pembury TN2 ....160 C6
 Rochester ME2 ....52 F7
 5 Royal Tunbridge Wells
 TN1 ....159 B3
 Sevenoaks TN13 ....92 A3
 7 Sidcup DA14 ....30 A4
Mewsend TN16 ....72 D1
Meyer Rd DA8 ....14 D8
Micawber Cl ME5 .....68 A1
Michael Gdns DA12 ...36 E3
Michael Marshall Ho
 SE9 ....29 C6
Michaels La DA3,TN15 ..62 C5
Michele Cotts ME3 ....38 C6
Mickleham Cl BR5 .....44 A7
Mickleham Rd BR5 ....44 A7
Mid Comp Cotts TN15 .95 E6
Mid Kent Bsns Pk ME6 .82 B7
Mid Kent Coll (City Way Ctr)
 ME1 ....53 D4
Mid Kent Coll of H & F Ed
 ME16 ....99 C3
Mid Kent Coll of Higher & F
 Ed ME5 ....67 E6
Mid Kent Sh Ctr The
 ME16 ....99 C7
Middle Field TN2 ....160 E8
Middle Garth ME17 ..179 D4
Middle La TN15 ....92 F6
Middle Mill Rd ME19 ..97 F7
Middle Park Ave SE9 ..28 E8
Middle Park Prim Sch
 SE9 ....28 D8
Middle Rd TN3 ......174 A5
Middle Row **6** ME4 ...99 F4
Middle St **4** ME7 .....54 A6
Middle Wlk TN2 .....159 E8
Middlefields ME8 ......70 A8
Middleham Ct **26** DA2 ..16 B1
Middlesex Rd ME15 ..116 D7
Middleton Ave DA14 ..30 C3
Middleton Cl ME8 .....69 E4
Middleton Ct **18** BR1 ..28 B1
Middlings Rise TN13 ..91 F1
Middlings The TN13 ...91 F2
Middlings Wood TN13 .92 A2
Midfield Ave Bexley DA7 ..14 C4
 Hextable BR8 ....32 B2
Midfield Prim Sch BR5 .30 A1
Midfield Way BR5 .....44 B8
Midhurst Ct ME15 ....100 A3
Midhurst Hill DA6 ....14 A2
Midley Cl ME16 ....99 C7
Midsummer Ct SE12 ..11 A3
Midsummer Rd ME6 ..81 E8
Midway The TN4 .....158 D2
Midwinter Cl **3** DA16 .13 A4
Miers Court Prim Sch
 ME8 ....69 F7
Mierscourt Cl ME8 ....70 A8
Mierscourt Rd ME8 ...69 E6
Mike Spring Ct DA12 ..36 D4
Milburn Rd ME7 ......54 C7
Mildmay Pl TN14 .....75 F8
Mildred Cl DA1 ....16 A1
Mildred Rd DA8 ....4 E1
Mile End Green Cotts
 DA3 ....48 D7
Mile La TN17 ....178 D7
Mile Oak Rd TN12 ...146 C3
Mile Stone Rd DA2 ....16 B1
Milebush La TN12 ....132 E1
Miles Dr SE28 ....2 E5
Miles Pl ME1 ....53 D3
Milestone Bldgs TN12 .149 F3
Milford Cl Bexley SE2 ..13 E3
 Maidstone ME16 ......99 D5
Military Rd ME4 ......53 F5
Milk House Cotts TN17 .180 A4
Milk St Bromley BR1 ...28 B2
 Newham E16 ....2 B5
Milking La
 Biggin Hill,Downe BR6 .....72 E7
 Biggin Hill,Leaves Green
 BR2 ....72 D8
Mill Bank Headcorn TN27 151 C6
 Tonbridge TN9 ......127 C2
Mill Brook Rd BR5 ....44 C5
Mill Cl Lenham ME17 ..120 C4
 Rochester ME2 ....39 B1
Mill Cotts ME15 ......114 B6
Mill Cres TN9 ....127 C6
Mill Ct Sutton at H DA4 ..47 C2
 14 Woolwich SE28 .....3 B6
Mill Hall Bsns Est The
 ME20 ....82 D2
Mill Hall Rd ME20 ....82 C3
Mill Hill TN9 ....138 D7
Mill Hill La DA12 .....37 D3
Mill House Cl DA4 .....46 E1
Mill La Benover ME18 .131 A7
 Chatham,Bluebell Hill ME5 .67 D1
 Chatham,Luton ME5 ..54 C1
 Coxheath ME17 ......115 D4
 Eynsford DA4 ....46 E1
 Farthing Street BR6 ..57 B1
 Frittenden TN17 .....166 D8
 Hartlip ME9 ....70 E6
 Hildenborough TN11,TN15 109 C2
 Horsmonden TN12 ...147 B1
 Ightham TN15 ....94 E5
 Maidstone ME14 ......99 F6
 Oxted RH8 ....104 A1
 Sevenoaks TN14 ......92 D6
 Shoreham TN14 ....59 F1
 Sissinghurst TN17 ...179 F8

Mill La continued
 Smarden TN27 ....153 A2
 Snodland ME6 ....82 B8
 Tenterden TN30 .....183 B1
 The Chart RH8 ....104 F4
 Tonbridge TN9 ......127 C2
 Wateringbury ME18 ..113 D7
 West Thurrock RM20 ..17 D3
 Westerham TN16 ....105 C5
 Woolwich SE18 ....2 A1
Mill Pl Chislehurst BR7 ..43 B8
 Crayford DA1 ....15 A3
Mill Pond Cl TN14 .....92 D6
Mill Pond Rd DA1 .....15 E1
Mill Rd Erith DA8 ......14 C7
 Gillingham ME7 ....54 C6
 Hawley DA2 ....32 F4
 Newham E16 ....1 B5
 Northfleet DA11 ......35 E8
 Rochester ME2 ....53 B8
 Sevenoaks TN13 ......91 E6
Mill Row DA5 ....31 B8
Mill St East Malling ME19 .97 F7
 Iden Green TN17,TN18 ..190 C3
 Loose ME15 ....115 F5
 Maidstone ME15 ......99 F4
 Snodland ME6 ....82 B8
 Westerham TN16 ....105 D8
Mill Stone Cl DA4 .....47 C7
Mill Stream Jun Sch
 ME19 ....97 F7
Mill Stream Pl TN9 ...127 D3
Mill Vale BR2 ....42 A7
Mill View TN11 ......111 D1
Mill Wlk ME16 ....99 A3
Millais Pl RM18 ....19 A7
Millars Mdw SE12 .....11 A3
Millars Rd SE12 ......11 A2
Millbank BR8 ....46 A8
Millbro BR8 ....46 A8
Millbrook ME5 ....81 D1
Millbrook Ave DA16 ..12 D3
Millbrook Cl ME15 ....99 F1
Millcroft Rd ME3 ......22 B4
Millen Ct DA4 ....47 C5
Millennium Cl E16 ......1 B7
Miller Cl BR1 ....28 B3
Miller Ct DA7 ....14 B4
Miller Rd DA12 ....37 A4
Miller Way ME2 ....39 D2
Millers Cotts TN11 ...144 C3
Millers Wharf **1** ME15 ..99 E2
Millers Wlk DA13 ......64 A7
Millersthumb TN17 ...165 C4
Millfield
 High Halden TN26 ...183 D7
 New Ash Green DA3 ...62 E8
Millfield Dr DA11 ......35 E6
Millfield La DA3 ....62 E8
Millfield Rd TN15 ......61 D4
Millfields ME5 ....68 D2
Millfields Cl BR5 ......44 B5
Millfields Cotts BR5 ...44 B5
Millfordhope Rd ME2 ..52 C7
Millhall ME20 ....82 E2
Millhouse La ME19 ....80 D3
Millman Ct SE3 ....11 B7
Millpond Cl ME2 ......53 B8
Millpond La TN30 ....182 D2
Mills Cres TN15 ......92 F8
Mills Rd ME20 ....98 E7
Mills Terr ME4 ....54 A3
Millside Ind Est DA1 ..15 D3
Millstock Terr **2** ME15 .99 E2
Millstone Mews DA4 ..47 C8
Millstream Ct TN3 ...156 D2
Millwood Ct **4** ME4 ..53 F4
Millwood Ho **1** SE28 ...2 D3
Millwood Rd BR5 .....44 C6
Milne Gdns SE9 ....11 E2
Milne Ho **11** SE18 ......1 F2
Milner Rd ME7 ....54 D7
Milner Wlk SE9 ....29 D7
Milners ME17 ....117 C7
Milroy Ave DA11 ......35 E6
Milstead Ct ME14 ....100 C3
Milsted Rd ME8 ....55 C3
Milton Ave
 Badgers Mount TN14 ..59 B1
 Cliffe Woods ME3 .....39 B8
 Gravesend DA12 ......36 C7
Milton Cl Gravesend DA12 .36 C6
 Kings Hill ME18 ......97 A3
Milton Dr TN2 ....159 D7
Milton Gdns Tilbury RM18 .19 B8
 Tonbridge TN9 ......142 F7
Milton Hall Rd DA12 ..36 D7
Milton Ho DA1 ....14 E2
Milton La ME18 ....97 B3
Milton Lodge **9** DA14 .30 A4
Milton Pl DA12 ....19 C1
Milton Rd Bexley DA16 .12 F6
 Erith DA17 ....4 A2
 Gillingham ME7 ....54 C3
 Gravesend DA12 ......36 C8
 Sevenoaks TN13 ......91 E6
 Swanscombe DA10 ...17 C1
Milton Rd Bsns Pk **4**
 DA12 ....36 C8
Milton St Maidstone ME16 .99 C2
 Swanscombe DA10 ...17 D1
Milverton Way SE9 ....29 A4
Milward Wlk **12** SE18 .12 A8
Mimosa Cl BR6 ....58 C8
Mincers Cl ME5 ....68 C6
Mineral St SE18 ....2 E2
Minerva Cl DA14 ......29 E4
Minerva Rd ME2 ......53 A8
Ministry Way SE9 .....28 F6

Minshaw Ct DA14 . . . . .29 F4
Minster Rd Bromley BR1 . . .28 B1
Gillingham ME8 . . . . .55 C3
Mint Bsns Pk E16 . . . . .1 A8
Minters Orch TN15 . . . . . .95 B7
Miranda Ho 6 DA17 . . . . . . .4 A1
Mirfield St SE7 . . . . .1 D3
Miriam Ct DA14 . . . . .30 B4
Miriam Rd SE18 . . . . .2 E1
Mirror Path SE9 . . . . .28 C5
Miskin Cotts ME3 . . . . . . .22 B6
Miskin Rd Dartford DA1 . . .32 D8
Hoo St Werburgh ME3 . . . . .40 E5
Miskin Way DA12 . . . . .36 D2
Mitchell Ave Chatham ME4 53 F2
Northfleet DA11 . . . . .35 D6
Mitchell Cl Dartford DA1 . .32 E6
Erith DA17 . . . . .4 C3
Lenham ME17 . . . . .120 C5
Woolwich SE2 . . . . .3 C2
Mitchell Ho
Kings Hill ME19 . . . . .96 F2
Orpington BR6 . . . . .57 F6
Mitchell Way 5 BR1 . . . . .42 A8
Swanscombe DA10 . . . . . . .34 E8
Mitchem Cl TN15 . . . . .61 E3
Mitre Ct 5 Erith DA17 . . . . .4 A2
Tonbridge TN9 . . . . .127 C2
Mitre Rd ME1 . . . . .53 B4
Moat Ct Orpington BR6 . . .57 F4
Sevenoaks TN13 . . . . .91 D5
Moat Croft DA16 . . . . .13 C4
Moat Ct Eltham SE9 . . . . . .11 F1
Sidcup DA15 . . . . .29 F5
Moat Farm TN2 . . . . .173 A2
Moat Farm Rd ME3 . . . . . .24 D6
Moat La Cowden TN8 . . . . .155 E7
Erith DA8 . . . . .15 A6
Moat Rd TN27 . . . . .151 B5
Moatbridge Sch SE9 . . . . .11 D1
Mockbeggar La TN17,
TN27 . . . . .181 C4
Model Farm Cl SE9 . . . . . .28 C5
Modest Cnr TN4 . . . . .142 E1
Moira Rd SE9 . . . . .11 F3
Molash Rd BR5 . . . . .44 D5
Molehill Copse Prim Sch
ME15 . . . . .116 D7
Moles Mead TN8 . . . . . . .122 C4
Molescroft SE9 . . . . .29 C5
Molescroft Way TN9 . . . . .142 F7
Mollison Rise DA12 . . . . . .36 E3
Molyneux Almshouses
TN4 . . . . .158 B4
Molyneux Ct TN4 . . . . . . .158 F4
Molyneux Park Gdns
TN4 . . . . .158 F4
Molyneux Park Rd TN4 .158 F4
Monarch Cl Chatham ME5 .68 A6
Tilbury RM18 . . . . .19 B5
Monarch Dr E16 . . . . .1 D8
Monarch Rd 8 DA17 . . . . . .4 A3
Monarch Terr ME18 . . . . . .97 C3
Monckton's Ave ME14 . . . .99 F7
Monckton's Dr ME14 . . . . .99 F7
Monckton's La ME14 . . . . .99 F7
Moncrieff Cl 5 E6 . . . . . . .1 E7
Moncrif Cl ME14 . . . . . . .101 B4
Monds Cotts TN14 . . . . . . .90 E3
Monica James Ho 12
DA14 . . . . .30 A5
Monk Dr E16 . . . . .1 A6
Monk St SE18 . . . . .2 A2
Monk's Well DA9 . . . . .17 C3
Monkdown ME15 . . . . . . .101 A1
Monkreed Villas DA3 . . . . .49 D4
Monks Cl SE2 . . . . .3 D2
Monks La Limpsfield TN8 .121 E6
Newbury's TN5 . . . . .185 B8
Monks Orch DA1 . . . . .32 D6
Monks Way BR5 . . . . .43 D1
Monks Wlk
Northfleet DA13 . . . . .35 A2
6 Tonbridge TN9 . . . . . . .143 B8
Monkton Rd Bexley DA16 .12 F5
Borough Green TN15 . . . . . .94 F7
Monkwood Cl ME1 . . . . . . .67 B8
Monmouth Cl
Bexley DA16 . . . . .13 A3
Gillingham ME8 . . . . .55 D2
Mons Way BR2 . . . . .42 E3
Monson Rd TN1 . . . . .159 B4
Monson Way 5 TN1 . . . . .159 B4
Mont St Aignan Way
TN8 . . . . .138 C8
Montacute Gdns TN2 . . . .158 F2
Montacute Rd TN2 . . . . . .159 A1
Montague Ct 13 DA15 . . . .30 A5
Montague Pl BR8 . . . . .45 F5
Montague Terr 1 BR2 . . . .42 A5
Montbelle Prim Sch SE9 .29 B5
Montbelle Rd SE9 . . . . . . .29 B5
Montbretia Cl BR5 . . . . . .44 C5
Montcalm Cl BR2 . . . . . . .42 A3
Montcalm Rd SE7 . . . . . . .11 D7
Monteith Cl TN3 . . . . .158 A3
Monterey Cl DA5 . . . . .31 C6
Montfort Dr ME19 . . . . . . .97 A2
Montfort Rd Chatham ME5 67 F2
Kemsing TN15 . . . . .76 E2
Rochester ME2 . . . . .53 A8
Montgomery Ave ME5 . . . .68 A7
Montgomery Cl DA15 . . . .12 F1
Montgomery Rd
Gillingham ME7 . . . . .54 C1
Royal Tunbridge Wells
TN4 . . . . .159 B7

Montgomery Rd continued
Sutton at H DA14 . . . . .47 D8
Montpelier Ave DA5 . . . . . .30 D8
Montpelier Gate ME16 . . . .99 B5
Montreal Rd
Sevenoaks TN13 . . . . .91 E4
Tilbury RM18 . . . . .19 A5
Montrose Ave
Bexley DA16 . . . . .12 E4
Gillingham ME5 . . . . .54 E2
Sidcup DA15 . . . . .30 A8
Montrose Cl DA16 . . . . . . .12 F4
Monypenny TN17 . . . . . . .191 F3
Monypenny TN11 . . . . . . .128 D8
Moon Ct SE12 . . . . .11 A3
Moon's La
Edenbridge RH7 . . . . .138 A1
Edenbridge RH7 . . . . .138 B1
Moonstone Dr ME5 . . . . . .68 B2
Moor Hill TN18 . . . . .194 F8
Moor La TN18 . . . . .138 A4
Moor Park Cl ME8 . . . . . . .70 A4
Moor Rd The TN14 . . . . . . .92 C7
Moor St ME8 . . . . .70 B8
Moor The TN18 . . . . .194 F8
Moorcroft Gdns BR2 . . . . .42 E4
Moorden La TN11 . . . . . . .125 A1
Moordown SE18 . . . . .6 A8
Moore Ave Grays RM20 . . .17 E8
Tilbury RM18 . . . . .19 B5
Moore Cl DA2 . . . . .33 D6
Moore Rd DA10 . . . . .17 E1
Moore St ME2 . . . . .53 A8
Mooreland Rd 1 BR1 . . . . .42 A8
Moorfield Rd BR6 . . . . . . .44 A2
Moorhead Way SE3 . . . . . .11 B4
Moorhen Cl DA8 . . . . .9 B7
Moorhouse Cotts TN16 . .105 A7
Moorhouse Rd RH8,
TN16 . . . . .105 A6
Mooring Rd ME1 . . . . .53 D1
Moorings The E16 . . . . .1 C8
Moorlands BR7 . . . . .29 B1
Moorside Rd BR1 . . . . .28 A4
Morants Court Cross
TN14 . . . . .75 C1
Morants Court Rd TN13 . .91 C8
Morden Rd SE3 . . . . .11 A5
Morden Road Mews SE3 .11 A5
Morden St ME1 . . . . .53 C4
More Park RC Prim Sch
ME19 . . . . .97 D8
Morebreddis Cotts
TN17 . . . . .164 A1
Morel Ct TN13 . . . . .92 B5
Morella Wlk ME17 . . . . . .120 C5
Morello Cl BR8 . . . . .45 D5
Morement Rd ME3 . . . . . . .40 D6
Moreton DA14 . . . . .30 A3
Moreton Almhouses 3
TN16 . . . . .89 D1
Moreton Ct DA1 . . . . .14 E4
Moreton Ind Est BR8 . . . . .26 A7
Morewood Cl TN13 . . . . . .91 F4
Morgan Dr DA9 . . . . .23 E8
Morgan Rd Bromley BR1 . .28 A1
Rochester ME2 . . . . .53 A8
Morgan St E16 . . . . .1 A8
Morhen Cl ME6 . . . . .81 E7
Morland Ave DA1 . . . . .15 B2
Morland Dr
Lamberhurst TN3 . . . . .176 B5
Rochester ME2 . . . . .39 A1
Morland Ho 4 BR7 . . . . . . .43 A8
Morley Bsns Ctr TN9 . . . .127 D1
Morley Cl BR6 . . . . .57 B8
Morley Dr TN12 . . . . .163 A6
Morley Rd Chislehurst BR7 43 C8
Tonbridge TN9 . . . . .127 D1
Morley's Rd TN14 . . . . . . .108 D2
Morne Cotts TN14 . . . . . . .75 F8
Morning Cross Cotts
ME3 . . . . .22 B4
Mornington Ave BR1 . . . . .42 C6
Mornington Cl TN16 . . . . . .72 D2
Mornington Ct DA5 . . . . . .31 D7
Morris Cl
Maidstone ME17 . . . . .116 D5
Orpington BR6 . . . . .57 F7
West Malling ME19 . . . . . . .81 F1
Morris Gdns DA1 . . . . .16 A2
Morry La ME17 . . . . .135 D7
Morston Gdns SE9 . . . . . . .28 F4
Mortgramit Sq SE18 . . . . . .2 A3
Mortimer Rd
Biggin Hill TN16 . . . . .72 C7
Erith DA8 . . . . .14 D8
Orpington BR6 . . . . .44 A1
Mortimers Ave ME3 . . . . . .39 A8
Mortlake Rd E16 . . . . .1 B7
Mortley Cl TN9 . . . . .127 C2
Morton Cl
Maidstone ME15 . . . . .116 D6
Swanley BR8 . . . . .45 E7
Morvale Cl DA17 . . . . .3 F2
Moselle Rd TN16 . . . . .72 F1
Mosquito Rd ME19 . . . . . . .96 F3
Moss Way DA2 . . . . .33 D4
Mossbank ME5 . . . . .68 A3
Mossdown Cl DA17 . . . . . . .4 A1
Mosslea Rd Bromley BR2 .42 D4
Orpington BR6 . . . . .57 C7
Mossy Glade ME8 . . . . . . .69 E6
Mostyn Rd ME14 . . . . .100 C4
Mosul Way BR2 . . . . .42 E3
Mosyer Dr BR5 . . . . .45 D8
Mote Ave ME15 . . . . .100 B3
Mote Cotts TN15 . . . . .110 A7

Mote Hall Villas ME14 . .101 C4
Mote Ho ME15 . . . . .100 D2
Mote Rd Maidstone ME15 100 A3
Shipbourne TN15,TN11 . . .110 A7
Mote The DA3 . . . . .62 F8
Motherwell Way RM20 . . . .17 A8
Mottingham St SE9 . . . . . .28 F7
Mottingham Gdns SE9 . . .28 D7
Mottingham La
Bromley SE12,SE9 . . . . . . .28 C8
Eltham SE12 . . . . .28 C8
Mottingham Prim Sch
SE9 . . . . .28 F5
Mottingham Rd SE9 . . . . . .28 F5
Mottingham Sta SE9 . . . . .28 F7
Mottisfont Rd SE2 . . . . .3 B2
Mouat Ct ME5 . . . . .68 A3
Mouchotte Cl TN16 . . . . . .72 C7
Moultain Hill BR8 . . . . .46 A5
Mound The SE9 . . . . .29 A5
Mount Ave ME18 . . . . .114 A1
Mount Castle La ME17 . . .120 F1
Mount Cl Bromley BR1 . . . .42 E8
Sevenoaks TN13 . . . . .91 F4
Mount Culver Ave DA14 . .30 D2
Mount Dr Bexley DA6 . . . . .13 E2
Maidstone ME14 . . . . .101 A4
Mount Edgcumbe Rd
TN4 . . . . .159 A3
Mount Ephraim TN4 . . . . .159 A4
Mount Ephraim Ct TN4 . .158 F4
Mount Ephraim Rd TN1 159 A4
Mount Harry Rd TN13 . . . .92 B4
Mount La Hartlip ME9 . . . . .70 D4
Maidstone ME14 . . . . .101 B4
Mount Lodge ME1 . . . . . . .53 B2
Mount Pleasant
Aylesford ME20 . . . . .83 A3
Biggin Hill TN16 . . . . .72 D2
Chatham ME5 . . . . .54 B3
Durgates TN5 . . . . .184 E5
Ide Hill TN14 . . . . .106 F4
Lamberhurst TN3 . . . . .175 E6
Paddock Wood TN12 . . . . .145 F7
Tenterden TN30 . . . . .193 C8
The Moor TN18 . . . . .194 F8
Tonbridge TN11 . . . . .126 D6
Mount Pleasant Ave 2
TN1 . . . . .159 B3
Mount Pleasant Ct
TN11 . . . . .126 D6
Mount Pleasant Dr
ME14 . . . . .101 A5
Mount Pleasant La TN3 176 A6
Mount Pleasant Pl SE18 . .2 D2
Mount Pleasant Rd
Dartford DA1 . . . . .15 F1
Royal Tunbridge Wells
TN1 . . . . .159 A3
Sevenoaks Weald TN14 . . .108 B2
Mount Pleasant Terr
ME17 . . . . .119 E2
Mount Pleasant Wlk DA5 .14 C5
Mount Rd Bexley DA6 . . . . .13 E2
Chatham ME4 . . . . .53 F3
Crayford DA1 . . . . .14 F1
Rochester ME1 . . . . .53 B2
Mount Sion TN1 . . . . .159 A2
Mount The Bexley DA6 . . . .14 B2
3 Chislehurst BR7 . . . . . . .43 A8
Mount View Ct 3 ME4 . . . .53 F3
Mountain Cl TN15 . . . . . . .78 F3
Mountbatten Ave
Chatham ME5 . . . . .68 A7
Higham ME3 . . . . .38 C4
Mountbatten Cl SE18 . . . .12 E8
Mountfield TN15 . . . . .95 A7
Mountfield Cl DA13 . . . . . .63 F2
Mountfield Ct 4 TN1 . . . . .159 B3
Mountfield Gdns TN1 . . . .159 B3
Mountfield Pk TN9 . . . . . .143 C8
Mountfield Rd TN1 . . . . . .159 B3
Mountfield Way 1 BR5 . . .44 C5
Mounthurst Rd BR2 . . . . . .42 A2
Mountjoy Cl SE2 . . . . .3 B4
Mounts Hill TN17 . . . . . . .190 B7
Mounts La TN17 . . . . .192 A3
Mounts Rd DA9 . . . . .17 B1
Mountsfield Cl ME16 . . . . .99 D5
Mountview Rd BR6 . . . . . . .44 A4
Moyle Cl ME8 . . . . .69 D4
Mozart St ME4 . . . . .53 E3
Muir Rd ME15 . . . . .100 A2
Muir St E16 . . . . .1 E5
Mulbarton Ct BR7 . . . . . . .29 D2
Mulberry Cl
Gillingham ME7 . . . . .69 A4
Greenwich SE7 . . . . .11 D8
Meopham Sta DA13 . . . . . .50 B3
Royal Tunbridge Wells
TN4 . . . . .143 D1
Mulberry Ct Bexley DA16 .12 F5
Maidstone ME14 . . . . .100 B5
Mulberry Rd DA11 . . . . . . .35 A4
Mulberry Way DA17 . . . . . .4 C4
Mulgrave Ho 18 SE18 . . . . .1 F2
Mulgrave Prim Sch SE18 . .2 B3
Mulgrave Rd SE18 . . . . . . .2 A2
Mullein Ct 7 RM17 . . . . . .18 D8
Mullender Ct DA12 . . . . . . .37 A7
Muller Ho SE18 . . . . .2 A1
Multon Rd TN15 . . . . .61 E4
Munday Bois Cotts
TN27 . . . . .153 F8
Munday Bois Rd TN27 . . .137 E1
Munday Rd E16 . . . . .1 A7
Munday Works Est TN9 127 C1
Munford Dr DA10 . . . . .34 E8

Mungeam Ho ME1 . . . . . . .53 C4
Mungo Park Rd DA2 . . . . . .36 D3
Mungo Park Way BR5 . . . .44 D2
Munn's La ME9 . . . . .70 E6
Munnery Way BR6 . . . . . . .57 B8
Munnings Ho E16 . . . . .1 B5
Munsgore La ME9 . . . . . . .71 C6
Murchison Ave DA5 . . . . . .30 E7
Murrain Dr ME15 . . . . . . .101 A1
Murray Ave BR1 . . . . .42 B7
Murray Bsns Ctr BR5 . . . .44 B6
Murray Ho 15 SE18 . . . . . .1 F2
Murray Lodge TN2 . . . . . .159 D2
Murray Rd Orpington BR5 .44 B6
Rochester ME2 . . . . .53 C8
Murray Sq E16 . . . . .1 B6
Murton-Neale Cl 3
TN18 . . . . .189 A2
Mus of Artillery in the
Rotunda★ SE18 . . . . .1 F1
Muscovy Ho DA18 . . . . .3 E3
Museum of Kent Rural Life★
ME14 . . . . .83 D1
Museum St ME14 . . . . . . .99 F4
Muskerry Ct TN4 . . . . . . .158 B4
Musket La
Eyhorne Street ME17 . . . . .102 C2
Leeds ME17 . . . . .102 A2
Mussenden La DA3,DA4 . .47 E3
Mustang Rd ME19 . . . . . . .96 F3
Mycenae Rd SE3 . . . . .11 A8
Mynn Cres ME14 . . . . . . .101 A4
Myra St SE2 . . . . .3 A2
Myrtle Alley SE18 . . . . .2 A3
Myrtle Cl DA8 . . . . .14 E6
Myrtle Cres ME5 . . . . .67 F5
Myrtle Pl DA2 . . . . .13 B8
Myrtle Rd DA1 . . . . .32 D6
Myrtledene Rd SE2 . . . . . . .3 A1

N

Nadine St SE7 . . . . .1 C1
Nag's Head La
Bexley DA16 . . . . .13 B4
Rochester ME1 . . . . .53 D4
Nagpur Ho 4 ME15 . . . . . .116 E5
Nairn Ct RM18 . . . . .18 F5
Nansen Rd DA12 . . . . .36 D4
Napier Com Sch ME7 . . . . .54 D4
Napier Ct
2 Lewisham SE12 . . . . . . .28 B5
Maidstone ME14 . . . . .99 F7
Napier Rd Bromley BR2 . . .42 B5
Erith DA17 . . . . .7 F2
Gillingham ME7 . . . . .54 D4
Northfleet DA11 . . . . .35 F7
Royal Tunbridge Wells
TN2 . . . . .159 D2
Napoleon Dr TN12 . . . . . .148 D5
Napoleon Wlk ME17 . . . . .120 C5
Napwood Cl ME8 . . . . .69 D6
Nares Rd ME8 . . . . .69 D4
Narrow Boat Cl SE28 . . . . .2 D4
Narrow Way BR2 . . . . .42 E3
Naseby Ct DA14 . . . . .29 F4
Nash Bank DA13 . . . . .49 F7
Nash Cl ME5 . . . . .68 C2
Nash Cl 16 DA14 . . . . .30 A5
Nash Croft DA11 . . . . .35 E4
Nash Gn BR1 . . . . .28 A2
Nash La BR2 . . . . .56 A4
Nash St DA13 . . . . .50 A7
Nashden Farm La ME1 67 A8
Nashenden La ME1 . . . . . .52 F1
Nassau Path 6 SE28 . . . . .2 C5
Natal Rd ME4 . . . . .54 A3
Nathan Way SE28,SE18 . . .2 E3
Naylor's Cotts ME7 . . . . . .69 B1
Neal Rd TN15 . . . . .61 E5
Neale St ME4 . . . . .53 F2
Neatscourt Rd E6 . . . . .1 D8
Neills Rd TN3 . . . . .175 D2
Nellington Ct TN4 . . . . . . .158 B4
Nellington Rd TN3,TN4 . .158 B4
Nelson Ave TN9 . . . . .127 A1
Nelson Cl TN16 . . . . .72 C2
Nelson Ct ME5 . . . . .54 C1
Nelson Ho
8 Maidstone ME15 . . . . . .116 F5
Swanscombe DA9 . . . . . . .17 D2
Nelson Mandela Rd SE3 .11 C4
Nelson Rd Bromley BR2 . . .42 C5
Dartford DA1 . . . . .15 C1
Erith DA17 . . . . .3 F1
Gillingham ME7 . . . . .54 D4
Northfleet DA11 . . . . .35 F6
Royal Tunbridge Wells
TN2 . . . . .159 D2
Sidcup DA14 . . . . .30 A4
Wouldham ME1 . . . . .66 C5
Nelson Terr ME5 . . . . .54 C1
Nepicar Farm★ TN15 . . . . .79 D1
Nepicar La TN15 . . . . .79 D3
Neptune Bsns Pk ME2 . . .53 E7
Neptune Cl ME2 . . . . .53 E7
Neptune Way ME2 . . . . . . .53 E6
Neptune Wlk DA8 . . . . .4 D2
Nesbit Rd SE9 . . . . .11 D3
Nesbitt Ho DA6 . . . . .14 B2
Ness Rd DA8 . . . . .15 D8
Nestor Ct ME18 . . . . .114 A8
Nethercombe Ho 4 SE3 .11 A8
Nethewode Ct DA17 . . . . . .4 B3
Netley Cl ME14 . . . . .100 D6
Nettlestead Cotts TN12 146 A4
Nettlestead Ct ME18 . . . .113 C5

Nettlestead La ME18 . . . .113 A6
Nevill Ct ME19 . . . . .81 C1
Nevill Gate TN2 . . . . .159 B1
Nevill Lodge TN2 . . . . . . .159 C4
Nevill Pk TN4 . . . . .158 E3
Nevill Pl ME6 . . . . .82 A7
Nevill Ridge TN4 . . . . .158 D3
Nevill St TN2 . . . . .159 A2
Nevill Terr TN2 . . . . .158 F2
Neville Cl
Maidstone ME14 . . . . .100 B8
Sidcup DA15 . . . . .29 F4
Neville Rd ME4 . . . . .53 E2
New Acres SE28 . . . . .2 E4
New Ash Green Prim Sch
DA3 . . . . .62 F8
New Barn Pk BR8 . . . . . . .45 E8
New Barn Rd
Northfleet DA13 . . . . .35 C3
Sutton Valence ME17,
TN12 . . . . .134 C2
Swanley BR8 . . . . .45 F8
New Barn St E13 . . . . .1 B8
New Barns Rd ME14 . . . . .100 A8
New Bassetts Cotts
TN12 . . . . .163 B5
New Beacon Sch TN14 . .107 F8
New College of Cobham
DA12 . . . . .51 A5
New Cotts Bean DA2 . . . . .34 B5
Shipbourne TN11 . . . . .110 D5
The Moor TN18 . . . . .194 B7
Tilbury RM16 . . . . .19 B1
New Covenant Pl 4 ME1 53 D4
New Ct 3 TN9 . . . . .127 C2
New Cut Chatham ME4 . . .53 F4
East Farleigh ME15 . . . . . .115 D7
New Cut Rd ME14 . . . . . .100 D5
New Delhi Ho 5 ME15 . . .116 E5
New Eltham Sta SE9 . . . . .29 C7
New England Rd TN4 . . . .159 A7
New Farm Ave BR2 . . . . . .42 A5
New Ferry App SE18 . . . . . .2 A3
New Hall Farm La ME3 . . .25 B6
New House La DA11 . . . . . .36 A6
New Hythe La ME20 . . . . . .82 B3
New Hythe Sta ME20 . . . . .82 C4
New Inn Cotts ME15 . . . . .115 C7
New Lydenburg Commercial
Est SE7 . . . . .1 C3
New Lydenburg St SE7 . . .1 C3
New Mill Rd BR5 . . . . .44 C8
New Pond Rd TN17 . . . . . .190 D6
New Pound La ME15 . . . . .96 C1
New Rd Bexley DA16 . . . . .13 B5
Burham ME1 . . . . .66 F1
Chatham ME4 . . . . .53 F4
Cliffe ME3 . . . . .22 A4
Cranbrook TN17 . . . . .179 B4
Ditton ME20 . . . . .82 C1
East Malling ME19 . . . . . . .98 A8
Egerton TN27 . . . . .137 F3
Erith DA8 . . . . .3 D1
Fordcombe TN11 . . . . .141 A1
Gravesend DA11 . . . . .19 B1
Grays RM17 . . . . .18 B8
Headcorn TN27 . . . . .151 D5
Hextable BR8 . . . . .31 F1
Langley ME17 . . . . .117 C5
Limpsfield RH8 . . . . .104 B5
Meopham Sta DA13 . . . . . .49 F4
Orpington BR6 . . . . .44 A2
Paddock Wood TN12 . . . . .146 A6
Rochester ME1 . . . . .53 D4
Sundridge TN14 . . . . .90 E2
Sutton at H DA4 . . . . .47 D7
Swanley BR8 . . . . .45 F6
New Road Ave ME4 . . . . . .53 E4
New Road Hill BR2,BR4 . .56 F2
New Road Sch ME4 . . . . . .54 D4
New Sch at West Heath The
TN13 . . . . .108 B4
New St Chatham ME4 . . . . .53 E3
New Street TN15 . . . . .63 D4
Westerham TN16 . . . . .105 C8
New Street Hill BR1 . . . . . .28 C3
New Street Sta DA13,TN15 63 D4
New Strs ME4 . . . . .53 F6
New Swan Yd 8 DA12 . . . .19 B1
New Tavern Fort★ DA12 . .19 C1
New Town Cotts TN11 . . . .125 A2
New Villas ME15 . . . . .115 C7
New Wharf Rd TN9 . . . . . .127 B1
New Wlk TN15 . . . . .78 F3
New Years La BR6,TN14 . .74 A5
Newark Ct 1 ME2 . . . . . . .53 B7
Newark Knok E6 . . . . .2 A7
Newark Yd ME2 . . . . .53 B7
Newbarn La TN14,TN16 . . .73 C2
Newbery Rd DA8 . . . . .14 F6
Newborough Ct TN10 . . . .127 C6
Newbridge Pk TN12 . . . . .130 A1
Newbury Ave ME16 . . . . . .99 C6
Newbury Cl
Cliffe Woods ME3 . . . . .39 B8
Dartford DA1 . . . . .33 B8
Newbury Cotts TN15 . . . .185 B8
Newbury Ct DA14 . . . . . . .29 F4
Newbury La TN5 . . . . .185 C8
Newbury Rd BR2 . . . . .42 A6
Newcomen Rd TN4 . . . . . .159 A5
Newenden Cl ME14 . . . . . .100 D6
Newenden Rd ME2 . . . . . .39 C2

Newham Coll of FE (Royal
Docks Campus) E16 .....2 C5
Newham Way E13 ....1 B8
Newhaven Gdns SE9 ....11 D3
Newhaven La 4 E16 ....1 A8
Newhouse Terr TN8 ......122 C3
Newick Cl DA5 ....14 B1
Newing Gn BR1 ....28 D1
Newington CE Prim Sch
ME9 ....71 B7
Newington Ct TN5 ......186 E1
Newington Ent Ctr ME9 .71 C8
Newington Ho 9 BR5 ...44 D1
Newington Ind Est ME9 .70 F6
Newington Sta ME9 ....71 B6
Newington Wlk ME14 ...100 C6
Newitt Rd ME3 ....40 E5
Newland Green La
TN27 ....153 D8
Newland St E16 ....1 F5
Newlands TN3 ....158 A3
Newlands Ct 8 SE9 .....12 A1
Newlands Farm Rd ME4 .24 B4
Newlands La DA13 ....63 F1
Newlands Lodge DA8 ....14 D8
Newlands Rd TN4 ....159 B7
Newlands Rise TN4 .....159 A6
Newlands Way TN4 .....159 B7
Newling Cl E6 ....1 F7
Newlyn Cl BR6 ....58 A6
Newlyn Ct 1 ME14 .....100 A4
Newlyn Dr TN12 ....149 F5
Newlyn Rd DA16 ....12 F5
Newman Ct 11 BR1 ......42 A8
Newman Ho SE18 ....12 A7
Newman Rd BR1 ....42 A8
Newman's Rd DA11 ......35 F6
Newman Ho SE18 ....12 A7
Newmarket Gn SE9 ......28 D8
Newmarsh Rd SE28 ....2 F5
Newnham Cl ME8 ....55 C2
Newnham Lodge DA17 ....4 A1
Newnham St ME4 ....54 B3
Newnhams Cl BR1 ....42 F6
Newports BR5 ....22 D2
Newstead Ave BR6 ......57 E8
Newstead Wood Sch for Girls
BR6 ....57 D7
Newton Abbot Rd DA11 .35 F6
Newton Ave TN10 ......127 E7
Newton Cl Chatham ME5 .68 C2
  1 Maidstone ME16 .....99 E3
Newton Gdns TN12 ....145 F7
Newton Ho
  Swanscombe DA9 ....17 D2
  Woolwich SE2 ....3 C1
Newton Rd Bexley DA16 .13 A4
  Royal Tunbridge Wells
  TN1 ....159 B4
  Tilbury RM18 ....19 A5
Newton Terr BR2 ....42 D3
Newton Willows TN3 ...171 C7
Newtown Cotts TN12 ..149 E6
Niagara Ct ME18 ....97 B3
Nichol La BR1 ....28 A1
Nicholas Cl ME16 ....99 A3
Nicholas Ct SE12 ....28 A7
Nicholas Stacey Ho 4
  SE7 ....1 B1
Nicholson Ho SE18 ......11 E7
Nickelby Cl SE28 ....3 C7
Nicklaus Dr ME5 ....67 F3
Nickleby Cl ME1 ....53 C2
Nickleby Rd DA12 ....37 A7
Nicola Terr DA7 ....13 E6
Nicolson Rd BR5 ....44 D2
Nicolson Way TN13 ......92 D5
Nigeria Rd SE7 ....11 D7
Nightingale Cl
  Biggin Hill TN16 ....72 C4
  Gillingham ME8 ....69 E6
  Larkfield ME20 ....81 F2
  Northfleet DA11 ....35 E4
Nightingale Cnr BR5 ....44 D5
Nightingale Ct ME2 ......52 C6
Nightingale Gr 3 DA1 ..16 A3
Nightingale Ho SE18 .....2 A1
Nightingale La
  Bromley BR1 ....42 D7
  Goathurst Common TN14 .107 B5
Nightingale Pl SE18 ....12 B8
Nightingale Prim Sch
  SE18 ....2 B1
Nightingale Rd
  Kemsing TN15 ....76 C2
  Orpington BR5 ....43 C3
Nightingale Vale SE18 ..12 A8
Nightingale Way
  Newham E6 ....1 E8
  Swanley BR8 ....45 E6
Nightingales The
  Royal Tunbridge Wells
  TN4 ....159 A5
  Sissinghurst TN27 ....180 F8
Nile Path 6 SE18 ....12 A8
Nile Rd ME7 ....54 C4
Nimrod Ho E16 ....1 B8
Nine Acres Rd ME2 ......52 B3
Nine Elms Gr DA11 ......36 A8
Nine Hams Rd TN16 ......88 D6
Nineveh La TN17,TN18 ..189 E6
Ninhams Wood BR6 ......57 A6
Nita Ct SE12 ....28 A7
Nithdale Rd SE18 ....12 C3

Niven Cl ME3 ....39 C3
Nizels La TN11 ....125 F8
No 1 St SE18 ....2 B3
Noah's Ark TN15 ....77 B1
Noble Tree Cross TN11 .126 B6
Noble Tree Rd TN11 ...126 B6
Noel Terr 15 DA14 ......30 B4
Nook The ME18 ....113 F7
Norah La ME3 ....38 B3
Nordenfeldt Rd DA8 ......9 F1
Nore Cl ME7 ....54 E1
Norfolk Cl Chatham ME5 .68 C3
  Dartford DA1 ....16 A2
  Gillingham ME8 ....55 D2
Norfolk Cres DA15 ......29 E8
Norfolk Gdns DA7 ....13 F6
Norfolk Pl DA16 ....13 A5
Norfolk Rd
  Gravesend DA12 ....36 D8
  Maidstone ME15 ....116 C8
  Royal Tunbridge Wells
  TN1 ....159 B2
  Tonbridge TN9 ....127 A1
Norham Ct 25 DA2 ......16 B1
Norheads La TN16 ....72 B2
Norlands Cres BR7 ......43 B8
Norman Cl Gillingham ME8 69 B5
  Kemsing TN15 ....76 D2
  Maidstone ME14 ......100 B6
  Orpington BR6 ....57 C7
  Rochester ME2 ....52 F4
Norman Ct TN8 ....122 B2
Norman Par DA14 ....30 D6
Norman Rd Dartford DA1 .32 E7
  Erith DA17 ....4 B3
  Erith DA17 ....4 B5
  Royal Tunbridge Wells
  TN1 ....159 B5
  Snodland ME6 ....82 A6
  West Malling ME19 .....97 B8
Norman Rise TN17 .....179 D4
Norman St TN14 ....106 F5
Norman Villas 4 TN18 .188 F2
Normandy Prim Sch DA7 14 D6
Normandy Terr E16 ......1 B7
Normandy Way DA2 .....14 E6
Normanhurst Ave TN7,
  DA16 ....13 D6
Normanhurst Rd
  Borough Green TN15 ....95 A7
  Orpington BR5 ....44 B7
Normans Cl DA11 ....36 A8
Norreys Rd ME8 ....49 E7
Norrington Rd ME15 ...116 B6
Norris Ho 14 SE7 ....11 C8
Norris Way DA1 ....14 F4
Norstead Gdns TN4 ...159 B8
Norsted La BR6 ....74 B8
North Ash Rd DA3 ....62 F7
North Bank Cl ME2 ......52 F5
North Beckton Prim Sch
  E6 ....1 F8
North Borough Jun Sch
  ME14 ....100 A6
North Cl DA6 ....13 D3
North Cray Rd DA14 .....30 E4
North Cres ME17 ....115 D4
North Ct 4 Bromley BR1 .42 B8
  2 Maidstone ME15 ....100 A1
North Dane Way ME5 ...68 C4
North Down TN12 ......149 E4
North Down View ME17 .119 F6
North Downs Bsns Pk
  TN13 ....75 C3
North Downs Terr ME19 .80 A5
North Dr BR6 ....57 F4
North End Farm DA13 ...34 F4
North End La BR6 ....57 B2
North End Trad Est DA8 .14 E6
North Farm La TN2 ....143 E2
North Farm Rd TN2 ....159 C8
North Folly Rd ME15 ...114 F3
North Frith Pk TN11 ...110 F1
North Glade The DA5 ...30 F7
North Hill Rd TN8 .....188 C1
North Kent Ave DA11 ...18 C1
North Lockside Rd ME4 .54 D8
North Mdw ME18 ....96 D7
North Meadow Cotts
  ME19 ....96 D7
North Pk SE9 ....12 A1
North Pole La BR2 ......56 A4
North Pole Rd ME16,
  ME18 ....98 C2
North Pondside Rd ME4 .54 A8
North Rd Bromley BR1 ..42 B8
  Chatham ME4,ME7 .....54 B8
  Chatham ME4,ME7 .....54 A7
  Cliffe ME3 ....22 B6
  Dartford DA1 ....15 A1
  Goudhurst TN17 ....163 E1
  Woolwich SE18 ....2 E2
North Riding DA2 ....49 D6
North Side Three Rd
  ME4 ....54 C8
North St Bexley DA7 ....14 A3
  Biddenden TN27 ......168 A2
  Bromley BR1 ....42 A8
  Cowden TN8 ....155 A6
  Dartford DA1 ....32 D8
  Gravesend DA12 ....36 B8
  Headcorn TN27 ....151 C5
  Maidstone ME16 ....98 F2
  Rochester ME2 ....53 B7
  Royal Tunbridge Wells
  TN2 ....159 C3

North St continued
  Sutton Valence ME17 ..134 E8
North Street Cotts
  ME17 ....134 E8
North Terr ME3 ....39 F6
North View ME15 ....100 B1
North View Cotts ME15 .115 C7
North View Rd TN13,TN14 92 C6
North Way ME14 ....100 B7
North West Kent Coll
  DA12 ....36 F7
North West Kent College
  (Dartford Campus) DA1 32 C6
North Woolwich Old Sta
  Mus★ E16 ....2 A4
North Woolwich Rd E16 ..1 A5
North Woolwich Rdbt E16 1 D5
North Woolwich Sta E16 .2 A4
Northall Rd DA7 ....14 C5
Northbourne BR2 ....42 A2
Northbourne Rd ME8 ....55 B4
Northcote Rd
  Northfleet DA11 ....35 F7
  Rochester ME2 ....53 A7
  Sidcup DA14 ....29 E4
  2 Tonbridge TN9 ......127 B1
Northcourt Prim Sch
  DA12 ....36 E7
Northdown ME9 ....86 D8
Northdown Bsns Pk
  ME17 ....120 F6
Northdown Cl
  Lenham ME17 ....120 F6
  Maidstone ME14 ......100 B7
  Paddock Wood TN12 ..145 F6
Northdown Rd
  Bexley DA16 ....13 C5
  Kemsing TN15 ....76 E2
  Longfield DA3 ....48 E7
Northend Prim Sch DA8 .14 F6
Northend Rd DA8 ....14 F6
Northfield DA3 ....48 F6
Northfield Ave BR5 .....44 C3
Northfield Cl BR1 ....42 E8
Northfields
  Maidstone ME16 ....98 F2
  Speldhurst TN3 ....158 A8
Northfleet Cl ME14 ....100 C5
Northfleet Ind Est DA11 .17 F3
Northfleet Sch for Girls
  DA11 ....35 D6
Northfleet Sta DA11 ....18 B1
Northfleet Tech Coll
  DA11 ....35 D7
Northgate ME1 ....53 C6
Northgrove Rd 9 TN18 .188 F2
Northiam Sta★ TN31 ..197 C2
Northlands 5 BR1 ......42 C7
Northlands Ave BR6 ....57 E6
Northlands Cotts TN32 .195 C1
Northleigh Cl ME15 ....116 A6
Northolme Rise BR6 ....57 E8
Northover BR1 ....28 A4
Northpoint 12 BR1 ......42 A8
Northpoint Bsns Est ME2 53 D8
Northridge Rd ME12 ....36 C5
Northside Rd BR1 ....42 A8
Northumberland Ave
  Bexley DA16 ....12 E4
  Gillingham ME8 ....54 F5
Northumberland Cl DA17 .4 C7
Northumberland Ct
  Bexley DA8 ....14 C6
  Maidstone ME15 ......116 D7
Northumberland Gdns
  BR1 ....43 A5
Northumberland Heath Prim
  Sch DA8 ....14 B7
Northumberland Pk DA8 14 C7
Northumberland Rd
  Istead Rise DA13 ......35 F1
  Maidstone ME16 ......116 D8
  Newham E6 ....1 F7
Northumberland Way
  DA8 ....14 D6
Northview BR8 ....45 E7
Northview Ave RM18 ....19 A6
Northward Hill Nature
  Reserve★ ME23 ....23 E5
Northwood Ave ME23 ...23 E4
Northwood Pl DA18 ......3 F3
Northwood Prim Sch
  DA18 ....3 F3
Northwood Rd TN10 ...127 C6
Norton Cres TN10 .....127 B7
Norton Gr ME5 ....67 E3
Norton Rd
  Five Oak Green TN12 ..117 D1
  Royal Tunbridge Wells
  TN4 ....143 A1
Nortons La TN30 ......182 E5
Nortons Way TN12 ....145 B7
Norvic Ho ME8 ....14 F7
Norwich Ave TN10 .....127 D5
Norwich Cl ME2 ....52 E6
Norwich Pl 7 DA6 ......14 A3
Norwood Ct ME3 ....22 B4
Norwood Ct 5 DA1 .....16 A3
Norwood La DA13 ....50 B3
Notre Dame RC Prim Sch
  SE18 ....12 B8
Nottidge Rd TN4 ......158 D1
Nottingham Ave
  Maidstone ME15 ......116 D7
  Newham E16 ....1 C7
Nottingham Wlk ME2 ...52 D6
Novar Cl BR6 ....43 F2

Novar Rd SE9 ....29 C7
Nower The TN14,TN16 ..89 F8
Nuffield Hospl TN2 ....159 C3
Nuffield Rd BR8 ....32 A2
Nugent Ind Pk BR5 .....44 C5
Nunappleton Way RH8 .104 A3
Nunnery La TN11 ......156 F8
Nunnington Cl SE9 .....28 E5
Nursery Ave Bexley DA7 .13 F4
  Maidstone ME8 ....69 D8
  Maidstone,Bearsted ME14 101 B3
Nursery Cl Dartford DA2 .33 C8
  Flimwell TN5 ....187 B3
  Orpington BR6 ....44 A2
  Sevenoaks TN13 ....92 C5
  Swanley BR8 ....45 C7
  Tonbridge TN9 ....127 C1
Nursery Gdns
  Chislehurst BR7 ....29 B2
  Hoo St Werburgh ME3 ..40 E5
Nursery Ho DA4 ....47 C5
Nursery Pl TN13 ....91 D4
Nursery Rd Ditton ME20 .82 C1
  Gillingham ME8 ....69 D8
  Meopham Sta DA13 ....50 A4
  Paddock Wood TN12 ..145 F8
  Royal Tunbridge Wells
  TN4 ....159 B8
Nursery The DA8 ....14 F7
Nurstead Ave DA3 ......49 D6
Nurstead Church La
  DA13 ....50 A5
Nurstead La DA3,DA13 .49 D5
Nurstead Rd DA8 ....14 A4
Nut Tree Cl BR6 ....58 D7
Nutfield Cl ME5 ....68 B8
Nutfield Ct 7 BR1 ......42 A6
Nutfield Way BR6 ....57 B8
Nutfields TN15 ....94 B4
Nuthatch DA3 ....49 B7
Nuthatch Gdns SE28 .....2 D8
Nutley Cl BR8 ....45 F8
Nutmead Cl DA5 ....31 C7
Nuttall Ct BR5 ....44 B6
Nutwood Ct ME14 .....100 E4
Nuxley Rd DA17 ....4 A1
Nyanza St SE18 ....12 D8

O

O'Neill Path 11 SE18 ...12 A8
Oak Apple Ct SE12 .....28 A7
Oak Ave Biddenden TN27 .182 D7
  Gillingham ME7 ....54 E6
  Sevenoaks TN13 ......108 B7
Oak Cl Crayford DA1 ....14 F3
  Hoo St Werburgh ME3 ..40 E3
Oak Cotts TN8 ....123 B6
Oak Ct BR1 ....42 F7
Oak Dr Higham ME3 .....38 B4
  Larkfield ME20 ....82 B2
Oak End Cl TN4 ....143 A2
Oak Farm Gdns TN27 ..151 D6
Oak Farm La TN15 ......63 E1
Oak Hill Rd TN13 ....92 A2
Oak Ho 6 Chatham ME5 .67 F4
  3 Royal Tunbridge Wells
  TN2 ....159 C7
  13 Sidcup DA15 ....30 A5
Oak La Gillingham ME8 ..70 D8
  Headcorn TN27 ....151 D5
  Sevenoaks TN13 ......108 A8
Oak Lodge
  Royal Tunbridge Wells
  TN2 ....159 D2
  Sevenoaks TN13 ....93 A3
Oak Lodge La TN16 .....89 D2
Oak Rd Erith DA8 ....15 A5
  Erith,Northumberland Heath
  DA8 ....14 C7
  Five Oak Green TN12 ..145 B7
  Grays RM17 ....18 C8
  Gravesend DA12 ....36 C4
  Hoo St Werburgh ME3 ..40 E3
  Orpington BR6 ....58 A3
  Rochester ME2 ....52 E6
  Royal Tunbridge Wells
  TN2 ....159 D7
  Stone DA9 ....16 E1
  Westerham TN16 ....89 D2
Oak Terr 3 TN18 ......188 F2
Oak Tree Ave
  Maidstone ME15 ......116 C4
  Stone DA9 ....33 F8
Oak Tree Cl
  Marden TN12 ....148 D5
  Royal Tunbridge Wells
  TN2 ....159 A1
Oak Tree Gdns BR1 .....28 B3
Oak Trees Com Sch
  ME15 ....116 C7
Oak View TN8 ....122 B2
Oak Warren TN13 ......108 A6
Oakapple Ho 10 ME16 ..99 A3
Oakapple La ME16 ......99 A3
Oakbrook Cl BR1 ....28 B4
Oakcroft 3 SE12 ....28 B5
Oakdale La TN8 ....105 C3
Oakdale Rd TN4 ....158 F4
Oakdene Ave
  Chislehurst BR7 ....29 A3
  Erith DA8 ....14 C8
Oakdene Rd
  Orpington BR5 ....44 A3
  Sevenoaks TN13 ....92 A5
Oakenden La TN8 ......140 C2
Oakenden Rd DA13 .....50 E1

Oakenholt Ho 1 SE2 ....3 D4
Oakes Cl E6 ....1 F7
Oakfield Hawkhurst TN18 .188 F2
  Rolvenden TN17 ......192 A1
Oakfield Cotts TN17 ...190 D4
Oakfield Court Rd TN2 .159 B3
Oakfield Inf Sch DA1 ...32 D6
Oakfield Jun Sch DA1 ..32 D6
Oakfield La
  Dartford DA1,DA2 .....32 B6
  Orpington BR2 ....56 B6
Oakfield Park Rd DA1 ..32 D6
Oakfield Pl DA1 ....32 D6
Oakfield Rd
  Marlpit Hill TN8 ......122 B5
  Matfield TN12 ....161 D8
Oakfields TN13 ....92 B1
Oakham Dr BR2 ....42 A5
Oakhill Ho BR5 ....44 A8
Oakhill Rd BR6 ....57 F8
Oakhouse Rd DA6 ......14 A2
Oakhurst Ave DA7 ......13 C4
Oakhurst Cl Bromley BR7 .42 F8
  Chatham ME5 ....67 F3
Oakhurst Gdns DA7 ....13 E7
Oakland Cl ME5 ....67 F3
Oakland Villas TN3 ....171 B6
Oaklands Chislehurst BR7 .29 D2
  Cranbrook TN17 ......179 D4
Oaklands Ave DA15 .....29 D4
Oaklands Cl Bexley DA6 .13 F2
  Orpington BR5 ....43 C3
  West Kingsdown TN15 ..61 E4
Oaklands Ct BR6 ....57 C8
Oaklands Inf & Jun Sch
  ME5 ....67 F4
Oaklands Inf Sch TN16 .72 C3
Oaklands Jun Sch TN16 .72 C3
Oaklands La TN16 ......72 C5
Oaklands Rd Bexley DA6 .13 F2
  Groombridge TN3 .....171 B6
  Hawkhurst TN18 ......189 C1
  Northfleet DA11 ....35 F4
Oaklands Way TN11 ...126 F4
Oaklea Rd TN12 ....145 F6
Oakleigh Cl Chatham ME5 .67 E2
  Swanley BR8 ....45 C6
Oakleigh Ct TN12 .....162 F6
Oakleigh Gdns BR6 ....57 E6
Oakleigh Park Ave BR7 .43 A8
Oakley Cl 8 Newham E6 ..1 F7
  West Thurrock RM20 ...17 C8
Oakley Ct DA1 ....33 B7
Oakley Dr Orpington BR2 .56 D7
  Sidcup SE9 ....29 D7
Oakley Lodge SE12 .....28 A8
Oakley Pk DA5 ....30 C8
Oakley Rd BR2 ....56 E8
Oakmead Meopham DA13 .64 D8
  Tonbridge TN10 ......127 C6
Oakmead Ave BR2 ......42 A3
Oakmere Rd SE2 ....13 A8
Oakmont Pl 6 BR6 .....43 D1
Oaks Bsns Village The
  ME5 ....68 C1
Oaks Dene ME5 ....67 F1
Oaks Forstal TN18 ....196 C5
Oaks Rd TN30 ....193 B8
Oaks The Aylesford ME20 .82 E1
  Dartford DA2 ....16 B1
  Smarden TN27 ....152 F2
  Swanley BR8 ....45 E7
  Woolwich SE18 ....2 C1
Oakum Ct ME4 ....54 B2
Oakway Ct DA1 ....13 C1
Oakways SE9 ....12 B1
Oakwood Ave BR2 ......42 B6
Oakwood Cl
  Chislehurst BR7 ....29 A2
  Dartford DA1 ....33 B7
Oakwood Ct
  Maidstone ME16 ....99 D3
  Swanley BR8 ....45 C7
Oakwood Dr Bexley DA7 .14 C3
  Sevenoaks TN13 ....92 B4
Oakwood Gdns BR6 ....57 C8
Oakwood Ind Est DA11 .18 A2
Oakwood Park Gram Sch
  ME16 ....99 C3
Oakwood Rd
  Maidstone ME16 ....99 D3
  Orpington BR6 ....57 C8
Oakwood Rise
  Longfield DA3 ....48 E6
  Royal Tunbridge Wells
  TN2 ....159 E7
Oakwood Sch DA7 ......14 D3
Oasis The 7 BR1 ....42 C7
Oast Cl TN2 ....159 D7
Oast Ct ME18 ....113 F1
Oast Ho The 3 ME8 ....69 F8
Oast House Way BR5 ...44 B5
Oast La TN10 ....127 A4
Oast View TN12 ......163 A6
Oast Way DA3 ....48 E3
Oastfield Ct TN15 ......92 C2
Oasts The ME14 ......101 C4
Oastview ME8 ....70 A8
Oatfield Cl TN17 ......179 C5
Oatfield Dr TN17 ......179 C5
Oatfield Rd BR6 ....43 F1
Occupation La SE18 ....12 B6
Ocelot Ct 6 ME4 ....54 B3
Ockham Dr BR5 ....30 A1
Ockley Ct DA14 ....29 E5
Ockley La TN18 ....189 A3
Ockley Rd TN18 ....189 A2

Octavia Ct ME5 . . . . .68 B3
Octavia Way **12** SE28 . . . .3 B6
Odeon Ct **1** E16 . . . . .1 E3
Odeon Par SE9 . . . . .11 E3
Odiham Dr ME16 . . . . .99 C7
Offen's Dr TN12 . . . . .149 E3
Offenham Rd SE9 . . . . .28 F4
Officers Terr ME4 . . . . .53 F7
Officers' Rd ME4 . . . . .54 B8
Ogilby St SE18 . . . . .1 E2
Okehampton Cres DA16 . .13 C6
Okemore Gdns BR5 . . . . . .44 C5
Old Ashford Rd ME17 . . . .120 C5
Old Bailey The ME17 . . . . .119 E6
Old Barn Cl
  Gillingham ME7 . . . . .68 F6
  Kemsing TN15 . . . . .77 A2
  Tonbridge TN9 . . . . .142 F8
Old Barn Rd ME17 . . . . .81 E2
Old Barn Way DA7 . . . . .14 D4
Old Bexley Bsns Pk DA5 .31 B8
Old Bexley CE Prim Sch
  DA5 . . . . .30 F7
Old Bexley La DA5 . . . . .31 E6
Old Carriageway The
  Gillingham ME7 . . . . .68 F4
  Sevenoaks TN13 . . . . .91 C5
Old Castle Wlk ME8 . . . . . . .69 D4
Old Chapel Rd BR8 . . . . . . .45 C2
Old Chatham Rd
  Kit's Coty ME20 . . . . .83 D6
  Sandling ME14 . . . . .83 F1
Old Church La TN12 . . . . . .112 E4
Old Church Rd
  Burham ME1 . . . . .66 C1
  Mereworth ME18,TN12 . . . .112 D5
  Pembury TN2 . . . . .144 F2
Old Clem Sq **12** SE18 . . . .12 A8
Old Coach Rd TN15 . . . . . . .78 E5
Old Corn Stores The
  ME14 . . . . .101 C4
Old Court Ho The TN13 . . . .92 C3
Old Ctyd The BR1 . . . . .42 B8
Old Dairy The TN12 . . . . . .129 C6
Old Dartford Rd DA4 . . . . . .46 F3
Old Dover Rd SE3 . . . . .11 B7
Old Downs DA3 . . . . .48 E4
Old Downs The DA3 . . . . . . .48 E4
Old Dr ME15 . . . . .115 F6
Old Farm Ave DA15 . . . . . . .29 E6
Old Farm Gdns BR8 . . . . . . .45 F6
Old Farm Rd E DA15 . . . . . .30 A6
Old Farm Rd W DA15 . . . . .29 F6
Old Farmhouse The BR8 . . .31 E1
Old Fire Sta The SE18 . . . . .12 B7
Old Forge La ME9 . . . . .86 F3
Old Forge Way DA14 . . . . . .30 B4
Old Gardens Cl TN2 . . . . . .173 B8
Old Gdn The TN13 . . . . .91 D4
Old George Ct ME3 . . . . . . .39 F4
Old Hadlow Rd TN10 . . . . .127 F4
Old Ham La ME17 . . . . .120 A4
Old Hill Chislehurst BR7 . . . .43 A8
  Orpington BR6 . . . . .57 E4
Old Homesdale Rd BR2 . . .42 C5
Old House La Hartlip ME9 . .70 E4
  Langton Green TN3 . . . . . .157 D4
Old Kent Rd TN12 . . . . . . .146 A6
Old La Ightham TN15 . . . . . .94 C4
  Tatsfield TN16 . . . . .88 D6
Old Lain ME17 . . . . .119 F6
Old London Rd
  Badgers Mount TN14 . . . . .59 A1
  Halstead TN14 . . . . .74 E4
  Tonbridge TN10 . . . . .127 C4
  Wrotham TN15 . . . . .78 F4
Old Loose Cl ME15 . . . . . . .115 F5
Old Loose Hill ME15 . . . . .115 F4
Old Maidstone Rd
  Keycol ME9 . . . . .71 C7
  Sidcup DA14 . . . . .30 F1
Old Manor Dr DA12 . . . . . . .36 C7
Old Manor Way
  Bexley DA7 . . . . .14 D5
  Bromley BR7 . . . . .28 E7
Old Mill Cl DA4 . . . . .46 E1
Old Mill La ME20 . . . . .83 C3
Old Mill Rd
  Maidstone ME17 . . . . .101 F1
  Woolwich SE18 . . . . .12 D8
Old Oast Bsns Ctr The
  ME20 . . . . .83 A4
Old Orch Charcott TN11 . . .125 A3
  Sandhurst TN18 . . . . .196 B6
Old Orch The ME8 . . . . .70 A8
Old Orchard La ME19 . . . . .81 D1
Old Otford Rd TN14 . . . . . . .76 B1
Old Park Rd SE2 . . . . .3 A1
Old Parsonage Ct ME19 . . .97 C7
Old Pattens La ME4 . . . . . . .53 D2
Old Perry St
  Chislehurst BR7 . . . . .29 E1
  Northfleet DA11 . . . . .35 E4
Old Polhill TN14 . . . . .75 D4
Old Post Office La SE3 . . . .11 B4
Old Rd Chatham ME4 . . . . . .53 F4
  Crayford DA1,DA7 . . . . . . .14 D3
  East Peckham TN12 . . . . .130 A4
  Wateringbury ME18 . . . . .113 C7
Old Rd E DA12 . . . . .36 D7
Old Rd W DA11 . . . . .36 A7
Old Regent Dr TN17 . . . . . .191 E3
Old Riding School The
  TN3 . . . . .171 B2
Old Saw Mill The TN15 . . . .95 D5

Old Sch The BR6 . . . . .57 B5
Old School Cl ME17 . . . .120 D4
Old School Ct
  Chattenden ME3 . . . . .39 F4
  Egerton TN27 . . . . .137 F3
  Swanley BR8 . . . . .45 E7
Old School Ho The **3**
  TN8 . . . . .122 C1
Old School La ME19 . . . . . .80 F4
Old School Pl ME14 . . . . .100 A5
Old School The
  Goudhurst TN17 . . . . .177 E8
  Maidstone ME16 . . . . .98 E1
Old School Yd DA12 . . . . . .36 E8
Old Soar Manor* TN15 . . . .95 B1
Old Soar Rd TN15 . . . . .95 C1
Old Station Rd SE18 . . . . .184 E6
Old Tannery Cl TN30 . . . . .192 F7
Old Terry's Lodge Rd
  TN15 . . . . .78 A4
Old Timber Top Cotts The
  TN13 . . . . .92 C4
Old Tovil Rd ME15 . . . . . . .100 A2
Old Trafford Cl ME16 . . . . . .99 B6
Old Tramyard SE18 . . . . .2 E2
Old Tree La ME17 . . . . .116 D3
Old Tye Ave TN16 . . . . .72 E3
Old Vicarage The DA13 . . . .50 A1
Old Wardsdown TN5 . . . . .187 B3
Old Watling St
  Gravesend DA11 . . . . .36 A3
  Rochester ME2 . . . . .52 B8
Old Weavers Cotts
  TN17 . . . . .190 D5
Old Whetsted Rd TN12 . . .130 A3
Old White Hart Cotts
  TN16 . . . . .90 C3
Old Wik The TN16 . . . . .76 C2
Old Yard The TN16 . . . . . . .90 C3
Old Yews The DA3 . . . . .49 B6
Oldborough Manor Com Sch
  ME15 . . . . .116 B6
Oldbury Cl Oldbury TN15 . . .94 B5
  Orpington BR5 . . . . .44 D5
Oldbury Cotts TN15 . . . . . . .94 B6
Oldbury La TN15 . . . . .94 B6
Oldchurch Ct **3** ME16 . . .99 E3
  Gillingham ME8 . . . . .69 D8
  Maidstone ME15 . . . . .100 E1
Oldfield Cl Bromley BR1 . . .42 F5
  Bromley BR1 . . . . .42 F5
Oldfield Dr ME1 . . . . .66 C5
Oldfield Rd Bexley DA7 . . . .13 E6
Oldman Ct SE12 . . . . .28 B6
Oleander Cl BR6 . . . . .57 D5
Olive Rd DA1 . . . . .32 D7
Oliver Cl Chatham ME4 . . . .54 C5
  West Thurrock RM20 . . . . .16 F7
Oliver Cres DA4 . . . . .46 F2
Oliver Ct SE18 . . . . .2 C2
Oliver Gdns E6 . . . . .1 D8
Oliver North Ho ME15 . . . .114 E7
Oliver Rd
  Staplehurst TN12 . . . . . . .149 E4
  Swanley BR8 . . . . .45 D6
  West Thurrock RM20 . . . . .16 F7
  West Thurrock RM20 . . . . .17 A7
Oliver Twist Cl ME1 . . . . . . .53 B4
Olivers Mill DA3 . . . . .62 E8
Olivers Row ME14 . . . . . . .101 C4
Olivier Dr ME2 . . . . .39 F4
Olivine Cl ME5 . . . . .84 A8
Olliffe Cl ME5 . . . . .67 F2
Olron Cres DA6 . . . . .13 E2
Olven Rd SE18 . . . . .12 C8
Olyffe Ave DA16 . . . . .13 A5
Onslow Cres BR7 . . . . .43 B8
Onslow Dr DA14 . . . . .30 D6
Onslow Rd ME1 . . . . .53 D3
Opal Cl E16 . . . . .1 D7
Opal Gn ME5 . . . . .68 B2
Openshaw Rd SE2 . . . . .3 B2
Orache Dr ME14 . . . . .100 E5
Orange Court La BR6 . . . . . .57 A2
Orange Terr ME1 . . . . .53 D6
Orangery La SE9 . . . . .11 F2
Orbit Cl ME5 . . . . .84 A8
Orbital One DA1 . . . . .33 B6
Orchard Ave
  Aylesford ME20 . . . . .82 E1
  Bexley DA17 . . . . .13 F8
  Dartford DA1 . . . . .32 B7
  Gravesend DA11 . . . . .36 B3
  Rochester ME2 . . . . .38 F1
Orchard Bank ME17 . . . . .117 B1
Orchard Bsns Ctr
  Maidstone ME16 . . . . .99 C8
  Paddock Wood TN12 . . . .146 A8
Orchard Cl Bexley DA7 . . . .13 E6
  Coxheath ME17 . . . . .115 C3
  Edenbridge TN8 . . . . .122 B2
  Horsmonden TN12 . . . . . .162 F6
  Langley Heath ME17 . . . .117 E4
  New Barn DA3 . . . . .49 B7
  Royal Tunbridge Wells
    TN2 . . . . .159 D6
  Sevenoaks TN14 . . . . .92 C7
Orchard Cotts
  Chislehurst BR7 . . . . .29 E2
  East Farleigh ME16 . . . . .115 A8
  Nettlestead Green ME18 . .113 C1
Orchard Cres
  Horsmonden TN12 . . . . . .163 A6
  Wateringbury ME18 . . . . .113 D6

Orchard Ct
  Benenden TN17 . . . . .190 D6
  Sidcup DA15 . . . . .12 F2
Orchard Dr
  Edenbridge TN8 . . . . .122 B2
  Maidstone ME14 . . . . . . .100 E4
  Meopham Sta DA13 . . . . .49 F4
  Newington ME9 . . . . .71 A5
  Tonbridge TN10 . . . . .127 E5
Orchard Glade TN27 . . . . .151 E5
Orchard Gn Bromley BR1 . .42 C8
  Orpington BR6 . . . . .57 E8
Orchard Gr Larkfield ME20 .82 B2
  Orpington BR6 . . . . .43 F1
  Royal Tunbridge Wells
    TN1 . . . . .159 B5
Orchard Hill DA1 . . . . .14 E2
Orchard Ho DA8 . . . . .14 F6
Orchard Ind Est ME15 . . . .116 F3
Orchard Lea TN11 . . . . . . .126 F5
Orchard Pl Keston BR2 . . . .56 D2
  Maidstone ME16 . . . . .99 E3
  2 Maidstone ME16 . . . .99 E3
  Orpington BR5 . . . . .44 C6
  Sundridge TN14 . . . . .90 D3
Orchard Prim Sch DA14 . . .30 B3
Orchard Rd Bexley DA16 . . .13 B4
  Bromley BR1 . . . . .42 C8
  East Peckham TN12 . . . . .130 A6
  Erith DA17 . . . . .4 A2
  Northfleet DA11 . . . . .35 C6
  Orpington BR6 . . . . .57 B5
  Otford TN14 . . . . .75 F3
  Pratt's Bottom BR6 . . . . . .58 C1
  Sevenoaks TN13 . . . . .91 E5
  Sidcup DA14 . . . . .29 E4
  Swanscombe DA10 . . . . . .17 E2
  Tenterden TN30 . . . . .183 A3
Orchard Rise DA14 . . . . . .171 B7
Orchard Rise E DA15 . . . . .12 F2
Orchard Rise W DA15 . . . . .12 E2
Orchard St Dartford DA1 . . .15 E1
  Gillingham ME8 . . . . .69 E8
  Maidstone ME15 . . . . .100 A3
Orchard Terr DA9 . . . . .16 E2
Orchard The
  Maidstone ME14 . . . . . . .101 B4
  Sevenoaks TN13 . . . . .91 E6
  Swanley BR8 . . . . .45 D7
Orchard View
  Detling ME14 . . . . .101 A8
  Tenterden TN30 . . . . .193 C8
Orchard Villas
  Chainhurst TN12 . . . . . . .132 A4
  1 Chatham ME4 . . . . . .53 F3
  Chislehurst BR7 . . . . .29 E1
  Sidcup DA14 . . . . .30 C2
Orchard Way
  Cranbrook TN17 . . . . .179 B4
  Dartford DA2 . . . . .32 D5
  Horsmonden TN12 . . . . . .163 A6
  Kemsing TN15 . . . . .77 A2
  Oxted RH8 . . . . .104 A2
  Snodland ME6 . . . . .81 F7
Orchardlea DA13 . . . . .34 F3
Orchards Sh Ctr The DA1 .15 E1
Orchid Cl **1** Newham E6 . . .1 E8
  Rochester ME2 . . . . .52 C6
Orchidhurst TN2 . . . . .159 D7
Ordnance Rd
  Gravesend DA12 . . . . .19 C1
  Woolwich SE18 . . . . .12 A8
Ordnance St ME4 . . . . .53 E3
Ordnance Terr **9** ME4 . . .53 E4
Oregon Sq BR6 . . . . .43 D1
Orford Ct **7** DA2 . . . . . . .16 B1
Oriental Rd E16 . . . . .1 D5
Oriole Way Larkfield ME20 .81 F2
  Woolwich SE28 . . . . .3 B6
Orion Rd ME1 . . . . .67 C7
Orissa Rd SE18 . . . . .2 E1
Orlestone Gdns BR6 . . . . . .58 E5
Orlick Rd DA12 . . . . .37 B7
Ormiston Rd SE10 . . . . .1 A1
Ormonde Ave BR6 . . . . .57 C8
Ormsby Gdns ME8 . . . . .69 E3
Ormsby Point **8** SE18 . . . .2 B2
Orpines The ME18 . . . . . . .113 F7
Orpington By-Pass TN14 .59 A2
Orpington Coll of Further
  Education BR6 . . . . .44 A1
Orpington Hospl BR6 . . . . .57 F6
Orpington Rd BR7 . . . . .43 E6
Orpington Sta BR6 . . . . .57 E8
Orpington Trad Est **10**
  BR5 . . . . .44 C5
Orwell Cl Lunsford ME20 . . .81 F3
  Rainham RM13 . . . . .4 D8
Orwell Spike ME19 . . . . . . .97 A5
Osberton Rd SE12 . . . . .11 A2
Osborne Rd Bexley DA17 . .13 F8
  Gillingham ME7 . . . . .54 C5
Osbourne Rd DA2 . . . . .16 B1
Osgood Ave BR6 . . . . .57 F5
Osgood Gdns **1** BR6 . . . .57 F5
Oslin Wlk ME20 . . . . .97 C2
Osmers Hill TN5 . . . . .184 F7
Osmunda Ct TN2 . . . . .159 C4
Osney Ho **4** SE2 . . . . .3 D4
Osney Way DA12 . . . . .36 F6
Osprey Ave ME5 . . . . .54 C5
Osprey Cl E6 . . . . .1 E8
Osprey Wlk ME20 . . . . .81 F1
Ospringe Ct SE9 . . . . .12 D1
Ospringe Pl TN2 . . . . .159 F6
Osterberg Rd DA1 . . . . .15 F3
Osterley Cl BR5 . . . . .44 A8
Ostlers Ct **2** ME6 . . . . . . .82 F2

Otford Cl Bromley BR1 . . . .43 A6
  Sidcup DA5 . . . . .14 B1
Otford Court (St Michael's
  Sch) TN14 . . . . .76 E4
Otford La TN14 . . . . .75 B6
Otford Prim Sch TN14 . . . .76 B3
Otford Rd TN14 . . . . .76 B3
Otford Sta TN14 . . . . .76 C3
Otham La ME15 . . . . .101 C2
Otham St
  Maidstone ME15 . . . . .101 C2
  Otham ME15 . . . . .117 B7
Otley Rd E16 . . . . .1 C7
Otlinge Rd BR5 . . . . .44 D5
Ottawa Rd RM18 . . . . .19 A5
Otterbourne Pl ME15 . . . . .100 E1
Otterden Ct ME16 . . . . .57 E6
Otteridge Rd ME14 . . . . . .101 A3
Otters Cl BR5 . . . . .44 D5
Ottershaw Ho BR5 . . . . .44 B8
Otway Terr **1** ME4 . . . . . .54 A3
  Gillingham ME4 . . . . .54 D6
Otway St Chatham ME4 . . . .54 A3
Oulton Cl SE28 . . . . .3 C7
Our Lady of Grace RC Prim
  Sch SE7 . . . . .11 B8
Our Lady of Hartley RC Prim
  Sch DA3 . . . . .48 F4
Our Lady of the Rosary RC
  Prim Sch DA16 . . . . .12 C1
Our Lady's RC Prim Sch
  DA1 . . . . .15 D1
Oval The New Barn DA3 . . .49 C6
  Sidcup DA15 . . . . .30 A8
Ovenden Rd
  Sevenoaks TN14 . . . . .90 F6
  Sundridge TN14 . . . . .90 D6
Over Minnis DA3 . . . . .62 F7
Overcliffe DA11 . . . . .19 A1
Overcourt Cl DA15 . . . . .13 B1
Overdale TN14 . . . . .108 B2
Overmead Eltham DA15 . . .29 D8
  Swanley BR8 . . . . .45 E4
Overton Rd SE2 . . . . .3 D3
Overy Liberty DA1 . . . . .32 E8
Overy St DA1 . . . . .15 E1
Owen Cl East Malling ME19 .97 F8
  Woolwich SE28 . . . . .3 C5
Owenite St SE2 . . . . .3 B2
Owens Way **7** ME4 . . . . . .55 A6
Owl House Gdns* TN3 . . . .175 F7
Owletts* DA12 . . . . .50 F6
Owletts Cl ME15 . . . . .116 D8
Ox La TN30 . . . . .183 B2
Ox Lea TN3 . . . . .158 A3
Oxenden Wood Rd BR6 . . .58 C4
Oxenhill Rd TN15 . . . . .76 E2
Oxenhoath Rd TN11 . . . . .111 D4
Oxfield TN8 . . . . .122 D3
Oxford Cl DA12 . . . . .36 F6
Oxford Ct DA14 . . . . .29 E4
Oxford Mews ME5 . . . . .31 A8
Oxford Rd Gillingham ME7 .54 D3
  Maidstone ME15 . . . . .116 D8
  Sidcup DA14 . . . . .30 B3
Oxford St ME6 . . . . .82 A8
Oxhawth Cres BR2 . . . . . . .43 B3
Oxleas E6 . . . . .2 B7
Oxleas Cl DA16 . . . . .12 D5
Oxleas Wood Nature
  Reserve* SE18 . . . . .12 C4
Oxley Shaw La ME19 . . . . .81 E2
Oyster Catchers Cl E16 . . . .1 B7
Ozolins Way E16 . . . . .1 A7

P

Pacific Cl DA10 . . . . .17 E2
Pacific Rd E16 . . . . .1 A7
Packer Pl ME5 . . . . .68 A8
Packham Cl BR6 . . . . .58 C7
Packham Rd DA11 . . . . .35 F5
Packhorse Rd TN13 . . . . . . .91 C4
Packmores Rd SE9 . . . . . . .12 C2
Pad's Hill ME15 . . . . .100 A4
Padbrook RH8 . . . . .104 A6
Padbrook Cl RH8 . . . . .104 B6
Paddock Cl
  Fordcombe TN3 . . . . .157 B5
  Greenwich SE3 . . . . .11 A5
  Limpsfield RH8 . . . . .104 A4
  Orpington BR6 . . . . .57 B6
  Platt TN15 . . . . .95 C6
  Sutton at H DA4 . . . . .47 C8
Paddock Rd DA6 . . . . .13 E3
Paddock The
  Ashurst TN3 . . . . .156 F5
  Chatham ME4 . . . . .53 F4
  Dartford DA2 . . . . .33 E6
  Farthing Street BR2 . . . . . .56 E2
  Hadlow TN11 . . . . .111 E1
  Pembury TN2 . . . . .160 C6
  Vigo Village DA13 . . . . . . .79 F7
  Westerham TN16 . . . . .89 C1
Paddock Way BR7 . . . . .29 D1
Paddock Wood Bsns Ctr
  TN12 . . . . .146 A7
Paddock Wood Prim Sch
  TN12 . . . . .146 A6
Paddock Wood Sta
  TN12 . . . . .146 A7
Paddocks Cl BR5 . . . . .58 D8
Paddocks The
  Cowden TN8 . . . . .155 D7
  Gillingham ME7 . . . . .69 A5

Oct – Par 229

Paddocks The continued
  Sevenoaks TN13 . . . . .92 D3
Padsole La ME15 . . . . .100 A4
Padstow Cl **3** ME7 . . . . . .57 F6
Padstow Manor **1** ME7 . .54 C6
Page Cl DA2 . . . . .34 C5
Page Cres DA8 . . . . .14 F7
Page Heath La BR1 . . . . . . .42 D6
Page Heath Villas BR1 . . . .42 D6
Pageant Cl RM18 . . . . .19 C6
Pagehurst Rd TN12 . . . . . .149 B3
Paget Gdns BR7 . . . . .43 B8
Paget Rise SE18 . . . . .12 A7
Paget Row ME7 . . . . .54 C5
Paget St ME7 . . . . .54 C5
Paget Terr SE18 . . . . .12 B8
Pagitt St ME4 . . . . .53 E3
Paiges Farm Cl TN14 . . . .108 C2
Pains Hill RH8 . . . . .104 C4
Painters Ash La DA11 . . . . .35 D5
Painters Ash Prim Sch
  DA11 . . . . .35 D5
Palace Ave ME15 . . . . .100 A4
Palace Ct **5** Bromley BR1 .42 B8
  Eltham SE9 . . . . .11 F1
  Gillingham ME5 . . . . .54 D2
Palace Gr BR1 . . . . .42 B8
Palace Ind Est ME15 . . . . .116 F4
Palace Rd Bromley BR1 . . . .42 B8
  Hill Park TN16 . . . . .89 A6
Palace View Bromley BR1 . .42 B6
  Lewisham SE12 . . . . .28 A6
Palace Wood Inf Sch
  ME16 . . . . .99 C6
Palace Wood Jun Sch
  ME16 . . . . .99 C6
Palewell Cl BR5 . . . . .44 B7
Pallant Way BR6 . . . . .57 A7
Pallet Way SE18 . . . . .11 E6
Palm Ave DA14 . . . . .30 D2
Palmar Cres DA7 . . . . .14 A5
Palmar Rd Bexley DA7 . . . .14 A5
  Maidstone ME16 . . . . .99 D6
Palmarsh Rd BR5 . . . . .44 D5
Palmeira Rd DA7 . . . . .13 D4
Palmer Ave DA12 . . . . .36 D4
Palmers Brook TN11 . . . . .111 F2
Palmers Green La TN12 . .146 D3
Palmers Orch TN14 . . . . . .75 F8
Palmers Yd TN27 . . . . .151 E5
Palmerston Cres SE18 . . . .12 C8
Palmerston Rd
  Chatham ME4 . . . . .53 F1
  Grays RM20 . . . . .17 D8
  Orpington BR6 . . . . .57 C5
Pamela Ct ME7 . . . . .54 D5
Panbro Ho SE18 . . . . .11 F6
Panfield Rd SE2 . . . . .3 A3
Pankhurst Ave E16 . . . . .1 B5
Pankhurst Ho SE18 . . . . . . .12 A7
Pankhurst Rd ME3 . . . . .40 D6
Pannell Rd ME3 . . . . .27 A6
Panter's BR8 . . . . .31 F1
Pantiles The
  Bexley DA7 . . . . .13 F7
  Bromley BR5 . . . . .42 E6
  20 Royal Tunbridge Wells
    TN2 . . . . .159 A2
Panton Cl ME5 . . . . .68 C4
Pantyles The TN14 . . . . . . .107 B5
Papillons Wlk SE3 . . . . .11 A4
Papion Gr ME5 . . . . .67 E2
Parade The Crayford DA1 . .14 A1
  Gravesend DA12 . . . . .36 D6
  Kemsing TN15 . . . . .76 E2
  Meopham Sta DA13 . . . . .50 A2
  Rochester ME2 . . . . .52 E8
  Staplehurst TN12 . . . . . . .149 F3
  Swanscombe DA10 . . . . . .17 F2
Paradise Cotts ME9 . . . . . . .70 E5
Paradise Path SE28 . . . . .3 A5
Paradise Pl **14** SE18 . . . . .1 A7
Paragon Cl E16 . . . . .1 A7
Paragon The SE3 . . . . .11 A5
Parbrook Rd ME3 . . . . .24 B2
Parham Rd ME4 . . . . .53 F2
Parish CE Prim Sch BR1 . .28 A1
Parish Gate Dr DA15 . . . . .12 E1
Parish Wharf **5** SE18 . . . .1 E7
Park App DA16 . . . . .13 B3
Park Ave Bromley BR1 . . . . .28 A2
  Edenbridge TN8 . . . . .122 B2
  Gillingham ME7 . . . . .54 D3
  Gravesend DA12 . . . . .36 C7
  Maidstone ME17 . . . . .115 E2
  Maidstone, Penenden Heath
    ME14 . . . . .100 B6
  Northfleet DA11 . . . . .35 E7
  Orpington BR6 . . . . .58 B7
  Orpington BR6 . . . . .57 A8
  Tonbridge TN11 . . . . .126 F5
  West Thurrock RM20 . . . . .17 B8
Park Barn Rd ME17 . . . . . .118 C5
Park Cliff Rd DA9 . . . . .17 C3
Park Corner Rd DA13 . . . . .34 F4
Park Cotts
  8 Hawkhurst TN18 . . . .189 A2
  Sevenoaks TN13 . . . . .92 C2
Park Cres Chatham ME4 . . .67 F8
  Erith DA8 . . . . .14 D8
Park Crescent Rd DA8 . . . .14 D8
Park Dr Longfield DA3 . . . . .48 E6
  Woolwich SE7 . . . . .11 E8
Park Farm Houses ME20 . .98 B8
Park Farm Rd
  Bromley BR1 . . . . .42 D8

Park Farm Rd *continued*
Ryarsh ME19 80 F6
Park Gdns DA8 4 D2
Park Gr Bexley DA7 14 C3
Bromley BR1 42 B8
Park Hill Bromley BR1 42 F5
Meopham Sta DA13 49 F5
Park Hill Rd TN14 76 E2
Park Ho Maidstone ME14 100 B6
Sevenoaks TN13 92 C5
Sidcup DA14 30 A3
Park House Cotts DA4 60 F5
Park House Gdns TN4 143 A2
Park La
Gill's Green TN17,TN18 188 D7
Godden Green TN15 93 A4
Kemsing TN15 77 A1
Maidstone, Cock Stone ME17 116 D2
Maidstone, Ringlestone ME14 99 F7
Sevenoaks TN13 92 C3
Swanley Village BR8 46 C7
Park Manor ME7 54 B5
Park Mead DA15 13 B1
Park Mews BR7 29 B2
Park Pl 8 Bromley BR1 42 B8
Gravesend DA12 36 C8
Hever TN8 139 D4
Sevenoaks TN13 91 D4
Park Rd Addington ME19 80 C3
Bromley BR1 42 B8
Chislehurst BR7 29 B2
Dartford DA1 33 A8
Dunk's Green TN11 111 C5
Gravesend DA11 36 B7
Leybourne ME19 81 D3
Limpsfield RH8 104 A8
Marden Thorn TN12 149 A4
Mereworth TN12 112 F5
Orpington BR5 44 C4
Royal Tunbridge Wells TN4 159 B5
Royal Tunbridge Wells,Southborough TN4 143 A2
Swanley BR8 45 F5
Swanscombe DA10 17 E1
Park Road Ind Est BR8 45 F6
Park St TN2 159 C3
Park Terr Sundridge TN14 90 D3
Swanscombe DA9 17 B2
Park The DA14 30 A3
Park View
Hodsoll Street TN15 63 C2
Sevenoaks TN13 92 C3
Park View Cl TN8 122 B2
Park View Ct
2 Lewisham SE12 28 C5
Maidstone ME15 100 E1
Park View Rd DA16 13 C4
Park View Terr 2 TN30 193 A7
Park Villas ME14 100 E4
Park Way Coxheath ME17 115 D3
Joyden's Wood DA5 31 E5
Maidstone ME15 100 B1
Park Way Prim Sch ME15 100 B1
Park Wood Gn ME8 69 D5
Park Wood La TN12 150 C1
Park Wood Par ME15 116 F5
Park Wood Trad Est
Maidstone ME15 116 F4
Otham ME15 117 A4
Parkdale Rd SE18 2 E1
Parker Ave RM18 19 C6
Parker Cl Gillingham ME8 69 E5
Newham E16 1 E5
Parker Ho 4 SE18 2 B1
Parker Ind Ctr DA1 33 C7
Parker Rd RM17 17 F8
Parker St E16 1 E5
Parker's Cnr ME3 9 C2
Parkfield Hartley DA3 48 E5
Sevenoaks TN15 92 F4
Parkfield Rd ME8 55 F1
Parkfield Way BR2 42 F4
Parkfields ME2 52 C7
Parkgate Cotts BR6 59 C6
Parkgate Rd BR6 59 C6
Parkhill Rd Sidcup DA15 29 E5
Sidcup, Old Bexley DA5 30 F8
Parkhurst Gdns 2 DA5 31 A8
Parkhurst Rd DA5 31 A8
Parkland Cl TN13 108 D6
Parklands TN4 158 E8
Parkmore BR7 29 B1
Parkside Cliffe Woods ME3 39 B7
Halstead TN14 74 F6
Sidcup DA14 30 B6
Parkside Ave
Bexley DA1,DA7 14 E5
Bromley BR1 42 E5
Tilbury RM18 19 B5
Parkside Cotts TN16 88 E6
Parkside Cross DA7 14 E5
Parkside Ct TN30 192 F7
Parkside Lodge DA17 4 C1
Parkside Par DA1 14 F5
Parkside Rd DA17 4 C2
Parkview TN2 159 D4
Parkview Ct DA11 36 A6
Parkview Rd SE9 29 B6
Parkway Erith DA18 3 E3
Tonbridge TN10 127 D5
Parkway Prim Sch DA18 3 E3
Parkwood Cl TN2 159 C6
Parkwood Hall Sch BR8 46 B6
Parkwood Inf Sch ME8 69 E5
Parkwood Jun Sch ME8 69 E5
Parkwood Rd
Biggin Hill TN16 88 F6
Sidcup DA5 30 F8
Paroma Rd DA17 4 A3
Parr Ave ME7 54 D6
Parr Ct DA10 34 E8
Parrock Ave DA12 36 C7
Parrock Rd DA12 36 C7
Parrock St DA12 36 B8
Parrock The DA12 36 C7
Parrs Head Mews ME1 53 C6
Parry Ave E6 1 F7
Parry Pl SE18 2 B2
Parson's Croft TN8 139 C5
Parsonage Cl TN4 158 B5
Parsonage La
Cold Harbour ME9 71 F8
Lamberhurst TN3 176 B6
Rochester ME2 53 C8
Sidcup DA14 30 F4
Sutton at H DA4 33 B2
Parsonage Manorway DA17 14 A8
Parsonage Rd
Rusthall TN4 158 B5
West Thurrock RM20 17 C8
Parsons La Dartford DA2 32 B5
Stansted TN15 62 E1
Partridge Ave ME20 81 F3
Partridge Cl 1 E16 1 D8
Partridge Dr
Orpington BR6 57 C7
St Mary's Island ME4 40 B1
Partridge Gn SE9 29 A5
Partridge Rd DA14 29 E4
Partridge Sq 3 E6 1 E8
Pasadena Cvn Pk TN15 61 B1
Pasley Rd ME4,ME7 54 A7
Pasley Rd E ME7 54 B7
Pasley Rd N ME4 54 B7
Pasley Rd W ME7 54 A7
Passey Pl SE9 11 F1
Passfield Ho SE18 2 D2
Passfield Path 13 SE28 3 B6
Pastens Rd RH8 104 C4
Paston Cres SE12 28 B8
Pat Bassant Row DA10 34 E8
Pat Drew Ho BR1 42 C8
Patagonia Ho TN2 159 C3
Patch The TN13 91 E5
Patience Cotts TN14 108 B2
Patricia Ct Bexley SE2 13 B7
Chislehurst BR7 43 D8
Patrixbourne Ave ME8 55 C2
Pattenden Gdns TN12 130 A7
Pattenden La TN12 148 C7
Pattens Gdns ME1 53 E2
Pattens La ME1,ME4 53 E1
Pattens Pl ME1 53 D2
Patterdale Rd DA2 33 D7
Patterson Ct DA1 16 A2
Pattinson Point 14 E16 1 A8
Pattison Wlk SE18 2 C1
Paulinus Cl BR5 44 C6
Pavement The TN30 183 B3
Pavilion Gdns TN13 92 C3
Pavilion La ME18 113 A8
Pavilion The 5 TN9 127 B1
Pavings The ME17 102 C2
Paxton Ct 5 SE12 28 C5
Paxton Rd BR1 28 A1
Payne's La ME15 116 B7
Paynes Cotts TN13 75 D1
Paynesfield Rd
Tatsfield TN16 88 D7
Tatsfield TN16 88 D8
Peace Cotts ME15 131 D7
Peace St SE18 12 A8
Peach Croft DA11 35 E4
Peach Hall TN10 127 C6
Peacock Mews 7 ME16 99 E4
Peacock Rise ME5 68 A4
Peacock St DA12 36 C8
Peacock Wlk E16 1 B7
Peal Cl ME3 40 E5
Pear Tree Ave ME20 82 C1
Pear Tree Cl
Cranbrook TN17 179 D3
Swanley BR8 45 D7
Pear Tree La
Gillingham ME7 68 E7
Loose ME15 116 B6
Pear Tree Pl ME3 38 B3
Pear Tree Row ME17 117 B5
Pear Tree Wlk ME9 71 A5
Peareswood Rd DA8 14 F6
Pearl Cl E6 2 A7
Pearl Way ME18 97 C3
Pearse Pl TN3 176 B5
Pearson Way DA1 32 F6
Pearson's Green Rd TN12 146 D5
Pearson's Green Rd TN12 146 F3
Peartree Cl DA8 14 D6
Peartree Cotts ME8 70 B8
Peartree La DA12 38 A2
Peartree Way SE10 1 A2
Pease Hill TN15 62 F4
Peasley La TN17 177 D6
Peat Way ME3 10 D1
Peatfield Cl DA15 29 E5
Pebble Hill Cotts RH8 104 B6
Peckham Cl ME2 53 C8
Peckham Ct TN12 129 F6
Peckham Ho 6 BR5 44 D1
Peckham Hurst Rd TN11 111 E7
Pedham Place Est BR8 46 A4
Peel Rd BR6 57 C5
Peel St ME14 100 A6
Peel Yates Ho 12 SE18 1 E2
Peens La ME17 133 C7
Pegasus Ct DA12 36 C5
Peggoty Cl ME3 38 B3
Pegley Gdns SE12 28 A6
Pegwell St SE18 12 E7
Pelham Cotts DA5 31 B7
Pelham Ct 19 DA14 30 A5
Pelham Prim Sch DA7 14 A4
Pelham Rd Bexley DA7 14 A4
Gravesend DA11 36 A8
Pelham Rd S DA11 35 F7
Pelham Terr 4 DA11 35 F8
Pelican Cl ME2 52 C6
Pelican Ct ME18 113 E7
Pell Cl TN5 185 A6
Pellipar Gdns SE18 1 F1
Pellipar Rd SE18 1 F1
Pells La TN15 78 A7
Pemberton Gdns BR8 45 E7
Pemberton Sq 4 ME2 53 C8
Pemble Cl TN12 145 A7
Pembroke ME4 54 B8
Pembroke Cl DA8 4 D2
Pembroke Ct ME4 54 A4
Pembroke Gdns ME8 69 E4
Pembroke Par DA8 4 C1
Pembroke Pl DA4 47 B8
Pembroke Rd
Bromley BR1 42 D7
Coxheath ME17 115 C3
Erith DA8 4 D2
Newham E6 1 F8
Sevenoaks TN13 92 B2
Tonbridge TN9 127 A1
Pembroke Rise ME4 54 A7
Pembury Cl TN2 160 D7
Pembury Cres DA14 30 E6
Pembury Gdns ME16 99 D3
Pembury Gr TN9 143 C8
Pembury Grange TN2 160 A6
Pembury Hall Rd TN11, TN2 144 C3
Pembury Hospl TN2 160 B7
Pembury Rd Bexley DA7 13 E8
Pembury TN11 144 A2
Royal Tunbridge Wells TN2 159 E4
Tonbridge TN11,TN9 143 D7
Pembury Sch TN2 160 D8
Pembury Vineyard* TN2 144 F1
Pembury Way ME8 55 E2
Pembury Wlks TN11, TN2 144 C2
Pen Way TN10 127 E5
Pencroft Dr DA1 32 C8
Penda Rd DA8 14 B7
Pendant Ct BR6 58 A5
Pendennis Rd
Orpington BR6 58 C8
Sevenoaks TN13 92 B4
Penderel Mews TN30 193 B8
Pendlebury Gn SE18 11 E6
Pendragon Rd BR1,SE12 28 A5
Pendragon Sch BR1 28 A5
Pendrell St SE18 12 D8
Pendrill Pl TN5 184 F5
Penenden DA3 62 F8
Penenden Ct ME14 100 B7
Penenden Heath Rd ME14 100 C7
Penenden St ME14 100 A6
Penfold Cl Chatham ME5 68 B7
Maidstone ME15 116 E5
Penfold Hill ME17 118 B8
Penfold Ho 14 SE18 12 B8
Penfold La DA5 30 D7
Penfold Way ME15 115 F6
Penfolds Cl TN10 127 C5
Penford Gdns SE9 11 D4
Pengarth Rd DA5 13 D1
Penguin Cl ME2 52 D6
Penhale Cl BR6 58 A6
Penhall Rd SE7 1 D2
Penhill Rd DA5 30 C8
Penhurst Cl ME14 100 F5
Peninsular Park Rd SE7 1 A2
Penlee Cl TN8 122 C2
Penmon Rd SE2 3 A3
Penn Gdns BR7 43 B7
Penn La Bexley DA5 13 D1
Ide Hill TN14 106 E8
Penn Yd TN2 160 C6
Pennant Rd ME1 67 C7
Penney Cl DA1 32 D8
Pennine Way Bexley DA7 14 E6
Maidstone ME15 101 A1
Northfleet DA11 35 E5
Pennine Wlk TN2 159 D5
Pennington Manor 1 TN4 142 F2
Pennington Pl TN4 143 B1
Pennington Rd TN4 143 A2
Pennington Way SE12 28 B6
Penns Yd TN2 160 C6
Penny Cress Gdns ME16 99 C3
Penny Spring Farm (Cvn Pk) ME14 85 B2
Pennyfields TN17 179 D4
Pennyroyal Ave E6 2 A7
Penpool La DA16 13 B4
Penrith Ct ME7 55 A5
Penryn Manor 4 ME7 54 C6
Penshurst Ave DA15 13 A1
Penshurst CE Prim Sch TN11 141 A4
Penshurst Cl
Gillingham ME8 55 E2
New Barn DA3 49 D7
West Kingsdown TN15 61 E4
Penshurst Enterprise Ctr TN11 141 C4
Penshurst Pl* TN11 141 B4
Penshurst Rd Bexley DA7 13 F6
Penshurst TN3,TN11 141 A5
Poundsbridge TN11,TN3 157 E8
Penshurst Sta TN11 124 F1
Penshurst Vineyard* TN11 140 F2
Penshurst Way BR5 44 C5
Penstocks The ME15 99 D2
Pentagon Sh Ctr ME4 53 F4
Penton Ho 3 SE2 3 D4
Pentstemon Dr DA10 17 E2
Penventon Ct 3 RM18 19 A5
Pepingstraw Cl ME19 96 D7
Pepper Cl E6 1 F8
Pepper Hill DA11 35 C5
Pepperhill La DA11 35 C5
Pepy's Way ME2 52 F8
Pepys Cl 4 Dartford DA1 16 A3
Northfleet DA11 35 D5
Tilbury RM18 19 C6
Pepys Cres E16 1 A5
Pepys Rise BR6 43 F1
Perch La TN3 161 D1
Percival Rd BR6 57 B8
Percy Rd DA7 13 E5
Percy St 13 RM17 18 C8
Percy Terr TN4 159 A6
Peregrine Ct DA16 12 F6
Peregrine Rd ME19 97 A2
Peridot Ct ME15 116 E5
Peridot St E6 1 E8
Perie Row 9 ME7 54 A6
Perimeter Rd ME20 82 C3
Periton Rd SE9 11 D3
Perkins Cl DA9 16 F2
Perpins Rd SE9 12 E1
Perran Cl DA3 48 F5
Perry Gr DA1 16 A3
Perry Hall Cl BR6 44 A2
Perry Hall Prim Sch BR6 43 F3
Perry Hall Rd BR6 44 A2
Perry Hill ME3 22 C1
Perry Ho DA14 30 A3
Perry St Chatham ME4 53 E3
Chislehurst BR7 29 E2
Crayford DA1 14 E4
Maidstone ME14 99 F6
Northfleet DA11 35 F7
Perry Street Gdns BR7 29 E2
Perryfield St ME14 99 F6
Perrys La BR6,TN14 74 C6
Perth Ho 4 RM18 19 A5
Pescot Ave DA3 49 B6
Pested Bars Rd ME17 116 D5
Petchart Cl ME2 52 C3
Peter St 5 DA12 36 B8
Peterborough Gdns ME2 52 C6
Peters Cl DA16 12 E5
Petersfield TN2 160 E7
Petersfield Dr DA13 63 F1
Petersham Dr BR5 44 A6
Petersham Gdns BR5 43 F7
Peterstone Rd SE2 3 B4
Petham Court Cotts BR8 45 F4
Petham Gn ME8 55 C2
Petlands ME17 116 D5
Petrie Ho 3 SE18 12 A8
Pett La ME9 87 B7
Pett St SE18 1 E2
Petten Cl BR5 44 D1
Petten Gr BR5 44 D1
Petteridge La TN12 161 F7
Pettits Row TN12 147 D8
Pettman Cres SE28,SE18 2 D3
Petts Wood Rd BR5 43 D4
Petts Wood Sta BR5 43 C4
Petworth Rd DA6 14 A2
Peverel E6 2 A7
Peverel Dr ME14 101 A5
Peverel Gn ME8 69 D4
Peveril Ct 15 DA2 16 B1
Phalarope Way ME4 40 C2
Pheasant Cl E16 1 B7
Pheasant La ME15 116 B8
Pheasant Rd ME4 54 C2
Phelps Cl TN15 61 E4
Philimore Cl SE18 2 E1
Philip Ave BR8 45 D5
Philipot Almshouse SE9 11 F1
Philipot Path SE9 11 F1
Philippa Gdns SE9 11 D2
Phillips Cl DA1 15 B1
Phillips Ct ME8 55 B2
Philpots La TN11 125 E6
Philpott's Cross TN18 188 E2
Phineas Pett Rd SE9 11 E4
Phipps Ho 1 SE7 1 B1
Phoenix Cotts ME18 113 D6
Phoenix Ct 11 ME7 54 C6
Phoenix Dr Orpington BR2 56 D7
Wateringbury ME18 113 E7
Phoenix Ind Est ME2 53 D7
Phoenix Pk ME15 116 F4
Phoenix Pl DA1 32 D8
Phoenix Rd ME5 68 B2
Phoenix Yard Cotts ME18 97 F1
Picardy Manorway DA17 4 B3
Picardy Rd DA17 4 A2
Picardy St DA17 4 A3
Piccadilly Apartments 4 ME5 54 B3
Pickering Ct 20 DA2 16 B1
Pickering Ho 4 SE18 2 A2
Pickering St ME15 116 B6
Pickford Cl DA7 13 E5
Pickford La DA7 13 E5
Pickford Rd DA7 13 E4
Pickforde La TN5 186 D1
Pickhill Oast TN30 193 B4
Pickhurst La BR2 42 A1
Pickle's Way ME3 22 A6
Pickmoss La TN14 76 A3
Pickwick Cres ME1 53 C3
Pickwick Ct SE9 28 F7
Pickwick Gdns DA11 35 D5
Pickwick Ho DA11 35 D5
Pickwick Way BR7 29 C2
Piedmont Rd SE18 2 D1
Pier Approach Rd ME7 54 D7
Pier Par 3 E16 2 A5
Pier Pl ME2 40 A3
Pier Rd Erith DA8 14 F8
Gillingham ME7 54 E7
Newham E16 2 A4
Northfleet DA11 18 F1
Swanscombe DA9 17 B3
Pier Rd Ind Est ME7 54 D7
Pier Way SE28 2 D3
Pierce Mill La TN11 129 C6
Piermont Pl BR1 42 E7
Pigdown La TN8 139 D4
Piggott's Cross TN8 123 D7
Pigsdean Rd DA13 51 B2
Pike Cl Bromley BR1 28 B3
New Hythe ME20 82 A4
Pikefields ME8 55 C2
Pikefish La TN12,ME18 130 F2
Pikey La ME19 97 E5
Pile La TN12 150 A5
Pilgrim's Way Cotts TN15 77 A2
Pilgrims Ct Dartford DA1 16 A2
Greenwich SE3 11 A6
Pilgrims La RH8 88 D3
Pilgrims Lakes ME17 119 E6
Pilgrims Rd
Upper Halling ME2 65 F6
Wouldham ME1 66 E5
Pilgrims View
Sandling ME14 83 E3
Swanscombe DA9 17 C1
Pilgrims Way Boxley ME14 84 E3
Broad Street ME14,ME17 102 C6
Cuxton ME2 52 C3
Dartford DA1 33 B8
Detling ME14 85 B1
Eccles ME20 83 B6
Hollingbourne ME17 102 F3
Lenham ME17 120 B7
Thurnham ME14 101 E8
Upper Halling ME2,ME6, ME19 65 D3
Vigo Village ME19 80 B7
Wrotham TN15 79 A3
Wrotham TN15 79 C4
Pilgrims Way E TN14 76 D3
Pilgrims Way W TN14 75 E3
Pilgrims' Rd DA10 17 E3
Pilgrims' Way TN16 89 B4
Pilgrims' Way TN14,TN15 77 C3
Pilkington Rd BR6 57 C8
Pillar Box La
Crouch TN11 111 D5
Oldbury TN15 93 E5
Pilot Rd ME1 67 C8
Pilots Pl DA12 19 C1
Pimp's Court Cotts ME15 115 E6
Pimp's Court Farm Ctr ME15 115 E6
Pimpernel Cl ME14 101 B4
Pimpernel Way ME5 67 E4
Pinchbeck Rd BR6 57 F4
Pincott Rd DA6 14 A3
Pincroft Wood DA3 49 C6
Pine Ave DA12 36 D7
Pine Cl Larkfield ME20 82 A2
Swanley BR8 45 F5
Pine Cotts ME14 99 E8
Pine Glade BR6 56 F6
Pine Gr Edenbridge TN8 122 B2
Gillingham ME7 69 A5
Maidstone ME14 100 B6
Pine Ho 3 Chatham ME5 67 F5
5 Maidstone ME14 100 B4
Pine Lodge ME16 99 C3
Pine Lodge Touring Pk ME17 101 F2
Pine Pl ME15 99 E1
Pine Rd ME2 52 F6
Pine Ridge TN10 127 B6
Pine Rise DA13 50 A3
Pine Tree La TN15 94 A2
Pine View TN15 95 C7
Pinecrest Gdns BR6 57 B6
Pinecroft DA16 13 A7
Pinehurst Chislehurst BR7 29 B2
Sevenoaks TN14 92 E6
Pinehurst Wlk 4 BR6 43 D1
Pineneedle La TN13 92 B4
Pines Rd BR1 42 E7
Pinesfield La ME19 80 B6
Pinewood BR7 29 A2

Pinewood Ave
Sevenoaks TN13 .92 D6
Sidcup DA15 .29 E7
Pinewood Cl
Orpington BR6 .43 D1
Paddock Wood TN12 .145 F6
Pinewood Ct TN4 .143 A1
Pinewood Dr
Chatham ME5 .84 D8
Orpington BR6 .57 E5
Pinewood Gdns TN4 .143 A1
Pinewood Pl DA2 .31 E6
Pinewood Rd Bexley SE2 .13 D8
Bromley BR2 .42 A5
Royal Tunbridge Wells TN2 .159 D5
Pinkham TN12 .130 A5
Pinkham Gdns TN12 .130 A6
Pinks Hill BR8 .45 E4
Pinnacle Hill DA7 .14 B3
Pinnacle Hill N DA7 .14 B3
Pinnacles The ME4 .40 C1
Pinnell Rd SE9 .11 D3
Pinnock La TN12 .149 E1
Pinnock's Ave DA11 .36 B7
Pintail Cl Grain ME3 .27 B6
Newham E6 .1 E8
Pintails The ME4 .40 B1
Pinto Way SE3 .11 B3
Pinton Hill TN5 .186 B3
Pioneer Cotts TN11 .141 A1
Pioneer Ct 5 DA11 .19 A1
Pioneer Way BR8 .45 E6
Pip's View ME3 .22 F5
Piper's Green Rd TN16 .106 B7
Pipers Cl TN5 .185 A4
Pipers La TN16 .106 A8
Pippenhall SE9 .12 B1
Pippin Cl ME17 .115 B2
Pippin Croft ME7 .69 A6
Pippin Rd TN12 .129 F6
Pippin Way ME19 .97 A2
Pippins The DA13 .50 A3
Pirbright Cl ME5 .68 D2
Pirie St E16 .1 B5
Pirrip Cl DA12 .36 F6
Pit La TN8 .122 C4
Pitchfont La RH8 .104 B8
Pitfield DA3 .48 F5
Pitfield Cres SE28 .3 A5
Pitfield Dr DA13 .63 F7
Pitfold Cl SE12 .11 B1
Pitfold Rd SE12 .11 A1
Pitt Rd
Chartway Street ME17 .118 A2
Maidstone ME16 .99 B1
Orpington BR6 .57 C6
Pittlesden TN30 .193 A7
Pittlesden Pl 1 TN30 .193 A7
Pittsmead Ave BR2 .42 A2
Pittswood Cotts TN11 .128 A8
Pix's La TN17 .192 A3
Pixot Hill TN12 .146 B2
Pizien Well Rd ME18 .113 B7
Place Farm Ave BR6 .43 D1
Place La ME9 .70 D4
Plain Rd TN12 .148 C4
Plain The TN17 .177 E8
Plains Ave ME15 .100 C1
Plaistow Gr BR1 .28 B1
Plaistow La BR1 .42 C8
Plaistow Sq ME14 .100 C6
Plane Ave DA11 .35 D8
Plane Tree Ho SE7 .1 D1
Plane Wlk TN10 .127 C7
Plantagenet Ho SE18 .1 F3
Plantation Cl DA9 .16 F1
Plantation Dr BR5 .44 D1
Plantation La ME14 .101 A3
Plantation Rd Erith DA8 .15 A6
Gillingham ME7 .55 A6
Hextable BR8 .32 A2
Plantation The SE3 .11 A5
Plat The TN8 .122 D1
Platt CE Prim Sch TN15 .95 C7
Platt Comm TN15 .95 C7
Platt House La TN15 .79 C6
Platt Ind Est TN15 .95 C8
Platt Mill Cl TN15 .95 B7
Platt Mill Terr TN15 .95 B7
Platt The Frant TN3 .173 B1
Sutton Valence ME17 .134 E7
Platt's Heath Prim Sch ME17 .119 F2
Platters The ME8 .69 C7
Plaxdale Green Rd TN15 .78 D7
Plaxtol Cl BR1 .42 C8
Plaxtol La TN15,TN11 .110 D8
Plaxtol Prim Sch TN15 .110 E7
Plaxtol Rd DA8 .14 A7
Playstool Cl ME9 .71 B6
Playstool Rd ME9 .71 A6
Pleasance Rd BR5 .44 B6
Pleasant Row 10 ME7 .54 A6
Pleasant Valley La ME15 .115 B4
Pleasant View 15 Erith DA8 .4 E1
Orpington BR6 .57 C5
Pleasaunce Ct SE9 .11 F3
Pleasure House La ME17 .135 A8
Plewis Ho ME7 .54 E7
Plomley Cl ME8 .69 D4
Plough Cotts ME17 .117 D2
Plough Hill TN15 .94 F4
Plough Wents Rd ME17 .117 B2
Plough Wlk TN8 .122 C3
Ploughmans Way
Chatham ME5 .68 A1
Gillingham ME8 .69 E6
Plover Cl Chatham ME5 .68 D1
Marlpit Hill TN8 .122 C3
Plover Rd ME20 .81 F2
Plowenders Cl ME19 .80 D2
Pluckley Cl ME8 .55 C3
Pluckley Rd TN27 .153 D2
Plug La DA13 .64 D5
Plum La SE18 .12 C7
Plum Tree Cotts TN18 .194 E8
Plum Tree La ME9 .86 B8
Plumcroft Prim Sch SE18 .12 C8
Plumey Feather Cotts TN6 .170 E3
Plummer La TN30 .192 F6
Plummers Croft TN13 .91 E6
Plumpton Wlk 9 ME15 .116 F6
Plumstead Common Rd SE18 .12 C8
Plumstead High St SE18, SE2 .2 E2
Plumstead Manor Sch SE18 .12 D8
Plumstead Rd SE18 .2 C2
Plumstead Sta SE18 .2 D2
Plumtree Gr ME7 .69 A4
Plumtree Rd TN27 .150 F7
Plumtrees ME16 .99 A2
Plymouth Dr TN13 .92 C3
Plymouth Pk TN13 .92 C3
Plymouth Rd Bromley BR1 42 B8
Newham E16 .1 A8
Plympton Cl 8 DA17 .3 E3
Plymstock Rd DA16 .13 C7
Poachers Cl ME5 .68 C5
Pochard Cl ME4 .40 B1
Pocket Hill TN13 .108 A7
Pococks Bank TN8 .123 C3
Podkin Wood ME5 .83 F8
Pointer Cl SE28 .3 D7
Pointer Sch The SE3 .11 A7
Polebrook Rd SE3 .11 C4
Polegate Cotts RM17 .17 E8
Polesden Rd TN2 .159 D2
Polesteeple Hill TN16 .72 D2
Polhill TN13,TN14 .75 C4
Polhill Dr ME5 .67 F2
Police Station Rd ME19 .97 C8
Pollard Cl E16 .1 A6
Pollard Ct ME7 .54 C5
Pollard Wlk DA14 .30 C2
Pollards Oak Cres RH8 .104 A3
Pollards Oak Rd RH8 .104 A3
Pollards Wood Hill RH8 104 B5
Pollards Wood Rd RH8 .104 B4
Polley Cl TN2 .160 D7
Pollyhaugh DA4 .60 E7
Polperro Cl BR6 .43 F3
Polthorne Gr SE18 .2 D2
Polytechnic St 14 SE18 .2 A2
Pond Cl SE3 .11 A5
Pond Farm Rd
Hucking ME17 .86 D1
Oad Street ME9 .71 F1
Pond Hill ME3 .22 B6
Pond La TN15 .93 E2
Pond Path BR7 .29 B2
Pondfield La DA12 .37 E1
Pondfield Rd BR6 .57 B7
Pondwood Rise BR6 .43 E2
Pontefract Rd BR1 .28 A3
Pontoise Cl TN13 .91 F5
Pook La TN27 .168 D3
Poona Rd TN1 .159 B2
Pootings Rd TN8 .122 E7
Pope Dr TN12 .149 E4
Pope House La TN30 .183 B4
Pope Rd BR2 .42 D4
Pope St ME16 .99 C2
Pope Street Ct SE9 .28 F7
Popes La RH8 .121 A8
Popes Row Cotts TN17 .176 F2
Popes Wood ME14 .100 F6
Poplar Ave
Gravesend DA12 .36 C4
Orpington BR6 .57 B8
Poplar Cl
Hoo St Werburgh ME3 .40 E3
Rochester ME2 .52 F5
Poplar Field TN30 .199 D4
Poplar Gr ME16 .99 C5
Poplar Mount DA17 .4 C2
Poplar Pl SE28 .3 C6
Poplar Rd Rochester ME2 .52 E5
Wittersham TN30 .199 D4
Poplar Wlk DA13 .50 B3
Poplars Cl DA3 .49 C6
Poplars The DA12 .36 E8
Poplicans Rd ME2 .52 B3
Poppy Cl Erith DA17 .4 B4
Gillingham ME7 .54 E5
Maidstone ME16 .99 D3
Porchester Cl Hartley DA3 48 F5
Loose ME15 .116 A6
Porchfield Cl DA12 .36 C6
Porcupine Cl SE9 .28 E6
Porrington Cl BR7 .43 A8
Port Ave DA9 .17 B1
Port Cl Chatham ME5 .68 B3
Maidstone ME14 .101 A5
Port Hill BR6 .74 B7
Port Rise ME4 .53 F3
Port Victoria Rd ME3 .27 C4
Porter Cl RM20 .17 C8
Porter Rd E6 .1 F7
Porters Cl TN12 .161 F6
Porters Wlk ME17 .117 E4
Porters Wood TN12 .161 E6
Porteus Ct DA1 .32 D6
Porthkerry Ave DA16 .13 A3
Portland Ave
Gravesend DA12 .36 B6
Sidcup DA15 .13 A1
Portland Cl TN10 .127 D7
Portland Cres SE9 .28 E6
Portland Pl 1 ME6 .82 A8
Portland Rd
Bromley,Mottingham SE9 .28 E6
Bromley,Sundridge BR1 .28 C3
Gillingham ME7 .54 E6
Gravesend DA12 .36 B7
Northfleet DA11 .18 D1
Wouldham ME1 .66 C4
Portland St 1 ME4 .54 B2
Portland Villas DA12 .36 B7
Portman Cl Bexley DA7 .13 E4
Maypole DA5 .31 E7
Portman Pk TN9 .127 C3
Portmeadow Wlk SE2 .3 D4
Portobello Par TN15 .62 A2
Portree Mews ME7 .54 E3
Portsdown Cl ME16 .99 B2
Portsea Rd RM18 .19 C6
Portsmouth Cl ME2 .52 D6
Portsmouth Mews E16 .1 B5
Portway Gdns SE18 .11 D7
Portway Rd ME3 .39 B7
Post Barn Rd ME4 .53 F2
Post Office Rd 12 TN18 .188 F2
Post Office Sq TN1 .159 A3
Postern La TN9,TN11 .127 E1
Postley Commercial Ctr ME15 .100 A2
Postley Rd ME15 .100 A1
Postmill Dr ME15 .99 F1
Pot Kiln La TN26 .169 E4
Potash La TN15 .95 C6
Potter's La TN18 .189 A6
Pottery Rd Coldblow DA5 .31 C6
Hoo St Werburgh ME3 .40 D5
Potyn Ho ME1 .53 C4
Poulters Wood BR2 .56 D5
Pound Bank Cl TN15 .61 F2
Pound Cl BR6 .57 D8
Pound Court Dr BR6 .57 D8
Pound Green Ct 4 DA5 .31 A8
Pound Ho TN11 .128 E8
Pound La Halstead TN14 .74 D4
Sevenoaks TN13 .92 C3
Pound Park Rd SE7 .1 D2
Pound Pl SE9 .12 A1
Pound Rd TN12 .129 F6
Poundfield Rd TN18 .196 B5
Poundsbridge Hill TN11, TN3 .157 D7
Poundsbridge La TN11 .141 D2
Pounsley Rd TN13 .91 E6
Pout Rd ME6 .81 F7
Poverest Prim Sch BR5 .44 A4
Poverest Rd BR5 .44 A4
Povey Ave ME2 .39 C2
Powder Mill La
Dartford DA1 .32 F6
Leigh TN11 .126 B1
Royal Tunbridge Wells TN4 .159 B8
Tonbridge TN11 .126 E2
Powdermill Cl TN4 .159 C8
Powell Ave DA2 .33 E6
Powell Cl ME20 .83 A3
Power Ind Est DA8 .15 A6
Power Station Rd ME3 .27 B4
Powerscroft Rd DA14 .30 C2
Powis St SE18 .2 A3
Powlett Rd ME2 .39 C1
Powster Rd BR1 .28 B3
Powys Cl DA7 .13 D8
Poynder Rd RM18 .19 B6
Poynings Cl BR6 .58 C8
Poyntell Cres BR7 .43 D8
Poyntell Rd TN12 .149 F4
Pragnell Rd SE12 .28 B6
Prall's La TN12 .145 E2
Pratling St ME20 .83 C4
Pratts Bottom Prim Sch TN14 .74 C8
Premier Bsns Ctr ME4 .54 C1
Premier Par ME20 .82 E1
Prentiss Ct SE7 .1 D2
Prescott Ave BR5 .43 B3
Presentation Ho 9 DA12 36 B8
Prestbury Sq SE9 .28 F4
Preston Ave ME7 .54 E1
Preston Ct DA14 .29 F4
Preston Dr DA7 .13 D6
Preston Hall Hospl ME20 82 F1
Preston Ho
Sutton at H DA4 .47 D7
1 Woolwich SE18 .2 A2
Preston Rd
Northfleet DA11 .35 E7
Tonbridge TN9 .127 A1
Preston Way ME8 .55 B2
Prestons Rd BR2 .56 A8
Prestwood Cl SE18 .13 A8
Pretoria Ho 4 Erith DA8 .14 E7
8 Maidstone ME15 .116 E5
Pretoria Rd Chatham ME4 .53 F2
Gillingham ME7 .54 D3
Prettymans La TN8 .122 F4
Pridmore Rd ME6 .81 F8
Priest Hill RH8 .104 B6
Priest's Wlk DA12 .37 A6
Priestdale Ct ME4 .53 E3
Priestfield Rd ME7 .54 E5
Priestfield Stad (Gillingham FC) ME7 .54 E5
Priestfields ME1 .53 B3
Priestlands Park Rd DA15 .29 F5
Priestley Dr
Lunsford ME20 .81 F4
Tonbridge TN10 .127 E7
Priestwood Rd DA13 .64 C5
Primmett Cl TN15 .61 E4
Primrose Ave ME8 .69 B5
Primrose Cl ME4 .67 E7
Primrose Dr ME20 .82 D1
Primrose Ho 10 ME15 .116 E7
Primrose Rd ME2 .65 E5
Primrose Terr DA12 .36 C7
Primrose Wlk TN12 .146 A5
Prince Arthur Rd ME7 .54 B6
Prince Charles Ave
Chatham ME5 .68 B4
Sutton at H DA4 .47 D7
Prince Consort Dr BR7 .43 D8
Prince Henry Rd SE7 .11 D7
Prince Imperial Rd
Chislehurst BR7 .29 B1
Woolwich SE18 .11 F6
Prince John Rd SE9 .11 E2
Prince Michael of Kent Ct DA1 .15 A5
Prince Of Wales Rd SE3 .11 A6
Prince Phillip Lodge The ME20 .82 F1
Prince Regent La E16 .1 C7
Prince Regent Sta E16 .1 C6
Prince Rupert Rd SE9 .11 F3
Prince's Plain BR2 .42 E1
Prince's St Rochester ME1 53 C4
Royal Tunbridge Wells TN2 .159 C3
Princes Ave Chatham ME5 .68 B5
Dartford DA2 .33 B7
Orpington BR5 .43 E4
Princes Cl DA14 .30 D5
Princes Plain Prim Sch BR2 .42 E2
Princes Rd Dartford DA1 .32 D7
Dartford,Fleet-Downs DA1 .33 C7
Gravesend DA12 .36 C5
Hextable BR8 .32 A2
Princes St
Gravesend DA11 .19 B1
Maidstone ME14 .100 A5
Princes View DA1 .33 A7
Princes Way ME14 .85 A1
Princess Alice Way SE28 .2 D4
Princess Cl SE28 .3 D7
Princess Margaret Rd RM18 .20 D7
Princess Mary Ave ME4 .54 B7
Princess Par BR6 .57 A7
Princess Royal University Hospl BR6 .57 A6
Princess St DA7 .13 F4
Prinys Dr ME8 .69 C4
Priolo Rd SE7 .1 C1
Prior's Way TN8 .155 A6
Prioress Cres DA9 .17 C3
Priors Heath TN17 .177 C2
Priorsdean Cl ME16 .98 E1
Priorsford Ave BR5 .44 B5
Priory Ave BR5 .43 D3
Priory Cl Bromley BR7 .42 F6
Dartford DA1 .15 D2
East Farleigh ME15 .115 B8
Priory Ct 5 Dartford DA1 .15 D1
Gillingham ME8 .55 A2
Rochester ME1 .53 D5
Priory Ctr The DA1 .32 E8
Priory Dr SE2 .3 D1
Priory Fields DA4 .60 F8
Priory Gate 4 ME14 .100 A5
Priory Gdns Dartford DA1 .15 D2
★ Orpington BR6 .44 B2
Priory Gr Aylesford ME20 .82 D1
Tonbridge TN9 .143 B8
Priory Hill DA1 .15 D1
Priory Ho 4 SE7 .11 C8
Priory Hospl Hayes Grove The BR2 .56 A8
Priory La DA4 .46 F1
Priory Leas SE9 .28 E7
Priory Mews DA2 .33 C8
Priory Pl DA1 .15 D1
Priory Rd Dartford DA1 .15 D1
Dartford DA1 .15 D2
Gillingham ME8 .55 A2
Maidstone ME15 .100 A3
Rochester ME2 .53 A6
Tonbridge TN9 .143 C8
Priory Retail Pk DA1 .15 D2
Priory Sch The BR5 .44 C1
Priory St TN9 .143 B8
Priory Way TN30 .193 C7
Priory Wlk TN9 .143 B8
Pristling La TN12 .165 B8
Pritchard Ct ME7 .54 C3
Progress Est The ME15 .117 A4
Prospect Ave ME2 .53 B8
Prospect Cl DA17 .4 A2
Prospect Cotts
Lamberhurst TN3 .176 A3
Pratt's Bottom BR6 .58 C2
Prospect Gr DA12 .36 D8
Prospect Pk TN4 .142 F1
Prospect Pl Bromley BR2 .42 B6
Collier Street TN12 .131 C2
Prospect Pl *continued*
Dartford DA1 .15 F1
Gravesend DA12 .36 D8
Grays RM17 .18 B8
Maidstone ME16 .99 E3
Prospect Rd
Royal Tunbridge Wells TN4 .158 F8
Royal Tunbridge Wells,Camden Park TN2 .159 C3
Sevenoaks TN13 .92 C4
Prospect Row
Chatham ME4 .54 A3
Chatham ME7 .54 A6
Prospect Vale SE18 .1 E2
Prospero Ho 7 DA17 .4 A1
Provender Way ME14 .100 E5
Providence Chapel TN12 .148 C6
Providence Cotts
Groombridge TN3 .171 C7
Higham ME3 .38 B2
Providence Pl TN27 .151 A7
Providence St DA9 .17 A2
Prudhoe Ct 27 DA2 .16 B1
Pucknells Cl BR8 .45 C8
Pudding La
Maidstone ME14 .99 F4
Seal TN15 .92 F6
Pudding Rd ME8 .69 F8
Puddingcake La TN17 .192 C5
Puddledock La
Hextable BR8,DA2 .31 F2
Toy's Hill TN16 .106 A3
Puffin Rd ME3 .27 B5
Pullington Cotts TN17 .190 E6
Pullman Mews SE12 .28 B5
Pullman Pl SE9 .11 E2
Pump Cl ME19 .81 D1
Pump La Chelsfield BR6 .59 B5
Gillingham ME7,ME8 .55 D3
Pump Terr TN1 .159 B4
Punch Croft DA3 .62 E7
Purbeck Rd ME4 .53 E2
Purcell Ave TN10 .127 F6
Purfleet By-Pass RM19 .16 D8
Purland Rd SE28 .2 F4
Purneys Rd SE9 .11 D3
Purrett Rd SE18 .2 F1
Purser Way ME7 .54 C7
Pursey Cl TN15 .61 E4
Puttenden Rd TN11 .110 F3
Pym Orch TN16 .90 C3
Pynham Cl SE2 .3 B3
Pyrus Cl ME5 .84 A8

Q

Quadrant The DA7 .13 D7
Quaggy Wlk SE3 .11 A3
Quaker Cl TN13 .92 D4
Quaker Dr TN17 .179 D6
Quaker La TN17 .179 D6
Quaker's Hall La TN13 .92 C5
Quakers Cl DA3 .48 E6
Quantock Cl TN2 .159 D5
Quantock Rd DA1 .14 E5
Quarries The ME17 .116 C4
Quarry Bank TN9 .143 A7
Quarry Cotts
Rockrobin TN5 .184 D7
Sevenoaks TN13 .92 A4
Quarry Hill TN15 .92 D4
Quarry Hill Par 3 TN9 .143 B8
Quarry Hill Rd
Borough Green TN15 .94 F6
Tonbridge TN9 .143 B8
Quarry Rd
Maidstone ME15 .100 A2
Royal Tunbridge Wells TN1 .159 B5
Quarry Rise TN9 .143 A7
Quarry Sq ME14 .100 A5
Quarry Wood Ind Est ME20 .98 E8
Quay La DA9 .17 B3
Quayside ME4 .54 B8
Quebec Ave TN16 .89 D1
Quebec Cotts 9 TN16 .89 D1
Quebec Ho★ TN16 .89 D1
Quebec Rd RM18 .19 A5
Quebec Sq 10 TN16 .89 D1
Queen Anne Ave BR2 .42 A6
Queen Anne Gate DA7 .13 D4
Queen Anne Rd ME14 .100 B4
Queen Borough Gdns BR7 .29 D2
Queen Elizabeth Military Hospl The SE18 .11 E7
Queen Elizabeth Sq ME15 .116 D6
Queen Mary's Hospl DA14 .30 A2
Queen Mother Ct The ME1 .53 B4
Queen St Bexley DA7 .13 F4
Chatham ME4 .54 A4
Erith DA8 .14 E8
Gravesend DA12 .19 B1
Kings Hill ME18 .97 B3
Paddock Wood TN12 .146 D7
Rochester ME1 .53 C4
Sandhurst TN18 .196 B5

Queen's Ave
Maidstone ME16 . . . .**99** D5
Snodland ME6 . . . .**82** A8
Queen's Dr TN14 . . . .**92** C7
Queen's Farm Rd DA12 . . . . .**37** E7
Queen's Gdns TN14 . . . . . .**159** B6
Queen's Mews 12 TN18 . . .**189** A2
Queen's Pas BR7 . . . .**29** B2
Queen's Rd Bexley DA16 . . . .**13** B5
Bromley BR1 . . . .**42** A7
Chatham ME5 . . . .**54** D1
Chislehurst BR7 . . . .**29** B2
Gillingham ME7 . . . .**54** C4
Hawkhurst TN18 . . . .**189** A2
Maidstone ME16 . . . .**99** C4
Royal Tunbridge Wells
TN4 . . . .**159** B6
Snodland ME6 . . . .**82** A8
Queenbridge Ind Pk
RM20 . . . .**17** A8
Queendown Ave ME8 . . . . . .**69** D5
Queens Cotts TN5 . . . .**184** E6
Queens Ct
Edenbridge TN8 . . . .**122** D1
Gillingham ME8 . . . .**70** A8
11 Hawkhurst TN18 . . . .**189** A2
1 Sidcup DA14 . . . .**30** A4
Queens Gate Gdns BR7 . . . .**43** D8
Queens Gdns DA2 . . . .**33** B7
Queens Ho ME16 . . . .**99** B3
Queens Rd Erith DA8 . . . . . .**14** E8
Gravesend DA12 . . . .**36** C5
Queens Way ME14 . . . .**85** A1
Queenscroft Rd SE9 . . . .**11** D1
Queensland Ct RM18 . . . . . .**18** F5
Queensland Ho 2 E16 . . . . . .**2** A5
Queensway
Allhallows-on-S ME3 . . . .**9** D3
Hayes BR2,BR4 . . . .**56** A6
Orpington BR5 . . . .**43** C3
Queenswood Rd
Kit's Coty ME20 . . . .**83** D7
Sidcup DA15 . . . .**12** F1
Quentins Rd TN16 . . . .**73** B3
Quern The ME15 . . . .**99** E1
Quernmore Cl BR1 . . . .**28** A2
Quernmore Rd BR1 . . . .**28** A2
Quested Way ME17 . . . .**119** C6
Quickrells Ave ME3 . . . .**22** B5
Quickthorn Cres ME5 . . . . . .**67** E5
Quiet Nook BR2 . . . .**56** D7
Quilter Rd BR5 . . . .**44** D1
Quilter St SE18 . . . .**2** F1
Quincewood Gdns TN10 **127** B7
Quinion Cl ME5 . . . .**84** A8
Quinnell St ME8 . . . .**55** E1
Quixote Cres ME2 . . . .**39** B1

R

Rabbits Rd DA4 . . . .**47** E7
Rablus Pl ME4 . . . .**46** F3
Racefield Cl DA12 . . . .**37** E1
Rackham Cl DA16 . . . .**13** B5
Radburn Pl DA10 . . . .**17** E2
Radfield Way DA15 . . . .**29** D8
Radland Rd E16 . . . .**1** A7
Radleigh Gdns ME1 . . . .**53** E1
Radley Ho 13 SE2 . . . .**3** D4
Radnor Ave DA16 . . . .**13** B2
Radnor Cl Chislehurst BR7 . . .**29** E2
Maidstone ME14 . . . .**99** E7
Radnor Cres SE18 . . . .**13** A7
Radzan Cl DA2 . . . .**31** E6
Raeburn Ave DA1 . . . .**15** B2
Raeburn Cl TN10 . . . .**127** E6
Raeburn Rd DA15 . . . .**12** E1
Rafford Way BR1 . . . .**42** B6
Rag Hill TN16 . . . .**88** E6
Rag Hill Cl TN16 . . . .**88** E6
Rag Hill Rd TN16 . . . .**88** E6
Raggatt Pl ME15 . . . .**100** B2
Ragge Way TN15 . . . .**92** F7
Raggleswood BR7 . . . .**43** A4
Raglan Ct SE12 . . . .**11** A2
Raglan Prim Sch BR2 . . . . . .**42** D5
Raglan Rd Bromley BR2 . . . . .**42** C5
Erith DA17 . . . .**3** F2
Woolwich SE18 . . . .**2** C1
Ragstone Rd ME20 . . . .**98** C8
Ragstone Rd ME15 . . . .**101** A2
Railway Cotts
Cowden TN8 . . . .**155** D8
Marden TN12 . . . .**148** D6
Railway Pl Erith DA17 . . . .**4** A3
21 Gravesend DA12 . . . .**19** B1
Railway Sidings The
DA13 . . . .**50** A4
Railway St Chatham ME4 . . . .**53** F4
Gillingham ME7 . . . .**54** C6
Northfleet DA11 . . . .**18** A2
Railway St Ind Pk ME7 . . . . .**54** D6
Railway Terr ME1 . . . .**89** D1
Rainham Cl
Maidstone ME15 . . . .**100** A1
Sidcup SE9 . . . .**12** L1
Rainham Mark Gram Sch
ME8 . . . .**55** D2
Rainham Rd ME5 . . . .**54** C1
Rainham Sch for Girls
ME8 . . . .**69** C8
Rainham Sh Ctr 2 ME8 . . . . .**55** F1
Rainham Sta ME8 . . . .**55** F1

Rainton Rd SE7 . . . .**1** A1
Raleigh Cl Chatham ME5 . . . .**68** A6
Erith DA8 . . . .**14** F8
Raleigh Mews 6 BR6 . . . . . .**57** F5
Ramac Ind Est SE7 . . . .**1** B1
Ramac Way SE7 . . . .**1** B1
Ramillies Cl ME5 . . . .**68** A6
Ramillies Rd DA15 . . . .**13** B1
Rammell Mews TN17 . . . . . .**179** D4
Rampion Cl ME14 . . . .**100** E5
Ramsden Cl ME5 . . . .**44** C1
Ramsden La TN17 . . . .**190** F4
Ramsden Rd Erith DA8 . . . . . .**14** D7
Orpington BR5 . . . .**44** B1
Ramsgate Cl E16 . . . .**1** B5
Ramslye Rd TN4 . . . .**172** E8
Ramus Wood Ave BR6 . . . . . .**57** E5
Rance Ho 11 SE18 . . . .**1** E2
Rancliffe Gdns SE9 . . . .**11** E3
Randall Cl DA8 . . . .**14** C8
Randall Hill Rd TN15 . . . .**78** F3
Randall Rd ME4 . . . .**53** E1
Randall St ME14 . . . .**99** F6
Randalls Row ME15 . . . .**115** F5
Randle's La TN14 . . . .**74** D5
Randolph App E16 . . . .**1** C7
Randolph Cl DA7 . . . .**14** C4
Randolph Cotts ME2 . . . .**39** B1
Randolph Ho ME7 . . . .**54** C5
Randolph Rd
Gillingham ME7 . . . .**54** C5
Orpington BR2 . . . .**42** F1
Ranelagh Gdns DA11 . . . .**35** F8
Range Rd DA12 . . . .**36** E8
Rangefield Rd BR1 . . . .**28** A3
Rangeworth Pl DA15 . . . .**29** F5
Rankine Rd TN2 . . . .**159** D7
Ranleigh Gdns DA7 . . . .**13** F7
Ranmore Path BR5 . . . .**44** A5
Ranscombe Cl ME2 . . . .**52** D5
Ranscombe Farm Cotts
ME2 . . . .**52** C4
Ransom Rd 1 SE7 . . . .**1** C1
Ranters La TN17 . . . .**177** C7
Ranworth Rd DA7,DA8 . . . . . .**14** E5
Raphael Ave RM18 . . . .**19** B7
Raphael Cl TN11 . . . .**126** E7
Raphael Rd DA12 . . . .**36** D8
Rashleigh Way DA4 . . . .**47** C5
Ratcliffe Cl SE12 . . . .**28** A8
Ratcliffe Highway
High Halstow ME3 . . . .**24** D5
Hoo St Werburgh ME3 . . . . . .**40** C6
Rathmore Rd
Gravesend DA11 . . . .**36** B8
Greenwich SE7 . . . .**1** B1
Raven Cl ME20 . . . .**82** A1
Raven's Hoe DA14 . . . .**30** A3
Ravens Dane Cl ME15 . . . . .**101** A1
Ravens Knowle ME1 . . . .**66** D4
Ravens Way SE12 . . . .**11** A2
Ravens Wood Sch for Boys
BR2 . . . .**56** D7
Ravensbourne Coll of Design
& Communication BR7 . . .**28** F3
Ravensbourne Ct 23 BR5 .**44** D1
Ravensbourne Rd
Bromley BR1 . . . .**42** A6
Crayford DA1 . . . .**15** A4
Ravensbourne Sch The
BR2 . . . .**42** B5
Ravensbury Rd BR5 . . . .**44** A5
Ravenscourt Rd BR5 . . . .**44** B7
Ravenscroft Cl 5 E16 . . . .**1** A8
Ravenscroft Cres SE9 . . . . . .**28** F5
Ravenscroft Rd E16 . . . .**1** A8
Ravenshill BR7 . . . .**43** B8
Ravensleigh Gdns BR1 . . . . . .**28** B3
Ravensquay Bsns Ctr
BR5 . . . .**44** B4
Ravenswood DA5 . . . .**30** C7
Ravenswood Ave
Rochester ME2 . . . .**39** B1
Royal Tunbridge Wells
TN2 . . . .**159** D6
Ravensworth Rd SE9 . . . .**28** F7
Ravine Gr SE18 . . . .**12** E8
Rawdon Rd ME15 . . . .**100** A3
Rawlings Cl BR6 . . . .**57** F5
Rawsthorne Cl E16 . . . .**1** F5
Ray Lamb Way DA8 . . . .**15** B7
Rayfield Cl BR2 . . . .**42** E3
Rayfield Ct ME6 . . . .**66** B1
Rayford Cl DA1 . . . .**15** C2
Rayleas Cl SE18 . . . .**12** B6
Rayleigh Cl ME16 . . . .**99** D7
Rayleigh Ho 2 ME15 . . . .**116** D8
Rayleigh Rd E16 . . . .**1** B5
Raymer Rd ME14 . . . .**100** B8
Raymere Gdns SE18 . . . .**12** E7
Raymond Postgate Ct 5
SE28 . . . .**3** B6
Raynehurst Jun & Inf Sch
DA12 . . . .**36** F5
Rayners Ct DA11 . . . .**18** B1
Raynham Villas TN12 . . . . . .**132** A4
Rays Hill DA4 . . . .**47** C4
Read Way DA12 . . . .**36** E3
Reader's Bridge Rd
TN30 . . . .**182** E4
Readers Ct ME18 . . . .**104** A8
Reading Ho 4 ME15 . . . .**116** F5
Readscroft Rd ME8 . . . .**69** D5
Rebecca Cl DA14 . . . .**30** B4
Recreation Ave ME6 . . . .**82** A8
Recreation Cl ME14 . . . .**100** B6
Recreation Ground Rd
TN30 . . . .**193** B7

Rectory Bsns Ctr 2
Rectory Cl Crayford DA1 . . . .**14** E3
Sidcup DA14 . . . .**30** B4
Snodland ME6 . . . .**82** A8
Wouldham ME1 . . . .**66** C5
Rectory Ct 3 RM17 . . . .**18** D8
Rectory Dr TN3 . . . .**142** D3
Rectory Field Cres SE7 . . . . .**11** C7
Rectory Fields TN17 . . . .**179** D5
Rectory Grange ME1 . . . .**53** C2
Rectory La Brasted TN16 . . . .**90** C3
Harrietsham ME17 . . . .**119** E5
Ightham TN15 . . . .**94** C5
Maidstone ME16 . . . .**99** A1
Sevenoaks TN13 . . . .**92** C1
Sidcup DA14 . . . .**30** C4
Sutton Valence ME17 . . . . . .**134** C6
Sutton Valence ME17 . . . . . .**134** F7
Titsey TN16 . . . .**88** E4
Rectory La N ME17 . . . .**81** E2
Rectory La S ME19 . . . .**81** E1
Rectory Mdw DA13 . . . .**35** A2
Rectory Paddock Sch
BR5 . . . .**44** C7
Rectory Park Rd TN12 . . . . .**163** A2
Rectory Pl SE18 . . . .**2** A2
Rectory Rd Cliffe ME3 . . . . . .**22** A3
New Ash Green TN15 . . . .**63** C5
Orpington BR2 . . . .**56** D3
Swanscombe DA10 . . . .**34** E8
West Tilbury RM18 . . . .**19** D8
Reculver Wlk ME15 . . . .**116** F7
Red Barracks Rd 4 SE18 . . .**1** F2
Red Cedars Rd BR6 . . . .**43** E2
Red Hill Chislehurst BR7 . . . .**29** B2
Red Hill ME18 . . . .**97** F1
Red Hill Prim Sch BR7 . . . . .**29** B3
Red Ho * DA6 . . . .**13** E3
Red Ho The RH8 . . . .**104** C5
Red House Gdns ME18 . . . .**113** C7
Red House La DA6 . . . .**13** C4
Red La Limpsfield RH8 . . . . . .**121** B7
Oxted RH8 . . . .**104** B2
Red Lion Cl BR5 . . . .**44** C3
Red Lion La SE18 . . . .**12** A6
Red Lion Pl SE18 . . . .**12** A6
Red Lion Sq TN15 . . . .**110** E8
Red Lodge Cres DA5 . . . .**31** E5
Red Lodge Rd DA5 . . . .**31** D5
Red Oak TN18 . . . .**194** E6
Red Oak Cl BR6 . . . .**57** B8
Red Oast Cotts TN5 . . . .**187** C3
Red Robin Cotts ME9 . . . .**71** B6
Red St DA13 . . . .**35** B2
Redbank ME19 . . . .**81** E2
Redbourne Dr SE28 . . . .**3** D7
Redbridge Cl ME5 . . . .**68** C4
Redcliffe La ME14 . . . .**100** B7
Redding Cl DA2 . . . .**33** D8
Redding Ho SE18 . . . .**1** E3
Reddy Rd DA8 . . . .**14** F8
Rede Court Rd ME2 . . . .**52** E8
Rede Wood Rd ME16 . . . .**98** F3
Redfern Ave ME7 . . . .**54** E5
Redfern Ho ME2 . . . .**65** F5
Redgate Dr BR2 . . . .**56** B8
Redhill Rd DA3 . . . .**62** F6
Redhill Wood DA3 . . . .**63** A7
Redhouse Rd TN16 . . . .**88** C6
Redland Shaw ME4 . . . .**53** E1
Redlands Rd TN13 . . . .**91** F3
Redlane Cotts RH8 . . . .**104** B2
Redleaf Cl Erith DA17 . . . .**14** A8
Royal Tunbridge Wells
TN2 . . . .**159** D6
Redmans Ind Est RM18 . . . . .**20** A8
Redmans Rd BR6,TN14 . . . . .**59** E4
Redpoll Way SE28 . . . .**3** D3
Redpoll Wlk TN12 . . . .**146** A5
Redruth Manor 3 ME7 . . . . .**54** C6
Redsells Cl ME15 . . . .**101** A1
Redshank Rd ME4 . . . .**40** B1
Redstart Cl E6 . . . .**1** E8
Redvers Rd ME4 . . . .**54** A2
Redwall La ME15,ME17 . . . . .**132** C6
Redwell Gr ME18 . . . .**97** C2
Redwell La TN15 . . . .**94** B4
Redwing Cl ME20 . . . .**82** A2
Redwing Path SE28 . . . .**2** D4
Redwing Rd ME5 . . . .**68** B7
Redwings La TN3 . . . .**144** E2
Redwood Cl Chatham ME5 . . .**68** B2
Sidcup DA15 . . . .**30** A7
Redwood Ct DA1 . . . .**16** A1
Redwood Pk TN12 . . . .**145** A5
Reed Ave BR6 . . . .**57** E7
Reed Cl Eltham SE12 . . . .**11** A2
New Hythe ME20 . . . .**82** A5
Newham E16 . . . .**1** A8
Reed Court Cotts TN12 . . . .**132** A5
Reed Court Farm Trail★
TN12 . . . .**132** A5
Reed St ME3 . . . .**22** B6
Reedham Cres ME3 . . . .**39** C7
Reeds La TN11 . . . .**110** E5
Reeves Cl TN12 . . . .**149** E4
Reeves Cres BR8 . . . .**45** D6
Reeves Ct Ditton ME19 . . . . . .**82** A1
Fordcombe TN3 . . . .**157** B5
Reeves Rd SE18 . . . .**12** B8
Reeves Terr TN5 . . . .**186** E1
Reflection The E16 . . . .**2** B1
Reform Rd ME4 . . . .**54** B2
Regency Cl
Gillingham ME8 . . . .**69** C3
West Kingsdown TN15 . . . . . .**61** E4

Regency Hall 21 TN2 . . . . . .**159** A2
Regency Ho TN2 . . . .**159** B2
Regency Way DA6 . . . .**13** E4
Regent Dr ME15 . . . .**116** A8
Regent Pl TN2 . . . .**159** D3
Regent Rd ME7 . . . .**54** C4
Regent Sq DA17 . . . .**4** B2
Regent St TN17 . . . .**191** E4
Regent Way ME18 . . . .**97** C3
Regent's Pl SE3 . . . .**11** A5
Regents Ct 3 DA11 . . . .**19** B1
Regents Dr BR2 . . . .**56** D5
Regina Ct TN4 . . . .**158** F4
Reginald Ave ME2 . . . .**52** C3
Reginald Rd ME16 . . . .**99** E3
Reidhaven Rd SE18 . . . .**2** F2
Reigate Rd BR1,SE12 . . . .**28** A5
Reinckendorf Ave SE9 . . . . . .**12** D1
Reinden Gr ME15 . . . .**100** F1
Rembrandt Cl TN10 . . . .**127** E6
Rembrandt Dr DA11 . . . .**35** E5
Remington Rd E6 . . . .**1** E7
Rendlebury Ho 12 SE18 . . . . .**1** F2
Renfrew Cl E6 . . . .**2** A6
Rennets Cl SE9 . . . .**12** E2
Rennets Wood Ho SE9 . . . . .**12** D2
Rennets Wood Rd SE9 . . . . .**12** D2
Renovation The E16 . . . .**2** B4
Renown Rd ME5 . . . .**68** C2
Renshaw Cl 7 DA17 . . . .**13** F8
Renton Dr BR5 . . . .**44** D2
Repository Rd SE18 . . . .**1** F1
Repton Rd BR6 . . . .**58** A6
Repton Way ME5 . . . .**67** F4
Reservoir Cl DA9 . . . .**17** C1
Resolution Cl ME5 . . . .**68** A6
Resolution Wlk SE18 . . . .**1** F3
Restavon Cvn Pk TN16 . . . . .**73** B3
Restharrow Rd ME14 . . . . . .**100** E4
Restharrow Way ME4 . . . .**40** C1
Restmore Cl ME3 . . . .**22** A4
Restons Cres SE9 . . . .**12** E1
Retreat Cvn Pk The
ME18 . . . .**113** D6
Retreat The Grays RM17 . . . . .**18** B8
Orpington BR6 . . . .**58** B4
Platt TN15 . . . .**95** D8
Revell Rise SE18 . . . .**12** F8
Revenge Rd ME5 . . . .**84** C8
Reventlow Rd SE9 . . . .**29** C7
Reynard Cl BR1 . . . .**43** A6
Reynolah Gdns 3 SE7 . . . . . .**1** B1
Reynolds Cl TN10 . . . .**127** E6
Reynolds Fields ME3 . . . .**38** C6
Reynolds La TN4 . . . .**158** F7
Reynolds Pl SE3 . . . .**11** B7
Rhode St ME4 . . . .**54** A4
Rhodes Ho 5 ME5 . . . .**54** C2
Rhodewood Rd ME15 . . . . . .**101** A1
Rhododendron Ave DA13 . . .**64** A2
Ribblesdale Rd DA2 . . . .**33** C7
Ribston Cl BR2 . . . .**42** F1
Ribston Gdns TN12 . . . .**145** F7
Ricardo Path 5 SE28 . . . .**3** C5
Rice Par BR5 . . . .**43** D4
Richard Beau Nash
Apartments 4 TN1 . . . . .**159** B4
Richard Cl SE18 . . . .**12** E2
Richard House Dr E16 . . . .**1** E7
Richard Neve Ho SE18 . . . . . .**2** E2
Richard St Chatham ME4 . . . .**53** F4
Rochester ME1 . . . .**53** C3
Richard's Cl TN11 . . . .**124** F2
Richardson Cl 7 DA9 . . . .**17** A2
Richardson Rd TN4 . . . .**159** A5
Richborough Cl BR5 . . . .**44** D5
Richborough Drive ME2 . . . . .**39** A1
Richings Ho BR5 . . . .**44** A8
Richmer Rd DA8 . . . .**15** A7
Richmond Cl
Biggin Hill TN16 . . . .**88** B8
Chatham ME5 . . . .**68** B4
Rochester ME2 . . . .**39** C1
Richmond Ct Bromley BR1 . . .**28** B1
Sevenoaks TN13 . . . .**92** B4
Richmond Dr DA12 . . . .**36** E6
Richmond Inf Sch ME7 . . . . .**54** C6
Richmond Pl
Royal Tunbridge Wells
TN2 . . . .**159** B1
Woolwich SE18 . . . .**2** C2
Richmond Rd
Gillingham ME7 . . . .**54** C7
1 Grays RM17 . . . .**18** C8
Richmond Way ME15 . . . . . .**116** A8
Richmount Gdns SE3 . . . .**11** A4
Ricketts Hill Rd TN16 . . . . . .**88** E7
Rickyard Path SE9 . . . .**11** E3
Riddlesdale Ave TN4 . . . . . .**159** A6
Riddons Rd SE12 . . . .**28** C4
Rideout St SE18 . . . .**1** F2
Rider Cl DA15 . . . .**12** E1
Ridge Ave DA1 . . . .**14** F1
Ridge Cl SE28 . . . .**2** D4
Ridge La DA13 . . . .**64** A2
Ridge Meadow Prim Sch
ME5 . . . .**67** F6
Ridge The
Groombridge TN3 . . . .**171** A6
Orpington BR6 . . . .**57** D8
Sidcup DA5 . . . .**30** F8
Ridge View Sch TN10 . . . . . .**127** D5
Ridge Way Crayford DA1 . . . . .**14** F1
Marlpit Hill TN8 . . . .**122** D4
Ridgebrook Rd SE3 . . . .**11** D4
Ridgecroft Cl DA5 . . . .**31** C7
Ridgelands TN3 . . . .**142** C4
Ridgeway Dartford DA2 . . . . . .**33** E3

Ridgeway continued
Hayes BR2 . . . .**56** A8
Hurst Green TN19 . . . .**194** A3
Pembury TN2 . . . .**160** D7
The Moor TN18 . . . .**194** E8
Ridgeway Ave DA12 . . . .**36** B5
Ridgeway Bglws DA12 . . .**37** F1
Ridgeway Cres
Orpington BR6 . . . .**57** E2
Tonbridge TN10 . . . .**127** D4
Ridgeway Crescent Gdns
BR6 . . . .**57** E2
Ridgeway Dr BR1 . . . .**28** B4
Ridgeway E DA15 . . . .**12** F2
Ridgeway The
Chatham ME4 . . . .**67** E7
Gillingham ME7 . . . .**54** C7
Shorne DA12 . . . .**37** E3
Tonbridge TN10 . . . .**127** D4
Ridgeway W DA15 . . . .**12** E2
Ridgeways The TN4 . . . .**143** B1
Ridgewood DA3 . . . .**49** C7
Ridgway ME16 . . . .**99** B2
Ridgwell Rd E16 . . . .**1** C8
Ridgy Field Cl TN15 . . . .**79** C2
Riding La TN11 . . . .**109** D2
Riding Pk TN11 . . . .**126** D7
Ridings The
Biggin Hill TN16 . . . .**72** E2
Paddock Wood TN12 . . . . . .**146** A7
Royal Tunbridge Wells
TN2 . . . .**159** F6
Ridlands Gr RH8 . . . .**104** E5
Ridlands La RH8 . . . .**104** E5
Ridlands Rise RH8 . . . .**104** E4
Ridley Cl BR6 . . . .**57** C6
Ridley Rd Bexley DA16 . . . . . .**13** B6
Bromley BR2 . . . .**42** A6
Rochester ME1 . . . .**53** B4
Riefield Rd SE9 . . . .**12** C2
Riggall Ct ME2 . . . .**52** A3
Riggs Way TN15 . . . .**78** F3
Ring Cl BR1 . . . .**28** B1
Ringden Ave TN12 . . . .**145** F6
Ringer's Ct 5 BR1 . . . .**42** A6
Ringer's Rd BR1 . . . .**42** A6
Ringle Gn TN18 . . . .**196** C5
Ringlestone Cres ME14 . . . . .**99** F8
Ringlestone Rd ME17 . . . . . .**103** D4
Ringlet Cl E16 . . . .**1** B8
Ringlet Rd ME4 . . . .**40** B2
Ringmer Way BR1 . . . .**42** F4
Rings Hill TN11 . . . .**126** B4
Ringshall Rd BR5 . . . .**44** A6
Ringside TN8 . . . .**122** C2
Ringwood Ave BR6 . . . .**58** C1
Ringwood Cl ME8 . . . .**69** D8
Ringwood Rd ME15 . . . .**116** C8
Ripley Cl BR1 . . . .**42** F4
Ripley Rd Erith DA17 . . . .**4** A2
Newham E16 . . . .**1** C7
Ripleys Market DA1 . . . .**32** E8
Ripon Cl ME8 . . . .**55** D3
Ripon Rd SE18 . . . .**12** B8
Rippersley Rd DA16 . . . .**13** A6
Rippolson Rd SE18 . . . .**2** F1
Risden La TN18 . . . .**195** D7
Rise The Chatham ME4 . . . . . .**54** A7
Crayford DA1 . . . .**14** F3
Gillingham ME7 . . . .**69** A3
Gravesend DA12 . . . .**36** E4
Rochester ME1 . . . .**53** D3
Sevenoaks TN13 . . . .**108** C7
Sidcup DA5 . . . .**30** C8
Riseden Rd TN5 . . . .**184** C1
Ritch Rd ME6 . . . .**81** E8
Ritter St SE18 . . . .**12** A8
Ritz Blgs TN1 . . . .**159** A3
Rivendell Cl ME3 . . . .**27** B5
River Bank Cl 8 ME15 . . . . .**100** B4
River Cl ME15 . . . .**115** A7
River Cotts BR5 . . . .**44** C7
River Ct TN13 . . . .**91** E5
River Dr ME2 . . . .**52** E7
River Lawn Rd TN9 . . . .**127** B1
River Park View BR6 . . . .**44** B2
River Rd IG11 . . . .**3** A8
River St 6 ME7 . . . .**54** A6
River View Gillingham ME8 **55** D3
Greenwich SE7 . . . .**1** C3
Maidstone ME15 . . . .**99** F2
River View Cl 4 ME4 . . . .**53** F3
River Way ME20 . . . .**82** B4
River Wlk TN9 . . . .**127** B1
Riverbank Rd BR1 . . . .**28** A5
Riverdale Est TN9 . . . .**143** D8
Riverdale Rd Erith DA8 . . . . . .**4** C1
Sidcup DA5 . . . .**13** F1
Woolwich SE18 . . . .**2** F1
Riverhead Cl ME16 . . . .**99** D6
Riverhead Ho TN13 . . . .**91** E5
Riverhead Inf Sch TN13 . . . . .**91** E4
Riverhill TN15 . . . .**108** E4
Riverhill Cotts TN15 . . . .**108** E5
Riverhill House Gdns★
TN15 . . . .**108** E5
Riverhope Mans SE18 . . . .**1** E3
Rivermead ME4 . . . .**40** C2
Rivermead Sch ME7 . . . .**54** E6
Rivers Cl ME18 . . . .**113** E7
Rivers Wlk ME17 . . . .**120** C5
Riversdale DA11 . . . .**35** E5
Riverside Edenbridge TN8 . . .**122** C1
Eynsford DA4 . . . .**60** D8
Greenwich SE7 . . . .**1** B3
Riverside Cl BR5 . . . .**44** C7

Riverside Cotts TN14 ...59 F1
Riverside Ct
2 Orpington BR5 ...44 C4
Tonbridge TN9 ...127 C1
Riverside Ctry Pk & Visitor Ctr★ ME7 ...55 D5
Riverside East Rd ME4 ...40 C1
Riverside Ind Est DA1 ...15 E2
Riverside Pk ME16 ...115 A8
Riverside Rd DA14 ...30 E6
Riverside Ret Pk TN14 ...92 C8
Riverside Way DA1 ...15 E2
Riverston Sch SE12 ...11 A2
Riverview 6 DA1 ...16 A3
Riverview Ct 16 Erith DA17 ...4 A1
Stone DA9 ...16 F1
Riverview Hts SE18 ...12 B7
Riverview Inf Sch DA12 ...36 E4
Riverview Jun Sch DA12 ...36 E4
Riverview Rd DA9 ...17 A2
Riverwood La BR7 ...43 D8
Rixon Ho SE18 ...12 B8
Roach St ME2 ...53 A7
Roan Ct ME2 ...52 F8
Robert Napier Sch The ME7 ...54 E3
Robert St Newham E16 ...2 B5
Woolwich SE18 ...2 D2
Roberton Dr BR1 ...42 C8
Roberts Cl Eltham SE9 ...29 D7
8 Orpington BR5 ...44 C4
Roberts Ho SE18 ...11 E6
Roberts Mews BR6 ...44 A1
Roberts Orchard Rd ME16 ...98 F3
Roberts Rd Erith DA17 ...4 A1
Gillingham ME8 ...69 E8
Snodland ME6 ...81 F8
Robertson Ho SE18 ...11 F6
Robin Cres E6 ...1 D8
Robin Ct 6 ME1 ...53 D4
Robin Hill Dr BR7 ...28 E2
Robin Ho 5 ME16 ...99 E4
Robin Hood Gn BR5 ...44 A4
Robin Hood La
Bexley DA6 ...13 E2
Chatham ME5 ...67 D1
Robin Hood Lane (Lower) ME5 ...67 F2
Robin Hood Lane (Upper) ME5 ...67 E1
Robin Way BR5 ...44 B6
Robina Cl DA6 ...13 D3
Robina Ct BR8 ...46 A5
Robinia Ave DA11 ...35 D8
Robins Ave ME17 ...120 C5
Robins Cl ME17 ...120 C4
Robins Ct Lewisham SE12 ...28 C5
Maidstone ME14 ...100 B7
Robins Gr BR4 ...56 A7
Robinwood Dr TN15 ...92 F8
Robson Cl E6 ...1 E7
Robson Dr Aylesford ME20 82 D2
Hoo St Werburgh ME3 ...40 D6
Robson Ho SE18 ...12 A7
Robyn Cotts TN26 ...183 E8
Robyns Croft 6 DA11 ...35 E5
Robyns Way
Edenbridge TN8 ...138 D8
Sevenoaks TN13 ...91 F5
Rocfort Rd ME6 ...82 A8
Rochdale Ho TN1 ...159 C5
Rochdale Rd
Royal Tunbridge Wells TN1 ...159 C6
Woolwich SE2 ...3 B2
Rochester Airport ME1, ME5 ...67 C6
Rochester Airport Ind Est ME1 ...67 C5
Rochester Ave
Bromley BR1 ...42 B7
Rochester ME1 ...53 C4
Rochester Castle★ ME1 ...53 C6
Rochester Cath★ ME1 ...53 C6
Rochester Cl 1 DA15 ...13 B1
Rochester Cres ME3 ...40 D6
Rochester Ct ME2 ...53 E8
Rochester Dr DA5 ...14 A1
Rochester Gate ME1 ...53 D5
Rochester Gram Sch for Girls The ME1 ...53 C2
Rochester Ho 1 ME15 ...116 D7
Rochester Ind Coll ME1 ...53 D4
Rochester Rd
Burham ME1 ...66 E2
Chalk DA12 ...37 B6
Chatham ME1,ME5 ...67 C4
Dartford DA1 ...33 A8
Pratling Street ME20 ...83 B4
Rochester ME2 ...52 D4
Tonbridge TN10 ...127 D4
Rochester St ME4 ...53 E3
Rochester Sta ME1 ...53 D5
Rochester Way
Dartford DA1 ...31 F8
Eltham SE9 ...12 B4
Eltham,Kidbrooke SE3,SE9 ...11 D4
Rock Ave ME7 ...54 C3
Rock Cotts TN3 ...173 B1
Rock Farm Oasthouse ME18 ...113 C6
Rock Hill BR6 ...59 B4
Rock Hill Rd TN27 ...137 E2
Rock Rd
Borough Green TN15 ...94 F7
Maidstone ME14 ...100 A6
Rock Villa Rd TN1 ...159 A4
Rockdale TN13 ...92 B2
Rockdale Rd TN13 ...92 C2
Rockliffe Manor Prim Sch SE18 ...12 F8
Rockmount Rd SE18 ...2 F1
Rocks Cl ME19 ...98 A6
Rocks Hill TN17 ...166 A4
Rocks Rd The ME19 ...98 B6
Rocky Hill ME16 ...99 E4
Rocky Hill Terr 2 ME16 ...99 E4
Rodeo Cl DA8 ...15 B6
Roding Rd E6 ...2 B8
Rodmell Rd TN2 ...159 A2
Rodney Ave TN10 ...127 E4
Rodney Gdns BR4 ...56 A6
Rodway Rd BR1 ...42 B8
Roebourne Way E16 ...2 A5
Roebuck Ho ME1 ...53 E5
Roebuck Rd ME1 ...53 C5
Roedean Cl BR6 ...58 B6
Roedean Rd TN2 ...159 A1
Roehampton Cl DA12 ...36 E8
Roehampton Dr BR7 ...29 C2
Roethorne Gdns TN30 ...193 B8
Roffen Rd ME1 ...53 C2
Rogers Ct BR8 ...46 A5
Rogers Rough Rd TN17 ...177 B2
Rogers Wood La DA3 ...62 B6
Rogersmead TN30 ...193 A7
Rogley Hill TN27 ...181 B6
Rogues Hill TN11 ...141 C3
Rokesby Cl DA16 ...12 D5
Rolinsden Way BR2 ...56 D6
Rollesby Way SE28 ...3 C7
Rolleston Ave BR5 ...43 B3
Rolleston Cl BR5 ...43 B2
Rollo Rd BR8 ...31 F1
Rolvenden Ave ME8 ...55 C3
Rolvenden Gdns BR1 ...28 D1
Rolvenden Hill TN17 ...192 C5
Rolvenden Prim Sch TN17 ...191 E3
Rolvenden Rd
Rochester ME2 ...39 C2
Tenterden TN30 ...192 E7
Rolvenden Sta★ TN17 ...192 D6
Roman Cl ME5 ...67 D1
Roman Hts ME14 ...100 C6
Roman Rd
Edenbridge TN8 ...138 D5
Northfleet DA11 ...35 C5
Snodland ME6 ...81 F8
Roman Sq SE28 ...3 A5
Roman Villa Rd DA2,DA4 ...33 C2
Roman Way Crayford DA1 ...14 E2
Rochester ME2 ...52 F4
Romany Ct ME5 ...54 D1
Romany Rd ME8 ...55 C2
Romany Rise BR5 ...43 C1
Romden Rd
Smarden,Haffenden Quarter TN27 ...169 B8
Smarden,Romden TN27 ...153 D1
Rome Terr ME4 ...53 F4
Romero Sq SE3 ...11 C3
Romford Rd TN2 ...160 F7
Romney Cl ME14 ...101 A3
Romney Dr BR1 ...28 D1
Romney Gdns DA7 ...13 F6
Romney Pl ME15 ...100 A4
Romney Rd Chatham ME5 ...68 B5
Northfleet DA11 ...35 E5
Woolwich SE2 ...2 C3
Romney St TN15 ...77 A7
Romney Street Cvn Pk TN15 ...77 A7
Romney Way TN10 ...127 E5
Romsey Cl Orpington BR6 ...57 C6
Rochester ME2 ...52 E8
Ron Green Ct DA8 ...14 D8
Ronald Ho SE3 ...11 C3
Ronalds Rd BR1 ...42 A8
Ronaldstone Rd DA15 ...12 E1
Ronfearn Ave BR5 ...44 D4
Ronver Rd SE12 ...28 A7
Roodlands La TN8 ...123 D6
Rook La ME9 ...71 F6
Rook Wlk 2 E6 ...1 E7
Rookdean TN13 ...91 C5
Rookery Cres ME3 ...22 B6
Rookery Ct RM20 ...17 A8
Rookery Dr BR7 ...43 A8
Rookery Gdns BR5 ...44 C4
Rookery Hill ME6 ...81 F8
Rookery La BR2 ...42 D3
Rookery Lodge ME3 ...22 C5
Rookery Rd BR6 ...57 A1
Rookery The RM20 ...17 A8
Rookery View RM17 ...18 D8
Rookesley Rd BR5 ...44 D2
Rookley Cl TN2 ...159 D2
Rooks Hill TN15 ...109 D6
Roopers TN3 ...158 A7
Roosevelt Ave ME5 ...68 A8
Rope Wlk Chatham ME4 ...53 F5
Cranbrook TN17 ...179 C5
Rope Wlk The TN18 ...196 B5
Rope Yard Rails SE18 ...2 B3
Ropemakers Ct ME4 ...54 A1
Roper Cl ME8 ...69 C3
Roper St 1 SE9 ...12 A1
Roper's Gate TN2 ...158 E1
Roper's Green La ME3 ...24 B2
Roper's La ME3 ...40 F8
Ropery Bsns Pk SE7 ...1 C2
Rose Ave DA12 ...36 E7
Rose Bruford Coll DA15 ...30 B7
Rose Cotts
Lamberhurst TN3 ...176 A5
Rochester ME2 ...52 B8
St Mary Hoo ME3 ...24 E6
Rose Ct ME17 ...115 D1
Rose Dale BR6 ...57 B8
Rose Hill Sch TN4 ...158 E5
Rose St Northfleet DA11 ...18 B1
Rochester ME1 ...53 D3
Tonbridge TN9 ...143 C8
Rose Terr ME19 ...96 D7
Rose Way SE12 ...11 A2
Rose Yd ME14 ...100 A4
Roseacre RH8 ...104 A1
Roseacre Gdns ME14 ...101 A3
Roseacre Jun Sch ME14 ...101 A4
Roseacre La ME14 ...101 A4
Roseacre Rd DA16 ...13 B4
Rosebank Gdns DA11 ...35 E7
Rosebank Wlk 13 SE18 ...1 E2
Roseberry Gdns
Dartford DA1 ...32 C8
Orpington BR6 ...57 E7
Rosebery Ave DA15 ...29 E8
Rosebery Ct DA11 ...35 F7
Rosebery Rd
Chatham ME4 ...53 E2
Gillingham ME7 ...54 D7
Grays RM17 ...17 E8
Rosecroft Cl
Biggin Hill TN16 ...72 F1
Orpington BR5 ...44 C3
Rosedale Cl Dartford DA2 ...33 B8
Woolwich SE2 ...3 B3
Rosedale Cnr BR7 ...42 F8
Rosedene Cl DA1 ...32 C8
Rosefield Sevenoaks TN13 ...92 A3
15 Sidcup DA14 ...30 A4
Rosegarth DA13 ...49 E8
Rosehill Rd TN16 ...72 C2
Rosehill Wlk TN1 ...159 A3
Roseholme ME16 ...99 D2
Roselare Cl TN16 ...89 D1
Roseleigh Ave ME16 ...99 C5
Rosemary Cl
4 Chatham ME5 ...67 F4
Oxted RH8 ...104 A2
Rosemary Ct 1 ME1 ...53 D4
Rosemary La
Flimwell TN5 ...187 A5
Hodsoll Street TN15 ...63 D3
Swift's Green TN27 ...152 F5
Rosemary Rd Bexley DA16 12 F6
Maidstone ME15 ...101 A3
West Malling ME19 ...81 F1
Rosemead Gdns TN27 ...151 B7
Rosemount Cl ME15 ...115 F4
Rosemount Ct ME2 ...39 A1
Rosemount Dr BR1 ...42 F5
Rosenheath Cl BR6 ...58 C3
Rosetta Prim Sch E16 ...1 B8
Roseveare Rd SE12 ...28 C4
Rosewood DA2 ...31 E4
Rosewood Cl DA14 ...30 C5
Rosewood Ct BR1 ...42 D8
Rosher Ho DA11 ...18 F1
Rosherville CE Prim Sch DA11 ...18 E1
Rosherville Way DA11 ...18 E1
Roslin Way BR1 ...28 A3
Ross Ct BR7 ...28 F1
Ross Ho SE18 ...11 E6
Ross Rd DA1 ...15 A1
Ross St ME1 ...53 D4
Ross Way SE9 ...11 E4
Rossdale TN2 ...159 D5
Rosse Mews SE3 ...11 B6
Rossland Cl DA6 ...14 B2
Rosslyn Gn ME16 ...99 B5
Rossmore DA14 ...30 A3
Rother Ct 24 BR5 ...44 D1
Rother Rd TN10 ...127 C5
Rother Vale ME5 ...68 C3
Rothermere Cl TN17 ...190 E6
Rothesay Ct 6 SE12 ...28 B5
Rothley Cl TN30 ...193 B8
Rouge La DA12 ...36 B7
Rougemont ME18 ...97 C2
Roughetts Rd ME19 ...80 F3
Roughway La TN11 ...111 C7
Round Ash Way DA3 ...48 E3
Round Green Cotts TN17 ...164 F4
Round St DA12,DA13 ...50 D5
Round Wood Cl ME5 ...68 A1
Roundel Way TN12 ...148 D5
Roundhay ME19 ...81 E1
Roundhill Rd TN2 ...159 D1
Roundlyn Gdns BR5 ...44 B5
Roundtable Rd BR1 ...28 A5
Roundway TN16 ...72 D4
Roundwell ME14 ...101 D3
Roundwood BR7 ...43 B7
Routh St E6 ...1 F8
Rover Rd ME5 ...68 B2
Row The DA3 ...62 F8
Rowan Cl Aylesford ME20 ...82 E1
Meopham Sta DA13 ...50 B3
Paddock Wood TN12 ...145 F5
Rowan Cres DA1 ...32 C7
Rowan Ct 2 SE12 ...28 A8
Rowan Ho
4 Chatham ME5 ...67 F5
7 Maidstone ME16 ...99 A3
Royal Tunbridge Wells TN4 ...158 E4
Sidcup DA14 ...29 F5
Rowan Lea ME5 ...54 B1
Rowan Rd Bexley DA7 ...13 E4
Swanley BR8 ...45 D6
Rowan Shaw TN10 ...127 D6
Rowan Tree Rd TN2 ...158 E1
Rowan Wlk Chatham ME4 ...53 E3
Orpington BR2 ...56 F7
Rowans Cl DA3 ...48 D7
Rowanwood Ave DA15 ...30 A7
Rowbrocke Cl ME8 ...69 D3
Rowdow La TN14,TN15 ...76 E5
Rowe Pl ME20 ...82 F6
Rowenden Vineyard★ TN17 ...191 B2
Rowfield 6 TN8 ...122 D3
Rowhill Cotts DA2 ...31 E2
Rowhill Rd DA2 ...32 A3
Rowhill Sch DA2 ...32 C4
Rowland Ave ME7 ...54 E2
Rowland Cl
Gillingham ME7 ...54 E1
Maidstone ME16 ...99 E3
Rowlands Manor BR5 ...44 C3
Rowlatt Cl DA2 ...32 C4
Rowlatt Rd DA2 ...32 C5
Rowley Ave DA15 ...30 B8
Rowley Hill TN2 ...144 D1
Rowmarsh Cl DA11 ...35 D4
Rowntree Path 1 SE28 ...3 B5
Rowton Rd SE18 ...12 C7
Rowzill Rd BR8 ...31 F2
Royal Albert Sta E16 ...1 E6
Royal Albert Way
Newham E16 ...1 E6
Newham,Cyprus E6 ...2 A6
Royal Ave TN9 ...143 D8
Royal Chase TN4 ...158 F4
Royal Cl BR6 ...57 B6
Royal Connaught Apartments E16 ...1 D5
Royal Ct SE9 ...28 F7
Royal Docks Com Sch The E16 ...1 C7
Royal Docks Rd E6 ...2 B7
Royal Eagle Cl ME2 ...53 E7
Royal Engineers Mus★ ME7 ...54 B6
Royal Engineers' Rd ME14 ...99 F7
Royal Oak Cotts TN8 ...105 C2
Royal Oak Rd DA6 ...13 F3
Royal Oak Terr DA12 ...36 C7
Royal Par BR7 ...29 C1
Royal Parade Mews BR7 ...29 C1
Royal Park Prim Sch DA14 ...30 E5
Royal Pier Rd DA12 ...19 C1
Royal Rd Newham E16 ...1 D7
Sidcup DA14 ...30 D5
Sutton at H DA2 ...33 A3
Royal Rise TN9 ...143 C8
Royal Sch of Military Engineering ME3 ...39 C4
Royal Sovereign Ave ME4 ...54 B7
Royal Star Arc 5 ME14 ...99 F4
Royal Tunbridge Wells Bsns Pk TN2 ...143 D1
Royal Victoria Pl
Newham E16 ...1 B5
Royal Tunbridge Wells TN1 ...159 B4
Royal Victoria Sq E16 ...1 B6
Royal Victoria Sta E16 ...1 A6
Royal West Kent Ave TN10 ...127 D4
Roydene Rd SE18 ...2 E1
Roydon Hall★ TN12 ...112 F4
Roydon Hall Rd TN12 ...112 F4
Royston Rd Crayford DA1 ...14 F1
Maidstone ME15 ...101 A3
Roystons Cl ME8 ...55 F2
Royton Ave ME17 ...120 D5
Rubin Pl ME19 ...97 B3
Ruck La TN12 ...162 E3
Ruckinge Way ME8 ...55 C3
Ruddstreet Cl SE18 ...2 C2
Rudge Cl ME5 ...68 D2
Rudland Rd DA7 ...14 B4
Ruegg Ho 5 SE18 ...12 A8
Ruffet Ct TN2 ...158 E1
Ruffets Wood DA12 ...36 C2
Rugby Cl ME5 ...67 F4
Ruggles Cl ME23 ...23 E3
Rumania Wlk DA12 ...36 F5
Rumstead La ME17,ME9 ...86 D4
Rumstead Rd ME9 ...86 E4
Rumwood Ct ME17 ...117 B5
Runciman Cl BR6 ...58 C1
Runham La ME17 ...119 E3
Running Horse Rdbt The ME14 ...83 E1
Runnymede Ct DA2 ...33 C7
Runnymede Gdns ME15 116 A8
Rural Vale DA11 ...35 E8
Ruscombe Cl TN4 ...142 F2
Rush Cl ME5 ...68 A3
Rushbrook Rd SE9 ...29 C6
Rushdean Rd ME2 ...52 D5
Rushdene SE2 ...3 D3
Rushdene Wlk TN16 ...72 D2
Rushes The ME20 ...82 B4
Rushet Rd BR5 ...44 A7
Rushetts TN3 ...157 F4
Rushetts Rd TN15 ...61 E3
Rusheymead Ho 5 SE18 ...2 F1
Rushford Cl TN27 ...151 D5
Rushgrove St SE18 ...1 F2
Rushley Cl BR2 ...56 E6
Rushlye Cl TN3 ...173 F5
Rushmead Dr ME15 ...116 A7
Rushmere Ct TN15 ...94 D7
Rushmore Cl BR1 ...42 E6
Rushmore Hill BR6,TN14 ...74 D6
Rushymead TN15 ...77 A1
Ruskin Ave DA16 ...13 A5
Ruskin Cl ME19 ...97 F8
Ruskin Ct SE9 ...11 F1
Ruskin Dr Bexley DA16 ...13 A4
Orpington BR6 ...57 E7
Ruskin Gr Bexley DA16 ...13 A5
Dartford DA1 ...16 A2
Ruskin Rd DA17 ...4 A2
Ruskin Wlk BR2 ...42 F3
Rusland Ave BR6 ...57 D7
Russell Cl Bexley DA7 ...14 A3
Crayford DA1 ...15 A3
Greenwich SE7 ...11 C7
Russell Ct ME4 ...54 B3
Russell House Sch TN14 ...76 C3
Russell Pl DA4 ...47 A8
Russell Quay 2 DA11 ...19 A1
Russell Rd
Gravesend DA12 ...19 D1
Kit's Coty ME20 ...83 D7
Newham E16 ...1 B7
Tilbury RM18 ...18 F5
Tilbury RM18 ...18 F6
Russell Sq DA3 ...48 D6
Russell Terr DA4 ...47 C5
Russells Ave ME8 ...70 A8
Russells Yd TN17 ...179 D4
Russet Cl ME2 ...52 E8
Russet Ct Coxheath ME17 115 C3
17 Erith DA17 ...4 A1
Russet Ho RM17 ...18 C7
Russet Way ME19 ...96 F2
Russets The
Maidstone ME16 ...99 B5
Meopham Sta DA13 ...50 A3
Russett Cl Ditton ME20 ...98 E8
Orpington BR6 ...58 B5
Russett Rd TN12 ...129 F6
Russett Way BR8 ...45 D8
Rusthall Grange TN4 ...158 D4
Rusthall Pk TN4 ...158 D4
Rusthall Rd TN4 ...158 D4
Rustic Wlk E16 ...1 B7
Ruston Rd SE18 ...1 E3
Rustwick TN4 ...158 D4
Ruth Ho 2 ME16 ...99 E5
Ruth St ME4 ...54 A2
Rutherford Way TN10 ...127 D7
Rutherglen Rd SE2 ...13 A8
Ruthin Rd SE3 ...11 A8
Rutland Ave DA15 ...30 A8
Rutland Cl Dartford DA1 ...32 D8
Sidcup DA5 ...30 D7
Rutland Ct Chislehurst BR7 43 A8
Sidcup SE9 ...29 C6
Rutland Gate DA17 ...4 B1
Rutland Ho 10 SE18 ...1 F2
Rutland Pl ME8 ...69 C3
Rutland Way
Maidstone ME15 ...116 E8
Orpington BR5 ...44 C3
Ruxley Cl DA14 ...30 E2
Ruxley Cnr DA14 ...30 E2
Ruxley Corner Ind Est DA14 ...30 D2
Ruxley Ct 1 BR1 ...42 C7
Ruxton Cl BR8 ...45 E6
Ruxton Ct 5 BR8 ...45 E6
Ryan Cl SE3 ...11 C3
Ryan Dr ME15 ...101 A2
Ryarsh Cres BR6 ...57 E6
Ryarsh La ME19 ...81 B1
Ryarsh Pk ME19 ...80 F4
Ryarsh Prim Sch ME19 ...81 A4
Ryarsh Rd ME19 ...81 B5
Rycault Cl 4 ME16 ...99 E3
Rycaut Cl ME8 ...69 D3
Rycroft La TN14 ...107 E5
Rydal Cl TN4 ...158 E5
Rydal Dr Bexley DA7 ...14 A6
Royal Tunbridge Wells TN4 ...158 E5
Rydal Ho ME15 ...116 E7
Ryde Cl ME5 ...68 B8
Rydens Ho SE9 ...28 C5
Ryder Cl BR1 ...28 B3
Ryders TN3 ...158 A3
Rydons Cl SE9 ...11 E4
Rye Cl DA5 ...14 B1
Rye Cres BR5 ...44 D1
Rye Field 25 BR5 ...44 D1
Rye La Otford TN14 ...76 A2
Sevenoaks TN13,TN14 ...91 F7
Rye Rd Four Throws TN18 195 D8
Hawkhurst TN18 ...189 B1
Rye Wood Cotts TN14 ...91 F7
Ryecroft Gravesend DA12 ...36 E3
New Barn DA3 ...49 D5
Ryecroft Rd
Orpington BR5 ...43 D3
Otford TN14 ...76 A2
Ryedale Ct TN13 ...91 E6
Ryegrass Cl ME5 ...68 C6
Ryelands Cres SE12 ...11 C1
Rymers Cl TN2 ...159 D7
Rymill St E16 ...2 A5
Rysted La TN16 ...89 D1

S

Sabre Ct ME7 . . . . .55 A1
Sackville Ave BR2 . . . . . . .42 A1
Sackville Cl TN13 . . . . .92 B5
Sackville Rd DA2 . . . . .32 E6
Sackville Sch TN11 . . . . . .126 C6
Sacred Heart Sch TN5 . . .184 D5
Saddington St DA12 . . . . .36 C8
Saddler's Pk DA4 . . . . .60 D7
Saddlers Cl ME14 . . . . . . .100 E5
Sadlers Cl ME5 . . . . .67 D2
Saffron Cl ME5 . . . . .99 B3
Saffron Way **1** ME5 . . . .67 F5
Sage Cl **7** E6 . . . . .1 F8
Sage Rd ME1 . . . . .53 B3
Saigasso Cl E16 . . . . .1 D7
Sailfield St ME4 . . . . .53 F7
Sailmakers Ct **5** ME4 . . .54 B2
St Mary Magdalene CE
   Prim Sch SE18 . . . . .2 A2
Saints Hill TN11 . . . . .157 A8
St Aidan's Way DA12 . . . . .36 E5
St Alban's Cl DA12 . . . . . .36 D5
St Alban's Gdns DA12 . . . .36 D5
St Alban's Rd DA1 . . . . . . .15 F1
St Alban's Rd Inf Sch
   DA1 . . . . .15 F1
St Albans Cl ME7 . . . . .54 E7
St Albans Rd BR2 . . . . .52 D6
St Alfege Rd SE7 . . . . .11 D8
St Andrew's Cl ME16 . . . . .99 A2
St Andrew's Ct **4** BR8 . . .45 E6
St Andrew's Rd
   10 Gravesend DA12 . . . .36 B8
   Maidstone ME16 . . . . . . .99 A3
   Tilbury RM18 . . . . .18 E5
St Andrew's Wlk ME3 . . . . .9 D2
St Andrews Cl Erith SE28 . . .3 D7
   Paddock Wood TN12 . . . .146 A6
St Andrews Ct
   26 Gravesend DA12 . . . .19 B1
   Royal Tunbridge Wells
   TN4 . . . . .143 A1
St Andrews Dr BR5 . . . . . .44 B2
St Andrews Ho ME1 . . . . . .28 B2
St Andrews Mews SE3 . . . .11 A7
St Andrews Park Rd
   TN4 . . . . .143 A1
St Andrews Pk ME16 . . . . .99 A3
St Andrews Rd
   Gillingham ME7 . . . . .54 D7
   Paddock Wood TN12 . . . .146 A6
   Sidcup DA14 . . . . .30 D5
St Andrews Sch ME1 . . . . .53 C4
St Andrews Way RH8 . . . .104 F4
St Ann's Green La TN12 . .148 F8
St Annes Ct ME16 . . . . . . .99 E4
St Anns Way TN16 . . . . . . .73 B3
St Anselm's RC Prim Sch
   DA1 . . . . .16 A2
St Anthony's Ct BR6 . . . . .57 B8
St Aubyns Cl BR6 . . . . . . .57 F7
St Aubyns Gdns BR6 . . . . .57 F8
St Audrey Ave DA7 . . . . . . .8 A6
St Augustine Ho **1** TN9 143 B8
St Augustine of Canterbury
   RC Prim Sch ME8 . . . . . .69 D3
St Augustine's Ave BR2 . .42 E4
St Augustine's of Canterbury
   CE Prim Sch DA17 . . . . . .3 F2
St Augustine's RC Prim Sch
   TN4 . . . . .159 A4
St Augustine's Rd DA17 . . .3 F2
St Barnabas CE Prim Sch
   TN1 . . . . .159 B5
St Barnabas Cl
   Gillingham ME7 . . . . .54 D3
   Maidstone ME16 . . . . . . .99 C8
St Barnabas' Cl TN1 . . . .159 B5
St Bartholomew's Hospl
   ME1 . . . . .53 E4
St Bartholomew's La **4**
   ME1 . . . . .53 E4
St Bartholomew's Terr **2**
   ME1 . . . . .53 E4
St Bartholomews RC Prim
   Sch BR8 . . . . .45 E6
St Benedict Rd ME6 . . . . . .81 C5
St Benedict's Ave DA12 . . .36 E6
St Benedicts RC Prim Sch
   ME5 . . . . .68 C2
St Benets Ct TN30 . . . . . .193 B8
St Benets Way TN30 . . . . .193 B8
St Benjamins Dr BR6 . . . . .58 C2
St Bernards Rd TN10 . . . .127 C6
St Blaise Ave BR1 . . . . . . .42 B7
St Boltophs Cl TN13 . . . . .92 B3
St Botolph's Rd DA11 . . . . .35 D5
St Botolph's Rd TN13 . . . . .92 A3
St Botolph's CE Prim Sch
   DA11 . . . . .35 D5
St Botolph's Rd TN13 . . . . .92 B3
St Brelade's Ct TN8 . . . . .122 A3
St Brides Cl DA18 . . . . .3 D4
St Catherine's Hospl
   ME1 . . . . .53 D4
St Catherine's RC Sch for
   Girls DA6 . . . . .14 B2
St Catherines Ct ME1 . . . . .53 D5
St Chad's Dr DA12 . . . . . . .36 E5
St Chad's Rd RM18 . . . . . .19 A7
St Chad's Sch RM18 . . . . .19 A6

St Clement's Ave RM20 . . .17 B8
St Clement's Ho ME1 . . . . .53 D5
St Clement's Rd RM20 . . . .17 C7
St Clement's Way RM20 . .16 F8
St Clements Cl DA11 . . . . .35 F5
St Clements Ct RM17 . . . . .17 F8
St Clere Hill Rd TN15 . . . . .77 F7
St Columba's Cl DA12 . . . .36 E5
St Columba's RC Boys Sch
   DA6 . . . . .14 B2
St David's Bridge TN17 . .179 D4
St David's Cres DA12 . . . . .36 D4
St David's Rd
   Allhallows ME3 . . . . .9 D2
   Hextable BR8 . . . . .31 F1
   Royal Tunbridge Wells
   TN4 . . . . .159 B6
St Davids Gate ME16 . . . . .99 A2
St Domingo Ho SE18 . . . . . .1 F7
St Dunstan's Dr DA12 . . . .36 E5
St Dunstans Wlk TN17 . . .179 D4
St Edith's Rd TN15 . . . . . . .77 A2
St Edmund Ho SE2 . . . . . .13 D8
St Edmund's Cotts TN15 . .62 A2
St Edmund's Ct TN15 . . . . .62 A2
St Edmunds Cl DA18 . . . . . .3 D4
St Edmunds Rd DA1 . . . . . .16 A3
St Faith's La ME14 . . . . . .101 B4
St Faith's St ME14 . . . . . . .99 F4
St Fidelis RC Prim Sch
   . . . . .14 C8
St Fidelis' Rd DA8 . . . . .4 D1
St Francis Ave DA12 . . . . . .36 E4
St Francis Cl
   Maidstone ME14 . . . . . . .100 B7
   Orpington BR6 . . . . .43 E3
   Rochester ME2 . . . . .52 E6
St Francis RC Prim Sch
   ME15 . . . . .99 C4
St Francis Rd DA13 . . . . . .64 B3
St Francis' Rd DA8 . . . . .4 D2
St George's Bickley CE Prim
   Sch BR1 . . . . .42 D7
St George's CE Prim Sch
   TN15 . . . . .78 F3
St George's CE Sch DA11 36 A6
St George's Cres DA12 . . . .36 D4
St George's Ct TN15 . . . . . .78 F3
St George's Ctr DA11 . . . . .19 B1
St George's Pk TN2 . . . . .172 F8
St George's Rd
   Gillingham ME7 . . . . .54 C6
   Sevenoaks TN13 . . . . .92 B5
   Sidcup DA14 . . . . .30 D2
St George's Sq ME16 . . . . .99 E3
St George's Wlk ME3 . . . . . .9 D2
St Georges Cl SE28 . . . . . . .3 D7
St Georges Ct TN4 . . . . . .159 A5
St Georges Mews **11**
   TN9 . . . . .143 B8
St Georges Rd
   Bromley BR1 . . . . .42 F6
   Orpington BR5 . . . . .43 D3
   Swanley BR8 . . . . .45 F5
St Georges Rd W BR1 . . . .42 E7
St Georges Sq DA3 . . . . . .48 E6
St German's Pl SE3 . . . . . .11 A6
St Giles Cl BR6 . . . . .57 D5
St Gregory's Cres DA12 . . .36 E6
St Gregory's Ct DA12 . . . . .36 E6
St Gregory's RC Comp Sch
   TN4 . . . . .159 A7
St Helens DA14 . . . . .30 B5
St Helens CE Prim Sch
   ME3 . . . . .22 B5
St Helens Cotts ME15 . . . .114 E8
St Helens La ME15 . . . . . .114 E8
St Helens Rd Cliffe ME3 . . .22 B5
   7 Erith DA18 . . . . .3 D4
St Helier's Cl ME16 . . . . . .99 B2
St Hilary Ho SE2 . . . . .13 D8
St Hilda's Way DA12 . . . . . .36 E5
St Hildas TN15 . . . . .110 F8
St James Cl
   East Malling ME19 . . . . . .97 F8
   Grain ME3 . . . . .27 B6
   Tonbridge TN10 . . . . . . .127 D7
St James Ct
   3 Bromley BR2 . . . . .42 A7
   Greenwich SE3 . . . . .11 B6
   Stone DA9 . . . . .16 F1
St James Oaks DA11 . . . . .36 A8
St James Pl DA11 . . . . .15 D1
St James RC Prim Sch
   BR5 . . . . .43 B4
St James Rd ME3 . . . . .27 B5
St James Sq DA3 . . . . .48 E6
St James Way DA14 . . . . . .30 E3
St James' CE Inf Sch
   TN2 . . . . .159 C4
St James' CE Jun Sch
   TN2 . . . . .159 C4
St James' CE Prim Sch
   ME3 . . . . .27 B6
St James' Inf Sch ME19 . .97 F8
St James' La DA9 . . . . .33 E8
St James' Pk TN1 . . . . . . .159 C5
St James' Rd TN1 . . . . . . .159 C5
St James's Ave DA11 . . . . .36 A8
St James's Cl SE18 . . . . . . .2 C1
St James's Ct TN1 . . . . . .159 B4
St James's Rd
   Gravesend DA11 . . . . . . .19 A1
   Sevenoaks TN13 . . . . .92 B5
St James's St DA11 . . . . . .19 A1
St Joachim's RC Prim Sch
   E16 . . . . .1 C7

St John Fisher RC Comp
   (Lower) Sch ME4 . . . . . . .53 F2
St John Fisher RC Comp Sch
   ME4 . . . . .53 E3
St John Fisher RC Prim Sch
   DA18 . . . . .3 E3
St John's CE Inf Sch
   ME4 . . . . .53 E3
St John's CE Prim Sch
   ME14 . . . . .100 E4
St John's CE Prim Sch
   TN4 . . . . .159 B7
St John's CE Prim Sch
   TN15 . . . . .92 D4
St John's Cl ME3 . . . . .38 C4
St John's Ct TN13 . . . . .92 C5
St John's Hill TN13,TN14 . .92 C5
St John's Jerusalem *
   DA4 . . . . .33 B1
St John's La DA3 . . . . .48 F3
St John's Par **4** DA14 . . .30 B4
St John's Pk
   Greenwich SE3 . . . . .11 A7
   Royal Tunbridge Wells
   TN4 . . . . .159 A8
St John's RC Comp Sch
   DA12 . . . . .36 D7
St John's RC Prim Sch
   BR5 . . . . .44 C3
St John's Rd Bexley DA16 .13 B4
   Dartford DA2 . . . . .33 C8
   Erith DA8 . . . . .4 D1
   Gillingham ME7 . . . . .54 C3
   Gravesend DA12 . . . . .36 D8
   Higham ME3 . . . . .38 C4
   Newham E16 . . . . .1 A7
   Orpington BR5 . . . . .43 B3
   Royal Tunbridge Wells
   TN4 . . . . .159 A6
   Sevenoaks TN13 . . . . .92 C5
   Sidcup DA14 . . . . .30 B4
St John's Terr SE18 . . . . . .12 D8
St Johns Cl DA8 . . . . .4 D1
St Johns Rd ME3 . . . . .40 E6
St Johns Way
   Edenbridge TN8 . . . . . . .122 C3
   Rochester ME1 . . . . .53 A2
St Joseph's RC Prim Sch
   Bromley BR1 . . . . .28 B1
   Crayford DA1 . . . . .14 E3
   Northfleet DA11 . . . . .35 D8
St Josephs Cl BR6 . . . . . . .57 F6
St Josephs Ct **4** SE12 . . .28 B5
St Josephs Prep Sch
   DA12 . . . . .36 C6
St Justin Cl BR5 . . . . .44 D6
St Katharine's Knockholt CE
   Prim Sch TN14 . . . . .74 B2
St Katherine's La ME6 . . . .81 F7
St Katherine's Sch ME6 . . .81 F7
St Katherines Cotts DA12 37 E4
St Katherines Rd DA18 . . . .3 D4
St Keverne Rd SE9 . . . . . . .28 E4
St Kilda Rd BR6 . . . . .43 F1
St Laurence Ave ME16 . . . .99 E8
St Laurence Cl BR5 . . . . . .44 D6
St Lawrence Ave TN4 . . . .142 D3
St Lawrence CE Prim Sch
   TN15 . . . . .93 E3
St Lenard's Twr * TN4 . . . .97 A7
St Leonard's St ME19 . . . . .97 F2
St Leonards Ave ME4 . . . . .53 F2
St Leonards Cl
   4 Bexley DA16 . . . . .13 A4
   Grays RM17 . . . . .17 F4
St Leonards Rd ME16 . . . . .99 C8
St Leonards Rise BR6 . . . . .57 E6
St Luke's Ave ME14 . . . . .100 B5
St Luke's CE Inf Sch
   TN4 . . . . .159 C7
St Luke's Rd
   Maidstone ME14 . . . . . . .100 B5
   Royal Tunbridge Wells
   TN4 . . . . .159 B6
St Luke's Way ME3 . . . . . . .9 D2
St Lukes Cl Dartford DA2 . .33 E3
   Swanley BR8 . . . . .45 D7
St Lukes Cotts BR8 . . . . . .45 D7
St Lukes Ct ME14 . . . . . . .100 A6
St Margaret Clitherow RC
   Prim Sch
   Tonbridge TN10 . . . . . . .127 B6
   Woolwich SE28 . . . . .3 B5
St Margaret's at Troy Town
   CE Prim Sch ME1 . . . . . .53 D4
St Margaret's Banks ME1 53 D5
St Margaret's CE Jun Sch
   ME8 . . . . .69 E8
St Margaret's CE Prim Sch
   SE18 . . . . .2 C1
St Margaret's Cl DA2 . . . . .33 D6
St Margaret's Cres DA12 . .36 E5
St Margaret's Ct **6** ME8 . .69 E8
St Margaret's Ct ME23 . . . .23 E3
St Margaret's Gr **8** SE18 .12 C8
St Margaret's Inf Sch
   ME8 . . . . .69 E8
St Margaret's Mews ME1 53 C5
St Margaret's Rd
   Dartford DA2,DA4 . . . . . .33 E2
   Northfleet DA11 . . . . .35 E7
St Margaret's St ME1 . . . . .53 C5
St Margaret's Terr SE18 . . . .2 C1
St Margarets Ave DA15 . . .29 D5
St Margarets CE Prim Sch
   TN12 . . . . .131 D1
St Margarets Cl
   Maidstone ME16 . . . . .99 B2

St Margarets Cl continued
   Orpington BR6 . . . . .58 B6
St Margarets Dr ME8 . . . . .69 C5
St Margarets Villas
   TN12 . . . . .147 D8
St Mark's Ave DA11 . . . . . .35 F8
St Mark's CE Prim Sch
   Bromley BR2 . . . . .42 A6
   Royal Tunbridge Wells
   TN4 . . . . .158 D1
St Mark's Rd Bromley BR2 42 A6
   Royal Tunbridge Wells
   TN2 . . . . .172 F7
St Marks CE Prim Sch
   ME20 . . . . .82 A6
St Marks Ct ME20 . . . . . . .82 F6
St Marks Ho ME7 . . . . .54 C5
St Marks Ind Est ME16 . . . .1 D5
St Martin's Cl ME14 . . . . . .85 A1
St Martin's Dr DA4 . . . . . . .60 D7
St Martin's Rd DA1 . . . . . . .15 F1
St Martins Erith DA18 . . . . . .3 D4
St Martins Mdw TN16 . . . . .90 C4
St Mary & St Joseph's RC Sch
   DA14 . . . . .30 A3
St Mary Cray Prim Sch
   BR5 . . . . .44 C3
St Mary Cray Sta BR5 . . . .44 B5
St Mary St SE18 . . . . .2 A2
St Mary's ME3 . . . . .24 D5
St Mary's Abbey ME19 . . . .97 C8
St Mary's CE Prim Sch
   BR8 . . . . .45 E5
St Mary's Church Rd
   TN14 . . . . .90 F2
St Mary's Cl
   Gravesend DA12 . . . . .36 C6
   Grays RM17 . . . . .18 D8
   Laddingford ME18 . . . . . .130 E4
   Orpington BR5 . . . . .44 C7
   Platt TN15 . . . . .95 C7
   Ticehurst TN5 . . . . .186 D1
St Mary's Ct Erith DA17 . . .3 D2
   5 Westerham TN16 . . . .89 D1
St Mary's Dr TN13 . . . . . . .91 E4
St Mary's Gdns ME4 . . . . . .54 B7
St Mary's Gn TN16 . . . . . . .72 C1
St Mary's Gr TN16 . . . . . . .72 C1
St Mary's Island CE Prim Sch
   ME4 . . . . .40 B2
St Mary's La
   Newington ME9 . . . . .71 C7
St Mary's Pl Eltham SE9 . . .12 A1
   Newington ME9 . . . . .71 C7
St Mary's Prim Sch ME2 . .53 B7
St Mary's RC Prim Sch
   Eltham SE9 . . . . .12 A2
   Gillingham ME7 . . . . .54 D6
   Tilbury RM18 . . . . .18 F5
St Mary's Rd
   Coldblow DA5 . . . . .31 C7
   Gillingham ME7 . . . . .54 C6
   Rochester ME2 . . . . .53 B7
   Stone DA9 . . . . .16 E2
   Swanley BR8 . . . . .45 E5
   Tonbridge TN9 . . . . .143 B7
   Wrotham TN15 . . . . .79 A2
St Mary's View ME9 . . . . . .71 C7
St Mary's Wlk ME1 . . . . . . .66 F1
St Marys Ct SE7 . . . . .11 D7
St Marys Way DA3 . . . . . . .48 E6
St Matthew's CE Inf Sch
   ME1 . . . . .53 A2
St Matthew's Cl ME9 . . . . .71 C7
St Matthew's High Brooms CE
   Prim Sch TN4 . . . . .159 B8
St Matthew's Way ME3 . . . .9 D2
St Matthews Dr
   Bromley BR1 . . . . .42 F6
   Rochester ME1 . . . . .53 A2
St Mellion Cl SE28 . . . . .3 D7
St Merryn Cl SE18 . . . . . . .12 D7
St Michael's CE Inf Sch
   ME16 . . . . .99 E3
St Michael's CE Prim Sch
   TN30 . . . . .183 A3
St Michael's Cl
   Chatham ME4 . . . . .53 F3
   Erith DA18 . . . . .3 D4
St Michael's Ct **6** ME2 . .53 B8
St Michael's East Wickham
   CE Prim Sch DA16 . . . . . .13 C6
St Michael's Prim Sch
   TN7 . . . . .170 B5
St Michael's RC Prim Sch
   ME4 . . . . .53 F7
St Michael's Rd
   Bexley DA16 . . . . .13 B4
   Maidstone ME16 . . . . .99 D3
   Royal Tunbridge Wells
   TN4 . . . . .159 B7
St Michael's Rise DA16 . . .13 B6
St Michael's Terr TN30 . . .183 A3
St Michaels RH8 . . . . .104 A5
St Michaels Cl
   Bromley BR1 . . . . .42 E6
   4 Newham E16 . . . . .1 D8
   Pratling Street ME20 . . . . .83 C3
St Michaels Ct TN11 . . . . .126 E7
St Michaels Dr TN14 . . . . . .76 E3
St Mildred's Cl **4** TN30 193 A7
St Mildreds Rd **5** SE12 . .28 A8
St Nicholas CE Inf Sch
   ME2 . . . . .53 A7
St Nicholas Ct TN13 . . . . . .92 B1
St Nicholas Dr TN13 . . . . . .92 C1

St Nicholas Gdns ME2 . . .52 F7
St Nicholas Rd SE18 . . . . . .2 F2
St Nicolas La BR7 . . . . . . .42 E8
St Olave's & St Saviour's
   Gram Sch BR6 . . . . .58 B7
St Olaves Prep Sch SE9 . . .29 B6
St Patrick's Gdns DA12 . . .36 D5
St Patrick's RC Prim Sch
   SE18 . . . . .2 D2
St Paul's CE Prim Sch
   BR8 . . . . .46 B8
St Paul's Cl Greenwich SE7 .1 D1
   Rochester ME2 . . . . .52 D5
   Swanscombe DA10 . . . . . .34 E8
St Paul's Cray CE Prim Sch
   BR5 . . . . .44 D6
St Paul's Cray Rd BR5,
   BR7 . . . . .43 D8
St Paul's Ct TN4 . . . . .158 C4
St Paul's RC Sch SE2 . . . .13 A8
St Paul's Rd DA8 . . . . .14 C7
St Paul's Sq BR2 . . . . .42 A4
St Paul's St TN4 . . . . .158 C4
St Paul's Wood Hill BR5 . . .43 F4
St Paulinus Ct DA1 . . . . . .14 E3
St Paulinus' CE Prim Sch
   DA1 . . . . .14 E3
St Pauls CE Inf Sch TN4 158 B4
St Pauls CE Jun Sch
   TN4 . . . . .158 B4
St Pauls Cl TN10 . . . . .127 D5
St Pauls Inf Sch ME14 . . .100 A7
St Peter & St Paul RC Prim
   Sch BR5 . . . . .43 F7
St Peter Ave TN16 . . . . . . .73 B3
St Peter Chanel RC Prim Sch
   DA14 . . . . .30 C3
St Peter St ME1 . . . . .53 D4
St Peter's Bridge ME14 . . .99 F4
St Peter's CE Prim Sch
   Aylesford ME20 . . . . .83 A3
   Royal Tunbridge Wells
   TN2 . . . . .159 C3
St Peter's Cl TN10 . . . . . . .34 F8
St Peter's Cl ME20 . . . . . . .82 C1
St Peter's Inf Sch ME1 . . . .53 C3
St Peter's Path ME1 . . . . . .53 D5
St Peter's RC Prim Sch
   SE18 . . . . .2 B2
St Peter's St TN2 . . . . . . .159 C3
St Peters Cl
   Chislehurst BR7 . . . . .29 D1
   Ditton ME20 . . . . .82 B1
St Peters La BR5 . . . . .44 A7
St Peters Pl ME20 . . . . . . .82 F6
St Peters Rd ME20 . . . . . . .82 B1
St Peters Row TN3 . . . . . .157 F5
St Peters St ME16 . . . . . . .99 F4
St Philip's Ave ME15 . . . .100 B1
St Philips Ct TN2 . . . . . . .159 D6
St Philomena's RC Prim Sch
   BR5 . . . . .44 C2
St Quentin Rd DA16 . . . . . .12 F4
St Ronan's Cl ME15 . . . . .116 C7
St Ronan's Sch TN18 . . . .189 D2
St Saviours Rd ME15 . . . .116 D6
St Simon Stock Sch
   ME16 . . . . .99 C4
St Stephen's Cl ME9 . . . . .71 C7
St Stephen's Cotts
   TN1 . . . . .159 B5
St Stephen's Ct TN1 . . . .159 B5
St Stephen's Prim Sch
   TN9 . . . . .143 D8
St Stephen's RC Prim Sch
   DA16 . . . . .13 A5
St Stephen's Sq ME15 . . . .99 E2
St Stephen's St TN9 . . . . .143 B8
St Stephens Mews ME1 . . .67 E8
St Thomas Ct DA5 . . . . . . .31 A8
St Thomas More RC Prim Sch
   Bexley DA7 . . . . .13 F5
   Chatham ME5 . . . . .68 A5
   Eltham SE9 . . . . .11 E4
St Thomas More RC Sec Sch
   SE9 . . . . .12 A1
St Thomas of Canterbury RC
   Prim Sch ME8 . . . . .55 B2
St Thomas RC Prim Sch
   TN13 . . . . .92 B2
St Thomas Rd Erith DA17 . .4 C4
   Newham E16 . . . . .1 A7
   Northfleet DA11 . . . . .35 E6
St Thomas' Dr BR5 . . . . . .43 C1
St Thomas' Rd RM17 . . . . .18 C8
St Thomas's Almshouses
   DA11 . . . . .36 B7
St Thomas's Ave DA11 . . .36 B7
St Thomas's Pl **15** RM17 .18 C8
St Thomas-a-Becket RC Prim
   Sch SE2 . . . . .3 A3
St Timothy's Mews **3**
   BR1 . . . . .42 B8
St Vincents Ave DA1 . . . . . .16 A2
St Vincents La ME19 . . . . . .80 A2
St Vincents RC Prim Sch
   SE9 . . . . .28 E4
St Vincents Rd DA1 . . . . . .16 A1
St Welcume's Way
   ME17 . . . . .119 E6
St Werburgh Cres ME3 . . . .40 D5
St Werburgh Ct ME3 . . . .40 D5
St William of Perth RC Prim
   Sch ME1 . . . . .53 B2
St William's Way ME1 . . . . .53 D2
St Winifred's Rd TN16 . . . . .72 F1
Sala Ho SE3 . . . . .11 B3

Salomons Way RM13 .....4 E7
Salcote Rd DA12 ......36 E3
Salem Pl DA11 ......35 D8
Salem St ME15 ......100 A3
Salhouse Cl SE28 ......3 C7
Salisbury Ave
 Gillingham ME8 ......69 D8
 Swanley BR8 ......46 A5
Salisbury Cl TN10 ......127 D5
Salisbury Ho **4** ME15 ..116 D7
Salisbury Mews BR2 ...42 E4
Salisbury Rd Bromley BR2 .42 E4
 Chatham ME4 ......54 A3
 Dartford DA2 ......33 C7
 2 Grays RM17 ......18 C8
 Kit's Coty ME20 ......83 D7
 Langton Green TN3 ...157 F3
 Maidstone ME14 ......100 A6
 Northfleet DA11 ......35 F7
 Royal Tunbridge Wells
 TN4 ......159 C8
 Sidcup DA5 ......31 A7
 Tonbridge TN10 ......127 D4
Salix Rd RM17 ......18 D8
Sallow Cl ME4 ......40 C1
Sallows Shaw DA13 ......50 C4
Sally Port ME7 ......54 A6
Sally Port Gdns ME7 ..54 B6
Salmon Rd Dartford DA1 .15 F4
 Erith DA17 ......4 A1
Salomons Rd Newham E13 .1 C8
 Rusthall TN4 ......158 C4
Salt La ME3 ......21 F4
Salt's Ave ME15 ......115 F3
Saltash Rd ME16 ......13 C6
Saltbox Hill TN16 ......72 B6
Saltcote Cl DA1 ......14 E1
Salter's Cross ME18 ...114 A1
Saltford Cl **2** DA8 ......4 E1
Saltings Rd ME6 ......82 A7
Saltley Cl E6 ......1 E7
Saltwood Cl BR6 ......58 C6
Saltwood Rd ME15 ......99 F1
Salvadori St ME7 ......160 D6
Sam Bartram Cl SE7 ....1 C1
Samara Cl ME5 ......68 A1
Samphire Cl ME14 .....100 E4
Samphire Ct ME17 ......18 E8
Samphire Way ME4 ......40 E2
Sampson Cl DA17 ......3 D3
Samson Ho SE1 ......2 C1
Samuel Cl SE18 ......1 E2
Samuel Palmer Ct BR6 ..44 A2
Samuel St SE18 ......1 F2
Sanctuary Cl DA1 ......15 D1
Sanctuary Rd ME8 ......55 A3
Sanctuary The DA5 ......13 D1
Sand La TN17 ......166 F4
Sandalwood Ho DA15 ..29 F5
Sandbanks Hill DA2 ....34 B2
Sandbourne Dr ME14 ..83 F1
Sandby Gn SE9 ......11 E4
Sandcliff Rd DA8 ......4 D1
Sanderling Ct SE28 .....3 C6
Sanderling Way TN9 ....17 A1
Sanderson Way TN14 ..59 B1
Sandersons Ave TN14 ..59 B1
Sandstead Rd BR5 ......44 B3
Sandfield Rd TN11 .....157 A7
Sandford Rd
 Bexley DA7,DA6 ......13 E4
 Bromley BR2 ......42 A5
Sandgate Ct ME8 ......69 F4
Sandgate Rd DA16 ......13 C7
Sandham Point SE18 ....2 B2
Sandhill La ME3 ......38 D6
Sandhole Cotts TN12 ..161 C4
Sandhurst Ave TN2 ....160 E5
Sandhurst Cl
 Gillingham ME8 ......55 C3
 Royal Tunbridge Wells
 TN2 ......159 C6
 Sandhurst Cross TN18 ..196 A4
Sandhurst Cross TN12 .150 F1
Sandhurst Ho TN2 .....159 D5
Sandhurst La TN17 .....191 B2
Sandhurst Pk TN2 .....159 C6
Sandhurst Prim Sch
 TN18 ......196 C5
Sandhurst Rd Bexley DA5 .13 D2
 Orpington BR6 ......58 A6
 Royal Tunbridge Wells
 TN2 ......159 D6
 Sidcup DA15 ......30 A5
 Tilbury RM18 ......19 C5
Sandhurst Vineyards★
 TN18 ......196 E5
Sandilands TN13 ......91 D5
Sandling Cl ME14 .....100 B7
Sandling La ME14 .....100 A8
Sandling Prim Sch
 ME14 ......100 B8
Sandling Rd
 Maidstone ME14 ......99 F6
 Maidstone,Ringlestone
 ME14 ......99 F7
Sandling Rise SE9 ......29 A5
Sandling Way ME4 ......40 E1
Sandown Cl TN2 ......159 F6
Sandown Dr ME8 ......69 D7
Sandown Gr TN2 ......159 F6
Sandown Pk TN2 ......159 F6
Sandown Rd
 Gravesend DA12 ......36 C2
 West Malling ME19 ....97 B8

Sandpiper Cl DA9 ......17 A1
Sandpiper Dr DA8 ......15 B7
Sandpiper Rd ME5 ......68 C2
Sandpiper Way BR5 ....44 D6
Sandpipers The DA12 ..36 D6
Sandpit Pl SE7 ......1 E1
Sandpit Rd DA1 ......15 C3
Sandra Ct **5** ME2 ......53 B8
Sandringham Ct ME19 ..97 A1
Sandringham Dr
 Bexley DA16 ......12 E5
 Maypole DA2 ......31 E6
Sandringham Ho ME1 ..53 B4
Sandringham Mews
 TN4 ......159 A5
Sandringham Rd
 Bromley BR1 ......28 A3
 Gillingham ME8 ......69 E3
Sandrock Ho TN2 .....159 D4
Sandrock Rd TN2 .....159 C4
Sandrock Villas TN18 .188 F3
Sandshaw Ct DA3 ......48 E4
Sandstone Rd SE12 .....28 B6
Sandstone Rise ME5 ...84 C8
Sandtoft Rd SE7 ......11 B8
Sandway Path **6** BR5 ....44 C5
Sandway Rd
 Harrietsham ME17 .....119 F4
 Orpington BR5 ......44 C5
Sandy Bank Rd DA12 ..36 B7
Sandy Bury BR6 ......57 D7
Sandy Dell ME7 ......69 A3
Sandy Hill Ave SE18 ....2 B1
Sandy Hill La SE18 .....2 B2
Sandy Hill Rd SE18 .....2 B1
Sandy La Bean DA13,DA2 .34 D5
 Ightham TN15 ......94 B3
 Limpsfield RH8 ......104 E1
 Maidstone,Harbourland
 ME14 ......100 C8
 Maidstone,Penenden Heath
 ME14 ......100 C7
 Maidstone,Ware Street
 ME14 ......101 B5
 New Town ME19 ......81 A1
 Orpington BR6 ......44 A2
 Ruxley BR5 ......44 D8
 Sevenoaks TN13 ......92 C4
 Snodland ME6,ME19 ...81 E6
 Tenterden TN30 ......193 B7
 Tilbury RM16 ......19 B8
 West Thurrock RM20 ..17 B8
 Westerham TN16 ......89 D2
 Wrotham Heath TN15,ME19 .79 F1
Sandy Mount ME14 ...101 B5
Sandy Ridge
 Borough Green TN15 ..95 A7
 Chislehurst BR7 ......29 A2
Sandycroft SE2 ......13 A8
Sandycroft Rd ME2 ....38 F1
Santana Ho SE18 ......12 B7
Santer Ho TN18 ......194 E8
Sapho Pk DA12 ......36 F4
Saphora Cl BR6 ......57 D5
Sapphire Cl E6 ......2 A7
Sara Cres DA9 ......17 E5
Sara Ho **1** DA8 ......14 E7
Sara Pk DA12 ......36 E4
Sara Turnbull Ho **3** SE18 .1 F2
Saracen Cl ME7 ......55 A1
Saracen Fields ME5 ....84 C8
Sarafand Ho ME1 ......53 B4
Sarah Ct **7** DA6 ......13 E3
Sark Wlk E16 ......1 B7
Sarsen Hts ME5 ......67 F1
Sarsens Cl DA12 ......50 F6
Sassoon Cl ME20 ......82 A4
Satanita Cl E16 ......1 D7
Saunder's Cross TN14 ..59 A3
Saunders Cl DA11 ......35 E6
Saunders Rd
 Royal Tunbridge Wells
 TN4 ......158 E1
 Woolwich SE18 ......2 F1
Saunders St
 7 Chatham ME4 ......53 F3
 Gillingham ME7 ......54 C6
Saunders Way
 Dartford DA1 ......32 F6
 Woolwich SE28 ......3 B6
Savage Gdns E6 ......1 F7
Savage Rd ME5 ......68 B3
Saville Cl TN10 ......127 D7
Saville Ho E16 ......2 B5
Saville Rd E16 ......1 E5
Savoy Rd DA1 ......15 D2
Sawyers Ct ME4 ......54 B2
Saxby Wood TN11 ....125 F1
Saxbys Rd TN15 ......93 D5
Saxon Cl Kings Hill ME19 .96 F2
 Northfleet DA11 ......35 C5
 Otford TN14 ......75 F2
 Rochester ME2 ......53 A8
Saxon Pl Horton Kirby DA4 .47 C4
 Rochester ME2 ......52 F5
Saxon Rd Bromley BR1 ..28 A1
 Hawley DA2 ......32 E4
Saxon Way Prim Sch
 ME7 ......54 E6
Saxon Wlk DA14 ......30 C2
Saxons Dr ME14 ......100 B7
Saxton St ME7 ......54 C5
Saxville Rd BR5 ......44 B6
Sayer Cl DA9 ......17 A2
Sayers La **6** TN30 ....193 A7
Sayes Court Rd BR5 ....44 B5

Scabharbour Rd TN14 .108 C1
Scadbury Gdns BR5 ....44 A7
Scadbury Park Nature
 Reserve★ BR7 ......29 F2
Scads Hill Cl BR6 ......43 F3
Scarborough Cl TN16 ..72 C1
Scarborough La ME1 ..66 D2
Scarlet Cl BR5 ......44 B5
Scarlett Cl ME5 ......68 C5
Scarsbrook Rd SE3 .....11 D4
Schofield Wlk SE3 .....11 B4
Scholars Rise ME2 .....52 D7
Scholey Cl ME2 ......66 B4
School App ME15 ......94 F7
School Ave ME7 ......54 E4
School Cl DA13 ......50 A2
School Cotts Bromley BR1 .28 A1
 Crockenhill BR8 ......45 D2
 Seal TN15 ......92 F6
 Sidcup DA14 ......30 C3
School Cres DA1 ......14 F3
School Field TN8 .....122 C4
School Hill TN3 ......176 B6
School House La TN12 .163 E7
School La Bean DA13 ...34 C5
 Bexley DA16 ......13 B4
 Chestnut Street ME9 ...71 F4
 Culverstone Green DA13 .64 A2
 Hadlow TN11 ......128 E8
 Hextable BR8 ......32 B1
 Higham ME3 ......38 C5
 Horton Kirby DA3,DA4 ..47 E4
 Knockmill TN15 ......77 F8
 Maidstone ME15 ......100 E1
 Newington ME9 ......71 B7
 Platt's Heath ME17 ....119 F2
 Plaxtol TN11,TN15 ....110 E6
 Seal TN15 ......92 F6
 Sutton Valence ME17 ..134 E7
 Trottiscliffe ME19 ......80 A5
 Wouldham ME1 ......66 D5
School Rd Chislehurst BR7 .29 C1
 Gravesend DA12 ......36 C5
School Rise TN2 ......158 F1
School Terr **6** TN18 ..188 F2
School Villas ME18 ....113 D5
Schoolfield Rd RM20 ..17 A8
Schooner Ct DA2 ......16 C3
Schooner Ho **11** DA8 ....4 E1
Schooner Wlk ME7 ....39 F3
Schrieber Mews ME7 ..54 D5
Scilla Cl **11** RM17 ......18 D8
Scimitar Cl ME7 ......55 A1
Scords La TN16 ......106 C4
Scotby Ave ME5 ......68 B4
Scotland La SE12 ......50 F6
Scotney Castle★ TN3 ..176 D3
Scotney Castle Gdns★
 TN3 ......176 D3
Scotney Cl BR6 ......57 A6
Scotney Ho ME2 ......39 C1
Scotsdale Cl BR5 ......43 E5
Scotsdale Rd SE12 .....11 B2
Scott Ave ME8 ......70 A8
Scott Cl ME20 ......98 C8
Scott Cres DA8 ......14 F6
Scott Ho **4** DA17 ......3 F1
Scott Rd Gravesend DA12 .36 D3
 Tonbridge TN9 ......142 F7
Scott St ME14 ......99 F6
Scott Wilkie Prim Sch
 E16 ......1 C7
Scott's Terr ME4 ......53 F3
Scotteswood Ave ME4 .53 F2
Scotts Ho ME16 ......13 C6
Scotts Park Prim Sch
 BR1 ......42 C8
Scotts Pas **11** SE18 .....2 B2
Scotts Rd BR1 ......28 A1
Scotts Terr SE9 ......28 E6
Scotts Way
 Royal Tunbridge Wells
 TN2 ......172 E8
 Sevenoaks TN13 ......91 E5
Scoulding Rd E16 ......1 A7
Scragged Oak Cvn Pk
 ME14 ......85 B2
Scragged Oak Rd
 Detling ME14 ......85 C5
 Hucking ME17 ......86 C1
Scratchers La DA3 ......61 E7
Scratton Fields DA12 ..50 D4
Scrubbs La ME16 ......99 D4
Scudders Hill DA3 .....48 C3
Seabrook Rd TN10 ....127 A3
Seabrooke Rise RM17 ..18 B8
Seacourt Rd SE2 ......3 D4
Seaford Ct ME1 ......53 B5
Seagull La E16 ......1 A6
Seagull Rd ME2 ......52 D6
Seal CE Prim Sch TN15 .92 F7
Seal Dr TN15 ......92 F6
Seal Ho TN15 ......92 F6
Seal Hollow Rd TN13 ..92 D4
Seal Rd TN13,TN14,TN15 .92 D6
Sealand Ct ME1 ......53 B5
Sealcroft Cotts TN15 ..92 F8
Seamew Ct ME2 ......52 C7
Searles Dr E6 ......2 B8
Seaton Rd Bexley DA16 .13 C7
 Dartford DA1 ......32 A8
 Gillingham ME7 ......54 E3
Seaview ME3 ......27 B5
Seaview Rd ME7 ......54 C4
Second Ave Chatham ME4 .54 C1
 Gillingham ME7 ......54 E3
 West Thurrock RM20 ..17 A8
Secretan Rd ME1 ......53 B1

Sedcombe Cl DA14 .....30 C4
Sedge Cres ME5 ......67 E4
Sedgebrook Rd SE3 ....11 D4
Sedgemere Rd SE2 ......3 C3
Sedgemoor Ho ME1 ....53 E5
Sedley Cl Aylesford ME20 .82 F2
 Cliffe Woods ME3 ......39 C7
 Gillingham ME8 ......69 C3
Sedley Dr DA13 ......35 A3
Sedley's CE Prim Sch
 DA13 ......35 A3
Sefton Cl BR5 ......43 F5
Sefton Rd BR5 ......43 F5
Sejant Ho **4** RM17 ....18 B8
Selah Dr BR8 ......45 C8
Selborne Ave DA5 ......30 E7
Selborne Rd DA14 ......30 B4
Selbourne Cl DA3 ......49 D6
Selbourne Rd ME7 .....54 D7
Selbourne Wlk ME15 ..116 F6
Selby Cl Chislehurst BR7 .29 A2
 14 Newham E6 ......1 E8
Selby Rd Maidstone ME15 116 A4
 Newham E13 ......1 B8
Select Bsns Ctr TN12 ..149 E5
Selkirk Dr DA8 ......14 E6
Sellbourne Pk TN3 ....173 C4
Sellinge Gn ME8 ......55 C3
Sellwood Ct DA1 ......33 B7
Selsey Cl DA16 ......13 B3
Selsted Cl ME8 ......55 C2
Selwood Ho BR7 ......29 C2
Selwyn Cres DA16 .....13 B3
Selwyn Pl **1** BR5 ......44 B6
Selwyn Rd RM18 ......18 F5
Semple Gdns ME4 .....53 E3
Senacre La ME15 ......116 E6
Senacre Sq ME15 ......116 F7
Senacre Tech Coll
 ME15 ......116 D6
Senacre Wood Prim Sch
 ME15 ......116 F7
Senator Wlk **4** SE28 ..2 D3
Sencler Ho Bexley SE2 ..13 D8
 Erith SE2 ......3 D1
Senlac Pl TN3 ......171 C7
Senlac Rd SE12 ......28 B7
Sennen Wlk SE9 ......28 E5
Sennocke Ct TN13 ......92 B2
Sequoia Gdns BR6 .....43 F2
Sermon Dr BR8 ......45 C6
Serpentine Ct TN13 ...92 D5
Serpentine Rd TN13 ...92 D4
Serviden Dr BR1 ......42 D8
Sessions House Sq ME14 99 F5
Setford Rd ME1 ......66 C6
Settington Ave ME5 ...54 C1
Seven Acres
 Crockenhill BR8 ......45 D3
 New Ash Green DA3 ..62 E7
Seven Mile La
 Kings Hill ME18 ......96 A3
 Mereworth TN11,TN12 ..112 E3
 Wrotham Heath TN15 ..95 F7
Seven Wents TN15 .....94 A4
Sevenoaks Bsns Ctr
 TN14 ......92 C6
Sevenoaks By-Pass
 TN13,TN14 ......107 F7
Sevenoaks Cl DA7 ......14 B3
Sevenoaks Hospl TN13 .92 C6
Sevenoaks Mus & Gallery★
 TN13 ......92 C2
Sevenoaks Prep Sch
 TN13 ......93 A1
Sevenoaks Prim Sch
 TN13 ......92 B5
Sevenoaks Rd
 Borough Green TN15 ..94 F3
 Ightham TN15 ......94 A4
 Orpington BR6 ......57 F6
 Otford TN14 ......76 B3
 Pratt's Bottom BR6,TN14 ..58 C2
Sevenoaks Sch TN13 ..92 C1
Sevenoaks Sch Int Ctr
 TN13 ......92 B1
Sevenoaks Sta TN13 ..92 B3
Sevenoaks Way BR5 ...44 C7
Sevenoaks Way Ind Est **1**
 BR5 ......44 C6
Sevenoaks Wildfowl
 Reserve★ TN14 ......92 A7
Severn Cl TN10 ......127 C5
Severn Rd ME5 ......68 C5
Sevington Pk ME15 ...115 F6
Sewell Rd SE2 ......3 B4
Sextant Pk ME2 ......53 E6
Sexton Rd RM18 ......18 F6
Seymour Dr BR2 ......42 F1
Seymour Rd
 1 Chatham ME5 ......54 B3
 Gillingham ME8 ......70 C8
 Northfleet DA11 ......35 F6
 Tilbury RM18 ......18 F6
Seymour St SE18 ......2 C3
Seymour Wlk DA10 ....34 E8
Shacklands Rd TN14 ..59 D1
Shackleton Cl ME5 ....68 B6
Shades The ME2 ......52 C7
Shaftesbury Cl ME19 ..81 F1
Shaftesbury Ct Erith DA8 .14 F6
 3 Woolwich SE28 .....3 C5
Shaftesbury Dr ME16 ..99 C4
Shaftesbury La DA1 ...16 B3
Shaftesbury Rd TN4 ..159 A5
Shaftesbury Ct **2** 27 A7
Shakespeare Ave RM18 .19 B6

Sal – She 235

Shakespeare Farm Rd
 ME3 ......24 F7
Shakespeare Ho **1** DA17 .3 F1
Shakespeare Rd
 Bexley DA7 ......13 E6
 Dartford DA1 ......16 A3
 Gillingham ME7 ......54 C3
 Tonbridge TN9 ......142 F8
Shalder Ho ME2 ......54 D7
Shalfleet Cl **1** ME5 ....68 A7
Shalford Cl BR6 ......57 C6
Shallons Rd SE9 ......29 B4
Shambles The TN13 ....92 C2
Shamel Bsns Ctr ME2 .53 C7
Shamley Rd ME5 ......68 D2
Shamrock Rd DA12 ....36 F8
Shandon Cl TN2 ......159 C4
Shanklin Cl ME5 ......68 C8
Shannon Ct BR6 ......44 A2
Sharfleet Dr ME2 ......52 B7
Sharland Rd DA12 .....36 C6
Sharman Ct DA14 ......30 A4
Sharnal La ME6 ......82 A7
Sharnal St ME3 ......24 A2
Sharnbrooke Cl DA16 .13 C4
Sharon Cres ME5 ......67 F4
Sharon Ct **10** DA14 ....30 B4
Sharp Way DA1 ......15 F4
Sharp's Field TN27 ....151 E5
Sharps Gn ME8 ......55 D5
Sharsted Way
 Gillingham ME7 ......69 A3
 Maidstone ME14 ......101 B5
Shaw Cl Cliffe Woods ME3 .39 B8
 Maidstone ME14 ......100 C7
 Woolwich SE28 ......3 B5
Shaw Cres RM18 ......19 B6
Shaw Ho **6** Erith DA17 ..3 F1
 5 Newham E16 ......2 A5
Shaw Rd TN16 ......88 C7
Shaw The TN2 ......159 C2
Shawbrooke Rd SE9 ...11 D3
Shawbrooke Pk BR1 ...42 D7
Shawhill Ho ME19 ......80 B1
Shaws Way ME1 ......53 C3
Shawstead Rd ME7,ME7 .68 D5
Sheafe Dr TN17 ......179 C5
Sheal's Cres ME15 .....100 A2
Sheals Ct ME15 ......100 A2
Shearers Cl ME14 .....100 E4
Shears Cl DA2 ......32 C6
Shears Green Ct DA11 .36 A6
Shears Green Inf Sch
 DA11 ......35 F5
Shears Green Jun Sch
 DA11 ......35 F5
Shearwater
 Maidstone ME16 ......99 B5
 New Barn DA3 ......49 B6
Shearwater Cl ME2 ....52 C7
Shearwood Cres DA1 ..15 A4
Sheen Rd BR5 ......43 F5
Sheepbarn La TN16 ....72 A7
Sheepcote La BR5,BR8 ..44 F4
Sheephurst La TN12 ..147 E5
Sheerness Harbour Est
 ME12 ......27 F3
Sheerness Mews E16 ..2 B4
Sheerwater Rd E16 .....1 D8
Sheet Hill TN15 ......94 D2
Sheffield Rd **4** TN4 ..142 F2
Sheilings The TN15 ....92 F7
Shelbury Cl DA14 ......30 A5
Shelden Dr ME8 ......69 F8
Sheldon Bsns Ctr ME6 .53 D8
Sheldon Cl SE12 ......11 B2
Sheldon Rd DA7 ......13 F6
Sheldon Way ME20 ....82 B3
Sheldrake Cl E16 ......1 F5
Sheldwich Terr BR2 ...42 E3
Shell Cl BR2 ......42 E3
Shellbank La DA2 ......34 B4
Shelldrake Cl ME3 ......27 B5
Shelley Cl BR6 ......57 E7
Shelley Dr DA16 ......12 E6
Shelley Ho DA1 ......14 E2
Shelley Pl RM18 ......19 B6
Shelley Rd ME15 ......99 C2
Shelley Rise ME1 ......53 A3
Shelleys La TN14 ......74 A3
Shelton Cl TN10 ......127 C5
Shenden Cl TN13 ......108 C7
Shenden Way TN13 ...108 C7
Shenfield Rd SE18 .....11 D7
Shenley Gr ME14 ......83 F2
Shenley Rd DA1 ......33 A8
Shenstone Cl DA1 .....14 D3
Shenstone Sch DA1 ...14 D3
Shepherd St DA11 .....35 D8
Shepherds Cl BR6 ......57 F7
Shepherds Gate ME7 ..68 F5
Shepherds Gate Dr
 ME14 ......100 E6
Shepherds Gn BR7 ....29 D1
Shepherds La
 Dartford DA1 ......32 B8
 Woolwich SE28 ......3 A6
Shepherds Leas SE9 ..12 D3
Shepherds Way
 Langley Heath ME17 ..117 E4
 Lower Stoke ME3 ......25 C4
Shepherds Wlk TN2 ..159 D4
Shepherdsgrove La
 RH19 ......154 A4
Sheppards Coll **8** BR1 .42 A8

Shepperton Cl ME5 . . . . . . .68 C4
Shepperton Rd BR5 . . . . . .43 C3
Sheppey Cl DA8 . . . . .15 B7
Sheppey Rd ME15 . . . . . .116 A7
Sheppey Ho **1** BR1 . . . . .28 B1
Sheppey Pl DA12 . . . . . . .36 B8
Shepway Cl ME15 . . . . . .116 C8
Shepway Inf Sch ME15 . .116 E8
Shepway Jun Sch ME15 116 E8
Sherard Mans SE9 . . . . . . .11 F2
Sherard Rd SE9 . . . . .11 E2
Sheraton Ct ME4 . . . . . . .67 F1
Sherborne Gr TN15 . . . . . .77 A2
Sherborne Rd BR5 . . . . . .43 F4
Sherbourne Cl
  Royal Tunbridge Wells
  TN2 . . . . .159 D2
  West Kingsdown TN15 . . . .61 E4
Sherbourne Dr
  Maidstone ME16 . . . . .99 B2
  Rochester ME2 . . . . .39 A1
Sherbrooke Cl DA7 . . . . . .14 A3
Sherenden La TN12 . . . .164 D8
Sherenden Pk TN11 . . . .129 A5
Sherenden Rd TN11 . . . .144 D7
Sherfield Rd RM17 . . . . . .18 B8
Sheridale Bsns Ctr ME2 . .53 A6
Sheridan Cl Chatham ME5 .68 C7
  Maidstone ME14 . . . . .99 E8
  Swanley BR8 . . . . .45 F6
Sheridan Cres BR7 . . . . . .43 B7
Sheridan Ct Dartford DA1 .16 A3
  Rochester ME1 . . . . .53 A2
Sheridan Lodge **1** BR2 . .42 C5
Sheridan Rd Bexley DA7 . . .3 A4
  Erith DA17 . . . . .4 A2
Sheriff Dr ME5 . . . . .68 A2
Sheringham Cl ME16 . . . . .99 D7
Sheringham Ho **5**
  ME15 . . . . .116 D8
Sherington Prim Sch
  SE7 . . . . .11 B8
Sherington Rd SE7 . . . . . .11 B8
Sherlies Ave BR6 . . . . . . .57 E8
Sherman Cl ME7 . . . . .55 B1
Sherman Rd BR1 . . . . .42 A8
Shernden La TN8 . . . . . .138 C4
Shernold Sch ME16 . . . . . .99 D5
Shernolds ME15 . . . . . . .116 B7
Sherway Cl TN27 . . . . . . .151 E5
Sherway Rd TN27 . . . . . .152 D6
Sherwin Knight Inf Sch
  ME2 . . . . .52 E5
Sherwin Knight Jun Sch
  ME2 . . . . .52 E5
Sherwood Ave ME5 . . . . . .68 A2
Sherwood Cl DA5 . . . . . . .13 C1
Sherwood Ho
  Chatham ME5 . . . . .68 A3
  Erith DA8 . . . . .14 E8
Sherwood Park Ave
  DA15 . . . . .13 B1
Sherwood Park Com Prim
  Sch TN2 . . . . .159 D6
Sherwood Park Prim Sch
  DA15 . . . . .13 B1
Sherwood Pl TN3 . . . . . .157 E3
Sherwood Rd Bexley DA16 12 E4
  Royal Tunbridge Wells
  TN2 . . . . .159 E5
Sherwood Way TN2 . . . .159 D6
Shieldhall St SE2 . . . . .3 C2
Shillingheld Cl ME14 . . . .100 A5
Shinecroft TN14 . . . . .76 A3
Shingle Barn La ME15 . .114 C3
Shinglewell Rd DA8 . . . . . .14 A7
Ship Field Cl TN16 . . . . . .88 C6
Ship Hill TN16 . . . . .88 D6
Ship La Rochester ME1 . . .53 E4
  Sutton at H BR8,DA4 . . . . .46 E8
Shipbourne Rd
  Shipbourne TN11 . . . . . .110 D2
  Tonbridge TN10 . . . . . . .127 C5
Shipbourne Sch TN11 . .110 C4
Shipley Ct ME14 . . . . . . .100 A4
Shipley Hills Rd DA13 . . .49 E1
Shipman Rd E16 . . . . .1 C7
Shipwrights Ave ME4 . . . .54 B2
Shire Ct DA18 . . . . .3 D3
Shire La
  Farthing Street BR6 . . . . . .57 C3
  Orpington BR6 . . . . .57 E5
Shirebrook Rd SE3 . . . . . .11 D4
Shirehall Rd DA2 . . . . . . .32 E4
Shires The TN12 . . . . . . .146 A7
Shirley Ave Chatham ME5 .67 D5
  Sidcup DA5 . . . . .30 D7
Shirley Cl Chalk DA12 . . . .37 B6
  Dartford DA1 . . . . .15 C4
Shirley Ct ME15 . . . . . . .116 E5
Shirley Gdns TN4 . . . . . .158 C5
Shirley Gr TN4 . . . . .158 C5
Shirley House Dr SE7 . . . .11 C7
Shirley Hts **5** DA6 . . . . .13 E3
Shirley Rd DA15 . . . . .29 E5
Shirley Way ME15 . . . . . .101 A3
Sholden Gdns BR5 . . . . . .44 C4
Sholden Rd ME2 . . . . .39 C1
Shooters Hill SE18 . . . . . .12 A6
Shooters Hill Rd SE18,
  SE3 . . . . .11 D6
Shore The Northfleet DA11 18 C2
  Northfleet,Rosherville DA11 18 F1
Shoreham Aircraft Mus★
  TN14 . . . . .75 F8

Shoreham Cl DA5 . . . . . . .30 D7
Shoreham Ho TN14 . . . . . .76 A8
Shoreham La
  Badgers Mount TN14 . . . . .75 A7
  Chelsfield BR6 . . . . .59 A3
  Sevenoaks TN13 . . . . .91 F4
  Tenterden TN30 . . . . . . .183 A3
Shoreham Pl TN14 . . . . . .76 A7
Shoreham Rd
  Orpington BR5 . . . . .44 B7
  Otford TN14 . . . . .76 B5
Shoreham Sta TN14 . . . . .76 B8
Shoreham Village Sch
  TN14 . . . . .75 F8
Shoreham Way BR2 . . . . . .42 A3
Shoreham Wlk ME15 . . . .116 F7
Shorehill Ct TN15 . . . . . . .76 F2
Shorehill La TN15 . . . . . . .76 F4
Shorland Ct ME1 . . . . .53 B5
Shorne CE Prim Sch
  DA12 . . . . .37 E3
Shorne Cl Orpington BR5 . .44 D5
  3 Sidcup DA15 . . . . . . .13 B1
Shorne Ifield Rd DA12 . . .37 C2
Shorne Wood Ctry Pk★
  DA12 . . . . .37 C1
Shornefield Cl BR1 . . . . . .43 A6
Shornells Way SE2 . . . . . . .3 C1
Short La RH8 . . . . .104 B3
Short Path SE18 . . . . .12 B8
Short St **3** ME4 . . . . . . .54 B3
Shortlands Cl DA17 . . . . . . .3 F3
Shortlands Gn ME15 . . . .116 F5
Shorts Way ME1 . . . . .53 A3
Shortway SE9 . . . . .11 E4
Shottenden Rd ME7 . . . . . .54 D7
Shottery Cl SE9 . . . . .28 E5
Showfields Rd TN2 . . . . .158 F1
Shrapnel Cl SE18 . . . . . . .11 E7
Shrapnel Rd SE9 . . . . .11 F4
Shrewsbury La SE18 . . . . .12 B6
Shroffold Rd BR1 . . . . . . .28 A5
Shropshire Terr **1**
  ME15 . . . . .116 E7
Shrubbery Rd
  Gravesend DA12 . . . . .36 C2
  Sutton at H DA4 . . . . .47 D8
Shrubcote TN30 . . . . . . .193 C7
Shrublands Ct
  Royal Tunbridge Wells
  TN2 . . . . .159 C4
  1 Tonbridge TN9 . . . . .127 C2
Shrubsall Cl SE9 . . . . .28 E7
Shrubshall Mdw TN15 . .111 A8
Shrubsole Dr ME14 . . . . . .83 F3
Shurlock Ave BR8 . . . . . . .45 D1
Shurlock Dr BR6 . . . . .57 C6
Shuttle Cl
  Biddenden TN27 . . . . . . .168 A2
  Sidcup DA15 . . . . .29 F8
Shuttle Rd DA1 . . . . .15 A4
Shuttlemead DA5 . . . . . . .30 F8
Sibley Cl DA6 . . . . .13 E2
Sibthorpe Rd SE12 . . . . . .28 C8
Sidcup By Pass Rd
  Orpington BR5,BR7,DA14 . .30 B1
  Sidcup DA14 . . . . .29 E4
Sidcup Hill DA14 . . . . . . .30 B3
Sidcup Hill Gdns DA14 . . .30 C3
Sidcup Pl DA14 . . . . .30 A3
Sidcup Rd SE12,SE9 . . . . .28 D7
Sidcup Sta DA15 . . . . .30 A6
Sidcup Tech Ctr DA14 . . . .30 D2
Sidewood Rd SE9 . . . . . . .29 D7
Sidmouth Ct DA1 . . . . . . .33 B7
Sidmouth Rd Bexley DA16 13 C7
  Orpington BR5 . . . . .44 B5
Sidney Cl TN2 . . . . .172 F8
Sidney Gdns TN14 . . . . . .76 C2
Sidney Ho SE18 . . . . .11 F6
Sidney Rd Gillingham ME7 .54 C7
  Rochester ME1 . . . . .53 A2
Sidney St ME16 . . . . .99 C2
Siebert Rd SE3 . . . . .11 A8
Siedle Ho **9** SE18 . . . . .12 A8
Siemens Rd SE18 . . . . .1 D3
Signal Ct **6** ME4 . . . . . . .55 F1
Silchester Ct ME14 . . . . .100 C7
Silecroft Rd DA7 . . . . .14 A6
Silk Cl SE12 . . . . .11 A1
Silk Mills Cl TN13 . . . . . . .92 C6
Silver Bank ME5 . . . . .68 A6
Silver Birch Cl
  Joyden's Wood DA2 . . . . . .31 E4
  Woolwich SE28 . . . . .3 A5
Silver Birch Wlk ME18 . . .113 D6
Silver Birches ME5 . . . . . .68 A3
Silver Cl TN9 . . . . .143 B6
Silver Hill Chatham ME4 . .53 F3
  Hurst Green TN19 . . . . . .194 B1
  Rochester ME1 . . . . .52 F2
  Tenterden TN30 . . . . . . .183 B1
Silver Hill Gdns **4** ME4 .53 F3
Silver Rd DA12 . . . . .36 E6
Silver Spring Cl DA8 . . . . .14 B8
Silver St ME9 . . . . .87 F5
Silver Tree ME5 . . . . .68 B1
Silverdale Hartley DA3 . . .48 F5
  Maidstone ME16 . . . . .99 A2
Silverdale Dr Bromley SE9 28 E6
  Gillingham ME8 . . . . .69 F7
Silverdale La
  Royal Tunbridge Wells
  TN4 . . . . .159 B6
  Sandhurst Cross TN18 . . .195 F5
Silverdale Rd Bexley DA7 .14 B5
  Orpington,Petts Wood BR5 .43 C5

Silverdale Rd continued
  Orpington,St Paul's Cray
  BR5 . . . . .44 A6
  Royal Tunbridge Wells
  TN4 . . . . .159 B6
Silverden Cotts TN18 . . .195 F4
Silverhurst Dr TN10 . . . .127 C7
Silverland St E16 . . . . .1 F5
Silverlocke Rd RM17 . . . . .18 D8
Silverspot Cl ME8 . . . . . . .69 F7
Silversted La TN16 . . . . . .89 D6
Silverstone Ct **10** BR1 . .42 C7
Silvertown Sta E16 . . . . . . .1 E5
Silvertown Way E16 . . . . . .1 A5
Silverweed Rd ME5 . . . . . .67 F4
Silwood Cl TN2 . . . . .159 F7
Simmonds Ct TN4 . . . . . .158 B4
Simmonds Dr DA3 . . . . . . .49 A4
Simmonds La ME15 . . . . .117 B6
Simmons Rd SE18 . . . . .2 B1
Simnel Rd SE12 . . . . .28 B8
Simon Ct **5** SE28 . . . . . . .3 B5
Simone Cl BR1 . . . . .42 D8
Simpson Rd ME6 . . . . .82 A6
Simpson's Cotts BR2 . . . . .56 C7
Simpson's Rd BR1,BR2 . . .42 A6
Simpsons Pl **6** ME4 . . . . .42 A6
Sinclair Cl ME8 . . . . .69 E5
Sinclair Way DA2 . . . . .33 D4
Sindal Shaw Ho ME5 . . . . .67 E4
Singapore Dr ME7 . . . . . . .54 B5
Single St TN16 . . . . .73 B4
Single's Cross TN14 . . . . .74 D4
Single's Cross La TN14 . . .74 C5
Singlewell Prim Sch
  DA12 . . . . .36 D2
Singlewell Rd DA11 . . . . . .36 B4
Sinkerweazel TN17 . . . . .179 E2
Sion Wlk **8** TN1 . . . . . .159 A2
Sir David's Pk TN4 . . . . .142 E1
Sir Evelyn Rd ME1 . . . . . . .53 B1
Sir John Hawkins Hospl
  ME4 . . . . .53 E4
Sir John Hawkins Way
  ME4 . . . . .53 F4
Sir Joseph Williamson's
  Mathematical Sch ME1 .53 C1
Sir Martin Bowes Ho **11**
  SE18 . . . . .2 A2
Sir Thomas Longley Rd
  ME2 . . . . .53 E6
Sirdar Strand DA12 . . . . . .36 F3
Siscup Cl SE9 . . . . .29 B6
Siskin Gdns TN12 . . . . . .146 A5
Siskin Wlk ME20 . . . . .81 F2
Sissinghurst Castle Gdns★
  TN17 . . . . .166 D1
Sissinghurst CE Prim Sch
  TN17 . . . . .180 B8
Sissinghurst Dr ME16 . . . .99 B4
Sissinghurst Rd
  Biddenden TN27 . . . . . . .167 C2
  Sissinghurst TN17,TN27 . .180 D8
Sittingbourne Rd
  Maidstone,Detling ME14 . .100 E8
  Maidstone,Penenden Heath
  ME14 . . . . .100 B6
Siward Rd BR2 . . . . .42 C6
Six Bells La TN13 . . . . . . .92 C5
Six Fields Path TN30 . . . .193 A7
Six Penny Cl TN8 . . . . . .138 C8
Skeet Hill La BR5,BR6 . . . .58 E8
Skeffington St SE18 . . . . . .2 C3
Skeynes Rd TN8 . . . . . . .122 B1
Skibbs La BR5,BR6 . . . . . .58 E7
Skinner Gdns TN17 . . . . .180 A4
Skinner St Chatham ME4 . .53 F3
  Gillingham ME7 . . . . .54 C7
Skinner Street Prim Sch
  ME7 . . . . .54 C6
Skinner's Terr **15** TN9 . .143 B8
Skinner's Way ME17 . . . .117 E4
Skinners Cl ME20 . . . . . . .83 A6
Skinners La TN8 . . . . . . .122 D2
Skinners' Sch The TN4 . .159 A6
Skinney La DA4 . . . . .47 D6
Skippers Cl DA9 . . . . .17 B2
Skua Ct ME2 . . . . .52 C7
Sky Studios E16 . . . . .2 A4
Skye Cl ME15 . . . . .116 A7
Slade Cl ME5 . . . . .68 B2
Slade Gdns DA8 . . . . .14 F6
Slade Green Inf Sch DA8 15 A7
Slade Green Jun Sch
  DA8 . . . . .15 A7
Slade Green Rd DA8 . . . . .15 A7
Slade Green Sta DA8 . . . . .15 A6
Slade Prim Sch TN9 . . . .127 B2
Slade The
  Lamberhurst TN3 . . . . . .176 A3
  Tonbridge TN9 . . . . .127 B2
  Woolwich SE18 . . . . .12 E8
Sladebrook Rd SE3 . . . . . .11 D4
Sladedale Rd SE18 . . . . . . .2 E1
Slades Dr BR7 . . . . .29 C4
Slaney Rd TN12 . . . . . . .149 F4
Slater Cl **9** SE18 . . . . . . .2 A2
Slaters TN8 . . . . .123 F2
Slatin Rd ME2 . . . . .53 B8
Sleeches Cross TN3 . . . . .178 B7
Sleepers Stile Rd TN5 . . .175 B1
Slicketts Hill ME4 . . . . . . .54 A4
Slip Mill Rd TN18 . . . . . .188 E4
Slip The TN16 . . . . .89 C1
Slipway Rd E16 . . . . .1 B5
Sloane Gdns BR6 . . . . . . .57 C5
Sloane Sq DA3 . . . . .48 E6
Slocum Cl SE28 . . . . .3 C6

Small Bridge Cotts
  TN17 . . . . .163 B2
Small Bridge Rd TN12,
  TN17 . . . . .163 B2
Small Grains DA3 . . . . . . .62 B7
Small Hythe Cl ME15 . . . .101 B2
Small Hythe Rd TN30 . . .193 B4
Small Profits ME18 . . . . . .114 A4
Smallhythe Pl★ TN30 . . . .193 C1
Smallhythe Place (Mus)★
  TN30 . . . . .199 C8
Smarden Bsns Est TN27 168 D7
Smarden Cl **8** DA17 . . . . .4 A1
Smarden Gr SE9 . . . . .28 F4
Smarden Prim Sch
  TN27 . . . . .153 A1
Smarden Rd
  Standen TN27 . . . . .168 B6
  Swift's Green TN27 . . . . .152 B4
Smarts Cotts ME14 . . . . .101 C4
Smarts Hill TN11 . . . . . . .141 A1
Smarts Rd DA12 . . . . .36 C6
Smetham Gdns ME2 . . . . .39 B1
Smith Rd ME5 . . . . .68 B3
Smith St ME2 . . . . .53 A6
Smith's Hill ME15 . . . . . .114 C5
Smithers Cl TN11 . . . . . . .111 E1
Smithers Ct TN12 . . . . . .130 A7
Smithers La TN12 . . . . . .130 A7
Smithfield Rd ME3 . . . . . .27 C5
Smithies Rd SE2 . . . . .3 B2
Smiths La TN8 . . . . .105 C2
Smiths Orch ME9 . . . . . . .87 F5
Smithy Field **7** TN8 . . . .122 D3
Smithy The TN5 . . . . .184 A3
Smugglers TN18 . . . . . . .189 A1
Smugglers Wlk DA9 . . . . .17 B2
Smythe Cl TN4 . . . . .142 E3
Smythe Rd DA4 . . . . .47 A8
Snag La TN14 . . . . .73 D7
Snape La TN5 . . . . .184 D1
Snape View TN5 . . . . . . .184 F4
Snelling Ave DA11 . . . . . .35 F6
Snipe Cl Erith DA8 . . . . . .15 B7
  Pembury TN2 . . . . .160 E8
Snipe Ct ME2 . . . . .52 C7
Snoad La TN12 . . . . .165 A8
Snodhurst Ave ME5 . . . . . .67 E5
Snodhurst Ho **2** ME5 . . . .68 A7
Snodland CE Prim Sch
  ME6 . . . . .81 F8
Snodland Rd ME19 . . . . . .81 D7
Snodland Sta ME6 . . . . . . .82 B8
Snodlands Cl BR6 . . . . . . .57 A1
Snoll Hatch Rd TN12 . . . .129 F5
Snow Ho ME7 . . . . .54 E7
Snowdon Ave ME14 . . . . .100 B5
Snowdon Cl ME5 . . . . .68 B7
Snowdon Par ME14 . . . . .100 C5
Snughorne La TN27 . . . . .168 D8
Sobraon Villas TN15 . . . . .95 C7
Sole Fields TN13 . . . . . . .108 C8
Sole St DA12,DA13 . . . . . .50 D4
Sole Street Farm ME3 . . . .39 B3
Sole Street Sta DA13 . . . . .50 D4
Solefield Prep Sch
  TN13 . . . . .108 C8
Solefields Rd TN13 . . . . .108 C8
Solent Gdns ME5 . . . . . . .68 B8
Soleoak Dr TN13 . . . . . . .108 B8
Solomon Rd
  Gillingham ME8 . . . . .70 A8
  Rainham ME8 . . . . .55 F1
Solomons Rd ME4 . . . . . . .53 F4
Somerden Rd BR5 . . . . . . .44 D2
Somerfield Cl ME16 . . . . . .99 D5
Somerfield Hospl The
  ME16 . . . . .99 E5
Somerfield La ME16 . . . . . .99 D4
Somerfield Rd ME16 . . . . . .99 D4
Somerhill Ave DA15 . . . . . .24 B8
Somerhill Rd Bexley DA16 13 B5
  Tonbridge TN9 . . . . .143 D8
Somerset Ave DA16 . . . . . .12 F3
Somerset Cl ME5 . . . . .68 C8
Somerset Ct Dartford DA1 32 B8
  Maidstone ME15 . . . . . . .116 C8
  Orpington BR6 . . . . .44 A2
  Royal Tunbridge Wells
  TN4 . . . . .159 A6
Somerset Villas TN3 . . . .171 C2
Somersham Rd DA7 . . . . . .13 E5
Somertrees Ave SE12 . . . .28 B6
Somerville Gdns TN4 . . . .158 F4
Somerville Rd DA1 . . . . . .15 F1
Somner Wlk ME15 . . . . . .116 F4
Sonnet Wlk TN16 . . . . . . .72 C1
Soper's La TN18 . . . . . . .188 D4
Sophia Rd E16 . . . . .1 B7
Sophurst La TN12 . . . . . .161 C5
Sopurst Wood TN12 . . . .161 D5
Sopwith Cl TN16 . . . . . . .72 D3
Sorrel Cl SE28 . . . . .3 A5
Sorrel Ct **8** RM17 . . . . . .18 D8
Sorrel Gdns E6 . . . . .1 E8
Sorrell Cl **4** TN8 . . . . . .122 D3
Sorrell Rd ME5 . . . . .67 F4
Sorrell Way DA11 . . . . . . .35 F2
Sortmill Rd ME6 . . . . .82 B7
Sounds Lodge BR8 . . . . . .45 C3
South Ash Rd TN15 . . . . . .62 E4
South Ave ME8 . . . . .55 B2
South Aylesford Ret Pk
  ME20 . . . . .98 E8
South Bank Cliffe ME3 . . .22 B2
  Staplehurst TN12 . . . . . .149 E2
  Sutton Valence ME17 . . . .134 E7

South Bank continued
  Westerham TN16 . . . . . . .89 D1
South Borough Prim Sch
  ME15 . . . . .100 A2
South Brook La TN8 . . . . .123 C7
South Bush La ME8 . . . . . .70 B6
South Cl DA6 . . . . .13 D3
South Cres ME17 . . . . . . .115 C4
South Ct TN4 . . . . .159 A6
South Dr BR6 . . . . .57 E5
South Eastern Rd ME2 . . .53 C7
South Frith TN4 . . . . .143 A6
South Gipsy Rd DA16 . . . .13 D4
South Glade The DA5 . . . .30 F7
South Gr TN1 . . . . .159 A2
South Green La ME9 . . . . .86 F6
South Hall DA4 . . . . .46 F2
South Hill BR7 . . . . .28 F2
South Hill Rd DA12 . . . . . .36 C7
South Kent Ave DA11 . . . .18 C1
South La ME17 . . . . .134 E6
South Molton Rd E16 . . . . .1 A7
South Park Bsns Village
  ME15 . . . . .100 A1
South Park Rd ME15 . . . .100 C1
South Pk TN13 . . . . .92 B2
South Pondside Rd ME4 . .54 A8
South Rd Chatham ME4 . . .54 B7
  Chatham ME4,ME7 . . . . . .54 A7
  Erith DA8 . . . . .14 F7
  Marden TN12 . . . . .148 E5
South Ridge BR2 . . . . .42 C5
South Rise Prim Sch SE18 2 D1
South Rise Way SE18 . . . . .2 D2
South Row Greenwich SE3 11 A5
  Penshurst TN8 . . . . .140 D5
South Side Three Rd
  ME4 . . . . .54 C8
South St Bromley BR1 . . . .42 A7
  Gravesend DA12 . . . . .36 B8
  Maidstone ME16 . . . . .98 E1
South Street Rd ME9 . . . .86 C7
South Terr
  Chattenden ME3 . . . . .39 F6
  Farningham DA4 . . . . .46 F2
South View Bromley BR1 . .42 C7
  Oxted RH8 . . . . .104 A2
South View Cl DA5 . . . . . .13 F1
South View Ct **11** BR1 . . .42 C7
South View Rd
  Dartford DA2 . . . . .32 D3
  Royal Tunbridge Wells
  TN4 . . . . .159 A6
  Turner's Green TN5 . . . . .184 F6
  West Thurrock RM20 . . . . .17 C8
South View Terr TN17 . . .177 E8
Southampton Mews E16 . .1 A5
Southborough CE Prim Sch &
  Tunbridge Wells Language
  Unit TN4 . . . . .158 F8
Southborough Ct TN4 . . .143 A2
Southborough La BR2 . . . .42 F4
Southborough Prim Sch
  BR2 . . . . .43 A4
Southborough Rd BR1 . . . .42 E5
Southbourne BR2 . . . . . . .42 A2
Southbourne Gdns SE12 . .11 B3
Southbourne Gr ME5 . . . . .68 A4
Southcroft Ave DA16 . . . . .12 C4
Southcroft Rd BR6 . . . . . . .57 E7
Southdene TN14 . . . . .74 F6
Southend Cl SE9 . . . . .12 B1
Southend Cres SE9 . . . . . .12 B1
Southern Pl BR8 . . . . .45 E5
Southernden Rd TN27 . . .136 E1
Southey Mews E16 . . . . . . .1 A5
Southey Way **1** ME20 . . .81 F4
Southey Wlk RM18 . . . . . .19 B6
Southfield Ct DA1 . . . . . . .15 F4
Southfield Rd
  Orpington BR7 . . . . .44 A6
  Royal Tunbridge Wells
  TN4 . . . . .159 A6
Southfield Shaw DA13 . . .64 B1
Southfields Hextable BR8 .31 F1
  Rochester ME1 . . . . .53 C3
  Speldhurst TN3 . . . . .158 A7
  Turner's Green TN5 . . . . .184 F6
Southfields Rd TN15 . . . . .61 F2
Southfields Sch DA11 . . . .36 C3
Southfields Way TN4 . . . .159 B8
Southfleet Ave SE3 . . . . . .49 B7
Southfleet Rd Bean DA2 . .34 C4
  8 Northfleet DA11 . . . . .37 F7
  Orpington BR6 . . . . .57 E6
  Swanscombe DA10 . . . . . .35 A7
Southgate TN4 . . . . .158 F3
Southgate Rd TN30 . . . . .193 C7
Southill Rd Bromley BR7 . .28 F1
  Chatham ME4 . . . . .53 F3
Southland Rd SE18 . . . . . .12 F7
Southlands Ave BR6 . . . . .57 E5
Southlands Ct BR2 . . . . . .42 D5
Southlands Gr BR1 . . . . . .42 E6
Southlands Rd BR1,BR2 . .42 D5
Southlees La ME9 . . . . . . .86 F3
Southold Rise SE9 . . . . . .28 F5
Southover BR1 . . . . .28 A3
Southport Rd SE18 . . . . . . .2 D1
Southspring DA15 . . . . . . .29 D8
Southview Ave RM18 . . . . .19 A6
Southview Cl BR8 . . . . . . .46 A5
Southview Hts RM20 . . . . .17 C8
Southwark Pl BR1 . . . . . . .42 F6
Southwark Rd ME2 . . . . . .52 D6
Southway BR2 . . . . .42 A2
Southways ME17 . . . . . . .134 E7
Southwell Rd ME2 . . . . . . .52 D6

Southwold Rd DA5 14 B1
Southwood ME16 98 F2
Southwood Ave TN4 159 A6
Southwood Bldgs TN4 158 B4
Southwood Cl BR1 42 F5
Southwood Ho SE9 29 B6
Southwood Rd Eltham SE9 29 B6
Rusthall TN4 158 B5
Woolwich SE28 3 B5
Sovereign Bvd ME7,ME8 55 A2
Sovereign Ct Bromley BR2 42 F5
Sutton at H DA4 47 B8
Sovereign Ho SE18 1 F3
Sovereign Way TN9 127 C1
Sovereigns The ME16 99 D4
Sovereigns Way TN12 148 C6
Soverign Ho BR7 29 D1
Sowerby Cl SE9 11 F2
Spa Ind Pk TN2 159 E8
Spa Valley Rly★ TN3 171 D7
Spade La ME9 70 C6
Spar Cl TN11 111 F1
Sparepenny La DA4 46 E1
Sparkes Cl BR2 42 B5
Sparkeswood Ave TN17 191 F3
Sparkeswood Cl TN17 191 F3
Sparrow Dr BR5 43 D1
Sparrow's Farm L Ctr
SE9 29 C8
Sparrows Green Rd
TN5 184 F5
Sparrows La SE9 29 C7
Spearhead Rd ME14 99 F7
Spearman St 8 SE18 12 A8
Spectrum Bsns Ctr ME2 53 E8
Spectrum Bsns Est
ME15 116 F4
Speedgate Farm DA3 61 F8
Speedgate Hill DA3 62 A8
Speedwell Ave ME5 67 F4
Speedwell Cl
Gillingham ME7 54 E5
Maidstone ME14 100 E5
5 Marlpit Hill TN8 122 D3
Speedwell Ct RM17 18 E7
Spekehill SE9 28 F5
Spekes Rd ME7 69 B6
Speldhurst CE Prim Sch
TN3 158 A7
Speldhurst Ct ME16 99 D4
Speldhurst Hill TN3 158 B8
Speldhurst Rd
Langton Green TN3 157 F5
Royal Tunbridge Wells
TN3,TN4 158 E8
Spelmonden Rd TN12 162 F2
Spembley Ct ME4 53 E4
Spencer Cl Chatham ME5 68 A5
Orpington BR6 57 F8
Spencer Ct 5 BR6 57 C5
Spencer Flats ME5 68 B8
Spencer Gdns SE9 11 F2
Spencer Mews
10 Royal Tunbridge Wells
TN1 159 B4
6 Royal Tunbridge
Wells,Mount Sion TN1 159 A2
Spencer St DA11 36 A8
Spencer Way ME15 116 E7
Spencer Wlk RM18 19 B5
Spenlow Dr ME5 84 A8
Spenny La TN12 147 B7
Speranza St SE18 2 F1
Speyside TN10 127 B5
Spielman Rd DA1 15 F3
Spiers The ME7 55 C5
Spillway The ME15 99 D2
Spindle Cl SE18 1 E3
Spindle Glade ME14 100 C5
Spindle Ho 8 DA15 30 A5
Spindles RM18 19 A7
Spindlewood Cl ME5 68 B3
Spinel Cl SE18 2 F1
Spinnaker Ct 4 ME1 53 C1
Spinnens Acre Com Jun Sch
ME5 68 C1
Spinners Cl TN27 168 A2
Spinners Wents TN11 111 D8
Spinney Oak BR1 42 E7
Spinney The Chatham ME5 68 B1
Maidstone ME15 100 B2
Sidcup DA14 30 E3
Swanley BR8 45 E7
Tonbridge TN9 143 A7
Spinney Way TN14 73 D8
Spinneys The BR1 42 F7
Spire Cl DA12 36 B7
Spires The Dartford DA1 32 D6
Maidstone ME16 99 D4
Rochester ME2 52 D5
Spital St DA1 15 D1
Spitfire Cl ME5 68 B6
Spitfire Rd ME19 96 F3
Spode La TN8 155 A7
Sponden La TN18 196 A7
Spongs La TN17 166 A1
Sportsfield ME14 100 B5
Sportsmans Cotts ME19 97 B5
Spot La ME15 101 A2
Spout La Brenchley TN12 162 C5
Crockham Hill TN8 105 C1
Spray Hill TN3 176 B4
Spray St SE18 2 B2
Sprig The ME14 101 A4
Spring Cott DA1 32 D8
Spring Cross DA3 63 A7
Spring Ct 17 DA15 30 A5
Spring Gdns
Biggin Hill TN16 72 C1
Orpington BR6 58 B4
Rusthall TN4 158 B4
Spring Gr DA12 36 B7
Spring Head Rd TN15 76 F2
Spring Hill TN11,TN3 157 A7
Spring La
Bidborough TN3 142 D3
Oldbury TN15 94 B5
Spring Lodge 3 BR5 44 C4
Spring Shaw Rd BR5 44 A8
Spring Vale Bexley DA7 14 B3
Dartford DA1 32 D8
Maidstone ME16 99 E4
Swanscombe DA9 17 C1
Spring Vale Cl BR8 45 F8
Spring Vale N DA1 32 D8
Spring Vale S DA1 32 D8
Springcroft DA3 49 A4
Springdale Cotts ME3 39 A3
Springett Almshouses
TN18 194 E8
Springett Cl ME20 82 F6
Springett Way ME17 115 D3
Springfield Ave
Maidstone ME14 99 F7
Swanley BR8 45 F5
Tenterden TN30 183 C2
Springfield Cotts TN12 162 F5
Springfield Gdns BR1 42 F5
Springfield Gr SE7 11 C8
Springfield Ind Est
TN18 188 F3
Springfield Rd
Bexley,Bexleyheath DA7 14 B3
Bexley,Welling DA16 13 B4
Bromley BR1 42 F5
Edenbridge TN8 122 B1
Gillingham ME7 54 E6
Groombridge TN3 171 C7
Lunsford ME20 81 F4
Royal Tunbridge Wells
TN4 142 F1
Springfield Terr 7 ME4 53 F4
Springfield Wlk 3 BR6 43 D1
Springfields TN5 186 E1
Springhead TN2 159 D5
Springhead Ent Pk DA11 35 C7
Springhead Rd Erith DA8 14 F8
Northfleet DA11 35 C7
Springholm Cl TN16 72 C1
Springrove Cotts TN12 148 B5
Springshaw Cl TN13 91 D4
Springvale ME8 69 C6
Springvale Ct Eltham SE12 11 A3
Northfleet DA11 35 C6
Springvale Ret Pk 2
BR5 44 C6
Springvale Way BR5 44 C6
Springview Apartments
TN2 159 D6
Springwater Cl SE18 12 A6
Springwell Rd TN9 143 B8
Springwood Cl 1 ME16 99 A3
Springwood Hall TN11 110 D1
Springwood Rd ME16 99 A3
Sprivers Gdns★ TN12 162 E4
Spruce Cl ME20 82 B2
Spruce Ho TN4 158 E4
Spruce Rd TN16 72 D3
Sprucedale Cl BR8 45 E7
Spur Rd BR6 58 A8
Spurgeon Cl RM17 18 C8
Spurgeons Cotts ME17 115 E2
Spurrell Ave DA5 31 D4
Spurway ME14 101 A4
Square Hill ME15 100 B4
Square Hill Rd ME15 100 B4
Square The Cowden TN8 155 B6
Hadlow TN11 128 E8
Hunton ME15 131 D7
Leigh TN11 125 F1
Lenham ME17 120 D5
Sevenoaks TN13 91 E5
Swanley BR8 45 D6
Tatsfield TN16 88 C7
Wadhurst TN5 185 A4
Squerryes Ct★ TN16 105 C7
Squerryes Mede TN16 105 C8
Squires Cl ME2 52 B7
Squires Field BR8 45 F8
Squires Ho 3 SE18 12 B8
Squires Way DA2 31 D4
Squires Wood Dr BR7 28 F1
Squirrel Way TN2 159 E5
Stable Cl ME5 68 C5
Stabledene Way TN2 160 D6
Stables End BR6 57 C7
Stables The TN18 194 E8
Stace Cl TN30 193 C8
Stacey Cl DA12 36 E3
Stacey Rd TN10 127 A4
Staceys St ME14 99 F5
Stack La DA3 48 F4
Stack Rd DA4 47 D5
Stackfield 1 TN8 122 D3
Stacklands Cl TN15 61 E4
Stadium Rd SE18 11 F8
Stadium Way DA1 14 E2
Stadler Cl ME16 99 D7
Staffa Rd ME15 116 A7
Staffhurst Wood Rd
TN8,RH8 121 C6
Stafford Cl DA9 16 F2
Stafford Rd
Royal Tunbridge Wells
TN2 159 E4
Stafford Rd *continued*
Sidcup DA14 29 E4
Tonbridge TN9 127 B2
Stafford St ME7 54 C5
Stafford Way TN13 108 C8
Stag Rd Chatham ME5 68 B5
Royal Tunbridge Wells
TN2 159 D8
Stagshaw Cl ME15 100 A2
Stainer Ho SE3 11 C3
Stainer Rd TN10 127 F6
Staines Wlk DA14 30 C2
Stainmore Cl BR7 43 D8
Stair Rd TN10 127 F4
Stairfoot La TN13 91 C5
Stake La ME2 66 A6
Staleys Rd TN15 94 F7
Stalham Ct ME7 69 B4
Stalin Ave ME5 68 B8
Stalisfield Pl BR6 57 A1
Stampers The ME15 99 D2
Stan La ME18 112 A7
Stanam Rd TN2 160 E6
Stanbridge Rd TN8 122 B2
Stanbrook Rd
Northfleet DA11 35 F8
Woolwich SE2 3 B4
Standard Ind Est E16 1 F4
Standard Rd Bexley DA6 13 E3
Erith DA17 4 A1
Farthing Street BR6 57 A1
Standen Cl ME8 69 E4
Standen St
Benenden TN17,TN18 190 D2
Royal Tunbridge Wells
TN4 159 A5
Standen Street TN17 196 E8
Standings Cross TN12 145 E1
Standish Ho SE3 11 B3
Stane Way SE18 11 E7
Stanford Dr ME16 99 C3
Stanford La TN11 112 C2
Stanford Way ME2 52 C2
Stangate Rd Birling ME19 81 B8
Rochester ME2 52 C7
Stangrove Rd TN8 122 C1
Stanham Pl DA1 15 A3
Stanham Rd DA1 15 C2
Stanhill Cotts DA2 31 D2
Stanhope Ave BR2 42 A1
Stanhope Cl ME14 99 E7
Stanhope Rd Bexley DA7 13 E5
Rochester ME2 53 A7
Royal Tunbridge Wells
TN1 159 C5
Sidcup DA15 30 A4
Swanscombe DA10 17 F1
Stanhope Way TN13 91 D5
Stanhopes RH8 104 B7
Stanley Cl
Staplehurst TN12 149 E4
Stone DA9 16 E2
Stanley Cotts DA2 33 E3
Stanley Cres DA12 36 D3
Stanley Glyn Ct BR7 29 A3
Stanley Holloway Ct E16 1 A7
Stanley Rd Bromley BR2 42 C5
Chatham ME5 68 C6
Gillingham ME7 54 C6
Grays RM17 18 B8
Marden TN12 148 D5
Northfleet DA11 35 E7
Orpington BR6 43 F1
Royal Tunbridge Wells
TN1 159 B5
Sidcup DA14 30 A5
Swanscombe DA10 17 F1
Stanley Way BR5 44 B4
Stanmore Ho SE12 28 B7
Stanmore Rd DA17 4 C2
Stansfeld Rd E16 1 D7
Stansted CE Prim Sch
TN15 62 F1
Stansted Cl ME16 99 D7
Stansted Cres DA5 30 D7
Stansted Hill TN15 63 A1
Stansted La TN15 62 C1
Stanton Cl BR5 44 C2
Stanton Ct
9 Bromley BR1 42 C7
5 Sidcup DA15 30 A5
Staple Cl DA5 31 D5
Staple Dr TN12 149 F4
Stapleford Ct TN13 91 F4
Staplehurst Ho BR5 44 C4
Staplehurst Rd
Bogden TN12 133 C2
Frittenden TN12,TN17 150 D1
Gillingham ME8 55 B3
Staplehurst Sch TN12 149 E5
Staplehurst Sta TN12 149 E5
Staplers Ct ME14 100 B8
Staples Ho E6 2 A7
Staples The BR8 46 B8
Stapleton Rd Bexley DA7 13 F8
Orpington BR6 57 F7
Stapley Rd DA17 4 A1
Star Bsns Ctr RM13 4 D8
Star Hill Crayford DA1 14 E2
Rochester ME1 53 D5
Star Hill Rd TN14 75 A2
Star Ho TN3 176 B5
Star La Gillingham ME7 69 A7
Orpington BR5,BR8 44 E5
Star Mill Ct ME5 54 D2
Star Mill La ME5 54 D2
Starboard Ave DA9 17 B1
Starling Cl DA3 49 B6
Starnes Ct 5 ME14 100 A5
Starr Cotts TN12 131 C2
Starts Cl BR6 57 A7
Starts Hill Ave BR6 57 B6
Starts Hill Rd BR6 57 B6
Starve Goose La TN17 178 E4
State Farm Ave BR6 57 C6
Stately Pk ME18 113 C1
Station App
Bexley,Barnehurst DA7 14 C5
Bexley,Bexleyheath DA7 13 E5
Bexley,Welling DA16 13 A5
Borough Green TN15 94 F7
Bromley BR7 28 E2
Chelsfield BR6 58 B5
Chislehurst BR7 43 A7
Dartford DA1 15 E1
Edenbridge TN8 122 C2
Grays RM17 18 A8
Greenwich SE3 11 B4
Halling ME2 66 A5
Hayes BR2 42 A1
Maidstone ME16 99 F3
Orpington BR6 57 F8
Orpington,St Mary Cray BR5 44 B5
Otford TN14 76 C3
Paddock Wood TN12 146 A7
Staplehurst TN12 149 E5
Swanley BR8 45 E5
Station Cotts
Gill's Green TN18 188 F5
Hartley TN17 178 E2
Horsmonden TN12 163 B5
Station Cres SE3 1 A1
Station Ct TN15 94 F7
Station Hill
Chiddingstone Causeway
TN11 141 A8
Hayes BR2 56 A8
Station Hill Cotts ME15 115 A7
Station Mews 3 TN30 193 A7
Station Par
Sevenoaks TN13 92 A3
Sidcup DA15 30 A6
Station Rd Aylesford ME20 82 E2
Betsham DA13 35 A4
Bexley DA7 13 E4
Borough Green TN15 94 F7
Brasted TN16 90 B4
Bromley BR1 42 A8
Cliffe ME3 22 B3
Crayford DA1 14 F1
Cuxton ME2 52 C2
East Farleigh ME15 115 A7
East Tilbury RM18 20 B7
Edenbridge TN8 122 C2
Erith DA17 4 A3
Eynsford DA4 60 D7
Goudhurst TN17 177 C7
Groombridge TN3 171 C7
Halstead TN14 74 F8
Harrietsham ME17 119 D6
Headcorn TN27 151 D5
Hurst Green TN19 194 A3
Longfield DA3 48 E6
Maidstone ME14 99 F5
Meopham Sta DA13 50 A4
Nettlestead Green ME18 113 C1
Newington ME9 71 B6
Northfleet DA11 18 B1
Northiam TN31 197 C1
Orpington BR6 57 F8
Orpington,St Mary Cray BR5 44 C5
Otford TN14 76 C3
Paddock Wood TN12 145 F7
Rainham ME8 55 F1
Rochester ME2 53 C7
Rockrobin TN5 184 C6
Sevenoaks TN13 91 E7
Shoreham TN14 76 A7
Sidcup DA14,DA15 30 A5
Staplehurst TN12 149 F5
Stone DA9 17 A2
Sutton at H DA4 47 B7
Swanley BR8 45 E5
Tenterden TN30 193 A7
Withyham TN7 170 B5
Station Rd N DA17 4 B3
Station Sq BR5 43 C4
Station St E16 2 B5
Steadman Cl ME3 38 C6
Stede Hill ME17 103 F3
Stedley 17 DA14 30 A4
Stedman Cl DA5 31 E5
Steele Ave DA9 17 A2
Steele St ME2 53 A8
Steele Wlk DA8 14 B7
Steele's La DA13 64 A6
Steellands Rise TN5 186 F1
Steep Cl BR6 57 F4
Steephill Sch DA3 48 D5
Steeple Heights Dr TN16 72 D2
Steerforth Cl ME1 53 C2
Steers Pl TN11 111 E2
Stella Cl TN12 148 D5
Stelling Rd DA8 14 D7
Stenning Ct TN10 127 C4
Stephen Cl BR6 57 F7
Stephen Rd DA7 14 C4
Stephen's Rd TN4 159 B6
Stephenson Ave RM18 19 A6
Stephenson Ho SE2 3 D1
Stepneyford La TN17 191 C7
Steps Hill Rd ME9 86 D6
Sterling Ave ME16 99 C5
Sterling Ho SE3 11 B3
Sterndale Rd DA1 32 F8
Sterry Gdns ME15 116 E7
Stevanne Ct 1 DA17 4 A1
Stevedale Rd DA16 13 C5
Steven Cl ME4 54 A3
Stevens Cl Dartford DA2 33 E3
Egerton TN27 137 F3
Joyden's Wood DA5 31 D4
Snodland ME6 82 A8
Stevens Cotts TN30 193 A7
Stevens Rd ME20 82 F6
Stevenson Cl Erith DA8 15 B7
Maidstone ME15 99 F3
Stevenson Way ME20 81 F4
Stewart Cl BR7 29 B4
Stewart Ho ME3 39 F6
Stewart Rd TN4 159 C7
Steyning Gr SE9 28 F4
Steynton Ave DA5 30 D6
Stickens La ME19 97 E7
Stickfast La ME17 135 D3
Stickland Rd 2 DA17 4 A2
Stilebridge La
Underling Green ME17 133 A5
Underling Green TN12 132 E3
Stiles Cl Bromley BR2 42 F3
Erith DA8 4 B1
Still La TN4 142 F2
Stillwater Mews ME4 40 B2
Stirling Cl Gillingham ME8 69 E4
Rochester ME1 53 A3
Sidcup DA14 29 F4
Stirling Dr BR6 58 B5
Stirling Ho 5 SE18 2 B1
Stirling Rd ME19 96 F3
Stisted Way TN27 137 F3
Stock Hill TN16 72 D2
Stock La DA2 32 C4
Stockbury Dr ME16 99 D7
Stockbury Ho 7 BR5 44 D1
Stockenbury TN12 129 F6
Stockett La ME15 115 D6
Stockland Green Rd
TN3 158 B8
Stocks Green Prim Sch
TN11 126 E5
Stocks Green Rd TN11 126 C5
Stocks Rd TN30 199 F3
Stockton Cl ME14 100 B8
Stockwell Cl BR1 42 B7
Stofield Gdns SE9 28 D5
Stoke Com Sch ME3 25 C5
Stoke Rd Allhallows ME3 9 C1
Hoo St Werburgh ME3 40 F6
Kingsnorth ME3 41 C8
Lower Stoke ME3 24 E1
Stokesay Ct 14 DA2 16 B1
Stone Cotts TN3 175 F4
Stone Court La TN2 160 E8
Stone Cross Rd TN5 185 A4
Stone Crossing Halt DA9 16 E2
Stone Ct DA8 4 F1
Stone Hill Rd TN27 137 F2
Stone House Hospl DA2 16 C1
Stone Lake Ind Pk SE7 1 C2
Stone Lake Ret Pk SE7 1 C2
Stone Lodge Farm Pk★
DA2 16 D1
Stone Pit La TN18 196 E5
Stone Place Rd DA9 16 E2
Stone Rd BR2 42 A5
Stone Row TN3 157 B5
Stone Row Cotts TN3 157 D1
Stone St Cranbrook TN17 179 D5
Gravesend DA11 19 B1
Royal Tunbridge Wells
TN1 159 B4
Stone Street Rd TN15 93 E2
Stone Wood DA2 34 C5
Stone, St Mary's CE Prim Sch
DA9 33 E8
Stoneacre★ ME15 117 B7
Stoneacre Cl ME8 69 D5
Stoneacre Ct 7 ME15 100 A1
Stoneacre La ME15 117 B7
Stonebridge Green Rd
TN27 137 F4
Stonebridge Rd DA11 18 B2
Stonechat Sq 6 E6 1 E8
Stonecroft DA13 80 A8
Stonecroft Rd DA8 14 C7
Stonecrop Cl ME4 40 C1
Stonecross Lea ME5 54 C1
Stonefield Cl DA7 14 A4
Stonefield Way SE7 11 D7
Stonegate Cl BR5 44 C6
Stonegate Rd TN5 185 C1
Stonehill Woods Pk
DA14 31 B2
Stonehorse Ct ME3 39 A3
Stonehorse La ME2 39 A2
Stonehouse Cnr RM19 16 E8
Stonehouse La
Halstead TN14 74 E8
Pratt's Bottom TN14 58 E1
Purfleet RM19 16 E8
Stonehouse Rd BR6,TN14 58 D1
Stoneings La TN14 89 F8
Stoneleigh Rd RH8 104 E5
Stoneness Rd RM20 17 C7
Stones Cross Rd BR8 45 C4
Stones Rdbt ME4 40 B1
Stonestile Bsns Pk
TN27 151 A7
Stonestile Rd TN27 151 A7
Stoneswood Rd RH8 104 B5
Stonewall E6 2 A8

Stonewall Park Rd TN3 .157 F3
Stonewood St TN4 ......159 A8
Stonewood Rd DA8 ....4 E1
Stoney Alley SE18 ......12 A5
Stoney Bank ME7 ....54 F1
Stony Cnr DA13 ....49 E6
Stony La ME1 ....67 C5
Stonyfield TN8 ....122 D3
Stopford Rd ME7 ....54 D4
Store Rd E16 ....2 A4
Storehouse Wharf ME12 .27 F3
Storey St E16 ....2 A4
Stornaway Strand DA12 .36 F4
Stotfold BR1 ....42 E8
Stour Cl Orpington BR2 .56 C6
Rochester ME2 ....52 F7
Tonbridge TN10 ....127 B5
Stour Ct **22** BR5 ....44 D1
Stour Rd DA1 ....15 A4
Stow Ct DA2 ....33 C8
Stowe Rd BR6 ....58 B6
Stowting Rd BR6 ....57 E6
Strait Rd E6 ....1 F6
Strand Approach Rd ME7 54 E7
Strand Cl DA13 ....50 A3
Strand Ct SE18 ....2 E1
Strand Rdbt The ME7 ...54 E7
Strandfield Cl SE18 .....2 E1
Stratfield Ho SE12 .....28 A6
Stratford Ave ME8 .....69 D8
Stratford Dr ME15 ....116 D6
Stratford House Ave BR1 42 E6
Stratford La **2** ME8 .69 F8
Stratford Rd ME19 .....97 A8
Stratford St TN1 ......159 C5
Strathaven Rd SE12 ....11 B1
Stratheden Par SE3 ....11 A7
Stratheden Rd SE3 .....11 A7
Stratton Cl DA7 ....13 E4
Stratton Rd DA7 ....13 E4
Stratton Terr TN16 ...105 C8
Straw Mill Hill ME15 ...99 E1
Strawberry Cl TN2 ....172 E7
Strawberry Fields BR8 .45 E7
Strawberry Vale TN9 ..127 C1
Stream La TN18 ....195 A7
Stream Pit La TN18 ...196 B5
Stream Side TN10 ....127 D6
Stream The ME20 ....82 C1
Stream Way DA17 ......14 A8
Streamdale SE2 ....13 B8
Streamside ME20 ......82 B1
Streamside Cl BR2 ....42 A5
Streatfeild TN8 ......122 D1
Streatfield Ho ME19 ...89 C1
Street End Rd ME5 .....54 B1
Street Farm Cotts ME3 40 F6
Street The Ash TN15 ...62 E5
Benenden TN17 ....190 D6
Boxley ME14 ....84 C3
Bredhurst ME7 ....69 B1
Cobham DA12 ....50 F6
Detling ME14 ....85 A1
Egerton TN27 ....137 F3
Frittenden TN17 .....166 E7
Hartlip ME9 ....70 D5
High Halstow ME23 ....23 E3
Horton Kirby DA4 .....47 C5
Ightham TN15 ....94 D6
Maidstone ME14 .....101 C4
Meopham DA13 ....50 A1
Mereworth ME18 .....112 D8
Plaxtol TN15 ....110 F7
Ryarsh ME19 ....80 F4
Shorne DA12 ....37 E3
Silver Street ME9 .....87 F5
Sissinghurst TN17 ...180 B8
Smarden TN27 ....153 A1
Stockbury ME9 ....86 E8
Teston ME18 ....114 A7
Trottiscliffe ME19 ....80 A5
Ulcombe ME17 ....135 F7
Upper Halling ME7 ....65 E5
Wittersham TN30 ....199 D3
Wormshill ME9 ......103 F7
Streetfield ME17 .....135 F7
Streetfield Mews SE3 ..11 A4
Streetfield Rd ME8 ....55 F1
Strettitt Gdns TN12 ..129 F5
Strickland Ave DA1 ....15 F4
Strickland Way **5** BR6 .57 F6
Strongbow Cres SE9 ...11 F2
Strongbow Rd SE9 .....11 F2
Strood Ret Pk ME2 ....53 B7
Strood Sta ME2 ....53 C7
Strover St ME7 ....54 C7
Struttons Ave DA11 ....35 F6
Stuart Ave BR2 ....42 A1
Stuart Cl Hextable BR8 .32 A1
Maidstone ME14 .....100 C6
Royal Tunbridge Wells
TN2 ....172 F8
Stuart Evans Cl DA16 ..13 C4
Stuart Mantle Way DA8 .14 E7
Stuart Rd Bexley DA16 .13 B6
Gillingham ME7 ....54 D3
Gravesend DA11 ......19 A1
Stubbs Hill BR6,TN14 ..74 C6
Studios The DA3 ....62 F8
Studland Dr DA15 .....29 F5
Studley Cres DA3 .....49 C7
Studley Ct DA14 ......30 B3
Stumble Hill TN11 ....110 C5
Sturdee Ave ME7 ......54 E4
Sturdee Cotts ME3 ....41 A6

Sturges Field BR7 .....29 D2
Sturla Rd ME4 ....54 A3
Sturmer Ct ME19 ......97 A2
Sturry Way ME8 ....55 C2
Styants Bottom Rd TN15 .93 F5
Style Cl ME8 ....69 E4
Styles Cl TN8 ....123 B5
Styles Cotts TN8 ....123 B5
Styles Ct TN12 ....145 F7
Styles La ME14 ....84 C3
Sudbury E6 ....2 A7
Sudbury Cres BR1 .....28 A3
Suffolk Ave ME8 ......55 F1
Suffolk Cl **7** ME8 ..55 F1
Suffolk Mews **1** TN1 159 A4
Suffolk Rd Dartford DA1 .15 E1
Gravesend DA12 ....19 D1
Maidstone ME15 .....116 D8
Sidcup DA14 ....30 C2
Suffolk Way TN13 .....92 C2
Sullivan Ave E16 ....1 D8
Sullivan Cl DA1 ......32 C8
Sullivan Rd Tilbury RM18 .19 A6
Tonbridge TN10 .....127 E5
Sultan Mews ME5 ......68 C2
Sultan Rd ME5 ....68 C2
Summer Cl TN30 .....183 C1
Summer Hill BR7 ......43 A7
Summerfield
  6 Bromley BR1 .....42 B8
  Marden TN17 ....164 B6
Summerfield St **9** SE12 .28 A8
Summerhill TN27 .....151 A6
Summerhill Ave TN4 ..142 F1
Summerhill Cl BR6 ....57 E7
Summerhill Rd
  Bogden TN12 ....133 C1
  Dartford DA1 ....32 D8
Summerhill Villas BR7 .43 B8
Summerhouse Dr DA2,
  DA5 ....31 D4
Summerlands Lodge
  BR6 ....57 A6
Summerton Way SE28 ...3 D7
Summervale Rd TN4 ..158 C1
Sumner Cl Orpington BR6 .57 C6
  Rolvenden TN17 ....191 F3
Sun Ct DA8 ....14 F5
Sun Hill DA3 ....62 A8
Sun La Gravesend DA12 .36 C6
  Greenwich SE3 ....11 B7
Sun Rd DA10 ....17 F1
Sun Terr ME5 ....68 B4
Sunburst Cl TN12 ....148 D5
Sunbury St SE18 ....1 F3
Sunderland Cl ME1 ....53 A3
Sunderland Dr ME8 ....70 A8
Sunderland Ho **3** ME7 .54 C7
Sunderland Point E16 ...2 C5
Sundew Ct **9** RM17 ..18 D8
Sundorne Rd SE7 ....1 C1
Sundridge & Brasted CE Prim
  Sch TN14 ....90 E2
Sundridge Ave
  Bexley DA16 ....12 D4
  Bromley BR1 ....42 D8
Sundridge Cl DA1 .....16 A1
Sundridge Ct **10** BR1 .28 B1
Sundridge Dr ME5 .....68 A4
Sundridge Hill
  Cuxton ME2 ....52 C3
  Halstead TN14 ....74 C1
Sundridge Ho BR1 ....28 B3
Sundridge La TN14 ....74 D2
Sundridge Park Sta BR1 .28 B1
Sundridge Rd TN14 ....91 B8
Sunfields Pl SE3 ......11 B7
Sunhill Ct TN2 ....160 C6
Sunland Ave DA6 .....13 E3
Sunningdale Cl Erith SE28 .3 E7
  Gillingham ME8 ....69 D6
Sunningdale Cl ME15 .100 B4
Sunningdale Dr ME8 ...69 D6
Sunningdale Rd BR1 ..42 E4
Sunningvale Ave TN16 .72 D3
Sunningvale Cl TN16 ..72 D3
Sunnybank TN5 ......187 E3
Sunnydale BR6 ....57 A8
Sunnydale Rd SE12 ...11 B2
Sunnyfield Rd BR7 ....44 A6
Sunnyfields ME8 .....69 E8
Sunnymead Ave ME7 ..54 E5
Sunnyside TN8 ......122 B3
Sunnyside Rd TN4 ...158 C4
Sunray Ave BR2 ......42 F3
Sunset Cl DA8 ....15 B7
Sunset Rd SE28 ....3 A5
Sunshine Ct **1** ME8 .69 F8
Superabbey Est ME20 .83 B2
Superior Dr **4** BR6 .57 F4
Surlingham Cl SE28 ....3 D6
Surrenden Rd TN12 ..149 E3
Surrey Cl TN2 ....172 E8
Surrey Rd ME15 .....116 D8
Susan Rd SE3 ....11 B5
Susan Wood BR7 .....43 A8
Sussex Cl TN2 ....159 C1
Sussex Dr ME5 ....68 A4
Sussex Mews **19** TN2 159 A2
Sussex Rd Dartford DA1 .33 A8
  Erith DA8 ....14 B7
  Maidstone ME15 ....116 D8
  Orpington BR5 ......44 C3
  Sidcup DA14 ....30 B3
  Tonbridge TN9 .....143 A8
Sussex Road Prim Sch
  TN9 ....143 A8

Sutcliffe Rd Bexley DA16 .13 C5
  Woolwich SE18 ......12 E8
Sutherland Ave
  Bexley DA16 ....12 E3
  Biggin Hill TN16 ....72 E1
  Orpington BR5 ......43 F4
Sutherland Cl Chalk DA12 .37 B6
  Stone DA9 ....16 F2
Sutherland Gdns ME8 .69 E6
Sutherland Ho ME8 ...11 F6
Sutherland Rd Erith DA17 .4 A3
  Royal Tunbridge Wells
  TN1 ....159 B3
Sutlej St SE7 ....11 C7
Sutton at Hone CE Prim Sch
  DA4 ....33 A1
Sutton Cl ME8 ....70 A8
Sutton Ct TN12 ......148 C5
Sutton Forge TN12 ...148 D5
Sutton Rd Langley ME17 .117 C5
  Maidstone ME15 ....116 D6
Sutton St ME14 ......101 D4
Sutton Valence Castle★
  ME17 ....134 F7
Sutton Valence Prep Sch
  ME17 ....134 C7
Sutton Valence Prim Sch
  ME17 ....134 E7
Sutton Valence Sch
  ME17 ....134 E7
Swadelands Cl ME17 .120 C5
Swadelands Sch ME17 120 C5
Swaffield Rd TN13 ....92 C5
Swain Cl ME2 ....52 F8
Swain Rd Gillingham ME8 .69 B6
  Tenterden TN30 ....183 D3
Swaisland Rd DA1 .....15 B1
Swaislands Dr DA1 ....14 F2
Swale Rd Crayford DA1 .15 A3
  Rochester ME2 ......52 C7
Swaledale Rd DA2 ....33 C7
Swallow Cl Bexley DA8 .14 E6
  Stone DA9 ....16 F2
Swallow Ct **3** SE12 ..28 A8
Swallow Dr TN2 ......159 F6
Swallow Ho **4** ME16 .99 E4
Swallow Rd ME20 .....81 F2
Swallow Rise ME5 ....68 A5
Swallow St E6 ....1 E8
Swallowfield Rd SE7 ...1 B1
Swallowfields **2** DA11 .35 E5
Swallowtail Cl BR5 ...44 D5
Swan Apartments **12**
  ME15 ....116 E5
Swan App E6 ....1 E8
Swan Bsns Pk DA1 ....15 C3
Swan Cl BR5 ....44 A6
Swan Cotts TN30 ....199 D3
Swan La Brandfold TN17 .163 F3
  Dartford DA1 ....31 F8
  Marlpit Hill TN8 ....122 C4
Swan Rd SE18 ....1 D3
Swan Ridge TN8 .....122 B4
Swan St
  West Malling ME19 ..97 C8
  Wittersham TN30 ..199 C3
Swan Valley Com Sch
  DA10 ....34 F8
Swanbridge Rd DA7 ...14 B6
Swanland Dr TN9 ....142 F7
Swanley Ctr BR8 .....45 E6
Swanley La BR8 ......45 F6
Swanley New Barn Rly★
  BR8 ....45 E8
Swanley Rd DA16 ....13 C6
Swanley Sch BR8 .....45 E6
Swanley Sta BR8 .....45 E6
Swanley Village Rd BR8 .46 B8
Swanmead Way TN9 .127 D2
Swanscombe Bsns Ctr
  DA10 ....17 E2
Swanscombe Ho **1** BR5 .44 B7
Swanscombe Inf Sch
  DA10 ....34 F8
Swanscombe St DA10 .17 F1
Swanscombe Sta DA10 .17 F2
Swansea Ct E16 ....2 B4
Swanton Rd Erith DA8 .14 B7
Swanzy Rd SE14 ......92 C7
Sward Rd BR5 ....44 A3
Swattenden La TN17 .179 B1
Swaylands DA17 ......14 A8
Swaynesland Rd RH8 .104 F1
Sweeps Hill Cl TN2 ...160 D7
Sweeps La BR5 ....44 B5
Sweet Briar Cr ME6 ...99 D5
Sweetings La TN3,TN5 .175 D1
Sweetlands La TN12 ..150 A5
Sweets La ME19 ....98 A4
Swetenham Wlk SE18 ...2 C1
Sweyn Pl SE3 ....11 A5
Sweyne Jun Sch The
  DA10 ....34 F8
Sweyne Rd DA10 ......17 E1
Swievelands Rd TN16 .72 C1
Swift Cl Larkfield ME20 .82 A2
  Woolwich SE28 ....3 B6
Swift Cres ME5 ....68 C6
Swift Ho **6** ME16 ...99 E4
Swifts View TN17 ....179 D6
Swiller's La DA12 .....37 E3
Swinburne Gdns RM18 .19 B5
Swingate Ave ME3 ....22 B6
Swingate Cl ME5 .....68 B2
Swingate Inf Sch ME5 .68 C1
Swingate La SE18 .....12 E7
Swingfield Ct BR2 ....42 D4

Swinton Ave ME3 .....39 F5
Swires Shaw BR2 .....56 D6
Swithland Gdns SE9 ..29 A4
Syamore Mews DA8 .....4 D1
Sycamore Ave DA15 ..12 F1
Sycamore Cl Eltham SE9 .28 E6
  Gravesend DA12 .....36 D8
  Tilbury RM18 ....19 A5
Sycamore Cotts
  Bidborough TN3 ....142 D3
  Pembury TN2 ....160 C6
Sycamore Cres ME16 .99 C5
Sycamore Rd Erith DA8 ..4 D1
  Stone DA9 ....33 E8
Sycamore Dr
  Aylesford ME20 .....82 E1
  Swanley BR8 ....45 E7
Sycamore Gdns ME12 145 F5
Sycamore Lodge BR6 .57 F8
Sycamore Rd
  Dartford DA1 ....32 D7
  Rochester ME2 ......52 E5
Sychem La TN12 .....145 A6
Sychem Pl TN12 .....145 A7
Sydenham Cotts SE12 .28 C6
Sydney Cotts **11** BR5 .44 C6
Sydney Rd Bexley DA6 .13 D3
  Chatham ME4 ....54 A3
  Erith SE2 ....3 D3
  Sidcup DA14 ....29 E4
  Tilbury RM18 ....19 A5
Sydney Terr TN18 ....188 F3
Sylewood Cl ME1 .....67 B8
Sylvan Cl RH8 ....104 B6
Sylvan Glade ME5 ....84 A8
Sylvan Mews DA9 .....17 B3
Sylvan Rd ME8 ....69 C8
Sylvan Wlk BR1 ......42 F6
Sylvester Ave BR7 ....28 F2
Sylvestre Cl ME2 .....66 A4
Sylvestres TN13 ....91 E6
Symonds Cl TN15 .....61 E5
Symonds La ME18 ...130 F6
Symons Ave ME4 ......54 A2
Syon Lodge **11** SE12 .28 A8
Syringa Ct **10** RM17 .18 D8

T

Tabor Ct TN12 ....163 A6
Tadburn Gn ME5 ......68 B4
Taddington Wood La
  ME5 ....67 E2
Tadley Ct Gillingham ME7 .54 C7
  Rochester ME1 ......67 C8
Tail Race The ME15 ...99 E2
Tainter Rd TN11 .....111 E1
Talbot Pk TN2 ....159 D5
Talbot Rd Maidstone ME16 99 C6
  The Moor TN18 .....194 F8
Tall Trees Cl ME17 ..118 D2
Tallents Cl DA4 ......33 B1
Tallis Cl E16 ....1 D7
Tallis Gr SE7 ....11 B8
Tally Rd RH8 ....104 E4
Tamar Dr ME2 ....52 F7
Tamar Rd TN10 .....127 B5
Tamar St E16 ....1 E2
Tamarind Cl ME7 .....69 A4
Tamesis Strand DA12 .36 E3
Tan Yard La DA5 .....31 A8
Tandridge Dr BR6 ....43 D1
Tandridge Pl **2** BR6 .43 D1
Tangier La TN3 ......173 B6
Tangleberry Cl BR1 ...42 F5
Tanglewood Cl ME8 ..69 C6
Tanglewood Ct BR5 ..44 C6
Tangmere Cl ME7 .....54 F5
Tanhurst Wlk SE2 ......3 D3
Tankerton Mead TN8 122 C1
Tanner Ho ME8 ....69 D6
Tanners Mead TN8 ..122 C1
Tannery Rd TN9 .....127 C1
Tansy Cl E6 ....2 A7
Tanyard Rolvenden TN17 .191 E4
  Sandhurst TN18 ....196 B5
Tanyard Cotts DA12 ..37 E1
Tanyard Hill DA12 ....37 E2
Tanyard La TN4 ......142 F1
Tanyard The TN17 ...179 D4
Tappan Dr ME4 ....40 B2
Tapsell's La TN5 .....184 D5
Tarbutts TN17 ....179 D4
Tarland Ho TN2 .....159 D3
Tarling Cl DA14 ......30 B5
Tarnwood Pk SE9 .....28 F7
Tarragon Rd ME16 ....99 B3
Tarr Ho TN2 ....159 D3
Tasker Cl ME15 ......101 B3
Tasman Wlk E16 ....1 D7
Tasmania Ho RM18 ...19 A6
Tassell Cl ME19 ......82 A1
Tate Rd E16 ....1 F5
Tates TN17 ....189 A1
Tates Orch DA3 ......48 F3
Tatler Cl ME5 ....68 D2
Tatsfield Cl ME8 .....55 A2
Tatsfield La
  Biggin Hill TN16 ....88 F6
  Hill Park TN16 ......89 A6
Tatsfield Prim Sch TN16 88 D6
Tattersall Cl SE9 .....11 E2
Tattershall Ct **22** DA2 16 B1
Tattershall Rd ME15 .100 A1
Tattlebury La TN17 ..163 F1
Tattlebury Rd TN27 ..151 C8
Taunton Cl Bexley DA7 .14 D5

Taunton Cl continued
  Maidstone ME15 ....116 F6
Taunton Rd DA11 .....18 A2
Taunton Vale DA12 ...36 D5
Tavern Cl ME15 ......94 F7
Tavern Cotts TN15 ...93 A3
Taverners Rd ME8 ....69 E7
Tavistock Cl Chatham ME5 67 F1
  Gillingham ME8 ......69 E7
Tavistock Rd Bexley DA16 .13 C6
  2 Bromley BR2 ....42 A5
Tavy Bridge SE2 ....3 C4
Tawney Rd SE28 ....3 B6
Tay Cl ME5 ....68 B5
Tayfields TN12 ......150 C6
Taylor Cl
  Harrietsham ME17 ..119 D6
  4 Orpington BR6 ..57 F6
Taylor Ct **1** TN2 ...159 C7
Taylor Rd ME6 ....81 F8
Taylor Row DA2 ......32 C5
Taylor St TN4 ....159 A8
Taylor's Bldgs SE18 ...2 B2
Taylor's La Higham ME3 .38 B5
  Rochester ME2 ......53 B7
Taylors Cl DA14 ......29 F4
Taylors La ME19 ......79 F6
Taylors Pl ME19 ......79 E5
Tea Garden La TN3 ..158 C2
Teakcroft Ctr RM13 ...4 D7
Teal Ave BR5 ....44 D5
Teal Cl Grain ME3 ....27 B5
  Newham E16 ....1 D8
Teapot La ME20 ......82 E1
Teardrop Ctr BR8 ....46 C4
Teasaucer Hill ME15 115 F8
Teasel Cl ME14 ......100 F4
Teasel Cres SE28 ......2 E5
Teasel Rd ME5 ....67 F4
Teasels TN27 ....168 A1
Teasley Mead TN3 ..156 C1
Tebbs Way TN15 ......94 C3
Tedder Ave ME5 ......68 D4
Tedder Rd TN4 ......159 B7
Teesdale Rd DA2 ......33 C7
Teeswater Ct DA18 ....3 D3
Teign Mews SE9 ......28 E6
Teignmouth Rd DA16 .13 C5
Teise TN2 ....159 D2
Telegraph Hill ME3 ...38 C5
Telemann Sq SE3 .....11 B4
Telford Ho Erith DA17 ..4 A3
  1 Maidstone ME14 100 A1
Telford Rd SE9 ....29 D6
Tellson Ave SE18 .....11 E6
Telscombe Cl BR6 ....57 E8
Telston Ct TN14 ....75 F2
Temeraire Manor **2**
  ME7 ....54 A6
Tempest Rd ME19 ....96 F3
Templar Dr Erith SE28 ..3 D7
  Gravesend DA11 .....36 A3
Templars Ct **11** TN8 122 D3
Templars Pl SE28 ......2 C3
Temple Gdns ME2 ....53 A6
Temple Hill DA1 ......15 F2
Temple Hill Com Prim Sch
  DA1 ....16 A2
Temple Hill Sq DA1 ...15 F2
Temple Manor★ ME2 .53 A6
Temple Mill Prim Sch
  ME2 ....39 B1
Temple Rd TN16 ......72 D2
Temple Sch ME2 ......39 B2
Temple Way ME19 ....81 F1
Templemore DA14 ....30 B3
Tenby Rd DA16 ....13 D6
Tenchley's La
  Limpsfield RH8 ....104 D4
  The Chart RH8 .....104 E3
Tenney Ho RM17 .....18 D4
Tennyson Ave ME3 ...39 B7
Tennyson Cl DA16 ....12 F6
Tennyson Ho **2** DA17 ..3 F1
Tennyson Rd
  Dartford DA1 ....16 A2
  Gillingham ME7 .....54 C3
Tennyson Wlk
  Northfleet DA11 .....35 D5
  Tilbury RM18 ....19 B5
Tensing Ave DA11 ....35 E5
Tent Peg La BR5 ......43 C4
Tenterden & District Mus★
  TN30 ....193 A7
Tenterden CE Jun Sch
  TN30 ....193 C8
Tenterden Cl SE9 .....28 E8
Tenterden Inf Sch TN30 193 B7
Tenterden Rd
  Biddenden TN27 ....182 B7
  Chatham ME5 ....68 B5
  Fosten Green TN27 .181 F4
  Rolvenden TN17 ....192 A3
Tenterden Station Est
  TN30 ....193 A8
Tenterden Town Sta★
  TN30 ....193 A8
Tenterden Vineyard★
  TN30 ....193 C1
Tenzing Cres SE9 .....28 C6
Terance Butler Ave ME2 .53 E8
Terence Cl Chatham ME4 .54 A2
  Gravesend DA11 .....36 F6
Terence Ct **6** DA17 ..13 F8
Terminus Rd ME16 ....99 A2
Tern Cres ME2 ....52 C6
Terrace Rd ME16 .....99 E3
Terrace St DA12 ......19 B1

Terrace The
25 Gravesend DA12 . . . . .19 B1
Rochester ME1 . . . . .53 C5
Sevenoaks TN13 . . . . . . .91 D5
Terraces The DA2 . . . . .33 C8
Terry Wlk ME19 . . . . .81 E2
Terry's Lodge Rd TN15 . .78 C6
Testers Cl RH8 . . . . .104 B3
Teston Ho ME18 . . . . . .114 A7
Teston La ME15,ME18 . .114 C7
Teston Rd Kings Hill ME19 .97 B5
Offham ME19 . . . . .96 C7
Red Hill ME18 . . . . .97 E2
West Malling ME19 . . . . .97 A6
Tetty Way BR1,BR2 . . . . .42 A7
Teviot Cl DA16 . . . . .13 B6
Tewson Rd SE18 . . . . .2 E1
Teynham Gn
Gillingham ME8 . . . . . . .55 A4
Hayes BR2 . . . . .42 A4
Teynham Ho SE9 . . . . . . .12 D1
Teynham Rd DA2 . . . . . . .33 C8
Thackeray Ave RM18 . . . .19 B6
Thackeray Rd ME20 . . . . .81 F3
Thames Ave
Gillingham ME8 . . . . . . .69 E8
High Halstow ME23 . . . . .23 E4
Thames Barrier Visitor Ctr★
SE18 . . . . .1 D3
Thames Gate DA1 . . . . . .16 A3
Thames Rd Crayford DA1 .15 A4
Grays RM17 . . . . .18 B7
Newham E16 . . . . .1 D5
Tonbridge TN10 . . . . . . .127 C5
Thames Road Ind Est E16 .1 D4
Thames Terr ME3 . . . . . .22 B6
Thames View ME3 . . . . . .39 C7
Thames View Cotts ME3 .38 D3
Thames View Inf Sch
ME8 . . . . .55 D2
Thames View Jun Sch
ME8 . . . . .55 D2
Thames Way
Gravesend DA11 . . . . . . .19 A1
Northfleet DA11 . . . . . . .35 E7
Thamesbank Pl SE28 . . . . .3 C7
Thamesgate Sh Ctr 20
DA11 . . . . .19 B1
Thameside Ind Est E16 . .1 D4
Thameside Inf & Jun Schs
RM17 . . . . .18 C8
Thamesmead Sh Ctr 3 A6
Thamesmere Dr SE28 . . . . .3 A6
Thamesview DA9 . . . . . . .17 C2
Thamesview Sch DA12 . . .36 F5
Thanet Dr BR2 . . . . .56 D7
Thanet Ho
7 Maidstone ME15 . . . .116 F5
7 Northfleet DA11 . . . . .35 F7
Thanet Rd Erith DA8 . . . .14 E7
Sidcup DA5 . . . . .31 A8
Thanington Ct SE9 . . . . .12 E1
Thatch Barn Rd TN27 . . .151 D6
Thatcher Ct DA1 . . . . . . .32 D8
Thatcher Rd TN12 . . . . .149 E4
Thatchers La ME3 . . . . . .22 B5
Thatchers The ME16 . . . .99 B5
Thaxted Rd SE9 . . . . . . .29 C6
Theatre Sq 7 TN30 . . . .193 A7
Thelma Cl DA12 . . . . . . .36 F3
Thelma Gdns SE3 . . . . . .11 E6
Theobalds TN18 . . . . . . .188 F2
Theobalds Cl TN15 . . . . .77 A1
Theodore Cl TN2 . . . . . .159 E7
Theodore Pl ME7 . . . . . .54 C5
Thicketts TN13 . . . . .92 C4
Third Ave Chatham ME5 . .54 C1
Gillingham ME7 . . . . . . .54 F4
West Thurrock RM20 . . . .17 A8
Third St TN3 . . . . .157 F3
Thirlemere Cl ME16 . . . . .99 D8
Thirlmere Cl
Gillingham ME7 . . . . . . .55 A5
Rochester ME2 . . . . .39 C1
Thirlmere Rd Bexley DA7 .14 C6
Royal Tunbridge Wells
TN4 . . . . .158 E5
Thirsk Ho 6 ME15 . . . . .116 F6
Thirza Rd DA1 . . . . .15 F1
Thistle Cl DA1 . . . . .33 B7
Thistle Rd DA12 . . . . . . .36 E8
Thistlebank ME5 . . . . . . .68 A3
Thistlebrook SE2 . . . . . . .3 C4
Thistlebrook Ind Est SE2 .3 C4
Thistledown
Gravesend DA12 . . . . . . .36 D2
Maidstone ME14 . . . . . .100 F4
Thistledown Cl ME7 . . . . .69 A4
Thistlefield Cl DA5 . . . . .30 D7
Thistlemead BR7 . . . . . . .43 B7
Thomas Aveling Sch The
ME1 . . . . .67 C8
Thomas Cotts DA13 . . . . .35 B1
Thomas Cribb Mews E6 . .2 A7
Thomas Dinwiddy Rd
SE12 . . . . .28 B6
Thomas Dr DA12 . . . . . . .36 D6
Thomas Dunk Almshouses 13
TN18 . . . . .189 A2
Thomas Shearley Ct DA5 31 B8
Thomas St Rochester ME1 .53 C3
Royal Tunbridge Wells
TN4 . . . . .159 A5
Woolwich SE18 . . . . .2 A2
Thomas Tallis Sch SE3 . . .11 A4
Thomas Wyatt Way TN15 78 F3
Thompson Cl ME8 . . . . . .70 A8

Thomson Cl ME6 . . . . . . .66 A1
Thong La Basted TN15 . . .94 F5
Gravesend DA12 . . . . . . .37 A2
Thorn Cl Bromley BR2 . . . .43 A3
Chatham ME5 . . . . .67 D1
Thorn Rd TN12 . . . . . . .148 E4
Thorn's Mdw TN16 . . . . .90 C4
Thorndale BR7 . . . . .28 F1
Thorndale Cl ME5 . . . . . .67 D4
Thorndale Ct TN17 . . . . .198 A8
Thornden La
Rolvenden TN17 . . . . . .192 A1
Rolvenden Layne TN17 . .198 A8
Thorndike Cl ME4 . . . . . .67 F8
Thorndike Ho ME4 . . . . . .67 F8
Thorndon Ct TN17 . . . . . .43 F7
Thorndon Rd BR5 . . . . . .43 F7
Thorndyke Way TN15 . . . .78 F3
Thorne Cl Erith DA8 . . . . .14 B8
Newham E16 . . . . .1 A7
Thornet Wood Rd BR1 . . .43 A6
Thorney Croft Cl ME17 . .118 D2
Thornfield Gdns TN2 . . . .159 F5
Thornham Rd ME8 . . . . . .55 C3
Thornhill Ave SE18 . . . . .12 E7
Thornhill Rd ME14 . . . . .100 A6
Thornton Dene DA14 . . . .30 A3
Thornton Rd Bromley BR1 28 A3
Erith DA17 . . . . .4 B2
Thorntree Prim Sch SE7 . .1 D1
Thorntree Rd SE7 . . . . . . .1 D1
Thorold Rd ME5 . . . . . . .54 B3
Thorpe Ave TN10 . . . . . .127 C5
Thorpe Cl BR6 . . . . .57 E8
Thorpe Wlk ME8 . . . . . . .69 D3
Thrale Way ME8 . . . . . . .69 E4
Three Corners DA7 . . . . .14 B5
Three Elm La TN11 . . . . .128 D5
Three Gates Rd DA3 . . . . .48 A2
Three Leg Cross Rd
TN5 . . . . .186 D3
Three Oaks La TN15 . . . .184 D7
Thresher Field TN8 . . . . .140 A6
Threshers Dr ME14 . . . . .100 E5
Thrift The DA2 . . . . .34 C5
Throckmorten Rd E16 . . . .1 B7
Throwley Cl SE2 . . . . .3 C3
Thrush Cl ME5 . . . . .68 B2
Thunderer Rd RM9 . . . . . . .3 F8
Thurnham CE Inf Sch
ME14 . . . . .101 A4
Thurnham Ho 5 BR5 . . . .44 D1
Thurnham La ME14 . . . . .101 C7
Thurrock Bsns Ctr RM20 .16 F8
Thurrock Ent Ctr RM18 . .18 A8
Thurrock Park Way
RM17 . . . . .18 D7
Thursland Rd DA14 . . . . .30 E3
Thursley Rd SE9 . . . . . . .28 F5
Thurston Dr ME2 . . . . . . .52 D7
Thurstone Ct ME14 . . . . .99 F6
Thwaite Cl DA8 . . . . .14 C8
Thyer Cl BR6 . . . . .57 C6
Thyme Cl SE3 . . . . .11 C4
Thyme Wlk ME16 . . . . . . .99 B3
Tibbs Court La TN12 . . . .162 A6
Ticehurst Cl BR5 . . . . . . .30 A1
Tichborne Cl ME16 . . . . . .99 C6
Tickford Cl SE2 . . . . .3 C4
Tidal Basin Rd E16 . . . . . .1 A8
Tidebrook Ct 4 BR5 . . . . .44 C5
Tidelock Ho SE28 . . . . . . .2 D4
Tideside Ct SE18 . . . . . . .1 E3
Tideway The ME1 . . . . . .67 C8
Tidford Rd DA16 . . . . . . .12 F5
Tiger La BR2 . . . . .42 B5
Tilbrook Rd SE3 . . . . . . .11 D4
Tilbury Cl BR5 . . . . .44 B7
Tilbury Fort★ RM18 . . . .19 C3
Tilbury Manor Inf Sch
RM18 . . . . .19 B7
Tilbury Manor Jun Sch
RM18 . . . . .19 B7
Tilbury PRU RM18 . . . . . .18 F5
Tilbury Town Sta RM18 . .18 F5
Tilden Cl TN26 . . . . .183 D7
Tilden Ct TN26 . . . . .183 E7
Tilden Gill Rd TN30 . . . .193 C7
Tilden La TN12 . . . . .132 C3
Tilden Rd ME17,TN27 . . .135 E2
Tile Farm Rd BR6 . . . . . .57 D7
Tile Fields ME17 . . . . . .102 D2
Tile Kiln La Coldblow DA5 .31 C6
Dartford DA2,DA5 . . . . . .31 F5
Tilebarn Cnr TN10 . . . . .127 E4
Tilehurst Point 2 SE2 . . .3 C4
Tilghman Way ME6 . . . . .66 B1
Till Ave DA4 . . . . .46 F2
Tilley Cl ME3 . . . . .40 D5
Tillingbourne Gn BR5 . . . .44 A5
Tillmans Mead DA4 . . . . .47 A2
Tilsden La TN17 . . . . . . .179 E3
Tilt Yard App SE9 . . . . . .11 F1
Tilton Rd TN15 . . . . .94 F7
Timber Bank DA13 . . . . . .79 F8
Timber Cl BR7 . . . . .43 A7
Timber Ct RM17 . . . . . . .18 A8
Timber Tops ME5 . . . . . .84 D8
Timberbank ME5 . . . . . . .68 A6
Timbercroft La SE18 . . . . .12 E7
Timbercroft Prim Sch
SE18 . . . . .12 E7
Timbertop Rd TN16 . . . . .72 C1
Timothy Cl DA6 . . . . .13 E3
Timothy Ho DA18 . . . . . . .3 E4
Tinker Pot La TN15 . . . . .77 D6
Tinker's Alley ME4 . . . . . .53 F7

Tinkerpot Rise TN15 . . . .77 C5
Tinkers St TN15 . . . . . . .186 E3
Tintagel Gdns ME2 . . . . .52 F7
Tintagel Manor 6 ME7 . .54 C6
Tintagel Rd BR5 . . . . . . .44 C1
Tintern Rd ME16 . . . . . . .99 D7
Tippens Cl TN17 . . . . . . .179 D4
Titan Rd RM17 . . . . .18 B8
Titchfield Cl 5 ME15 . . .116 F6
Titchfield Rd ME15 . . . . .116 F6
Tithe Yd ME17 . . . . .120 D5
Titmuss Ave SE28 . . . . . . .3 B6
Titsey Cnr RH8 . . . . .104 B7
Titsey Hill CR6,RH8 . . . . .88 B4
Titsey Pl★ RH8 . . . . .88 B3
Titsey Rd Limpsfield RH8 .104 B8
Titsey RH8 . . . . .88 B1
Tiverton Dr SE9 . . . . .29 C7
Tivoli Gdns
Gravesend DA12 . . . . . . .36 B7
Woolwich SE18 . . . . .1 C6
Tobruk Way ME5 . . . . . . .67 F6
Toby Gdns TN11 . . . . . . .128 E8
Tockwith Ct TN13 . . . . . .92 D4
Toddington Cres ME5 . . . .67 D1
Toke Pl ME17 . . . . .132 E8
Tolcairn Ct 2 DA17 . . . . . .4 A1
Tolgate La ME2 . . . . .53 B7
Tolgate Way ME14 . . . . . .83 E4
Tolhurst Rd TN12 . . . . . .145 A7
Tollgate Mews TN15 . . . .95 A8
Tollgate Pl TN27 . . . . . . .151 E5
Tollgate Rd Dartford DA2 .33 D8
Newham E6 . . . . .1 E8
Tolsey Mead TN15 . . . . . .95 A8
Tom Coombs Cl SE9 . . . . .11 E3
Tom Cribb Rd SE28 . . . . . .2 D3
Tom Jenkinson Rd E16 . . .1 A5
Tom Joyce Cl ME6 . . . . . .81 F7
Tomlin Cl Snodland ME6 . .82 A8
Staplehurst TN12 . . . . . .149 E4
Tonbridge By-Pass
Tonbridge TN4,TN9,TN11 .143 C6
Tonbridge,Stocks Green
TN11,TN9,TN14,TN15 126 B5
Tonbridge Castle★ TN9 127 B2
Tonbridge Chambers 10
TN9 . . . . .143 B8
Tonbridge Cottage Hospl
TN11 . . . . .143 C6
Tonbridge Ct ME2 . . . . . .39 C1
Tonbridge Gram Sch for Girls
TN9 . . . . .143 C7
Tonbridge Rd
Hadlow TN11 . . . . .128 C7
Ightham TN15 . . . . .94 C3
Little Mill TN11,TN12 . . .129 D4
Maidstone,East Barming
ME16 . . . . .98 E1
Maidstone,Upper Fant
ME16 . . . . .99 C3
Pembury TN2 . . . . .160 A7
Sevenoaks TN13,TN15 . .108 C3
Tonbridge TN11 . . . . . .126 E5
Wateringbury ME18 . . . .113 C8
Tonbridge Sch TN10 . . . .127 C3
Tonbridge Sta TN9 . . . . .127 B1
Tong La TN12 . . . . .162 B2
Tong Rd TN12,TN3 . . . . .162 A4
Tongswood Dr TN18 . . . .189 C1
Tony Law Ho SE12 . . . . . .11 A2
Tooley St DA11 . . . . .35 D8
Top Dartford Rd BR8,DA2 32 A2
Topcliffe Dr BR6 . . . . . . .57 D6
Topley Dr ME23 . . . . . . .23 E3
Topley St SE9 . . . . .11 D3
Tor Gr SE28 . . . . .2 E5
Tor Rd DA16 . . . . .13 C6
Torbay Rd TN12 . . . . . . .130 E5
Torbrook Cl DA5 . . . . . . .13 E1
Tormount Rd SE18 . . . . . .12 E8
Toronto Rd
Gillingham ME7 . . . . . . .54 E4
Tilbury RM18 . . . . .19 A5
Torrens Wlk DA12 . . . . . .36 E3
Torrington Cl ME18 . . . . .112 D8
Torver Way BR6 . . . . . . .57 D7
Totnes Rd DA16 . . . . .13 C7
Tovil Gn ME15 . . . . .99 E2
Tovil Green Bsns Pk
ME15 . . . . .99 E1
Tovil Hill ME15 . . . . .99 E2
Tovil Rd ME15 . . . . .99 F2
Tovil, St Stephen's CE Inf Sch
ME15 . . . . .99 E2
Tower Cl Gravesend DA12 .36 E3
Orpington BR6 . . . . .57 F7
Tower Croft DA4 . . . . . . .60 E8
Tower Gdns ME14 . . . . .101 B4
Tower Hill ME19 . . . . . . .96 D7
Tower Ind Est TN15 . . . . .78 D5
Tower La ME14 . . . . . . .101 B4
Tower Park Rd DA1 . . . . .14 F2
Tower Rd Bexley DA7 . . . .14 A3
Dartford DA1 . . . . .15 C1
Erith DA17 . . . . .4 C2
Orpington BR6 . . . . .57 F7
Tower Ret Pk DA1 . . . . . .14 F2
Tower View ME19 . . . . . .97 B3
Towerfields BR2 . . . . . . .56 E6
Towers Point ME1 . . . . . .53 B4
Towers Wood DA4 . . . . . .47 D8
Town Acres TN10 . . . . . .127 C4
Town Hill
Lamberhurst TN3 . . . . . .176 A4
West Malling ME19 . . . . .81 C1
Town Hill Cl ME19 . . . . . .81 C1

Town Lock Ho 4 TN9 . . .127 C2
Town Mdw ME17 . . . . . . .179 D4
Town Pier Sq 5 DA11 . . . .19 B1
Town Rd ME3 . . . . .39 A6
Town Sq DA8 . . . . .14 E8
Town Square Cres DA9 . .33 F8
Town Station Cotts
TN8 . . . . .122 D1
Towncourt Cres BR5 . . . . .43 D5
Towncourt La BR5 . . . . . .43 D5
Townfield Cnr DA12 . . . . .36 D7
Towngate Wood Pk Mobile
Home Pk TN10 . . . . . .127 E7
Townland Cl TN27 . . . . . .168 A2
Townlands Rd TN5 . . . . .184 F4
Townley Gram Sch for Girls
DA6 . . . . .13 F2
Townley Rd DA6 . . . . . . .13 F2
Townsend Rd ME6 . . . . . .81 F8
Townsend Sq ME19 . . . . .97 A2
Townshend Cl DA14 . . . . .30 C2
Townshend Ho 14 SE18 . . .1 C7
Townshend Rd BR7 . . . . .29 B3
Toy's Hill TN16,TN8 . . . .106 C3
Toynbec Cl BR7 . . . . .29 B4
Tracies The ME9 . . . . . . .71 C6
Trader Rd E6 . . . . .2 B7
Tradescant Dr DA13 . . . . .50 B3
Trafalgar Rd Dartford DA1 32 E6
Gravesend DA11 . . . . . . .36 A8
Wouldham ME1 . . . . . . .66 C5
Trafalgar St ME7 . . . . . . .54 C5
Tramways ME5 . . . . .54 C2
Tranquil Rise DA8 . . . . . . .4 E1
Transfesa Rd TN12 . . . . .146 A7
Transmere Cl BR5 . . . . . .43 C5
Transmere Rd BR5 . . . . . .43 C5
Transom Ho 3 ME1 . . . . .53 C1
Trapfield Cl ME14 . . . . . .101 C4
Trapfield La ME14 . . . . . .101 C4
Trapham Rd ME16 . . . . . .99 D5
Trasa Ct 10 RM17 . . . . . .18 C8
Travers Gdns ME9 . . . . . .87 F5
Travertine Rd ME5 . . . . . .68 B1
Trebble Rd DA10 . . . . . . .17 E1
Trebilco Cl TN2 . . . . .159 D7
Tredegar Rd DA2 . . . . . . .32 A5
Tredwell Cl BR1 . . . . .42 A5
Tree La TN15 . . . . .110 E8
Tree Rd E16 . . . . .1 C7
Treebourne Rd TN16 . . . . .72 C1
Treetops Gravesend DA12 .36 B4
Kemsing TN15 . . . . .77 A2
Tonbridge TN9 . . . . .143 B7
Treetops Cl SE2 . . . . .3 E1
Treewall Gdns BR1 . . . . .28 B4
Trefoil Ho Erith DA18 . . . .3 E4
Grays RM17 . . . . .18 A7
Tregony Rd BR6 . . . . .57 F6
Trelawn Cres ME5 . . . . . .68 B2
Trellyn Cl ME14 . . . . .98 F2
Trench Rd TN10 . . . . . . .127 C6
Trenear Cl TN6 . . . . .58 A6
Trent Rd ME5 . . . . .68 B5
Trentham Dr BR5 . . . . . . .44 A5
Trenton Cl ME16 . . . . . . .99 B7
Trevale Rd ME1 . . . . .53 B1
Trevelyan Cl DA1 . . . . . . .15 F3
Trevereux Hill RH8 . . . . .104 F4
Trevino Dr ME5 . . . . .67 F2
Trevithick Dr DA1 . . . . . .15 F3
Trevor Cl BR2 . . . . .42 A2
Trevor Dr ME16 . . . . .99 C5
Trewin Cl ME20 . . . . .82 D2
Trewsbury Ho 2 SE2 . . . . .3 D4
Triangle Ct E16 . . . . .1 C8
Triangle The DA15 . . . . . .30 A8
Tricorn Ho SE28 . . . . .2 D5
Trident Cl ME2 . . . . .53 E7
Trinity Cl Orpington BR2 . .42 E1
Royal Tunbridge Wells
TN2 . . . . .159 D4
Trinity Ct Aylesford ME20 . .83 A3
Dartford DA1 . . . . .33 B7
Eltham SE9 . . . . .12 B1
Trinity Gdns DA1 . . . . . . .15 C1
Trinity Mews SE9 . . . . . .12 D1
Trinity Pl DA1 . . . . .13 F3
Trinity Rd Gillingham ME7 .54 C6
Gravesend DA12 . . . . . . .36 C8
Trinity Sch ME1 . . . . .53 D4
Trinity Sch, Belvedere
DA17 . . . . .4 C2
Trinity St 12 E16 . . . . .1 A8
Tristan Gdns TN4 . . . . . .158 D4
Triton Lodge 9 DA8 . . . . . .4 E1
Triumph Rd E6 . . . . .1 F7
Trivett Cl DA9 . . . . .17 A2
Trolling Down Hill DA2 . .33 C6
Troodos Hill ME14 . . . . . .99 F8
Troon Cl SE28 . . . . .3 D7
Trosley Ave DA11 . . . . . . .36 B6
Trosley Ctry Pk★ ME19,
DA13 . . . . .80 A7
Trosley Ctry Pk Visitor Ctr★
DA13 . . . . .79 F7
Trosley Rd DA17 . . . . .4 A8
Trottiscliffe CE Prim Sch
ME19 . . . . .80 A5
Trottiscliffe Rd ME19 . . . .80 D3
Trotts La TN16 . . . . .105 C8
Trotwood Cl ME5 . . . . . . .84 A8
Troughton Rd SE7 . . . . . . .1 B1
Troutbeck Ho ME20 . . . . .82 C1
Troy Ct 6 SE18 . . . . .2 B2
Troy La TN8 . . . . .121 F4
Troy Mews ME1 . . . . .53 C4
Troys Mead ME17 . . . . . .102 D2

Trubridge Rd ME3 . . . . . .40 E5
Truro Cl ME8 . . . . .55 D3
Truro Rd DA12 . . . . .36 D5
Truro Wlk TN10 . . . . . . .127 C5
Trusedale Rd E6 . . . . .1 F7
Trycewell La TN15 . . . . . .94 D6
Tuam Rd SE18 . . . . .12 D8
Tubbenden Cl BR6 . . . . . .57 E7
Tubbenden Dr BR6 . . . . . .57 D6
Tubbenden Inf & Jun Sch
BR6 . . . . .57 D6
Tubbenden La BR6 . . . . . .57 E7
Tubbenden La S BR6 . . . . .57 D5
Tubs Hill TN13 . . . . .92 B3
Tubs Hill Par TN13 . . . . . .92 A3
Tudeley La
Tonbridge TN9 . . . . .143 D7
Tonbridge, Tudeley TN11,
TN9 . . . . .144 B8
Tudor Ave ME14 . . . . . . .100 B6
Tudor Cl Bromley BR7 . . . .42 F8
Dartford DA1 . . . . .15 B1
Northfleet DA11 . . . . . . .35 E7
Tudor Cres TN14 . . . . . . .76 D3
Tudor Ct Biggin Hill TN16 .72 F2
Crockenhill BR8 . . . . . . .45 C2
Royal Tunbridge Wells
TN2 . . . . .158 E1
Sidcup DA14 . . . . .30 A5
Tudor Dr TN14 . . . . .76 C3
Tudor Gr Chattenden ME3 .39 F4
Gillingham ME8 . . . . . . .69 F8
Tudor Par SE9 . . . . .11 B3
Tudor Way BR5 . . . . .43 D3
Tudor Wlk DA5 . . . . .13 E1
Tudway Rd SE3 . . . . .11 C3
Tufa Cl ME5 . . . . .68 B1
Tuffs Cotts ME3 . . . . .25 C3
Tufnail Rd DA1 . . . . .15 F1
Tufton Mews ME8 . . . . . . .55 F1
Tufton St ME14 . . . . .100 A4
Tugboat St SE28 . . . . .2 E4
Tugmutton Cl BR6 . . . . . .57 B6
Tulip Cl 5 E6 . . . . .1 F8
Tulip Tree Cl TN9 . . . . . .143 B8
Tumblefield Est TN15 . . . .78 F8
Tumblefield Rd TN15 . . . .78 E7
Tumblers Hill ME17 . . . . .127 E3
Tunbridge Wells Girls' Gram
Sch TN4 . . . . .159 A6
Tunbridge Wells Gram Sch
for Boys TN4 . . . . . . .159 A7
Tunbridge Wells High Sch
TN2 . . . . .159 F5
Tunbridge Wells Ind Hospl
The TN3 . . . . .157 B3
Tunbridge Wells Mus &
Gall★ TN1 . . . . .159 B4
Tunbridge Wells Sta
TN1 . . . . .159 A3
Tunbridge Wells Trad Pk
TN2 . . . . .159 D8
Tunbridge Wells West Sta★
TN2 . . . . .158 F1
Tunbury Ave ME5 . . . . . . .67 F1
Tunbury Ave S ME5 . . . . .67 F1
Tunbury Prim Sch ME5 . . .67 F1
Tunnan Leys E6 . . . . .2 A7
Tunnel Ave 1 SE10 . . . . . .1 A1
Tunnel Cotts RM20 . . . . . .17 A8
Tunnel Est RM20 . . . . . . .16 F8
Tunnel Rd TN1 . . . . .159 B4
Tunstall Cl BR6 . . . . .57 E6
Tunstock Way DA17 . . . . . .3 E3
Tupman St ME1 . . . . .53 B4
Tuppy St SE28 . . . . .2 C3
Turgis Rd ME17 . . . . . . .117 E4
Turks Hall Pl ME2 . . . . . .65 E5
Turley Cotts TN3 . . . . . . .158 A8
Turnberry Way BR6 . . . . .43 D1
Turnbull Cl DA9 . . . . .33 E8
Turnbury Cl SE28 . . . . .3 D7
Turnden Rd TN17 . . . . . .179 A3
Turner Ave TN17 . . . . . . .179 D3
Turner Cl TN16 . . . . .72 C1
Turner Ct DA1 . . . . .15 C2
Turner Ho
Gravesend DA12 . . . . . . .36 C6
5 Greenwich SE7 . . . . .11 B8
Turner Rd Bean DA2 . . . . .34 B5
Tonbridge TN10 . . . . . . .127 B5
Turner St ME3 . . . . .22 B5
Turner's Oak DA3 . . . . . .62 E7
Turners Ave TN30 . . . . . .193 B8
Turners Gdns TN13 . . . . .108 C2
Turners Green La TN5 . . .184 F6
Turners Green Rd TN5 . . .184 F6
Turners Pl DA4 . . . . .47 C8
Turnpike Cl DA6 . . . . .13 D3
Turnpike Dr BR6 . . . . . . .58 D2
Turnpike La RM18 . . . . . .19 D8
Turnstone DA3 . . . . .49 A7
Turnstone Rd ME5 . . . . . .68 C1
Turnstones The DA12 . . . .36 D6
Turpin La SE3 . . . . .15 A8
Turpington Cl BR2 . . . . . .42 E2
Turpington La BR2 . . . . . .42 E3
Turton Ho 5 SE18 . . . . . .12 B8
Tuscan Dr ME5 . . . . .68 C1
Tuscan Rd SE18 . . . . .2 D1
Tutsham Way TN12 . . . . .145 F6
Tuxford Rd TN4 . . . . . . .158 B5
Tweed Rd TN10 . . . . . . .127 C5
Tweedy Rd BR1 . . . . .42 A5
Twigg Cl DA8 . . . . .14 E7

Twin Tumps Way SE28 ....3 A6
Twisden Rd ME19 ....97 F8
Twiss Ho 6 SE18 ....2 B1
Twistleton Ct DA1 ....15 D1
Twitton La TN14 ....75 E3
Twitton Mdws TN14 ......75 E3
Two Gates Hill ME3 ......38 F5
Twydall Ent Ctr ME8 .....55 C4
Twydall Gn ME8 ....55 B3
Twydall Inf Sch ME8 ......55 B2
Twydall Jun Sch ME8 .....55 B2
Twydall La ME8 ....55 B2
Twyford Ct ME14 ....100 D6
Twyford Rd TN11 ....111 E1
Twysden Cotts TN18 ....196 A4
Tydeman Rd ME15 ......100 F2
Tye La BR6 ....57 C5
Tyeshurst Cl SE2 ....3 E1
Tyland Barn Wildlife Conservation Ctr★ ME14 ....83 E3
Tyland La ME14 ....83 F3
Tyler Cl East Malling ME19 .97 F8
Erith DA8 ....14 B7
Tyler Dr ME8 ....69 E4
Tyler Gr DA1 ....15 F3
Tylers Green Rd BR8 ....45 C2
Tylney Rd BR1 ....42 D7
Tyndall Rd DA16 ....12 F4
Tyne Cl ME5 ....68 C5
Tyne Rd TN10 ....127 B5
Tynedale Cl DA2 ....33 D7
Tynemouth Cl E6 ....2 B7
Tynemouth Rd SE18 ......2 E1
Typhoon Rd ME19 ....96 F3
Tyron Way DA14 ....29 F3
Tyrrell Ave DA16 ....13 B2
Tyrrells Hall Cl 5 RM17 .18 D8
Tyrwhitt-Drake Mus of Carriages★ ME15 .....100 A3

U

Uckfield La TN8 ....139 D4
Udall Cotts DA15 ....29 E5
Ufton Cl ME15 ....100 E1
Ulcombe CE Prim Sch ME17 ....135 F6
Ulcombe Hill ME17 .....118 F1
Ulcombe Rd
Headcorn TN27 ....151 C6
Langley Heath ME17 .....117 E3
Ullswater Ho 5 ME15 ...116 E7
Underdown Ave ME4 .....53 F1
Underlyn Ind Est TN12 ..132 F2
Underlyn La TN12 ......132 D1
Underriver House Rd TN15 ....109 D5
Underwood ME19 ....96 D7
Underwood Cl ME15 .....99 F2
Underwood The SE9 .....28 F6
Unicorn Wlk DA9 ....16 F2
Unicumes La ME16 ......99 C2
Union Pk ME15 ....116 F4
Union Pl ME4 ....54 A4
Union Rd BR2 ....42 D4
Union Sq 22 TN2 ....159 A2
Union St Chatham ME4 ...54 A3
Flimwell TN5 ....187 B3
Maidstone ME14 ....100 A5
Rochester ME1 ....53 C5
Unity Way SE18 ....1 D3
Univ of East London E16 ..2 A6
Univ of Greenwich ME4 ..54 B8
Univ of Greenwich Avery Hill Campus (Mansion Site) SE9 ....12 C1
Univ of Greenwich Avery Hill Campus (Southwood Site) SE9 ....12 D1
Univ of Greenwich Avery Hill Campus Southwood Site SE9 ....29 D8
University Gdns DA5 .....30 F8
University Pl DA8 ....14 C7
University Way
Dartford DA1 ....15 E4
Woolwich E16 ....2 B6
Unwin Cl ME20 ....83 A3
Upbury Arts Coll ME7 ...54 B4
Upbury Way ME4 ....54 A4
Upchat Rd ME2,ME3 .....39 F3
Updale Rd DA14 ....29 F4
Upland Prim Sch DA7 ....13 F4
Upland Rd DA7 ....13 F4
Uplands SE18 ....2 B1
Uplands Cl Rochester ME2 52 D6
Sevenoaks TN13 ....91 F4
Uplands Com Tech Coll TN5 ....185 A4
Uplands Rd BR6 ....44 B1
Uplands Way TN13 ......91 F4
Upnor Castle★ ME2 .....39 F2
Upnor Ho ME15 ....116 E8
Upnor Rd ME2 ....39 E2
Upper Abbey Rd DA17 ....4 A2
Upper Austin Lodge Farm Cotts DA4 ....60 E3
Upper Austin Lodge Rd DA4 ....60 D4
Upper Ave DA13 ....49 E8
Upper Bank Hill ME15 ..114 E3
Upper Britton Pl ME7 ....54 B5
Upper Bush Rd ME2 .....51 F2
Upper Church Hill DA9 ..16 E2
Upper Cumberland Wlk TN1 ....159 B1
Upper Dr TN16 ....72 C1
Upper Dunstan Rd TN4 .159 B6
Upper East Rd ME4 .....54 B8
Upper Fant Rd ME16 ....99 D2
Upper Green La TN11 ..110 D5
Upper Green Rd TN11 ..110 D5
Upper Grosvenor Rd TN1,TN4 ....159 B6
Upper Grove Rd DA17 ...13 F8
Upper Haysden La TN11, TN9 ....142 E6
Upper Holly Hill Rd DA17 .4 B1
Upper Hunton Hill ME15 ....115 A3
Upper Luton Rd ME5 ....54 C2
Upper Mill ME18 ....113 D8
Upper Nellington TN3 ..158 B4
Upper Park Rd
Bromley BR1 ....42 C8
Erith DA17 ....4 B2
Upper Platts TN5 ......186 F1
Upper Profit TN3 ......158 A3
Upper Rd ME15 ....100 B2
Upper Ruxley Cotts DA14 31 A1
Upper Sheridan Rd DA17 .4 A2
Upper Spring La TN15 ...94 B5
Upper St
Hollingbourne ME17 .....102 E3
Leeds ME17 ....117 F5
Rusthall TN4 ....158 D4
Upper Stephens TN3 ...158 A3
Upper Stone St ME15 ..100 A3
Upper Street N DA3 .....62 F8
Upper Street S DA3 .....62 F8
Upper Wickham La DA16 13 B6
Upperton Rd DA14 ......29 F3
Upton Cl DA5 ....13 F1
Upton Day Hospl DA6 ...13 E3
Upton Prim Sch DA6 ....13 F2
Upton Quarry TN3 .....157 F3
Upton Rd Bexley DA5,DA6 .13 E2
Woolwich SE18 ....12 C8
Upton Rd S DA5 ....13 F1
Upton Villas 4 DA6 .....13 E3
Uptons TN27 ....151 C6
Upwood Rd SE12 ....11 A1
Uridge Cres TN10 ......127 C4
Uridge Rd TN10 ....127 C4
Urquhart Cl ME5 ....68 A5
Ursula Lodges DA14 .....30 B3
Usborne Cl TN12 ......149 E3

V

Vaizeys Wharf SE7 ....1 B3
Vale Ave
Royal Tunbridge Wells,Mount Sion TN1 ....159 A3
Royal Tunbridge Wells,Southborough TN4 .142 F1
Vale Cl BR6 ....57 A6
Vale Cotts ME9 ....87 A8
Vale Ct TN4 ....143 A2
Vale Dr ME5 ....67 E6
Vale Rd Bromley BR1 .....43 A7
Dartford DA1 ....32 B7
Hawkhurst TN18 ....188 F3
Maidstone ME15 ....115 E4
Northfleet DA11 ....35 E7
Royal Tunbridge Wells,Mount Sion TN1 ....159 A3
Royal Tunbridge Wells,Southborough TN4 .142 F1
Tonbridge TN9 ....127 C1
Vale Rise TN9 ....143 E8
Valence Ho ME15 ......116 C7
Valence Rd DA8 ....14 D7
Valence Sch TN16 ....89 F1
Valence View TN17 ....166 E7
Valenciennes Ho ME4 ...54 A4
Valentine Ave DA5 ......30 E7
Valentine Cl ME7 ....55 A1
Valentine Dr ME23 ......23 E4
Valentine Rd ME15 .....116 E7
Valerian Cl ME5 ....67 E4
Valetta Way ME1 ....53 B4
Valiant Ho 5 SE7 ....1 C1
Valiant Rd ME5 ....68 C2
Valiant Way E6 ....1 F8
Valley (Charlton Athletic FC) The SE7 ....1 C1
Valley Cl DA1 ....14 F1
Valley Dr
Gravesend,Riverview Park DA12 ....36 D4
Gravesend,Singlewell DA12 .36 E1
Maidstone ME15 ....115 F6
Sevenoaks TN13 ....92 B1
Valley Forge Cl TN10 ...127 F4
Valley Gdns DA9 ....17 B1
Valley Gr SE7 ....1 C1
Valley Hts DA1 ....15 F3
Valley Industries TN11 ..128 B7
Valley L Ctr SE9 ....29 C8
Valley La DA13 ....64 B2
Valley Mushroom Farm TN16 ....72 D1
Valley Park Com Sch ME14 ....100 C4
Valley Rd Crayford DA1 ...14 F1
Erith DA8 ....4 D2
Fawkham Green DA3 .....48 C2
Gillingham ME7 ....54 E4
Orpington BR5 ....44 B8
Valley Rd *continued*
Rusthall TN4 ....158 D4
Valley Rise ME5 ....67 F1
Valley The ME17 ....115 D3
Valley View
Biggin Hill TN16 ....72 D1
Royal Tunbridge Wells TN4 ....143 A2
Swanscombe DA9 ....17 B1
Valley View Rd ME1 .....53 B1
Valley View Terr DA4 ....46 F1
Valleyside SE7 ....1 D1
Valliers Wood Rd DA15 ..29 E7
Vambery Rd SE18 ....12 C8
Vanbrugh Cl 2 E16 ....1 D8
Vanbrugh Pk SE3 ....11 A7
Vanburgh Cl BR6 ....43 E1
Vancouver Cl BR6 ....58 A6
Vancouver Dr ME8 ......55 C1
Vandome Cl E16 ....1 B7
Vandyke Cross SE9 ......11 E2
Vanessa Cl DA17 ....4 A1
Vanessa Way DA5 ....31 D5
Vanessa Wlk DA12 ......36 F3
Vange Cottage Mews ME1 ....53 B4
Vanguard Cl E16 ....1 A8
Vanguard Way ME2 .....53 E8
Vanity La ME17 ....115 D1
Vanoc Gdns BR1 ....28 A4
Vanquisher Wlk DA12 ...36 F5
Varley Rd E16 ....1 B7
Varnes St ME20 ....82 F6
Vaughan Ave TN10 .....127 E6
Vaughan Rd DA16 ....12 F5
Vauxhall Cl DA11 ....35 F8
Vauxhall Cres ME6 ......82 A6
Vauxhall Gdns TN9 ....143 C7
Vauxhall La
Bidborough TN11,TN4 ...143 B4
Tonbridge TN11 ....143 D6
Vauxhall Pl DA1 ....32 E8
Veitchil Barn BR8 ....45 F8
Veles Rd ME6 ....81 F8
Venmead Ct 4 DA17 ......4 A2
Venners Cl DA7 ....14 E5
Ventnor Cl ME5 ....68 C8
Venture Cl DA5 ....30 E8
Venture Ct SE12 ....28 A8
Venus Rd SE18 ....1 F3
Verdun Rd SE18,SE2 .....13 A8
Vermont Rd TN4 ....158 C4
Vernham Rd SE18 ....12 C8
Vernon Cl Orpington BR5 ..44 B6
West Kingsdown TN15 .....61 F2
Vernon Rd
Royal Tunbridge Wells TN1 ....159 C6
Swanscombe DA10 ....17 F1
Veroan Rd DA7 ....13 E5
Verona Gdns DA12 ......36 E4
Verona Ho DA8 ....14 F7
Vert Ho RM17 ....18 C7
Veryan Cl BR5 ....44 C5
Vesper Ct TN27 ....153 A1
Vestry Cotts
New Barn DA3 ....49 C5
Sevenoaks TN14 ....92 C8
Vestry Rd TN14 ....92 C8
Via Romana DA12 ....37 B7
Viaduct Terr DA4 ....47 C7
Vicarage Ave SE3 ....11 A7
Vicarage Cl
Aylesford ME20 ....82 F3
Erith DA8 ....14 C8
Halling ME2 ....66 A5
Stoke ME3 ....25 A3
Vicarage Ct Chalk DA12 ..37 A7
Newington ME9 ....71 B7
Vicarage Dr DA11 ....18 C1
Vicarage Hill TN16 ......89 D1
Vicarage La Chalk DA12 ..37 A6
East Farleigh ME15 ....115 B6
Hoo St Werburgh ME3 ....40 E4
Sevenoaks TN13 ....91 D8
Vicarage Pk SE18 ....2 C1
Vicarage Rd Coldblow DA5 31 B7
Gillingham ME7 ....54 C5
Halling ME2 ....65 F5
Rochester ME2 ....53 B8
Royal Tunbridge Wells TN4 ....142 F2
Woolwich SE18 ....2 C1
Yalding ME18 ....114 A1
Vicarage Row ME3 ......38 C4
Vicarage Sq RM17 ....18 A8
Vicarage Way TN19 ....194 A3
Vicary Way ME16 ....99 D5
Vickers Rd DA8 ....4 D1
Victor Mills Cotts DA14 ..31 A1
Victoria Ave 3 DA12 .....36 B8
Victoria Bglws DA14 ....30 F1
Victoria Bsns Ctr DA16 ..13 B5
Victoria Cl Chatham ME5 ..67 D2
Edenbridge TN8 ....138 C8
Victoria Cotts
Cranbrook TN17 ....179 D5
Edenbridge TN8 ....138 C8
Victoria Ct 6 ME16 .....99 E3
Victoria Dock Rd E16 ....1 B6
Victoria Dr Kings Hill ME19 96 F1
Sutton at H DA4 ....47 D7
Victoria Gdns TN16 .....72 C4
Victoria Hill Rd BR8 .....46 A8
Victoria Ind Pk DA1 .....15 E2
Victoria Orch ME16 .....99 B3
Victoria Rd Bexley DA6 ...14 A3
Bromley BR2 ....42 D4
Victoria Rd *continued*
Chatham,Luton ME4 ......54 B2
Chatham,Walderslade ME5 .67 E3
Chislehurst BR7 ....29 A3
Dartford DA1 ....15 E2
Edenbridge TN8 ....138 C8
Erith DA8 ....14 E8
Golden Green TN11 .....128 F6
Northfleet DA11 ....35 F7
Royal Tunbridge Wells TN1 ....159 B4
Royal Tunbridge Wells,Southborough TN4 .142 E1
Sevenoaks TN13 ....92 B2
Sidcup DA15 ....30 A5
Victoria Scott Ct DA1 ....14 F4
Victoria St Eccles ME20 ..82 F6
Erith DA17 ....3 F1
Gillingham ME7 ....54 D6
Maidstone ME16 ....99 E3
Rochester ME1 ....53 D5
Rochester,Strood ME2 ....53 B7
Victoria Terr ME1 ....53 A2
Victoria Way SE7 ....1 B1
Victoria Wharf DA1 ......15 E2
Victory Cotts TN14 .....108 C2
Victory Lodge 10 DA8 .....4 E1
Victory Manor 1 ME7 ...54 A6
Victory Pk ME2 ....53 E7
Victory Terr ME17 ......134 E8
Victory Way DA2 ....16 C3
Vidal Manor ME7 ....54 C5
Vidgeon Ave ME3 ....40 D6
View Cl TN16 ....72 C3
View Rd ME3 ....39 B7
View The SE2 ....3 E1
Viewfield Rd DA5 ....30 C7
Viewland Rd SE18 ....2 F1
Viewlands ME5 ....54 C3
Viewlands Ave TN16 .....89 F7
Viewpoint ME14 ....100 C8
Viewpoint Ct DA3 ....48 F5
Vigilant Way DA12 ......36 F3
Vigo Hill ME19,TN15 .....79 E6
Vigo Rd TN15 ....79 C7
Vigo Village Sch DA13 ...80 A8
Viking Cl ME2 ....52 F4
Viking Ho 3 SE18 ....1 E2
Viking Rd DA11 ....35 C5
Viking Way Erith DA8 .....4 C3
West Kingsdown TN15 .....61 E5
Villa Cl DA12 ....37 B6
Villa Ct DA1 ....32 E6
Villa Rd ME3 ....38 B3
Villacourt Rd SE18,SE2 ..13 A8
Village Green Ave TN16 ..72 E2
Village Green Rd DA1 ...15 A3
Village Green Way TN16 .72 E2
Village The SE7 ....11 D8
Village View ME5 ....54 C2
Villas Rd SE18 ....2 C2
Vincent Cl Bromley BR2 ...42 B5
Sidcup DA15 ....29 E7
Vincent Rd
Kit's Coty ME20 ....83 C7
Woolwich SE18 ....2 B2
Vincent Sq TN16 ....72 C6
Vincent St 13 E16 ....1 A8
Vine Ave TN13 ....92 B3
Vine Court Rd TN13 .....92 C4
Vine Ct
16 Gravesend DA11 ......19 B1
Staplehurst TN12 ....149 F3
Wateringbury ME18 .....113 D8
Vine Lodge TN13 ....92 C3
Vine Rd BR6 ....57 F4
Vine The TN13 ....92 C3
Vine Wlk TN12 ....149 E3
Vineries The ME7 ....54 E5
Vines La
Hildenborough TN11 ....109 C1
Rochester ME1 ....53 C5
Viney's Gdns TN30 .....183 C1
Vineyard La TN5 ....186 C2
Vinson Cl BR6 ....44 A1
Vinson Ct DA15 ....30 A6
Vinters Rd ME14 ....100 B4
Vintners Way ME14 ....100 E4
Viola Ave SE2 ....3 B1
Violet Cl ME5 ....84 A8
Violets The TN12 ......146 A5
VIP Trad Est SE7 ....1 C2
Virginia Rd ME7 ....54 C7
Virginia Wlk DA12 ....36 E2
Viscount Dr E6 ....1 F8
Vista The Eltham SE9 ....28 E8
Sidcup DA14 ....29 F3
Vixen Cl ME5 ....68 C6
Voce Rd SE18 ....12 D7
Vogue Ct 11 BR1 ....42 B8
Voyagers Cl SE28 ....3 C7
Vulcan Cl Chatham ME5 ..68 B7
Newham E6 ....2 A7
Vyne The DA7 ....14 B4
Vyvyan Cotts TN17 .....190 C3
Vyvyan Ho SE18 ....12 A6

W

Wadard Terr BR8 ....46 C4
Wade Ave BR5 ....44 D2
Wadeville Cl DA17 ....4 A1
Wadhurst Bsns Pk TN5 .184 B7
Wadhurst CE Prim Sch TN5 ....184 F5
Wadhurst Rd TN3 ......173 D1
Wadhurst Sta TN5 .....184 C6
Wadlands Rd ME3 ....22 B5
Waghorn Rd ME6 ....82 A8
Waghorn St ME4 ....54 B2
Wagon La TN12 ....130 C1
Wagoners Cl ME14 .....100 E4
Wagtail Way BR5 ....44 D5
Waid Cl DA1 ....15 F1
Wainhouse Cl TN8 .....122 D3
Wainscott Prim Sch ME2 39 D2
Wainscott Rd ME2 ....39 D2
Wainscott Wlk ME2 ......39 D3
Waite Davies Rd 8 SE12 28 A8
Wake Rd ME1 ....67 C8
Wakefield Cl ME2 ....52 D6
Wakefield Rd DA9 ....17 C2
Wakehurst Cl ME17 ....115 B3
Wakeleys Cotts ME8 .....70 B8
Wakely Cl TN16 ....72 C1
Wakerley Cl 6 E6 ....1 F7
Waldair Ct E16 ....2 B4
Waldeck Rd DA1 ....16 A1
Waldegrave Rd BR1 .....42 F5
Walden Ave BR7 ....28 F4
Walden Cl DA17 ....3 F1
Walden Par BR7 ....28 F2
Walden Rd BR7 ....28 F2
Waldenhurst Rd BR5 ....44 D2
Waldens Cl BR5 ....44 D2
Waldens Rd BR5 ....44 E3
Waldens The ME17 .....118 E2
Walderslade Ctr ME5 ....68 A3
Walderslade Girls Sch ME5 ....67 F5
Walderslade Prim Sch ME5 ....68 A3
Walderslade Rd ME5 ....67 F6
Walderslade Woods ME5 67 E2
Waldo Ind Est BR1 ......42 D6
Waldo Rd BR1 ....42 D6
Waldrist Way DA18 ....3 F4
Waldron Dr ME15 ......115 F6
Waldstock Rd SE28 ....3 A6
Walk The ME17 ....118 E2
Walkden Rd BR7 ....29 A3
Walker Cl Crayford DA1 ..14 F4
Woolwich SE18 ....2 C2
Walker Pl TN15 ....94 D6
Walkhurst Cotts TN17 ..190 F7
Walkhurst Rd TN17 ....190 F7
Walkley Rd DA1 ....15 B2
Walks The TN3 ....171 C8
Wall Cl ME3 ....40 D7
Wallace Cl Erith SE28 .....3 D6
Royal Tunbridge Wells TN2 ....173 A8
Wallace Gdns DA10 .....17 E1
Wallace Rd ME1 ....67 E8
Wallace Terr TN15 ......62 E4
Waller Hill TN17 ....166 B5
Wallers TN3 ....158 A8
Wallhouse Rd DA8 ......15 C7
Wallis Ave ME15 ......116 E5
Wallis Cl DA2 ....31 F5
Wallis Field TN3 ....171 B6
Wallis Pk DA11 ....18 B2
Walmer Cl BR6 ....57 D6
Walmer Ct 3 ME14 ....100 A5
Walmer Ho ME2 ....39 C1
Walmer Terr SE18 ....2 D2
Walmers Ave ME3 ....38 A4
Walnut Cl Chatham ME5 ..68 B8
Eynsford DA4 ....60 D7
Paddock Wood TN12 ....146 A6
Yalding ME18 ....113 F1
Walnut Hill Rd DA13 ....49 E6
Walnut Tree Ave
Dartford DA1 ....32 E6
Loose ME15 ....116 A5
Walnut Tree Cl
Chislehurst BR7 ....43 C8
Westerham TN16 ....89 D1
Walnut Tree Ct ME20 ....82 B1
Walnut Tree La ME15 ..116 A5
Walnut Tree Rd DA8 ......4 E1
Walnut Tree Way DA13 ...50 B3
Walnut Way
Royal Tunbridge Wells TN4 ....159 D8
Swanley BR8 ....45 D7
Walnuts Rd BR6 ....44 B1
Walnuts The BR6 ....44 A1
Walpole Cl ME19 ....81 F1
Walpole Ho 4 BR7 ......43 D8
Walpole Pl SE18 ....2 B2
Walpole Rd BR2 ....42 D4
Walsham Cl SE28 ....3 D6
Walsham Rd ME5 ....67 F1
Walshaw Ho 2 ME14 ...100 A6
Walsingham Cl ME8 .....69 D3
Walsingham Ho 3 ME14 ....100 A6
Walsingham Pk BR7 ....43 D7
Walsingham Rd BR5 .....44 B8
Walsingham Wlk DA17 ...14 A8
Walter Burke Ave ME1 ...66 C5
Walter's Farm Rd TN9 ..127 C1
Walters Green Rd TN11 .156 F6
Walters Ho SE18 ....12 A7
Walters Rd ME3 ....40 E6
Walters Yd BR1 ....42 A7
Walterstown Ct DA1 .....32 D8
Waltham Cl Dartford DA1 .15 A1
27 Orpington BR5 ....44 D1
Waltham Rd ME8 ....55 C3
Walthamstow Hall TN13 .92 C4
Walthamstow Hall (Nursery Unit) TN13 ....92 B5
Walton Rd Sidcup DA14 ...30 C5

Walton Rd *continued*
Tonbridge TN10 . . . . .127 F6
Walwyn Ave BR1 . . . . .42 D6
Wanden La TN27 . . . . . .153 C8
Wansbury Way BR8 . . . . .46 A5
Wanstead Cl BR1 . . . . . . .42 C7
Wanstead Rd BR1 . . . . . . .42 C7
Wansunt Rd DA5 . . . . .31 C7
Warberry Park Gdns
TN4 . . . . .158 E4
Warblers Cl 3 ME2 . . . . . .53 A7
Ward Cl Durgates TN5 . . .184 E5
Erith DA8 . . . . .14 D8
Ward's La TN5 . . . . .185 E4
Warde's ME18 . . . . .113 F2
Warden Cl ME16 . . . . .99 C4
Warden Mill Cl ME18 . . . .113 E7
Warden Rd ME1 . . . . .53 C2
Wardens Field Cl 2 BR6 . .57 F4
Wardona Ct DA10 . . . . . . .17 F1
Wardour Ct 11 DA2 . . . . . .16 B1
Wards Wharf App E16 . . . .1 D4
Wardwell La ME9 . . . . . . .71 C8
Ware St ME14 . . . . .101 A5
Warepoint Dr SE28 . . . . . . .2 D4
Warham Rd TN14 . . . . . . .76 B3
Waring Cl BR6 . . . . .58 A4
Waring Dr BR6 . . . . .58 A4
Waring Rd DA14 . . . . .30 C2
Warland Rd
West Kingsdown TN15 . . . . .61 F2
Woolwich SE18 . . . . .12 E7
Warmlake ME17 . . . . . . .117 F1
Warmlake Bsns Est
ME17 . . . . .117 E1
Warmlake Rd ME17 . . . .117 C1
Warne Pl 4 DA15 . . . . .13 B1
Warner St ME4 . . . . .53 F3
Warnett Ct ME6 . . . . .66 A1
Warnford Gdns ME15 . . .116 A8
Warnford Rd BR6 . . . . . . .57 F5
Warren Ave BR6 . . . . .57 F5
Warren Cl DA6 . . . . .14 A2
Warren Cotts TN11 . . . . .141 A3
Warren Ct TN15 . . . . .92 C3
Warren Dr BR6 . . . . .58 B5
Warren Farm La TN3 . . .172 B4
Warren Gdns BR6 . . . . . . .58 A5
Warren Hastings Ct DA11 18 F1
Warren La Oxted RH8 . . .104 A1
Woolwich SE18 . . . . .2 B3
Yelsted ME9 . . . . .70 C3
Warren Rd Bexley DA6 . . .14 A2
Dartford DA1 . . . . .32 E5
Hayes BR2 . . . . .56 A8
Kit's Coty ME5 . . . . .83 D7
Luddesdown ME2 . . . . .51 D3
Northfleet DA13 . . . . .35 B3
Orpington BR6 . . . . .58 C5
Sidcup DA14 . . . . .30 C5
Warren Ridge TN3 . . . . .173 C3
Warren Road Prim Sch
BR6 . . . . .57 F6
Warren The
Gravesend DA12 . . . . .36 D4
2 Greenwich SE7 . . . . .11 C8
Penshurst TN11 . . . . .141 A4
Ticehurst TN5 . . . . .186 E1
Warren View DA12 . . . . . .37 E2
Warren Wlk 1 SE7 . . . . . . .11 C8
Warren Wood Cl BR2 . . . .56 A8
Warren Wood Com Prim Sch
& Language Unit ME1 . . .67 C8
Warren Wood Rd ME1 . . .67 C7
Warrens The DA3 . . . . . . .48 F3
Warrington Rd TN12 . . . .146 A6
Warrior Ave DA12 . . . . . . .36 C4
Warsop Trad Est TN8 . . .138 D8
Warspite Rd SE18 . . . . .1 E3
Warwall E6 . . . . .2 B7
Warwick Cl Orpington BR6 58 A7
Sidcup DA5 . . . . .30 F8
Warwick Cres ME1 . . . . . .52 F2
Warwick Ct 8 DA8 . . . . . .14 F7
Warwick Gdns DA13 . . . . .64 A8
Warwick Pk TN2 . . . . . . .159 B1
Warwick Pl
Maidstone ME16 . . . . .99 E3
Northfleet DA11 . . . . .18 B2
Warwick Rd Bexley DA16 .13 C4
4 Royal Tunbridge Wells
TN1 . . . . .159 A2
Sidcup DA14 . . . . .30 B3
Warwick Terr SE18 . . . . . .12 D8
Warwick Way DA1 . . . . . . .32 E6
Washington Ho ME15 . . .116 E5
Washneys Rd BR6 . . . . . . .74 B6
Washwell La TN5 . . . . . .184 F3
Wassall La TN17 . . . . . . .197 E7
Wat Tyler Way ME15 . . . .100 A4
Watchgate DA2 . . . . .33 E3
Watchmans Terr 6 ME5 .54 C2
Water La
Harrietsham ME17 . . . . . .119 B5
Hawkhurst TN18 . . . . .189 B4
Headcorn TN17,TN27 . . . .151 A4
Hunton ME15 . . . . .131 D6
Kingswood ME17 . . . . . . .118 F3
Limpsfield RH8 . . . . .104 A8
6 Maidstone ME15 . . . . . .100 A4
Maidstone,Bearsted ME14 101 E6
Shoreham TN14 . . . . .75 F6
Sidcup DA14 . . . . .30 F6
Smarden TN27 . . . . .152 F2
West Malling ME19 . . . . . . .97 C8
Water Mill Way DA4 . . . . .47 B7
Water Slippe TN11 . . . . .111 D1
Watercress Cl TN14 . . . . .92 C7
Watercress Dr TN14 . . . . .92 C7
Watercroft Rd TN14 . . . . .58 F1
Waterdale Rd SE2 . . . . . . .13 A8
Waterdales DA11 . . . . . . .35 D7
Waterdown Rd TN4 . . . .158 E1
Waterfield TN2 . . . . .173 A7
Waterfield Cl Erith DA17 . . .4 A3
Woolwich SE28 . . . . .3 B5
Waterfrets Cotts TN3 . . .157 F5
Waterfront Studios Bsns Ctr
E16 . . . . .1 A5
Watergate Ho 5 SE18 . . . .2 A2
Waterglade Ind Pk RM20 .16 F8
Waterhead Cl DA8 . . . . . .14 E7
Waterhouse Cl E16 . . . . . .1 D8
Wateringbury CE Prim Sch
ME18 . . . . .113 E6
Wateringbury Cl BR5 . . . .44 B7
Wateringbury Rd ME19 . .97 F3
Wateringbury Sta ME18 113 E6
Waterlakes TN8 . . . . . . .138 C8
Waterloo Pl
Cranbrook TN17 . . . . .179 D5
Tonbridge TN9 . . . . .143 B8
Waterloo Rd
Cranbrook TN17 . . . . .179 D6
Gillingham ME7 . . . . .54 C4
Tonbridge TN9 . . . . .143 B8
Waterloo St
1 Gravesend DA12 . . . . . .36 C8
Maidstone ME15 . . . . .100 A3
Waterlow Rd
Maidstone ME14 . . . . .100 A6
Vigo Village DA13 . . . . . . .79 F7
Waterman's La TN12 . . .146 B3
Watermans Way DA9 . . . .17 B3
Watermeadow Cl
Erith DA8 . . . . .15 B6
Gillingham ME7 . . . . .68 F6
Watermill Cl
Maidstone ME16 . . . . .99 B5
Rochester ME2 . . . . .53 C8
Watermint Cl BR5 . . . . . . .44 D5
Waters Cotts TN5 . . . . . .185 A4
Waters Edge ME15 . . . . . .99 F2
Waters Edge Ct DA8 . . . . .4 F1
Waters Pl ME7 . . . . .69 A6
Waterside Crayford DA1 . .14 F2
Maidstone ME14 . . . . .99 F5
Waterside Ct
Leybourne ME19 . . . . .81 E2
Rochester ME2 . . . . .53 E6
Waterside Gate ME16 . . . .99 F5
Waterside La ME7 . . . . . .54 F7
Waterside Mews ME18 . .113 D6
Waterside Sch SE18 . . . . . .2 D1
Watersmeet Cl ME15 . . .100 A1
Watersmeet Way SE28 . . .3 D7
Waterton BR8 . . . . .45 D5
Waterton Ave DA12 . . . . .36 E8
Waterworks Cotts TN14 . .92 B6
Watery La
Heaverham TN15 . . . . .93 D7
Sidcup BR5,DA14 . . . . .30 B2
Watford Rd E16 . . . . .1 A8
Watkins Cl TN12 . . . . . . .149 E5
Watling Ave ME5 . . . . . . .54 D2
Watling Ho 10 SE18 . . . . .12 A8
Watling St Bexley DA6,DA7 14 C3
Dartford DA1,DA2 . . . . . . .33 C8
Gillingham ME5 . . . . .54 D2
Gravesend DA11,DA12 . . . .36 C2
Northfleet DA11,DA13 . . . .35 C5
Rochester ME2 . . . . .52 D7
Watson Ave ME5 . . . . .67 D5
Watson Cl RM20 . . . . .17 A6
Watt Ho SE2 . . . . .3 C1
Watt's Cross Rd TN11 . .126 B6
Watt's La BR7 . . . . .43 C8
Watts Cl Snodland ME6 . . .82 B8
Wadhurst TN5 . . . . .184 F4
Watts' Ave ME1 . . . . .53 C4
Watts' St ME4 . . . . .53 E3
Wavell Dr DA15 . . . . .12 E1
Waveney Rd TN10 . . . . .127 B5
Waverley Cl Bromley BR2 .42 D4
Chatham ME5 . . . . .68 D2
Coxheath ME17 . . . . .115 C3
Waverley Cres
Woolwich SE18 . . . . .12 D8
Woolwich SE18 . . . . .2 D1
Waverley Dr TN2 . . . . . .159 F6
Waverley Gdns E6 . . . . . . .1 E8
Waverley Rd SE18 . . . . . . .2 D1
Way Volante DA12 . . . . . .36 E4
Wayfield Com Prim Sch
ME5 . . . . .68 A7
Wayfield Link SE9 . . . . . .12 D1
Wayfield Rd ME5 . . . . . . .68 A7
Waylands BR8 . . . . .45 F5
Waylands Cl TN14 . . . . . .74 E4
Wayne Cl BR6 . . . . .57 F7
Wayne Ct ME2 . . . . .39 D2
Wayside
3 Chislehurst BR7 . . . . . . .43 D8
Tenterden TN30 . . . . .183 B2
Wayside Ave TN30 . . . . .183 B3
Wayside Dr TN8 . . . . . . .122 D3
Wayside Flats TN30 . . . .183 B2
Wayside Gr SE9 . . . . .28 F4
Wayville Rd DA1 . . . . .33 B8
Weald Cl Istead Rise DA13 35 E1
Maidstone ME15 . . . . .116 C6
Orpington BR2 . . . . .56 E8
Sevenoaks Weald TN14 . .108 C2
Weald Com Prim Sch
TN14 . . . . .108 B2
Weald Ct TN11 . . . . .126 D6
Weald of Kent Gram Sch for
Girls The TN9 . . . . .143 C7
Weald Rd TN13 . . . . .108 B7
Weald The BR7 . . . . .28 F2
Weald View
Frittenden TN17 . . . . .166 E6
Paddock Wood TN12 . . . . .146 E1
Turner's Green TN5 . . . . .184 F6
Weald View Rd TN9 . . . .143 B7
Wealden Ave TN30 . . . . .183 B1
Wealden Cl TN11 . . . . . .126 E5
Wealden Ct 5 ME5 . . . . . .54 B3
Wealden Pl TN13 . . . . . . .92 D6
Wealden View TN17 . . . .177 E8
Wealden Way ME20 . . . . .98 E7
Weardale Ave DA2 . . . . . .33 C7
Weare Rd TN4 . . . . .159 C8
Weatherly Cl ME1 . . . . . .53 C4
Weathersfield Ct SE9 . . . .11 F1
Weaver Cl E6 . . . . .2 B6
Weaver's Orch DA13 . . . .35 A2
Weavering Cl ME2 . . . . . .39 B2
Weavering Cotts ME14 . .100 E3
Weavering St ME14 . . . .100 F4
Weavers Cl
Gravesend DA11 . . . . .36 A7
Staplehurst TN12 . . . . . . .149 F4
Weavers Cotts TN17 . . . .177 E8
Weavers La TN14 . . . . . . .92 C6
Weavers The
Biddenden TN27 . . . . .168 A1
Maidstone ME16 . . . . .99 B5
Webb Cl ME3 . . . . .40 D6
Webb Ct 6 SE28 . . . . .3 B6
Webb's Mdw TN15 . . . . . .92 C2
Webber Cl DA8 . . . . .15 B7
Webster Rd ME8 . . . . .55 F1
Wedgewood Cl ME16 . . . .99 B5
Wedgewood Ct DA5 . . . . .30 F8
Wedgewood Dr ME5 . . . . .68 A7
Wedgwoods TN16 . . . . . . .88 C6
Weeds Wood Rd ME5 . . . .67 F4
Week St ME14 . . . . .100 A4
Weeks La TN27 . . . . .168 A5
Weigall Rd SE12,SE3 . . . . .11 A3
Weir Mill ME19 . . . . .97 F7
Weir Rd DA5 . . . . .31 B8
Weird Wood DA3 . . . . . . .49 C6
Welbeck Ave Bromley BR1 28 A4
Royal Tunbridge Wells
TN4 . . . . .159 C8
Sidcup DA15 . . . . .30 A7
Welcombe Ct ME8 . . . . . .69 D8
Weld Cl TN12 . . . . .149 F4
Weldstock Ho 2 SE28 . . . .2 D3
Well Cl TN11 . . . . .125 F1
Well Field DA3 . . . . .48 F5
Well Hall★ SE9 . . . . .11 E3
Well Hall Par SE9 . . . . . . .11 F3
Well Hall Rd SE18,SE9 . . . .11 F5
Well Hill BR6 . . . . .59 B5
Well Hill La BR6 . . . . .59 B4
Well Hill Nursery BR6 . . . .59 C4
Well Penn Rd ME3 . . . . . .22 C3
Well Rd Maidstone ME14 .100 A5
Otford TN14 . . . . .76 C3
Well St East Malling ME19 .97 E6
Maidstone ME15,ME17 . . .115 E4
Wellan Cl DA16 . . . . .13 B2
Welland Rd TN10 . . . . . .127 B4
Wellands Cl BR1 . . . . .42 F7
Wellbrook Rd BR6 . . . . . .57 A6
Wellcome Ave DA1 . . . . . .15 E3
Weller Ave ME1 . . . . .53 D2
Weller Pl BR6 . . . . .73 A8
Weller Rd TN4 . . . . .158 C4
Wellers Cl TN16 . . . . . . .105 C8
Wellesley Cl 7 SE7 . . . . . .1 C1
Welling High St DA16 . . . .13 B4
Welling Sch DA16 . . . . . . .13 B6
Welling Sta DA16 . . . . . . .13 A5
Welling Way DA16 . . . . . .12 D4
Wellingfield Ct 1 DA16 . .13 A4
Wellington Ave
Sidcup DA15 . . . . .13 A1
Woolwich SE18 . . . . .2 B3
Wellington Cotts
Gill's Green TN18 . . . . . . .188 E4
Meopham DA13 . . . . .64 A7
Wellington Gdns SE7 . . . . .1 C1
Wellington Ho 6 ME15 .116 E5
Wellington Mews SE7 . . . .11 C8
Wellington Par DA15 . . . .13 A2
Wellington Pl
Maidstone ME14 . . . . .99 F6
Sparrow's Green TN5 . . . .184 F5
Wellington Rd Bexley DA5 13 D2
Bromley BR2 . . . . .42 C5
Dartford DA1 . . . . .15 C1
Erith DA17 . . . . .3 F1
Gillingham ME7 . . . . .54 C4
Orpington BR5 . . . . .44 C3
Tilbury RM18 . . . . .19 A5
Wellington St
Gravesend DA12 . . . . .36 C8
Woolwich SE18 . . . . .2 A2
Wellington Way ME19 . . . .96 F3
Wellingtonia Way TN8 . .122 C2
Wellmeade Dr TN13 . . . .108 B8
Wells Cl
Royal Tunbridge Wells
TN1 . . . . .159 A3
Tenterden TN30 . . . . .193 B8
Tonbridge TN10 . . . . .127 D4
Westerham TN16 . . . . . . .105 C8
Wells Cotts ME18 . . . . . .113 C2
Wells Ct ME2 . . . . .52 D5
Wells Ho Bromley BR1 . . . .28 B3
Wells Ho *continued*
Royal Tunbridge Wells
TN4 . . . . .158 F4
Wells Rd Bromley BR1 . . . .42 F7
Rochester ME2 . . . . .52 D5
Wellsmoor Gdns BR1 . . . .43 A6
Welton Cl TN9 . . . . .142 F7
Welton Rd SE18 . . . . .12 E7
Wemmick Cl ME1 . . . . . . .67 D7
Wendover Cl ME2 . . . . . . .66 B5
Wendover Ct BR2 . . . . . . .42 B6
Wendover Rd
Bromley BR1,BR2 . . . . .42 B6
Eltham SE9 . . . . .11 D4
Wendover Way
Bexley DA16 . . . . .13 A3
Orpington BR6 . . . . .44 A3
Wensley Cl SE9 . . . . .11 F1
Wents Wood ME14 . . . . .100 F5
Wentworth Cl Erith SE28 . .3 D7
Gravesend DA11 . . . . .36 A3
Hayes BR2 . . . . .56 A8
Orpington BR6 . . . . .57 E5
Wentworth Dr
Cliffe Woods ME3 . . . . .39 B8
Dartford DA1 . . . . .15 A1
Gillingham ME8 . . . . .69 E7
Wentworth Ho 3 SE3 . . .11 A7
Wentworth Prim Sch
DA1 . . . . .32 A8
Wenvoe Ave DA7 . . . . . . .14 B5
Wernbrook St SE18 . . . . .12 C8
Wesley Ave E16 . . . . .1 B5
Wesley Cl Maidstone ME16 98 F3
Orpington BR5 . . . . .44 C6
Wesley Ho BR1 . . . . .42 D6
Wessex Dr DA8 . . . . .14 E6
Wessex Wlk DA2 . . . . .31 E6
West App BR5 . . . . .43 C4
West Borough Prim Sch
ME16 . . . . .99 B3
West Brow BR7 . . . . .29 B3
West Common Rd BR2 . . .56 B7
West Crescent Rd DA12 .19 C1
West Cross TN30 . . . . . .192 F7
West Cross Gdns TN30 .192 F7
West Ct 3 ME15 . . . . . . .100 A1
West Dr Chatham ME5 . . . .67 D5
Sutton Valence ME17 . . . .135 B7
West End Brasted TN16 . . .90 B2
Kemsing TN15 . . . . .77 A2
Marden TN12 . . . . .148 C6
West Hallowes SE9 . . . . . .28 E7
West Heath Cl DA1 . . . . . .14 F1
West Heath La TN13 . . .108 B7
West Heath Rd
Bexley SE2 . . . . .13 D8
Crayford DA1 . . . . .14 F1
West Hill Biggin Hill BR6 . .72 F7
Dartford DA1 . . . . .15 D1
West Hill Dr DA1 . . . . . . .15 C1
West Hill Prim Sch DA1 .15 C1
West Hill Rise DA1 . . . . . .15 D1
West Holme DA8 . . . . .14 C6
West Kent Ave DA11 . . . . .18 C1
West Kent Coll TN9 . . . .143 A7
West Kingsdown CE Prim Sch
TN15 . . . . .62 A2
West Kingsdown Ind Est
TN15 . . . . .61 F2
West La ME3 . . . . .26 F6
West Lodge Prep Sch
DA14 . . . . .30 A5
West Malling CE Prim Sch
ME19 . . . . .97 B8
West Malling Ind Pk
ME19 . . . . .80 E2
West Malling Sta ME19 . .97 D8
West Mersea Cl E16 . . . . . .1 B5
West Mill DA11 . . . . .18 F1
West Mill Rd ME20 . . . . .82 C4
West Motney Way ME8 . .55 F3
West Park Ave TN4 . . . . .142 F1
West Park Rd ME15 . . . .100 B2
West Parkside SE10 . . . . . .1 A2
West Pk SE9 . . . . .28 E7
West Rd Chatham ME4 . . . .54 A7
Goudhurst TN17 . . . . .177 E8
Kilndown TN17 . . . . .176 F3
West Shaw DA3 . . . . .48 D7
West St Bexley DA7 . . . . . .13 F4
Bromley BR1 . . . . .42 A7
Erith DA8 . . . . .4 E1
Gillingham ME7 . . . . .54 D6
Gravesend DA11 . . . . .19 B1
Grays RM17 . . . . .18 A8
Harrietsham ME17 . . . . . .119 C6
Hunton ME15 . . . . .131 D7
Rochester ME2 . . . . .39 B1
West Malling ME19 . . . . . . .97 B8
Woodside Green ME17 . . .120 E8
Wrotham TN15 . . . . .78 F3
West Terr DA15 . . . . .29 E7
West Thurrock Prim Sch
RM20 . . . . .17 A8
West Thurrock Way
RM20 . . . . .17 B8
West View Hospl TN30 . .192 E6
West View Rd
Crockenhill BR8 . . . . .45 D3
Dartford DA1 . . . . .15 F1
Swanley BR8 . . . . .46 A5
West Way BR5 . . . . .43 D4
West Wlk ME16 . . . . .99 B3
West Wood Cott BR6 . . . .59 B4
West Wood Rd ME9 . . . . .86 B8
West Woodside DA5 . . . . .30 E7
West Yoke TN15 . . . . .62 D7
Westbere Ho BR5 . . . . . . .44 C4
Westbourne Rd DA7 . . . . .13 E7
Westbrook Ct SE3 . . . . . . .11 B6
Westbrook Dr BR5 . . . . . .44 D1
Westbrook Rd SE3 . . . . . .11 B6
Westbrook Terr TN2 . . . .159 D1
Westbrooke Cl ME4 . . . . .54 A2
Westbrooke Cres DA16 . .13 C4
Westbrooke Rd
Bexley DA16 . . . . .13 C4
Sidcup DA15 . . . . .29 D6
Westbrooke Sch DA16 . . .13 D4
Westbury Ct 5 DA14 . . . .30 A4
Westbury Rd BR1 . . . . . . .42 D8
Westbury Terr TN16 . . . .105 C8
Westcombe Hill SE3 . . . . .11 A8
Westcombe Park Rd SE3 11 A7
Westcombe Park Sta SE3 .1 A1
Westcott Ave DA11 . . . . . .36 A5
Westcott Cl BR1 . . . . .42 F4
Westcourt Prim Sch
DA12 . . . . .36 E6
Westcourt Rd ME7 . . . . . .54 A6
Westdale Rd SE18 . . . . . .12 B8
Westdean Ave SE12 . . . . .28 C7
Wested Farm Cotts BR8 .45 F2
Wested La BR8 . . . . .46 A3
Westerdale Rd 5 SE10 . . .1 A1
Westergate Rd Bexley SE2 13 E8
Rochester ME2 . . . . .38 F1
Westerham Cl ME8 . . . . . .55 B3
Westerham Dr DA15 . . . . .13 C1
Westerham Hill TN16 . . . .89 B5
Westerham Rd
Brasted TN16 . . . . .90 A2
Limpsfield RH8,TN16 . . . .104 C6
Orpington BR2 . . . . .56 D4
Sevenoaks TN13 . . . . .91 C4
Westerham TN16 . . . . . . .105 A8
Westerhill Rd ME17 . . . .115 C1
Western Ave
Chatham ME4 . . . . .54 A8
7 Hawkhurst TN18 . . . . . .188 F2
Western Beach Apartments
E16 . . . . .1 A5
Western Cross Cl DA9 . . .17 C1
Western Gateway E16 . . . .1 A6
Western Rd
Borough Green TN15 . . . . . .94 F7
Hawkhurst TN18 . . . . .188 F2
Maidstone ME16 . . . . .99 C2
Royal Tunbridge Wells
TN1 . . . . .159 C5
Royal Tunbridge
Wells,Southborough TN4 .143 A1
Turner's Green TN5 . . . . . .184 F6
Western Way SE28 . . . . . . .2 E4
Westfield
New Ash Green DA3 . . . . . .62 F6
1 Orpington BR6 . . . . .57 C5
Sevenoaks TN13 . . . . .92 C5
Westfield Bsns Ctr ME2 . .53 C7
Westfield Cl DA12 . . . . . . .36 C2
Westfield Cotts
Cudham TN14 . . . . .73 D3
West Kingsdown TN15 . . . . .61 F4
Westfield Gdns ME9 . . . . .71 C3
Westfield Ho TN30 . . . . .192 F7
Westfield Rd DA7 . . . . . . .14 C4
Westfield Sole Rd ME5,
ME14 . . . . .84 D8
Westfield St SE18 . . . . .1 D3
Westfield Terr TN17 . . . .178 F1
Westfield Villas TN12 . . .148 B5
Westgate Ct SE12 . . . . . . .28 A7
Westgate Ho 6 DA1 . . . . .15 D1
Westgate Prim Sch DA1 .32 D8
Westgate Rd DA1 . . . . . . .15 D1
Westharold BR8 . . . . .45 D6
Westhill Cl DA12 . . . . . . .36 B7
Westholme BR6 . . . . .43 F2
Westhorne Ave SE12,SE9 .11 C2
Westhurst Dr BR7 . . . . . . .29 B3
Westland Ho 1 E16 . . . . . .2 A5
Westland Lodge 2 BR1 . .42 C7
Westleigh Dr BR1 . . . . . . .42 E8
Westmarsh Cl ME15 . . . .116 F7
Westmead ME20 . . . . .82 C4
Westminster Ind Est SE18 .1 D3
Westminster Sq ME16 . . .99 B4
Westmoor St SE7 . . . . .1 D3
Westmore Rd TN16 . . . . . .88 C7
Westmoreland Ave DA16 .12 E3
Westmoreland Pl 9 BR1 .42 A6
Westmoreland Rd BR2 . . .42 A5
Westmorland Cl ME15 . .116 E7
Westmorland Gn ME15 . .116 E7
Westmorland Rd ME15 .116 E7
Westmount Ave ME4 . . . . .53 F3
Westmount Rd SE9 . . . . . .12 A3
Weston Ave RM20 . . . . . . .16 F8
Weston Rd ME2 . . . . .53 A8
Westree Ct 7 ME16 . . . . .99 E3
Westree Rd ME16 . . . . . . .99 E3
Westrise TN9 . . . . .143 A7
Westview ME4 . . . . .40 B2
Westway Coxheath ME17 .115 C3
Pembury TN2 . . . . .160 D7
Westways
Edenbridge TN8 . . . . .122 C2
Westerham TN16 . . . . .89 C1
Westwell Cl BR5 . . . . .44 D1
Westwell Ct TN30 . . . . . .192 F7
Westwell Ho TN30 . . . . .192 F7
Westwood Cl BR1 . . . . . . .42 D6

Westwood Farm DA13 ...34 D2
Westwood La DA16 ......12 F4
Westwood Rd
 Betsham DA13 ....34 E2
 East Peckham TN12 ...129 E6
 Loose ME15 ....116 A7
 Rusthall TN4 ....158 C5
Westwood Tech Coll
 DA16 ....12 E3
Westwood Way TN13 ....91 F5
Westwood Wlk ME9 ......71 B7
Wetheral Dr ME5 ....68 B4
Wey Cl ME5 ....68 C5
Weybridge Cl ME5 ....68 C4
Weyhill Cl ME14 ....100 C6
Weyman Rd SE3 ....11 C6
Weymouth Cl E6 ....2 B7
Wharf La ME3 ....22 B6
Wharf Rd
 Gillingham ME7 ....54 C7
 Gravesend DA12 ....19 E1
 Grays RM17 ....17 F8
 Maidstone ME15 ....99 E2
Wharf Rd S RM17 ....17 F8
Wharfedale Rd DA2 ......33 C7
Wharfside Cl DA8 ....4 F1
Wharnecliffe Ho DA9 ....17 B1
Wharton Rd BR1 ....42 B8
Whatcote Cotts TN15 ...95 C7
Whatman Cl ME14 ....100 C6
Wheatcroft DA12 ....36 C7
Wheatcroft Gr ME8 ......69 F7
Wheatear Way ME5 ......68 B7
Wheatfield ME19 ....81 E1
Wheatfield Cl TN17 ....179 C5
Wheatfield Dr TN17 ....179 C5
Wheatfield Lea TN17 ...179 C5
Wheatfield Way TN17 ..179 C5
Wheatfields Chatham ME5 68 D2
 Maidstone ME14 ....100 D4
 Newham E6 ....2 B7
Wheatley Cl DA9 ....17 A2
Wheatley Terrace Rd
 DA8 ....14 F8
Wheatsheaf Cl ME15 ...116 B8
Wheatsheaf Hill
 Chelsfield TN14 ....58 F2
 Ide Hill TN14 ....106 F4
Wheatsheaf Way TN10 .127 D6
Wheatstone Rd DA8 ......4 D1
Wheelbarrow Park Est
 TN12 ....148 B7
Wheeler Pl ME18 ....97 A2
Wheeler St
 Headcorn TN27 ....151 E5
 Maidstone ME14 ....100 A5
Wheeler's La ME17 .....132 E7
Wheelers The ME8 ....69 B6
Wheelock Cl DA8 ....14 B7
Wheelwrights The
 ME17 ....119 D6
Wheelwrites TN15 .....110 E7
Whenman Ave DA5 ....31 C5
Whernside SE28 ....3 C6
Whetsted Rd
 Five Oak Green TN12 ..145 C8
 Whetsted TN12 ....129 F1
Whetstone Rd SE3 ......11 D6
Whiffen Wlk ME19 ....82 B1
Whiffen's Ave ME4 .....53 F5
Whiffen's Ave W ME4 ...53 F5
Whimbrel Cl SE28 ....3 C6
Whimbrel Gn ME20 ......81 F2
Whimbrel Wlk ME5 ......68 C1
Whimbrels The ME4 .....40 B1
Whinchat Rd SE28 ....2 D3
Whinfell Way DA12 .....36 F4
Whinyates Rd SE9 ......11 E4
Whippendell Cl BR5 ....44 B8
Whippendell Way BR5 ..44 B7
Whistler Rd TN10 .....127 D6
Whitby Cl Biggin Hill TN16 .72 B1
 Stone DA9 ....17 A2
Whitby Rd SE18 ....1 F2
Whitchurch Cl ME4 .....99 E4
Whitcombe Cl ME5 ......68 C3
White Ave DA11 ....35 F5
White Bear Pas 3 TN1 .159 A2
White Cottage Rd TN10 127 D6
White Gate ME2 ....52 F8
White Gates DA14 ....30 A3
White Hart Cl TN13 ...108 C7
White Hart Par TN13 ...91 E5
White Hart Rd
 Orpington BR6 ....44 A2
 Woolwich SE18 ....2 E2
White Hart Wood TN13 .108 C6
White Hart Yd 10 DA11 ..19 B1
White Hill Rd ME9,ME14 .69 F1
White Horse Hill BR7,SE9 29 A4
White Horse La
 Harvel DA13 ....64 C2
 Otham Hole ME15 .....117 A6
White Horse Rd DA13 ...64 E1
White House Cl ME3 ....40 E4
White House La TN14 ..107 F5
White House Rd TN14 .107 F5
White La RH8,TN16 ......88 B3
White Lodge TN1 ......159 C4
White Lodge Cl TN13 ...92 B4
White Oak Cl 13 TN9 ...143 B8
White Oak Gdns DA15 ..29 F8
White Oak Prim Sch BR8 45 E7
White Oak Sq 3 BR8 ...45 E6
White Post
 Four Elms TN8 ....123 A6

White Post continued
 Hollingbourne ME17 ..103 B5
White Post Cnr TN11 ..110 F5
White Post Hill DA4 ....47 A2
White Post La
 Culverstone Green DA13 ..63 F2
 Sole Street DA13 ......50 B5
White Rd ME4 ....54 A2
White Rock Ct ME16 ....99 E3
White Rock Pl 5 ME16 ..99 E3
White's La TN18 ......189 B2
White's Mdw BR1 ....43 A5
Whitebeam Ave BR2 .....43 A3
Whitebeam Cl TN15 .....77 A2
Whitebeam Dr ME17 ...115 B3
Whitebine Gdns TN12 .130 A6
Whitebread La TN31 ...197 D1
Whitecroft BR8 ....45 E7
Whitefield Cl BR5 .....44 C6
Whitefield Rd TN4 ....159 A6
Whitefriars TN13 .....108 A8
Whitefriars Wharf TN9 127 C1
Whitegate Cl TN4 .....159 A8
Whitegate Ct ME8 ......69 D5
Whitegates Ave TN15 ..61 E4
Whitegates La TN5 ....184 D8
Whitehall Dr ME17 ....118 D3
Whitehall La Erith DA8 ..14 F5
 6 Grays RM17 ....18 C8
Whitehall Rd
 Broad Street ME14 ...102 A6
 Bromley BR2 ....42 D5
Whitehaven Cl BR2 .....42 A5
Whitehaven Ct 6 DA6 ..13 E3
Whitehead Cl DA2 ......32 C5
Whiteheads La ME14 ..101 B4
Whitehill TN15 ....79 B3
Whitehill Inf Sch DA12 ..36 C5
Whitehill Jun Sch DA12 .36 C5
Whitehill La DA12 ......36 D5
Whitehill Par DA12 ....36 C5
Whitehill Rd Dartford DA1 15 A2
 Gravesend DA12 ....36 C6
 Longfield,Whitehill DA13 ..48 D8
 Meopham DA13 ....64 B7
Whitehorse Hill ME5 ...54 B3
Whitehouse Cres ME1 ..83 A8
Whitelake Rd TN10 ...127 C5
Whiteleaves Rise ME2 ..52 B3
Whitelimes TN18 .....188 D8
Whiteoak Ct 1 BR8 ....45 E6
Whitepost La DA13 .....80 A8
Whites Cl DA9 ....17 C1
Whitewall Ctr ME2 .....53 D8
Whitewall Rd ME2 .....53 D7
Whitewall Way ME2 ....53 D7
Whitewebbs Way BR5 ..43 F8
Whitewell La TN17 ....179 D7
Whitewood Cotts TN16 .88 C7
Whitfield Cres DA2 ....33 C8
Whitfield Rd DA7 ....13 F7
Whitings Way E6 ....2 B8
Whitmore St ME16 .....99 D2
Whitney Wlk DA14 ......30 E2
Whittaker St ME4 ......54 A4
Whitworth Rd SE18 ....12 A7
Whybourne Crest TN2 .159 D1
Whyman Ave ME4 ....54 A1
Wichling Cl BR5 ....44 D1
Wicken Ho ME16 ....99 E4
Wickenden Rd TN13 ....92 C5
Wickens Pl ME19 ....97 C8
Wickets The TN14 ....108 C2
Wickham Cl ME9 ......71 B6
Wickham Common Prim Sch
 BR4 ....56 A6
Wickham Ct DA16 ......12 E5
Wickham Field TN14 ...75 F3
Wickham La SE2,SE18 ...13 A8
Wickham Pl ME17 .....120 D5
Wickham St Bexley DA16 .13 A6
 Rochester ME1 ....53 D3
Wickhams Way ME3 .....48 F4
Wickhurst Rd TN14 ...107 F3
Wicks Cl SE9 ....28 D4
Wicksteed Cl DA5 ......31 D5
Widbury TN3 ....157 F3
Widecombe Rd SE9 .....28 E5
Widgeon Cl E16 ....1 B7
Widgeon Path SE28 .....2 D3
Widgeon Rd Erith DA8 ..15 B7
 Rochester ME2 ....52 D6
Widmore Lodge Rd BR1 .42 D7
Widmore Rd BR1 ....42 C7
Wierton Hill ME17 ....133 D7
Wierton La ME17 .....116 E1
Wierton Rd ME17 .....133 E8
Wigmore Rd ME8 ....69 B4
Wilberforce Ct 2 SE28 ..3 C5
Wilberforce Rd ME17 .115 D3
Wilberforce Way DA12 ..36 D3
Wilde Cl RM18 ....19 C5
Wilde Rd DA8 ....14 B7
Wilden Park Rd TN12 .164 E7
Wilderness Rd BR7 .....29 B1
Wilderness Ave TN15 ..92 F5
Wilderness Mount
 TN13 ....92 D5
Wildernesse Sch The
 TN13 ....92 E6
Wildfell Cl ME5 ....84 C8
Wildman Cl ME8 ....69 D3
Wildwood Cl
 Kingswood ME17 ......118 E2
 1 Lewisham SE12 ....28 A8
Wildwood Glade ME7 ...69 B4
Wilford Ho 3 SE18 ......2 B1

Wilfred St 23 DA12 ......19 B1
Wilkins Way TN16 ......90 B3
Wilkinson Cl 1 DA1 ...16 A3
Wilkinson Pl ME18 .....97 A2
Wilkinson Rd E16 ....1 C7
Wilks Ave DA1 ....32 F6
Will Adams Ct 9 ME7 ..54 C6
Will Adams Rdbt ME8 ..54 C5
Will Adams Way ME8 ...54 F1
Will Crooks Gdns SE9 ..11 D3
Will Thorne Pav The E16 ..1 E7
Willenhall Rd SE18 ......2 B1
Willersley Ave
 Orpington BR6 ....57 D7
 Sidcup DA15 ....29 F7
Willersley Cl DA15 .....29 F7
Willesley Gdns TN17 ..179 D6
Willett Cl BR5 ....43 E3
Willett Way BR5,BR6 ...43 E3
Willetts Cotts TN3 ...156 C4
Willetts La TN3 ......156 C4
William Baker Ho ME20 .98 F8
William Barefoot Dr SE9 .29 A5
William Ho 4 DA12 ....36 B8
William Judge Cl TN30 .193 D7
William Luck Cl TN12 ..129 E6
William Rd ME2 ....52 C2
William Smith Ho 10 DA17 4 A3
William St
 Gravesend DA12 ....36 B8
 Grays RM17 ....18 C8
 Royal Tunbridge Wells
 TN4 ....159 A5
Williams Way DA2 ......31 D6
Willicombe Ho TN2 ...159 D4
Willicombe Pk TN2 ...159 D4
Willington Gn ME15 ..116 E7
Willington St ME15 ...100 F2
Willis Ho ME1 ....53 C4
Willis Rd DA8 ....4 D2
Willoughby Way SE7 ....1 B2
Willow Ave
 Hoo St Werburgh ME3 ..40 E3
 Sidcup DA15 ....13 A1
 Swanley BR8 ....45 B1
Willow Cl Bromley BR2 ..42 F4
 Orpington BR5 ....44 B2
 Sidcup DA5 ....13 F1
Willow Cres
 Five Oak Green TN12 .145 B7
 Staplehurst TN12 ....149 F5
 Loose ME15 ....116 A6
Willow Dene Sch SE18 ..12 E6
Willow Gr BR7 ....29 B2
Willow Grange DA14 ...30 B5
Willow Ho
 2 Chatham ME5 ....67 F5
 8 Maidstone ME16 ....99 A3
Willow La
 Paddock Wood TN12 ..146 E6
 Woolwich SE18 ....2 A2
Willow Lea TN10 ......127 C7
Willow Lodge TN4 ....158 E4
Willow Pk TN14 ....75 F2
Willow Rd Dartford DA1 ..32 C7
 Erith DA8 ....15 A6
 Larkfield ME20 ....81 F3
 Rochester ME2 ....52 E6
Willow Rise ME15 ....100 F1
Willow Terr DA4 ....60 E8
Willow Tree Ct DA14 ...29 F3
Willow Tree Rd TN2 ..158 F1
Willow Tree Wlk BR1 ..42 B8
Willow Vale BR7 ....29 B2
Willow Way
 Biddenden TN27 ......182 D7
 Maidstone ME15 ......100 B3
Willow Wents ME18 ....96 D1
Willow Wlk
 Culverstone Green DA13 ..63 F3
 Orpington BR6 ....57 B7
 Royal Tunbridge Wells
 TN2 ....159 E8
Willow Wood Rd DA13 ..63 F2
Willowbank Ct 12 ME15 .100 B4
Willowbank Dr ME23 ....2 E3
Willowby Gdns ME8 ....69 E4
Willowfields Cl 1 SE18 ..2 C1
Willowherb Cl ME4 ....40 C1
Willowmead ME19 ......81 E2
Willows The
 Gillingham ME8 ....55 E2
 Grays RM17 ....18 D8
 Newington ME9 ....71 B6
Willowside ME6 ....66 A1
Willrose Cres SE2 ......3 B1
Wilman Rd TN4 ....159 B7
Wilmecote Ct ME8 .....69 D8
Wilmington Ave BR6 ...58 C8
Wilmington Court Rd
 DA2 ....32 A6
Wilmington Gram Sch for
 Boys DA2 ....32 B5
Wilmington Hall Sch
 DA2 ....32 B5
Wilmington Ho DA2 ....32 D6
Wilmington Prim Sch
 DA2 ....32 B5
Wilmington Way ME8 ...55 B2
Wilmot Rd DA1 ....15 B2
Wilmount St SE18 ....2 B2
Wilson Ave ME1 ....67 E7
Wilson Cl
 Maidstone ME15 ......116 E7
 Tonbridge TN11 ......126 E5
Wilson Ct ME18 ....114 A1

Wilson Ho 3 SE7 ......11 C8
Wilson La DA4 ....47 F7
Wilson Rd TN10 ......127 E5
Wilsons La ME15 ......115 A5
Wilsons Way DA13 .....63 F3
Wilton Dr ME20 ....98 B3
Wilton Ho 2 BR7 ......43 D8
Wilton Rd SE2 ....3 C2
Wiltshire Cl Chatham ME5 68 C8
 Dartford DA2 ....33 D8
Wiltshire Rd BR6 ......44 A2
Wiltshire Way
 4 Maidstone ME15 ...116 E8
 Royal Tunbridge Wells
 TN2 ....159 D7
Wimborne 6 DA14 .....30 B4
Wimborne Ave BR7 .....43 F6
Wimborne Ho DA12 ....36 D5
Wimbourne Dr ME8 ....69 D6
Wimpole Cl BR2 ....42 C5
Win'freds Cl TN17 ...191 E3
Winch Cl TN17 ....179 D3
Winch's Garth TN12 ..149 F5
Winchcomb Gdns SE9 ..11 D4
Winchelsea Ave DA7 ...13 F7
Winchelsea Rd ME5 ....68 B5
Winchester Ave ME5 ...67 F4
Winchester Cl 11 E6 ....1 F7
Winchester Cres DA12 ..36 D5
Winchester Ct 14 DA17 ..4 A1
Winchester Gr TN13 ...92 B4
Winchester Ho
 3 Maidstone ME15 ...116 D7
 Woolwich SE18 ....11 D7
Winchester Pl 9 ME14 .100 A5
Winchester Rd
 Bexley DA7 ....13 D5
 Hawkhurst TN18 .....189 A2
 Orpington BR6 ....58 C6
 Tonbridge TN10 ......127 D5
Winchester Way ME8 ...70 A8
Wincliff Rd TN9 ......143 B8
Wincrofts Dr SE9 ......12 D3
Windermere Cl
 Dartford DA1 ....32 B7
 Orpington BR6 ....57 B7
Windermere Dr ME8 ....69 D7
Windermere Ho 4
 ME15 ....116 E7
Windermere Rd DA7 ...14 C5
Windhover Way DA12 ...36 E4
Windmill Cl ME2 ....39 B1
Windmill Cotts
 Cranbrook TN17 ......179 D6
 Lower Stoke ME3 ......25 C5
Windmill Ct
 Maidstone ME17 .....116 B3
 Royal Tunbridge Wells
 TN2 ....159 C3
Windmill Dr BR2 ....56 C6
Windmill Grange ME15 .61 F3
Windmill Hill
 Brenchley TN12 ......146 B1
 Platt TN15 ....95 D7
 Pye Corner ME17 ....136 E2
Windmill Hts ME14 ...101 B4
Windmill La
 Cousley Wood TN5 ...185 C8
 Durgates TN5 ....184 E4
Windmill La E ME19 ...97 C6
Windmill La W ME19 ...97 A6
Windmill Manor ME7 ...54 C4
Windmill Pk TN15 ......95 E7
Windmill Rd
 Gillingham ME7 ....54 C4
 Sevenoaks TN13 .....108 B6
 Sevenoaks Weald TN14 ..108 B2
Windmill Row ME17 ...117 D2
Windmill St
 Gravesend DA12 ....36 B7
 Rochester ME2 ....39 B1
 Royal Tunbridge Wells
 TN2 ....159 C3
Windrush Ct 8 DA8 .....4 E1
Windrush Prim Sch SE28 .3 B5
Windsor Ave ME4 ......53 F2
Windsor Cl
 Chislehurst BR7 ....29 B3
 Maidstone ME14 ......100 B6
Windsor Ct
 1 Bromley BR1 ....42 E6
 Gillingham ME7 ....54 D5
 18 Sidcup DA14 ....30 A4
Windsor Dr Dartford DA1 .15 A1
 Orpington BR6 ....58 A4
Windsor Hall E16 ....1 B5
Windsor Rd Bexley DA6 ..13 E3
 Gillingham ME7 ....54 D5
 Gravesend DA12 ....36 B4
Windward Rd ME1 ......53 C1
Windy Ridge BR1 ......42 E8
Windyridge ME7 ....54 E1
Winfield La TN15 ....94 E3
Winford Mews ME1 ....53 A2
Wingate Rd DA14 ......30 C2
Wingfield Ct DA15 .....29 F7
Wingfield Prim Sch SE3 .11 B4
Wingfield Rd DA12 .....36 B8
Wingham Cl
 Gillingham ME8 ....55 C3
 Maidstone ME15 ......116 F7
Wingrove Dr
 Maidstone ME14 ......100 C5
 Rochester ME2 ....53 C7
Winifred Rd Dartford DA1 .15 B2
 Erith DA8 ....4 E1
 Maidstone ME15 ......100 F3

Winifred St E16 ....1 F5
Winn Common Rd SE18 .12 E8
Winn Rd SE12,SE9 .....28 B7
Winnipeg Dr 3 BR6 ....57 F4
Winser Rd TN17 ......192 A1
Winsor Prim Sch E6 .....2 A7
Winsor Terr E6 ....2 A8
Winston Ave ME18 .....97 B3
Winston Cl DA9 ....16 F1
Winston Ct 10 BR1 .....42 B8
Winston Dr ME2 ....39 D2
Winston Rd ME2 ....52 D5
Winstone Scott Ave
 TN3 ....157 E4
Winterborne Ave BR6 ..57 D7
Winterfield La ME19 ...97 E8
Wintergarden Cres DA9 .34 A8
Wintergreen Cl
 8 Maidstone ME16 ....1 E8
 St Mary's Island ME4 ..40 C1
Winters Croft DA12 ....36 D2
Winterton Ct 8 TN16 ..89 D1
Winton Ct BR8 ....45 E5
Winton Rd BR6 ....57 B6
Wireless Rd TN16 .....72 D4
Wirral Wood Cl BR7 ...29 A2
Wirrals The ME5 ....68 A4
Wise Ho ME5 ....12 A7
Wise's La TN15 ....62 E2
Wiseacre TN3 ....176 A3
Wishart Rd SE3 ....11 D5
Wisley Rd BR5 ....30 E1
Wistaria Cl BR6 ....57 B8
Wisteria Gdns BR8 ....45 D7
Wisteria Ho 11 ME15 .116 E7
Witches La TN13 ....91 D4
Witham Way ME2 ......52 F7
Withens Cl BR5 ....44 C5
Witherston Way SE9 ...29 A5
Withyham Rd TN3 ....171 B7
Wittersham CE Prim Sch
 TN30 ....199 D2
Wittersham Cl ME5 ....68 D5
Wittersham Ho 2 BR5 .44 D1
Wittersham Rd
 Wittersham TN30 ....199 C5
 Wittersham,Potman's Heath
 TN17,TN30 ....198 D4
Wittersham Road Sta★
 TN17 ....198 D6
Wixom Ho SE3 ....11 C3
Woburn Cl SE28 ....3 D7
Woburn Ct 1 DA6 .....13 E3
Wodehouse Cl ME20 ...81 F4
Wodehouse Rd DA1 ....16 A3
Woldham Pl BR2 ....42 C5
Woldham Rd BR2 ......42 C5
Wolds Dr BR6 ....57 A6
Wolf Ho ME4 ....54 B8
Wolf's Cnr RH8 ......104 A4
Wolf's Hill RH8 ......104 A4
Wolf's Rd RH8 ....104 B5
Wolf's Row RH8 ......104 B6
Wolfe Cl BR2 ....42 A3
Wolfe Cres SE7 ....1 D1
Wolfe Rd ME16 ....99 B2
Wolfs Wood RH8 .....104 A3
Wollaston Cl ME8 .....69 D3
Wolseley Rd TN4 .....159 C7
Wolsey Ct SE9 ....11 F1
Wolsey Mews BR6 .....57 F5
Wolsley Cl DA1 ....14 E2
Wolsley Ho DA1 ....14 E2
Wolvercote Rd SE2 .....3 C4
Wombwell Gdns DA11 ..35 E6
Wood Cl Ditton ME20 ..98 B3
 Joyden's Wood DA5 ...31 E5
Wood Dr Bromley BR7 ..28 E2
 Sevenoaks TN13 ....91 F1
Wood End BR8 ....45 C5
Wood La Dartford DA2 ..33 C4
 East End TN17 ....181 C3
Wood Lodge Gdns BR1 .28 E1
Wood Lodge Grange
 TN13 ....92 C5
Wood Pl DA13 ....30 A3
Wood Point 10 E16 .....1 A8
Wood Rd TN16 ....72 C1
Wood Retreat SE18 ....12 D7
Wood Ride BR5 ....43 E5
Wood St Chatham ME7 ..54 A6
 Cuxton ME2 ....52 B2
 9 Grays RM17 ....18 C8
 Royal Tunbridge Wells
 TN1 ....159 B4
 Swanley Village BR8 ..46 D8
Wood View Cl TN15 ....61 E3
Wood Way BR6 ....57 A8
Woodberry Gr DA5 ....31 D5
Woodbine Cotts ME2 ...65 E5
Woodbine Rd DA15 ....29 E7
Woodbridge Dr ME15 ..99 F1
Woodbrook Rd SE2 ....13 B8
Woodbury Cl
 Biggin Hill TN16 ......72 F1
 Royal Tunbridge Wells
 TN4 ....159 A5
Woodbury Gdns SE28 ..28 A4
Woodbury La TN30 ...193 A7
Woodbury Park Gdns
 TN4 ....159 A5
Woodbury Park Rd TN4 159 B5
Woodbury Rd
 Chatham ME5 ....67 F1
 Hawkhurst TN18 .....189 A2
Woodchurch Cl
 Chatham ME5 ....68 B5
 Sidcup DA14 ....29 D5

Woodchurch Cres ME8 ..55 C2
Woodchurch Ct **1** BR5 ..44 C4
Woodchurch Dr BR1 ...28 D1
Woodchurch Ho ME8 ...55 C2
Woodchurch Rd TN30 .193 D8
Woodclyffe Dr BR7 ....43 A7
Woodcock La
  Grafty Green ME17 ...136 E5
  Iden Green TN17 .....190 E3
Woodcocks
  Headcorn TN27 ....151 D5
  Newham E16 ....1 D8
Woodcote Dr BR6 ......43 D2
Woodcroft SE9 ....28 F5
Woodcut ME14 ....100 A8
Woodfall Dr DA1 ......14 F3
Woodfalls Ind Est ME18 130 D6
Woodfield Ave
  Gravesend DA11 ......36 B6
  Tonbridge TN11 ......126 E5
Woodfield Rd TN9 .....143 B8
Woodfield Way ME3 ....39 E4
Woodfields TN13 ......91 D4
Woodford Gr ME18 .....97 B3
Woodford Ho **13** SE18 ...12 B8
Woodford Rd ME16 .....99 B2
Woodgate La ME9 ......71 C2
Woodgate Rd ME19 .....80 D4
Woodgate Way TN9,
  TN11 ....143 E7
Woodgates CI TN26 ...183 D7
Woodgers Gr BR8 ......45 F7
Woodget CI E6 ....1 E7
Woodhatch CI E6 ......1 E8
Woodhayes BR7 ....29 B2
Woodhead Dr BR6 ......57 E8
Woodhill SE18 ....1 E2
Woodhill Pk TN2 .....160 C6
Woodhill Prim Sch SE18 .1 E2
Woodhurst ME5 ....67 D4
Woodhurst Ave BR5 ....43 C3
Woodhurst CI ME2 .....52 B2
Woodhurst Rd SE2 .....3 A2
Woodington CI SE9 ....12 A1
Woodknoll Dr BR7 .....42 F8
Woodland Ave DA3 ....48 F5
Woodland CI
  New Barn DA3 ....49 C6
  Royal Tunbridge Wells
    TN4 ....159 C7
  West Malling ME19 ...97 A8
Woodland Dr TN8 .....122 D3
Woodland Rd TN4 .....159 C7
Woodland Rise TN15 ...92 E4
Woodland Terr SE7 ....1 E2
Woodland View TN30 ..199 E4
Woodland Way
  Bidborough TN4 .....142 D3
  Erith SE2 ....3 D2
  Maidstone ME14 .....100 B7
  Orpington BR5 ....43 C4
  Swanscombe DA9 .....17 A3
Woodlands Bexley DA6 ..14 B2
  Chatham ME5 ....68 A2
  Coxheath ME17 ......115 B3
  Cranbrook TN17 .....179 D6
  Paddock Wood TN12 ..145 F7
  Pembury TN2 ....160 F7
  Royal Tunbridge Wells
    TN4 ....143 A2
Woodlands Ave
  Sidcup DA15 ....29 E7
  Snodland ME6 ....81 F8
Woodlands CI
  Bromley BR1 ....42 F7
  Maidstone ME14 .....100 B7
  Swanley BR8 ....45 F7
  Teston ME18 ....114 B8
Woodlands Ct ME5 .....67 F3
Woodlands Farm DA16 ..12 C5
Woodlands Inf & Jun Schs
  TN10 ....127 E6
Woodlands La DA12 ....37 E1
Woodlands Par ME20 ...98 D8
Woodlands Pk DA5 .....31 D4
Woodlands Pk (Cvn Pk)
  TN27 ....182 D7

Woodlands Prim Sch
  ME7 ....54 F4
Woodlands Rd Bexley DA7 13 E4
  Bromley BR1 ....42 F7
  Ditton ME20 ....98 D8
  Gillingham ME7 ......54 F4
  Orpington BR6 ....58 A4
  Tonbridge TN9 ......143 A7
Woodlands Rise BR8 ...45 F7
Woodlands Terr
  Crockenhill BR8 .....45 B3
  Gillingham ME7 ......54 F3
Woodlands The BR6 ....58 B4
Woodlands View TN14 ..59 A1
Woodlark Rd ME4 ......40 B1
Woodlea Leybourne ME19 .81 F2
  New Barn DA3 ....49 C6
Woodleas ME16 ....98 F2
Woodley Rd BR6 ....58 C8
Woodman Par **4** E16 ...2 A5
Woodman St E16 ....2 A5
Woodmere SE9 ....28 F7
Woodmount ME8 ....45 D2
Woodpecker CI **1** TN8 .122 D3
Woodpecker Glade ME8 .69 D6
Woodpecker Rd
  Larkfield ME20 ......81 F1
  Woolwich SE28 ....3 C6
Woodrow SE18 ....1 F2
Woodrush PI ME4 ......40 B1
Woods Green Cotts TN5 184 F7
Woodsgate Way TN2 ..160 B6
Woodside Gillingham ME8 .69 C6
  Kilndown TN17 ......176 F2
  Orpington BR6 ....58 B5
  Vigo Village DA13 ...79 F8
Woodside Ave BR7 .....29 C3
Woodside CI Crayford DA7 14 D3
  Pembury TN2 ....160 E6
Woodside Cres DA15 ...29 E5
Woodside Dr DA2 ......31 E4
Woodside Gn ME3 ......39 B7
Woodside La DA5 ......13 D1
Woodside Par DA15 ....29 E5
Woodside Rd Bromley BR1 42 E4
  Crayford DA7 ....14 D3
  Maidstone ME15 .....116 C7
  Pembury TN2 ....160 E6
  Rusthall TN4 ....158 D4
  Sevenoaks TN13 ......92 B4
  Sidcup DA15 ....29 E5
  Sundridge TN14 ......90 E3
  Tonbridge TN9 ......143 B7
Woodside Sch DA17 ....4 B2
Woodstock CI DA5 .....30 F7
Woodstock CI SE12 ....11 A1
Woodstock Rd ME2 .....53 A7
Woodvale Ct BR1 ......42 B8
Woodview CI BR6 ......57 C8
Woodview Cres TN11 ..126 F5
Woodview Rd BR8 .....45 D7
Woodview Rise ME2 ....38 F1
Woodville SE3 ....11 B6
Woodville CI SE12 ....11 A2
Woodville Gr **2** DA16 ..13 A4
Woodville PI DA12 ....36 B8
Woodville Rd ME15 ...100 A2
Woodville St **15** SE18 ...1 E2
Woodward Terr DA9 ...16 E1
Woodyates Rd
  Eltham SE12 ....28 B8
  Lewisham SE12 ....11 A1
Woolacombe Rd SE3 ...11 C5
Woolaston CI ME15 ....99 F1
Woolbrook Rd DA1 ....14 E1
Wooldeys Rd ME8 .....55 F2
Woolf CI SE28 ....3 B5
Woolf Wlk RM18 ......19 C5
Woollett CI DA1 ......15 A3
Woollett St ME14 ....100 A5
Woolley CI TN4 ......142 F1
Woolley Rd
  Maidstone ME15 .....116 F7
  Royal Tunbridge Wells
    TN4 ....142 F1
Woolpack Cnr TN27 ...182 A7
Woolpack Cotts TN27 .182 A7

Woolwich Arsenal Sta
  SE18 ....2 B2
Woolwich Church St SE18 1 E3
Woolwich CI ME5 ......68 A7
Woolwich Comm SE18 ..12 A8
Woolwich Dockyard Ind Est
  SE18 ....1 E3
Woolwich Dockyard Sta
  SE18 ....1 D1
Woolwich High St SE18 ..2 A3
Woolwich Manor Way E6 .2 A7
Woolwich Manorway E16 .2 A8
Woolwich New Rd SE18 ..2 B2
Woolwich Polytechnic Sch
  for Boys SE28 ....3 A5
Woolwich Rd Bexley DA7 .14 A4
  Erith DA8 ....3 E1
  Greenwich SE10,SE7 ..1 C2
Wootton Gn ME8 ......55 D3
Wootton Ho SE9 ......12 D1
Wopsle CI ME1 ....67 D7
Worcester Ave ME19 ...97 A2
Worcester CI
  Istead Rise DA13 ....35 F1
  Rochester ME2 ....52 E8
  Swanscombe DA9 .....17 B3
Worcester Rd ME15 ...116 D7
Wordsworth CI
  Chatham ME5 ....68 C7
  Tilbury RM18 ....19 C5
Wordsworth Ho **15** SE18 .12 A8
Wordsworth Rd
  Bexley DA16 ....12 E6
  Maidstone ME14 .....100 B7
Wordsworth Way
  Dartford DA1 ....16 A3
  New Hythe ME20 .....82 A4
Workhouse La
  Coxheath ME15 ......115 C4
  Sutton Valence ME17 .135 A8
Workhouse Rd ME19 ...80 F4
World of Silk★ DA1 ...14 E2
Worlds End La BR6 ....58 B3
Wormdale Hill ME9 ....71 B3
Wormdale Rd ME9 .....71 B4
Worsenden TN27 .....167 E1
Worsfold Ct **5** ME15 ..100 A1
Worships Hill TN13 ...91 A4
Worth CI BR6 ....57 E6
Worthing Ct RM17 ....17 E8
Wotton CI ME15 ......116 E5
Wotton Gn BR5 ....44 D5
Wouldham All Saints CE Prim
  Sch ME1 ....66 C5
Wouldham Rd
  Grays RM17,RM20 ....17 E8
  Rochester ME1 ....52 E1
Wouldham Terr **3** BR5 ..44 B6
Wrangleden CI ME15 ..116 E5
Wrangleden Rd ME15 ..116 E5
Wrangling La DA13 ....64 F3
Wrekin Rd SE18 ......12 C7
Wren CI Larkfield ME20 ..81 F1
  Orpington BR5 ....44 D6
Wren Ind Est ME15 ...116 F4
Wren Path SE28 ....2 D4
Wren Rd DA14 ....30 C5
Wren Way ME5 ....68 B6
Wren Wlk RM18 ....19 B7
Wren's Cross ME15 ...100 A3
Wren's Croft DA11 ....35 E4
Wrens Rd ME9 ....87 F6
Wricklemarsh Rd
  Greenwich SE3 ......11 B6
  Greenwich SE3 ......11 D6
Wright CI Gillingham ME8 .55 C2
  Swanscombe DA10 ....17 D1
Wrights CI TN30 .....193 A8
Wrotham Hill Rd TN15 ..79 A6
Wrotham Rd Bexley DA16 .13 C6
  Borough Green TN15 ..95 A8
  Culverstone Green DA13 .63 F4
  Gravesend DA11,DA13 .36 A4
  Meopham Sta DA13 ...50 A3
Wrotham Road Prim Sch
  DA11 ....36 B8
Wrotham Sch TN15 ....79 A1

Wrotham Water La ME19,
  TN15 ....79 E5
Wrotham Water Rd TN15,
  ME19 ....79 E4
Wrott & Hill Ct DA4 ..47 B8
Wrottesley Rd SE18 ...12 C8
Wroxham Rd SE28 .....3 D6
Wulfred Way TN15 ....77 B1
Wyatt CI TN15 ....94 F7
Wyatt Ho **1** ME2 ....53 A7
Wyatt PI ME2 ....53 A7
Wyatt Rd DA1 ....14 F4
Wyatt St ME14 ....100 A4
Wyborne Prim Sch SE9 .29 B7
Wyborne Rise TN2 ....173 B8
Wybournes La ME23 ...23 C3
Wycliffe CI DA16 .....12 F6
Wycliffe Ho **6** DA11 ..35 F7
Wycliffe Row DA11 ...35 F7
Wycombe Ct SE3 ......11 A7
Wydeville Manor Rd
  SE12 ....28 B4
Wye CI BR6 ....43 F2
Wye Rd
  Borough Green TN15 ..95 A8
  Gravesend DA12 ......36 D6
  Tonbridge TN10 .....127 C5
Wyfold Ho **10** SE2 .....3 C4
Wyke Manor Rd ME14 .100 A4
Wykeham CI DA12 .....36 E2
Wykeham Cotts ME17 .115 F2
Wykeham Ct BR7 ......29 E2
Wykeham Gr ME17 ....118 A7
Wykeham St ME2 ......53 B8
Wyles Rd ME4 ....53 E2
Wyles St ME7 ....54 C7
Wylie Ho ME3 ....39 F6
Wylie Rd ME3 ....40 D6
Wyncham Ave DA15 ....29 E7
Wyncroft CI BR1 .....42 F6
Wyndcliff Rd SE3,SE7 ..11 B8
Wyndham Ave TN11 ...125 F1
Wyndham CI Leigh TN11 .125 F1
  Orpington BR6 ....43 C1
Wyndham Rd ME4 .....53 E2
Wyndham Way SE9 ....28 F5
Wynn's Ave DA15 .....13 A2
Wytchlings The ME17 .118 D2
Wythens Wlk SE9 .....12 B1
Wytherling CI ME14 ..100 F5
Wythes CI BR1 ....42 F7
Wythes Rd E16 ....1 E5
Wythfield Rd SE9 .....11 F1
Wyvern CI Dartford DA1 .32 C8
  Orpington BR6 ....58 B7
  Snodland ME6 ....82 A7
Wyvern Ho **3** RM17 ...18 B8
Wyvill CI ME5 ....69 E5

Y

Yalding CI ME2 ....39 B1
Yalding Gr BR5 ....44 D5
Yalding Hill ME18 ...114 A3
Yalding Organic Gdns★
  ME18 ....130 F7
Yalding St Peter & St Paul CE
  Prim Sch ME18 .....114 A1
Yalding Sta ME18 ....113 D1
Yantlet Dr ME2 ......52 C7
Yard The ME5 ....68 B3
Yardley CI TN9 ......127 D3
Yardley Court Prep Sch
  TN11 ....143 F7
Yardley Park Rd TN9 .127 D3
Yarnton Way SE2,DA18 ..3 E4
Yarrow Cres E6 ....1 E8
Yarrow Ct ME14 ......100 F5
Yarrow Rd ME5 ....67 F4
Yateley St SE18 ......1 D3
Yaugher La ME9 ......70 C3
Ye Olde Tudor Ct BR7 .29 B3
Yelsted La Chatham ME14 .84 D7
Yelsted ME9 ....70 A1

Yelsted Rd ME9 ....86 A7
Yeoman CI E6 ....2 B6
Yeoman Ct ME14 .....101 B3
Yeoman Dr ME7 ....54 F1
Yeoman Gdns TN12 ...145 F6
Yeoman Ho ME1 ....53 D4
Yeoman La ME14 .....101 B4
Yeoman Pk ME15 .....101 A2
Yeoman Way ME15 ...101 A2
Yeoman's Mdws TN13 ..92 A1
Yeovil CI BR6 ....57 E8
Yester Dr BR7 ....28 E1
Yester Pk BR7 ....28 F2
Yester Rd BR7 ....28 F1
Yew Rd ME3 ....40 E3
Yew Tree CI
  Aylesford ME20 ......82 E1
  Bexley DA16 ....13 A6
  Chatham ME5 ....68 D1
  New Barn DA3 ....49 D7
  Sevenoaks TN13 ......91 D4
Yew Tree Cotts
  Groombridge TN3 ...171 F8
  Halstead TN14 ....74 F7
  Sandling ME14 ....83 F1
Yew Tree Green Rd
  TN12 ....147 A1
Yew Tree Mews TN16 .105 D8
Yew Tree PI ME7 .....69 B1
Yew Tree Rd TN4 ....159 B8
Yews The DA12 ....36 D7
Yewtree Ho **2** ME1 ...53 D4
Yewtree Ind Est ME20 .82 D2
Yoke CI ME2 ....53 B8
Yokosuka Way ME7,ME8 .55 A7
Yolande Gdns SE9 ....11 E2
Yopps Gn TN15 ....94 E1
York Ave Chatham ME5 ..67 F3
  Gillingham ME7 ......54 C4
  Sidcup DA15 ....29 F6
York CI E6 ....1 F7
York Hill ME5 ....54 C2
York Par TN10 ......127 C6
York PI RM17 ....18 A8
York Rd Biggin Hill TN16 .88 B8
  Dartford DA1 ....32 F8
  Gravesend DA12 ......36 C5
  Maidstone ME15 ....100 C2
  Northfleet DA11 .....35 D8
  Rochester ME1 ....53 C3
  Royal Tunbridge Wells
    TN1 ....159 A4
  Tonbridge TN10 ....127 D5
York Rise BR6 ....57 E8
York Road Jun Sch DA1 .32 F8
York Terr DA8 ....14 C6
Yorkland Ave DA16 ...12 F3
Youens PI ME3 ....38 B3
Young Rd E16 ....1 C7

Z

Zambra Way TN15 .....92 F7
Zangwill Rd SE18,SE3 ..11 D6
Zealand Ho SE18 ......1 E2
Zelah Rd BR5 ....44 C2
Zetland Ave ME7 .....54 E2
Zillah Gdns ME8 .....69 C6
Zion PI DA12 ....36 B8
Zion St TN15 ....92 F6

Addresses

Name and Address	Telephone	Page	Grid reference

Name and Address	Telephone	Page	Grid reference

NG NH NJ NK
NM NN NO NP
NR NS NT NU
NX NY NZ
SC SD SE TA
SH SJ SK TF TG
SM SN SO SP TL TM
SR SS ST SU TQ TR
SW SX SY SZ TV

Any feature in this atlas can be given a unique reference to help you find the same feature on other Ordnance Survey maps of the area, or to help someone else locate you if they do not have a Street Atlas.

The grid squares in this atlas match the Ordnance Survey National Grid and are at 500 metre intervals. The small figures at the bottom and sides of every other grid line are the National Grid kilometre values (**00** to **99** km) and are repeated across the country every 100 km (see left).

To give a unique National Grid reference you need to locate where in the country you are. The country is divided into 100 km squares with each square given a unique two-letter reference. Use the administrative map to determine in which 100 km square a particular page of this atlas falls.

The bold letters and numbers between each grid line (**A** to **F**, **1** to **8**) are for use within a specific Street Atlas only, and when used with the page number, are a convenient way of referencing these grid squares.

Example The railway bridge over DARLEY GREEN RD in grid square B1

Step 1: Identify the two-letter reference, in this example the page is in **SP**

Step 2: Identify the 1 km square in which the railway bridge falls. Use the figures in the southwest corner of this square: Eastings **17**, Northings **74**. This gives a unique reference: **SP 17 74**, accurate to 1 km.

Step 3: To give a more precise reference accurate to 100 m you need to estimate how many tenths along and how many tenths up this 1 km square the feature is (to help with this the 1 km square is divided into four 500 m squares). This makes the bridge about **8** tenths along and about **1** tenth up from the southwest corner.

This gives a unique reference: **SP 178 741**, accurate to 100 m.

Eastings (read from left to right along the bottom) come before Northings (read from bottom to top). If you have trouble remembering say to yourself "Along the hall, THEN up the stairs"!

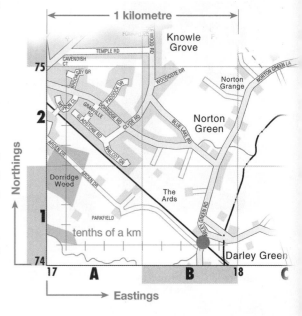